COPING AND EMOTION IN SPORT

The emotional highs and lows of competitive sport, whether experienced as a competitor, spectator or coach may be the essential ingredient that gives sport its universal and compelling appeal. Emotion is clearly a pervasive force within competitive sport, and this is reflected in the burgeoning interest over recent decades in athletes' emotions and strategies for coping with these emotions. The interplay between emotion and coping is a critical factor in determining, through its influence on key psychological functions, an athlete's potential success in competitive sport. This fully revised and updated edition of the original text on coping and emotion in sport goes further than any other book in examining the central role that these two factors play in sports performance.

The book explores theory and measurement, current research, and contemporary issues and special populations. Each chapter closely integrates cutting-edge research themes with discussion of practical and applied issues, and case studies and reflections from practitioners working in elite sport are woven throughout the book. With contributions from leading international scholars and consultant psychologists, this book is vital reading for all students and professionals working in sport psychology.

Joanne Thatcher is a Senior Lecturer in Sport and Exercise Psychology at Aberystwyth University. She has published over 30 academic papers and books. She is a Chartered Psychologist (BPS), a registered Sport and Exercise Psychologist (HPC) and past chair of the BPS Division of Sport & Exercise Psychology.

Marc Jones is a Reader in Sport and Exercise Psychology at Staffordshire University and has published over 40 academic papers, mostly in the area of stress and emotion. He is a Chartered Psychologist (BPS) and a registered Sport and Exercise Psychologist (HPC).

David Lavallee is Professor and Head of the School of Sport at the University of Stirling. He is an editorial board member of several journals, including *International Review of Sport & Exercise Psychology, Psychology of Sport & Exercise, Sport & Exercise Psychology Review* and *Qualitative Research in Sport & Exercise*.

COPING AND EMOTION IN SPORT

Second Edition

Edited by Joanne Thatcher, Marc Jones and David Lavallee

Routledge
Taylor & Francis Group

LONDON AND NEW YORK

First Published in 2004
By Nova Science Publishers

This edition published 2012
by Routledge
2 Park Square, Milton Park, Abingdon, Oxon OX14 4RN

Simultaneously published in the USA and Canada
by Routledge
711 Third Avenue, New York, NY 10017

Routledge is an imprint of the Taylor & Francis Group, an informa business

British Library Cataloguing in Publication Data
A catalogue record for this book is available from the British Library

Library of Congress Cataloging in Publication Data
A catalogue record for this book has been requested from the Library of Congress.
Coping and emotion in sport / edited by Joanne Thatcher, Marc Jones and David Lavallee.
p. cm.
Sports--Psychological aspects. 2. Adjustment (Psychology) 3. Athletes--Psychology.
I. Lavallee, David, Ph. D. II. Thatcher, Joanne. III. Jones, Marc V.
GV706.4.C684 2011
796.01--dc22
2011004752

ISBN: 978-0-415-57818-9 (hbk)
ISBN: 978-0-415-57819-6 (pbk)
ISBN: 978-0-203-85229-3 (ebk)

Typeset in Bembo by Saxon Graphics Ltd, Derby

MIX
Paper from
responsible sources
FSC
www.fsc.org   FSC® C004839

Printed and bound in Great Britain by
CPI Antony Rowe, Chippenham, Wiltshire

CONTENTS

LIST OF FIGURES

LIST OF TABLES

CONTRIBUTORS

Dr Megan Babkes Stellino School of Sport and Exercise Science, University of Northern Colorado

Dr Chris Beedie School of Sport, Performing Arts and Leisure, University of Wolverhampton

Peter Clarke Chartered Psychologist

Dr Melissa Day Sport, Exercise and Health Sciences, University of Chichester

Dr Tracey Devonport School of Sport, Performing Arts and Leisure, University of Wolverhampton

Dr Paul Freeman School of Sport and Health Sciences, University of Exeter

Professor Sheldon Hanton University of Wales Institute, Cardiff

Dr Marc Jones Department of Sport, Exercise and Health, Staffordshire University

Professor Andrew Lane School of Sport, Performing Arts and Leisure, University of Wolverhampton

Professor David Lavallee School of Sport and Exercise Science, University of Stirling

Dr Jeffrey Martin Kinesiology, Health and Sport Studies, Wayne State University

Dr Paul McCarthy School of Life Sciences, Department of Psychology, Glasgow Caledonian University

Dr Stephen D. Mellalieu School of Engineering, Swansea University

Dr Kristina Moore School of Sport and Exercise Science, University of Northern Colorado

Professor Aidan Moran School of Psychology, University College, Dublin

Dr Rich Neil Cardiff School of Sport, University of Wales Institute, Cardiff

Dr Julie Partridge Department of Kinesiology, Southern Illinois University

Professor Remco Polman Institute of Sport, Exercise and Active Living, Victoria University, Australia

Dr Tim Rees School of Sport and Health Sciences, University of Exeter

Dr Corinne Reid Department of Psychology, Murdoch University, Australia

Dr Hugh Richards Department of Physical Education, Sport and Leisure, The University of Edinburgh

Dr Joanne Thatcher Department of Sport and Exercise Science, Aberystwyth University

Dr Mark Uphill Department of Sport Science, Tourism and Leisure, Canterbury Christchurch University

Dr Christopher R. D. Wagstaff Sport and Exercise Science, University of Portsmouth

Dr Natalie Walker School of Health, University of Northampton

Dr Neil Weston Sport and Exercise Science, University of Portsmouth

PREFACE

Joanne Thatcher, Marc Jones and David Lavallee

Just before the fight, when the referee was giving us instructions, Liston was giving me that stare. And I won't lie I was scared. Sonny Liston was one of the greatest fighters of all time. He was one of the most scientific boxers who ever lived; he hit hard; and he was fixing to kill me. It frightened me, just knowing how hard he hit. But I was there; I didn't have no choice but to go out and fight .... Everyone predicted that Sonny Liston would destroy me. And he was scary. But it's a lack of faith that makes people afraid of meeting challenges, and I believed in myself. I was confident I could whup him. So what I did was, I studied his style, I trained hard, and I watched Liston outside the ring. I went to his training camp and tried to understand what went on inside his head, so later on I could mess with his mind. And all the time, I was talking, talking. That way, I figured Liston would get so mad that, when the fight came, he'd try to kill me and forget everything he knew about boxing.

Muhammad Ali (taken from Hauser, 1997, p. 74)

It may come as a shock to some but possibly the most supremely confident athlete of modern times, Muhammad Ali, experienced emotions prior to competing that all of us can recognize. It is also apparent, given Ali's legendary status as a sportsman, that he was able to cope with these emotions, clearly crucial in a sport such as boxing where failure to do so could have substantial consequences for the athlete. The emotional highs and lows of competitive sport, whether experienced as a competitor, spectator or coach, may be the essential ingredient that gives sport its universal and compelling appeal. Who could fail to share the intense excitement and infectious joy when Usain Bolt won gold and broke world records in the 100 m and 200 m at the Beijing Olympics in 2008?

Emotion is clearly a pervasive force within competitive sport, and this is reflected in its academic study, with a burgeoning interest over recent decades in athletes' emotions and strategies for coping with these emotions. A search of 'Web of Science' showed that since the publication of the first edition of this book in 2004 to the present day (2010) 302 articles have been published in the area of coping, emotion and sport. Research in this area is clearly still flourishing, and the body of literature and thus our understanding of coping and emotion in sport have increased substantially since 2004. We therefore felt it was timely to update the first edition to reflect contemporary developments in the area of coping and emotion in sport.

In the introduction to the first edition we suggested that in the coming years sport psychology researchers and practitioners would add considerably to our knowledge of coping and emotion in sport. Thankfully, it appears that we have not been proved wrong! Also, in the final chapter of the first edition we offered some suggestions for moving this field forward, and contributions in this second edition reflect some of the developments we hoped to see in this field. For instance, inquiry has increasingly extended to other emotions besides anxiety (see Chapter 9), to understanding cognitive processes involved in the generation of emotions (see Chapter 3) and to the positive emotions experienced in sport (see Chapter 9).

A now well-accepted axiom is that stress, coping and emotion are intertwined, and only in research efforts to understand them further can and should we consider these individually (Lazarus, 1999). Stress remains a central theme in this second edition, reflecting the continued interest in explaining and understanding competitive stress in sport. Lazarus and Folkman's (1984) transactional model of stress still dominates this field of inquiry, and as such this approach permeates throughout the chapters of this book. Lazarus's (2000) cognitive motivational relational theory has also gained prominence in this field, and accordingly underpins discussion of a range of topics covered here. Reflecting the now mature standing of sport and exercise psychology within the parent discipline of psychology sport psychologists are increasingly offering theoretical explanations of various phenomena themselves. In this field, Jones and colleagues introduced their theory of challenge and threat states in athletes in 2009. Research is clearly yet to fully test its proposals and application, but its sport-specific psychophysiological approach is a welcome addition to the field and initial results are promising.

Much of the flavour and content of the original edition are retained here, as many of the central issues and concerns highlighted in the first edition remain, for instance, understanding the antecedents and consequences of emotions in sport (see Jones and Uphill, Chapter 3). Changes from the first edition to the current one reflect emerging developments within coping and emotion in sport, for instance, an increased focus on well-being, and not just in athletes, but in others in the sporting environment (see Day, Chapter 4). Many of these themselves reflect developments in the wider field of psychology, for example, the growth of the Positive Psychology movement (see McCarthy, Chapter 9) and increased knowledge of and interest in human performance in extreme and hostile environments (see Weston, Chapter 16). Although these developments illustrate that the field of coping and emotion in sport is keeping pace with contemporary themes within the wider field of psychology, further reciprocity between the two would still seem appropriate. It will be interesting to see whether and how, for instance, Rees and colleagues' work on social support (see Chapter 6) and Mellalieu and Hanton's work on facilitative anxiety interpretations (see Chapter 8) is received and applied in investigations into coping and emotion in other subdisciplines of psychology.

The first edition of this book was purposely divided into distinct sections with distinct emphases: theory, research, and specific issues and populations. In this second edition we have removed these sections to reflect one of its key aims. This is to offer greater integration of theory, research and application in relation to specific populations and contexts and the general athletic population as a whole. A second key aim of this second edition is to provide a more integrated consideration of coping and emotion in sport. Such integration is difficult in some areas at present, reflecting the lack of research that has examined these constructs in relation to each other and therefore identifying a clear need to do so in future investigations (see Rees and Freeman, Chapter 6). We are extremely grateful to the authors of all the chapters in this second edition for so eloquently addressing these two aims of achieving greater integration of constructs and of the theoretical, practical and empirical perspectives on coping and emotion in sport. We hope that in doing so, this book makes a significant contribution to this field for both academics and practitioners. In an applied field of study such as sport and exercise psychology, direct and clear integration of theory, research and practice is of clear value, and we hope that this book achieves this.

We feel very privileged to have been exposed to the thoughts, arguments, data and personal insights of such a range of international experts as these have emerged with the development of each author's contribution to this book. We hope readers will share our excitement. Our thanks go to Routledge for supporting the production and publication of this second edition of *Coping and Emotion in Sport*.

References

Hauser, T. (1997). *Muhammad Ali*. London: Pan Books.

Jones, M. V., Meijen, C., McCarthy, P. J. and Sheffield, D. (2009). A theory of challenge and threat states in athletes. *International Review of Sport and Exercise Psychology, 2*, 161–180.

Lazarus, R. S. (1999). *Stress and emotion: A new synthesis*. London: Springer.

Lazarus, R. S. (2000). How emotions influence performance in competitive sports. *The Sport Psychologist, 14*, 229–252.

Lazarus, R. S. and Folkman, S. (1984). *Stress, appraisal, and coping*. New York: Raven.

1

COPING PROCESSES IN SPORT

Hugh Richards, The University of Edinburgh

> Unless he is already doomed, fortune favours the man who keeps his nerve.
>
> (from Beowulf, 8th century [modified quote])

Introduction

In this chapter theoretical and empirical developments in coping are examined. The chapter presents an appraisal-based model to illustrate the fundamental relationship between emotion and coping. The interactions between these key constructs offer a comprehensive explanation of how performers respond to the combined challenges and threats of competition. Adopting a perspective of coping as a process (Lazarus and Folkman, 1984) selected recent empirical research is reviewed to summarize current understanding of coping in sport, the impact of relevant individual differences such as optimism, and approaches to train coping and assess coping effectiveness. Throughout, the chapter explains some of the key considerations in coping research in terms of design and measurement, and it concludes with suggested future developments for sport coping research.

Coping and sport performance

Coping can be explained as any changes in thoughts or behaviours that are made to manage the perceived demands of a situation (Lazarus and Folkman, 1984). Coping lies at the very heart of competitive sport, and the way in which performers cope with challenges, success and failure provides the human story that brings spectators to modern professional sport. Consider for example the Tour de France champion, enduring three weeks of riding over 3,600 kilometres before claiming his prize. Or the Formula 1 driver, sustaining gravitational forces of up to 5G and average heart rates of 170 bpm whilst driving at speeds that can reach 350 kph. Or the Olympic sprinter for whom the outcome of hours of training, years of competition, a professional life and sometimes their very identity, all hang, ready to be judged by millions, on less than 10 seconds. When performers produce results in situations like these, questions of interest are often not just about their skill or physical prowess, but also about how they coped with such demands.

For sport psychologists this key question has been unpacked in several ways. What do we mean by coping? What exactly are performers coping with? What different kinds of coping responses are used? Are some types of coping better than others? Are some people better at coping than others? How can performers be helped to cope better? This chapter summarizes the current, empirically based knowledge and understanding in response to each of these questions. Scientific understanding of coping is based on work emanating from other areas in psychology. From the 1960s and 1970s research focused on coping with issues associated with illnesses, medical conditions and treatments, dying and bereavement as well as professional stressors such as combat stress in the military and occupational stress and burnout. More recently sport-based research on coping has developed, so that there is significant and sufficient literature on coping in sport to warrant specific reviews (Nicholls and Polman, 2007) and book chapters (Richards, 2004, 2011) on the subject. Although this chapter focuses on coping in sport it also draws from evidence and ideas from the broader psychology literature. The chapter therefore is not a systematic review of all sport coping research, or one that is limited to exclusively sports-based research. Instead it is focused on providing answers to the important issues identified by the questions at the start of this paragraph.

What is coping?

Coping has traditionally been studied using two approaches, which are described as coping *style* and coping *process* approaches (Lazarus, 1993). Coping style is defined as 'the preferred set of coping strategies that remain relatively fixed across time and circumstances' (Carver, Scheier and Weintraub, 1989, p. 270). These authors distinguish between this definition of coping style and one in which personality characteristics, such as monitoring (seeking information) or blunting (distancing self from information), might predispose individuals to cope in certain ways (Kaissidis-Rodafinos, Anshel and Porter, 1997). In contrast the coping process approach is defined as the 'process of constantly changing cognitive and behavioral efforts to manage specific external and/or internal demands or conflicts appraised as taxing or exceeding one's resources' (Lazarus and Folkman, 1984, p. 141).

Definitions of coping have consistently emphasized that it involves deliberate and effortful responses, and have described coping as 'efforts to manage' (Lazarus and Folkman, 1984, p. 141), 'cognitions and behaviors ... consciously decided' (Cox and Ferguson, 1991, p. 23), 'a response aimed' (Snyder and Dinoff, 1999, p. 5), and 'a deliberate process involving thoughts and actions' (Kowalski and Crocker, 2001, p. 136). Some studies are not consistent with this view: for example Gould, Eklund and Jackson (1993a) found successful (medal-winning) Olympic wrestlers reported their coping was well practised, internalized and *automatic*. In psychological terms an automatic skill is one that requires little mental effort (Schmidt, 1991) or working memory. However, confusion about automaticity of coping in this case may have arisen from taking verbatim comments from interviews with athletes, for whom the term 'automatic' might have simply meant well-learned responses. It is logical that any skill must be well learned and practised to be effectively used in time urgent, pressurized situations.

Some responses, for example defence mechanisms such as repression, occur to protect the individual, and are not under conscious control. Responses not consciously recognized by the person are categorically distinct from conscious coping. Furthermore such responses require investigation with methods quite different from the self-report that characterizes the vast majority of sport coping research. Therefore within this chapter, and in keeping with recent reviews in this area (Carver and Connor-Smith, 2010) the definition of coping adopted excludes automatic and involuntary responses.

Coping occurs in response to perceived changes in the environment or self that are evaluated as requiring alteration. Based on established theory (Lazarus, 1999), coping can be best described through an integrated model in which appraisal, coping and emotion can be identified and their relationship to each other illustrated. However, an analytical model can fail to adequately illustrate the interconnectivity that exists between the different factors. So in reviewing and using this model the reader is asked to consider the following two key points. First, the model separates out constituent parts, but in reality performers' thoughts, emotions and responses are blended together. Second, whilst the model appears like a circuitry diagram that might suggest a temporal organisation, the speed with which thoughts operate means that absolute time is not relevant to discriminating the processes. The model is shown in Figure 1.1.

Central to the model is the concept of cognitive appraisal (Lazarus and Folkman, 1984), widely accepted as an explanation for the transaction that occurs between person and environment. Coping occurs following primary appraisal in which a situation is identified as relevant to the individual and presenting threat, harm, challenge or loss *and* following a second appraisal where an imbalance between the demands of the situation and their resources is perceived. It should be noted that recently it has been questioned whether challenge should be considered a type of stress (Blascovich, 2008; Carver and Connor-Smith, 2010). The outcomes of the two appraisal stages are significant determinants of whether an individual applies effort to cope with the perceived demand (Aldwin, 1994). Despite their names, primary and secondary appraisals are thought to occur relatively 'instantaneously' (Lazarus, 1999). Furthermore, Lazarus suggests that the emotion that results from appraisal is part of this instantaneous process.

Understanding how performers appraise stressors is vital to understand the coping response. For example, Hoar, Crocher, Holt, and Tamminen (2010) suggest inconsistencies in findings on gender differences in coping may be due to a failure to assess appraisal. A further important additional component within this model,

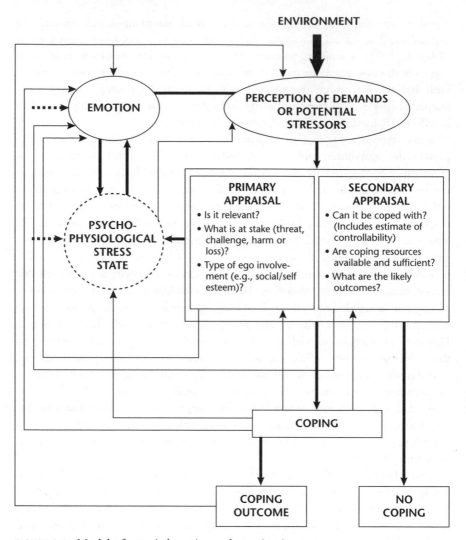

FIGURE 1.1 Model of appraisal, coping and emotion in sport

which differs from previous models (e.g. Hardy, Jones and Gould, 1996), is the emphasis that the demands are *perceived* by the individual. This is central to a transactional view of stress that proposes that two individuals might perceive the same situation quite differently, and that consequently this might have different effects.

The transaction that occurs through appraisal is important to the complete model, and research that assumes a named event, for example the Olympics, presents the same meaning to all athletes, has significant limitations. Consider the difference between two hypothetical athletes, one of whom is returning to the Olympics as a reigning champion and clear favourite who has competed at the top level for ten years, whereas the other athlete is a complete newcomer to international-level competition, a surprise selection with no previous form or expectation about their performance. It would seem likely that the relational meaning of competing in the Olympics might be very different to each of these athletes. For the first athlete there might be pressure to perform and maintain the existing position as world number one, as was found in a study on successful athletes (Kreiner-Phillips and Orlick, 1993). The situation might present little opportunity to increase standing but represent a real threat of losing that position. In contrast, the inexperienced performer might be more likely to perceive the situation as one in which there was little to lose (low threat) and everything to gain (challenge). That an event can be appraised quite differently and represent two different meanings to two performers, demonstrates the crucial role appraisal has in relation to emotion and coping. Research designs that assume that an event (such as the Olympics) or an overt outcome (such as win/loss, or a medal) represent similar experiences to participants are inherently flawed.

The position of the psycho–physiological stress state is also different from other, more linear models. In this model it is not placed between appraisal and coping but is influenced by many factors within the model. Also included within the model is a 'no coping' option that might follow from appraising that a situation is not relevant and requires no response. No coping is categorically distinct from any coping, which most definitions agree involves 'effort'. Finally, it is clear from the literature that dimensions of personality are likely to affect all stages of this model (see Table 1.1 for examples and suggested elements of the model to which they are thought to relate).

Recent empirical research on the two main approaches to coping in sport, style and process, is discussed in the following sections, leading to the progressive view that reconciliation between these approaches is possible, justified and necessary to develop our understanding of coping. However, before moving to this section, we also need to answer the question of what it is exactly that sports individuals are coping with. The answer lies in the relationship between coping and emotion.

Coping and emotion

The unique focus of this book is that coping and emotion in sport are considered throughout in relation to each other. Relating coping with emotion is not a new concept; Folkman and Lazarus (1988) stated that coping affects emotion just as emotion affects coping. Furthermore in his cognitive-motivational-relational theory (CMR) of emotion, Lazarus (1999) presents emotion as the 'superordinate system that includes motivation (an individual's goals), appraisal, stress, emotion and coping as component parts', and continued by emphasizing that 'coping, along with appraisal is, in effect, a mediator of the emotional reaction' (p. 101).

A further link between emotion and coping is also apparent in relation to different types of coping. One distinction found in the coping literature (Folkman and Lazarus, 1985) is between coping responses designed to deal with the problem or to address emotions. However, some authors (Cox and Ferguson, 1991) perceive

TABLE 1.1 Examples of influence of specific personality variables on different components of the model of appraisal, coping and emotion in sport

Component	Personality variables	Theoretical link
Perceived demands	Repression Trait-anxiety	Repressors show different attentional patterns to threatening stimuli from non-repressors (Langens and Mörth, 2003). Trait-anxious more likely to interpret neutral stimuli negatively (Eysenck, 1997).
Appraisal	Optimism Locus of control	Positive expectancies and perception that one can influence situation influence decisions on coping (Cox and Ferguson, 1991; Grove and Heard, 1997).
Psycho-physiological stress state	Trait-anxiety	Heightened response in stressful situations (Eysenck, 1992).
Emotion	Emotional control	Differentiated emotional response (Roger and Najarian, 1989).
Coping	Learned resourcefulness	Propensity to delay gratification and to maintain coping efforts for longer term gains (Rosenbaum, 1988).

that addressing emotion is the primary purpose of all coping efforts, making the link between coping and emotion relevant to all instances of coping. Empirical support for the relationship between coping and emotion was provided by Pensgaard and Duda (2003), who found that the coping effectiveness reported by Olympic athletes was significantly and positively related to positive emotions.

A final link between emotion and coping is based on shared resources. The focus of coping in this chapter is on voluntary, conscious and effortful responses. Coping responses, defined in these terms, demand mental activity that must take place within the architecture of a cognitive processing system such as working memory (assumed to take place primarily in the prefrontal cortices; Kane and Engle, 2005). Furthermore this activity also places demand on resources necessary for controlling (selecting) attention and resisting interference (Jonides and Nee, 2006). Theoretical and empirical evidence links both coping responses and emotion to the same expendable psychological resource, usually considered in relation to self-regulation (Baumeister and Heatherton, 1996; Richards and Gross, 2000). What this means in practice is that a performer who experiences emotion, such as frustration due to their immediate goals being blocked, has reduced resources available to cope with subsequent situations.

Therefore the relation between coping and emotion can be considered to be multifaceted. There is a theoretical link through the hypothesized process combining coping, appraisal and emotion that suggests coping impacts on emotion and that emotion, through perception, impacts on coping (Folkman and Lazarus, 1988; Lazarus, 1999). Coping is also linked to emotion, as empirical evidence shows that emotion is a primary orientation for coping efforts (Folkman and Lazarus, 1985; Cox and Ferguson, 1991). Finally empirical evidence supports the view that both coping responses and emotional regulation are connected in that they draw on a single psychological resource. Interdependence occurs because this resource is limited, and depletion, through any activity such as emotional control, physical effort, thought control, persistence or suppression, will temporarily reduce ability in any subsequent attempts that also make demands on the same resource (Schmeichel and Baumeister, 2004).

Recognizing the interrelationship between coping and emotion is important to provide a realistic understanding of the performer's coping responses. Although very commonly associated with stress and anxiety, coping may occur in relation to any kind of emotion. A performer whose competition requires travelling around the world may have to cope with feeling homesick, lonely and sad, whilst another performer may have to cope with feelings of guilt and responsibility if they believe their opportunity for success has been underpinned by sacrifices made by parents and family. Similarly performers may experience boredom in the holding camp before a major games, endure the relentless monotony of off-season heavy training blocks or frustration of failing to reach performance standards, which may all require coping. The content of coping, what performers actually report doing to cope, is examined in the next section, which reviews research that has adopted a perspective of coping as a process.

The coping process

The coping process approach, which is the dominant perspective held by sports psychology research (Nicholls and Polman, 2007; Gaudreau, Nicholls and Levy, 2010; Richards, 2011), views coping as a dynamic event in which deliberate, conscious attempts at coping are made in response to perceived demands. The empirical basis for the process perspective emanated from the work of Folkman and Lazarus (1985), who found self-report coping was different before and after an exam and at a third point after exam results were posted. They argued that the changes in responses confirmed that coping was a dynamic changing *process*.

Gaudreau, Lapierre and Blondin (2001) mirrored this design, measuring coping at 2 hours prior to, and 1 and 24 hours after, a golf competition. They found coping changes across time in the use of six of the twelve strategies that were measured. In finding evidence of coping changes, measurements in these two studies occurred at the same time as the context and nature of the situation across the three time points changed. This suggests an alternative explanation for the findings. The principle of Occam's razor, a scientific rule of thumb, proposes that the simplest explanation should be considered most likely. In these studies the most straightforward reason for the changes in coping was that the situation had changed. For example, Folkman and Lazarus (1985) found that self-isolation decreased from before the exam to after. With no more revision to do this would seem quite logical. Using this evidence to support a theoretical view that coping is naturally dynamic and changing ignores the simple and logical alternative explanation.

Across these two studies it is really only the changes in coping found between 1 hour-post and 24 hours-post a golf competition, where there was relatively little unchanged in the context of the situation, which is genuinely supportive of a process perspective. Noting the extent to which different coping behaviours were used at the different times, Gaudreau et al. (2001) concluded that the data showed partial support for the process approach to coping. However, their analysis also demonstrated some support for individual consistency or the existence of a coping style, in that each athlete retained the same relative position in the group with respect to the extent to which they used a specific coping behaviour.

A further research design issue is of importance here. Gaudreau et al. found golfers reported using more behavioural disengagement (for instance, 'I gave up trying to get what I want out of my performance') during competition than before or in the 24 hours after competition. They suggested that a golfer playing below desired levels might attempt to disengage from their goal in order to lessen negative emotions. However, it is unlikely that all of the golfers assessed were dissatisfied with their performance, and it would be theoretically inconsistent for golfers who performed well to score highly on behavioural disengagement. The finding is probably due to those golfers who under-performed scoring very highly on behavioural disengagement and skewing the group score. The problem is that aggregating all participants' coping responses, when they might be cognitively appraising situations differently and consequently experiencing different emotions, is a flawed approach to understanding coping. Analysing the coping of a group without considering what they were coping with may obscure significant patterns of behaviour.

The coping process perspective has received wide support from studies using qualitative analysis of interviews with performers. For example Gould et al. (1993a) found Olympic wrestlers used combinations of coping, sometimes targeted to more than one aim, supporting a process approach. Further retrospective interview data, supportive of a coping process perspective, has been found with US national figure skaters coping with the rigours of training and competition (Gould, Finch, and Jackson, 1993b), the US alpine and freestyle ski team's coping with season-ending injuries (Gould et al., 1997), Australian Olympic medallists coping with success (Jackson, Mayocchi and Dover, 1998), elite US decathletes coping with competition (Dale, 2000), Korean national athletes coping with national level status (Park, 2000), female soccer players coping with the World Cup finals (Holt and Hogg, 2002) elite athletes and performing artists coping with failure and success

(Poczwardowski and Conroy, 2002), and in non-elite golfers (Giacobbi, Foore and Weinberg, 2004).

Nicholls et al. (2005b) used a diary method, which overcomes the limitations of retrospective recall, with eleven adolescent golfers over thirty-one days, and found forty different coping responses to stressors. Interestingly just four stressors accounted for 75 per cent of the total reported stressors. With a small number of stressors but large variety in coping, the evidence for coping as a dynamic, changing process is strong. Extended diary data across a season with female adolescent basketball players further supports the process view of coping. Tamminen and Holt (2010) found 'multiple coping responses that were mixed and selectively applied ... to deal with stressors' (p. 112).

While these studies provide confirmatory support for the process approach, they were not designed specifically to test it by uncovering patterns of coping responses consistent with the coping style approach. Much of the early work was characterized by a perception that a named event, for example the Olympics, presented the same meaning to all athletes. Given the transactional model of stress and the central role of appraisal described previously in this chapter, this perception is incorrect, and to find different coping occurring when appraisal also might be different is weak evidence of process. More recently researchers have tried to make sure coping responses have been assessed in relation to specific stressors (Nicholls et al., 2007). It is perhaps even more informative when research directly assesses the relationship between appraisal and coping. Gaudreau and Blondin (2004) found quantitative data that athletes (N = 148) reporting high task-oriented coping had significantly greater 'experience of control' than either athletes who reported high use of all types of coping, or athletes who just reported high disengagement coping.

A critical aspect of the appraisal model is that coping is influenced by the perceived demands of the situation. Whilst it seems self-evident that athletes will perceive situations differently from each other, research has suggested that certain situational features are likely to elicit certain types of coping behaviour more than others. For example, Dugdale, Eklund and Gordon (2002) found that athletes competing at the 1998 Commonwealth Games who experienced unexpected stressors appraised them as more threatening and were more likely to hold back from a desired course of action than athletes who experienced expected stressors. It is important to note that Dugdale et al. (2002) grouped situations based on how athletes perceived them (expected or unexpected). This approach would appear to be more logical with respect to the transactional model of appraisal than would grouping situations on the basis of external, objective names or classes (such as poor officiating).

One further important issue emanating from the existing research on coping is the relevance of cultural influences on coping behaviour. Yoo (2001) identified *transcendental control* as a 'culturally specific psychological control mechanism used by Koreans when dealing with adversity' (p. 291). Evidence of these differences resulting from cultural influences and from the perceived nature of the stressor (for instance, unexpected) point to the types of situational characteristics that may offer some positive contribution in interpreting the coping research data.

To date, research on the coping process in sport has been generally confirmatory. Athletes have reported using different coping responses over time and across situations, and successful athletes report having well-practised skills. Furthermore coping responses may be used in combination and applied flexibly to a single stressor. Finally different coping responses may have differential impact on outcomes since an athlete may use some strategies regularly but might have used a specific strategy once to win a competition. Simple Likert scales will not easily determine the balance between frequency of use versus importance, and so this data collection method limits knowledge development of coping. Although there is clearly strong support for viewing coping as a process, some studies have found evidence of consistent patterns either in the relative amounts of coping behaviours used across time (e.g. Gaudreau et al., 2001) or in situations where stressors were likely to be very stable, such as training (e.g. Crocker and Isaak, 1997). Consistency of coping behaviour across time or situation lends some credence to the view that individuals may have particular coping styles.

Coping style

Traditionally, psychological research has examined coping style by two means. The first dichotomously groups individuals based on the way in which they deal with or perceive information, to see if such groupings reflect stylistic patterns of coping. Of all the perceptual styles (see Aldwin, 1994, for more in-depth coverage of different styles), 'blunting–monitoring' (Miller, 1980, cited in Aldwin, 1994) and 'approach-avoidance' (Roth and Cohen, 1986, cited in Aldwin, 1994) have been examined in the sport psychology literature. Anshel and Kaissidis (1997) assessed the coping style (monitoring–blunting) of male and female basketball players, and examined whether this style influenced the type of coping behaviour (classified as approach or avoidance) that was selected in response to four game-relevant, hypothetical stressful events. A blunting style is one in which an individual avoids information relating to the source of stress, whilst a monitoring style is one in which an individual 'is alert for and sensitised to threat-relevant information' (Kaissidis-Rodafinos et al., 1997, p. 428). Overall, in response to the selected stressful situations they found that basketball players used more approach than avoidance coping, but noted that participants used more avoidance strategies when perceived control over the situation was low, such as when receiving a bad call from the referee.

Although participants reported using more approach coping, there was little consistency in coping behaviour across situations. Individuals identified as predisposed to 'monitoring' tended to employ approach coping, whereas individuals predisposed towards 'blunting' used more avoidance coping. However, when they examined the relative contribution of situational and personal factors in determining coping, Anshel and Kaissidis (1997) found that whilst both contributed significantly, 69 per cent and 31 per cent respectively, situational factors were much better predictors of coping behaviour, which suggests the style difference of monitoring–

blunting was not the most significant factor in determining coping. Situation and preferred style influenced coping independently, and so the data supported an additive model, with each factor influencing coping directly and independently.

In this study participants were asked to indicate the extent to which they would use a limited number (five or eight) of coping responses in three or four specific situations, for example, 'receiving a bad call from a referee'. However in real situations differences in perceptual style might mean players would perceive and therefore experience situations differently, and this might impact on their coping responses. In this design in which the situations were clearly delineated by the researcher, there is much less opportunity for differences associated with perceptual style to be revealed. Finally, asking how a hypothetical situation would be coped with may bear little relevance to real coping response under pressure.

Anshel and Weinberg (1999) investigated whether a transactional model, emphasizing the influence of the situation, was better than a trait/dispositional model in determining coping behaviour. Basketball referees' coping responses to fourteen situations, previously identified as sources of stress, were content-analysed as approach or avoidant coping. Results showed coping style differed across different situations. The referees employed an approach style in response to controllable stressors and an avoidance style in response to situations low in controllability. Anshel and Weinberg (1999) suggested that either approach or avoidance coping style could be 'employed' by an individual according to the situation. The results of this study are more in keeping with discussing approach and avoidance as types of coping responses (or strategy) rather than as predisposing personality styles.

Giacobbi and Weinberg (2000) examined whether trait anxiety might influence whether athletes adopt stylistic patterns of coping response. Coping responses of 273 college athletes were measured three times using varied stems (instructions) on the same scale, once asking respondents 'what they usually do' (trait), and twice asking them to select situations they had really experienced from a list of common athletic encounters (state 1 and 2). In contrast with studies by Anshel and colleagues discussed previously, Giacobbi and Weinberg (2000) found moderate to high correlations between trait reports and state responses to the two specific situations.

The authors recognized the weakness of retrospective assessment because respondents asked about their coping in relation to a specific event (state) may actually have aggregated how they usually coped with this kind of event – in effect producing a situation-specific trait-like response and increasing the likelihood of a correlation with reports of non-specific generalized coping. Although this issue was raised as a difficulty with the study, the concept of situation-specific style may actually provide the solution to the style/process issue. Giacobbi and Weinberg (2000) acknowledged the perennial problem of retrospective reports associated with recall bias and errors, and recommended that repeated measures of coping are made as close to events as possible to increase the validity of investigations into coping. A final methodological confound in this study is that individual athletes' potentially different appraisals of the stressful encounters presented were not known.

The evidence regarding coping style is mixed, as Ptacek, Pierce and Thompson (2006) comment: 'although evidence for temporal and cross-situational consistency in coping is not compelling, neither is it totally lacking' (p. 1138). In their non-sport study with ninety-three university students, measures of trait coping were correlated with specific coping responses reported weekly, for ten weeks in response to the most stressful event of the week. They found significant correlations between dispositional coping and coping responses *aggregated* across six weeks. They argued that the limitation of coping style research is that it has not considered an aggregation of real coping responses. In other words coping style is unlikely to accurately predict a single specific instance of coping, but it does predict aggregations of responses.

An interesting addition to the measurement of coping style is that Ptacek et al. (2006) found a higher overall correlation between two aggregates formed from two randomly selected sets of three-week responses. The aggregate from one set of three weeks correlated more highly with the aggregate from the other set of three than did self-reports of coping style. The old adage in psychology, that the best predictor of behaviour is past behaviour, seems to hold in this case. Ptacek et al. (2006) suggest that coping style may be better determined by assessing real situation-specific coping responses repeatedly, over time, than by a single dispositional questionnaire.

The limitations of measuring coping style with a single self-report are also highlighted by Aldwin (1994), who suggested that there are 'concerns over whether individualised generalized descriptions of coping style actually describe specific coping behaviours' (p. 112) because people typically overestimate their ability to employ responses that they think are socially desirable. Aldwin also suggests that difficulty in establishing whether predictable patterns of coping behaviour exist might be due to applying incorrect levels of analysis. Attempts to predict specific coping responses are too specific and should instead look to predict general types of coping from broad identified styles.

Emanating from the work of Lazarus and Folkman (1984), one of the oldest typologies of coping is that of problem-oriented and emotion-oriented coping. It is often the case that problem-oriented coping is implicitly considered to be a more beneficial approach, even though it was not originally considered that one type of coping is better than the other. Furthermore comparing the two types of coping against each other ignores the fact that they were not proposed to occur independently from each other (most coping responses involve some of each).

Aldwin (1994) and Cox and Ferguson (1991) have suggested that the dichotomy of problem and emotion orientation is too simplistic and seemingly incomplete to offer any further contribution to analysing coping. Moos and Bilings (1982) and Pearlin and Schooler (1978) both suggested an appraisal (or re-appraisal) classification is added to the existing emotion- and problem-focused classifications. Endler and Parker (1990) suggested an alternative to the original classification, which included task-oriented (equivalent to problem-focused) and emotion-oriented (equivalent to emotion-focused), and added a third classification termed avoidance.

Avoidance coping might be very pertinent for sport because competitive stressors peak suddenly prior to the onset of an event and in many cases dissipate once the performance has begun. An athlete who can avoid the stressor for a short duration, knowing it will dissipate shortly afterwards, will experience less stress. Even during the event, avoidance coping can be effective. Krohne and Hindel (1988) found elite table-tennis players using cognitive avoidance experienced less anxiety and won more tie-breaks than players who did not use this strategy.

More recently it has been recommended by Skinner et al. (2003) that the dichotomous classifications of coping (problem–emotion, approach–avoid and cognitive–behavioural) should no longer be used, and instead thirteen families of coping were identified through confirmatory factor analysis on 400 ways of coping. The authors suggest that coping responds to situations and could be triggered by a) threat or challenge to competence, b) threat or challenge to attachment, or c) appraisal of autonomy. Furthermore the analysis supported a hierarchical multidimensional model of coping, with the distinction between engagement and disengagement coping at its apex (Carver and Connor-Smith, 2010; Connor-Smith and Flachsbart, 2007). There is a need therefore for sport coping research to move away from using categorisations that do not have empirical support.

Reconciling process and style approaches

Whilst both style and process approaches have been applied to research on coping in sport, recent systematic review shows that the significant majority of studies support a process approach (Nicholls and Polman, 2007). In part the reason for this is the inability of the style approach to empirically identify stable patterns of coping behaviour. This may be a failure in designs to adequately assess the appraised meaning of situations, instead assuming that named events can be considered equivalent to each other. For example, in their study on young competitive swimmers, Crocker and Isaak (1997) assessed coping behaviours across three different competitions and training sessions. Overall they found a degree of consistency in coping with training, perhaps not surprising if the training sessions were very similar, held in the same place with the same coach, and represented a single phase of the training programme. In contrast they found little consistency in the use of coping behaviours in competition, where perceived demands of each competition might vary in relation to importance, level of other competitors, and presence of significant others. Thus this explanation could be encapsulated within the idea of the relational meaning of an event (Lazarus, 2000). Crocker and Isaak concluded that the varied pattern of coping used in the three competitions provides evidence against the idea of coping styles. Inherent within this conclusion is the assumption that if a stylistic preference for coping did exist, it would emerge for every swimming meet. However, if each swimming meet had different relational meaning, then the meets cannot be assumed to be comparable to each other. The evidence from this study does not exclude the possibility that stylistic patterns of coping might still exist for swimming meets appraised as similar by these athletes.

Process and style approaches have often been set in opposition. However, even ardent advocates of a process approach to coping concede that process and style approaches 'are two sides of the same coin and both sides are usually relevant' (Lazarus, 1993, p. 236). The arguments against coping style are the same that have been offered against personality in general, which are centred around the paradox that the theory assumes distinctive qualities of personality are invariant across situations, yet the data show considerable behavioural variation. The Cognitive Affective Personality System (CAPS: Mischel and Shoda, 1995) describes an approach to studying patterns of behaviour linked coherently to elements of personality. An important feature of this theory is defining situations based not on nominal terms but on their psychological features as perceived by the individual concerned. This idea matches discussions put forward earlier in this chapter and elsewhere about the need to assess the way in which situations are appraised (e.g. Anshel, Jamieson and Raviv, 2001; Dugdale et al., 2002) and their relational meaning to the individual (Lazarus, 2000). Discussion in this chapter has identified that when individuals appraise situations, important psychological features are salient in influencing coping behaviour, including whether it was expected, whether it can be controlled or influenced, and whether it will be of short or long duration.

Mischel and Shoda (1995) presented data from a study on children in a summer camp showing intra-individual situation–behaviour profiles have stability across time but individuals do not behave in the same way in situations with different psychological features. Interpretation of, and emotional reaction to, situations are all components of describing the features of the situation, and are essential to understanding the meaning it has and consequently explaining observed behaviour. Psychological features of the situation then interact with the personality system, which is described as comprising cognitive-affective units which are one of five types: encodings, expectancies and beliefs, affects, goals and values, and competencies and self-regulatory plans. The cognitive-affective units become differentially activated by the situation. For example, during regular competition an athlete may have cognitive-affective units activated that concern their desired performance goals and plans to achieve these based on their *competencies*. If, however, an opponent were to commit an illegal and dangerous tackle, this change to the psychological features of the situation may activate their *expectancies* about what is acceptable in the sport and *beliefs* about what justice would be appropriate for the perpetrator. These changes to the psychological features of the situation would be likely to elicit two quite different sets of appraisal, coping and emotion.

The cognitive-affective theory is a significant development in explaining how stable units of personality are differentially activated by psychological features of the perceived situation to produce varied behaviours. However, the potential of this theoretical approach to studying coping in sport has not been realized. Recently Smith (2006) outlined how the CAPS approach could be used in sport research.

However he acknowledged many of the challenges including high complexity, limitations of statistical analysis, a focus on ideographic research (which might be afforded less weight than nomothetic research) and problems in determining psychological features of situations. Nevertheless this theory allows for a conceptualization of coping as dynamic and changeable between situations, as the research adopting a process approach has suggested, whilst at the same time recognizing that stable cognitive-affective units exist and that these influence the production of signature coping responses when psychological features are matched.

Coping and self-regulation

The process of coping has been defined as one that is deliberate (Kowalski and Crocker, 2001), effortful (Lazarus and Folkman, 1984), and is a consciously aimed response (Snyder and Dinoff, 1999). As such the cognitive activity of processing information, identifying if any response is required, deciding and selecting a response, and then enacting coping, must be considered essential mental activity that lies behind the appraisal and coping stages of the model shown in Figure 1.1. This background mental activity that takes place when a performer decides to cope can be best explained using the concept of self-regulation. Self-regulation is defined as 'self generated thoughts, feelings and actions that are strategically planned and adapted to the attainment of personal goals' (Zimmerman, 2006, p. 705), with cyclical feedback used to improve future performance. Early work in this area was based on the self-control model (Carver and Scheier, 1981, 1983), explained through cybernetic analogies such as thermostats. Self-regulation was proposed to operate through a negative feedback system in which inputted information (monitoring room temperature) was compared against a preordained target or benchmark (desired heat setting). Any mismatch (room too cold) would prompt a response (boiler on) and repeated monitoring would continue until the mismatch was removed and response action could cease (boiler switch off). This cyclical process is described as a negative feedback loop to emphasize that the regulation is aimed at reducing the discrepancy between perceived and desired states.

A case study of a world-class rugby union place kicker (Jackson and Baker, 2001) provides an example through qualitative analysis of the content of thought processes during kicking. This revealed that although the timing of routine changed with increased difficulty, the kicker was unaware of this and so this was not deliberate coping. His use of mental strategies, including deep breaths to relax, visualizing kicking without a crowd to block out this source of stress, and thought stopping, was under self-regulatory control. As the performer reported, 'I don't always do it because if things are going well … I've just got to keep going' (Jackson and Baker, 2001, p. 62). The comment reflects that the kicker has a *comparator* in order to recognize and respond when a discrepancy (negative feedback) occurs. This exemplifies good coping where basic coping skills, a well-learned routine, are combined with self-regulation that provides superordinate control – *'checks and corrects'* – as skill is deployed. Flexible coping (Cheng, 2001; Ptacek et al., 2006) is an effective approach to match coping to the constraints and appraisal of a situation. Furthermore flexible coping might provide a better assessment of coping ability and effectiveness than any of the typology-based approaches that have seen one type of coping type (task-oriented) recommended over others (Gaudreau et al., 2010).

Human-as-machine analogies are limited because humans have emotions and biases in perception and interpretation. Furthermore a thermostat works automatically without thought, but coping as defined earlier requires conscious cognition (Cox and Ferguson, 1991). A more 'humanized' version of the control model incorporating these limitations is shown in Figure 1.2. The model includes perceived information entering as input (subject to biases), and output selection, distinct from enacting the response, reflecting choices made in coping responses beyond the 'on–off' option from the thermostat analogy.

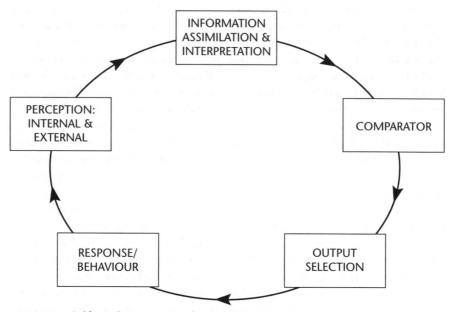

FIGURE 1.2 Self-regulation process for describing coping activity

The relationship between self-regulation and coping has been advocated by Baumeister and colleagues (Baumeister, Faber and Wallace, 1999; Muraven and Baumeister, 2000; Schmeichel and Baumeister, 1994), who propose that coping consumes self-regulatory resources, which are limited and become depleted. This weakens the ability to self-regulate until the resource has time to replenish. Schmeichel and Baumeister (2004) link activities of self-regulation to executive functions usually considered the preserve of cognitive and neuro-psychology. Specifically they suggest that to self-regulate a person must use executive abilities of planning and problem-solving, attentional switching and control, ignoring distraction, troubleshooting and performing novel tasks. This list of executive functions relates to the kinds of coping strategies assessed by validated coping questionnaires such as *effort* and *thought control* (from 'Coping inventory for competitive sport': Gaudreau, El Ali, and Marivain, 2005), and *suppression of competing activities* and *planning* (from MCOPE: Crocker and Graham, 1995).

The model of self-regulation (Figure 1.2) is also well suited to explain how self-regulatory failure might result in an athlete failing to cope. For example an athlete might fail to recognize their emotional state in the lead up to an event and once the event starts realize that they feel sluggish and slow. Here the error is in the perception phase. Alternatively an athlete just returning from injury may feel frustrated with their performance level and push too hard, because they have adopted an inappropriate comparator that does not accurately reflect their training and rehabilitation status. Detecting errors in self-regulation also leads to applied interventions – in the example above by readjusting goals to be more realistic.

Training on coping

The literature on coping in both sport and non-sport settings is dominated with research that helps us understand coping and to some extent predict it. Empirical information about interventions is scarce. This is a serious limitation in the current knowledge of sports-specific coping. Careful consideration of the limited pool of evidence does suggest some general principles to guide application and research.

When performers take action or control thoughts to cope with demanding situations, the things they think or do usually fall under the list of strategies discussed earlier, which are included in many mental skills programmes. Anshel (1990) trained college tennis players to cope with acute stress, and is a rare example of evidence-based information on coping training. Anshel lists a range of strategies that formed the content of coping training, from attribution training through imagery to assertiveness and relaxation. Strategies were applied according to a framework described by the mnemonic acronym COPE, which had four stages: Control emotions, Organize input, Plan response and Execute. Cognitive-behavioural strategies, learned in six sessions over three weeks, and used at each of the four stages of the COPE framework, were found to have a significant positive effect on performance and to reduce negative affect.

To cope effectively performers must know how to cope and have learned and practised the skills so they can be deployed reliably under serious competition pressure. Learning skills is familiar to performers and their coaches, and cognitive skills (such as cognitive restructuring) and physical skills (such as tennis serve) share many training principles (Rosenbaum et al., 2006; Rosenbaum, Carlson and Gilmore, 2001).

The basis of training lies in three elements: instruction, practice and feedback. The extensive literature on motor-control and learning (see Schmidt and Bjork, 1992, for a summary of key practice issues) provides excellent guidance on how these can be applied to produce different learning effects as required. For example rooming inexperienced and experienced performers together can provide a model of good 'coping' associated with planning and preparation. Similarly coping 'homework' on cognitive restructuring can use distributed rather than massed practice to enhance learning and retention. Sports performers are familiar with these principles applied to physical training and so sport psychologists may find their client population easier to manage through practice and learning of cognitive skills than in other domains of applied psychology. Learning skills, with repeated cycles of practice and feedback, distinguish genuine coping training from education-based support programmes.

In addition to instruction, practice and feedback, coping training must have progression to prepare performers to use coping skills in stressful situations. Progressive exposure is the hallmark of stress inoculation training (Meichenbaum, 1977), which was designed originally as a psychotherapeutic procedure but has successfully been applied to physical performance. Mace and Carroll (1985) trained novice abseilers, progressing from ground level, to training suspended from gymnasium wall bars, to abseiling from the roof of a building, practising using learned positive self-instruction at each stage. Progression can be achieved by manipulating pressure derived from any of a number of sources such as time urgency, increased complexity, evaluation, mock and real competitions at lower levels, frustrations, fatigue by exertion, general fatigue and non–sport stressors. In short anything that might make the coping practice harder can be conceived of as a means of providing progression within training.

A second aspect that is often considered as a form of progression is simulation. In sport performance, the sources of pressure can be hard to recreate for training purposes. How do you simulate a crowd of 80,000 spectators? One option is to utilize visualization as a means to help performers envisage how the coping skills might operate under real competition (Suinn, 2005). In other domains such as the military, emergency medicine, fire fighting, rescue, armed police response, aircraft safety and oil, gas and nuclear industry safety, considerable expenditure is made to achieve degrees of simulation, often through technology and machine-based simulators. The effort and expenditure devoted to achieving simulation emphasizes just how important it is thought to be in improving transfer from practice to reality (see for example Pizzi, Goldfarb and Nash, 2006; Salas et al., 1999). However, few sports, Formula 1 being an example of an exception, have the finance or training numbers to warrant proper simulator development. Furthermore since teams in some sports are competitors there is no advantage to pooling resources to aid development. Where simulation is not easily achievable the fallback position must be careful progression, in which the perceptual and cognitive challenges that performers experience are identified and then recreated in training.

Feedback is imperative to learning, and should be provided beyond basic coping skill learning, extending into use in real situations. Coping skills need to be reviewed, modified and adapted to suit the performer. For example a preparation plan can be reviewed, 'weeded' for unnecessary content and checked for completeness. The ability to regain focus after an unexpected delay in performance can be gauged based on the subsequent performance. Feedback can be aimed at both whether the skill was correctly used and whether it had the desired effect. This is equivalent to feedback on the process of the skill and the outcome. Outcome, or effectiveness, will be covered in the next section. Feedback on the process calls for performers to develop their awareness to evaluate coping alongside the skilled performance itself. Training and performance diaries or logs that incorporate critical reflection on coping can be used to develop awareness. Performer-centred and preferably performer-led debriefing sessions can also help generate the required awareness of 'how it went'. Training takes time, and realistic expectations should be set concerning the acquisition of coping skills, their impact, and how easy they will be to use. Initially coping may be hard to use, have little impact, and require high effort. Like all skills it will become more consistent, effective and easy to do with repeated practice. Performers who understand this, and that coping training follows the stages of 'adopt, adapt, adept', are more likely to persist and develop a good level of coping skills.

Effectiveness of coping

Definitions of coping distinguish coping responses from the outcome of attempts at coping, therefore research includes all responses, not just those elements that were successful. Unsuccessful attempts are still considered to be coping, and are distinct from the absence of any coping attempts. However the main reason for studying coping is to understand what is effective, and when, in order to inform beneficial interventions (Folkman and Moskowitz, 2004), and recent studies acknowledge the importance of measuring effectiveness (Nicholls et al., 2010). However, measuring effectiveness is not straightforward, and remains one of the most perplexing issues in coping research (Somerfield and McCrae, 2000).

Different approaches to assessing effectiveness of coping have been proposed and are briefly reviewed here. Originally, coping was dichotomized as adaptive or non-adaptive, terms used in animal studies where adaptation was construed in terms of biological survival. Effective adaptation was assessed in relation to physical health, illness and neuroendocrine markers (Steptoe, 1991). In sport, performance goals drive performers to undergo physical demands, and defining coping effectiveness based on biological adaptation is illogical. For example the most 'adaptive' coping behaviour for running a marathon would actually be to not run, save energy and physical resources, and avoid putting the whole system under stress. A better approach to coping effectiveness, adopted in the wider literature on coping, is to examine, in context, short and long-term outcomes.

Typically, research examining long-term outcome assesses general health indices, mood, satisfaction and well-being. However, sport coping research has predominantly focused on acute pressures in competition. Park (2000) emphasized the performance focus by defining effective coping as 'lessening anxiety, activating arousal or both for maintaining optimal performance' (p. 75). Whilst broad outcome measures such as health, well-being, satisfaction and mood might determine coping effectiveness in other domains, in sport these may be less important to athletes than achieving performance goals. In sport, long-term outcomes of coping responses have not been widely researched, although the stressors performers experience beyond competition, such as monotonous training, contract uncertainty, unfair management styles, travel and absence from family, have been recognized as significant career stressors that might be linked to some of the typical long-term outcome measures. In contrast to long-term outcomes, determining coping effectiveness based on short-term outcome considers whether coping alleviates the unpleasant emotion (including reducing duration or intensity) and/or addresses the specific problem. Ntoumanis and Biddle (1998) noted that sport research in this area was nonexistent. Currently the situation remains largely unchanged.

Most research addresses the complexity of measuring effectiveness simply by adding a Likert rating scale of effectiveness against reported coping responses (Nicholls and Polman 2007; Nicholls et al., 2009). Respondents are well placed to determine the effectiveness of their own coping, but what remains unknown from this measurement is what they were coping with. Grouping responses against labelled stressors, injury for example, does not reveal critical information concerning the individual's appraisal or significant contextual features. For example a player coping with injury by playing through, when they appraised it as not too serious or limiting to performance, and time left to play was short, might see this as effective. In contrast, appraising an injury as more serious, in terms of both limiting performance and increased potential damage, with significant performance time left, produces conditions under which the same coping (playing through) would be very ineffective. Without this detail, measurement of effectiveness is – ineffective.

In contrast to outcome approaches, the *goodness-of-fit approach* emphasizes that the quality of coping should be evaluated in terms of how well the coping response fits the appraised situation. This fit relates to both primary appraisal (was there a significant stressor?) and secondary appraisal (was it controllable?). A good fit is thought to occur when problem-oriented coping is selected when stressors are perceived as controllable, and emotion-oriented coping is used when stressors are uncontrollable. Although Kim and Duda (2003) found significant, but low magnitude, support for this model with a large cross-cultural (United States and Korea) sample of 722 athletes, they also concluded that the model needed more supporting evidence, challenging or modifying. Significantly they emphasized their support for Folkman's view that several approaches to evaluate effectiveness should be used.

An alternative to the goodness-of-fit approach is to consider certain types of coping to be more effective than others. Nicholls et al. (2010) have suggested, on the basis of evidence from their previous work, that task-oriented coping is more effective than distraction or disengagement-oriented coping. This view, favouring task or problem-oriented coping, is in accordance with culturally held and media-supported views of effective coping. However, whilst it can be easy to believe a view that conforms to a widely held norm, the quality of evidence supporting this is weakened by the absence of thorough measurement of coping effectiveness. For example when individual athletes are asked what coping responses were effective in relation to specific situations and performance goals, the data does not unequivocally support task-oriented coping. This was demonstrated by Nicholls et al. (2005a), who adopted an approach sensitive to individual experiences by interviewing eighteen golfers about coping in relation to handling competitive stressors either 'well' or 'not well'. Through qualitative analysis Nicholls et al. established that both emotion and problem-oriented coping were used. Surprisingly, rather more emotion than problem-oriented coping was associated with effective coping, and the reverse was true for ineffective coping. The authors recognized the need to understand the golfers' appraisals in order to fully explain what they were coping with, and emphasized the importance of measuring appraisal in future research to allow coping effectiveness to be evaluated. Appraisal is one of three important elements that need to be considered in determining effectiveness, as represented in Figure 1.3.

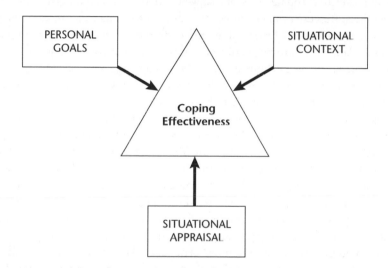

FIGURE 1.3 Factors required to determine effective coping in sport

The other two elements needed to judge effectiveness are knowledge about personal goals and the situational context. Situational context is important. If for example the stressor is of short duration, such as immediate pre-competition worry, avoidance might be very effective, but it would be much less so if worry occurs frequently. Equally, coping by accepting a frequently occurring stressor might not be as effective as resolving the problem itself. However, in a different situation, for example forced retirement, acceptance might be an essential component of effective coping. The importance of this aspect in determining coping effectiveness was emphasized by Folkman and Lazarus (1988), who advocated the 'goodness-of-fit' approach for effective coping, including both the individual's appraisal of the situation and the situational context.

It is also necessary to understand the personal goals of performers to frame judgements about coping effectiveness. Effective coping will help performers to meet specific personal goals that are not necessarily obvious ones such as winning or beating a personal best time. Goals, appraisal and situational context are all important to assess coping effectiveness, and measurement approaches that address this key issue thoroughly are necessary before evidence advocating specific coping strategies or types over others can be accumulated.

Determining effective coping should also avoid comparing mean effectiveness scores between different coping responses to different stressors (Nicholls et al., 2010). To evaluate the effectiveness of different coping responses it is necessary to compare how they are applied to same or equivalent stressors when appraisal was similar. With this level of information it would be possible to determine what coping responses are more effective than others. Current evidence that has not combined goals, personal appraisal and situational context to discriminate effective from non-effective coping does not support advocating certain types of coping above others. Because evidence shows that different coping responses are reported to be effective at different times and in different contexts, the empirically supported recommendation is to provide performers with a range of coping strategies. This is the position taken by Nicholls et al. (2006), who suggested practitioners teach three or four effective strategies including problem-focused, emotion-focused and avoidance, since all types are likely to have their uses.

This recommendation and the ambiguous evidence for effective coping raises one final point that is equally relevant to measuring and training effective coping, which relates to coping flexibility. In reviewing effective coping research, Folkman and Moskowitz (2004) emphasized the importance of flexible coping, where modifications to coping are made according to unfolding changes in the situation and appraisal. In non-sport research, flexible coping has been found to produce better strategy–situation fit, and greater effectiveness in using problem and emotion-oriented coping to achieve personal goals (Cheng, 2001). Flexible coping would require an individual to self-monitor, plan and take action to better adapt to circumstances, and so connects well with the earlier discussion on self-regulation and coping. Flexible coping is related to individual appraisal, particularly in relation to perceived controllability, and the variation in choice of coping that results from this. Current research has readily embraced the need to assess coping effectiveness. However, methods for assessing what coping works need to be enhanced to improve understanding and applied impact. These and other methodological and design issues are summarized in the final section of this chapter.

Sports coping research: issues of design and measurement

Throughout this chapter critical review of empirical research has identified several issues related to the design and measurement of coping. It is clear that further descriptions of the coping response of different groups of people (for example by age, sex, culture, ability or sport) using simple self-report questionnaires will serve little value. Equally the development of alternative measures with marginally better psychometric properties, or worded to suit specific situations, will do relatively little to advance sport coping research. In contrast future research that addressed some, or any, of the issues identified in the literature and summarized in this chapter, would help to significantly develop our knowledge of coping.

Issue 1: Appraisal and effectiveness

Early research in sport coping described coping in the absence of these two crucial pieces of information. Without knowing what performers were coping with, it was impossible to group findings together in a meaningful way. Two performers in the same situation but appraising it differently are not coping with the same experience, and might as well be in different situations. Sport-based research has devoted effort to describing coping across all kind of variables including age (Kristiansen and Roberts, 2010), skill level (Nicholls et al., 2007), gender (Anshel and Sutarso, 2007) culture (Yoo, 2001) sport type (cricket: Thelwell, Weston and Greenlees, 2007; golf: Giacobbi et al., 2004; rugby: Nicholls et al., 2006; volleyball: Holt, Berg and Tamminen, 2007), time (Gaudreau et al., 2001; Holt and Dunn, 2004), competition versus training (Nicholls et al., 2009), and success versus failure (Poczwardowski and Conroy, 2002). Some though by no means all have attempted to include an indication of what kinds or types of coping were effective. However, even with this vast knowledge describing coping there remains a significant gap when practising psychologists look to the research for guidance on how to help improve a performer's coping ability. There is also a limited value to generalized descriptions for applied sport psychology, where intervention works at an individualized level including individual assessment. It is unlikely that an intervention would be prescribed on the basis of general knowledge about coping by sport, age and gender when an interview with the client will provide precise and detailed information. The question 'What is the point of this research?' must be better answered through design, and research on the efficacy of interventions is perhaps the most pressing need for the future of sport coping research.

Issue 2: Retrospective information and questionnaires

There is a huge reliance in the literature on data that is collected retrospectively, with the time lapse between coping and recall in some cases being months. As time elapses memories will decay and possibly be recalled in biased ways according to outcomes or associated emotions. Furthermore data collected via questionnaire or checklist has limitations, including assessing only coping identified *a priori*, providing prompts that might lead responses, and being burdensome for frequent administration (Folkman and Moscowitz, 2004). Closing the gap between coping and reporting on that coping will be likely to improve accuracy, and if it is collected before a known outcome will avoid biases from this source. Coping diaries (Tamminen and Holt, 2010), think aloud protocols (Schomer, 1986) and momentary assessment have all been used in recent research, but these are still relatively unusual. More is needed.

Issue 3: Hypothetical and minimal coping

Some designs request respondents to report on coping with described situations. Even though the scenarios may have been identified as common stressors, it is not safe to assume that all respondents have actually experienced them. In essence these studies are asking respondents how they think they might respond to a situation they might not necessarily have experienced. The lack of real coping that is assessed in a design such as this leaves the data extremely weak because of very poor ecological validity. Other studies that have examined coping by diary have applied them to the season in the expectation that over its course, the respondents will be coping with *something*. The difficulty with this is that normal experiences may not really raise the need for coping so that it can be effectively studied. Without intense emotions such as stress, performers may be reporting 'coping' that is really relatively routine. Therefore coping research needs to distinguish times when respondents experience real pressure, where the outcome is personally salient, and consequently they have to use coping strategies as well as they can. Without these characteristics there is a risk that reported coping responses are just 'noise' in the data collection method.

Issue 4: Aggregation

Research design that aggregates reported coping from a sample of respondents often does not effectively account for underlying degrees of homogeneity or heterogeneity on relevant factors. Simple aggregation limits the ability to adequately investigate change or stability over time, since within the group these are often averaged out or masked. This issue is well demonstrated by Louvet et al. (2009), who used a statistical technique called 'latent class growth modelling' (LCGM) on 227 soccer referees coping at three times across the season. The LCGM identified different sub-groups for each of the three types of coping reported across the season, as can be seen in Figure 1.4.

The authors clearly illustrate the importance of avoiding the weak design of simple aggregations. For problem-focused coping the mean of the entire sample was 2.86, 2.82 and 2.84, for times 1, 2 and 3 respectively. This is essentially a straight line, and might suggest that all soccer referees use this consistently through the season. In contrast Figure 1.4 depicts five distinct sub-groups showing quite different trajectories across the season. This technique is just one that significantly advances research capacity and understanding.

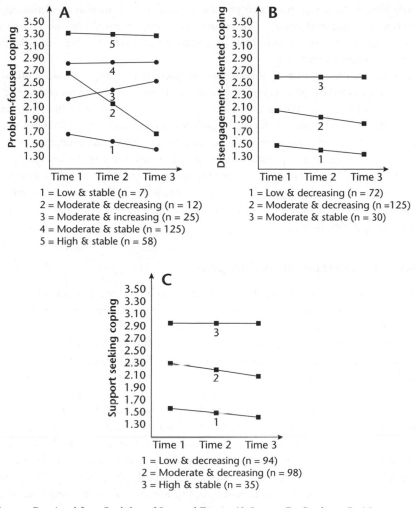

Source: Reprinted from *Psychology of Sport and Exercise*, 10, Louvet, B., Gaudreau, P., Menaut, A., Genty, J. and Deneuve, P. Revisiting the changing and stable properties of coping utilization using latent class growth analysis: a longitudinal investigation with soccer referees, 124-135, Copyright (2009), with permission from Elsevier.

FIGURE 1.4 Longitudinal trajectories of problem-focused, disengagement, and seeking support coping across three competitions

Issue 5: Ideographic versus nomothetic design

The issue of aggregation testifies to the potential limitation of failing to observe patterns in coping data. An alternative solution to more sophisticated statistical analysis is to use ideographic research techniques (Tennen et al., 2000). Holt and Dunn (2004) provided longitudinal analyses of appraisal and coping with four soccer players based on audio diary and interview data. Although such studies are clearly time-consuming, the value of such detailed data is to reveal relationships between appraisal and coping that recur and change throughout the six-week period. This relationship would have been difficult to establish using other design and measurement approaches.

An innovative alternative example of an ideographic approach to studying coping is provided by Nieuwenhuys, Hanin and Bakker (2008), who conducted a case study with an elite sailor and via semi-structured interviews were able to create composite sequence analyses for good and bad races, showing the connection, order of influence and effectiveness of in-competition experiences and coping. It is clear that an ideographic approach is essential to examine some of the key questions in sport coping, particularly with regard to patterns of stability and development. However there is a clear tension with such approaches in that they might fail to meet equivalent standards of scientific credibility, and be less publishable, because of limited generalizability.

Issue 6: Intervention versus description

There is very little recent published research outlining the efficacy of coping interventions based on knowledge about coping. Individual coping skills continue to be researched independently of coping specific theory or evidence. This criticism is not new to coping research, and Coyne and Racioppo (2000) were forthright in summing up their view of the mainstream psychology literature base: 'we are sceptical that the existing body of descriptive coping studies has made any significant, specific contribution to intervention research' (p. 658). It would seem that sport research has committed the same mistake, with relatively few empirical articles describing the procedure and outcome of interventions designed to enhance coping. Since the impact of and need for coping might vary dramatically between individuals, it may be that this issue relates to the ideographic one above. Nevertheless in order for the current knowledge to be properly extended to practical value, and to address more directly the issue of causality in terms of coping use and outcome, future research needs to adopt an intervention-based approach to investigating coping in sport.

Conclusion

From the discussion in this chapter, two main issues have emerged. First is the need for coping and emotion to be considered as constituent parts of an integrated process that includes appraisal. Research needs to progress from simply measuring aggregated coping responses of groups of athletes, and concurrently assess appraisal and the psychological features of the situation, which through identifying relational meaning, draws links to emotion. Research must also tackle the complexity of measuring coping effectiveness.

The second main issue concerns the idea that coping style and coping process can be reconciled within a single coherent framework by the cognitive-affective theory of personality presented by Mischel and Shoda (1995). Research on coping style has often been considered akin to traditional views of personality traits, and held to be the antithesis of a process approach, but this theory of personality incorporates both variation in behaviour (process) and stable elements of personality (style) that would allow some realistic predictive ability. Such prediction will come from building up intra-individual behaviour-situation profiles and then moving to identify individuals who share either common patterns of profiles or underlying cognitive-affective processing structures. The theory offers a much more sophisticated approach to understanding personality and behaviour. However, it is clear that research to achieve this requires lengthy periods of data collection, and the difficulties inherent in this may negatively impact on development in this area.

The chapter has also focused on two areas in which sport coping research can be developed. One is the clear theoretical overlap with work on self-regulation, which provides an effective organizing framework for training coping, identifying coping failures and explaining how it operates. The self-regulation construct is not just useful for applied and training purposes but also suggests some theoretical relationships that can be tested in research such as the resource depletion hypothesis. The second related area is the need for sport coping research to better reflect the close relationship with the practice of sport psychology, and to investigate the development of coping skills to contribute more effectively to the work of practitioners, coaches and athletes.

Finally, the research discussed in this chapter has identified a number of methodological issues for consideration in future research. These include advocating more ideographic approaches to research, adopting alternative approaches to data collection, and ensuring through design that real coping is reported on in response to meaningful, pressurized situations. As sport is often all about performance under pressure, there are many varied opportunities to further knowledge on this critical skill.

References

Aldwin, C. M. (1994). *Stress, coping and development: An integrated perspective.* New York: Guildford.

Anshell, M. H. (1990). Towards validation of a model of coping with acute stress in sport. *International Journal of Sport Psychology*, 21, 58–83.

Anshel, M. H. and Kaissidis, A. N. (1997). Coping style and situational appraisals as predictors of coping strategies following stressful events in sport as a function of gender and skill level. *British Journal of Psychology*, 88, 263–276.

Anshel, M. H. and Weinberg, R. S. (1999). Re-examining coping among basketball referees following stressful events: Implications for coping interventions. *Journal of Sport Behavior*, 22, 141–161.

Anshel, M. H., Jamieson, J. and Raviv, S. (2001). Cognitive appraisals and coping strategies following acute stress among skilled competitive male and female athletes. *Journal of Sport Behavior*, 24, 128–143.

Anshel, M. H. and Sutarso, T. (2007). Relationships between sources of acute stress and athletes' coping style in competitive sport as a function of gender. *Psychology of Sport and Exercise*, 8, 1–24.

Baumeister, R. F. and Heatherton, T. F. (1996). Self-regulation failure: An overview. *Psychological Inquiry,* 7, 1–15.

Baumeister, R. F., Faber, J. E. and Wallace, H. M. (1999). Coping and ego depletion: recovery after the coping process. In C. R. Snyder (ed.), *Coping: The psychology of what works.* New York: Oxford University Press.

Blascovich, J. (2008). Challenge and threat. In A. J. Elliot (ed.), *Handbook of approach and avoidance motivation* (pp. 431–45). New York: Psychology Press.

Carver, C. S. and Scheier, M. F. (1981). *Attention and self-regulation: A control-theory approach to human behavior.* New York: Springer-Verlag.

Carver, C. S. and Scheier, M. F. (1983). A control-theory approach to human behavior, and implications for problems in self-management. In P. C. Kendall (ed.), *Advances in cognitive-behavioral research and therapy* (Vol. 2, pp. 127–194). New York: Academic Press.

Carver, C. S., Scheier, M. F. and Weintraub, J. K. (1989). Assessing coping strategies: A theoretically based approach. *Journal of Personality and Social Psychology,* 56, 267–283.

Carver, C. S. and Connor-Smith, J. (2010). Personality and coping. *Annual Review of Psychology,* 61, 679–704.

Cheng, C. (2001). Assessing coping flexibility in real-life and laboratory settings: A multimethod approach. *Journal of Personality and Social Psychology,* 80, 814–833.

Connor-Smith, J. K. and Flachsbart, C. (2007). Relations between personality and coping: A meta-analysis. *Journal of Personality and Social Psychology,* 93, 1080–1107.

Cox, T. and Ferguson, E. (1991). Individual differences, stress and coping. In C. L. Cooper and R. Payne (eds), *Personality and stress: Individual differences in the stress process* (pp. 7–30). Chichester: John Wiley.

Coyne, J. C. and Racioppo, M. W. (2000). Never the twain shall meet? Closing the gap between coping research and clinical intervention research. *American Psychologist,* 55, 655–664.

Crocker, P. R. E. and Isaak, K. (1997). Coping during competitions and training sessions: Are youth swimmers consistent? *International Journal of Sport Psychology,* 28, 355–369.

Crocker, P. R. E. and Graham, T. R. (1995). Coping by competitive athletes with performance stress: Gender differences and relationships with affect. *Sport Psychologist,* 9, 325–338.

Dale, G. A. (2000). Distractions and coping strategies of elite decathletes during their most memorable performances. *Sport Psychologist,* 14, 17–41.

Dugdale, J. R., Eklund, R. C. and Gordon, S. (2002). Expected and unexpected stressors in major international competition: Appraisal, coping, and performance. *Sport Psychologist,* 16, 20–33.

Endler, N. and Parker, J. (1990). Multi-dimensional assessment of coping: A critical review. *Journal of Personality and Social Psychology,* 58, 844–854.

Eysenck, M. W. (1997). *Anxiety and cognition: A unified theory.* Hove UK: Psychology Press.

Folkman, S. and Lazarus, R. S. (1985). If it changes it must be a process: A study of emotion and coping during three stages of a college examination. *Journal of Personality and Social Psychology* 48, 150–170.

Folkman, S. and Lazarus, R. S. (1988). Coping as a mediator of emotion. *Journal of Personality and Social Psychology,* 54, 466–475.

Folkman, S. and Moskowitz, J. T. (2004). Coping: Pitfalls and promise. *Annual Review of Psychology,* 55, 745–774.

Gaudreau, P., Lapierre, A. M. and Blondin, J. P. (2001). Coping at three phases of a competition: Comparison between pre-competitive, competitive, and post-competitive utilization of the same strategy. *International Journal of Sport Psychology,* 32, 369–385.

Gaudreau, P. and Blondin, J. P. (2004). Different athletes cope differently during a sport competition: A cluster analysis of coping. *Personality and Individual Differences,* 36, 1865–1877.

Gaudreau, P., El Ali, M. and Marivain, T. (2005). Factor structure of the coping inventory for competitive sport with a sample of participants at the 2001 New York marathon. *Psychology of Sport and Exercise,* 6, 271–288.

Gaudreau, P., Nicholls, A. and Levy, A. R. (2010). The ups and downs of coping and sport achievement: An episodic process analysis of within-person associations. *Journal of Sport and Exercise Psychology*, 32, 298–311.

Giacobbi, P. R., Foore, B. and Weinberg, R. S. (2004). Broken clubs and expletives: The sources of stress and coping responses of skilled and moderately skilled golfers. *Journal of Applied Sport Psychology*, 16, 166–182.

Giacobbi, P. R. and Weinberg, R. S. (2000). An examination of coping in sports: Individual trait anxiety differences and situational consistency. *Sport Psychologist*, 14, 42–62.

Gould, D., Eklund, R. C. and Jackson, S. A. (1993a). Coping strategies used by U.S. Olympic wrestlers. *Research Quarterly for Exercise and Sport*, 64, 83–93.

Gould, D., Finch, L. M. and Jackson, S. A. (1993b). Coping strategies used by National Champion figure skaters. *Research Quarterly for Exercise and Sport*, 64, 453–468.

Gould, D., Udry, E., Bridges, D. and Beck, L. (1997). Coping with season-ending injuries. *Sport Psychologist*, 11, 379–399.

Grove, J. R. and Heard, N. P. (1997). Optimism and sport confidence as correlates of slump-related coping among athletes. *Sport Psychologist*, 11(4), 400–410.

Hardy, L., Jones, G. and Gould, D. (1996). *Understanding psychological preparation for sport: Theory and practice of elite performers*. Chichester UK: Wiley.

Hoar, S. D., Crocker, P. R. E., Holt, N. L. and Tamminen, K. A. (2010). Gender differences in adolescent athletes' coping with interpersonal stressors in sport: More similarities than differences? *Journal of Applied Sport Psychology*, 22, 134–149.

Holt, N. L. and Hogg, J. M. (2002). Perceptions of stress and coping during preparations for the 1999 women's soccer World Cup finals. *Sport Psychologist*, 16, 251–271.

Holt, N. L. and Dunn, J. G. H. (2004). Longitudinal idiographic analyses of appraisal and coping responses in sport. *Psychology of Sport and Exercise*, 5, 213–222.

Holt, N. L., Berg, K. J. and Tamminen, K. (2007). Tales of the unexpected: Coping among female collegiate volleyball players. *Research Quarterly for Exercise and Sport*, 78, 117–132.

Jackson, R. C. and Baker, J. S. (2001). Routines, rituals and rugby: Case study of a world-class goal kicker. *The Sport Psychologist*, 15, 48–65.

Jackson, S. A., Mayocchi, L. and Dover, J. (1998). Life after winning gold: II. Coping with change as an Olympic gold medallist. *Sport Psychologist*, 12, 137–155.

Jonides, J. and Nee, D. E. (2006). Brain mechanisms of proactive interference in working memory. *Neuroscience*, 139, 181–193.

Kaissidis-Rodafinos, A., Anshel, M. H. and Porter, A. (1997). Personal and situational factors that predict coping strategies for acute stress among basketball referees. *Journal of Sports Sciences*, 15, 427–436.

Kane, M. J. and Engle, R. W. (2002). The role of pre-frontal cortex in working memory capacity, executive attention, and general fluid intelligence: An individual differences perspective. *Psychonomic Bulletin and Review*, 9, 637–671.

Kim, M. S. and Duda, J. L. (2003). The coping process: Cognitive appraisals of stress, coping strategies and coping effectiveness. *The Sport Psychologist*, 17, 406–425.

Kowalski, K. C. and Crocker, P. R. E. (2001). Development and validation of the coping function questionnaire for adolescents in sport. *Journal of Sport and Exercise Psychology*, 23, 136–155.

Kreiner-Phillips, K. and Orlick, T. (1993). Winning after winning: The psychology of ongoing excellence. *Sport Psychologist*, 7, 31–48.

Kristiansen, E. and Roberts, G. C. (2010). Young elite athletes and social support: Coping with competitive organizational stress in Olympic competition. *Scandinavian Journal of Medicine and Science in Sports*, 20, 686–695.

Krohne, H. W. and Hindel, C. (1988). Trait anxiety, state anxiety, and coping behavior as predictors of athletic performance. *Anxiety Research*, 1, 225–234.

Langens, T. A. and Mörth, S. (2003). Repressive coping and the use of passive and active coping strategies. *Personality and Individual Differences*, 35(2), 461–473.

Lazarus, R. S. (1993). Coping theory and research: Past, present and future. *Psychosomatic Medicine*, 55, 234–247.

Lazarus, R. S. (1999). *Stress and emotion: A new synthesis*. New York: Springer.

Lazarus, R. S. (2000). How emotions influence performance in competitive sports. *The Sport Psychologist*, 14, 229–252.

Lazarus, R. S. and Folkman, S. (1984). *Stress appraisal and coping*. New York: Springer.

Louvet, B., Gaudreau, P., Menaut, A., Genty, J. and Deneuve, P. (2009). Revisiting the changing and stable properties of coping utilization using latent class growth analysis: A longitudinal investigation with soccer referees. *Psychology of Sport and Exercise*, 10, 124–135.

Mace, R. D. and Carroll, D. (1985). The control of anxiety in sport: Stress inoculation training prior to abseiling. *International Journal of Sport Psychology*, 16, 165–175.

Meichenbaum, D. H. (1977). *Cognitive behavior modification: An integrative approach*. New York: Plenum.

Mischel, W. and Schoda, Y. (1995). A cognitive-affective system theory of personality: Reconceptualizing situations, dispositions, dynamics, and invariance in personality structure. *Psychological Review*, 102, 246–268.

Moos, R. and Billings, A. (1982). Conceptualizing and measuring coping resources and processes. In L. Goldberger and S. Breznitz (eds), *Handbook of stress: Theoretical and clinical aspects*. New York: Free Press.

Muraven, M. and Baumeister, R. F. (2000). Self-regulation and depletion of limited resources: Does self-control resemble a muscle? *Psychological Bulletin*, 126, 247–259.

Nicholls, A. R., Holt, N. L. and Polman, R. C. J. (2005a). A phenomenological analysis of coping effectiveness in golf. *The Sport Psychologist*, 19, 111–130.

Nicholls, A. R., Holt, N. L., Polman, R. C. J. and James, D. W. G. (2005b). Stress and coping among international adolescent golfers. *Journal of Applied Sport Psychology*, 17, 333–340.

Nicholls, A. R., Holt, N. L., Polman, R. C. J. and Bloomfield, J. (2006). Stressors, coping, and coping effectiveness among professional rugby union players. *The Sport Psychologist*, 20, 314–329.

Nicholls, A. R. and Polman, R. C. J. (2007). Coping in sport: A systematic review. *Journal of Sports Sciences*, 25, 11–31.

Nicholls, A. R., Polman, R. C. J., Levy A. R., Taylor, J. and Cobley, S. (2007). Stressors, coping and coping effectiveness: Gender, type of sport and skill differences. *Journal of Sports Sciences*, 25, 1521–1530.

Nicholls, A. R., Polman, R. C. J., Morley, D. and Taylor, N. J. (2009). Coping and coping effectiveness in relation to a competitive sport event: Pubertal status, chronological age, and gender among adolescent athletes. *Journal of Sport and Exercise Psychology*, 31, 299–317.

Nicholls, A. R., Polman, R. C. J., Levy A. R. and Borkoles, E. (2010). The mediating role of coping: A cross-sectional analysis of the relationship between coping self-efficacy and coping effectiveness among athletes. *International Journal of Stress Management*, 17, 181–192.

Nieuwenhuys, A., Hanin, Y. L. and Bakker, F. C. (2008). Performance-related experiences and coping during races: A case of an elite sailor. *Psychology of Sport and Exercise*, 9, 61–76.

Ntoumanis, N. and Biddle, S. J. H. (1998). The relationship of coping and its perceived effectiveness to positive and negative affect in sport. *Personality and Individual Differences*, 24, 773–788.

Park, J. K. (2000). Coping strategies used by Korean national athletes. *Sport Psychologist*, 14, 63–80.

Pearlin, L. I. and Schooler, C. (1978). The structure of coping. *Journal of Health and Social Behavior*, 19, 2–21.

Pensgaard, A. M. and Duda, J. L. (2003). Sydney 2000: The interplay between emotions, coping and the performance of Olympic-level athletes. *The Sport Psychologist*, 17, 253–267.

Pizzi, L. Goldfarb, N. I. and Nash, D. B. Crew resource management and its application in medicine. http://www.ahrq.gov/clinic/ptsafety/chap44.htm [retrieved 25 Oct. 2006].

Poczwardowski, A. and Conroy, D. E. (2002). Coping responses to failure and success among elite athletes and performing artists. *Journal of Applied Sport Psychology*, 14, 313–329.

Ptacek, J. T., Pierce, G. R. and Thompson, E. L. (2006). Finding evidence of dispositional coping. *Journal of Research in Personality*, 40, 1137–1151.

Richards, H. (2004). Coping in sport. In D. Lavallee, J. Thatcher and M. V. Jones (eds), *Coping and emotion in sport*. New York: Nova.

Richards, H. (2011). Coping and mental toughness. In D. Collins, A. Button and H. Richards (eds), *Performance psychology: A practitioner's guide*. London: Elsevier.

Richards, J. M. and Gross, J. J. (2000). Emotion regulation and memory: The cognitive costs of keeping one's cool. *Journal of Personality and Social Psychology*, 79, 410–424.

Roger, D. and Najarian, B. (1989). The construction and validation of a new scale for measuring emotional control. *Personality and Individual Differences*, 10(8), 845-853.

Rosenbaum, D. A., Carlson, R. A. and Gilmore, R. O. (2001). Acquisition of intellectual and perceptual-motor skills. *Annual Review of Psychology*, 52, 453–470.

Rosenbaum, D. A., Augustyn, J. S., Cohen, R. G. and Jax, S. A. (2006). Perceptual motor expertise. In K. A. Ericsson, N. Charness, P. J. Feltovich and R. R. Hoffman (eds), *The Cambridge handbook of expertise and expert performance* (pp. 505–522). New York, NY: Cambridge University Press.

Rosenbaum, M. (1988). Learned resourcefulness, stress and self-regulation. In S. Fisher and J. Reason (Eds.), *Handbook of Life Stress, Cognition and Health* (pp. 483-493). Chichester: John Wiley.

Roth, S. and Cohen, L. J. (1986). Approach, avoidance and coping with stress. *American Psychologist*, 41, 813-819.

Salas, E., Prince, C., Bowers, C. A., Stout, R. J., Oser, R. L. and Cannon-Bowers, J. A. (1999). A methodology for enhancing crew resource management training. *Human Factors*, 41, 161–172.

Schmeichel, B. J. and Baumeister, R. F. (2004). Self-regulatory strength. In R. Baumeister and K. Vohs (eds), *Handbook of self-regulation: Research, theory and applications*. New York: Guildford Press.

Skinner, E. A., Edge, K., Altman, J. and Sherwood, H. (2003). Searching for the structure of coping: A review and critique of category systems for classifying ways of coping. *Psychological Bulletin*, 129, 216–269.

Schmidt, R. A. (1991). *Motor learning and performance: From principles to practice*. Champaign, IL: Human Kinetics.

Schmidt, R. A. and Bjork, R. A. (1992). New conceptualization of practice: Common principles in three paradigms suggest new concepts for training. *Psychological Science*, 3, 207–217.

Schomer, H. (1986). Mental strategies and the perception of effort of marathon runners. *International Journal of Sport Psychology*, 17, 41–59.

Smith, R. E. (2006). Understanding sport behavior: A cognitive-affective processing systems approach. *Journal of Applied Sport Psychology*, 18, 1–27.

Somerfield, M. R. and McCrae, R. R. (2000). Stress and coping research: Methodological challenges, theoretical advances, and clinical applications. *American Psychologist*, 55, 620–625.

Snyder, C. R. and Dinoff, B. L. (1999). Coping: Where have you been? In C. R. Snyder (ed.), *Coping: The psychology of what works* (pp. 3–19). New York: Oxford University Press.

Steptoe, A. (1991). Psychological coping, individual differences and physiological stress responses. In C. L. Cooper and R. Payne (eds), *Personality and stress: Individual differences in the stress process* (pp. 205–233). Chichester: John Wiley.

Suinn, R. (2005). Behavioral intervention of stress management in sports. *International Journal of Stress Management*, 12, 343–362.

Tamminen, K. A. and Holt, N. L. (2010). Female adolescents athletes' coping: A season-long investigation. *Journal of Sports Sciences*, 28, 101–114.

Tennen, H., Affleck, G., Armeli, S. and Carney, M. A. (2000). A daily process approach to coping: Linking theory research and practice. *American Psychologist*, 55, 626–636.

Thelwell, R. C., Weston, N. J. V. and Greenlees, I. A. (2007). Batting on a sticky wicket: Identifying sources of stress and associated coping responses for professional cricket batsmen. *Psychology of Sport and Exercise*, 8, 219–232.

Yoo, J. (2001). Coping profile of Korean competitive athletes. *International Journal of Sport Psychology*, 32, 290–303.

Zimmerman, B. J. (2006). Development and adaptation of expertise: The role of self-regulatory processes and beliefs. In K. A. Ericsson, N. Charness, P. J. Feltovich and R. R. Hoffman (eds), *The Cambridge handbook of expertise and expert performance*. New York: Cambridge University Press.

2

EMOTION IN SPORT

Antecedents and performance consequences

Marc Jones, Staffordshire University and
Mark Uphill, Canterbury Christ Church University

> My nerves were really bad when I got to the pool. I had to keep lying down because I thought I was going to be sick ... but as soon as you dive in, the only thing you think about is the strokes, consistency and telling yourself, 'Don't mess this up.'
>
> *Becky Adlington talking about how she felt before winning gold in the 800-metre freestyle in the 2008 Beijing Olympics (Adlington, 2008)*

Emotions pervade sport, and for psychologists, coaches, officials and athletes there is much to be gained by knowing how emotions arise and the impact they have on behaviour and ultimately performance. In the first part of this chapter we explore why athletes, coaches and officials respond emotionally in sport settings. Understanding how emotions arise can help psychologists in the development of strategies to help individuals to control emotions. The coping techniques outlined in the following chapters of this book provide an illustration of how this can be done. In the second part of this chapter we consider the processes by which emotions influence behaviour and sport performance. For example, we illustrate why a young soccer player who enjoys practice may attend more frequently, an anxious coach may influence their athletes' anxiety levels, and an injured official who feels dejected may not adhere to a rehabilitation programme.

Understanding emotion

Before considering how emotions arise it is necessary to define emotion. Yet defining emotion is a difficult task given the range and complexity of the different states (such as anger, happiness, anxiety, guilt) it must describe. Definitions however, are not invariant across time or theoretical orientation, but rather reflect a convention or points of convergence amongst experts (Ekkekakis and Petruzzello, 2000). Thus, although emotions seem to resist classical attempts at definition (Russell and Fehr, 1994), it is apparent that several distinctions have been made among cognitively oriented researchers.

What is an emotion?

Emotions are thought to be more transient and intense than moods (Jones, Mace and Williams, 2000), although the duration and magnitude of the emotional response are essentially descriptive markers (Davidson, 1994). A more accepted means of differentiating between mood and emotion is with regard to their respective antecedents. Specifically, although both mood and emotion are suggested to possess a cognitive origin (e.g. Lazarus, 1991), unlike emotion, mood is thought to lack a relationship with an object (Vallerand and Blanchard, 2000). An emotion can therefore be thought of as a response to an event or stimulus: for example, pride at winning a race, or happiness at making a free throw. In contrast mood is proposed to be a more enduring state where the individual does not know the causes of feelings experienced (Parkinson et al., 1996). While mood and emotion describe specific feeling states, affect is typically used in the literature as a broad term referring to all valenced responses including preferences, emotions and moods (Ekkekakis and Petruzzello, 2000; Rosenberg, 1998).

Although precise definitions of emotion vary among researchers, Fredrickson (2001) suggests there is a consensus that an emotion is a cognitively appraised response to an event, either conscious or unconscious, which 'triggers a cascade of response tendencies manifest across loosely coupled component systems, such as subjective experience, facial expression, cognitive processing and physiological changes' (p. 218). Some researchers also emphasize a behavioural aspect in the emotional response (e.g. Gross, 1998). To illustrate, imagine a rugby player who is the recipient of a late and dangerous tackle. The rugby player may experience an increase in heart rate, muscular tension, may feel angry, scowl, and retaliate by punching an opponent.

There may be a consensus of what constitutes an emotion (cf. Frederickson, 2001), but there are particular difficulties in distinguishing between emotion and mood. This is because both mood and emotion comprise changes in the way an individual feels. Therefore, in a practical sense a person may be unable to distinguish between feelings triggered in response to specific events and those already present as part of an underlying mood state (Lane and Terry, 2000). However, attempts at distinguishing between mood and emotion in sport settings have been made (e.g. Beedie, Lane and Terry, 2001), and these are discussed in more detail by Lane (Chapter 5). We now consider how emotions arise. There are a number of theories of emotion (see Dalgleish and Power, 1999; Lewis and Haviland-Jones, 1999). The next section focuses specifically on those that have been applied to sport settings.

How do emotions arise?

A number of approaches have been proposed to explain how emotions arise in sport settings. These include attribution-based approaches (Weiner, 1986; Vallerand, 1987), reversal theory (Apter, 1989; Kerr, 1997) and cognitive-motivational-relational theory (Lazarus, 1991, 1999, 2000a, 2000b). In this section we briefly review each approach before discussing common issues that emerge from these.

Attribution-based approaches

Weiner (1986) proposed that outcome-dependent emotions occur from an initial evaluation of the event (such as feeling happy after a win) while attribution-dependent emotions occur following consideration of possible reasons for success or failure. Attribution of success or failure occurs along three dimensions, stability (stable or unstable), locus of causality (internal or external) and controllability (in one's or another's control or out of one's or another's control). For example, an internal attribution of success may result in pride, whereas an internal attribution of failure may result in guilt or shame. Attribution-dependent emotions are more likely in situations where the outcome is unexpected, important or negative (Biddle, Hanrahan and Sellars, 2001), and are considered to be less intense than outcome-dependent emotions (Vallerand and Blanchard, 2000). Research evidence does show that attributions play a role in emotional responses to sport. For example, adolescent swimmers and track and field athletes experienced more intense positive emotions and less intense negative emotions following attributions to stable and personally controllable factors (Graham, Kowalski and Crocker, 2002), while team sport athletes who made attributions of team control after a victory experienced higher levels of happiness (Allen, Jones and Sheffield, 2009a). The attributions made after competition can also influence the temporal response of emotions, with amateur golfers experiencing anger for a longer period post-competition when they identified the cause of a poor performance as stable rather than unstable (Allen, Jones and Sheffield, 2009b).

Vallerand (1983, 1987) drew on aspects of Weiner's attribution theory and other appraisal models (Arnold, 1960; Lazarus, 1968; Schachter, 1964) to develop a model of emotion for sport settings. Vallerand suggested that emotions occurred after two types of appraisal: intuitive and reflective. Intuitive appraisal is similar to the process that results in Weiner's (1986) outcome-dependent emotions. Reflective appraisal involves attributions about the outcome in addition to other appraisals (such as intellectualization, comparison processes, information-processing functions and mastery-related cognitions), and is similar to the process that results in Weiner's attribution-dependent emotions. While intuitive appraisal is always thought to occur prior to an emotional response, reflective appraisal is not necessary to produce emotions. Rather it occurs following a mismatch between an individual's expectations and the actual outcome. There is some support for Vallerand's model, in that the major predictor of emotion following physical activity is intuitive appraisal, and not reflective appraisal, which typically explains a limited amount of variance in emotions experienced in sport (Biddle et al., 2001; Crocker et al., 2002; Vallerand and Blanchard, 2000).

One element of what could be considered part of Vallerand's reflective appraisal and which has been associated with emotional responses in sport is counterfactual thinking (generating thoughts of what might have been). For example, Olympic bronze medallists who were not expected to win a medal were rated as happier than Olympic silver medallists who were expected to have won gold, as the bronze medallists were likely to have made a downward counterfactual comparison (such as I could have left with nothing) that resulted in a positive emotional response (McGraw, Mellers and Tetlock, 2005). Counterfactual thoughts are often elicited in response to negative affect or unexpected outcomes, and are typically considered functional insofar as they help individuals regulate affect or enhance motivation (cf. Roese and Olson, 1997). Indeed, counterfactual thoughts are commonly experienced by athletes, and influence their emotional response, with upward counterfactuals associated with negative emotions and downward counterfactuals associated with positive emotions (Dray and Uphill, 2009).

Attribution-based approaches emphasize the role of performance evaluation as an antecedent of emotion. However, other antecedents are also important in generating emotions (Crocker et al., 2002). For example, a water polo player arriving to play in a competition may feel disappointment on seeing an umpire he believes penalizes him too often. Therefore, we turn to consider other approaches that more explicitly outline how a range of antecedents may be implicated in the generation of emotion.

Reversal theory

Apter's reversal theory (1989) states that emotions are a result of the various combinations of metamotivational states (or frames of mind) that an individual is in at any given time. There are four pairs of metamotivational states: telic–paratelic; conformist–negativistic; mastery–sympathy; autic–alloic. These pairs of opposite states exist in a bistable system. That is, when one of each pair is active, the other is inactive. For example, if someone is in a telic state they cannot be in a paratelic state. However, one can reverse (hence the name of the theory) between opposite states. Reversals occur in response to external events, frustration from not experiencing the goal of the current configuration of metamotivational states, and from satiation, which is being in the same metamotivational state for an extended period of time (Blaydon, Lindner and Kerr, 2000). Because there are four pairs of metamotivational states, at any given moment an individual is experiencing a total of four states (one from each pair). However, typically one or more of the states will be salient (Frey, 1999), reflecting a person's motives at a particular time. For example, when the telic state is most salient a person is goal-oriented and has a preference for low levels of arousal.

Eight somatic emotions (anxiety, anger, excitement, provocativeness, relaxation, placidity, boredom, sullenness) are generated from possible combinations of the telic–paratelic and negativism–conformity pairs of states in relation to the individual's felt level of arousal. For example, an individual experiencing high felt arousal in a telic–conformity state will be anxious, yet an individual experiencing high felt arousal in a paratelic–conformity state will experience excitement. Eight transactional emotions (humiliation, resentment, modesty, virtue, pride, gratitude, shame, guilt) are generated by possible combinations of the autic–alloic and mastery–sympathy pairs of states, and the levels of felt transactional outcome (net gain or net loss) at any time (Kerr, 1997). For example, an individual experiencing a net loss in an autic–mastery state will experience humiliation, yet an individual experiencing a net gain in the same autic–mastery state will experience pride.

Reversal theory research in sport has been led by the work of John Kerr and colleagues (Kerr, 1990, 1997). Research has shown that metamotivational states may be related to participation (e.g. Lindner and Kerr, 2000), change at different stages of competition (Males, Kerr and Gerkovich, 1998), be related to perceptual and cognitive responses to exercise (Thatcher, Kuroda, Thatcher and Legrand, 2010) and help explain athletes' emotional responses to injury (Thatcher, Kerr, Amies and Day, 2007). There is support for reversal theory in sport settings, then, although the combinations of the metamotivational states do not appear to account for all the emotions thought to be experienced by athletes. For example, there is no combination of metamotivational states that can account for happiness, an emotion thought to be related to sport performance (Jackson, 2000; Jones et al., 2005, Lazarus, 2000b).

Cognitive-motivational relational theory (CMRT)

In CMRT, emotions occur when events are appraised as having either positive or negative significance for well-being (relational meaning) in relation to goals. Emotion is part of a changing person–environment relationship, and three components central to this process are motivation, appraisal and coping. These combine and form core-relational themes for each emotion that describe the transaction between the individual and the environment. This provides an explanation of how each emotion arises. The core-relational themes for the eight emotions Lazarus (2000b) outlined as particularly relevant to sport are shown in Table 2.1

Motivation covers both an individual's goals (for instance, to win a tennis match) and how psychological and behavioural responses may be mobilized to achieve a goal (such as increase effort). Events are appraised through two processes, primary and secondary appraisal. Primary appraisal is concerned with the relevance of a stimulus to a person's well-being in terms of their goals. The three ways in which events are primarily appraised include goal relevance (is there anything at stake?), goal congruence or incongruence (is the stimulus beneficial or harmful?) and goal content (the kind of goal at stake, such as enhancing ego identity). An individual's goals are arranged hierarchically, and the more important the goal the more intense the emotion.

TABLE 2.1 Core-relational themes for sport-related emotions

Emotion	Core-Relational Theme
Anger	A demeaning offense against me and mine.
Anxiety	Facing uncertain, existential threat.
Shame	Failing to live up to an ego-ideal.
Guilt	Having transgressed a moral imperative.
Hope	Fearing the worst but yearning for better, and believing the improvement is possible.
Relief	A distressing goal-incongruent condition that has changed for the better or gone away.
Happiness	Making reasonable progress toward the realization of a goal.
Pride	Enhancement of one's ego-identity by taking credit for a valued object or achievement, either one's own or that of someone or a group with whom one identifies.

Source: Adapted from *Emotion and Adaptation* by Richard S. Lazarus, 1991. New York: Oxford University Press.

Secondary appraisal concerns coping options, which Lazarus defined as cognitive and behavioural efforts to manage demands that are appraised as taxing or exceeding the resources of that person. The three aspects of secondary appraisal include blame or credit (can responsibility for the harm or benefit be determined?), coping potential (is it possible to influence the person–environment relationship for the better?), and future expectations (whether things will improve or worsen). Coping efforts may be temporally antecedent to the occurrence of an emotion following primary appraisal and/or may be directed towards managing the emotion itself.

Because athletes' goals, appraisal of situations and coping strategies may vary both between and within individuals, CMRT provides a comprehensive theoretical account for the inter- and intra-individual differences that can be witnessed amongst athletes. Also, rapid vacillation between appraisals and/or an athlete's commitment to multiple goals may explain how the same stimulus can generate more than one emotion. For example, a boxer may want to win a contest, look stylish in doing so and not get hurt, thus a number of emotions could occur as a result of the same encounter. Accordingly, research has indicated that athletes may experience a range of feelings prior to and during competition (Jones et al., 2000; Mellalieu, Hanton and Jones, 2003).

The central tenets of CMRT have been supported in athletes. Uphill and Jones (2007) interviewed twelve international athletes about the emotions they experienced during competition. There was evidence of appraisals being central to emotion, and that the appraisal process comprised primary and secondary aspects. The findings on core-relational themes were mixed, with support for the core-relational themes of guilt, relief and shame, partial support for anxiety, happiness and sadness, and no support for the core-relational themes of anger and pride. It may be that the core-relational themes account for some emotions better than others (Bennett, Lowe and Honey, 2003) or that interviewing athletes does not yield a complete description of the appraisal process (Uphill and Jones, 2007). The applicability of CMRT to sport is also discussed in detail by Uphill and Jones in Chapter 10.

There has been limited consideration of CMRT in sport settings, but it does provide a framework for research into emotions. Importantly CMRT illustrates the complexity of the emotion process and the central role of cognition. In particular the role of coping is central to the appraisal process that illustrates the link between coping and emotion. Coping potential does not refer to actual coping, but an evaluation of prospects for coping (Lazarus, 1991). For example, a golfer who finds himself in a greenside bunker may have either a favourable or unfavourable coping expectancy depending on, for example previous outcomes of similar shots. Coping behaviours, in addition to coping expectancy, also play a role in CMRT, influencing the emotions experienced. Lazarus and colleagues (Folkman and Lazarus, 1988; Lazarus, 1991, 2000) suggest that coping behaviours can be classified into one of either two categories (see Chapter 3 for a detailed discussion of this issue). Problem-focused coping involves taking action to change an aspect of the person–environment relationship, either by altering an aspect of the environment itself, or by changing one's situation within it. For example, an ice skater struggling with a difficult move could remove herself from the rink and practise the movements on a training mat, or remove herself from the training environment to try to cope with her anger or disappointment. Coping behaviours act to mediate and change the emotional experience of athletes. Thus, relocating to the training mat may engender more positive feelings of relief or happiness at subsequent success, whilst leaving the training environment may elicit feelings of embarrassment or shame.

Emotion-focused coping on the other hand influences only what is in the mind of an athlete (Lazarus, 2000). Specifically, strategies to cope with a particular event can involve either a redirection of attention, or a reinterpretation (reappraisal) of the person–environment relationship. A basketball player jeered by a crowd may feel anxious. In this scenario, anxiety could be reduced by refocusing attention to task-relevant cues or by reappraising the situation more as a challenge to her psychological skills than as a threat to performing well.

What factors moderate the emotional response?

As an adjunct to research outlining how emotions arise, Cerin et al. (2000) have proposed an interactional model of stress, identifying factors that may moderate athletes' emotional responses to competition. Cerin et al. (2000) suggest that the factors that moderate emotional states can be divided into four categories: athletic competition (for instance demands, opportunities), personal factors (such as gender, age), situational factors (such as type of sport, level of competition), and behaviour/performance (for example, above or below average). Mellalieu (2003) has extended Cerin et al.'s (2000) model by proposing that mood state should be included as a factor that may moderate emotional response. For example, an athlete in a depressed mood is proposed to respond to competition with high levels of anger and tension and reduced vigour (Lane and Terry, 2000).

Core issues in approaches to emotion in sport

From the approaches to emotion outlined in the previous section a number of core issues appear central to the study of emotion in sport. These include the role of cognition in the generation of emotions, the transient nature of emotions and the multidimensional nature of the emotional response.

The importance of cognition

Theories of emotion applied to sport (e.g. Apter, 1989; Lazarus, 2000a; Vallerand, 1987; Weiner, 1986) emphasize the importance of cognition in the occurrence of emotions. However, it is not universally accepted that all emotions require cognitive processing (see Ekman and Davidson, 1994 for a discussion of this issue). Much of this debate centres on how cognition is defined. Using a broad definition of cognition which includes basic sensory information processing, the elicitation of most, if not all emotions, will involve at least some cognitive processing (Ellsworth, 1994). In short, cognition is seen to be central because one does not react in an emotional way to events perceived as meaningless. This cognitive processing may be unconscious and may manifest itself in a physiological response before awareness of the emotion. That a physiological response may precede conscious awareness of an emotional reaction is shown in a study by Bechara, Damasio, Tranei and Damasio (1997). Participants were asked to choose a card from one of four decks, two that would result in the loss of money in the long term, and two that would result in monetary gain in the long term. They displayed increased autonomic arousal when the choice concerned the loss of money. This increase in autonomic arousal preceded participants' abilities to articulate which decks were best. Even when participants were unable to explain why, they still chose more cards from the 'better decks', guided by their autonomic response.

Cognition is not only important in determining which emotions arise. There is a substantial body of literature in sport that outlines how the *perception* of an emotion is an important aspect. The control model of debilitative and facilitative competitive state anxiety outlines that athletes with a positive belief in their ability to cope, and to attain their goals, will interpret anxiety symptoms as facilitative (helpful), whereas those with negative expectancies will interpret symptoms as debilitative (unhelpful) to performance (Jones, 1995). Both elite and successful competitors have reported more facilitative perceptions of anxiety symptoms than did non-elite and unsuccessful competitors respectively, when no differences in anxiety intensity levels were present (Jones and Swain, 1995; Jones, Swain and Hardy, 1993). More recent work has extended this line of inquiry to consider a broader range of emotions. Athletes who perceive anxiety symptoms as facilitative to performance report more positive feelings (for instance excited, relaxed) and less negative feelings (such as tense, angry) than athletes who perceive their anxiety symptoms as debilitative to performance (Jones and Hanton, 2001; Mellalieu et al., 2003). Other negative emotions could also be perceived as helpful to performance, such as a boxer perceiving a high level of anger as useful for performance (Jones et al., 2009). In sum, research has generally supported the tenets of Jones's theory, and demonstrated that athletes with a positive perception of anxiety symptoms perform better (see Hanton, Neil and Mellalieu, 2008 for a review). Yet, the conceptual worth of this research has recently been questioned, and a positive perception of symptoms may simply represent the absence of any real levels of perceived anxiety (Lundqvist, Kentta and Raglin, 2010). That is, in a sample of eighty-four Swedish athletes Lundqvist et al. found that the majority of anxiety items identified as facilitative for performance were rated at an intensity of 'Not at all', and suggested this was the main reason the athletes in this sample rated these items as facilitative to performance.

A further important cognitive element of emotions is a person's goals. The importance of goals in influencing how emotions arise is supported by research (Graham et al., 2002). Broadly, achieving goals will lead to a positive emotional reaction while failure to achieve goals leads to a negative emotional response. Further, what an athlete is striving for is crucial to the emotion process, and emotions arise because encounters with the environment are appraised as having either a positive or negative significance for well-being in terms of a person's goals. The importance of an individual's goal determines the intensity of the emotional response (Lazarus, 1991). Of particular relevance to emotion are achievement goals. In general there is a positive association between approach goals, where the focus is on what can be achieved, and positive affect (e.g. Adie, Duda and Ntoumanis, 2008, 2010). Consideration of achievement goals may also help explain why some negatively valenced emotions can be considered helpful for performance. For example, participants playing a computer game had a stronger preference for fear when pursuing an avoidance goal, while excitement was the preferred emotion when adopting an approach goal (Tamir and Ford, 2009). This illustrates that fear may be perceived as a useful emotion if the goal is to avoid errors.

The role of cognition in the generation of emotions and the perception of physiological and cognitive symptoms has important implications for intervention techniques. By changing the importance of some goals, by altering the perception of an athlete's ability to cope, or by changing the way in which symptoms are perceived, it may be possible to develop a more appropriate emotional state for competition. See Jones (2003) and Uphill, McCarthy and Jones (2009) for a review of emotional control strategies.

The transient nature of emotion

Because athletes are continuously appraising stimuli before, during and after competition, emotions may change substantially during these periods. Although there is research focusing on the temporal patterning of anxiety, Cerin et al. (2000) have called for more research into the temporal patterning of other emotions. In one such study Jones et al. (2000) reported that international field hockey players experienced greater levels of annoyance and less tension during the game than immediately before. More recently Sève et al. (2007), using video-assisted recall, found that table tennis players' emotions influenced performance, and were influenced by performance (such as a set result) and the interpretation of the unfolding situation. Because of the transient nature of emotions, measures of emotional state during competition are likely to provide more valid data to assess the emotion–performance relationship and the efficacy of strategies developed for emotional control, than measures taken prior to competition. While the difficulties of assessing emotion during performance in some sports are obvious, where it is possible, this is an important area of future research.

The multidimensional nature of emotions

The complex nature of the emotional response is illustrated in Frederickson's definition cited at the start of the chapter. As emotions are commonly assessed using self-report measures, the research focus has frequently been on the subjective experience aspect of the emotional response. However, other aspects of the emotional response are important. For example, measures of competitive anxiety, such as the Competitive State Anxiety Inventory-2 (CSAI-2; Martens et al., 1990) and the Sport Anxiety Scale (SAS; Smith, Smoll and Schultz, 1990) include a somatic anxiety subscale, which provides information about an individual's perception of physiological changes, thought to accompany the anxiety response. Physiological changes are considered important because research has consistently shown them to play a role in determining the intensity of the emotion. For example, Wiens, Mezzacappa and Katkin (2000) classified participants into those who were readily able to perceive visceral feedback (heartbeat detection) and those who were less able to perform the same task. Those who were better at the heartbeat detection task tended to report more intense emotional responses than those less able to perform the task. In addition, Hohmann (1966) found that individuals with spinal cord injuries, which reduced feedback from the autonomic nervous system, did still experience emotions although they were described as less intense, with the intensity varying with the location of the point of damage on the spine. Similarly, physical exertion has been shown to intensify feelings of anger (Zillmann, Katcher and Milavsky, 1972). Physiological changes may also be unique to specific emotions (e.g. Ax, 1953). To illustrate, in comparison with fear, Ax (1953) found that anger is associated with a greater rise in diastolic blood pressure and muscle tension, a larger number of increases in skin conductance and a larger decrease in heart rate. In short, feedback from the autonomic nervous system is central to emotion (cf. Damasio, 2005).

Because of the potential impact upon others (such as team mates or the opposition), the display of emotions by individuals is an important component of the emotional response (cf. Kelly and Barsade, 2001), and one that has received comparatively little empirical attention in the sports literature to date. Moreover, the display of emotions may not just serve a communicative function to others; it may intensify the subjective experience of emotions (cf. Strack, Martin and Stepper, 1988). Understanding the emotional response is the first step in understanding how emotions impact behaviour. In the remainder of this chapter, we discuss how emotions influence performance, with the specific effects of particular emotions outlined where evidence permits.

Consequences of emotion

Emotion is a topic of interest in performance settings precisely because emotions influence performance, and because this influence can be so dramatic. There has been a substantial amount of research exploring the relationship between anxiety and performance. While anxiety is clearly a prevalent emotion in performance settings and does relate to performance (see Woodman and Hardy, 2001 for a review), in this section the focus is on those approaches that have considered the relationship between a broad range of emotions (including anxiety) and performance. It then discusses how emotions impact subcomponents of performance.

Emotions and overall performance levels

The mental health model (Morgan, 1968) and the Individual Zones of Optimal Functioning model (IZOF: Hanin, 2000a) approaches have dominated the sport literature in describing whether a particular affective pattern is associated with good or poor performance, and it is to these approaches that we now turn.

Mental health model

Based on his work exploring the personality characteristics of successful and unsuccessful athletes, Morgan (1968, 1980, 1985) proposed the 'iceberg profile', or mental health model of sport performance. In this model athletic success is associated with a higher than normal level of vigour and lower than normal levels of tension, depression, anger, fatigue and confusion, assessed by the Profile of Mood States (POMS; McNair, Lorr and Droppleman, 1971). When plotted graphically against normative values this pattern of data represents an iceberg with the higher than normal score on vigour representing the peak of the iceberg. We recognize that the mental health model refers to mood, not emotion, but the blurring of boundaries between mood and emotion is illustrated here. Because data using the POMS was often collected in relation to a specific competition it could be considered to represent emotion.

The number of studies utilizing the mental health model has provided sufficient data for two meta-analyses. In the first, Rowley et al. (1995) reported that the mental health model accounted for less than 1 per cent of the variance in sports performance. A second meta-analysis of the mental health model controlled for moderating factors such as type of sport and duration of competition, and found that vigour, depression, anger, anxiety and confusion did predict athletic performance in the direction proposed in the mental health model (Beedie, Terry and Lane, 2000).

The mental health model has more recently served as the basis for a conceptual model outlining the relationship between the six mood states assessed by the POMS and performance levels. In Lane and Terry's model (2000), depressed mood serves as a moderator for the effect of anger and tension on performance. Specifically, these emotions have curvilinear effects on performance (that is, they enhance performance up to a point) in the absence of a depressed mood, but reduce performance in the presence of a depressed mood.

The mental health model has been used extensively in sport yet it is based on data from the POMS, a measure developed for use with psychiatric patients which assesses predominantly negative moods (five) rather than positive moods (one). Further, sport is, at least for most, an enjoyable experience and a more balanced approach would appear appropriate. This more balanced approach to emotion and performance is observed in the IZOF.

Individualized Zones of Optimal Functioning (IZOF)

The IZOF model (Hanin, 2000a) was originally developed to explain the association between anxiety and sport performance (Hanin, 1989), but in recent years work has focused on a broader range of emotions (Hanin, 2000a, 2000b). The IZOF proposes an idiosyncratic relationship between emotional state (comprising a number of discrete emotions) and performance levels (Hanin, 2000a). For example, one athlete may perform well when tense and angry, whereas another may perform poorly when in the same state. In developing an IZOF profile athletes choose a list of positive and negative emotions, and their intensities, that relate to performance.

Hanin (2000a) provided a detailed description of the emotional response, and proposed that it could be classified along five dimensions. Three dimensions related to the structure of the subjective experience: form, content and intensity, whereas two dimensions related to the dynamics of the subjective experience: time and context. The form dimension describes the way in which emotions may be represented and includes cognitive, affective, motivational, somatic, kinesthetic, performance and communicative components. The content dimension describes the hedonic tone (pleasant–unpleasant) and impact of emotion on performance (optimal–dysfunctional), and the intensity dimension describes the strength of feeling. The time dimension refers to the temporal patterning of the emotion (such as pre, during or post competition) and the context dimension refers to the environmental characteristics (such as practice or competition).

The IZOF is a useful approach, particularly in consultancy, because it engages athletes in exploring the emotion–performance relationship. It also has intuitive appeal in that many athletes and coaches relate to the central idea that the emotion–performance relationship is idiosyncratic. While the utility of the IZOF has been demonstrated in sport settings, for example with karate athletes (Robazza, Bortoli and Hanin, 2004) and swimmers and track and field athletes (Robazza, Pellizzari, Bertollo and Hanin, 2008), some limitations have been noted. The IZOF uses a concept of emotional state comprising a range of discrete emotions, and how this occurs is not explained (Crocker et al., 2002). While conceptually distinct emotions (such as sadness and anger) have been reported to co-occur (Levine, 1996), it would appear unlikely that these are experienced simultaneously. Rather, an emotional state may best be conceptualized as a number of discrete emotions that occur sequentially over time, and not a number of discrete emotions that are experienced simultaneously. Also, both Crocker et al. (2002) and Lazarus (2000b) criticize some of the adjectives used to describe emotions in the IZOF (for example the terms confident and purposeful, which may describe cognitive states rather than emotions).

The mental health model and the IZOF model have both made substantial contributions to describing the link between emotion and performance. Yet as we have noted both approaches have limitations. Further, neither approach really provides a complete explanation of the mechanisms by which emotions may impact performance. We now move on to discuss these mechanisms.

How emotions influence aspects of performance

Emotions change not only the way we feel, but also the way we think, process information and behave. This has implications for the performances of coaches, officials and athletes, and the mental health model and the IZOF hypothesis have made substantial contributions in describing the link between emotion and performance. Besides observing that certain emotions are associated with a particular performance level, it is equally important to understand why that might be the case. Accordingly, understanding the impact of emotions requires a focus on the mechanisms by which change may occur. Collectively researchers agree that emotions are important for performance because of changes in an individual's physical and cognitive functioning, along with motivation levels (Botterill and Brown, 2002; Jones, 2003; Lazarus, 2000b; Uphill et al., 2009; Vallerand and Blanchard, 2000).

The physical effects of emotions

Physical changes may accompany some emotions, and in this section we consider the performance consequences of the two main physical changes that take place when emotions are experienced. The first is overt displays of emotion, such as changes in facial expression, and the second is activation of the autonomic nervous system – the fight or flight response.

Changes in facial expression accompany many emotions, and the universality of some emotional expressions has been demonstrated across cultures (Ekman, 1980). Other indicators of emotion are, for example, how an angry person may clench their fists, or an anxious performer may appear fidgety. Emotions indicate to others how we feel, and play a key role in social behaviour. Displays of emotion may maintain, enhance or impair social relationships. For example, a coach's look of anger after an error by a senior team member may lead to a breakdown in trust. A display of emotions (or otherwise) may also serve social-regulative purposes (Hackfort, 1993). For example, in cricket a batsman may consciously decide to appear calm and unruffled after missing the ball to appear confident to the bowler.

Displays of emotion not only influence how others perceive us, experienced emotions can also influence social interaction. Specifically, a positive affective state is associated with the liking of self and others, sociability and activity (Lyubomirsky, King and Diener, 2005) and pro-social behaviour (Platow et al., 1999). Emotional contagion can occur in social settings (Hatfield, Cacioppo and Rapson, 1994), whereby an emotion is 'transmitted' from one person to another via facial, verbal and behavioural expressions of emotion, suggesting that an 'emotional climate' may emerge, with many athletes within a team for instance experiencing the same emotion. To illustrate, Totterdell (2000) observed that members of a cricket team experienced considerable similarity in moods, independent of events occurring during a game.

Emotions may also be influenced by significant others in performance settings (such as the leader or coach). Behaviours reflecting a negative personal rapport positively predicted anxiety in varsity and regional athletes (Baker, Cote and Hawes, 2000). Athletes recognize the influence of significant others, and look to coaches to change emotions. Collegiate and varsity athletes indicated a preference for emotional content in a pre-game speech (say, by arousing phrases, appeals to emotions such as pride or anger) before a championship game, when competing against a higher-ranked opponent and when considered the underdogs (Vargas-Tonsing and Guan, 2007). Interestingly though it was the informational content (such as game plans) and not the emotional content of coaches' pre-game speeches that changed competitive soccer players' emotional states (Vargas-Tonsing, 2009).

Because sport performance is in part contingent upon those around us (such as team mates, opposition, officials), understanding how the display of emotions influences significant others' perceptions and behaviours is important. For example, a visibly angry player may cause fear in their opponents, a visibly anxious leader may increase the anxiety levels of their team, and a calm official may defuse a potentially explosive contest.

Many emotions, such as anxiety, excitement and anger, are accompanied by an increase in physiological arousal (Kerr, 1997) that has been defined as the level of neural excitation (Malmo, 1959). However, Hardy, Jones and Gould (1996) have outlined that arousal should not be considered as a unitary response. For example, it may involve an increase in activity in one part of the autonomic nervous system (such as the heart rate) but other parts (such as skin conductance) may be depressed. It is also important to recognize that an individual in a heightened state of arousal is not necessarily experiencing an emotion, and individuals may experience emotions without necessarily changing their level of arousal. Nevertheless, because of the importance of coping with the pressure of competition, and the apparently contrasting levels of arousal required to succeed at different sports (for instance, snooker versus weightlifting), the relationship between arousal and performance has led to a great deal of research interest. Broadly, the research suggests that arousal may influence performance by impacting both cognitive functioning (see next section) and physical functioning, as outlined in the remainder of this section.

High levels of arousal can increase anaerobic power, which may enhance performance on simple physical tasks such as jumping (e.g. Parfitt, Hardy and Pates, 1995; Parfitt and Pates, 1999). The effect of arousal may vary across emotions. For example, handgrip strength was significantly higher following imagery-induced excitement, compared with imagery-induced anxiety, which in turn produced higher performance than a control condition (Perkins, Wilson and Kerr, 2001). Imagery-induced anger was associated with enhanced muscular strength on an isometric extension of the right leg, in contrast to imagery-induced happiness, and this effect was moderated by personality, with imagery-induced anger leading to a greater increase in muscular strength in extroverts than introverts (Woodman et al., 2009).

While we should be cognizant that changes in arousal accompanying emotions may differ between individuals (Hardy et al., 1996) and also between emotions (Ax, 1953), the implication of these findings is that an increase in arousal accompanying some emotions could be positive for sports requiring anaerobic power. Yet caution is warranted in suggesting that emotions associated with high arousal can unequivocally improve performance in these sports, for two reasons. First, Murphy, Woolfolk and Budney (1988) found that fear and anger were not associated with an increase in handgrip dynamometer performance. Second, there are very few tasks where the sole requirement is strength, thus we also need to understand the impact of arousal on other functions in addition to anaerobic power. For example, even tasks such as weightlifting or scrummaging in rugby require attentional focus and coordination in order to be successful.

Increasing arousal could have a negative effect on fine motor tasks through increasing muscular tension that can impact fine motor control (Parfitt, Jones and Hardy, 1990). This is illustrated in research by Noteboom and colleagues (Noteboom, Barnholt and Enoka, 2001a; Noteboom, Fleshner and Enoka, 2001b). Participants performed a submaximal isometric pinch task where they were required to exert a constant force of 4 Newtons with the thumb and index finger of the right hand. Arousal was increased through the delivery of electric shocks (Noteboom et al., 2001a; Noteboom et al., 2001b) or asking participants to engage in a mental arithmetic task (Noteboom et al., 2001b). Increased arousal from the delivery of electric shocks was associated with a decrease in steadiness, that is, increased variation in the force exerted (Noteboom et al., 2001a; Noteboom et al., 2001b), although increased arousal from the mental arithmetic task did not affect performance (Noteboom et al., 2001b), possibly suggesting different effects of arousal induced by a stressful cognitive task from those of arousal induced by a physically threatening stressor. The impact of arousal on fine motor control has clear implications for success in some sports. For example, increased arousal may impact the success of 'touch shots' in sport such as a drop shot in tennis or a downhill putt in golf.

Increased arousal may also result in difficulties with coordination (Oxendine, 1970) and impact the movement patterns of athletes. Collins et al. (2001) reported that anxiety, which is often associated with an increase in arousal, impacted the movement patterns of soldiers required to perform a stepping task on two parallel bars 20 metres off the ground and weightlifters performing the snatch lift. There was less variability in the movement patterns of the soldiers on the parallel bars when performing the task at 20 metres (so anxious) in comparison with ground level, while the weightlifters reported that they consciously focused on task movement patterns when anxious. The implications for skilled performance are evident in that anxious athletes may move less freely than non-anxious athletes. For example, an anxious baseball or cricket batter may not strike the ball cleanly and 'snatch' at the shot. Further, changes in physical tension that can result from the stress response and make movement patterns less fluid are thought to predispose an athlete to injury (Williams and Andersen, 1998).

The research reviewed here clearly indicates the differential effects that arousal, which can accompany some emotions, may have on physical functioning. However, like much of the research in the sport literature the focus has been on the changes that accompany anxiety. The impact of arousal accompanying other high-intensity emotions (such as excitement or anger) on movement patterns and fine motor skills is yet to be more widely investigated.

The impact of emotion on cognitive functioning

Emotions may lead to changes in a range of cognitive functions that could impact performance, including attentional focus, perception, decision making and the recall of information. In general, positive emotions broaden attention whereas negative emotions narrow attention (Frederickson, 2001). Not only do positive emotions encourage a broader focus of attention, they also result in more creative thinking and approaches to problem solving (Fredrickson and Branigan, 2005), and this may be useful in sport settings, for example when a performer is trying to think of a novel game play or approach to break down the defence of a determined opponent.

Under high physiological arousal, which may accompany some emotions, an individual's attentional focus is proposed to be narrower than under conditions of low arousal (cf. Easterbrook, 1959). A consequence of this attentional narrowing is a positive effect on performance if it blocks out unimportant distractions for the performer, but a negative effect if an individual misses some task-relevant cues. However, the effect of high-arousal emotions like anxiety on attention is not always so clear-cut. Attentional control theory (ACT) outlines that a performer under high anxiety is more concerned with potential threats in the environment, and this may govern attention (Eysenck et al., 2007). There is sport-specific evidence to support this notion. For example, Moran, Byrne and McGlade (2002) presented members of the Irish National Gymnastic squad with three slides showing a gymnast performing a back flip. In the low-anxiety slide the back flip was performed on a low beam with safety mats, in the medium-anxiety slide it was performed on a low beam with no safety mats, and in the high-anxiety slide it was performed on the high beam with no safety mats. The participants were asked to imagine they were the gymnast in the slide, and their point of gaze was measured. The results demonstrated that the high-anxiety slide elicited significantly more fixations to peripheral areas than both the low-anxiety and medium-anxiety slides. Moran et al. (2002) noted that there were two possible explanations for these results. Because of attentional narrowing associated with anxiety, individuals may attempt to compensate by including more fixations in peripheral areas (illustrating that increased distractibility and attentional narrowing under high anxiety may not be incompatible hypotheses). Alternatively, in line with ACT the absence of crash mats was found threatening by the gymnasts (as it indicated the possibility of being hurt) and they focused their attention more on this aspect. Similar findings have been reported with soccer players: for example anxious participants taking a penalty kick fixated for longer on the goalkeeper (Wilson, Vine and Wood, 2009).

Interestingly, how anxiety is perceived may also be associated with attention. Eubank, Collins and Smith (2000, 2002) presented a series of words to high competitive-trait-anxious participants who were required to ignore the meaning of the word displayed to them and press a key depending on the colour in which the word was presented (the Stroop-colour word task). The length of time on this task was in part a reflection of the time taken to process the meaning of the word, with words that were considered more important taking longer to process. Athletes who perceived their anxiety symptoms as debilitative to performance allocated more resources to processing negative stimuli, whereas athletes who perceived their anxiety symptoms as facilitative for performance allocated more resources to processing positive stimuli (Eubank et al., 2000). When in a negative mood, athletes who perceived their anxiety symptoms as debilitative for performance took longer to process ambiguous words (such as result or score), than when in a positive or neutral mood, because they attached negative meaning and greater processing priority to those words (Eubank et al., 2002). Athletes who perceived their anxiety symptoms as facilitative for performance took longer to process ambiguous words when in a positive mood than when in a negative or neutral mood. This was thought to occur because the athletes attached a positive meaning to the ambiguous information (to protect against the possibility of interpreting the stimuli negatively) and thereby lengthened the time it took to process the information (Eubank et al., 2002). The findings of Eubank et al. suggest that the meaning attached to stimuli, and any subsequent emotional reaction, can be impacted by athletes' current mood state and the way in which they perceive anxiety symptoms.

If anxiety does lead to attentional narrowing, or greater fixations on peripheral or emotion congruent cues, this may have an impact on performance. Although some attentional narrowing may be beneficial if irrelevant cues are ignored, coaches, officials and athletes need to gather as much information as possible from the environment, and may suffer because of changes in attentional focus as a result of anxiety. For example, a rugby player may focus attention on the location of the defender (as they are fearful about being tackled hard) rather than on the team mate in possession of the ball; an official may miss a crucial decision because they were fixated on a threatening coach; or a coach may not gather sufficient tactical information because of attentional narrowing. While it is clear that anxiety can impact attentional focus, there is little research to date investigating whether other emotions have similar effects in sport settings. It is possible that a guilty individual may direct their attention to cues in the environment and internal thoughts that reinforce feelings of guilt. Also, as other emotions such as anger and excitement are proposed to lead to increases in physiological arousal (Kerr, 1997), these emotions may also result in some attentional narrowing.

Anxiety is thought to influence not only the pattern of attentional focus but also the efficiency with which information is processed. In ACT worry is proposed to impair the efficiency of cognitive functioning but not necessarily its effectiveness, provided that the performer can respond to this processing inefficiency by using compensatory strategies such as enhanced effort and use of processing resources. Other emotions may have similar effects, and Hanin (2000a) suggested that optimal emotions for performance ensure efficient use of available resources until task completion while dysfunctional emotions lead to an inefficient or inappropriate use of resources. Enhanced effort may however lead to worse performance on motor skills if attention is directed inwards in an attempt to consciously control the execution of a motor skill (Beilock and Carr, 2001; Masters and Maxwell, 2008).

Emotions may also impact memory. People are more likely to remember events that evoke greater emotional reactions, although memory may be enhanced for the salient parts of the event at the expense of peripheral details (Bower, 1994). Therefore, while a coach or athlete may remember the specific moment when they won an important competition or match clearly, memory of events leading up to this moment may be impaired. Also, the retrieval of a memory is enhanced if the individual is in an emotional state that corresponds to the particular memory (Bower, 1994). For example, athletes feeling sad and dejected may recall times when they lost or made errors, while athletes feeling happy and excited may find themselves recalling past success or times when they performed well. Thus, it is somewhat ironic that recalling previous good performances in detail in order to bolster confidence and improve emotional state is harder if a person is feeling sad and dejected, which is precisely when positive recollections may be needed the most.

Emotion-related changes in perception of stimuli may also extend to individuals' judgement of risk that may impact decision making in sport. Stefanucci et al. (2008) observed that fearful participants judged a hill to be steeper than did those who were unafraid. Indeed, Lerner and Keltner (2001) found that fearful people make pessimistic estimates of risk and risk–averse choices, whereas angry people make optimistic risk estimates and choices relating to risk seeking. To extrapolate these findings to sport settings, an angry golfer may be more inclined to play a risky approach shot to the green and a fearful coach may adopt conservative tactics going into an important game.

Finally, emotions may increase the speed of decision making and perception if accompanied by increases in arousal. A body of research indicates that decision making is quicker when exercising than when at rest (e.g. Adam et al., 1997; McMorris and Graydon, 1996a, 1996b; McMorris et al., 1999). Exercise is thought to improve decision making because it changes the arousal levels of the central nervous system, with increases in adrenaline and nor-adrenaline helping because of their role as neurotransmitters in the central nervous system (McMorris et al., 1999). If decision making is quicker under conditions of exercise-induced arousal, this may have implications for performance in aerobic sports (such as soccer, rugby, hockey and netball). It also suggests that the speed of decision making may be increased under conditions of high arousal resulting from an emotion, although this has yet to be tested empirically in a sport setting. Interestingly, in addition to decision making, perceptuo-motor speed may also be increased with somatic anxiety (Jones and Cale, 1989), while hope was associated with the immediate benefit of increasing reaction time in a computer-based soccer task (Woodman et al., 2009).

The impact of emotion on motivational aspects

Many theorists consider emotion to serve an adaptational function that can mediate and energize subsequent behaviours by ensuring people channel extra physical and mental resources towards a task (Vallerand and Blanchard, 2000). An emotion can lead individuals both toward and away from an object (Vallerand and Blanchard, 2000). Certain emotions could have either effect depending on the particular individual and the situation. For example, an individual feeling guilty about an error during a basketball match may try to stay away from the ball to avoid making further errors. Conversely, the individual may try to gain possession of the ball as much as possible in an attempt to improve performance and overcome feelings of guilt. Similarly, Hanin (2000a) suggested that optimal emotions for performance generate enough energy to initiate and maintain the required amount of effort for a task, whereas dysfunctional emotions result in an inappropriate amount of energy (too much or too little) being deployed. There is research evidence to suggest that emotions may impact motivation. Erez and Isen (2002) found that positive affect was associated with higher levels of effort, higher levels of motivation and greater persistence on cognitive tasks (such as solving anagrams). In performance settings a lack of perception of effort is observed in flow states, with movement often perceived as effortless (Jackson, 2000). More broadly, enjoyment is one of the most important predictors of sport commitment, and accordingly participation, in both youth athletes (e.g. Carpenter and Scanlan, 1998) and elite sport (e.g. Scanlan et al., 2003).

The impact of emotion on motivational aspects has implications not only for sport performance but also for participation in sport-related settings. For example, an athlete may use the anger experienced following an injury to increase effort during the rehabilitation programme, while conversely, feelings of depression may be associated with lower levels of adherence and effort.

Bringing it together: understanding psycho-physiological responses to competition

A recent theoretical approach has been proposed to explain how physiological responses and emotional responses to competition may be related, and how in turn performance may be affected. The Theory of Challenge and Threat States in Athletes (TCTSA: Jones et al., 2009), integrates the appraisal, emotional response (intensity and direction), autonomic arousal and performance consequences of responses to competition. The broad basis for this theory is that there is a dichotomy between individuals who perceive a competitive situation as a challenge (positively) and those who perceive it as a threat (negatively). This dichotomy is intuitively appealing because it supports the commonly held belief that some individuals will rise to the demands of competition and perform well, while some wilt and perform poorly.

The theory of challenge and threat states in athletes (TCTSA)

The TCTSA (Jones et al., 2009) draws predominantly on the biopsychosocial (BPS) model of challenge and threat (Blascovich and Mendes, 2000; Blascovich and Tomaka, 1996), the model of adaptive approaches to competition (Skinner and Brewer, 2004) and the control model of debilitative and facilitative competitive state anxiety (Jones, 1995) to understand athletes' responses to competition. See Figure 2.1.

Rather than discuss each element of the theory in detail, we outline those of particular relevance to this chapter: the changes in autonomic arousal, and emotions of challenge and threat states.

The cardiovascular responses described by Blascovich and colleagues (Blascovich and Mendes, 2000; Blascovich and Tomaka, 1996) in challenge and threat states are proposed to be indicative of differential activation of the sympathetic-adreno-medullary (SAM) and pituitary-adreno-cortical (PAC) axes. A challenge state is proposed to result from SAM activation producing greater cardiac activity (increased heart rate) and left-ventricular contractility which increases stroke volume. The combination of increased heart rate and enhanced left-ventricular contractility enhances cardiac output. SAM activation releases epinephrine, which

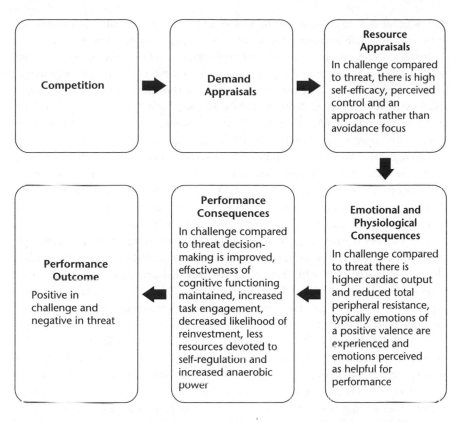

FIGURE 2.1 Comparison of challenge and threat responses in the theory of challenge and threat states in athletes (adapted from Jones et al., 2009).

causes vasodilation (widening of blood vessels resulting from relaxation of the muscular wall) and a decrease in systematic vascular resistance. Together these changes represent the efficient mobilization of energy for immediate action and coping (Blascovich et al., 1999), and consist of increased blood flow to the brain and muscles, higher blood glucose levels, which is the fuel of the nervous system, and an increase in free fatty acids that can be used by the muscles as fuel (cf. Dienstbier, 1989).

A threat state is proposed to result in an increase in both SAM and PAC activation. The activation of the PAC axis results in the release of adreno-corticotrophic hormone that causes the adrenal cortex to secrete corticosteroids into the bloodstream. Thus, although cardiac activity increases similar to a challenge condition, there is no corresponding decrease in systemic vascular resistance, and it may even increase (Dienstbier, 1989). As a result, blood pressure typically increases (Blascovich and Mendes, 2000; Blascovich and Tomaka, 1996). The combination of increased cardiac activity and stable, or increased, systemic vascular resistance represents a less efficient pattern for coping because, in this instance, the blood flow to the brain and muscles is not increased and while stored fat and protein are converted into usable energy, this occurs over a longer period of time.

In the TCTSA positive emotions will typically, but not exclusively, be associated with a challenge response, and negative emotions will typically, but not exclusively, be associated with a threat response. Challenge and threat reflect motivational states (Blascovich and Mendes, 2000) and thus are orthogonal to the valence of the emotion experienced (Mendes et al., 2008). High-intensity emotions of a negative valence, like anger, that can serve motivational functions could therefore occur in a challenge state. To illustrate, cardiovascular responses consistent with a challenge state were associated with higher levels of anger in participants who experienced social rejection (Mendes et al., 2008). Athletes will perceive their emotions in a challenge state as helpful for performance and their emotions in a threat state as unhelpful for performance, regardless of the valence of the emotion.

The TCTSA is a new approach yet to be fully tested in sport settings, although the cardiovascular responses aligned with challenge and threat states have been observed in baseball and softball athletes who provided a two-minute speech about a specific playing situation (Blascovich et al., 2004). The participants who experienced a challenge state during this task performed better during the subsequent season than players who experienced a threat state. In contrast, Williams, Cumming and Balanos (2010) were unable to find consistent differences in cardiac output between participants when using challenge or threat imagery, although the anxiety experienced during the challenge script was perceived as more helpful for performance. There may also be additional physiological changes that occur during performance settings not covered in the TCTSA. In particular, testosterone may be associated with a challenge state (Salvador and Costa, 2009), and this may be beneficial to performance in a number of ways, including increased dominance in face-to-face encounters, a greater willingness to take risks, improved reaction time, improved aspects of spatial ability and increased metabolic rate of muscles (Neave and Wolfson, 2003).

Concluding remarks

It is to be expected that on completing an overview of current theory and research pertaining to the antecedents and consequences of emotion in sport a number of areas for future research become apparent. Rather than focusing on what we do not know and where future research is needed (covered by Jones, Lavallee and Thatcher in Chapter 16), we focus here on what we do know from the research. First, the theories and research reviewed outline the importance of cognition in the occurrence of emotions, and this provides strong support for the development of cognitive techniques, such as reappraisal, for emotional control (Gross and John, 2003; Jones, 2003; Uphill et al., 2009). Second, emotional states are transient, which supports research exploring the relationship between emotions experienced during competition and performance (e.g. Jones et al., 2000; Smith et al., 2001) and the effectiveness of emotional control techniques during competition (e.g.

Jones et al., 2002). Third, the multidimensional nature of the emotional response means that a range of behavioural, cognitive and physical emotion-focused strategies can be utilized to control emotions and enhance performance. Finally, the multidimensional nature of the emotional response results in a number of consequences of emotion that may impact performance in sport settings.

It is clear that the many consequences of emotion make it difficult to develop a general model of how emotion may relate to sport performance, even if we focus on one emotion, such as anxiety. This is because sport encompasses a wide range of activities that place varying emphases on a range of different components (such as scanning for visual information, decision making, hand–eye coordination, strength, maintaining effort). What can be achieved is an understanding of how each emotion may impact each subcomponent of performance, which will facilitate an understanding of how each emotion relates to performance in each position (such as a prop or outside half in rugby), or task (such as tackling or passing in rugby). This is clearly a mammoth task, yet it is one that needs to be undertaken if we are to fully understand the consequences of emotion in sport settings. It is also possible to develop theories of athletes' responses to competition that incorporate the subjective, physiological, and cognitive elements and this has been done in the TCTSA although more research is needed to test this new approach.

References

Adam, J. J., Teeken, J. C., Ypelaar, P. J. C., Verstappen, F. T. J. and Pass, F. G. W. (1997). Exercise-induced arousal and information processing. *International Journal of Sport Psychology*, 28, 217–226.

Adie, J. W., Duda, J. L. and Ntoumanis, N. (2008). Achievement goals, competition appraisals, and the psychological and emotional welfare of sport participants. *Journal of Sport and Exercise Psychology*, 30, 302–322.

Adie, J. W., Duda, J. L. and Ntoumanis, N. (2010). Achievement goals, competition appraisals, and the well- and ill-being of elite youth soccer players over two competitive seasons. *Journal of Sport and Exercise Psychology*, 32, 555–579.

Adlington, R. (2008). Quoted in *Independent on Sunday*, 17 August, p. 4.

Allen, M. S., Jones, M. V. and Sheffield, D. (2009a). Causal attribution and emotion in the days following competition. *Journal of Sports Sciences*, 27, 461–468.

Allen, M. S., Jones, M. V. and Sheffield, D. (2009b). Attribution, emotion and collective efficacy in sports teams. *Group Dynamics: Theory, research, and practice*, 13, 205–217.

Apter, M. J. (1989). *Reversal theory: Motivation, emotion and personality*. London: Routledge.

Arnold, M. B. (1960). *Emotion and personality*. New York: Columbia Press.

Ax, A. F. (1953). The physiological differentiation between fear and anger in humans. *Psychosomatic Medicine*, 15, 433–422.

Baker, J., Cote, J. and Hawes, R. (2000). The relationship between coaching behaviours and sport anxiety in athletes. *Journal of Science and Medicine in Sport*, 3, 110–119.

Bechara, A., Damasio, H., Tranel, D. and Damasio, A. R. (1997). Deciding advantageously before knowing the advantageous strategy. *Science*, 275, 1293–1295.

Beedie, C. J., Lane, A. M. and Terry, P. C. (2001). Distinguishing emotion from mood in psychological measurement: a pilot study examining anxiety. *Journal of Sports Sciences*, 19, 69–70.

Beedie, C. J., Terry, P. C. and Lane, A. M. (2000). The Profile of Mood States and athletic performance: two meta-analyses. *Journal of Applied Sport Psychology*, 12, 49–68.

Beilock, S. L. and Carr, T. H. (2001). On the fragility of skilled performance: what governs choking under pressure? *Journal of Experimental Psychology – General,* 130, 701–725.

Bennett, P., Lowe, R. and Honey, K. (2003) Appraisals and emotions: a test of the consistency of reporting and their associations. *Cognition and Emotion,* 17, 511–520.

Biddle, S. J. H., Hanrahan, S. J. and Sellars, C. N. (2001). Attributions: Past, present and future. In R. N. Singer, H. A. Hausenblas and C. M. Janelle (eds), *Handbook of research on sport psychology,* (pp. 319–339). New York: J. Wiley and Sons.

Blascovich, J. and Mendes, W. B. (2000). Challenge and threat appraisals: the role of affective cues. In J. P. Forgas (ed.), *Feeling and thinking: The role of affect in social cognition* (pp. 59–82). Paris: Cambridge University Press.

Blascovich, J., Mendes, W. B., Hunter, S. B. and Salomon, K. (1999). Social 'facilitation' as challenge and threat. *Journal of Personality and Social Psychology,* 77, 68–77.

Blascovich, J., Seery, M. D., Mugridge, C. A., Norris, R. K. and Weisbuch, M. (2004). Predicting athletic performance from cardiovascular indexes of challenge and threat. *Journal of Experimental Social Psychology,* 40, 683–688.

Blascovich, J. and Tomaka, J. (1996). The biopsychosocial model of arousal regulation. *Advances in Experimental Social Psychology,* 28, 1–51.

Blaydon, M. J., Lindner, K. J. and Kerr, J. H. (2002). Metamotivational characteristics of eating-disordered and exercise-dependent triathletes: an application of reversal theory. *Psychology of Sport and Exercise,* 3, 223–236.

Botterill, C. and Brown, M. (2002). Emotion and perspective in sport. *International Journal of Sport Psychology,* 33, 38–60.

Bower, G. H. (1994). Some relations between emotions and memory. In P. Ekman and R. J. Davidson (eds), *The nature of emotion* (pp. 303–305). Oxford: Oxford University Press.

Carpenter, P. J. and Scanlan, T. K. (1998). Changes over time in the determinants of sport commitment. *Pediatric Exercise Science,* 10, 356–365.

Cerin, E., Szabo, A., Hunt, N. and Williams, C. (2000). Temporal patterning of competitive emotions: a critical review. *Journal of Sports Sciences,* 18, 605–626.

Collins, D., Jones, B., Fairweather, Doolan, S. and Priestley, N. (2001). Examining anxiety associated changes in movement patterns. *International Journal of Sport Psychology,* 31, 223–242.

Crocker, P. R. E., Kowalski, K. C., Graham, T. R. and Kowalski, N. P. (2002). Emotion in sport. In J. M. Silva III and D. E. Stevens (eds), *Psychological foundations of sport* (pp. 107–131). Boston, Mass.: Allyn & Bacon.

Dalgleish, T. and Power, M. J. (1999). *Handbook of cognition and emotion.* Chichester: Wiley.

Damasio, A. (2005). *Descartes' Error.* 10th Anniversary edition, with a new author preface. New York: Penguin Books.

Davidson, R. J. (1994). On emotion, mood, and related affective constructs. In P. Ekman and R. J. Davidson (eds), *The nature of emotion: Fundamental questions* (pp. 51–55). Oxford: Oxford University Press.

Dienstbier, R. A. (1989). Arousal and physiological toughness: Implications for mental and physical health. *Psychological Review,* 96, 84–100.

Dray, K. and Uphill, M. A. (2009). A survey of athletes' counterfactual thinking: precursors, prevalence, and consequences. *Sport and Exercise Psychology Review,* 5, 16–26.

Easterbrook, J. A. (1959). The effect of emotion on cue utilization and the organization of behavior. *Psychological Review,* 66, 183–201.

Ekkekakis, P. and Petruzzello, S. J. (2000). Analysis of the affect measurement conundrum in exercise psychology I. Fundamental issues. *Psychology of Sport and Exercise,* 1, 71–88.

Ekman, P. (1980). *The face of man: Expressions of universal emotions in a New Guinea village.* New York: Garland STPM Press.

Ekman, P. and Davidson, R. J. (1994). *The nature of emotion.* Oxford: Oxford University Press.

Ellsworth, P. C. (1994). Levels of thought and levels of emotions. In P. Ekman and R. J. Davidson (eds), *The nature of emotion: Fundamental questions* (pp. 192–196). Oxford: Oxford University Press.

Erez, A. and Isen, A. M. (2002). The influence of positive affect on the components of expectancy motivation. *Journal of Applied Psychology*, 87, 1055–1067.

Eubank, M., Collins, D. and Smith, N. (2000). The influence of anxiety direction on processing bias. *Journal of Sport and Exercise Psychology*, 22, 292–306.

Eubank, M., Collins, D. and Smith, N. (2002). Anxiety and ambiguity: It's all open to interpretation. *Journal of Sport and Exercise Psychology*, 24, 239–253.

Eysenck, M. W., Derakshan, N., Santos, R. and Calvo, M. G. (2007). Anxiety and cognitive performance: attentional control theory. *Emotion*, 7, 336–353.

Folkman, S. and Lazarus, R. S. (1988). Coping as a mediator of emotion. *Journal of Personality and Social Psychology*, 54, 466–475.

Fredrickson, B. L. (2001). The role of positive emotions in positive psychology – the broaden-and-build theory of positive emotions. *American Psychologist*, 56, 218–226.

Fredrickson, B. L. and Branigan, C. (2005). Positive emotions broaden the scope of attention and thought–action repertoires. *Cognition and Emotion*, 19, 313–332.

Frey, K. P. (1999). Reversal theory: basic concepts. In J. H. Kerr (ed.), *Experiencing sport: Reversal theory*. Chichester, UK: J. Wiley & Sons.

Graham, T. R., Kowalski, K. C. and Crocker, P. R. E. (2002). The contributions of goal characteristics and causal attributions to emotional experience in youth sport participants. *Psychology of Sport and Exercise*, 3, 273–291.

Gross, J. J. (1998). The emerging field of emotion regulation: an integrative review. *Review of General Psychology*, 2, 271–299.

Gross, J. J. and John, O. P. (2003). Individual differences in two emotion regulation processes: implications for affect, relationships, and well being. *Journal of Personality and Social Psychology*, 85, 348–362.

Hackfort, D. (1993). Functional attributions to emotions in sport. In J. R. Nitsch and R. Seiler (eds), *Movement in sport: Psychological foundations and effects*. Proceedings of the VIIIth European Congress of Sport Psychology, 1 (pp. 143–149). Sankt Augustin, Germany: Academia Verlag.

Hanin, Y. L. (1989). Interpersonal and intragroup anxiety in sports. In D. Hackfort and C. D. Spielberger (eds), *Anxiety in sports: An international perspective* (pp. 19–28). Washington, DC: Hemisphere.

Hanin, Y. L. (2000a). Individual zones of optimal functioning (IZOF) model: emotions–performance relationships in sport. In Y. L. Hanin (ed.), *Emotions in sport* (pp. 65–89). Champaign, Ill.: Human Kinetics.

Hanin, Y. L. (2000b). Successful and poor performance and emotions. In Y. L. Hanin (ed.), *Emotions in sport* (pp. 157–187). Champaign, Ill.: Human Kinetics.

Hanton, S., Neil, R. and Mellalieu, S. D. (2008). Recent developments in competitive anxiety direction and competition stress. *International Review of Sport and Exercise Psychology*, 1, 45–57.

Hardy, L., Jones, G. and Gould, D. (1996). *Understanding psychological preparation for sport: Theory and practice of elite performers*. Chichester: John Wiley & Sons.

Hatfield, E., Cacioppo, J. T. and Rapson, R. L. (1994). *Emotional contagion*. Cambridge: Cambridge University Press.

Hohmann, G. W. (1966). Some effects of spinal cord lesions on experiencing emotional feelings. *Psychophysiology*, 3, 143–156.

Jackson, S. A. (2000). Joy, fun, and flow state in sport. In Y. L. Hanin (ed.), *Emotions in sport* (pp. 135–155). Champaign, Ill.: Human Kinetics.

Jones, G. (1995). More than just a game: research developments and issues in competitive anxiety in sport. *British Journal of Psychology*, 86, 449–478.

Jones, G. and Cale, A. (1989). Relationships between multidimensional competitive state anxiety and cognitive and motor subcomponents of performance. *Journal of Sports Sciences*, 7, 229–240.

Jones, G. and Hanton, S. (2001). Pre-competitive feeling states and directional anxiety interpretations. *Journal of Sports Sciences*, 19, 385–395.

Jones, G. and Swain, A. B. J. (1995). Predispositions to experience debilitative and facilitative anxiety in elite and non-elite performers. *The Sport Psychologist*, 9, 201–211.

Jones, G., Swain, A. B. J. and Hardy, L. (1993). Intensity and direction dimensions of competitive state anxiety and relationships with performance. *Journal of Sports Sciences*, 11, 525–532.

Jones, M. V. (2003). Controlling emotions in sport. *The Sport Psychologist*, 17, 471–486.

Jones, M. V., Lane, A. M., Bray, S., Uphill, M. and Catlin, J. (2005). Development and validation of the Sport Emotion Questionnaire (SEQ). *Journal of Sport and Exercise Psychology*, 27, 407–431.

Jones, M. V., Mace, R. D., Bray, S. R., MacRae, A. and Stockbridge, C. (2002). The impact of motivational imagery on the emotional state and self-efficacy levels of novice climbers. *Journal of Sport Behavior*, 25, 57–73.

Jones, M. V., Mace, R. D. and Williams, S. (2000). Relationship between emotional state and performance during international field hockey matches. *Perceptual and Motor Skills*, 90, 691–701.

Jones, M. V., Meijen, C., McCarthy, P. J. and Sheffield, D. (2009). A theory of challenge and threat states in athletes. *International Review of Sport and Exercise Psychology*, 2, 161–180.

Kelly, J. R. and Barsade, S. G. (2001). Mood and emotions in small groups and work teams. *Organizational Behavior and Human Decision Processes*, 86, 99–130.

Kerr, J. H. (1990). Stress and sport: Reversal theory. In G. Jones and L. Hardy (eds), *Stress and performance in sport* (pp. 107–131). Chichester: J Wiley & Sons.

Kerr, J. H. (1997). *Motivation and emotion in sport*. East Sussex: Psychology Press.

Lane, A. M. and Terry, P. C. (2000). The nature of mood: development of a conceptual model with a focus on depression. *Journal of Applied Sport Psychology*, 12, 16–33.

Lazarus, R. S. (1968). Emotions and adaptation: Conceptual and empirical relations. In W. J. Arnold (ed.), *Nebraska symposium on motivation* (pp. 175–266). Lincoln: University of Nebraska Press.

Lazarus, R. S. (1991). *Emotion and adaptation*. Oxford: Oxford University Press.

Lazarus, R. S. (1999). *Stress and emotion: A new synthesis*. New York: Springer.

Lazarus, R. S. (2000a). Cognitive–motivational–relational theory of emotion. In Y. L. Hanin (ed.), *Emotions in sport* (pp. 39–63). Champaign, Ill.: Human Kinetics.

Lazarus, R. S. (2000b). How emotions influence performance in competitive sports. *The Sport Psychologist*, 14, 229–252.

Lerner, J. S. and Keltner, D. (2001). Fear, anger, and risk. *Journal of Personality and Social Psychology*, 81, 146–159.

Levine, L. J. (1996). Anatomy of disappointment: a naturalistic test of appraisal models of sadness, anger, and hope. *Cognition and Emotion*, 10, 337–359.

Lewis, M. and Haviland-Jones, J. M. (eds) (1999). *Handbook of emotions* (2nd edn). London: Guilford Press.

Lindner, K. J. and Kerr, J. H. (2000). Metamotivational orientations in sport participants and non-participants. *Psychology of Sport and Exercise*, 1, 7–25.

Lyubomirsky, S., King, L. and Diener, E. (2005). The benefits of frequent positive affect: does happiness lead to success? *Psychological Bulletin*, 131, 803–855.

Lundqvist, C., Kentta, G. and Raglin, J. S. (2010). Directional anxiety responses in elite and sub-elite young athletes: Intensity of anxiety symptoms matters. *Scandinavian Journal of Medicine and Science in Sports*. doi: SMS1102 [pii] 10.1111/j.1600–0838.2010.01102.x

Males, J. R., Kerr, J. H. and Gerkovich, M. M. (1998). Metamotivational states during canoe slalom competition: a qualitative analysis using reversal theory. *Journal of Applied Sport Psychology*, 10, 185–200.

Malmo, R. B. (1959). Activation: a neuropsychological dimension. *Psychological Review*, 66, 367–386.

Martens, R., Burton, D., Vealey, R. S., Bump, L. A. and Smith, D. E. (1990). Development and validation of the Competitive State Anxiety Inventory – 2. In R. Martens, R. S. Vealey and D. Burton (eds), *Competitive anxiety in sport* (pp. 117–190). Champaign, Ill.: Human Kinetics.

Masters, R. and Maxwell, J. (2008). The theory of reinvestment. *International Review of Sport and Exercise Psychology*, 1, 160–183.

McGraw, A. P., Mellers, B. A. and Tetlock, P. E. (2005). Expectations and emotions of Olympic athletes. *Journal of Experimental Social Psychology*, 41, 438–446.

McMorris, T. and Graydon, J. (1996a). Effect of exercise on the decision-making performance of experienced and inexperienced soccer players. *Research Quarterly for Exercise and Sport*, 67, 109–114.

McMorris, T. and Graydon, J. (1996b). Effect of exercise on soccer decision-making tasks of differing complexities. *Journal of Human Movement Studies*, 30, 177-193.

McMorris, T., Myers, S., MacGillivary, W. W., Sexsmith, J. R., Fallowfield, J., Graydon, J. and Forster, D. (1999). Exercise, plasma catecholamine concentrations and decision-making performance of soccer players on a soccer-specific test. *Journal of Sports Sciences*, 17, 667–676.

McNair, D. M., Lorr, M. and Droppleman, L. F. (1971). *Manual for the Profile of Mood States.* San Diego: Educational and Industrial Testing Service.

Mellalieu, S. D. (2003). Mood matters: But how much? A comment on Lane and Terry (2000). *Journal of Applied Sport Psychology*, 15, 99–114.

Mellalieu, S. D., Hanton, S. and Jones, G. (2003). Emotional labeling and competitive anxiety in preparation and competition. *The Sport Psychologist*, 17, 157–174.

Mendes, W. B., Major, B., McCoy, S. and Blascovich, J. (2008). How attributional ambiguity shapes physiological and emotional responses to social rejection and acceptance. *Journal of Personality and Social Psychology*, 94, 278–291.

Moran, A., Byrne, A. and McGlade, N. (2002). The effects of anxiety and strategic planning on visual search behavior. *Journal of Sports Sciences*, 20, 225–236.

Morgan, W. P. (1968). Personality characteristics of wrestlers participating in the world championships. *Journal of Sports Medicine and Physical Fitness*, 8, 212–216.

Morgan, W. P. (1980). The trait psychology controversy. *Research Quarterly for Exercise and Sport*, 51, 50–76.

Morgan, W. P. (1985). Selected psychological factors limiting performance: a mental health model. In D. H. Clarke and H. M. Eckert (eds), *Limits of human performance* (pp. 70–80). Champaign, Ill.. Human Kinetics.

Murphy, S. M., Woolfolk, R. L. and Budney, A. J. (1988). The effects of emotive imagery on strength performance. *Journal of Sport and Exercise Psychology*, 10, 334–345.

Neave, N. and Wolfson, S. (2003). Testosterone, territoriality, and the 'home advantage'. *Physiology and Behavior*, 78, 269–275.

Neumann, R. and Strack, F. (2000). 'Mood contagion': The automatic transfer of mood between persons. *Journal of Personality and Social Psychology*, 79, 211–223.

Noteboom, J. T., Barnholt, K. R. and Enoka, R. M. (2001a). Activation of the arousal response and impairment of performance increase with anxiety and stressor intensity. *Journal of Applied Physiology*, 91, 2093–2101.

Noteboom, J. T., Fleshner, M. and Enoka, R. M. (2001b). Activation of the arousal response can impair performance on a simple motor task. *Journal of Applied Physiology*, 91, 821–831.

Oxendine, J. B. (1970). Emotional arousal and motor performance. *Quest*, 13, 23–32.

Parfitt, C. G., Jones, J. G. and Hardy, L. (1990). Multidimensional anxiety and performance. In J. G. Jones and L. Hardy (eds), *Stress and performance in sport* (pp. 43–80). Chichester, England: Wiley.

Parfitt, G., Hardy, L. and Pates, J. (1995). Somatic anxiety and physiological arousal: their effects upon a high anaerobic, low memory demand task. *International Journal of Sport Psychology*, 26, 196–213.

Parfitt, G. and Pates, J. (1999). The effects of cognitive and somatic anxiety and self-confidence on components of performance during competition. *Journal of Sports Sciences*, 17, 351–356.

Parkinson, B., Totterdell, P., Briner, R. B. and Reynolds, S. (1996). *Changing moods: The psychology of mood and mood regulation*. London: Longman.

Perkins, D., Wilson, G. V. and Kerr, J. H. (2001). The effects of elevated arousal and mood on maximal strength performance in athletes. *Journal of Applied Sport Psychology*, 13, 239–259.

Platow, M. J., Durante, M., Williams, N., Garrett, M., Walshe, J., Cincotta, S., Lianos, G. and Barutchu, A. (1999). The contribution of sport fan social identity to the production of prosocial behavior. *Group Dynamics: Theory, research, and practice*, 3, 161–169.

Robazza, C., Bortoli, L. and Hanin, Y. (2004). Precompetition emotions, bodily symptoms, and task-specific qualities as predictors of performance in high-level karate athletes. *Journal of Applied Sport Psychology*, 16, 151–165.

Robazza, C., Pellizzari, M., Bertollo, M. and Hanin, Y. L. (2008). Functional impact of emotions on athletic performance: Comparing the IZOF model and the directional perception approach. *Journal of Sports Sciences*, 26, 1033–1047.

Roese, N. J. and Olson, J. M. (1993). Self-esteem and counterfactual thinking. *Journal of Personality and Social Psychology*, 65, 199–206.

Rosenberg, E. L. (1998). Levels of analysis and organization of affect. *Review of General Psychology*, 2, 247–270.

Rowley, A. J., Landers, D. M., Kyllo, L. B. and Etnier, J. L. (1995). Does the iceberg profile discriminate between successful and less successful athletes? A meta-analysis. *Journal of Sport and Exercise Psychology*, 17, 185–199.

Russell, J. A. and Fehr, B. (1994). Fuzzy concepts in a fuzzy hierarchy: Varieties of anger. *Journal of Personality and Social Psychology*, 67, 186–205.

Salvador, A. and Costa, R. (2009). Coping with competition: neuroendocrine responses and cognitive variables. *Neuroscience and Biobehavioral Reviews*, 33, 160–170.

Scanlan, T. K., Russell, D. G., Beals, K. P. and Scanlan, L. A. (2003). Project on elite athlete commitment (PEAK): II. A direct test and expansion of the Sport Commitment Model with elite amateur sportsmen. *Journal of Sport and Exercise Psychology*, 25, 377–401.

Schachter, S. (1964). The interaction of cognitive and physiological determinants of emotional state. In L. Berkowitz (ed.), *Advances in experimental and social psychology*, 1 (pp. 49–80). New York: Academic Press.

Sève, C. Ria, L., Poizat, G., Saury, J. and Durand, M. (2007). Performance-induced emotions experienced during high-stakes table tennis matches. *Psychology of Sport and Exercise*, 8, 25–46.

Skinner, N. and Brewer, N. (2004). Adaptive approaches to competition: Challenge appraisals and positive emotion. *Journal of Sport and Exercise Psychology*, 26, 283–305.

Smith, N., Bellamy, M., Collins, D. J. and Newell, D. (2001). A test of processing efficiency theory in a team sport context. *Journal of Sports Sciences*, 19, 321–332.

Smith, R. E., Smoll, F. L. and Schultz, R. W. (1990). Measurement and correlates of sport-specific cognitive and somatic trait anxiety: The sport anxiety scale. *Anxiety Research*, 2, 263–280.

Stefanucci, J. K., Proffitt, D. R., Clore, G. R. and Parekh, N. (2008). Skating down a steeper slope: fear influences the perception of geographical slant. *Perception*, 37, 321–323.

Strack, F., Martin, L. L. and Stepper, S. (1988). Inhibiting and facilitating conditions of the human smile: a non-obtrusive test of the facial feedback hypothesis. *Journal of Personality and Social Psychology*, 54, 768–777.

Tamir, M. and Ford, B. Q. (2009). Choosing to be afraid: Preferences for fear as a function of goal pursuit. *Emotion*, 9, 488–497.

Thatcher, J., Kerr, J., Amies, K. and Day, M. (2007). A Reversal Theory analysis of psychological responses during sports injury rehabilitation. *Journal of Sport Rehabilitation*, 16, 343–362.

Thatcher, J., Kuroda, Y., Thatcher, R. and Legrand, F. D. (2010). Perceptual and cognitive responses during exercise: relationships with metamotivational state and dominance. *European Journal of Sports Sciences*, 10, 188–207.

Totterdell, P. (2000). Catching moods and hitting runs: mood linkage and subjective performance in professional sport teams. *Journal of Applied Psychology*, 85, 848–859.

Uphill, M. A. and Jones, M. V. (2007). Antecedents of emotions in elite athletes: a cognitive motivational relational theory perspective. *Research Quarterly for Exercise and Sport,* 78, 79–89.

Uphill, M. A., McCarthy, P. J. and Jones, M. V. (2009). Getting a grip on emotion regulation in sport: conceptual foundations and practical application. In S. Mellalieu and S. Hanton (eds), *Advances in applied sport psychology* (pp. 162–194). London: Routledge.

Vallerand, R. J. (1983). On emotion in sport: theoretical and social psychological perspectives. *Journal of Sport Psychology,* 5, 197–215.

Vallerand, R. J. (1987). Antecedents of self-related affects in sport: preliminary evidence on the intuitive-reflective appraisal model. *Journal of Sport Psychology,* 9, 161–182.

Vallerand, R. J. and Blanchard, C. M. (2000). The study of emotion in sport and exercise: historical, definitional, and conceptual perspectives. In Y. L. Hanin (ed.), *Emotions in sport* (pp. 3–37). Champaign, Ill.: Human Kinetics.

Vargas-Tonsing, T. M. (2009). An exploratory examination of the effects of coaches' pre-game speeches on athletes' perceptions of self-efficacy and emotion. *Journal of Sport Behavior,* 32, 92–111.

Vargas-Tonsing, T. M. and Guan, J. (2007). Athletes' preferences for informational and emotional pre-game speech content. *International Journal of Sports Sciences and Coaching,* 2, 171–180.

Weiner, B. (1986). *An attributional theory of motivation and emotion.* New York: Springer-Verlag.

Wiens, S., Mezzacappa, E. S. and Katkin, E. S. (2000). Heartbeat detection and the experience of emotions. *Cognition and Emotion,* 14, 417–427.

Williams, J. M. and Andersen, M. B. (1998). Psychosocial antecedents of sport injury: Review and critique of the stress and injury model. *Journal of Applied Sport Psychology,* 10, 5–25.

Williams, S. E., Cumming, J. and Balanos, G. M. (2010). The use of imagery to manipulate challenge and threat appraisal states in athletes. *Journal of Sport and Exercise Psychology,* 32, 339–358.

Wilson, M. R., Vine, S. J. and Wood, G. (2009). The influence of anxiety on visual attentional control in basketball free throw shooting. *Journal of Sport and Exercise Psychology,* 31, 152–168.

Woodman, T., Davis, P. A., Hardy, L., Callow, N., Glasscock, I. and Yuill Proctor, J. (2009). Emotions and sport performance: An exploration of happiness, hope, and anger. *Journal of Sport and Exercise Psychology,* 31, 169–188.

Woodman, T. and Hardy, L. (2001). Stress and Anxiety. In R. N. Singer, H. A. Hausenblas and C. M. Janelle (eds), *Handbook of research on sport psychology,* (pp. 290–318.) New York: John Wiley & Sons.

Zillmann, D., Katcher, A. H. and Milavsky, B. (1972). Excitation transfer from physical exercise to subsequent aggressive behavior. *Journal of Experimental Social Psychology,* 8, 247–259.

3

COPING WITH TRAUMA IN SPORT

Melissa Day, University of Chichester

Like many trauma victims, when David Busst is asked to describe the events of Saturday, April 8, 1996, at Old Trafford, his mind's eye operates in slow motion.

> Eighty seconds gone and we force a corner …. I trot up from central defence to take up my usual position at the back post … the ball curls in …. Noel Whelan heads it goalwards …. Peter Schmeichel parries and I slide in with Brian McClair and Denis Irwin …. I manage to get my toe to the ball first … and that's when the screaming started.
>
> *(Philip, Daily Telegraph, 19 January 2005)*

Trauma in sport differs from many other sports stressors in that traumatic events can involve severe injury and even loss of life. As described by David Busst in his interview with the *Daily Telegraph*, traumatic events will often have a rapid onset and may also influence many individuals at once. The impact of Busst's injury was evident on those nearby, such as goalkeeper Peter Schmeichel who shielded his eyes with his hands. The events of the match in 1996 may have had far-reaching consequences, not only on Busst who nearly lost his leg, but also on those players who witnessed his injury.

The aim of this chapter is to examine the impact of such traumatic experiences in the sporting context. The chapter examines how research defining trauma and vicarious trauma in psychology can be applied to sport, identifying how an athlete is likely to react to traumatic experiences. It also examines psychological theories used to explain trauma responses, identifying the potential impacts of trauma and how trauma may change an athlete's approach to training and competition. Finally, this chapter examines effective and ineffective coping strategies when faced with trauma, and the implications for applied sport psychologists.

Defining trauma and its relevance to the sporting context

Given the wealth of research that has examined stress in the sport psychology literature, it is important to understand the distinction between a stressful event or situation and one that is traumatic. Early criteria used to define trauma-related pathologies in the *Diagnostic and Statistical Manual of Mental Disorders–III-R* (DSM: APA, 1987, p. 250) included the requirement that the traumatic experience be 'an event outside the range of usual human experience'. Later criteria eliminated this requirement, reflecting that although traumatic events are not a frequent occurrence, in reality such experiences are indeed within the realms of usual human experience. Cahill and Foa (2007) estimated from epidemiological studies in the United States that between 37 and 92 per cent of respondents (depending on the sample) report experiencing one or more events that can be categorized as traumatic. This includes experiences or events such as accidental injury (Scotti et al., 1995), domestic violence (Krause et al., 2008), and combat (Monson and Friedman, 2006).

In the sporting context Wippert and Wippert (2008) suggest that acute stress may be separated into normative and non–normative life events. Normative stressors may occur as part of natural, expected development in an athletic career. For example, the transition from youth to senior athlete may induce a number of stressors yet would be expected in the life cycle of an athlete. On the other hand non–normative events occur with less frequency and are typically unforeseen. For example, sudden career termination caused by injury may be unpredictable and unexpected. Indeed, in Dugdale, Eklund and Gordon's (2002) study of Olympic athletes, over two-thirds of interviewees indicated that their most stressful sporting experience was unexpected. This distinction between expected and unexpected stressors demonstrates the potentially more harmful consequences of unexpected or unplanned stressors. Early laboratory research using animals demonstrated a preference for predictable situations in which the stimulus is signalled as far as possible in advance (Weinberg and Levine, 1980). Lazarus and Folkman (1984) suggested that this preference for predictability is because it allows an anticipatory coping response: the individual can prepare in some way to reduce the adverseness of the stressor. This implies that when an individual has more time available to prepare for the stressor they may perceive a greater availability of coping resources and the resulting stress may be minimized. However, sudden and unpredictable situations only allow a limited preparation time to assess coping resources, and consequently require immediate coping strategies that may result in elevated stress perceptions. It is also important to highlight that not all unpredictable or unexpected events can be categorized as 'traumatic'. Instead this forms one possible feature of the event that may increase the likelihood that it is perceived as stressful or even traumatic.

One approach to categorizing both stress and trauma is the stimulus approach, based on identifying the environmental factors that may cause a stress response. For example, Holmes and Rahe's (1967) checklist of major life changes and their associated readjustment weights provided an early method of measuring stress.

Using this scale a number of life events could be categorized from most stressful to least stressful, based on the amount of readjustment required after each one. The most stressful events included the death of a loved one and divorce, while the lower end of the list included minor law violations and Christmas. Considering the impact that the environment may have on sports performance, it is not surprising that a substantial amount of research in sport has employed a stimulus-based approach to determine the most frequently cited sources of stress. One of the first examples was Gould, Jackson and Finch (1993), who examined sources of stress in national champion figure skaters. Features of the skating environment such as expected potential and environmental demands for instance, media exposure were highly cited sources of stress by the skaters. Gould et al. (1993) also demonstrated that the stimulus approach could be used effectively to identify commonly occurring stressors in sport.

According to Lazarus (1999), the idea that a stimulus is the cause of a stress reaction, which then results in a coping response, is an appealing and intuitive method of examining stress. However, whilst this approach may provide us with examples or lists of potential stressors in particular situations, even the most frequently cited environmental stressors will not be perceived as stressful by all individuals. Further, with regards to trauma, the list can never be exhaustive since traumatic experiences may be highly unexpected or unusual, and consequently may not be included in stimulus-based lists. This suggests that attempting to categorize trauma-based events using a stimulus approach may mean that many life events are not included on the list, particularly in the sporting context where stressors are generally categorized by commonality or frequency of occurrence. While it is possible to suggest that particular events have the potential to be traumatic, further insight to verify this may be gained by also focusing on the individual's reaction to the experienced event.

An alternative to the stimulus-based approach is provided by the response approach, defined through the troubled *reaction* to stressful stimuli. Traumatic pathologies such as post-traumatic stress disorder (PTSD) can be categorized using both a stimulus and a response approach. The essential criterion for the diagnosis of PTSD is the individual's exposure to an event (stimulus). The *DSM IV-TR* (APA, 2000) criterion for a diagnosis is that the individual 'experienced, witnessed or was confronted with an event or events that involved actual or threatened death or serious injury, or a threat to the physical integrity of self or other' (pp. 427–428). The criteria also specify a number of further symptoms that are experienced by the individual (response). First, the response must include intense fear, helplessness or horror. A number of response symptoms may also be experienced, including re-experiencing the event (for instance through dreams or flashbacks), persistent avoidance (such as avoiding places associated with the trauma), increased anxiety and arousal (such as poor concentration or insomnia), and social or occupational impairment (*DSM IV-TR,* APA, 2000).

The events that have previously been characterized as traumatic by the sporting literature include the sudden death of an athlete on the sports team (Vernacchia,

Reardon and Templin, 1997), hearing about the death of another athlete in an individual sport (Kerr, 2007), athlete suicide (Buchko, 2005), witnessing or hearing about the injury of a team mate (Day, Bond and Smith, in review; O'Neill, 2008), athletic career termination (Wippert and Wippert, 2008), and the transition from professional sport to retirement (Carless and Douglas, 2009; Douglas and Carless, 2009). Much of the research that focuses on trauma in sport is clustered around two main themes: death and serious injury in sport, and career termination. While research on death and injury in sport clearly fits the *DSM-IV-TR* criteria for trauma, it may be more difficult to assess whether career transitions are truly traumatic. Wippert and Wippert (2008) proposed that the degree of trauma or threat this causes is highly dependent on factors such as the evaluation process, the attribution of blame, and the perception of meaning associated with the event. They continue that for some athletes career transitions can lead to severe emotional disturbances and threaten their physical and psychological integrity. From this perspective, while career transitions do not involve injury or death they do threaten the integrity of the individual, and as such could be categorized as traumatic.

Vicarious trauma: its significance to the athlete and the sport psychologist

Trauma may result not only from actually experiencing an event but also from witnessing or even learning about an event without being personally involved. It has been well documented that psychologists and counsellors working with traumatized individuals may be at risk of vicarious trauma after listening to client accounts of traumatic experiences (e.g. Baird and Kracen, 2006; McCann and Pearlman, 1990). Research has demonstrated that symptoms almost identical to PTSD can be displayed in this situation (Wilson and Lindy, 1994). Herman (1997) explained this as a form of traumatic countertransference, in which the counsellor or psychologist experiences similar emotions to the client, albeit to a lesser degree. Often the client who has experienced trauma discusses the events in detail. For example, a severely injured athlete might give graphically detailed descriptions of the injury and the psychological and emotional aftermath. The visual images this creates for the psychologist and their empathic engagement with the athlete may leave the psychologist at risk of vicarious trauma. Consequently it is essential that support mechanisms such as supervision are in place for psychologists working with trauma.

A wider network of individuals surrounding the athlete may also be at risk of vicarious trauma. For example, a traumatic event may impact on coaches, team mates, friends and family, and even other athletes who have heard about the trauma. The indications from research (e.g. Holmes, Brewin and Henessey, 2004) are that individuals may have intrusive memories of traumatic events either from direct sensory experience (as a victim or witness) or from indirect experience such as audio accounts. The trauma film paradigm has been used to examine intrusive images after witnessing traumatic incidents. For example, Holmes et al. (2004)

reported a series of experimental studies in which nonclinical participants viewed a trauma film under several different encoding conditions. This well-established experimental model creates an analogue situation in which responses to witnessing trauma can be studied in the laboratory (Holmes et al., 2009). In general, participants are asked to view the trauma film and then record any subsequent intrusive thoughts in a diary (e.g. Holmes et al., 2004; Stuart, Holmes and Brewin, 2005). The research has suggested that individuals witnessing trauma may indeed experience intrusive images and recollections of the event (Holmes, 2004). Non-laboratory-based research has examined responses to actual trauma, such as the televized tragic events of 11 September 2001 (9/11). Holmes, Creswell and O'Connor (2007) suggested that a significant minority of their sample of London school children who had viewed the events of 9/11 on television reported PTSD symptoms such as re-experiencing and avoiding reminders of it two and six months after the events. These results indicate that PTSD symptoms can occur even in witnesses who have no direct connection to the victim(s).

The results from trauma film research have direct implications for the sporting context. At present, sport psychology research has tended to focus on the direct sensory victim of a traumatic event. For example, research on athletic injury centres on the psychological responses of the injured athlete and on their personal injury experiences (e.g. Udry et al., 1997). It rarely considers the responses of the coach, the officials, the remaining players or the audience. Yet trauma literature demonstrates that these witnesses may indeed develop trauma symptoms. O'Neill (2008) was one of few researchers to consider the impact of athletic injury from the perspective of the indirect witness. This longitudinal study examined the possible existence of injury contagion in sport. The results did not conclusively establish injury contagion, but did demonstrate that after witnessing the injury of another alpine ski racer, athletes used more fear-related words and phrases. O'Neill concluded that this supported the assertion that there was a psychological effect on team members after injury to a team mate. Based on the principle of emotional contagion (Hatfield, Cacioppo and Rapson, 1994), O'Neill had proposed that often after one athlete in a team sustains an injury, their team-mates are injured shortly afterwards. In the same way as emotional contagion can occur in a sports team (for example, an elated mood is communicated across the whole team; see Chapter 8), injury contagion may occur, with one player's injury drawing an emotional response from their uninjured team mates. This emotional response may include fear of a particular skill or part of a particular course (for example, a specific corner on a cycling course) or a general fear of injury. O'Neill (2008) explained that injury contagion may also occur when the emotional trauma of witnessing an injury causes the athlete to change their own performance tactics, thereby leading to an increased personal injury risk. For some individuals he proposed that an emotional response to witnessing injury could be conceptualized as a *forme frustre*, a subclinical form of PTSD. Similarly, Chase, Magyar and Drake (2005) proposed that a fear of injury might have a detrimental effect on performance since it may disrupt attention, inhibit movement, and disrupt skill mechanics (see Chapter 11).

Ironically, fear of injury and the strategies used to limit risk might actually create a greater risk of injury.

In addition to the traumatic effect of witnessing injury, research has demonstrated that hearing about the injury of a fellow athlete may result in symptoms of vicarious trauma. Krans et al. (2010) established that intrusive visual images could develop from listening to a traumatic verbal report. They found that after listening to a verbal report of a road-traffic accident, participants developed intrusive visual images and reported a significant emotional impact. In the sporting context Kerr (2007) presented a case study of a skydiver who withdrew from the sport after hearing about the accidental death of a fellow skydiver. She completed just one more skydive after hearing about the accident. She reported anxiety, depression and suicidal thoughts, and described how she felt unable to ensure her own safety when involved in the sport, and believed that others engaged in the sport could die at any moment.

Overall, research has demonstrated that vicarious trauma may impact on both the athlete and the applied sport psychologist. However, it is also noteworthy that despite these research findings, sports injury research has continued to focus on the experience of the initial victim, and to neglect the potential effects on direct and indirect witnesses.

Individual differences and susceptibility to trauma

While clinical definitions of trauma, vicarious trauma and PTSD have provided indications of potentially traumatic events, research has also focused on individuals who may be particularly susceptible to traumatic responses after experiencing such events. Wippert and Wippert (2008) suggested factors that determine whether an event is perceived as traumatic that support Lazarus's (1999) proposition that the degree and type of stress response will vary from person to person, meaning that the stimulus or response alone is insufficient to define stress. He proposed that the core element of stress is not found in either the environment or the individual, but in the relationship between the two. Research on factors that could trigger a trauma response is mostly longitudinal and retrospective in design, and generally examines the relation of risk factors to PTSD in a population exposed to trauma. Some studies have also included a control group who have not been exposed to trauma.

Brewin, Andrews and Valentine (2000) conducted a meta-analysis on fourteen separate risk factors for PTSD. This included results from seventy-seven articles from 1980 onwards. Their findings demonstrated that the severity of the traumatic event, lack of social support, and additional life stress had stronger effect sizes than other pretrauma factors. While trauma severity showed a greater likelihood of PTSD, Brewin et al. (2000) discussed the difficulty of collecting retrospective data on PTSD. They suggested that their retrospective research design might have resulted in an inflated report of the trauma severity. This is demonstrated by the significantly greater effect size in retrospective studies than in prospective studies.

Gender was also investigated as a moderator variable of PTSD symptomology. According to the APA (2000), in general females have a greater tendency to suffer from anxiety disorders. Brewin et al. (2000) found that women were more likely than men to develop PTSD, although this was not demonstrated in combat veterans. Despite this finding, overall results from the meta-analysis were that when the trauma event is held constant, women are at a greater risk of developing PTSD than men. O'Neill (2008) found that following the injury of a team mate, females showed a significant increase in the use of fear-related language. Males showed a higher baseline use of fear-related language but their increase in usage after the injury of a team mate was not significant.

There are a number of possible additional risk factors for PTSD. Age at the onset of trauma has been shown to be a significant risk factor in the military: the younger the individual is at the onset of the trauma experience, the greater their risk of developing PTSD. Education, previous trauma and general childhood adversity have also been found to predict PTSD to a varying extent, depending on the population. Less educated individuals are proposed to be at a greater risk of PTSD. This risk factor has been linked to early trauma experiences and general childhood adversity, which could in turn have a negative impact on school ability and consequently intelligence. At present, no research has examined the predictors of trauma in sport, although Day et al. (in review) suggest that factors such as personal injury experiences may impact on the level of vicarious trauma experienced when witnessing injury in others. As well as generally applicable factors such as age, trauma severity, lack of social support and additional life stress, there are some factors that may specifically apply to the sporting context such as ability level and athletic identity.

Psychological theories of trauma and PTSD

Following the inclusion of PTSD in the *DSM-III* a number of theories have been put forward to explain the natural course of post-trauma reactions and the specific symptoms of PTSD. Here I explain and review those theoretical explanations that are most relevant and applicable to the sporting context. The chapter discusses schema theory (Epstein, 1991; Horowitz, 1986), emotional processing theory (Foa and Riggs, 1993) and dual representation theory (Brewin, 2001).

Schema theories

Schemas represent general knowledge and core assumptions about objects, situations and events, which are then used to guide characteristic ways of attending, interpreting and responding to the world (McCann and Pearlman, 1990). Baird and Kracen (2006) explain that in most situations individuals believe that the world is safe and that they themselves are relatively free from harm. As individuals gain new everyday experiences information is automatically assimilated into existing schemas and pre-existing world views are restored. If everyday experiences support an individual's existing schemas, they serve to strengthen them. For example, an individual who thinks of themself as a talented swimmer and successfully completes a swimming event will have this assumption confirmed. Janoff–Bulman (1999) suggests that schemas include our fundamental assumptions about the nature of the external world, and our beliefs about ourselves. Most individuals' schemas assume that the world is benevolent and meaningful, and the self is worthy.

Two suggestions have been made for how trauma events may impact on an individual's schemas (Cahill and Foa, 2007). The first is that traumatic events will usually be discrepant with existing assumptions. Joseph and Linley (2005) supported this assertion. After witnessing or experiencing a traumatic event, the individual may be forced to question their beliefs, for example of invulnerability, as they realize that injury is possible and has occurred in others.

Second, Cahill and Foa (2007) suggested that processing a traumatic experience requires modification of existing assumptions through either accommodation or assimilation. If an individual accommodates the trauma information, they are said to have revised their schemas to take into account the new information. This accommodation of experiences could be in either a negative or a positive direction, depending on the meaning attributed to the traumatic event. Alternatively to assimilate the trauma information means that the individual perceives the new information to be consistent with their existing beliefs. Assimilation following trauma is in most cases not immediately possible since existing schemas provide no frame for understanding the traumatic experience. Payne, Joseph and Tudway (2007) provided an appealing analogy to the processes of accommodation and assimilation in picking up the pieces of a broken vase. The individual might choose to glue the vase back together (assimilation), although the result would be more fragile than the undamaged vase. Alternatively, the individual might discard the pieces and throw them away (negative accommodation) or use them as a mosaic to build something new (positive accommodation).

Schema theories may be useful in explaining why, when faced with identical situations, one individual may experience a trauma response whereas another may not. If the information received from the situation or event does not threaten the individual's schemas and worldviews, they may not experience this as traumatic and they may be able to assimilate this information. On the other hand, an event that does threaten an individual's pre–existing schemas may cause disruption as the individual attempts either to assimilate this information into the previous set of assumptions, or to change the assumptions so that the traumatic experience is accommodated. Although assimilating trauma information may be difficult, it is not impossible. For example, an athlete who has suffered a severe injury but who wishes to return to sport might blame the injury on her own behaviour and mistakes, and maintain the assumption that the sport is safe. An accommodating rather than assimilating response would be to recognize that the sport is associated with a high risk of injury. Consequently her revised schemas may cause her to become increasingly concerned about the risk of injury and disrupt her ability to perform.

Although schema theories offer a comprehensive explanation of post-traumatic reactions they have been criticized for failing to explain the experiences of individuals who suffer multiple traumas (Cahill and Foa, 2007). Research has demonstrated that many individuals experience multiple traumas, each of which may shatter their fundamental assumptions. In accordance with schema theory it might be expected that new traumas would no longer be able to violate the pre-existing schemas of safety and well-being. Any such initial schema would already have been shattered and accommodated to form new schemas that fit the trauma history. Consequently the individual may be expected to already hold schemas that are a comparatively good fit with the new trauma information, which would confirm their schemas rather than shatter them. It might therefore be expected that an individual who has experienced multiple traumas would recover quickly after a new trauma and demonstrate fewer trauma symptoms than an individual who has never experienced trauma. Yet research has opposed this suggestion, demonstrating that a history of previous trauma may actually be a predictor of PTSD (e.g. Breslau et al., 1999).

Emotion processing theory

Similar to schema theories, emotional processing theory also focuses on the pre-trauma beliefs of the individual. However, this theory suggests that those individuals who have rigid pre-trauma beliefs are the most vulnerable to PTSD. Foa and Rothbaum (1998) suggested that an individual's pre-trauma beliefs might be positive or negative. An example of positive pre-trauma beliefs was demonstrated in Kerr's (2007) case study of the skydiver who heard about the skydiving death of a friend. Until then she had believed that skydiving was a safe activity, that she was able to control the risks and take all the necessary safety precautions. The death of her friend contradicted this belief and destroyed her conviction that skydiving was essentially safe. An example of negative pre-trauma beliefs is an athlete who believes that his sport is dangerous, and is constantly afraid of injury. If he sustained or witnessed an injury it would reaffirm these beliefs. Thus emotion processing theory could explain why individuals who have experienced previous trauma and consequently already have negative assumptions about the world are at greater risk of developing PTSD symptoms. It demonstrates that it is the rigidity of beliefs that may be problematic, regardless of whether the beliefs are positive or negative.

Cahill and Foa (2007) asserted that the main premise of emotional processing theory is that anxiety disorders stem from fear structures in memory. These fear structures may include feared stimuli, fear responses, and their associated meanings. A fear structure is activated when information in the environment matches some of the information represented in the fear structure. Fear structures may form part of a normal and healthy reaction to harmful situations. For example, hearing a fire alarm may accurately represent a potentially dangerous situation and therefore prompt individuals to take action. Cahill and Foa (2007) continued, however, that in some individuals these fear structures might become maladaptive. This can be seen when avoidance responses are evoked by harmless stimuli, when responses are excessive and easily triggered, or when harmless stimuli are appraised as threatening. In the sporting context an athlete returning to sport following an injury may experience these avoidance responses when triggers of the injury scenario occur: for example, hearing a particular sound associated with the injury such as the noise of the whistle, or engaging in a particular activity such as a rugby scrum.

In order to change these maladaptive fear responses, emotional processing theory suggests that exposure to the feared stimulus must occur alongside new information that is incompatible with the erroneous information contained in the fear structure. Consequently the fear structure is activated but the corrective information provided lessens the fear response. For example, the rugby player might take part in a number of scrums without ill-effects, and this would help to replace the negative fear structures with a positive structure. Brewin and Holmes (2004) highlighted that emotional processing theory offers a sophisticated account of the mechanisms that may underlie the success of using prolonged exposure as a method of reducing symptoms of PTSD. Exposure therapies such as flooding have been used to treat phobias and PTSD symptoms by allowing the individual to experience the feared event or stimulus while affirming that no harm will occur, consequently changing negative fear structures to positive. Although emotional processing theory offers a comprehensive explanation for the fear responses that are often associated with trauma, it has been criticized for being too simplistic to allow understanding of more complex trauma. For example, this theory is unable to take into account that individuals recounting trauma may sometimes switch between emotion laden descriptions and more detached descriptions. Instead, emotion processing theory presumes that trauma information will result in strong associations for the individual, despite the inclusion of dissociation in PTSD symptoms. Thus it cannot be used to explain more complex cases of trauma in which the individual dissociates from the experience, or cases that involve post-trauma memory gaps or amnesia.

Dual representation theory

This is based on the hypothesis that people have two separate memory systems which operate in parallel, verbally accessible memory (VAM) and situationally accessible memory (SAM) (Stuart et al., 2005). VAM contains memories that can be accessed in words, whereas SAM contains information in the form of images. VAM is integrated with other autobiographical memories; it contains information that has received sufficient conscious processing to be transferred into a long-term memory store in a form that can easily be retrieved. In contrast the SAM system contains lower-level perceptual information that has not received much conscious attention, and has not been processed in sufficient depth to enter the VAM system. This may include sights, sounds, and information about bodily responses such as increased heart rate or temperature changes (Brewin and Holmes, 2003).

Dual representation theory (Brewin, Dalgliesh and Joseph, 1996) postulates that VAM and SAM take precedence over each other at different times (Brewin and

Holmes, 2003). Trauma memories may be represented both as ordinary episodic memories in the VAM and as image-based memories in the SAM. SAM memories may be difficult to control and difficult to communicate to others since the SAM system does not use a verbal code. It is when SAM memories are triggered that they are experienced as intrusive images, one of the main symptoms of PTSD. These can be defined as 'mental events which are perceived as interrupting a person's stream of consciousness by capturing the focus of attention' (Salkovskis, 1990, p. 91).

Research has suggested that a detailed VAM representation of the trauma is necessary to block the unwanted and automatic retrieval of SAM representations and the intrusive images that accompany these (Brewin, 2001). It has also been demonstrated that tasks that disrupt VAM encoding during a trauma will lead to increased intrusions, whereas disrupting the SAM system will lead to decreased intrusions. Suggested explanations for these effects are that processed VAM representations may inhibit lower-level SAM representations and disrupting VAM encoding will lead to increased SAM encoding and more intrusive images. Thus in order to lessen intrusions the SAM system should be disrupted. Holmes et al. (2004) used a variety of tasks to present such disruptions. Participants were asked to watch a trauma film and in the week after watching the film were asked to record the number of intrusions that occurred. They were randomly assigned to one of three groups, one control group and two groups who took part in a task while watching the film. One was a visuospatial tapping task: participants were asked to tap a sequence of five keys continuously on a keyboard that was concealed from view. The aim of this task was to impoverish SAM representations. In order to interfere with encoding into the VAM system participants in the third experimental group were taught how to dissociate from the trauma, and were required to do this while watching the film. Results demonstrated that participants who engaged in the visuospatial tapping task during the trauma film reported fewer intrusive memories than those who did not engage in this task. Further, those participants in the dissociation group experienced an increase in intrusive memories after watching the film. This supports the proposition that processes of encoding are critical in determining the likelihood of intrusive cognitions post trauma. By disrupting the SAM representations through the use of the visuospatial tapping task, the traumatic memories were less likely to intrude in the subsequent week. Alternatively, when the VAM system was impoverished the ability to suppress intrusive images was reduced.

Overall, dual representation theory has been well supported in the research literature, particularly by experimental research such as that by Holmes et al. (2003). However, there are some limitations to this research, particularly since trauma films are generally viewed in a remote and controlled experimental context. It is not clear how far results in the experimental context can be generalized to real-life traumatic experiences. Further, it is likely that the definition of trauma in the *DSM-V* will be revised so that exposure through electronic media such as television or films is no longer included. Yet this research does provide some important applied suggestions.

For example, during the individual final of the women's floor competition in the 2009 world gymnastics championships, one of the contestants landed on her head midway through a floor routine and incurred a serious spinal injury. This accident was seen by a number of gymnasts waiting to compete. BBC footage of the competition showed these witnesses, and illustrated a number of differing coping strategies. Some coaches turned their gymnasts away from the floor, engaging them in conversation and distracting them from the medical team attending to the injured gymnast. Dual representation theory suggests that this is an effective strategy. Other gymnasts stood and watched as the injured gymnast was placed on a spinal board. Interestingly, the title was won by the only athlete who had competed prior to the trauma. It is possible, though obviously not readily provable, that witnessing the accident affected the performances of the rest of the contestants.

Coping effectively with trauma and applied implications

Since trauma is no longer defined as outside the realms of usual human experience, it is important to recognize that helping an individual to cope with trauma may be an essential role of the applied sport psychologist. According to Sutton (2002), for the majority of individuals who encounter some kind of trauma, the more acute and distressing symptoms will occur during the 48-hour period after the trauma event. The immediate after-effects of trauma may include not only cognitive and emotional effects but also physiological symptoms such as nausea, cardiac symptoms, fatigue and increased muscle tension (Saari, 2005). For many individuals these will be temporary effects, part of a natural response to witnessing or experiencing a traumatic event.

The individual may cope with trauma using the two opposing strategies of denial or intrusive thoughts and images (Horowitz, 1986). Although intrusive images and thoughts may intuitively be considered harmful given their potential for eliciting negative emotions, some researchers suggest that these images allow the individual to process and reframe the trauma (Park and Ai, 2006). From a schema theory perspective, engaging with these memories will allow the individual to reframe the trauma, making meaning of the events and seeing its implications in a different and more acceptable way. Nonetheless Creamer (1995) warns that intrusive thoughts can be both adaptive and dysfunctional. Dysfunctional intrusions can prompt avoidance of the trauma, a high degree of arousal, and continuing intrusive cognitions over a period of time as experienced in PTSD. Further, dual representation theory posits that these intrusions will be present because the individual was unable to process the trauma sufficiently using the VAM system. The individual experiencing a high number of intrusions may find that these memories are more emotion laden, particularly with primary emotions that were experienced during the trauma. They may also find that these intrusions are difficult to control and difficult to communicate to others.

Strategies for coping with trauma have generally been categorized in the research literature into approach and avoidance based. While some individuals may attempt to suppress all images of the traumatic event and avoid conversation about them, others may actively seek support to cope with these events. Research has indicated that avoidance coping post-trauma may be positively associated with PTSD symptoms (e.g. Bryant and Harvey, 1995; Krause et al., 2008). In the sporting context Wippert and Wippert (2008) found that efforts to avoid trauma-related experiences in the time period immediately following the event might be closely related to the development of symptoms of traumatic stress. Interestingly, findings from their research also suggest that as time passes it is the perceived intrusiveness of trauma-related experiences that becomes increasingly relevant to the number of traumatic stress symptoms reported, while suppression attempts play a lesser role. Thus Wippert and Wippert suggest that it is early avoidance that is related to the development of posttraumatic symptoms, while intrusive thoughts may be related to the ongoing nature of these symptoms.

An alternative approach is suggested by Payne et al. (2007), who proposed that initially the environment might not be conducive to approach coping. For example, in the aftermath of a traumatic event support services may not be in place, other individuals in the athlete's usual support network may also have been involved in the traumatic event, or the athlete may feel too emotionally overwhelmed to discuss the trauma with others. Consequently the environment may not support the use of approach coping. Vernaccia et al. (1997) described the avoidance behaviours of a sports team following the death of a team mate. They commented that as a result of the trauma of losing a team mate, most of the athletes avoided the gym and playing or practising in it. Yet Payne et al. (2007) proposed that individuals would be inherently motivated to pursue well-being and fulfilment after trauma as long as that drive is supported by the social environment. Thus the availability of coping resources and a supportive environment will enable an individual to engage in approach coping behaviours. The main form of approach coping advocated in the research literature has been the use of social support following trauma. As highlighted by Rees, Smith and Sparkes (2003), social support can have a stress-buffering effect, protecting the individual from the effects of stressful events (see Chapter 6). It seems important therefore that the applied sport psychologist is aware of the important role of social support following trauma. Buchko (2005) emphasized that at times of crisis it is important to ensure that athletes are able to share their story, that their emotions are validated, and that the rules and roles of a support system are put in place.

Research in the sporting context highlights the importance of providing adequate support to athletes who have experienced or witnessed trauma. For example, O'Neill (2008) suggested that individual or team counselling could be made available for those individuals who desire it. Vernacchia et al. (1997) further highlight that following trauma the athletic team may close ranks and attempt to cope with the situation from within rather than seek outside help. It is important therefore for the sport psychology practitioner to recognize that they will be part of a support team that may also include coaches, athletic directors and medical staff. Finally, O'Neill also suggested that it might be possible to identify at-risk athletes by a history of family dysfunction, previous personal traumas, or a personal history of anxiety or depression. It is also important to ensure that sufficient support is made available to any individual who witnesses trauma in sport. It must also be acknowledged that this experience of vicarious trauma may not only include those who have been direct witnesses to trauma, but individuals who have heard reports about traumatic events. Vicarious trauma may also affect applied sport psychologists, who should ensure that they have adequate support mechanisms in place when working with clients who have experienced trauma.

Conclusions

While there has been a vast amount of research that has centred on stress and coping in the sporting context, few studies have examined trauma. As Lazarus (1999) suggests, this may be the difference between an individual feeling 'whelmed' and 'overwhelmed' (p. 129). He proposes that individuals will be able to cope with a certain amount of stress without developing serious symptoms; hence they are whelmed but not overwhelmed. It is after experiencing a traumatic situation that an individual may feel overwhelmed and consequently struggle to cope. Although this may not be a common occurrence in the sporting context, it is important to recognize the contribution of literature that allows us to understand the individual who has experienced trauma. Further, the past few years have seen an increase in the number of sports-related studies that are beginning to recognize the potential for trauma to occur in the sporting context. However, as with any emerging research topic there remain a number of unexplored avenues. As highlighted in this chapter in particular, this may include the impact of trauma and vicarious trauma in sport on all individuals in the sporting network, including athletes, coaches and spectators. While literature from other areas of psychology and from counselling demonstrates the potential for vicarious trauma in counsellors and psychologists, the impact on sport psychologists is currently unknown. Finally, one of the most frequently advocated methods of coping with trauma is social support, yet the most effective types and sources of support during sporting trauma remain unexamined.

Overall, there is a vast amount of literature that documents the impact of trauma and attempts to provide theoretical explanations for and justify effective strategies to cope with trauma. While such literature recognizes that trauma is inevitable in life, the sport psychology literature must begin to recognize that trauma is also inevitable in sport. It is constantly acknowledged that injury risk in sport is high. However the implications of witnessing or sustaining a severe injury that may lead to post-traumatic symptomology are not well developed in the literature. Further, other life events such as death, bereavement, and sudden retirement may also occur in the sporting context and may also be traumatic. Thus while at most times the sporting environment has the potential to enhance well-being, the need for research on trauma in the sporting context is clear in order to allow effective interventions to be put in place to help individuals cope.

References

American Psychiatric Association (1987). *Diagnostic and statistical manual of mental disorders* (3rd edn, rev.). Washington, DC: American Psychiatric Association.

American Psychiatric Association (2000). *Diagnostic and statistical manual of psychiatric disorders* (4th edn, rev.). Washington DC: American Psychiatric Association.

Baird, K. and Kracen, A. C. (2006). Vicarious traumatization and secondary traumatic stress: a research synthesis. *Counselling Psychology Quarterly*, 19, 181–188.

Breslau, N., Chilcoat, H. D., Kessler, R. C. and Davis, G. C. (1999). Previous exposure to trauma and PTSD effects of subsequent trauma: results from the Detroit Area Survey of Trauma. *American Journal of Psychiatry*, 156, 902–907.

Brewin, C. R. (2001). A cognitive neuroscience account of posttraumatic stress disorder and its treatment. *Behaviour Research and Therapy*, 39, 373–393.

Brewin, C., Andrews, B. and Valentine, B. (2000). Meta-analysis of risk factors for post traumatic stress disorder in trauma exposed adults. *Journal of Consulting and Clinical Psychology*, 68, 748–766.

Brewin, C. R., Dalgleish, T. and Joseph, S. (1996). A dual representation theory of posttraumatic stress disorder. *Psychological Review*, 103, 670–686.

Brewin, C. R. and Holmes, E. A. (2003). Psychological theories of posttraumatic stress disorder. *Clinical Psychology Review*, 23, 339–376.

Bryant, R. A. and Harvey, A. G. (1995). Avoidant coping style and post traumatic stress following motor vehicle accidents. *Behaviour Research and Therapy*, 33, 631–635.

Buchko, K. J. (2005). Team consultation following an athlete's suicide: A crisis intervention model. *The Sport Psychologist*, 19, 288–302.

Cahill, S. P. and Foa, E. B. (2007). Psychological theories of PTSD. In M. J. Friedman (ed.), *Handbook of PTSD: Science and practice*. New York: Guildford.

Carless, D. and Douglas, K. (2009). 'We haven't got a seat on the bus for you' or 'all the seats are mine': Narratives and career transitions in professional golf. *Qualitative Research in Sport and Exercise*, 1, 51–66.

Chase, M., Magyar, M. and Drake, B. (2005). Fear of injury in gymnastics: Self-efficacy and psychological strategies to keep on tumbling. *Journal of Sports Sciences*, 23, 465–475.

Creamer, M. (1995). A cognitive processing formulation of posttrauma reactions. In R. J. Kleber, C. R. Figley and B. P. R. Gersons (eds), *Beyond trauma: Cultural and societal dynamics*. New York: Plenum Press.

Day, M. C., Bond, K. and Smith, B. (in review). Holding it together: Coping with vicarious trauma in sport. *Psychology of Sport and Exercise*.

Douglas, K. and Carless, D. (2009). Abandoning the performance narrative: two women's stories of transition from professional sport. *Journal of Applied Sport Psychology*, 21, 213–230.

Dugdale, J. R., Eklund, R. C. and Gordon, S. (2002). Expected and unexpected stressors in major international competition: Appraisal, coping, and performance. *The Sport Psychologist*, 16, 20–33.

Epstein, S. (1991). The self-concept, the traumatic neurosis, and the structure of personality. In D. Ozer, J. M. Healy, Jr. and A. J. Stewart (eds), *Perspectives on personality* (Vol 3, part A) London: Jessica Kingsley.

Foa, E. B. and Riggs, D. S. (1993). Posttraumatic stress disorder in rape victims. In J. Oldham, M. B. Riba and A. Tasman (eds), *American Psychiatric Press review of psychiatry*, Vol. 12 (pp. 273–303). Washington, DC: American Psychiatric Press.

Foa, E. B. and Rothbaum, B. O. (1998). *Treating the trauma of rape: Cognitive behavioural therapy for PTSD*. New York: Guildford.

Gould, D., Jackson, S. A. and Finch, L. (1993). Sources of stress in national champion figure skaters. *Journal of Sport and Exercise Psychology*, 15, 134–159.

Hatfield, E., Cacioppo, J. and Rapson, R. (1994). *Emotional contagion: Studies in emotion and social interaction*. New York: Cambridge University Press.

Herman, J. (1997). *Trauma and recovery*. New York: Basic Books.

Holmes, E. A. (2004). Intrusive, emotional mental imagery and trauma: Experimental and clinical clues. *Imagination, Cognition and Personality*, 23, 147–154.

Holmes, E. A., Brewin, C. R. and Henessey, R. G. (2004). Trauma films, information processing, and intrusive memory development. *Journal of Experimental Psychology: General*, 133, 3–22.

Holmes, E. A., Creswell, C. and O'Connor, T. G. (2007). Post traumatic stress symptoms in London school children following September 11th 2001: An exploratory investigation of peritraumatic reactions and intrusive imagery. *Journal of Behaviour Therapy and Experimental Psychiatry*, 38, 474–490.

Holmes, E. A., James, E. L., Coode-Bate, T. and Deeprose, C. (2009). Can playing the computer game 'Tetris' reduce the build-up of flashbacks for trauma? A proposal from cognitive science. *PLoS ONE*, 4, 1–6.

Holmes, T. H. and Rahe, R. H. (1967). The social readjustment rating scale. *Journal of Psychosomatic Research*, 11, 213–218.

Horowitz, M. J. (1986). *Stress response syndrome* (2nd edn). Northvale, NJ: Jason Aronson.

Janoff-Bulman, R. (1999). Rebuilding shattered assumptions after traumatic life experiences. In C. R. Snyder (ed.), *Coping: The psychology of what works*. Cary, N.C.: Oxford University Press.

Joseph, S. and Linley, P. A. E. (2005). Positive adjustment to threatening events: An organismic valuing theory of growth through adversity. *Review of General Psychology*, 9, 262–280.

Kerr, J. H. (2007). Sudden withdrawal from skydiving: A case study informed by reversal theory's concept of protective frames. *Journal of Applied Sport Psychology*, 19, 337–351.

Krans, J., Näring, G., Holmes, E. A. and Becker, E. S. (2010). Motion effects on intrusion development. *Journal of Trauma and Dissociation*, 11, 73–82.

Krause, E. D., Kaltman, S., Goodman, L. A. and Dutton, M. A. (2008). Avoidant coping and PTSD symptoms related to domestic violence exposure: A longitudinal study. *Journal of Traumatic Stress*, 21, 83–90.

Lazarus, R. S. (1999). *Stress and emotion: A new synthesis*. London: Springer.

Lazarus, R. S. and Folkman, S. (1984). *Stress, appraisal, and coping*. New York: Raven.

McCann, L. and Pearlman, L. A. (1990). Vicarious traumatization: A framework for understanding the psychological effects of working with victims. *Journal of Traumatic Stress*, 3, 131–149.

Monson, C. M. and Friedman, M. J. (2006). Back to the future of understanding trauma: Implications for cognitive-behavioural therapies for trauma. In V. M. Follette (ed.), *Cognitive-behavioural therapies for trauma* (2nd edn). New York: Guildford.

O'Neill, D. (2008). Injury contagion in alpine ski racing: The effect of injury on teammates' performance. *Journal of Clinical Sport Psychology*, 2, 278–292.

Park, C. L. and Ai, A. L. (2006). Meaning making and growth: New directions for research on survivors of trauma. *Journal of Loss and Trauma*, 11, 389–407.

Payne, A. J., Joseph, S. and Tudway, J. (2007). Assimilation and accommodation processes following traumatic experiences. *Journal of Loss and Trauma*, 12, 73–89.

Philip, R. (2005). Busst counts his blessings and looks ahead. *Daily Telegraph*, 13 December.

Rees, T., Smith, B. and Sparkes, A. C. (2003). The influence of social support on the lived experiences of spinal cord injured sportsmen. *The Sport Psychologist*, 17, 135–156.

Saari, S. (2005). Processing a traumatic experience. In S. Saari (ed.), *Bolt from the blue: Coping with disasters and acute trauma*. London: Jessica Kingsley.

Salkovskis, P. M. (1990). Obsessions, compulsions and intrusive cognitions. In D. F. Peck and D. M. Shapiro (eds), *Measuring human problems*. Chichester: Wiley.

Scotti, J. R., Brach, B. K., Northrop, L. M. E., Rode, C. A. and Forsyth, J. P. (1995). The psychological impact of accidental injury: A conceptual model for clinicians and researchers. In J. Freedy and S. Hobfoll (eds), *Traumatic stress: From theory to practice*. New York: Plenum Press.

Stuart, A. D. P., Holmes, E. A. and Brewin, C. R. (2005). The influence of a visuospatial grounding task on intrusive images of a trauma film. *Behaviour Research and Therapy*, 44, 611–619.

Sutton, J. P. (2002). Trauma: trauma in context. In J. P. Sutton (ed.), *Music, music therapy and trauma: International perspectives*. Philadelphia, Pa.: Jessica Kingsley.

Udry, E., Gould, D., Bridges, D. and Beck, L. (1997). Down but not out: Athlete responses to season ending injuries. *Journal of Sport and Exercise Psychology*, 19, 229–248.

Vernacchia, R. A., Reardon, J. P. and Templin, D. P. (1997). Sudden death in sport: Managing the aftermath. *The Sport Psychologist*, 11, 223–235.

Weinberg, J. and Levine, S. (1980). Psychobiology of coping in animals: The effects of predictability. In S. Levine and H. Ursin (eds), *Coping and health*. New York: Plenum.

Wilson, J. and Lindy, J. (1994). Empathetic strain and countertransference. In J. Wilson and J. Lindy (eds), *Countertransference in the treatment of PTSD* (pp. 5–30). New York: Guilford.

Wippert, P. and Wippert, J. (2008). Perceived stress and prevalence of traumatic stress symptoms following athletic career termination. *Journal of Clinical Sport Psychology*, 2, 1–16.

4

MEASUREMENT ISSUES IN EMOTION AND EMOTION REGULATION

Andrew Lane, Chris Beedie and Tracey Devonport, University of Wolverhampton

Introduction

> A test is said to be valid if it measures what it claims to measure.
>
> *(Kline, 1994, p. 16)*

On the face of it, validity seems a straightforward concept, yet because psychological constructs such as mood, emotion and affect are not 'things' that can be picked up, but phenomena that we believe occur and exist, the process of establishing validity of their measurement is more involved. Psychologists tend to go to great lengths to investigate the validity of their measures. The often-lengthy process of validation leads researchers to address the more interesting questions such as 'Do emotions predict performance?' or 'How do we manage our emotions?' rather than 'Will this measure (typically a self-report questionnaire) assess accurately the concept it claims to?'

Mood, emotion, and affect have been studied extensively in the sport psychology literature (see Baron et al., 2009; Beedie, Terry and Lane, 2000; Hanin, 2000, 2003; Jones, 2003; Lane, 2007a; Lane and Devonport, 2009; Lane and Terry, 2000; Pensgaard and Duda, 2003; Robazza, Bortoli and Hanin, 2006; Ruiz and Hann, 2004). Recently, research has examined how people manage or regulate these states. It is generally accepted that most individuals actively monitor their feelings and develop self-regulating strategies to increase, decrease or maintain feelings in the belief that doing so will help performance (Hanin, 2000; Lane, 2007a). If researchers and practitioners alike are to study these issues, then they will need measures that are valid and reliable.

Ahead of any discussion of the measurement of emotion, mood and affect, it is important to clarify terminology. An examination of the literature in sport and elsewhere shows that these three terms have been used interchangeably. In fact some confusion exists, as questionnaires such as the Profile of Mood States (POMS) or its derivates (McNair, Lorr and Droppleman, 1971, 1992) and the Positive and Negative Affect Schedule (PANAS: Watson, Clark and Tellegen, 1988) have been used to assess mood in some studies, emotion in others, and affect in yet others (see Lane and Terry, 2000; Lane, Beedie and Stevens, 2005 for reviews). Therefore, despite differences in terminology, investigations of mood, emotion and affect might not be separate lines of enquiry per se. However, irrespective of what has gone before, conceptual clarity lies at the heart of the development of valid measures. Beedie, Terry and Lane (2005) examined distinctions between emotion and mood, as represented both in the scientific literature and in everyday language. Mood is generally proposed to be more enduring and less intense than emotion, and whilst emotions are about specific events or objects with immediate concern for the individual's goals (such as 'I am angry because …'), moods are more a reflection of the individual's resources in relation to more long-term, lifespan issues (such as 'I just feel a little down generally at the moment.'). Although most individuals are aware of the cause of emotions, the causes of moods are less obvious. Mood and emotions probably have different causes and different functions, thus theoretically they should be assessed using different scales. However, this is rarely the case, an issue addressed in more detail below. The term 'affect' is generally used by researchers who wish to avoid defining whether their construct is a mood or an emotion (e.g. Watson and Clark, 1997),[1] but for ease of comprehension, and in the absence of sufficient data to describe any one example as an emotion or a mood in most cases, the term 'emotion' will be used to represent emotion, mood and affect in this chapter.

Developing theory in this line of study depends partly on the availability of valid and reliable measures. Researchers wishing to test hypotheses using quantitative methods require tools that are fit for purpose. If researchers cannot trust the validity and reliability of their measures, then it follows that they cannot trust values derived from such measures when seeking to test theory. Issues of validity and reliability are also of concern for applied sport psychology practitioners. Validity determines how subscales on a questionnaire are calculated, which in turn will influence how practitioners interpret inventories in their work with athletes. For researchers and practitioners alike, self-report questionnaires should be rigorously validated.

A commonly accepted suggestion is that construct validity[2] is demonstrated by an accumulation of evidence that the construct the inventory purports to measure is related to other constructs consistent with theoretical predictions (Kline, 1994). It is however problematic to determine the amount of evidence required before validation is confirmed. Rather than view the validation process as complete, researchers should see it as an ongoing process, and that each time a measure is used, the validity of that measure is questioned (Anastasi and Urbina, 1997). It is healthy for scientific enquiry if researchers consider the extent to which the validity of measures used influenced the results, particularly self-report measures. Concepts such as emotion are inherently difficult to define and distinguish. As suggested above, the nature of emotion is still the subject of scholarly debate. Whilst the boundaries that help define the phenomenon continue to be debated (Gross, 2010; Parkinson, 2010), it follows that the way in which the construct is defined is subject to change.

This chapter focuses on measurement issues related to emotion, coping, and emotion regulation. Our chapter focuses on commonly used or recently developed measures. First, we review measures of emotion including the POMS (McNair, Lorr, and Droppleman, 1971) and the PANAS (Watson et al., 1988). We then explore a shortened version of the POMS, the Brunel Mood Scale (Terry et al., 1999; Terry, Lane and Fogarty, 2003). We conclude the review of emotion scales with the recently developed Sport Emotion Questionnaire (SEQ: Jones et al., 2005) and a new measure that distinguishes an anxious mood from an anxious emotion (Emotion and Mood Components of Anxiety Questionnaire: Beedie et al., 2011). Second, we explore measures of Emotional Intelligence (EI: Lane et al., 2009b; Schutte et al., 1998), and finally the recently developed Emotion Regulation of Others and Self scale (Niven et al., 2011).

Emotion scales used in the literature

In this section we focus on validity issues pertinent to commonly used scales. These include POMS (McNair et al., 1971) or shorter versions of POMS (Terry et al., 1999, 2003) and the sport-specific Sport Emotion Questionnaire (Jones et al., 2005).

Profile of Mood States

One of the most frequently used measures of emotion in sport psychology has been the POMS (McNair et al., 1971, 1992). POMS describes six dimensions: anger, confusion, depression, fatigue, tension and vigour. McNair et al. (1971, 1992) produced two versions of the POMS: one with sixty-five items and one with thirty items, with evidence to support the hypothesized six-factor structure in six factor analytical studies. McNair et al. (1971, 1992) selected items that were proposed to reflect the construct under examination, and allowed factor analysis to group items into factors. They found that the expected six-factor solution emerged in six different samples. This finding should be considered a strength of the possible six-factor model, as exploratory factor analysis notoriously produces factors unique to the sample (Thompson and Daniel, 1996). Further, POMS factors showed acceptable internal consistency coefficients and demonstrated acceptable criterion validity coefficients.

The initial rationale provided by sport researchers for using POMS was the validity of the questionnaire. Even though it was developed for a non-sporting/ non-athlete population, validation procedures reported by McNair et al. (1971) were considered rigorous at the time of publication. It should be noted that sport psychology researchers did not have an abundance of sport-specific measures, and so borrowing previously validated measures was judged the best way to initiate research. Once researchers started to use POMS to predict performance, the rationale for its use changed to testing the notion that successful sport performance is associated with an iceberg mood profile. An iceberg profile is typified by above-average scores for vigour and below-average anger, confusion, depression, fatigue and tension scores (Morgan, 1980). Athletes' POMS scores were compared against student norms, and clear situational differences exist.

Later research identified that an iceberg profile is the norm for athletes (Terry and Lane, 2000); hence, it should not be surprising that many studies found athletes reported this profile. Further, meta-analysis results show clear evidence that scores on the POMS do not distinguish athletes by level of competition (Beedie, Terry and Lane, 2000; Renger, 1993; Rowley et al., 1995). Terry (2000) argued that subsequent research should move beyond espousing the benefits of an iceberg profile.

The second of the two meta-analyses by Beedie et al. (2000) demonstrated that the POMS does have utility in the prediction of performance among athletes of similar standard. Although it is still a widely used measure in that context, using the original POMS presents several limitations in sport. The sixty-five-item version is extremely time-consuming to complete (Curren, Andrykowski and Studts, 1995; Grove and Prapavessis, 1992; Lane, 2007b; Shacham, 1983). Lane (2007b) argued that many sport scenarios require brief measures that athletes can complete quickly. Athletes are usually prepared to participate in research, even research that involves completing measures relatively close to competition, but their commitment to this process wanes if completing self-report measures is perceived as arduous. The relatively lengthy completion time contributed to the development of several shortened versions of the POMS (e.g. Grove and Prapavessis, 1992; Terry, 1995; Terry et al., 1999). Completion time is a function of the number of items and their comprehensibility. The original POMS also contains items with a North American orientation: for example, 'grovely' and 'blue' (Grove and Prapavessis, 1992), which athletes often ask the researcher to clarify. To address these issues, Terry and colleagues (Terry et al., 1999, 2003) sought to validate a twenty-four-item measure of the POMS factors, named the Brunel Mood Scale (BRUMS, in recognition of Brunel University where most of the work was completed). Terry et al. (1999, 2003) used confirmatory factor analysis to test the extent to which items support the hypothesized model proposed by McNair et al. (1971). By removing weak loading items from their intended factors, this eventually produced the twenty-four-item measure. Their 2003 study confirmed factorial validity[3] by multi-sample confirmatory factor analysis that showed invariance between items and factors and between factors across four disparate samples. Terry et al. (1999, 2003) went on to report criterion validity results for correlations between BRUMS and PANAS scores (Watson et al., 1988) and the State Anger-Expression Inventory (STAXI: Spielberger, 1991). Relationships were consistent with theoretical predictions, thereby providing evidence of criterion validity. Researchers have examined the validity of the BRUMS, conducting factor analytic studies with specific populations including adolescents with intellectual disability (Argus et al., 2004) and water-skiers (Fazackerley, Lane and Mahoney, 2003). Recent research has demonstrated that the scale is valid for use in other languages, namely Italian and Hungarian (Lane et al., 2007), and Malaysian (Hashim, Zulkifli and Ahmad, 2010).

Lane (2004, 2007a) acknowledged that a limitation of the BRUMS is that vigour is the only positive construct assessed. Recent research has extended validation of the scale to include calmness and happiness factors (Lane and Devonport, 2009; Lane and Jarrett, 2005; Lane and Godfrey, 2009; Lane, Thelwell and Devonport, 2009d; Lane et al., 2010a; Thelwell, Lane and Weston, 2007), resulting in a thirty-two-item, eight-factor scale. The subscales of happiness and calmness were taken from the UWIST Mood Adjective Check List (Matthews, Jones and Chamberlain, 1990). Eight dimensions are proposed to provide a more balanced assessment of positive and negative emotion. In a confirmatory factor analytic study, Lane et al. (2007) found support for factorial validity, including shortening each factor to three items.

A recent study that used the modified BRUMS investigated potential interactions between pleasant and unpleasant emotion. An emotional state which includes anxiety, excitement and vigour is often perceived to be helpful for performance (Hanin, 2000; Lane and Terry, 2000). Further, athletes report that anxiety direction is closely related to feeling excited (Jones and Uphill, 2004). Lane and Devonport (2009) examined the interaction between pleasant and unpleasant affect in relation to optimal performance among a sample of 222 male athletes. They also assessed relationships between emotions, trait EI and emotion regulation, asking athletes to complete a modified BRUMS to provide assessments on a range of pleasant and unpleasant emotions. Athletes also completed the trait Emotional Intelligence Scale (Schutte et al., 1998) along with the Emotion Regulation Questionnaire (Gross and John, 2003). Athletes rated their emotions in relation to how they felt before a performance when they performed at their best.

Lane and Devonport (2009) found that low scores for tension and anger correlated positively with happiness when athletes reported no other indicators of unpleasant emotions: that is, participants did not concurrently experience depression, confusion and fatigue. By contrast, when athletes reported feeling unpleasant emotions (anxious, tense, confused, depressed and fatigued), happiness and tension were inversely related. That is, the more anxious they felt, the more they also reported feeling confused, fatigued and depressed. These findings demonstrate why it might be important to look at the individual's overall emotional profile rather than focusing on one emotion. Lane and Devonport's finding suggests that when athletes experience tension coupled with other unpleasant emotions, they are less likely to experience pleasant emotions. In terms of relationships with EI, a concept we examine in more depth later in this chapter, Lane and Devonport found that vigour and happiness correlated with EI when experienced independently of negative emotions. Including a range of pleasant emotions and examining how they relate to unpleasant emotions allows researchers to investigate reasons why unpleasant emotions are associated with successful performance and well-being.

The Sport Emotion Questionnaire

Recent research developed and validated an SEQ (Jones et al., 2005) with the intention of producing a valid measure that has content and face validity.[4] Jones et al. found that emotions in sport are characterized by five factors: excitement, happiness, anger, anxiety and dejection. The qualitative stages used to develop the SEQ arguably represent an example of good practice. The first stage developed a set of suitable items that reflected each of the five emotional constructs that participants could easily understand. Adjectives and phrases that best described the emotions that they had experienced when competing in sport were reported by 264 athletes. A key feature of this stage of the process was the large sample size used. Rarely do qualitative studies use large sample sizes, possibly because of limitations and difficulties regarding data analysis.

Jones et al. (2005) found that athletes reported 548 separate adjectives and phrases. Frequency analysis indicated that fifty-two of the adjectives accounted for 73.3 per cent of the total number, therefore the fifty-two adjectives would appear to refer to emotions commonly experienced by athletes. Confirmatory factor analysis on responses to the SEQ from 518 athletes lent support for the factorial validity of a twenty-two-item measure, and the measure's internal validity was demonstrated. Criterion validity was investigated by examining relationships with the Test of Performance Strategies (TOPS: Thomas, Murphy and Hardy, 1999). Relationships between SEQ scores and the emotional control in competition sub-scale from the TOPS lent support for the construct validity of the SEQ. High scores on psychological skills to control emotions during competition were associated with low scores of anger and dejection and high scores of excitement and happiness. These findings lend support for the notion that psychological skills to control emotions before competition are related to pre-competition emotions with the exception of anxiety, which showed a weak non-significant relationship.

Evaluation of the concurrent validity of the measure demonstrated strong positive relationships between corresponding BRUMS and SEQ scores for anger, tension and anxiety, depression and dejection. The relationship between vigour and excitement was stronger than the relationship between vigour and happiness; hence it showed a strong overlap between the two scales. Jones et al. acknowledged the similarity between the two scales but suggested the SEQ is different in a number of ways. First, the SEQ was developed to provide a measure that was grounded in the experience of athletes, and whilst it does share some items with the BRUMS, most are unique. Second, a limitation of the BRUMS is that the factor structure was based on that in the POMS, which was specifically developed for use with clinical populations and contained sub-scales assessing fatigue, confusion and depression. The SEQ measures two positive states (excitement, happiness) in comparison to the BRUMS which only measures one (vigour), although the revised BRUMS also includes happiness and calmness. Recent research has provided evidence of the utility of the SEQ for use in sport investigating changes in emotion and relationships with cognitive factors such as attributions and self-efficacy (Allen, Jones and Sheffield, 2009, 2010).

In conclusion, the SEQ is a sport-specific measure of pre-competition emotion grounded in the experience of athletes, assessing: anger, anxiety, dejection, excitement, and happiness. This measure shows good evidence of validity and reliability and represents a wider range of emotions than its predecessor.

Positive Affect and Negative Affect Schedule

The PANAS (Watson et al., 1988) is a commonly used scale in psychology. As the title suggests, the scale assesses two higher-order generic constructs: positive affect and negative affect (essentially positive emotions and negative emotions, respectively). Validation studies using 3,554 responses indicated support for a twenty-item questionnaire. Further, and importantly for the present chapter, recent research using confirmatory factor analysis has demonstrated factorial validity of the PANAS among athletes (Crocker, 1997).

Research that has examined relationships between PANAS scores and sport performance has however produced equivocal results. Findings indicate that positive emotion is associated with facilitated performance in the sport of wrestling (Treasure, Monson and Lox, 1996). Such findings are consistent with the notion that vigour and positive emotion are similar constructs. Results relating to the influence of negative emotion on performance were less clear. Using the PANAS, Treasure et al. (1996) found that negative emotion was a poor predictor of performance. Treasure et al. examined emotion and performance relationships in the sport of wrestling, and their findings contrast with those reported by Terry and Slade (1995) in karate. Terry and Slade (1995) found that negative emotion was an effective predictor of performance, with losers reporting significantly higher confusion, depression, fatigue and tension, and lower anger than winners. Findings indicating that anger can be facilitative for performance question the appropriateness of examining this emotion as part of a general negative emotion construct (Watson and Tellegen, 1985). According to the conceptual model proposed by Lane and Terry (2000), the balance of positive and negative emotion dimensions experienced is influenced by scores on the Depression subscale. In this model anger, tension and vigour are associated with facilitated performance when these are experienced in the absence of depression. Therefore, there are three emotions associated with positive performance (anger, tension and vigour) and two emotions associated with negative performance (confusion and fatigue) among participants who report zero on the depressed mood scale. In the presence of depression, the balance of positive (vigour) and negative mood (anger, confusion, depression, fatigue and tension) is five to one. Collectively, it is suggested that using the PANAS model to predict performance may result in a loss of information.

In conclusion to this discussion of the validity of measures of emotion used in sport, we suggest that the SEQ (Jones et al., 2005) and BRUMS (Terry et al., 1999, 2003) represent examples of scales that have been validated using procedures currently accepted as good practice. However, as science strives for increasingly rigorous methods of validation, there is a need to reanalyse well-used scales, thereby demonstrating the validity process in action. The SEQ and BRUMS assess emotion using single-adjective checklists, and the use of each adjective can change over time. For example, during the validation of the BRUMS with adolescents, Terry et al. note that the item 'sad' was removed as it had become colloquially used as an insult. It is possible that other items might adopt different meanings in specific groups. We argue that data collectors in research programmes are likely to pick up such trends, and such information needs to be considered when looking to utilise these measures in sport psychology research.

The Emotion and Mood Component of Anxiety Questionnaire (EMCA-Q)

Having justified the use of the term 'emotion' as a cover-all for emotion, mood and affect above, we now report on the development of a scale that seeks to distinguish mood from emotion. Previous approaches to distinguishing emotion from mood in the academic literature have focused on structural distinctions, such as contrasting the brief intensity of an emotion with the more enduring and diffuse nature of a mood (Watson and Clark, 1997; Watson, 2000). Jones et al. (2005) argued that their measure assessed emotion rather than mood, as they asked participants to rate how they felt before competing, rather than 'How do you feel right now?' as used by Terry et al. (1999, 2003). However, if athletes respond to items using the 'right now' response timeframe before competition, then it is likely that preparing to compete will influence their feelings, and therefore the subsequent measure will contain a mixture of emotions and mood. Equally, an athlete who is in an unpleasant mood before going to a competition and then reports feeling anxious before competition on the SEQ is reporting a mix of moods and emotions. As Lane and Terry (2000) and later Lane et al. (2005) indicated, distinguishing mood from emotion before competition can be challenging.

In search of conceptual clarity, Beedie et al. (2005) conducted a content analysis of sixty-five published works that offered distinctions between emotion and mood. They also used qualitative methods to investigate emotion–mood distinctions among a sample of 106 non-academic participants, arguing for the utility of folk theory in conceptual development, which is briefly defined as common-sense theories; those based on 'the assumptions, hypotheses and beliefs of ordinary people about behaviour and mental experience' (Colman, 2001, p. 283). The authors reported a high level of agreement between academic and non-academic opinions, in both the nature and direction of potential distinguishing criteria. They identified eight distinguishing themes, with *duration, intentionality, cause, consequences* and *function* cited most frequently, and *intensity, physiology* and *awareness* of cause cited less frequently. In summarizing, the authors proposed that emotion and mood could be distinguished empirically if the subjective context of the affective responses (that is, the individual's awareness of the antecedents, focus and likely consequences) is also assessed in line with theoretical distinctions.

Following on from this, Beedie (2007) proposed that the subjective context in which an individual experiences feelings such as anxiety or anger determines whether they are interpreted as emotions or moods. This proposal extended the views of Clore (1994), who explained how emotion and mood could feel the same but still be perceived as different constructs. Subjective context also influences the availability of strategies to regulate such feelings. For example, if an athlete feels angry following an argument with a coach, the meaning attached to the feeling will be constrained, and the range of judgements it colours will be limited. By contrast, if the athlete feels angry but cannot identify a cause of those feelings, its focus will be unconstrained.

When the criteria identified by Beedie et al. (2005) are applied to existing measures, it is apparent why no published data are available to demonstrate emotion and mood differences. Most scales use single-adjective items that assess affective responses without providing any contextual information (see Power, 2006). Although it is tempting to infer emotion–mood distinctions from structural information relating to duration or intensity of feelings, which is included in some scales, this is not reliable. Using anxiety as an example, irrespective of whether the response timeframe suggests short duration (*how do you feel right now?*) or enduring feelings (*how have you felt this week?*), no information as to whether the anxiety is an emotion or a mood is available. A right-now format does not distinguish between a current mood and a current emotion, and using a 'past week' format does not clarify whether the respondent has been in the same anxious mood or emotionally anxious about the same thing during that period. Likewise the intensity of responses is unhelpful; although it is tempting to assume that low-intensity anxiety is a mood and high-intensity anxiety an emotion, the respondent could be mildly emotionally anxious or in an intensely anxious mood.

Beedie et al. (2011) sought to develop and validate the EMCA-Q based on a subjective-contextual model of emotion–mood distinctions, which specifies that differentiation of the emotion of anxiety from an anxious mood should be based on an individual's awareness of the context in which the respective feeling states occur. In stage 1, they conducted an empirical investigation of the factors that might distinguish emotion from mood (Beedie et al., 2005). This was followed by a philosophical enquiry into the nature of these factors (Beedie, 2007). Next, they utilized rigorous test development procedures to ensure the content validity of the EMCA-Q, after which confirmatory factor analysis was used to demonstrate factorial validity in two independent samples. In sample 1, 190 athletes reported anxious emotion and anxious mood in response to feelings shortly before competition. In sample 2, 300 students completed an exam-specific version of the EMCA-Q approximately an hour before competition. Confirmatory factor analysis showed that the hypothesized model was supported. In the next stage, they demonstrated that emotion and mood factors behave differently in relation to a stressor. Taken collectively, they provided initial evidence of construct validity, whilst acknowledging that scale validation is an ongoing process (Anastasi and Urbina, 1997) and tests of criterion validity have yet to be conducted. Thus research should continue the validation process. Research could look to develop a scale that assesses other affective states, possibly those identified by Jones et al. (2005). However, a limitation of such a scale would be its length, and so test constructors should be mindful of feedback from test administrators on how long completion takes, and be prepared to shorten the scale if athlete feedback is excessively negative.

In conclusion to this section, we have reviewed several measures of emotion. The past ten years have seen considerable developments in validation procedures, which have prompted researchers to test (and retest) the validity of commonly used scales. Newly developed scales are currently basking in the safety of conforming to current procedures, although at the time of writing, a new approach that seeks to distinguish mood from emotion might be gathering momentum. In the fullness of time the resulting measure may become the test of choice within the mood and emotion literature.

The next section looks at individual difference variables that influence emotional responses, and strategies people use to regulate their emotions. It is worth pointing out that our choice of scales is selective. Recent years have seen the expansion of coping research and along with this, the development of a number of scales. Coping has featured as the topic of several textbooks (including this one), which illustrates the increased interest in the subject. Coping and emotion regulation overlap because coping involves emotion regulation. However, coping occurs in response to negative events, and involves more than mood and emotion, whereas emotion regulation is specifically directed at changing emotion. Given the overlap between these constructs, we focus on a selection of measures rather than attempt to provide a comprehensive review. We examine EI and emotion regulation as we feel these scales are not reviewed comprehensively elsewhere, and we also provide an overview of coping measures.

Emotional intelligence

EI has emerged as a key concept among researchers and practitioners alike, and is subject to growing interest in sport psychology (Lane et al., 2009d; Meyer and Fletcher, 2007; Meyer and Zizzi, 2007; Thelwell et al., 2008; Zizzi, Deaner and Hirschhorn, 2003). Further to this, meta-analysis results indicate positive relationships between EI, health-related variables (Schutte et al., 2007) and performance variables (Van Rooy and Viswesvaran, 2004). Recent research points to encouraging results, with Zizzi et al. finding EI was associated significantly with sport performance, Thelwell et al. found that EI related with perceptions of coaching effectiveness, and Lane, Thelwell, et al. found EI correlated with psychological skills use. More recently, studies show that EI is related to emotional states associated with successful performance (Lane and Devonport, 2009; Lane et al., 2010a; Lane et al., 2009d).

Evidence also shows that EI relates to emotions experienced in competition (Lane et al., 2009d), and directly predicts performance (Zizzi et al., 2003). Lane et al. (2009d) found athletes reporting high levels of EI also reported higher scores on pleasant and lower scores on unpleasant emotions before performance. Lane, Devonport and Stevens (2010b) found EI correlated with pleasant emotions before and after 10-mile running. Recent research in sport has offered an insight into this trend, with evidence demonstrating that EI relates to psychological skills use (Lane et al., 2009c), whereby athletes high in EI reported more frequent use of psychological skills. It could be argued that participants with high EI are more likely to utilize psychological skills, possibly because such individuals can foresee their value with regards to regulating and managing emotions (Lane et al., 2009c).

EI can be defined as 'the ability to carry out accurate reasoning about emotions and the ability to use emotions and emotional knowledge to enhance thought' (Mayer, Roberts and Barsade, 2008, p. 111), and is assessed using either an objective performance-based measure (the Mayer-Salovey-Caruso Emotional Intelligence Test, MSCEIT: Mayer, Caruso and Salovey, 1999) or a subjective self-report measure (Emotional Intelligence Scale: EIS: Schutte et al., 1998) (see Meyer and Zizzi, 2007 for a review). In a performance test, individuals are asked to answer questions for which there are correct answers: for example correctly identifying a face showing an angry person. In self-report tests, individuals are asked to reflect on emotional experiences across different situations and report their subjective perceptions. These perceptions are indicative of an individual's predispositions or traits. It should be noted that the MSCEIT is a licensed test, and researchers and practitioners would need to undertake a training course before using it, and pay for each administration. For these reasons, we suggest that the MSCEIT is less likely to be used than self-report measures that are free to use. It should be noted that the norm in sport and exercise psychology is to develop a test that requires minimal training on the part of test administrators and is free to use (Lane, 2007b).

One commonly used measure of self-reported EI is the EIS (Schutte et al., 1998). This is a 33-item measure designed to assess an individual's perceptions of the extent to which they can identify, understand, harness and regulate emotions in self and others. Schutte et al. used a set of 62 items derived from Salovey and Mayer's model (1990). Exploratory factor analysis on data from 346 participants yielded a four-factor model. The authors argued that removing twenty-nine items and reanalysing data produced an adequate one-factor solution. Schutte et al. reported adequate internal consistency reliability ($\acute{\alpha} = 0.87$ to .90) and acceptable test–retest reliability ($r = 0.78$). In a subsequent study, Petrides and Furnham (2000) identified four factors: optimism/mood regulation, appraisal of emotions, social skills and utilization of emotions. Similarly, Saklofske, Austin and Minski (2003) subjected the EIS to confirmatory factor analysis (CFA) and found moderate support in terms of the strengths of fit indices for the four-factor model. With the view of reducing socially desirable responses by including a greater number of reverse scoring items, Besharat (2007) found support for a forty-one-item four-factor model among a population of Iranian students. By contrast, Gignac et al. (2005) tested several competing models for the EIS, finding some support for a four-factor model that describes appraisal of emotions in the self, appraisal of emotions in others, emotional regulation of the self, and utilization of emotions in problem solving. Gignac et al. argued that further validation work on the scale was needed if the intention of the scale is to assess the theoretical model proposed by Salovey and Mayer (1990).

Lane et al. (2009b) examined the validity of EIS for use in sport. A content analysis study identified thirteen items lacking a direct assessment of emotional experiences. Given the definition of EI presented previously, each item should contain reference to emotional experiences. For example, the item, 'I find it hard to understand the non-verbal messages of other people' assesses perceived difficulties in assessing non-verbal messages that might include emotions, but also might not. The item might be better phrased as 'I become tense (emotional content) in situations when I feel I need to understand the non-verbal messages of other people.'

After removing nineteen items, CFA on 1,681 athletes demonstrated acceptable fit indices. Lane et al. (2009b) tested two models: a single-factor model in which all items load onto one scale, which is the way EI is typically assessed in the EI literature, and a five-factor model (we discarded optimism because it is a personality trait rather than an aspect of EI). Recent research has shown the utility of the nineteen-item EIS. Lane et al. (2010a) found EIS scores related to emotional states associated with successful performance. Lane et al. (2010b) found EIS scores associated with emotional states before and after running. A key question is whether the shortened version is a significant improvement on the thirty-three-item version. It seems when using a single factor scale that there appear to be minimal differences in terms of relationships with emotional states experienced during competition. The advantage of the nineteen-item EIS possibly lies in shorter completion time and the removal of some items that might appear meaningless to athletes.

The quest to develop scales that could be used to examine EI in pre-competition scenarios contributed to the development of a much shorter version of the EIS. Davies, Lane and Devonport (2010) found support for a ten-item version for use with athletes. CFA results yielded good fit indices for the ten-item scale, suggesting the measure is suited for use in situations where brevity is important.

Emotion regulation

Emotion regulation of others and self

Emotion regulation is defined as a set of automatic and controlled processes involved in the initiation, maintenance and modification of the occurrence, intensity and duration of feeling states (Eisenberg et al., 2000; Gross, 2007; Gross and Thompson, 2007). Emotion regulation is relevant to many aspects of daily life, including family, work and sport (Gross, 2007). While emotion regulation can occur automatically, it is also performed in a more controlled manner, through the use of affect regulation strategies that are characterized by intent and awareness on the part of the agent. Measuring people's use of affect regulation strategies is important because the strategies that people choose can have benefits or costs for their well-being, performance and relationships (Gross and John, 2003; Lane and Devonport, 2009; Niven, Totterdell and Holman, 2009).

Recent research has developed a new conceptual framework and tool for assessing emotion regulation, proposing that regulatory behaviours can be dichotomized as emotion-improving and emotion-worsening strategies. Furthermore, Niven et al. (2011) argued that a limitation of existing scales is that they usually only assess strategies intended to improve affect. However, there is evidence in general life and sport that individuals also try to worsen their own (Parrott, 1993) and other people's affect (Niven et al., 2009), often for instrumental purposes. For example, an athlete might wish to get angry if they believe this helps performance, or a coach might show anger in a team talk in order to motivate their players.

Niven et al. (2011) developed and validated a scale to assess strategies designed to improve emotion and worsen emotion in others and self. They named this the EROS scale: Emotion Regulation of Others and Self. Niven et al. report evidence demonstrating significant relationships between emotion-improving and emotion-worsening strategies and their intended emotions. They drew items from strategies identified in the Parkinson and Totterdell (1999) and Niven et al. (2009) frameworks. These frameworks used a comprehensive corpus of emotion regulation strategies collected from large and diverse samples. After establishing face validity, they explored factorial validity on two independent samples. Exploratory factor analysis and confirmatory factor analysis provided evidence supporting the hypothesized model. Niven et al. (2011) noted that a frequency analysis of the items revealed all emotion-worsening items were also positively skewed: that is, people respond by indicating 'not at all' to each item. Criterion validity was evidenced by demonstrating that relationships were consistent with theoretical predictions. They found that improving one's own emotion correlated strongly with other measures of functional strategies to improve one's emotion (such as reappraisal). The increasing one's own unpleasant emotions factor correlated with dysfunctional responses to emotions as well as poor emotion regulation ability, negative emotion, high neuroticism, low extraversion and low agreeableness.

Recent research has sought to extend validity to sport and exercise settings (Lane et al., in review). Preliminary evidence of factorial validity is demonstrated by CFA results showing strong support for intra-individual emotion regulation strategies on a sample of over 700 athletes. However, although factor analysis confirmed support for the hypothesized model, the process identified a limitation in the wording of some items. For example, items such as 'I thought about something nice to try to make myself feel better' and 'I did something I enjoy to try to improve how I felt', taken from the improving own emotions scale, are unlikely to be used by athletes before or during competition. The term 'nice' is not used to describe strategies athletes might use or states they aspire to when seeking to change emotions, particularly if the strategy to regulate emotions focuses on attempts to manage performance. Athletes will tend to use strategies that focus on ensuring they achieve their performance goals, and if such goals are achieved, then pleasant emotions follow.

Lane (2010) examined emotion regulation strategies and emotions in a sample of 1,100 runners before exercise. He reported low endorsement for emotion-worsening strategies, with 53 per cent of participants reporting that they did not use such strategies: that is, they reported zero for each item. Data were divided into an increasing unpleasant emotions group and non-worsening group. Runners reporting the use of strategies intended to worsen emotion reported significantly higher unpleasant emotions and lower pleasant emotions than runners who did not report using worsening strategies. That is, it would appear that engaging in strategies to increase unpleasant emotions leads to unpleasant emotions. What is not clear from this result is whether athletes are intending to increase unpleasant emotions for instrumental reasons. However, as recent research suggests, unpleasant emotions such as anxiety can correlate with pleasant emotions such as happiness when performing optimally (Lane and Devonport, 2009), possibly because increasing unpleasant emotions increases levels of activation, and once an athlete reaches a level of arousal where they feel ready for competition, this could correlate with feeling happy. In this instance, happiness is representing a belief that the athlete will perform successfully.

The profile of emotion regulation strategies reported by Lane (2010) provides an interesting observation on the interplay between strategies. Strategies to increase unpleasant emotions were associated with greater use of strategies to increase pleasant emotions. An athlete might seek to increase anxiety, possibly as a strategy to generate a sense of importance of the event and use the effects of unpleasant emotions to narrow concentration. However, strategies intended to worsen emotion need to be kept in check, and as such athletes should aim to switch their use of strategies from intending to worsen to intending to improve. Lane suggested that findings show that using strategies to increase unpleasant emotions leads to unpleasant emotions, which in turn brings about greater regulatory efforts to enhance emotions. Collectively, results lend support to the notion that regulatory beliefs play an important role in the influence of exercise as an emotion-regulating strategy. Lane suggested that interventions should be aimed at teaching athletes to manage their emotion regulation strategies to ensure they get into the best emotional state for performance.

The EROS scale has shown some utility using a within-subject design. Lane et al. (2009a) investigated the effect of situational and individual difference variables on individuals' emotions and emotion-regulation strategies. Eight participants, all regular exercisers, completed an emotion regulation scale, an emotion scale, and maintained an emotion diary for a 30-day period. A brief analysis of situational changes during the 30 days demonstrated that participants experienced a range of challenges both within sport and in life in general. Lane et al. found that participants experienced intense emotions in a range of situations such as athletic competition and training, along with social interactions within these situations. For example, one participant indicated reporting feeling angry following a discussion with an official at a duathlon event. Participants also reported feeling intense emotions in relation to everyday tasks and work-related tasks. As with sport, factors associated with intense emotions related to individual goals (such as wanting to perform well in a presentation) and social relationships (such as an argument with family member or confrontation at work). Lane et al. (2009a) argued that researchers should examine emotion, emotion regulation and coping holistically, rather than focusing only on sport-specific stressors.

The research in emotion regulation forms part of a much larger research network (www.erosresearch.org/) involving researchers from sport, social, developmental, neuropsychology, clinical and work psychology. The synergy of this research network might help develop a more comprehensive analysis of emotions and strategies to regulate emotions across a range of different settings, and as such might be able to move research forwards.

Review of coping measures

We conclude our chapter with a brief summary of coping scales commonly used in sport (see Table 4.1). Coping has primarily been measured in sport and physical activity research with modifications of Folkman and Lazarus's (1985) Ways of Coping Checklist (WCC), and Carver, Scheier and Weintraub's (1989) COPE instrument. Sport modifications of the WCC have not fared well, with different factor structures emerging across various studies (Crocker, 1992; Grove, Eklund and Heard, 1997). The factor structure of the COPE and a version modified for sport (MCOPE; Crocker and Graham, 1995) on the other hand, has received support (Eklund, Grove and Heard, 1998). COPE or its subscales have been used extensively in sport coping research, and have demonstrated acceptable reliability and validity (Eubank and Collins, 2000; Renk and Creasey, 2003). However, in research where brevity is important the BRIEF COPE inventory is considered a useful alternative (Carver et al., 1989).

TABLE 4.1 Coping scales commonly used in sport and physical activity

Name and authors of inventory	Coping scales	Number of items	Response scale	Validation population
Coping Orientation for Problem Experiences –COPE (Carver, Scheier and Weintraub, 1989)	15: Active coping; Planning; Suppression of competing activities; Restraint coping; Positive reinterpretation; Acceptance; Seeking social support for instrumental reasons; Seeking social support for emotional reasons; Religion; Venting emotions; Denial; Behavioural disengagement; Mental disengagement; Drug-alcohol use; Humour	60 items	4-point Likert scale	$N = 978$ University under-graduate students

Name and authors of inventory	Coping scales	Number of items	Response scale	Validation population
Brief COPE (Carver, 1997)	14: Active coping; Planning; Positive reframing; Self-distraction; Acceptance; Using instrumental support; Using emotional support; Religion; Venting; Denial; Behavioural disengagement; Substance use; Humour; Self Blame	28 items	4-point Likert scale	$N = 418$ Age not listed
Modified COPE (MCOPE; Crocker and Graham, 1995)	9: Active coping; Seeking social support for instrumental reasons; Planning; Seeking social support for emotional reasons; Behavioural disengagement; Suppression of competing activities; Venting of emotions; Humour; Denial	48 items	5-point Likert scale	377 athletes diverse; age, sport and competitive experience
Ways of Coping Checklist (Folkman and Lazarus, 1985)	8: Problem-focused coping; Wishful thinking; Detachment; Seeking social support; Focusing on the positive; Self-blame; Tension reduction; Keep to self	66 items	4-point Likert scale	108 undergraduate students
Ways of Coping Checklist-revised (Folkman, Lazarus, Dunkel-Schetter, DeLongis and Gruen, 1986)	8: Confrontive coping; Distancing; Self-controlling; Seeking social support; Accepting responsibility; Escape-avoidance; Planful problem solving; Positive reappraisal	66 items	4-point Likert scale	$N = 150$ married couples
Ways of Coping with Sport (WOCS) (Madden, Kirkby and McDonald, 1989)	8: Problem-focused coping; Seeking social support; General emotionality; Increased effort and resolve; Detachment; Denial; Wishful thinking; Emphasizing the positive	66 items	4-point Likert scale	$N = 133$ athletes

Name and authors of inventory	Coping scales	Number of items	Response scale	Validation population
l'Inventaire des Stratégies de Coping en Compétition Sportive (ISCCS: Coping strategies in Sport Competition Questionniare; Gaudreau and Blondin, 2002)	10: Thought control; Mental imagery; Relaxation; Effort expenditure; Logical analysis; Seeking support; Venting of unpleasant emotions; Mental Distraction; Disengagement/ resignation; Social withdrawal	39 items	5-point Likert scale	$N = 316$ Athletes of varying abilities and sports (M=17.4 years)
Coping Style Inventory for Athletes (CSIA: Anshel and Kaissidis, 1997)	2: Approach coping; Avoidance coping	16 items	5-point Likert scale	$N = 190$ athletes ranging in age from 18 to 44 years
Athletic Coping Skills Inventory-28 (ACSI-28; Smith, Schutz, Smoll and Ptacek, 1995)	7: Coping with adversity; Peaking under pressure; Goal Setting/ mental preparation; Concentration; Freedom from worry; Confidence and achievement motivation; Coachability	28 items	4-point Likert scale	$N - 637$ athletes

Concluding remarks

The ongoing nature of demonstrating validity and reliability cannot be emphasized strongly enough. Equally, because a test shows evidence of factorial validity via factor analysis studies, researchers should be cautioned about using the inventory in an unquestioning way. Schutz (1994) emphasized the importance of giving the selection of measures to be used due consideration before conducting the research. Validity of a measure should not be seen as sacred, and even though the measure is commonly used, there could still be doubts over its validity and improvements to the measure could be made.

Notes

1   In fact Dennett (1991) described affect as 'the awkward term [for emotion and mood] used by psychologists' (p. 45).
2   Construct validity is the degree to which test scores relate to behaviours they purport to represent. Construct validity is generally considered the 'gold standard' of questionnaire

validity in the trait-related approach to psychometrics (Rust and Golombok, 1999). The American Psychological Association (1985) stated that a test cannot be said to have demonstrated construct validity until it has demonstrated content, factorial, and criterion validity.

3   Factorial validity is described as the correlation of the scores for a questionnaire with the scores for each subscale (Anastasi and Urbina, 1997). The techniques traditionally used to demonstrate factorial validity are often those under the broad heading of 'factor analysis'.

4   Content validity refers to the degree to which a test provides an adequate sample of a particular content domain. Rust and Golombok (1999) suggested that demonstration of content validity is usually a qualitative process (e.g. expert opinion), as the form of any deviation from validity is more important than the degree. Murphy and Davidshofer (1998) stated that (to their knowledge) no single statistic can be used to measure content validity. Related to content validity is face validity, the degree to which a questionnaire *appears* to measure what it purports to measure *to the respondent*.

References

Allen, M. S., Jones, M. V. and Sheffield, D. (2009). Causal attribution and emotion in the days following competition. *Journal of Sports Sciences*, 27, 461–468.

Allen, M. S., Jones, M. V. and Sheffield, D. (2010). The influence of positive reflection on attributions, emotions, and self-efficacy. *Sport Psychologist*, 24, 211–226.

American Psychological Association (1985). *Standards for educational and psychological testing*. Washington, DC: APA.

Anastasi, A. and Urbina, S. (1997). *Psychological testing*, 7th edn. Upper Saddle River, N.J.: Prentice Hall.

Anshel, M. H. and Kaissidis, A. N. (1997). Coping style and situational appraisals as predictors of coping strategies following events in sport as a function of gender and skill level. *British Journal of Psychology*, 88, 263–276.

Argus, G. R., Terry, P. C., Bramston, P. and Dinsdale, S. L. (2004). Measurement of mood in adolescents with intellectual disability. *Research in Developmental Disabilities*, 25, 493–507.

Baron, B., Moullan, F., Deruelle, F. and Noakes, T. D. (2009). The role of emotions on pacing strategies and performance in middle and long duration sport events. *British Journal of Sports Medicine* [online] 23 June.

Beedie, C. J. (2007). Towards empirical distinctions between emotion and mood: a subjective contextual model. In A. M. Lane (ed.), *Mood and human performance: Conceptual, measurement, and applied issues* (pp. 63–88). Hauppauge, N.Y.: Nova Science.

Beedie, C. J., Terry, P. C., Devonport, T. and Lane, A. M. (2011). Is an emotion the same as a mood? Development of the emotion and mood components of anxiety questionnaire. *Personality and Individual Differences*, 50, 228–233.

Beedie, C. J., Terry, P. C. and Lane, A. M. (2005). Distinguishing mood from emotion. *Cognition and Emotion*, 19, 847–878.

Beedie, C. J., Terry, P. C. and Lane, A. M. (2000). The Profile of Mood States and athletic performance: two meta-analyses. *Journal of Applied Sport Psychology*, 12, 49–68.

Besharat, M. A. (2007) Psychometric properties of Farsi version of the Emotional Intelligence Scale-41 (FEIS-41). *Personality and Individual Differences*, 43, 991–1000.

Carver, C. S. (1997). You want to measure coping but your protocol's too long: consider the Brief COPE. *International Journal of Behavioral Medicine*, 4, 92–100.

Carver, C. S., Scheier, M. F. and Weintraub, J. K. (1989). Assessing coping strategies: a theoretically based approach. *Journal of Personality and Social Psychology*, 56, 267–283.

Colman, A. M. (2001). Intentionality. In *Oxford dictionary of psychology* (pp. 369–370). Oxford: Oxford University Press.

Clore, G. L. (1994). Why emotions are never unconscious. In P. Ekman and R. J. Davidson (eds), *The nature of emotion* (pp. 285–290). Oxford: Oxford University Press.

Crocker, P. R. E. (1992). Measuring stress by competitive athletes: ways of coping. *International Journal of Sport Psychology*, 23, 161–175.

Crocker, P. R. E. (1997). A confirmatory factor analysis of the Positive Affect Negative Affect Schedule (PANAS) with a youth sport sample. *Journal of Sport and Exercise Psychology*, 19, 91–97.

Crocker, P. R. E. and Graham, T. R. (1995). Coping by competitive athletes with performance stress: gender differences and relationships with affect. *The Sport Psychologist*, 9, 325–338.

Curren, S. L., Andrykowski, M. A. and Studts, J. L. (1995). Short form of the Profile of Mood States (POMS–SF): psychometric information. *Psychological Assessment*, 7, 80–83.

Davies, K., Lane, A. M. and Devonport, T. (2010). Validity and reliability of a Brief Emotional Intelligence Scale: the BEIS-10. *Journal of Individual Differences*, 31, 198–208.

Dennett, D. C. (1991). *Consciousness explained*. New York: Little, Brown.

Eklund, R. C., Grove, J. R. and Heard, N. P. (1998). The measurement of slump-related coping: factorial validity of the COPE and Modified-COPE inventories. *Journal of Sport and Exercise Psychology*, 20, 157–175.

Eisenberg, N., Fabes, R. A., Guthrie, I. K. and Reiser, M. (2000). Dispositional emotionality and regulation: their role in predicting quality of social functioning. *Journal of Personality and Social Psychology*, 78, 136–157.

Eubank, M. R. and Collins, D. J. (2000). Coping with pre- and in-event fluctuations in competitive state anxiety: a longitudinal approach. *Journal of Sports Sciences*, 18, 121–131.

Fazackerley, R., Lane, A. M. and Mahoney, C. (2003). Confirmatory factor analysis of the Brunel Mood Scale for use in water-skiing. *Perceptual and Motor Skills*, 97, 657–661.

Folkman, S. and Lazarus, R. S. (1985). If it changes it must be a process: study of emotions and coping during 3 stages of a college examination. *Journal of Personality and Social Psychology*, 48, 150–170.

Folkman, S., Lazarus, R. S., Dunkel-Schetter, C., DeLongis, A. and Gruen, R. (1986). The dynamics of a stressful encounter: cognitive appraisal, coping and encounter outcomes. *Journal of Personality and Social Psychology*, 50, 992–1003.

Gaudreau, P. and Blondin, J. P. (2002). Development of a questionnaire for the assessment of coping strategies employed by athletes in competitive sport settings. *Psychology of Sport and Exercise*, 3, 1–34.

Gignac, G. E., Palmer, B. R., Manocha, R. and Stough, C. (2005). An examination of the factor structure of the Schutte self-report emotional intelligence (SSREI) scale via confirmatory factor analysis. *Personality and Individual Differences*, 39, 1029–1042.

Gross, J. (2010). The future's so bright, I gotta wear shades. *Emotion Review*, 3, 212–216.

Gross, J. (ed.) (2007). *Handbook of emotion regulation*. New York: Guilford Press.

Gross, J. J. and John, O. P. (2003). Individual differences in two emotion regulation processes: implications for affect, relationships, and well-being. *Journal of Personality and Social Psychology*, 85, 348–362.

Gross, J. and Thompson, R. A. (2007). Emotion regulation: conceptual foundations. In J. Gross (ed.), *Handbook of emotion regulation* (pp. 3–26). New York: Guilford.

Grove, J., Eklund, R. and Heard, N. (1997). Coping with performance slumps: factor analysis of the Ways of Coping in Sport Scale. *Australian Journal of Science and Medicine in Sport*, 29, 99–105.

Grove, J. R. and Prapavessis, H. (1992). Preliminary evidence for the reliability and validity of an abbreviated Profile of Mood States. *International Journal of Sport Psychology*, 23, 93–109.

Hanin, Y. L. (2000). Individual zones of optimal functioning (IZOF) model: emotion–performance relationships in sports. In Y. L. Hanin (ed.), *Emotions in sport* (pp. 65–89). Champaign, Ill.: Human Kinetics.

Hanin, Y. L. (2003). Performance related emotional states in sport: A qualitative analysis. *Forum: Qualitative Social Research Journal*, 4 (February). www.qualitative-research.net/fqs-texte/1-03/1-03hanin-e.htm (accessed 17 March 2011).

Hashim, H. A., Zulkifli, E. Z. and Ahmad, H. (2010). Factorial validation of Malaysian adapted Brunel Mood Scale in an adolescent sample. *Asian Journal of Sports Medicine*, 1(4), 185-194.

Jones, M. V. (2003). Controlling emotions in sport. *The Sport Psychologist*, 17, 471–486.

Jones, M. V., Lane, A. M., Bray, S. R., Uphill, M. and Catlin, J. (2005). Development and validation of the Sport Emotion Questionnaire. *Journal of Sport and Exercise Psychology*, 27, 407, 43.

Jones, M. V. and Uphill, M. (2004). Responses to the Competitive State Anxiety Inventory-2(d) by athletes in anxious and excited scenarios. *Psychology of Sport and Exercise*, 5, 201–212.

Kline, P. (1994). *The handbook of psychological testing*. London: Routledge.

Lane, A. M. (2004). Measures of emotions and coping in sport. In D. Lavallee, J. Thatcher and M. Jones (eds), *Coping and emotion in sport* (pp. 255–271). Hauppauge, N.Y.: Nova Science.

Lane, A. M. (2007a). The rise and fall of the iceberg: development of a conceptual model of mood–performance relationships. In A. M. Lane (ed.), *Mood and human performance: Conceptual, measurement, and applied issues* (pp. 1–34.). Hauppauge, N.Y.: Nova Science.

Lane, A. M. (2007b). Developing and validating psychometric tests for use in high performance settings. In L. Boyar (ed.), *Psychological tests and testing research* (pp. 203–213). Hauppage, N.Y.: Nova Publishers.

Lane, A. M. (2010). Emotion regulation and exercise: the effects of emotional regulation motives. Paper presented at the Division of Clinical Psychology Annual Conference 2010, 1–3 December, Lowry Hotel, Manchester.

Lane, A. M., Beedie, C. J.. Stanley, D. M. and Devonport, T. J. (in review). *Validity of the emotion regulation scale for use in sport.*

Lane, A. M., Beedie, C. J. and Stevens, M. J. (2005). Mood matters: a response to Mellalieu. *Journal of Applied Sport Psychology*, 17, 319–325.

Lane, A. M., Davis, P. and Devonport, T. (2009a). Situational variability in emotions and emotion regulation. Paper for the Variability in Emotion Regulation of Others and Self symposium, British Psychological Society Social Psychology Conference, Sheffield University, 16–17 September 2010.

Lane, A. M. and Devonport, T. J. (2009). Can anger and tension be helpful? Relationships between mood states and emotional intelligence during optimal performance. Paper presented at the Stress Anxiety Research Society Conference, Budapest, Hungary, July 16–18th, 2009.

Lane, A. M., Devonport, T. J., Soos, I., Leibinger, E., Karsai, I. and Hamar, P. (2010a). Emotional intelligence, mood states and successful and unsuccessful performance. *Journal of Sports Science and Medicine*, 9, 388–392.

Lane, A. M., Devonport, T. J. and Stevens, M. (2010b). Relationships between emotional intelligence, pre-race and post-race emotions in 10-mile runners. *Athletic Insight*, 2, www.athleticinsight.com/Vol12Iss3/Run.htm (accessed 17 March 2010).

Lane, A. M. and Godfrey, R. (2010). Emotional and cognitive changes during and post a near fatal heart attack and one-year after: a case study. *Journal of Sports Science and Medicine*, 9, 517–522.

Lane, A. M. and Jarrett, H. (2005). Mood changes following golf among senior recreational players. *Journal of Sports Science and Medicine*, 4, 47–51.

Lane, A. M., Meyer, B. B., Devonport, T. J., Davies, K., Thelwell, R., Gill, G. S., Diehl, C., Wilson, M. and Weston, N. (2009b). Validity of the Emotional Intelligence Scale for use in Sport. *Journal of Sports Science and Medicine*, 8, 289–295.

Lane, A. M., Soos, I., Leibinger, E., Karsai, I. and Hamar, P. (2007). Validity of the Brunel Mood Scale for use with UK, Italian and Hungarian athletes. In A. M. Lane (ed.), *Mood and human performance: Conceptual, measurement, and applied issues* (pp. 119–130). Hauppauge, N.Y.: Nova Science.

Lane, A. M. and Terry, P. C. (2000). The nature of mood: development of a conceptual model with a focus on depression. *Journal of Applied Sport Psychology*, 12, 16–33.

Lane, A. M., Thelwell, R. and Devonport, T. J. (2009d). Emotional intelligence and mood states associated with optimal performance. *E-journal of Applied Psychology*, 5, 67–73.

Lane, A. M., Thelwell, R. C., Lowther, J. and Devonport, T. J. (2009c). Emotional intelligence and psychological skills use among athletes. *Social Behavior and Personality*, 37, 195–201.

Madden, C. C., Kirkby, R. J. and McDonald, D. (1989). Coping styles of competitive middle distance runners. *International Journal of Sport Psychology*, 20, 287–296.

Matthews, G., Jones, D. M. and Chamberlain, A. G. (1990). Refining the measurement of mood: the UWIST Mood Adjective Checklist. *British Journal of Psychology*, 81, 17–42.

Mayer, J. D., Caruso, D. R. and Salovey, P. (1999). Emotional intelligence meets standards for traditional intelligence. *Intelligence*, 27, 267–298.

Mayer, J. D., Roberts, R. D. and Barsade, S. G. (2008). Human abilities: emotional intelligence. *Annual Review of Psychology*, 59, 507–536.

McNair, D. M., Lorr, M. and Droppleman, L. F. (1971). *Manual for the Profile of Mood States*. San Diego, CA: Educational and Industrial Testing Services.

McNair, D. M., Lorr, M. and Droppleman, L. F. (1992). *Revised Manual for the Profile of Mood States*. San Diego, CA: Educational and Industrial Testing Services.

Meyer, B. B. and Fletcher, T. B. (2007). Emotional intelligence: a theoretical overview and implications for research and professional practice in sport psychology. *Journal of Applied Sport Psychology*, 19, 1–15.

Meyer, B. B. and Zizzi, S. (2007). Emotional intelligence in sport: conceptual, methodological, and applied issues. In A. M. Lane (ed.), *Mood and human performance: Conceptual, measurement, and applied issues* (pp. 131–154.). Hauppauge, N.Y.: Nova Science.

Morgan, W. P. (1980). Test of champions: the iceberg profile. *Psychology Today*, 14, 92–108.

Murphy, K. R. and Davidshofer, C. O. (1998). *Psychological testing: Principles and applications*. Upper Saddle River, N.J.: Prentice Hall.

Niven, K., Totterdell, P. and Holman, D. (2009). A conceptual classification of controlled interpersonal affect regulation strategies. *Emotion*, 9, 498–509.

Niven, K., Totterdell, P. A., Stride, C. and Holman, D. (2011). Emotion Regulation of Others and Self (EROS): The development and validation of a new individual difference measure. *Current Psychology*, 30, 53–73.

Parkinson, B. (2010). Recognizing desirability: is goal comparison necessary? *Emotion Review*, 2, 159.

Parkinson, B. and Totterdell, P. (1999). Classifying affect regulation strategies. *Cognition and Emotion*, 13, 277–303.

Parrott, W. G. (1993). Beyond hedonism: motives for inhibiting good moods and for maintaining bad moods. In D. M. Wegner and J. W. Pennebaker (eds), *Handbook of mental control* (pp. 278–305). Englewood Cliffs, N.J.: Prentice-Hall.

Pensgaard, A. M. and Duda, J. L. (2003). Sydney 2000: the interplay between emotions, coping, and the performance of Olympic-level athletes. *Sport Psychologist*, 17, 253–267.

Petrides, K. and Furnham, A. (2000). On the dimensional structure of emotional intelligence. *Personality and Individual Differences*, 29, 313–320.

Power, M. J. (2006). The structure of emotion: an empirical comparison of six models. *Cognition and Emotion*, 20, 694–713.

Renger, R. (1993). A review of the Profile of Mood States (POMS) in the prediction of athletic success. *Journal of Applied Sport Psychology*, 5, 78–84.

Renk, K. and Creasey, G. (2003). The relationship of gender, gender identity, and coping strategies in late adolescents. *Journal of Adolescence*, 26, 159–168.

Robazza, C., Bortoli, L. and Hanin, Y. (2006). Perceived effects of emotion intensity on athletic performance: a contingency-based individualized approach. *Research Quarterly for Exercise and Sport*, 77, 372–385.

Rowley, A. J., Landers, D. M., Kyllo, L. B. and Etnier, J. L. (1995). Does the Iceberg Profile discriminate between successful and less successful athletes? A meta-analysis. *Journal of Sport and Exercise Psychology*, 16, 185–199.

Ruiz, M. C. and Hanin, Y. L. (2004). Metaphoric description and individualized emotion profiling of performance states in top karate athletes. *Journal of Applied Sport Psychology*, 16, 258–273.

Rust, J. and Golombok, S. (1999). *Modern psychometrics: The science of psychological assessment*. London: Routledge.

Saklofske, D. H., Austin, E. J. and Minski, P. S. (2003). Factor structure and validity of a trait emotional intelligence measure. *Personality and Individual Differences*, 34, 707–721.

Salovey, P. and Mayer, J. D. (1990). Emotional intelligence. *Imagination, Cognition and Personality*, 9, 185–211.

Schutte, N. S., Malouff, J. M., Hall, L. E., Haggerty, D. J., Cooper, J. T., Golden, C. J. and Dornheim, L. (1998). Development and validation of a measure of emotional intelligence. *Personality and Individual Differences*, 25, 167–177.

Schutte, N. S., Malouff, J. M., Thorsteinsson, E. B., Bhullar, N. and Rooke, S. E. (2007). A meta-analytic investigation of the relationship between emotional intelligence and health. *Personality and Individual Differences*, 42, 921–933.

Schutz, R. W. (1994). Methodological issues and measurement problems in sport psychology. In S. Serpa, J. Alves and V. Pataco (eds), *International perspectives on sport and exercise psychology* (pp. 35–57). Morgantown, W.V.: Fitness Information Technology.

Shacham, S. (1983). A shortened version of the Profile of Mood States. *Journal of Personality Assessment*, 47, 305–306.

Smith, R. E., Schutz, R. W., Smoll, F. L. and Ptacek, J. T. (1995). Development and validation of a multidimensional measure of sport-specific psychological skills: the Athletic Coping Skills Inventory–28. *Journal of Sport and Exercise Psychology*, 17, 379–398.

Terry, P. C. (1995). The efficacy of mood state profiling among elite competitors: a review and synthesis. *The Sport Psychologist*, 9, 309–324.

Terry, P. C. (2000). Introduction to the Special Issue: Perspectives on mood in sport and exercise. *Journal of Applied Sport Psychology*, 12, 1–4.

Terry, P. C. and Lane, A. M. (2000). Normative values for the Profile of Mood States for use with athletic samples. *Journal of Applied Sport Psychology*, 12, 93–109.

Terry, P. C., Lane, A. M. and Fogarty, G. J. (2003). Construct validity of the Profile of Mood States – Adolescents for use with adults. *Psychology of Sport and Exercise*, 2, 125–139.

Terry, P. C., Lane, A. M., Lane, H. J. and Keohane, L. (1999). Development and validation of a mood measure for adolescents. *Journal of Sports Sciences*, 17, 861–872.

Terry, P. C. and Slade, A. (1995). Discriminant capability of psychological state measures in predicting performance outcome in karate competition. *Perceptual and Motor Skills*, 81, 275–286.

Thelwell, R. C., Lane, A. M. and Weston, N. J. V. (2007). Mood states, self-set goals, self-efficacy and performance in academic examinations. *Personality and Individual Differences*, 42, 673–583.

Thelwell, R., Lane, A. M., Weston, N. J. V. and Greenlees, I. A. (2008). Examining relationships between emotional intelligence and coaching efficacy. *International Journal of Sport and Exercise Psychology*, 6, 224–235.

Thomas, P. R., Murphy, S. and Hardy, L. (1999). Test of Performance Strategies: development and preliminary validation of a comprehensive measure of athletes' psychological skills. *Journal of Sports Sciences*, 17, 697–711.

Thompson, B. and Daniel, L. G. (1996). Factor analytic evidence for the construct validity of scores: a historical overview and some guidelines. *Educational and Psychological Measurement,* 56, 197–208.

Treasure, D. C., Monson, J. and Lox, C. L. (1996). Relationship between self-efficacy, wrestling performance, and affect prior to competition. *The Sport Psychologist,* 10, 73–83.

Van Rooy, D. L. and Viswesvaran, C. (2004). Emotional intelligence: a meta-analytic investigation of predictive validity and nomological net. *Journal of Vocational Behavior,* 65, 71–95.

Watson, D. (2000). *Mood and temperament.* New York: Guilford Press.

Watson, D. and Clark, L. A. (1997). Measurement and mismeasurement of mood: recurrent and emergent issues. *Journal of Personality Assessment,* 68, 267–296.

Watson, D., Clark, L. A. and Tellegen, A. (1988). Development and validation of brief measures of positive and negative affect: the PANAS scales. *Journal of Personality and Social Psychology,* 54, 1063–1070.

Watson, D. and Tellegen, A. (1985). Toward a conceptual structure of mood. *Psychological Bulletin,* 98, 219–235.

Zizzi, S. J., Deaner, H. R. and Hirschhorn, D. K. (2003). The relationship between emotional intelligence and performance among college baseball players. *Journal of Applied Sport Psychology,* 15, 262–269.

5

COPING IN SPORT THROUGH SOCIAL SUPPORT

Tim Rees and Paul Freeman, University of Exeter

> I think it would be difficult if you were just totally on your own and never had anyone really helping you out and giving you support, basically. I think it's a big difference .... I can't see how you can totally do it on your own .... You do need encouragement and advice, and, good times, bad times, you need people to help you out. I think it's pretty hard to do it without them.
>
> *(Davis Cup tennis player quoted in Rees and Hardy, 2000, p. 342)*

Introduction

Increased awareness of its potential within sport (Holt and Hoar, 2006; Rees, 2007) has led to a proliferation of research examining effects of social support, and with good reason. As well as being noted in interviews about factors affecting Olympic performance (e.g. Gould et al., 1999) and with international-level performers from a number of different sports (Rees and Hardy, 2000), research has demonstrated that social support may account for as much as 24 per cent of the variance in objective performance, over and above the effects of stress (Freeman and Rees, 2008; Rees, Hardy and Freeman, 2007; Rees and Freeman, 2009). There has also been work demonstrating its links with self-confidence (Rees and Freeman, 2007), processes underpinning performance (Rees and Hardy, 2004), burnout (Gould et al., 1996), coping with competitive stress (Crocker, 1992), slumps in performance (Madden, Kirkby and McDonald, 1989), and psychological responses to injury (Rees et al., 2010). Given this, it is not surprising that researchers have for a long time been encouraging athletes to use social support as a resource (e.g. Richman et al., 1989). We would concur. In fact, understanding the role of social support is important both for researchers and practitioners. A solid foundation of theory-led research could help to guide the development of social support interventions. Given the importance of social support, the aim of this chapter is to provide an overview of social support research and outline implications for sport psychologists. We start by discussing early social support research, how support has been conceptualised, and theoretical approaches that have guided research. We then discuss how social support may operate, factors that influence the effectiveness of support, and relationships with coping and emotions. We finish by highlighting future research issues and implications for applied practice.

The origins of social support

Although there had been previous mention in sport of social support, one could argue that it was the psychologists Irwin Sarason, Barbara Sarason and Gregory Pierce who really brought the concept of social support to the attention of sport psychologists. In their 1990 address to the then Association for the Advancement of Applied Sport Psychology, they commented, 'While the concept of social support has been applied mainly to the areas of health, personal adjustment, and social competence, its potentiality for the domain of sports is intriguing' (1990b, p. 125). In their address, they offered a number of examples of how social support might be important for sport and for performance. These included the following: 'Knowing that other people are available to provide help in a particular situation might aid the individual in the coping process …. Knowing that a coach is available to assist in batting skills may provide the individual with an opportunity to pull out of his or her slump' (p. 120).

Sarason et al.'s interest stemmed from their own research in psychology. Indeed, the social support construct has been a prominent feature of the psychological research literature. The origins of social support are, however, normally credited to the sociologist Emile Durkheim, who drew the conclusion (1897/1951) that suicides were more prevalent among those with fewer social ties. Interest in and awareness of the relations between social ties and psychological and physical health and well-being were subsequently made more explicit in the general psychology research of the 1970s and 1980s. For example, in a seminal study, Berkman and Syme (1979) presented results of a nine-year prospective study of 6,298 adults from Alameda County, California. They found that those with fewer social ties at baseline were more likely to die during the nine-year follow-up period. Since that time, social support has been one of the most well-documented psychosocial factors affecting physical health outcomes and psychological health (see reviews by Berkman et al., 2000; Cohen, 1988, 2004; Cohen and Janicki-Deverts, 2009; Cohen and Wills, 1985; Cohen, Underwood and Gottlieb, 2000b; Heitzmann and Kaplan, 1988; House, Landis and Umberson, 1988; Sarason, Sarason and Pierce, 1990a; Seeman, 1996; Thoits, 1995; Uchino, 2004, 2009; Uchino, Cacioppo and Kiecolt-Glaser, 1996; Uchino et al., 2010; Veiel and Baumann, 1992). Compared with those with fewer social ties, more socially integrated people have been shown to live longer, be more likely to survive myocardial infarction, have lower mortality rates, especially from cardiovascular disease, cancer and infectious diseases, and be less likely to report being depressed. It would appear that the health risks of being socially isolated are akin to the risks from smoking, high blood pressure and obesity (Cohen, 2001). Despite the impressive evidence for the health benefits of social support, it should be noted that the conceptualisation and measurement of social support has been quite diverse.

What is social support?

Various terms have been used to describe social support, including social network size, social integration, quantity and quality of relationships, social resources, satisfaction with support, perceived and received support, and structural and functional elements of support (for reviews, see Cohen, 1988; Cohen et al., 2000b; Heitzmann and Kaplan, 1988; Sarason, Sarason and Pierce, 1990a; Veiel and Baumann, 1992). Although diversity clearly exists, these various conceptualisations suggest that social support is comprised of three major subconstructs (Lakey, 2010). *Social integration* (a structural form of support) reflects the number of different types of relationships in which recipients participate. *Perceived support* (a functional form of support) refers to one's potential access to social support, and is a support recipient's subjective judgement that friends, family, team mates and coaches would provide assistance if needed. Enacted support (a functional form of support) reflects the specific helping actions provided by friends, family, team mates and coaches, usually during a specific time frame. *Enacted support* may be assessed via objectively observable effortful supportive behaviours (Burleson, 2009; Burleson and MacGeorge, 2002; Shumaker and Brownell, 1984; Vangelisti, 2009), or via self-reported receipt of the type or amount of enacted support (often termed *received support*). In this chapter, we use the term 'received support', but it should be noted that the terms received and enacted support have often been used interchangeably in the social support literature.

Perceived and received support are conceptually related under some conditions and may interact in potentially important ways (Uchino, 2009), but are considered two key but separate constructs (Dunkel-Schetter and Bennett, 1990; Helgeson, 1993; Wethington and Kessler, 1986). The distinction between them is an important one, and they may share as little as 12 per cent of common variance (e.g. Haber et al., 2007). Generally, it is people's perception of their social support that has been noted as crucial for their mental health and emotional well-being (Cohen, 1988; Cohen, Gottlieb and Underwood, 2000a; Cohen and Wills, 1985; Wills and Shinar, 2000). On the other hand, evidence for the benefits of received support is mixed (Uchino, 2009) – such support can be associated with a beneficial effect, no effect, or even a detrimental effect on outcomes (e.g. Reinhardt, Boerner and Horowitz, 2006). Although there is evidence in sport that athletes' social support interactions are sometimes viewed as more negative than positive (Udry et al., 1997), the research literature in sport provides evidence for the benefits of both perceived and received support in relation to performance (e.g. see Freeman and Rees, 2008). To help understand and explain the different effects of social support, research has adopted a range of theoretical perspectives.

Theoretical perspectives

Lakey and Cohen (2000) outlined three key theoretical perspectives in research on social support: the social constructionist, relationship, and stress and coping perspectives.

The social constructionist perspective

Within the social constructionist perspective, perceptions of support availability are believed to influence thoughts about the self, and these thoughts may in turn impact on emotional distress. Alternatively, the extent to which someone is integrated in a broad social network should influence their sense of identity and self-esteem, and these aspects in turn impact on health and well-being.

The relationship perspective

The relationship perspective conceptualises social support as part of more generic relationship processes, suggesting that support may not necessarily be discriminated from other closely related concepts such as low conflict, companionship and intimacy.

The stress and coping perspective

The stress and coping perspective has been the most influential theoretical perspective on social support, and provides a backdrop for this chapter (see Figure 5.1). This perspective is linked closely with research and theory on stress and coping (Lazarus, 1966; Lazarus and Folkman, 1984). According to the stress and coping perspective, perceived and received support might play specific roles at several points along the causal chain linking stressors to outcomes in sport through appraisal and coping mechanisms.

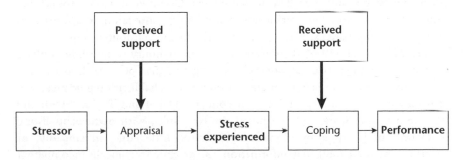

FIGURE 5.1 The differential impact of perceived and received support upon performance, and potential mechanisms

One way in which perceived support is hypothesised to lead to more favourable outcomes is through reducing the stress of situations (Barrera, 1986). More specifically, perceived support may be associated with appraisal mechanisms. Those who perceive themselves to have a lot of support available to them will tend to believe that they have the resources to cope with difficult situations and so are less likely to cognitively appraise those situations as stressful than individuals with low levels of perceived support (Bianco and Eklund, 2001). In health psychology, Bova (2001) found that the relationship between perceived support and both adjustment to illness and symptom experience was mediated by how the illness was cognitively appraised. In sport, Freeman and Rees (2009) demonstrated that perceived support was associated with appraising a competition as less of a threat. In line with Lazarus and Folkman's (1984) assertion that in stressful encounters, 'beliefs about control … play a major role in determining the degree to which a person feels threatened or challenged' (p. 76), Freeman and Rees also found that perceived support was positively associated with situational control, which was positively associated with challenge appraisals and negatively associated with threat appraisals. More favourable appraisals were in turn associated with better performance.

Similarly, Aspinwall and Taylor (1997) highlighted the potential influence of social support on proactive coping, which they define as 'efforts undertaken in advance of a potentially stressful event to prevent it or to modify its form before it occurs' (p. 417). Proactive coping refers to the development and acquisition of resources and skills that are not designed to specifically address any one stressor, but are instead designed to prepare in general for potential future stressors. Research into these stress prevention pathways is relatively scarce (Uchino, 2009), but these links may hold vital clues on how some individuals perform effectively in potentially demanding situations.

In contrast to perceived support, received support is more of a situational factor that arises in response to stressful circumstances. As we noted earlier, however, there is evidence that received support is associated with beneficial effects, no effects, and even detrimental effects. Gould et al. (1996) found that although friends were important for maintaining motivation, pressure from others, especially parents, played a major role in the burnout of junior tennis players. Udry et al. (1997) demonstrated in a sport-injury setting how athletes tended to view their social support as more negative than positive. In particular, they noted examples of inappropriate or insufficient rehabilitation guidance, lack of sensitivity to the injury, and lack of concern. Dakof and Taylor (1990) and Rees, Smith and Sparkes (2003) noted similar results, with participants listing these unhelpful actions by physicians: expressed little concern, empathy, or affection; provided insufficient information; and provided technically incompetent medical care. Given the potential for received support to be unhelpful, research has attempted to identify factors that may influence the effectiveness of received support.

When will received support be effective?

The effectiveness of received support may be affected by a number of different factors. These include:

- the type of support
- the match between the type of support and the needs arising as a result of a stressful situation
- the match between the type of support and the context
- the timing of support
- the support provider.

In relation to the type of support, it is important to note that social support is generally considered to be a multidimensional construct. Although debate has existed over how many dimensions comprise social support (Cutrona and Russell, 1990), there are certainly four dimensions that have regularly been noted: emotional, esteem, informational and tangible support. Rees and Hardy (2000) noted these four dimensions of support in their study of high-level athletes, drawing on the definitions of Cutrona and Russell (1990). Thus, in their simplest forms,

- **emotional support** refers to being there for comfort and security, leading to a person feeling loved and cared for
- **esteem support** refers to bolstering a person's sense of competence or self-esteem
- **informational support** refers to providing advice or guidance
- **tangible support** refers to providing concrete instrumental assistance.

Second, some authors have suggested the importance of a match between the type of support received and the needs of the individual (Cutrona and Russell, 1990). This 'optimal matching' model predicts that support will be more effective when it is matched to the needs arising from a stressful event. For example, having someone who would loan you money may be useful to help pay for training, but useless in the face of a recent loss of form. Optimal matching offers an eloquent explication of when *stress buffering* is likely to occur (i.e. at low levels of stress, level of social support is relatively unimportant; at high levels of stress, the detrimental relationship between stress and outcomes is reduced (buffered) for those with high social support compared to with those with low social support).

A key proposition of Cutrona and Russell (1990), who drew on the coping literature, is that the controllability or uncontrollability of the stressor determines support needs. According to this model, uncontrollable events lead to a need for forms of social support that foster emotion-focused forms of coping (such as emotional and esteem forms of support), and controllable events lead to a need for forms of social support that foster problem-focused coping (informational and tangible forms of support).

In a study demonstrating the stress–buffering effects of social support in relation to processes underpinning tennis performance, Rees and Hardy (2004) did indeed illustrate the importance of matching specific types of sport-relevant social support with the needs elicited by a stressor. At the same time, they argued that the effectiveness of the matching process was enhanced by paying close attention to the development of context-specific measures of stress and support. Despite this work from sport, in general, the optimal matching model has received little empirical support (Burleson, 2003; Burleson and MacGeorge, 2002). Instead, the same supportive behaviours often serve multiple functions, and different supportive behaviours can achieve similar objectives (Burleson and MacGeorge, 2002; Viswesvaran, Sanchez and Fisher, 1999). In fact, Cutrona and Russell (1990) recognise that specific forms of social support do not exclusively foster either emotion- or problem-focused coping, but can foster both. There is frequently a high degree of overlap between types (dimensions) of support in naturalistic settings (Cohen and Wills, 1985), such that attempts to bolster a person's sense of competence (esteem support) may also be interpreted as a sign of caring (emotional support).

Third, the effectiveness of received support may also depend on the context in which it is provided, with beneficial influences more likely when there is a match between the type of received support and the context (Berg and Upchurch, 2007). For example, in experimental situations there is evidence that emotional and esteem forms of received support may be beneficial in aiding performance on a golf-putting task (Rees and Freeman, 2010). In field studies, these forms of support have also been noted as useful in relation to confidence and performance (e.g. Freeman and Rees, 2009; Rees and Freeman, 2007; Rees et al., 2007). In performance contexts, it may be that such forms of emotional and esteem support may be considered more nurturing, less obtrusive, less controlling, and less likely to undermine important mediating mechanisms such as self-efficacy than informational (such as direct advice) and tangible (concrete instrumental assistance) forms of support (Bolger and Amarel, 2007; Trobst, 2000). This is because the receipt of informational and tangible support could undermine recipients' belief in their skills and competence to perform well in the absence of such help or advice.

Fourth, a key to the effectiveness of received support may be its timing. Bolger and Amarel (2007) discussed the implications of receiving support in what they termed the anterogatory and postrogotory periods. In the latter postrogotory period, the person has made an appraisal of the situational demands and has made the decision to ask for help. At this point, assuming it matches the needs of the recipient, received support can help them cope effectively with the situational demands. The situation is more complicated in the anterogatory period. Here, support is received before it has been requested. According to Bolger and Amarel (2007), support at this time is more likely to have negative influences on psychological mechanisms such as self-efficacy and emotions than during the postrogotory period. This has implications for sport, because much of the supportive communication of coaches is made in this anterogatory period. Being sensitive to the potential pitfalls of providing support at this point is therefore important. Bolger and Amarel have subsequently outlined that support will still have its intended effect in the anterogatory period (and not undermine self-efficacy) when it is delivered in such a way that the recipient does not notice it or interpret it as support. Bolger and Amarel refer to this as invisible support. For example, a player may assist a struggling team mate by requesting advice from the coach on a shared task. Alternatively, when a player sees a team mate struggling, he may highlight his 'own problem' and how he is overcoming it, rather than directly addressing the team mate's difficulties.

Finally, as Bianco (2001) noted in the context of injury, various network members tend to engage in the provision of various types of social support. Unfortunately, these people do not always provide their support well (Lehman, Ellard and Wortman, 1986), may differ in their expertise in providing specific types of support (Johnston and Carroll, 1998; Rees et al., 2003; Rosenfeld and Richman, 1997), and view the usefulness of their support differently than recipients (Coriell and Cohen, 1995). Thus, although the effectiveness of received support might depend on factors such as how well it is matched to stress, consideration of the providers of support may be equally important. Research using a social identity/self-categorisation perspective has demonstrated that only when the support is received from someone with whom one shares a common identity will the support have its intended impact (Haslam et al., 2004; Haslam et al., 2005). Other factors associated with effective support providers include their level of knowledge and expertise, the quality of relationship they share with the recipient, and whether they have experienced similar situations themselves (Bianco, 2001; Hardy and Crace, 1993; Suitor, Pillemer and Keeton, 1995). Research has also demonstrated that individuals' appraisals of others' supportiveness may reflect a unique matching (interaction) between the individual and the person providing the support (Lakey, Lutz and Scoboria, 2004). There may, then, be an interaction between the best-suited provider of support and the quality of the provision.

Social support and coping

Although coping is mentioned heavily in the social support literature and vice versa, the relationship between the two constructs is interpreted in different ways. First, the stress and coping theoretical perspective generally implies that received support initiates coping efforts. Indeed, Lakey and Cohen (2000) suggested that studies should examine whether coping mediates the relationship between received support and outcomes. Jones and Wirtz (2006) argued that cognitive reappraisal is one emotion-focused coping strategy, and demonstrated that person-centred emotional support facilitated the cognitive reappraisal of a stressful event, which in turn led to emotional improvement. Second, other researchers (e.g. Uchino, 2009) suggest that social support is one of many available coping strategies. This view appears to be reflected in coping questionnaires, such as the Modified-COPE (Crocker and Graham, 1995) and the Approach to Coping in Sport Questionnaire

(Kim and Duda, 2003), which include seeking support as subscales alongside other coping strategies. Third, Raedeke and Smith (2004) argued that social support is an external resource and coping behaviours are internal resources. Smith, Smoll and Ptacek (1990) found that social support and psychological coping skills were statistically distinct and that they operated in a conjunctive manner in relation to the stress–injury relationship. That is, only athletes low in both social support and coping skills displayed a significant relationship between stress and injury. Raedeke and Smith (2004) further examined this conjunctive relationship, but failed to replicate the finding in the context of the stress–burnout relationship. A greater understanding of the relationship between social support and coping is an important step to helping athletes perform effectively in demanding situations.

Social support and emotions

Research examining the relationship between social support and specific emotions in sporting contexts is scarce. Studies have noted, however, that social support may be an important resource during injury rehabilitation to generally help reduce distress and enhance emotional responses (e.g. Bianco, 2001). Athletes interviewed in a study by Rees and Hardy (2000) also highlighted that social support was useful when they felt down about their sport. In the work psychology literature, Mohr and Wolfram (2010) found that supervisor support was negatively associated with emotional irritation at work. Further, Van Steenbergen et al. (2008) examined the effects of received informational support on the cognitive appraisal of work–family demands and the emotions experienced. Results suggested that individuals who were provided with positively toned informational support appraised the task of combining their work and family roles more favourably and experienced more challenge-related emotions than individuals provided with negatively toned information. In a laboratory-based experiment, Jones and Wirtz (2006) found that emotional support was associated with emotional improvement, and this effect was partially mediated by support facilitating cognitive reappraisals of situations. Despite these findings, the relationship between social support and emotions has not always been found to be universally positive. For example, Neely et al. (2006) examined the correlations between social support and positive and negative affect in a laboratory experiment in which participants interacted with four different partners. In general, although support was significantly correlated with positive affect, it was not correlated with negative affect. Shrout, Herman and Bolger (2006) found evidence that received support might in fact be associated with emotional costs. Given these inconsistent findings, the influence of social support on emotions in sporting contexts would be an important avenue for future research.

Future research

Although the effects of social support in sport have become increasingly recognised, a number of areas warrant further research. The relationship between social support and coping is one such area. For example, does social support facilitate the adoption of effective coping strategies, or should social support be considered a coping strategy itself alongside other problem- and emotion-focused strategies? Research examining the links between social support and emotions in sport is also scarce. Given the influence of perceived support on cognitive appraisals, however, it is likely that high levels of support may lead to more positive emotional states.

There continues to be a pressing need to examine the mechanisms through which social support operates (Uchino, 2009). Studies have found that cognitive appraisal (Freeman and Rees, 2009) and self-efficacy (Rees and Freeman, 2009) might underpin the effects of support on performance, but research could examine other cognitive, emotional and behavioural mechanisms. Identifying the mechanisms that underpin the effects of social support will both enhance theory and help to develop effective theory-led support interventions (Thoits, 1995). Similarly, there is a need for a greater understanding of the various factors that influence the effectiveness of support. The notion of invisible support is interesting, and research into this concept may unveil subtler and more effective methods of providing support that avoid undermining the recipient's sense of competence and control.

Applied implications

The social support literature has demonstrated the potential importance of significant others for sportspeople. Athletes should be encouraged to be proactive in their use of social support, and along with all those in their support network, they should be helped to understand that such action is not a sign of weakness (Hardy, Jones and Gould, 1996). As highlighted in this chapter, however, social support is a complex construct, and various factors need to be considered in the development of effective support interventions. Hogan, Linden and Najarian (2002) noted that even the most well-intentioned professionally led support interventions can be experienced by the recipients as negative. For example, support may be ineffective, or even associated with negative outcomes if it reduces the recipient's sense of autonomy, control or self-efficacy (Gottlieb, 2000). Support interventions need to be carefully planned and implemented, based on theory and empirical evidence. A well-intentioned parent trying to help a child plan a training schedule could be perceived as over-controlling rather than supportive. Additionally, a well-intentioned coach trying to facilitate improvement may undermine an athlete's self-efficacy, if the coach focuses too much on weaknesses, particularly when support has not been solicited.

An important distinction exists between perceived and received support. As Bianco and Eklund (2001) noted, perceived support may exert beneficial effects through preventive pathways whereas received support may operate via palliative pathways, such as buffering stress and/or facilitating effective coping. Individuals with high perceived support are likely to experience less stress through appraisal and proactive coping mechanisms. As applied practitioners, sport psychologists could help provide a context for empowering individuals to purposefully develop and nurture the availability of social support. Interventions might focus on helping athletes fully understand how they can maximise the available support in their network and to learn the skills necessary to be proactive in using this resource. Providing opportunities for interactions may increase communication, strengthen bonds between network members, and improve individuals' sense of belonging to a supportive environment (Cutrona and Cole, 2000). Cutrona and Cole also suggested that cognitive therapy techniques may be useful in helping to change maladaptive beliefs, such as when athletes feel they must not request help and support.

In contrast to perceived support, received support is more of a situational factor that arises in response to stressful circumstances. The literature on received support has important implications for athletes and for all those involved with them. Various task-, recipient-, and provider-related factors may influence the effectiveness of received support. Understanding the need to match the correct support to the needs arising from stressors (Cutrona and Russell, 1990) is important for family, friends, team mates, coaches, managers, fitness trainers, physiotherapists and psychologists. Consideration should also be given to the most appropriate provider of support. Effective providers are likely to possess specific knowledge, experience and expertise – for example, informational and tangible support would need to come from those with specific expertise, whereas emotional support may be most effective from someone close to the athlete – and may share a common identity with the recipient. Applied practitioners might coordinate appropriate support behaviours to ensure the correct support is received from the right people. Further, the timing of support and how it is provided may be crucial. If an athlete has not actively engaged in seeking support, received support needs to be provided in a skilful or 'invisible' manner to avoid the recipient experiencing feelings of inefficacy. Sport psychologists may facilitate this process by educating providers and modelling appropriate methods of providing support. For example, sport psychologists could demonstrate alternative, indirect methods of providing advice to a player that could be used instead of overt instruction that may, at times, undermine self-efficacy.

A final point is that the beneficial effects of support interventions and manipulations may not be consistent across all athletes. For example, in a recent intervention study (Freeman, Rees and Hardy, 2009), golfers were provided with support though a focused professionally led intervention (cf. Hogan et al., 2002), instigated after a baseline period. An overall performance improvement was noted, but the effects were not statistically significant for all golfers. Rees and Freeman (2010) provided one potential explanation for this finding. In their study, the impact of the enacted support manipulation differed depending on whether individuals had high or low levels of levels of perceived support. Specifically, individuals with low perceived support benefited most from receiving support.

Conclusion

Research has demonstrated that social support is associated with a range of favourable outcomes in a sporting context. The concept of social support therefore holds strong appeal for researchers and applied practitioners alike. As outlined in this chapter, however, social support is a complex construct. This complexity needs to be recognised and understood to facilitate the development of theory and effective interventions. An important distinction exists between perceived and received support, and consideration needs to be given to factors that influence the effectiveness of support. Perceived support may exert beneficial effects through preventive pathways, including promoting favourable cognitive appraisals and proactive coping. Received support may arise in response to stressful circumstances, and either promote the use of effective coping strategies or act as a coping strategy itself. The effectiveness of received support is likely to be influenced by the dimension of support, the match to the needs elicited by the stressful situation and context, the timing of support, and the support provider. Further research into these factors will help refine theory, and in turn will inform the development of effective support interventions.

References

Aspinwall, L. G. and Taylor, S. E. (1997). A stitch in time: Self-regulation and proactive coping. *Psychological Bulletin*, 121, 417–436.

Barrera, M., Jr. (1986). Distinctions between social support concepts, measures, and models. *American Journal of Community Psychology*, 14, 413–445.

Berg, C. A. and Upchurch, R. (2007). A developmental–contextual model of couples coping with chronic illness across the lifespan. *Psychological Bulletin*, 133, 920–954.

Berkman, L. F., Glass, T., Brissette, I. and Seeman, T. E. (2000). From social integration to health: Durkheim in the new millennium. *Social Science and Medicine*, 51, 843–857.

Berkman, L. F. and Syme, S. L. (1979). Social networks, host resistance, and mortality: A nine-year follow-up study of Alameda County residents. *American Journal of Epidemiology*, 109, 186–204.

Bianco, T. (2001). Social support and recovery from sport injury: Elite skiers share their experiences. *Research Quarterly for Exercise and Sport*, 72, 376–388.

Bianco, T. and Eklund, R. C. (2001). Conceptual considerations for social support research in sport and exercise settings: The case of sport injury. *Journal of Sport and Exercise Psychology*, 23, 85–107.

Bolger, N. and Amarel, D. (2007). Effects of social support visibility on adjustment to stress: Experimental evidence. *Journal of Personality and Social Psychology*, 92, 458–475.

Bova, C. (2001). Adjustment to chronic illness among HIV-infected women. *Journal of Nursing Scholarship*, 33, 217–224.

Burleson, B. R. (2003). Emotional support skill. In J. O. Greene and B. R. Burleson (eds), *Handbook of communication and social interaction skills* (pp. 551–594). Mahwah, N.J.: Erlbaum.

Burleson, B. R. (2009). Understanding the outcomes of supportive communication: A dual-process approach. *Journal of Social and Personal Relationships*, 26, 21–38.

Burleson, B. R. and MacGeorge, E. L. (2002). Supportive communication. In M. L. Knapp and J. A. Daly (eds), *Handbook of interpersonal communication* (pp. 374–424). Thousand Oaks, Calif.: Sage Publications.

Cohen, S. (1988). Psychosocial models of the role of social support in the etiology of physical disease. *Health Psychology*, 7, 269–297.

Cohen, S. (2001). Social relationships and health: Berkman and Syme [1979]. *Advances in Mind–Body Medicine*, 17, 4–6.

Cohen, S. (2004). Social relationships and health. *American Psychologist*, 59, 676–684.

Cohen, S., Gottlieb, B. H. and Underwood, L. G. (2000a). Social support and health. In S. Cohen, L. G. Underwood and B. H. Gottlieb (eds), *Social support measurement and intervention: A guide for health and social scientists* (pp. 3–25). New York: Oxford University Press.

Cohen, S. and Janicki-Deverts, D. (2009). Can we improve our physical health by altering our social networks? *Perspectives on Psychological Science*, 4, 375–378.

Cohen, S., Underwood, L. G. and Gottlieb, B. H. (2000b). *Social support measurement and intervention: A guide for health and social scientists*. New York: Oxford University Press.

Cohen, S. and Wills, T. A. (1985). Stress, social support and the buffering hypothesis. *Psychological Bulletin*, 98, 310–357.

Coriell, M. and Cohen, S. (1995). Concordance in the face of a stressful event: When do members of a dyad agree that one person supported the other? *Journal of Personality and Social Psychology*, 69, 289–299.

Crocker, P. R. E. (1992). Managing stress by competitive athletes: Ways of coping. *International Journal of Sport Psychology*, 23, 161–175.

Crocker, P. R. E. and Graham, T. R. (1995). Coping with competitive athletes with performance stress: Gender differences and relationships with affect. *The Sport Psychologist*, 9, 325–338.

Cutrona, C. E. and Cole, V. (2000). Optimizing support in the natural network. In S. Cohen, L. G. Underwood and B. H. Gottlieb (eds), *Social support measurement and intervention: A guide for health and social scientists* (pp. 278–308). New York: Oxford University Press.

Cutrona, C. E. and Russell, D. W. (1990). Type of social support and specific stress: Toward a theory of optimal matching. In B. R. Sarason, I. G. Sarason and G. R. Pierce (eds), *Social support: An interactional view* (pp. 319–366). New York: Wiley.

Dakof, G. A. and Taylor, S. E. (1990). Victims' perceptions of social support: What is helpful from whom? *Journal of Personality and Social Psychology*, 58, 80–89.

Dunkel-Schetter, C. and Bennett, T. L. (1990). Differentiating the cognitive and behavioral aspects of social support. In B. R. Sarason, I. G. Sarason and G. R. Pierce (eds), *Social support: An interactional view* (pp. 267–296). New York: Wiley.

Durkheim, E. (1951). *Suicide*, trans. J. A. Spaulding and G. Simpson. New York: Free Press. (Original work published 1897)

Freeman, P. and Rees, T. (2008). The effects of perceived and received support on objective performance outcome. *European Journal of Sport Sciences*, 8, 359–368.

Freeman, P. and Rees, T. (2009). How does perceived support lead to better performance? An examination of potential mechanisms. *Journal of Applied Sport Psychology*, 21, 429–441.

Freeman, P., Rees, T. and Hardy, L. (2009). An intervention to increase social support and improve performance. *Journal of Applied Sport Psychology*, 21, 186–200.

Gottlieb, B. H. (2000). Selecting and planning support interventions. In S. Cohen, L. G. Underwood and B. H. Gottlieb (eds), *Social support measurement and intervention: A guide for health and social scientists* (pp. 195–220). New York: Oxford University Press.

Gould, D., Guinan, D., Greenleaf, C., Medbery, R. and Peterson, K. (1999). Factors affecting Olympic performance: Perceptions of athletes and coaches from more and less successful teams. *The Sport Psychologist*, 13, 371–394.

Gould, D., Tuffey, S., Udry, E. and Loehr, J. (1996). Burnout in competitive junior tennis players: II: Qualitative analysis. *Sport Psychologist*, 10, 341–366.

Haber, M., Cohen, J., Lucas, T. and Baltes, B. (2007). The relationship between self-reported received and perceived social support. *American Journal of Community Psychology*, 39, 133–144.

Hardy, C. J. and Crace, R. K. (1993). The dimensions of social support when dealing with sport injuries. In D. Pargman (ed.), *Psychological basis of sport injury* (pp. 121–144). Morgantown, W.V.: Fitness Information Technology.

Hardy, L., Jones, G. and Gould, D. (1996). *Understanding psychological preparation for sport: Theory and practice of elite performers.* Chichester: Wiley.

Haslam, S. A., Jetten, J., O'Brien, A. and Jacobs, E. (2004). Social identity, social influence, and reactions to potentially stressful tasks: Support for the self-categorization model of stress. *Stress and Health*, 20, 3–9.

Haslam, S. A., O'Brien, A., Jetten, J., Vormedal, K. and Penna, S. (2005). Taking the strain: Social identity, social support and the experience of stress. *British Journal of Social Psychology*, 44, 355–370.

Heitzmann, C. A. and Kaplan R. M. (1988). Assessment of methods for measuring social support. *Health Psychology*, 7, 75–109.

Helgeson, V. S. (1993). Two important distinctions in social support: Kind of support and perceived versus received. *Journal of Applied Social Psychology*, 23, 825–845.

Hogan, B. E., Linden, W. and Najarian, B. (2002). Social support interventions: Do they work? *Clinical Psychology Review*, 22, 381–440.

Holt, N. L. and Hoar, S. D. (2006). The multidimensional construct of social support. In S. Hanton and S. D. Mellalieu (eds), *Literature reviews in sport psychology* (pp. 199–225). Hauppauge, N.Y.: Nova Science.

House, J. S., Landis, K. R. and Umberson, D. (1988). Social relationships and health. *Science*, 241, 540–545.

Johnston, L. H. and Carroll, D. (1998). The provision of social support to injured athletes: A qualitative analysis. *Journal of Sport Rehabilitation*, 7, 267–284.

Jones, S. M. and Wirtz, J. G. (2006). How does the comforting process work? An empirical test of an appraisal-based model of comforting. *Human Communication Research*, 32, 217–243.

Kim, M. S. and Duda, J. L. (2003). The coping process: Cognitive appraisal of stress, coping strategies, and coping effectiveness. *The Sport Psychologist*, 17, 406–425.

Lakey, B. (2010). Social support: Basic research and new strategies for intervention. In J. E. Maddux and J. P. Tangney (eds), *Social psychological foundations of clinical psychology* (pp. 177–194). New York: Guilford.

Lakey, B. and Cohen, S. (2000). Social support theory and measurement. In S. Cohen, L. G. Underwood and B. H. Gottlieb (eds), *Social support measurement and intervention: A guide for health and social scientists* (pp. 29–52). New York: Oxford University Press.

Lakey, B., Lutz, C. J. and Scoboria, A. (2004). The information used to judge supportiveness depends on whether the judgment reflects the personality of perceivers, the objective characteristics of targets, or their unique relationship. *Journal of Social and Clinical Psychology*, 23, 796–814.

Lazarus, R. S. (1966). *Psychological stress and coping process.* New York: McGraw-Hill.

Lazarus, R. S. and Folkman, S. (1984). *Stress appraisal and coping.* New York: Springer.

Lehman, D. R., Ellard, J. H. and Wortman, C. B. (1986). Social support for the bereaved: Recipients' and providers' perspectives on what is helpful. *Journal of Consulting and Clinical Psychology*, 54, 438–446.

Madden, C. C., Kirkby, R. J. and McDonald, D. (1989). Coping styles of competitive middle distance runners. *International Journal of Sport Psychology*, 20, 287–296.

Mohr, G. and Wolfram, H. J. (2010). Stress among managers: The importance of dynamic tasks, predictability, and social support in unpredictable times. *Journal of Occupational Health Psychology*, 15, 167–179.

Neeley, L. C., Lakey, B., Cohen, J. L., Barry, R., Orehek, E., Abeare, C. A. and Mayer, W. (2006). Trait and social processes in the link between social support and affect: An experimental, laboratory investigation. *Journal of Personality*, 74, 1015–1045.

Raedeke, T. D. and Smith, A. L. (2004). Development and preliminary validation of an athlete burnout measure. *Journal of Sport and Exercise Psychology*, 23, 281–306.

Rees, T. (2007). Influence of social support on athletes. In S. Jowett and D. Lavallee (eds), *Social psychology in sport* (pp. 223–231). Champaign, Ill.: Human Kinetics.

Rees, T. and Freeman, P. (2009). Social support moderates the relationship between stressors and task performance through self-efficacy. *Journal of Social and Clinical Psychology,* 28, 245–264.

Rees, T. and Freeman, P. (2010). The effect of experimentally provided social support on golf-putting performance. *The Sport Psychologist,* 18, 333–348.

Rees, T. and Hardy, L. (2000). An investigation of the social support experiences of high-level sports performers. *Sport Psychologist,* 14, 327–347.

Rees, T. and Hardy, L. (2004). Matching social support with stressors: Effects on factors underlying performance in tennis. *Psychology of Sport and Exercise,* 5, 319–337.

Rees, T., Hardy, L. and Freeman, P. (2007). Stressors, social support and effects upon performance in golf. *Journal of Sports Sciences,* 25, 33–42.

Rees, T. J., Mitchell, I., Evans, L. and Hardy, L. (2010). Stressors, social support and psychological responses to sport injury in high and low-performance standard participants. *Psychology of Sport and Exercise,* 11, 505–512.

Rees, T., Smith, B. and Sparkes, A. (2003). The influence of social support on the lived experiences of spinal cord injured sportsmen. *Sport Psychologist,* 17, 135–156.

Reinhardt, J. P., Boerner, K. and Horowitz, A. (2006). Good to have but not to use: Differential impact of perceived and received support on well-being. *Journal of Social and Personal Relationships,* 23, 117–129.

Richman, J. M., Hardy, C. J., Rosenfeld, L. B. and Callanan, R. A. E. (1989). Strategies for enhancing social support networks in sport: A brainstorming experience. *Journal of Applied Sport Psychology,* 1, 150–159.

Rosenfeld, L. B. and Richman, J. M. (1997). Developing effective social support: Team building and the social support process. *Journal of Applied Sport Psychology,* 9, 133–153.

Sarason, B. R., Sarason, I. G. and Pierce, G. R. (1990a). *Social support: An interactional view.* New York: Wiley.

Sarason, I. G., Sarason, B. R. and Pierce, G. R. (1990b). Social support, personality and performance. *Journal of Applied Sport Psychology,* 2, 117–127.

Seeman, T. E. (1996). Social ties and health: The benefits of social integration. *Annals of Epidemiology,* 6, 442–451.

Shumaker, S. A. and Brownell, A. (1984). Toward a theory of social support: Closing conceptual gaps. *Journal of Social Issues,* 40, 11–36.

Shrout, P. E., Herman, C. M. and Bolger, N. (2006). The costs and benefits of practical and emotional support on adjustment: A daily diary study of couples experiencing acute stress. *Personal Relationships,* 13, 115–134.

Smith, R. E., Smoll, F. E. and Ptacek, J. T. (1990). Conjunctive moderator variables in vulnerability and resiliency research: Life stress, social support, coping skills, and adolescent sport injuries. *Journal of Personality and Social Psychology,* 58, 360–370.

Suitor, J. J., Pillemer, K. and Keeton, S. (1995). When experience counts: The effects of experiential and structural similarity on patterns of support and interpersonal stress. *Social Forces,* 73, 1573–1588.

Thoits, P. A. (1995). Stress, coping, and social support processes: Where are we? What next? *Journal of Health and Social Behavior* (Extra Issue), 53–79.

Trobst, K. K. (2000). An interpersonal conceptualization and quantification of social support transactions. *Personality and Social Psychology Bulletin,* 26, 971–986.

Uchino, B. N. (2004). *Social support and physical health: Understanding the health consequences of our relationships.* New Haven, Conn.: Yale University Press.

Uchino, B. N. (2009). Understanding the links between social support and physical health. *Perspectives on Psychological Science,* 4, 236–255.

Uchino, B. N., Cacioppo, J. T. and Kiecolt-Glaser, J. K. (1996). The relationship between social support and physiological processes: A review with emphasis on underlying mechanisms and implications for health. *Psychological Bulletin,* 119, 488–531.

Uchino, B. N., McKenzie, C., Birmingham, W. and Vaughn, A. A. (2010). Social support and the reactivity hypothesis: Conceptual issues in examining the efficacy of received support during acute psychological stress. *Biological Psychology* (online) http://pubget. com/search?q=authors%3A%22Allison%20A%20Vaughn%22 (accessed 18 March 2011).

Udry, E., Gould, D., Bridges, D. and Tuffey, S. (1997). People helping people? Examining the social ties of athletes coping with burnout and injury stress. *Journal of Sport and Exercise Psychology,* 19, 368–395.

Vangelisti, A. L. (2009). Challenges in conceptualizing social support. *Journal of Social and Personal Relationships,* 26, 39–51.

Van Steenbergen, E. F., Ellemers, N., Haslam, S. A. and Urlings, F. (2008). There is nothing either good or bad but thinking makes it so: Informational support and cognitive appraisal of the work–family interface. *Journal of Occupational and Organizational Psychology,* 81, 349–367.

Veiel, H. O. F. and Baumann, U. (1992). *The meaning and measurement of social support.* New York: Hemisphere.

Viswesvaran, C., Sanchez, J. I. and Fisher, J. (1999). The role of social support in the process of work stress: A meta-analysis. *Journal of Vocational Behavior,* 54, 314–334.

Wethington, E. and Kessler, R. C. (1986). Perceived support, received support and adjustment to stressful life events. *Journal of Health and Social Behavior,* 27, 78–89.

Wills, T. A. and Shinar, O. (2000). Measuring perceived and received social support. In S. Cohen, L. G. Underwood and B. H. Gottlieb (eds), *Social support measurement and intervention: A guide for health and social scientists* (pp. 86–135). New York: Oxford University Press.

6

SOCIAL INFLUENCE ON EMOTION IN SPORT

Megan Babkes Stellino, University of Northern Colorado, Julie Partridge, Southern Illinois University-Carbondale and Kristina Moore, University of Northern Colorado

> I always enjoyed being part of a team. I loved the camaraderie. It's what I loved about Davis Cup. It's what made doubles so important to me. If you're on a team, and you're angry or upset at something that happened in a game, you have people to share it with. It's the same thing when you win.
>
> *(John McEnroe; McEnroe and Kaplan, 2002, p. 29)*

Sporting emotions are central to the motivation and overall sport experience of all athletes regardless of age, competitive level, or type of sport. Emotional experiences associated with sport participation are influenced by many sources, and in turn meaningfully contribute to the nature of athletic involvement. Sport-related emotion result from interactions with the environment and, more importantly for the purposes discussed herein, social influences.

In this chapter we focus on how various social influences serve as sources that impact the athletes' emotional responses in sport. We begin with a brief description and definition of social influence, followed by explanation of the most commonly explored forms of emotional responses in sport: enjoyment and stress/anxiety. Next, we discuss the importance of investigations that focus on the connection between social influence and emotional responses in sport. Following this, we review research that has focused on how specific forms of social influence relate to athletes' emotional responses. We end with recommendations for practitioners and a discussion of future directions in this line of research.

Social influence in sport

The majority of sport contexts are inherently social in nature. Evaluation by others is often likely, and involvement usually requires the presence and participation of other individuals. One of the most distinguishing characteristics of sport, compared to other achievement realms (such as academia), is that it almost invariably occurs within a social atmosphere. It is, therefore, crucial to not only consider interpersonal factors such as motives and self-perceptions in examinations of individual sport participation experiences, but also to simultaneously consider social factors (Brustad and Babkes, 2004). While some athletes may train in isolation, competition and the vast majority of opportunities to engage in sport require an individual to demonstrate and display their ability in the presence of others. We must therefore include interpersonal influences to completely understand the achievement processes that occur in social environments (Cialdini and Trost, 1998).

The term 'social' is used in this chapter to reflect those components of life that involve, or are impacted by past, current, or anticipated relationships with others (Ruble and Goodnow, 1998). By 'social influence' we extend that definition to refer to the impact that those relationships may have on a particular dimension of an individual's experience. Consistent with the majority of current research in social and developmental sport psychology, we acknowledge that social influences combine with intrapersonal factors in an interactional manner (Lewin, 1951). As such, our focus in this chapter is on how interpersonal relationships and interactions impact sport participants' emotional experiences.

Many forms of social influence exist in the sport arena. The relationships and interactions that have an impact on the sport experiences of athletes exist within the sport environment, but may also include those that lie outside the boundaries of the athletic arena. Common forms of social influence within the sport environment include coaches, administrators, team mates, and opponents. Judges, officials/referees, and spectators can also be relevant forms of social influence for athletes. Family members, including parents and siblings, and peers or friends outside of the athletic environment are pertinent social influences as well. It is important to note that it is the athlete's perspective rather than an objective rating of others' influence that is often most relevant to the emotion experienced. The assessment of how social influences impact sport-related psychosocial processes and outcomes has therefore typically been in the form of perceived report from the perspective of the athlete. We now offer a brief introduction of emotion in sport in an effort to provide context for the subsequent review of literature on social influences as sources of enjoyment and stress/anxiety in the athletic domain.

Emotion in sport

While many emotional responses potentially relate to athletic endeavors, enjoyment and anxiety have emerged as two of the most meaningful and frequently researched.

Enjoyment

Regardless of age, type of sport participation, or competitive level, sport is often considered an enjoyable endeavor. Sport enjoyment has consistently been defined as 'a positive affective response to the sport experience that reflects generalized feelings such as pleasure, liking and fun' (Scanlan, Stein, and Ravizza, 1989, p. 65).

Scanlan and Simons (1992) further clarified that enjoyment is the most commonly assessed positive emotional response experienced by individuals in the sport domain. Enjoyment is considered to be a more specific emotional consequence than the general construct of experiencing positive affect, and broader than the specific momentary feeling of excitement or exhilaration.

The assessment of sport enjoyment has typically been via surveys to tap athletes' feelings of positive emotion. Surveys have included items specifically focused on liking sport (Brustad, 1988; Scanlan and Lewthwaite, 1986), fun (Scanlan and Lewthwaite, 1986; Wankel and Sefton, 1989) and enjoyment (Babkes and Weiss, 1999; Brustad, 1988; Raedeke, 1997; Wankel and Kreisel, 1985a, 1985b). Scanlan et al. (1993a) developed a four-item scale to enhance the psychometric properties of existing enjoyment scales by adding "happy" and "enjoy" to the earlier "liking" and "fun" items (Scanlan and Lewthwaite, 1986). Results from two separate factor analyses suggested that the four items form a single reliable scale (Scanlan et al., 1993a; Scanlan et al. 1993b), thereby establishing the necessary validity for use of this four-item measure of enjoyment that reflected the many ways positive emotion had previously been assessed in the literature.

Quantitative, qualitative, and mixed methods have been used to create a solid basis for comprehending and studying positive emotion in sport. Surveys and questionnaires were primarily used in the initial explorations that included the construct of enjoyment (Brustad, 1988; Csikszentimihalyi, 1975; Scanlan et al., 1993a; Scanlan and Lewthwaite, 1986; Wankel and Kreisel, 1985a; Wankel and Sefton, 1989). Other research by Scanlan and colleagues (Scanlan et al., 1989, Scanlan et al., 2003a; Scanlan et al., 2009; Scanlan et al., 2003b) has utilized a qualitative, or more inductive, approach in the form of structured interviews. While the quantitative research facilitated external validation of sources of enjoyment, the use of interviews revealed a more in-depth understanding of the factors related to positive emotion in sport, and allowed previously unidentified sources of enjoyment to emerge (Scanlan and Simons, 1992).

The literature on sport enjoyment includes research conducted with a variety of participants and in relation to various time periods. Sport enjoyment has been explored among males and females, racially and ethnically diverse groups, recreational and elite athletes, as well as young and experienced participants. Furthermore, enjoyment has been assessed in relation to specific time points, such as before and after a game, and long periods of time, such as the entire sport season or the most competitive years of an athlete's career. See the work of Scanlan and colleagues (Scanlan et al., 2003a, 2003b, 2005, 2009; Scanlan and Simons, 1992; Scanlan et al., 1993a) for more complete reviews of the breadth of literature on sport enjoyment.

Stress and anxiety

Stress has been defined as an individual's appraisal of a situation as too taxing or exceeding their resources and thus endangering their sense of well-being (Lazarus, 1967). According to Martens (1977), an athlete feels threatened in competitive sport when they perceive an imbalance between the performance demands and their capabilities to meet those demands under conditions where the consequences of failure are thought to be important. Of particular importance is the concept that it is the athlete's perceived imbalance coupled with the anticipation of negative consequences, not objective reality, that yields the stress process that has various emotional consequences in athletic situations. Anxiety, the most commonly examined negative emotional response to stress, has been examined among a variety of participants including youth, collegiate, adult recreational, and elite level athletes.

Measures of state anxiety have been the most commonly used mechanism for assessing negative emotion or stress in athletic situations (Scanlan, 1984). State anxiety measures typically seek to assess feelings of apprehension, tension, and autonomic nervous system activation that occur as immediate, "right now" reactions to situations that are perceived as threatening to one's self-esteem (Spielberger, 1966).

The importance of social influence on athlete emotion in sport

Now that we have presented brief introductions to social influence, enjoyment, and stress in the sport context, we address the next logical question: "Why do we care about social influences on emotion in sport?" We contend that the answer to this question is twofold and that both reasons are inextricably linked. First, the nature of the interpersonal relationships and interactions that athletes have with significant others has a well-documented impact on their emotional responses. Second, the emotional responses that an athlete experiences have an equally well substantiated impact on other achievement outcomes critical to healthy development and continued participation in sport, such as motivation (see Weiss and Amorose, 2008). An athlete's perception of social influence serves as a source of their emotional responses to sport involvement, which then leads to variations in their motivation. A positive perception of social influence conceivably leads to higher enjoyment and lower anxiety, which ultimately leads to continued involvement (Brustad, Babkes, and Smith, 2001; Partridge, Brustad, and Babkes Stellino, 2008; Weiss and Petlichkoff, 1989), whereas negative social influence may lead to lower enjoyment, higher debilitative stress and anxiety, and potential burnout or athletic dropout (Gould and Dieffenbach, 2000; Partridge et al., 2008; Smith, 1986). For example, if an individual perceives that their parent believes they are athletically competent and exerts low amounts of pressure, they would likely experience higher levels of enjoyment, feel less anxious in sport situations, and thus have the desire to continue involvement. Alternately, if an athlete receives little encouragement from the coach, they might report not having fun and feeling anxious in sport situations, and ultimately decide to quit.

The contribution of emotional responses in accounting for variations in sport motivation is well documented. Enjoyment or positive emotion, in particular, is frequently acknowledged as a central component in most theories that explain sport motivation (see Weiss and Amorose, 2008). It is for this reason that researchers have long attempted to determine what contributes to positive emotion. The nature of social influence consistently emerges as a critical source of positive, as well as negative, emotion. Therefore, we support the belief that social influence plays an essential role in the emotion experienced by athletes, and that this influence is furthermore critical to overall athletic motivation.

Research on social influence on athlete emotion

In this section, the extant research specifically focused on the relationships between various forms of social influence on emotion responses is systematically presented. Generally, the research suggests that enjoyment is likely when an athlete perceives feedback, reinforcement, and interactions with others to be positive. Stress and anxiety, however, can emerge when others are perceived as exerting too high expectations, providing too much evaluation and negative feedback, or contributing to an environment that emphasizes outcomes rather than engagement in the athletic process. In particular we highlight the research on parental, coach or leader, peer, and group influences on athlete enjoyment and anxiety.

Parental influence on athlete emotion

Mothers and fathers have long been considered some of the most important significant others in the youth sport context. Parents are typically credited with being the initial socializing agents who introduce youth to athletics, and are often found to have a critical role in providing them with the opportunity, transportation, equipment, and financial support necessary to play organized sport (Brustad and Partridge, 2002; Greendorfer, Lewko, and Rosengren, 2002; Partridge et al., 2008; Weiss and Amorose, 2008). As youths continue involvement in athletics, parents typically become a primary source of encouragement and support as well as models for interpreting athletic experiences. Depending on the children's perceptions, parental influence can have a positive or negative impact on the child. Here we focus on how various parental attitudes and behaviors affect young athletes' emotional responses. Specifically, a positive impact is considered one that increases enjoyment or decreases stress, while a negative impact is one that decreases enjoyment or increases stress.

It is important to recognize that a particular parental influence that is linked to an increase in a child's sport enjoyment does not necessarily mean that the absence of that parental factor is linked to a decrease in stress. Since stress and enjoyment are not opposites on a continuum, but rather exist separately from one another, significant others, including parents, influence them separately. That said, practically speaking it is no surprise that a parental form of influence such as emotional support is often reported to both increase enjoyment and decrease stress. However, we must be careful not to assume one in the instance of the other (Scanlan et al., 2005).

Parental influence as a source of athlete enjoyment

Many forms of parental influence have been identified as sources of athletes' enjoyment. Youth and elite-level sport participants' perceptions of positive parental beliefs, reactions, and interactions have often emerged in the literature as predictors of positive emotional responses (Babkes and Weiss, 1999; Scanlan and Lewthwaite, 1986; Scanlan et al., 1989). Wrestlers experienced greater seasonal enjoyment when they perceived that their parents were satisfied with their wrestling performance (Scanlan and Lewthwaite, 1986). Findings additionally indicated that higher season-long wrestling enjoyment was associated with fewer and less frequent negative maternal performance reactions. Babkes and Weiss (1999) found similar results in their study of competitive youth soccer players; higher perceived parental beliefs about competence and more frequent positive performance contingent responses were related to higher enjoyment. In-depth interviews with elite figure skaters also revealed that a source of enjoyment was the belief that their athletic achievement was a mechanism for bringing pleasure or pride to their families (Scanlan et al., 1989). More recently, Kanters, Bocarro, and Casper (2008) found that incongruent beliefs between parents and young male hockey players regarding the extent and nature of parental involvement was linked to children's reports of more positive feelings about their hockey participation. The authors suggested that rather than making inferences about the benefits of parents having inaccurate beliefs about their involvement compared with their child's perceptions of them, it is instead important to recognize athletes may provide higher reports of satisfaction and enjoyment in hockey if they think their parents expect them to report this. Parents and children perceiving similar levels of parental influence and involvement, therefore, appear to have important implications for athletes' positive affective responses in sport.

Level of perceived parental involvement has also been linked to athletes' positive emotion. Parental involvement has been defined as both physical involvement, where mothers and fathers demonstrate a presence in the sport context and contribute to their child's participation (as a coach or team parent), and emotional involvement, which reflects the provision of care. Research findings revealed that young competitive male wrestlers who reported more parental involvement in their sport participation enjoyed wrestling more than their counterparts whose parents were less involved (Scanlan and Lewthwaite, 1986). A positive relationship has also been found between perceived parental emotional involvement and enjoyment among adolescent soccer players from Norway (Ommundsen and Vaglum, 1991). In research that examined the influence of parental involvement on the athlete's positive emotional experience, among other psychosocial outcome variables, Babkes and Weiss (1999) found that perceptions of father involvement in particular were positively related to sport enjoyment levels. No significant relationship was found between mothers' involvement and athletes' enjoyment. More recently, study of sport enjoyment in two different age groups revealed that perceived positive parent involvement emerged as the most influential source of enjoyment for younger males and females and older females (McCarthy, Jones, and Clark-Carter, 2008).

Parental provision of encouragement and support for athletic endeavors has repeatedly been associated with positive emotional responses among young athletes in a variety of sports. The higher the perceived level of encouragement for pursuit of athletic endeavors, the more soccer participants reported satisfaction or positive emotion resulting from their playing (Green and Chalip, 1997). In a series of studies by Power and colleagues, conducted with young swimmers and soccer players, a positive relationship was consistently found between perceived parental support, especially from mothers, and the level of sport enjoyment (Averill and Power, 1995; Power and Woolger, 1994). A significant relationship has also been established between perceived parental support and greater sport enjoyment among male and female tournament tennis players (Hoyle and Leff, 1997; Leff and Hoyle, 1995). In a study of perceived parental support, pressure, and extracurricular activities in elementary-aged children, perceived parental support was significantly related to sports enjoyment (Anderson et al., 2003). Further evidence was revealed in focus groups with young participants in various sports, who reported that psychosocial support from their parents was an important source of enjoyment (McCarthy and Jones, 2007). Specifically, informational support, enhancement of self-worth, and extrinsic rewards contributed to enjoyment. On the other hand, inappropriate psychosocial support, including low informational support, low emotional support, and over-involved parents contributed to lack of enjoyment in the same youngsters.

Enjoyment levels among athletes are also associated with perceptions of pressure and expectations from their parents (Anderson et al., 2003; Averill and Power, 1995; Babkes and Weiss, 1999; Brustad, 1988; Green and Chalip, 1997; Hoyle and Leff, 1997; Leff and Hoyle, 1995; Power and Woolger, 1994; Scanlan and Lewthwaite, 1986). For the most part, lower levels of perceived parental pressure have been related to reports of higher levels of sport enjoyment. For example, Anderson et al. (2003) found that parental pressure negatively predicted sports enjoyment, particularly for young boys. Some parental gender differentiations have also emerged in terms of saliency of pressure from mothers and fathers. Babkes and Weiss (1999) found that lower perceived pressure from fathers in particular, was associated with high soccer enjoyment, and findings from Scanlan and Lewthwaite's (1986) study of young wrestlers revealed that lower levels of perceived maternal pressure were related to higher enjoyment. However, for some athletes, parental expectations are not necessarily negative, and instead are often linked to more positive emotional responses in sport situations. For example, studies have shown that high expectations are predictive of sport enjoyment among young soccer players (Averill and Power, 1994; Green and Chalip, 1997). Power and Woolger's (1994) findings of a curvilinear relationship between parental expectations and swimmers' enjoyment serve to somewhat clarify these other studies' results. It appears that perhaps there is a critical threshold of perceived parental expectations when emotional responses are considered. Continued exploration is necessary to identify how high is too high for expectations, and to determine when expectations turn to perceived pressure, and what the subsequent impact is on an athlete's positive sport emotion.

Parental influence as a source of athlete stress

Research on sources of stress in sport has repeatedly demonstrated that worry about negative evaluation, pressure, and expectations from parents are linked to a negative emotional experience in athletes across all ages and competitive levels. Stress-induced anxiety has been identified as a common response among young athletes who reported worrying about incurring negative parental evaluation. Findings suggest that an athlete's predisposition to be competitively anxious increases their likelihood of frequent worry about parents negatively evaluating their performance (Lewthwaite and Scanlan, 1989; Passer, 1983). Research conducted with young baseball and basketball players confirmed this prediction, and revealed that athletes higher in competitive trait anxiety were more likely to worry about negative evaluation from their parents and thus experienced more stress than their less anxious peers (Brustad, 1988; Brustad and Weiss, 1987). In subsequent studies, athletes from youth sport to elite levels have reported that negative performance evaluation, pre-competition worries related to receiving negative feedback, and striving to meet parental expectations were stressors (Bray, Martin, and Widemeyer, 2000; Cohn, 1990; Gould and Weinberg, 1985; Gould, Horn, and Spreemann, 1983; Pierce and Stratton, 1981; Scanlan et al., 1991). Shields et al. (2005) investigated the self-reported ethically relevant behaviors, expectations, and attitudes of youth, and adult sport-related influences. Of the youth respondents, 15 per cent indicated that their parents angrily criticize their sport performance. The authors suggest that this may account for the 21 per cent of athletes who preferred their parents not to watch their competitions, which sheds light on one of the risk factors for attrition during early adolescence.

Perceptions of parental pressure and high expectation for success in sport have been associated with negative emotional responses among athletes. A significant source of pre- and post-wrestling match stress for young athletes was perceived parental pressure to wrestle well (Bois, Lalanne, and Delforge, 2009; Gould et al., 1991a; Scanlan and Lewthwaite, 1984). Collins and Barber (2005) found that elite adolescent field hockey players who perceived their parents to place greater importance on performing well at the National Futures Tournament reported higher cognitive anxiety than those who perceived their parents to place less importance on success at the tournament. Further results revealed that young basketball and tennis players were significantly more anxious when both parents were present in the sport environment (Bois et al., 2009). Directive behaviors and pressure were positively related to anxiety for male and female tennis players, while praise and understanding were negatively associated with anxiety in only female tennis players. No significant relationships emerged between parenting practices and anxiety in basketball players, suggesting that type of sport may be an important variable for researchers to consider. Fear of failure has also been examined as a negative emotional response to parental practices. Sagar and Lavallee (2010) found that punitive behavior, controlling behavior, and high expectations from parents contributed to adolescent athletes' reported fear of failure.

In Hellstedt's (1990) research with highly competitive young ski racers, 72.8 percent of the athletes reported moderate to forceful levels of pressure to compete from their parents. High pressure among these athletes, like their counterparts in other sports, was associated with negative emotional reactions. Interestingly, given the level of their sport involvement, many of these athletes felt that this amount of pressure, although periodically a catalyst to stress, was beneficial for their athletic performance. These findings suggest that there may be an interactional effect between the level of sport participation, the emotional response that results from athletic involvement, and the degree of parental pressure, which has yet to be examined thoroughly.

Finally, VanYperen (1995) investigated the relationship between perceptions of parental influence and stress among elite-level Dutch soccer players. He specifically examined the mediational effects of parental support as a potential protective mechanism against other sources of stress, such as team and performance outcome issues. Findings revealed that when parental support was perceived as low, more negative emotions were experienced about the team following undesirable performances. When parental support was perceived as high, however, players did not experience negative feelings about the team. Similarly, although the study by Anderson et al. (2003) with young school-aged children revealed that perceived pressure from parents was not related to sports anxiety, findings also showed that parental support was negatively related to sports anxiety. These results provided some initial evidence that parental influence may not only directly impact on an athlete's emotional response to sport performances, but may in fact buffer the effects of stress as a result of outcomes or interactions with others that are less than desirable.

Coach influence on athlete emotion

In addition to the athlete's parents, other individuals in an athlete's life have also been found to impact sport stress and enjoyment levels. Engagement in sport often involves the proximal and relevant influence of coaches, as they are immediately present to observe and evaluate performance. Various aspects of coaching behavior and interactions with athletes have been found to significantly impact the emotional responses of participants in sport.

Coach influence as a source of athlete enjoyment

Given the variety of feedback and reinforcement provided by coaches, it is not surprising that they have the capacity to elicit positive emotions among athletes. Research consistently reveals that athletes who perceive their interactions and aspects of their relationship with their coach as favorable experience positive emotional outcomes. When coaches were perceived as giving positive appraisals of performance and support, athletes of varying skill levels reported higher levels of enjoyment (Scanlan and Lewthwaite, 1986; Scanlan et al., 1993a; Scanlan et al., 1989). Weiss and colleagues (Black and Weiss, 1992; Price and Weiss, 2000) examined the relationship between various perceived coach behaviors, leadership styles, and athlete enjoyment. Findings revealed that adolescent swimmers who perceived their coaches as providing frequent, but contingent, praise and technical information following desirable performances, and frequent encouragement plus information following undesirable performances, reported higher sport enjoyment (Black and Weiss, 1992). Price and Weiss (2000) found that in adolescent female soccer players, perceptions that their coaches provided greater training and instruction, social support, positive feedback, and had more democratic and less autocratic decision-making styles were associated with greater sport enjoyment. Similarly, adult male rugby union players who perceived their coaches as more oriented toward motivating athletes reported higher sport enjoyment (Boardley, Kavussanu, and Ring, 2008).

In their exemplar series of studies focused on youth sport coaching behaviors, Smith, Smoll and colleagues (Smith, Smoll, and Curtis, 1979; Smith et al., 1983) also repeatedly found that effective coaches, as determined by objective ratings and young athletes' perceptions, had players who experienced more fun in sport. In their initial study of Little League baseball coaches, findings revealed that children who had coaches who engaged in higher levels of reinforcement of both desirable performance and effort, and who responded to mistakes with encouragement and technical instruction, reported more season-long enjoyment (Smith et al., 1983). In subsequent experimental research, athletes who played for coaches who were trained to be effective in their provision of encouragement, feedback, and technical instruction enjoyed their sport experience more than athletes who played for untrained coaches (Smith et al., 1979). Recently, Smith, Smoll, and colleagues (Cumming et al., 2007; Smith, Cumming, and Smoll, 2008) have expanded their work on assessing coach influence on athlete experiences by creating and utilizing the Motivational Climate Scale for Youth Sports to examine the impact that coach-initiated motivational climates have on youth sport participants' experiences. Initial findings revealed, as anticipated, that male and female youth recreational basketball players who perceived that their coaches created a mastery-involving climate enjoyed their sport team experience more than their counterparts who perceived that their coaches created an ego-involving climate.

Researchers have also begun to acknowledge and examine the impact that more holistic coach–athlete relationships (Stuntz and Spearance, 2007) and non-sport-related interactions between coach and athlete (Stuntz and Spearance, 2010) have on athlete enjoyment. Findings suggest that coach cross-domain relationships with youth-sport and collegiate-level athletes, and athletes' perceptions that their coach cares about their entire life, including non-sport interests, predicted greater sport enjoyment. These results provide encouraging new directions for assessing how particular dimensions of coach influence impact athlete positive emotion.

Coaching influence as a source of athlete stress

Athletes' interactions with their coaches can result in stressful responses in sport situations. Scanlan and Lewthwaite (1984) found that young wrestlers who worried about receiving negative evaluations from coaches experienced significant amounts of pre-match stress. Interestingly, young male baseball players who played for coaches educated in the developmental model of Coach Effectiveness Training (CET) showed a decrease in sport performance anxiety during the season, whereas the anxiety level of the athletes who played for untrained coaches remained unchanged (Smith, Smoll, and Barnett, 1995). Baker, Cote, and Hawes (2000) found that late adolescent varsity-level athletes' perceptions of a negative personal rapport between themselves and their coach was a positive predictor of sport anxiety. Taken together, these findings suggest that if coaches are aware of their interactions with athletes, the stress response among athletes is reduced.

A link between concerns about meeting coach expectations, negative coach evaluations, and stress has been found in other studies of athletes from a wide range of competitive levels (Bray et al., 2000; Gould and Weinberg, 1985; Scanlan et al., 1991). Interviews conducted with elite athletes have revealed other stressful negative interactions with coaches. Specifically, high-level competitors cited coach communication problems, a lack of general social support from coaches, and interpersonal conflict with coaches as predictors of negative emotion (Gould, Eklund, and Jackson, 1991b, 1993; Gould, Jackson and Finch, 1993c; Scanlan et al., 1991).

The specific type of leadership style with which an athlete is confronted in sport is another important factor that may lead to negative emotional responses. Research has indicated that preferences for certain leadership styles, such as high levels of instructional and training behaviors, may relate to age (Chelladurai and Carron, 1983), gender (Chelladurai and Arnott, 1985; Terry, 1984), and task type (Riemer and Chelladurai, 1995). For example, compared with older athletes, male athletes or those with offensive team roles, younger athletes, female athletes, and defensive position players tend to have a preference for more democratic leadership styles. If an athlete has a coach with a leadership style that is inconsistent with the athlete's preferred style, this may lead to negative emotional responses. Lower levels of satisfaction, decreased intrinsic motivation, and lower levels of performance have all been associated with non-preferred leadership styles in coaches (Amorose and Horn, 2001; Chelladurai and Riemer, 1998; Dwyer and Fischer, 1990).

Peer influence on athlete emotion

Research on the impact of peers on athletes' emotional responses has continued to gain popularity in recent years and indicates that peers can be highly influential in facilitating enjoyment or creating stress. In a similar vein, the effect of the sporting group on an athlete and the climate of the sport environment have been shown to have an impact on individual participant's emotional responses.

Peer influence as a source of athlete enjoyment

Peers have the potential to be positive sources of emotion in sport. Affiliation-related aspects of sport have been found to be salient predictors of enjoyment for competitors at all levels of sport, and include such components as interactions with team mates, creating friendships, and the existence of a social support system (Csikszentmihalyi, 1975; Wankel and Kreisel, 1985a; Scanlan et al., 1993a; Weiss, Smith, and Theeboom, 1996). Similarly, friendships and other forms of positive peer relationships in sport such as high levels of peer acceptance have been found to lead to increased motivation, enjoyment, and continued involvement (Evans, 1985; Evans and Roberts, 1987; Smith, 1999; Smith, Balaguer, and Duda, 2006; Weiss and Smith, 1999, Zarbatany, Ghesquiere, and Mohr, 1992; Zarbatany, Hartmann, and Rankin, 1990). Peers have the opportunity to provide sport participants with several important elements of friendship (companionship, pleasant play, conflict resolution, and things in common) that increase enjoyment and commitment to sport (Weiss and Smith, 2002). Moreover, the opportunity to compare one's athletic skills to others has emerged as a source of enjoyment in sport. Elite athletes have spoken about performing better than others in competition and practices, or competitive achievement, as a key source of their sport enjoyment (Scanlan et al., 1989). Additionally, the competitive process has specifically been associated with positive emotion among male team sport athletes (Csikszentmihalyi, 1975; Wankel and Kreisel, 1985a), and the opportunity to experience positive team interactions and supportiveness, and develop friendships has been identified as a reason for sport enjoyment (Scanlan et al., 1993a).

Smith et al. (2006) investigated peer relationship variables in a sport sample (including perceived friendship quality, perceived peer acceptance, perceived competence, enjoyment, anxiety, self-presentational concerns, and self-determined motivation) in a sport sample. Results indicated five separate profiles that were consistent with previous work in developmental psychology (Seidman et al., 1999) and with theoretical expectations that more positive peer relationships increase psychological benefits (such as higher levels of perceived competence, lower anxiety, and lower self-presentational concerns), and that social factors impact motivation-related cognitions (such as self-determined motivation) and enjoyment.

Peer influence as a source of athlete stress

While peer relationships may lead to positive emotional experiences in sport, they have been found to be a source of negative social evaluation for athletes of all ages and competence levels, which in turn results in stress. Patrick et al. (1999) found that participation in a talent domain could lead to feelings of being ostracized by other members of a peer group because of the lack of popularity of a chosen activity. These negative social evaluations have the potential to increase levels of stress for the participants. Interviews conducted with elite Olympic wrestlers and figure skaters have revealed other stressful negative interactions. They cited team mate communication problems and a lack of general social support as predictors of negative emotion (Gould et al., 1991, 1993; Gould, Finch, and Jackson, 1993b). Similarly, Scanlan et al. (1991) found that interpersonal conflict between figure skating peers and the psychological warfare used by others were sources of stress in sport.

Another component of peer influence that is potentially detrimental to athletes' emotional responses to participation is peer victimization. Experiences in evaluative activities such as structured sport have been shown to be a consistent forum for negative peer interactions and negative affective reactions (Evans, 1985; Evans and Roberts, 1987; Kunesh, Hasbrook, and Lewthwaite, 1992; Partridge, 2003; Smith et al., 2009). Evans (1985) indicated that children playing in unstructured sports on school playgrounds at recess experienced negative affect when choosing sides for games because of its inherently evaluative component. Recent research conducted by Bray and colleagues (2000) found that young competitive skiers who reported more concerns about what their fellow competitors and friends thought of their general skiing ability than of evaluation of specific performances, experienced higher levels of pre-competition anxiety.

It is important to note that extensive research in developmental literature on peer victimization behaviors has found that these acts are mediated by gender. Patterns of aggressive/victimizing behaviors in children and adolescents suggest that while both genders may exhibit aggression toward one another, females are disproportionately likely to engage in what are termed "relationally aggressive" actions, wherein girls attempt to undermine or destroy another girl's social relationships through rumors, name-calling, and social isolation (Crick, Casas, and Mosher, 1997; Crick and Grotpeter, 1995; Currie, Kelly, and Pomerantz, 2007), all of which can cause negative emotional outcomes. Although victimization/ relational aggression has thus far received little attention in the sport domain, research in the developmental literature has demonstrated the impact of relational aggression and victimization behaviors on psychosocial outcomes in playground interactions with children (Braza et al., 2007; Ostrov and Keating, 2004), which suggests the viability of this topic for future study in sport.

Negative feelings and beliefs related to peer interactions or comparisons in the sport environment have also emerged as sources of stress for athletes. The guilt associated with potentially hurting opponents as a result of playing assertively was found to be a particularly salient source of stress for adult sport participants (Kroll, 1979). In Norwegian Olympic athletes, involvement in athletic arenas that have a performance-oriented climate, or one in which there is an emphasis on social comparison of skills, has also been show to create higher levels of stress than in mastery-oriented climates (Pensgaard and Roberts, 2000). Beliefs about the expectations of team mates' performances and athletic ability have been associated with emotional responses among sport participants. For example, male and female youth soccer players who reported that they had lower team expectancies experienced high stress prior to competition, whereas their more optimistic peers did not report significant levels of negative emotion (Scanlan and Passer, 1978, 1979).

These concerns about how peers view one's abilities are consistent with research on the experience of shame and embarrassment in sport. Shame is a negative emotion characterized by a pre-emptive concern being seen by others as something "less than" how one would like to be seen (in other words, devaluation: Elison, 2005; Partridge and Elison, 2009). This experience of devaluation has been shown to be central to fear of failure, as well as motive dispositions, such as avoidance behaviors in the sport domain (Conroy, 2004; Conroy, Willow, and Metzler, 2002).

Relevant 'others' in the sport environment and athlete emotion

The majority of literature in this area has focused on parents, coaches, and peers; however, other people conceivably have an influence on sport participants' emotional responses. Although limited to date, some research does exist to illuminate the influence that spectators, audience, or fans, and judges, referees, or officials, have on athlete emotion.

Spectator/audience/fan influence on athlete emotion

The influence of an audience on sport performance was first identified by Triplett (1898). Since that time, the impact of the presence of others has been well documented, and has been found to influence both physiological arousal (Mullen, Bryant, and Driskell, 1997) and cognitive processes (Baumeister and Cairns, 1992). Some evidence from previous research suggests that reactions from the audience were sources of enjoyment (Scanlan et al., 1989). Elite figure skaters noted that being able to share their talent and interact with spectators was a contributor to experiencing positive emotion. The social recognition indicated by audience standing ovations, and the glamour, prestige, and fame provided by the media, were specific sources of enjoyment mentioned by the athletes interviewed. Systematic research into the impact of an audience on the emotional state of the performer, however, has been less common, and has centered primarily on the impact of an audience on "home team" performers. The act of competing in front of a home audience has been found to be beneficial for competitive outcome, particularly during regular-season matches in many sports (Baumeister and Steinhilber, 1984, Brown et al., 2002; McAndrew, 2001). The impact of this audience effect on emotional outcomes has been less definitive. Some research has shown a positive impact of a home crowd on levels of anxiety, mood, motivation, and confidence (Bray, Jones, and Owen, 2002), but other studies have found no differences in psychological states between home and away competitions (Bray and Martin, 2003; Neave and Wolfson, 2003).

Judges/referees/officials' influence on athlete emotion

The influence of officials on emotional outcomes in sport has largely been ignored in the research to date. Scanlan and colleagues' (1991) finding that receiving biased or unfair judging contributed to stress among elite athletes provides a basis for exploring the influence that judges or officials have on the emotional responses of athletes. Jones, Bray, and Lavallee (2007) have more recently suggested that athletes may be affected by the behaviors of officials, such as perceived biases toward a home team (Nevill, Balmer, and Williams, 2002) or on the order in which athletes perform (Plessner, 1999). Therefore athletes should rehearse reacting to poor officiating calls during practice in order to be more emotionally prepared to deal with them. Further exploration of these forms of social influence on athletes' emotional responses is clearly required to more fully understand their potential impact.

Recommendations for practitioners

Based on the research reviewed, it is clear that some of the most important determinants of athletes' emotional responses to sport participation are their perceptions of social relationships and interactions. Therefore, we suggest strategies for practitioners who are interested in facilitating a favorable perception of social interactions in sport toward an end goal of increasing positive emotion and decreasing negative emotion.

For parents, who are the earliest and strongest social influences for children, there are several possible methods for improving young athletes' emotional responses in sport. First, parents should be encouraged to provide their children with indications that they are satisfied with performance. It is further recommended that parents become involved in their child's athletic endeavors. This may be accomplished in a variety of ways, including both behavioral (such as volunteering as a coach) and emotional (such as demonstrating appropriate emotional responses to child's sport experiences) strategies. It is important, however, for parents to remember that by creating a perception of pressure, enjoyment will be likely to decrease, and levels of stress will be likely to increase.

Several suggestions have been made to improve the perception of positive coaching styles. Research has indicated that coaches who are trained effectively in coaching effectiveness programs and who foster a mastery motivational climate have athletes who experience higher levels of enjoyment. Therefore, an important strategy for coaches could be to engage in a program, such as the CET program (Smith and Smoll, 1997), to be better prepared to engage in behaviors that will encourage positive emotional responses. Other recommendations for coaches include creating a mastery motivational climate and providing positive and supportive appraisals of an athlete's desired performance. Additionally, by providing an athlete with technical instruction following a mistake, a coach can send a message that mistakes can be corrected, and that the athlete is competent enough to make corrections. Overall, it is important for coaches to know the preferred coaching styles of their athletes, so that the coach may be more able to match coaching/leadership behaviors to their athletes' needs.

In order to facilitate positive peer relationships and resultant positive emotion, it is important for coaches, parents, administrators, and officials to make every possible effort to encourage sport participants to foster quality friendships on sport teams. Encouraging cooperation and teamwork in appropriate situations can facilitate the development of positive peer relationships in a team situation. Higher levels of peer acceptance and friendships have been linked to higher levels of enjoyment, while experiences of peer victimization are more likely to produce negative emotional outcomes and thus require further exploration. Therefore, parents, coaches, administrators, and officials should increase their awareness of the social dynamics of a sport situation in order to assess the occurrence of negative peer relationships. This may be another important step in promoting a positive experience for all individuals involved.

Future directions

The existing knowledge base concretely identifies how a variety of social influences impact athletes' emotion, but a number of potentially relevant others that might have an influence on emotion in sport remain either insufficiently explored or unexplored. These social influences may lie within the immediate sport context, or may be more secondary and tertiary to the athletic environment, but are still critical to the experiences of the athlete. Sport administrators, support staff (such as athletic trainers, strength and conditioning coaches, student-athlete advisors, and sport psychologists/consultants), and siblings are just a few of the potential social influences on enjoyment and stress that arguably deserve exploration.

The influence that athletic administrators exert warrants attention in the social influence on emotion in sport literature. Fletcher and Wagstaff (2009) identified the need for greater application of organizational psychology principles to increase understanding of the numerous organizational stressors that exist in sport. The individuals in charge of managing intercollegiate, interscholastic, and competitive youth sport environments have a central role in establishing the context in which athletes participate. The policies and standards set forth, and enforced, by administrators potentially impact the type of influence that coaches, as well as team captains, have on athletes' enjoyment and stress. It is conceivable that the emotional responses experienced by sport participants are a result of the influence that trickles down from administrators to coaches, thus creating a potential direct effect as well as an intervening effect on athletes' enjoyment and stress.

Athletic support staff may have a significant influence on the emotional outcomes for athletes. These individuals are often in contact with athletes for significant amounts of time and in a variety of situations, and thus may impact both enjoyment and stress in important ways. Future research should explore the nature and magnitude of these influences in order to more fully understand the entire sport experience.

Social influence that lies outside of the immediate sport context should also be examined in relation to emotional responses to athletic involvement. In particular, future research should extend its focus to the influence that family members have on individuals' emotion in sport, to include the impact that siblings have both on the athlete and on the nature of parents' influence. Research in developmental psychology suggests that the influence of siblings may both have a direct impact on athletes and have an impact mediated by parents (Eccles (Parson), 1983). Without accounting for how siblings influence one another's sport participation and achievement we are neglecting a critical aspect of family influence on athletes' enjoyment and stress.

The future of research on social influence on emotion would benefit greatly from the addition of studies that incorporate more diversity. The few studies that have examined the impact of parents, coaches, and peers on athletes' emotional responses have for the most part targeted upper-middle-class, primarily Caucasian, able-bodied and minded samples. The extant literature has established a strong foundation for understanding social influence on emotion; however the question of how significant others impact the emotions of athletes when race and ethnic, socio-economic background, and/or disability status are considered remains unanswered. To fully realize the influence that others have on an athletes' sport enjoyment and stress, considerable expansions in the breadth of participants sampled and the variety of forms of social influence must be included in future explorations.

Athletes' influence on the emotional experiences of others in sport is another area of research that warrants increased attention in future investigations. Very little research has focused on the athlete as the form of social influence on others (such as parents, coaches, and peers). Adopting this reverse-analysis of the roles and relationships within the study of social influence and emotion in sport reveals another important set of questions. For example, some recent research has examined how athletes influence the emotion experienced by sport parents (Fifer and Wiersma, 2008; Harwood and Knight, 2009). Findings from focus group interviews conducted by Wiersma and Fifer revealed that observation of the child's enjoyment was reported as an important source of youth sport parent enjoyment. This suggests that parents and children alike exert social influence on each other and their emotional responses. Harwood and Knight (2009) found that among the myriad of stressors experienced by parents due to their child's tennis competition, their child's emotions were in many cases the most highly reported. Some of the pertinent competition-related stressors that tennis-parents cited included the child's pre-match psychological state, emotional control and level of enjoyment during a match, perceiving a lack of skills to help their child manage emotions, as well as observing their child's emotional responses to a poor performance. These two studies exemplify a new line of research in the field of social influence on emotion in sport, which focuses on the emotional experience of the others most often previously examined as the source of social influence rather than the recipient of this influence.

Summary and conclusion

Athletes' emotional responses are profoundly affected by the nature and quality of social influence. An athlete's perception of these social relationships is the most meaningful determinant of that person's emotional responses in sport. To that end, a variety of methodologies (qualitative, quantitative, and a mixture of methods) have been employed to assess these perceptions. Enjoyment and anxiety are the most frequently assessed positive and negative emotion respectively in the sport domain, although a wider range of emotional responses should be examined in future research.

The influence of social relationships and interactions on athlete emotion has long been considered an important research topic in sport. Considerable research indicates that parents, coaches, and peers are all salient influences on athletes' positive and negative emotional responses in sport across gender, age, and experience level. Furthermore, specific findings reveal the particular aspects of parental, coach, and peer influences that have been found to increase or decrease athletes' enjoyment and/or stress.

Although social influence on athlete emotion has received ample attention in the psychology of sport literature, there are still several relevant others who have not been adequately examined (such as officials, spectators, siblings, trainers, and administrators). Moreover, utilization of more diverse samples will be critical to understanding the role of social influences on a wider variety of athletes, including individuals from different racial, socio-economic, physical, and psychological backgrounds.

Sports will always contain social mechanisms that influence participants' emotional experiences. Performance in a medium that often inherently exposes the participants to, or necessitates, evaluations by others will logically result in emotional outcomes that require understanding in order to create the most optimal situation for those individuals who engage in sports. Although a solid research base on emotion and social influences does currently exist, there are still significant voids that must be addressed before a complete understanding of these relationships and their consequences can be fully realized.

References

Amorose, A. J. and Horn, T. S. (2001). Pre- to post-season changes in the intrinsic motivation of first year college athletes: relationships with coaching behaviour and scholarship status. *Journal of Applied Sport Psychology,* 13, 355–373.

Anderson, J. C., Funk, J. B., Elliott, R. and Smith, P. H. (2003). Parental support and pressure and children's extracurricular activities: relationships with amount of involvement and affective experience of participation. *Applied Developmental Psychology*, 24, 241–257.

Averill, P. M. and Power, T. G. (1995). Parental attitudes and children's experiences in soccer: correlates of effort and enjoyment. *International Journal of Behavioral Development*, 18, 263–276.

Babkes, M. L. and Weiss, M. R. (1999). Parental influence on children's cognitive and affective responses to competitive soccer participation. *Pediatric Exercise Science*, 11, 44–62.

Baker, J., Cote, J. and Hawes, R. (2000). The relationship between coaching behaviours and sport anxiety in athletes. *Journal of Science and Medicine in Sport*, 3, 110–119.

Baumeister, R. F. and Cairns, K. J. (1992). Repression and self-presentation: when audiences interfere with self-deceptive strategies. *Journal of Personality and Social Psychology*, 62, 851–862.

Baumeister, R. F. and Steinhilber, A. (1984). Paradoxical effects of supportive audiences on performance under pressure: the home field advantage in sports championships. *Journal of Personality and Social Psychology*, 47, 85–93.

Black, S. J. and Weiss, M. R. (1992). The relationship among perceived coaching behaviors, perceptions of ability, and motivation in competitive age-group swimmers. *Journal of Sport and Exercise Psychology*, 14, 309–325.

Boardley, I. D., Kavussanu, M. and Ring, C. (2008). Athletes' perceptions of coaching effectiveness and athlete-related outcomes in rugby-union: An investigation based on the Coaching Efficacy Model. *The Sport Psychologist*, 22, 269–287.

Bois, J. E., Lalanne, J. and Delforge, C. (2009). The influence of parenting practices and parental presence on children's and adolescents' pre-competitive anxiety. *Journal of Sports Sciences*, 27, 995–1005.

Bray, S. R., Jones, M. V. and Owen, S. (2002). The influence of competition location on athletes' psychological states. *Journal of Sport Behavior*, 25, 231–242.

Bray, S. R. and Martin, K. A. (2003). The influence of competition location on individual sport athletes' performance and psychological states. *Psychology of Sport and Exercise*, 4, 117–123.

Bray, S. R., Martin, K. A. and Widemeyer, W. N. (2000). The relationship between evaluative concerns and sport competition state anxiety among youth skiers. *Journal of Sports Sciences*, 18, 353–361.

Braza, F., Braza, P., Carreras, M. R., Munoz, J. M., Sanchez-Martin, J. R., Azurmendi, A., Sorozabal, A., Garcia, A. and Cardas, J. (2007). Behavioral profiles of different types of social status in preschool children: an observational approach. *Social Behavior and Personality*, 35, 195–212.

Brown, T. D., VanRaalte, J. L., Brewer, B. W., Winter, C. R., Cornelius, A. E. and Andersen, M. (2002). World Cup soccer home advantage. *Journal of Sport Behavior*, 25, 135–144.

Brustad, R. J. (1988). Affective responses in competitive youth sport: the influence of intrapersonal and socialization factors. *Journal of Sport and Exercise Psychology*, 10, 307–321.

Brustad, R. J. and Babkes, M. L. (2004). Social influence on the psychological dimensions of physical activity involvement. In M. R. Weiss (ed.), *Developmental sport and exercise psychology: A lifespan perspective*. (pp. 317–336). Morgantown, W.V.: Fitness Information Technology.

Brustad, R. J., Babkes, M. L. and Smith, A. L. (2001). Youth in sport: psychological considerations. In R. N. Singer, H. Hausenblas, and C. Janelle (eds), *Handbook of research in sport psychology* (2nd ed., pp 604–635). New York: John Wiley & Sons.

Brustad, R. J. and Partridge, J. A. (2002). Parental and peer influence on children's psychosocial development through sport. In F. L. Smoll and R. E. Smith (eds), *Children and youth in sport: A biopsychosocial perspective* (2nd ed., pp. 187–210). Dubuque, Ind.: Kendall-Hunt Publishing.

Brustad, R. J. and Weiss, M. R. (1987). Competence perceptions and sources of worry in high, medium, and low competitive trait-anxious young athletes. *Journal of Sport Psychology*, 9, 97–105.

Chelladurai, P. and Arnott, M. (1985). Decision styles in coaching: preferences of basketball players. *Research Quarterly for Exercise and Sport*, 56, 15–24.

Chelladurai, P. and Carron, A. (1983). Athletic maturity and preferred leadership. *Journal of Sport Psychology*, 5, 371–380.

Chelladurai, P. and Riemer, H. A. (1998). Measurement of leadership in sport. In J. L. Duda (ed.), *Advances in sport and exercise psychology* (pp. 227–253). Morgantown, W.V.: Fitness Information Technology.

Cialdini, R. B. and Trost, M. R. (1998). Social influence: Social norms, conformity, and compliance. In D. T. Gilbert, S. T. Fiske, and G. Lindzey (eds), *The handbook of social psychology* (4th edn, pp. 151–192). New York: Oxford University Press.

Coakley, J. (1992). Burnout among adolescent athletes: a personal failure or social problem? *Sociology of Sport Journal*, 9, 271–285.

Cohn, P. J. (1990). An exploratory study on sources of stress and athlete burnout in youth golf. *The Sport Psychologist*, 4, 95–106.

Conroy, D. E. (2004). The unique psychological meanings of multidimensional fears of failing. *Journal of Sport and Exercise Psychology*, 26, 484–491.

Conroy, D. E., Willow, J. P. and Metzler, J. N. (2002). Multidimensional fear of failure measurement: the performance failure appraisal inventory. *Journal of Applied Sport Psychology*, 14, 76–90.

Collins, K. and Barber, H. (2005). Female athletes' perceptions of parental influences. *Journal of Sport Behavior*, 28, 295–314.

Crick, N. R., Casas, J. F. and Mosher, M. (1997). Relational and overt aggression in preschool. *Developmental Psychology*, 33, 579–588.

Crick, N. R. and Grotpeter, J. K. (1995). Relational aggression, gender, and social-psychological adjustment. *Child Development*, 66, 710–722.

Csikszentmihalyi, M. (1975). *Beyond boredom and anxiety*. San Francisco, Calif.: Jossey-Bass.

Cumming, S. P., Smoll, F. L., Smith, R. E. and Grossbard, J. R. (2007). Is winning everything? The relative contributions of motivational climate and won–lost percentage in youth sports. *Journal of Applied Sport Psychology*, 19, 322–336.

Currie, D. H., Kelly, D. M. and Pomerantz, S. (2007). 'The power to squash people': understanding girls' relational aggression. *British Journal of Sociology of Education*, 28, 23–37.

Dwyer, J. M. and Fischer, D. G. (1990). Wrestlers' perceptions of coaches' leadership as predictors of satisfaction with leadership. *Perceptual and Motor Skills*, 71, 511–517.

Elison, J. (2005). Shame and guilt: a hundred years of apples and oranges. *New Ideas in Psychology*, 23, 5–32.

Evans, J. R. (1985). The process of team selection in children's self-directed and adult-directed games. Unpublished doctoral dissertation, University of Illinois.

Evans, J. R. and Roberts, G. C. (1987). Physical competence and the development of children's peer relations. *Quest*, 39, 23–35.

Gould, D., Eklund, R., Petlichkoff, L., Peterson, K. and Bump, L. (1991a). Psychological predictors of state anxiety and performance in age-group wrestlers. *Pediatric Exercise Science*, 3, 198–208.

Gould, D., Eklund, R. C. and Jackson, S. A. (1991b). 1988 U.S. Olympic wrestling excellence: I Mental preparation, precompetitive cognition and affect. *The Sport Psychologist*, 6, 358–362.

Gould, D., Eklund, R. C. and Jackson, S. A. (1993a). Coping strategies used by U.S. Olympic wrestlers. *Research Quarterly for Exercise and Sport*, 64, 83–93.

Gould, D., Finch, L. M. and Jackson, S. A. (1993b). Coping strategies used by national champion figure skaters. *Research Quarterly for Exercise and Sport*, 64, 453–468.

Gould, D., Horn, T. and Spreemann, J. (1983). Sources of stress in junior elite wrestlers. *Journal of Sport Psychology*, 5, 159–171.

Gould, D., Jackson, S. A. and Finch, L. M. (1993c). Sources of stress in national champion figure skaters. *Journal of Sport and Exercise Psychology*, 15, 134–159.

Gould, D. and Weinberg, R. (1985). Sources of worry in successful and less successful intercollegiate wrestlers. *Journal of Sport Behavior*, 8, 115–127.

Gould, D., Wilson, C. G., Tuffey, S. and Lochbaum, M. (1993). Stress and the young athlete: the child's perspective. *Pediatric Exercise Science*, 5, 286–297.

Gould, D. and Dieffenbach, K. (2000). Psychological issues in youth sports: Competitive anxiety, overtraining, and burnout. In R. Malina and M. Clark (eds), *Youth sports in the*

21st century: Organized sports in the lives of children and adolescents. East Lansing, Mich.: Exercise Science Publications.

Greendorfer, S. L., Lewko, J. H. and Rosengren, K. S. (2002). Family and gender-based influences in sport socialization of children and adolescents. In F. L. Smoll and R. E. Smith (eds), *Children and youth in sport: A biopsychosocial perspective* (2nd edn, pp. 153–186). Dubuque, Ind.: Kendall-Hunt Publishing.

Green, B. C. and Chalip, L. (1997). Enduring involvement in youth soccer: the socialization of parent and child. *Journal of Leisure Research,* 29, 61–77.

Harwood, C. and Knight, C. (2009). Understanding parental stressors: an investigation of British tennis-parents. *Journal of Sports Sciences,* 27, 339–351.

Hellstedt, J. C. (1990). Early adolescent perceptions of parental pressure in the sport environment. *Journal of Sport Behavior,* 13, 135–144.

Hoar, S. D., Kowalski, K. C., Gaudreau, P. and Crocker, P. R. E. (2006). A review of coping in sport. In S. Hanton and S. Mellalieu (eds), *Literature reviews in sport psychology* (pp. 53–103). Hauppauge, N.Y.: Nova Science.

Hoyle, R. H. and Leff, S. S. (1997). The role of parental involvement in youth sport participation and performance. *Adolescence,* 32, 233–244.

Jones, M. V., Bray, S. R. and Lavallee, D. (2007). All the world's a stage: impact of an audience on sport performers. In S. Jowett and D. Lavallee (eds), *Social psychology in sport* (pp. 103–114). Champaign, Ill.: Human Kinetics.

Kanters, M. A., Bocarro, J. and Casper, J. (2008). Supported or pressured: an examination of agreement among parents and children on parent's role in youth sports. *Journal of Sport Behavior,* 31, 1–17.

Kroll, W. (1979). The stress of high performance athletics. In P. Klavora and J. V. Daniel (eds), *Coach, athlete and sport psychologists* (pp. 211–219). Champaign, Ill.: Human Kinetics.

Kunesh, M. A., Hasbrook, C. A. and Lewthwaite, R. (1992). Physical activity socialization: peer interactions and affective responses among a sample of sixth grade girls. *Sociology of Sport Journal,* 9, 385–396.

Lazarus, R. S. (1967). Cognitive and personality factors underlying threat and coping. In M. H. Appley and R. Trumbull (eds), *Psychological stress.* New York: Appleton-Century-Crofts.

Lazarus, R. S. and Folkman, S. (1984). *Stress, appraisal, and coping.* New York: Springer.

Leff, S. S. and Hoyle, R. H. (1995). Young athletes' perceptions of parental support and pressure. *Journal of Youth and Adolescence,* 24, 187–203.

Lewin, K. (1951). *Field theory in social science.* New York: Harper.

Lewthwaite R. and Scanlan, T. K. (1989). Predictors of competitive trait anxiety in male youth sport participants. *Medicine and Science in Sport and Exercise,* 21, 221–229.

Martens, R. (1977). *Sport competition anxiety test.* Champaign, Ill.: Human Kinetics.

Martens, R., Burton, D., Rivkin, F. and Simon, J. (1980). Reliability and validity of the Competitive State Anxiety Inventory (CSAI). In C. H. Nadeau, W. R. Halliwell, K. M. Newell, and G. C. Roberts (eds), *Psychology of motor behavior and sport–1979* (pp. 91–99). Champaign, Ill.: Human Kinetics.

Martens, R., Burton, D., Vealey, R. S., Bump, L. A. and Smith, D. E. (1990). Development and validation of the Competitive State Anxiety Inventory–2. In R. Martens, R. S. Vealey, and D. Burton (eds), *Competitive anxiety in sport* (pp. 117–190). Champaign, IL: Human Kinetics.

Martens, R. and Gill, D. (1976). State anxiety among successful and unsuccessful competitors who differ in competitive trait anxiety. *Research Quarterly,* 47, 698–708.

McAndrew, F. T. (2001). The home advantage in individual sports. *Journal of Social Psychology,* 133, 401–403.

McCarthy, P. J. and Jones, M. V. (2007). A qualitative study of sport enjoyment in the sampling years. *The Sport Psychologist,* 21, 400–416.

McCarthy, P. J., Jones, M. V. and Clark–Carter, D. (2008). Understanding enjoyment in youth sport: a developmental perspective. *Psychology of Sport and Exercise,* 9, 142–156.

McEnroe, J. and Kaplan, J. (2002). *Serious.* London, UK: Little, Brown.

Milne, A. A. (1928). *The house at Pooh Corner* (p. 120). New York: E. P. Dutton .

Mullen, B., Bryant, B. and Driskell, J. E. (1997). Presence of others and arousal: an integration. *Group Dynamics,* 1, 52–64.

Neave, N. and Wolfson, S. (2003). Testosterone, territoriality, and the "home advantage." *Physiology and Behavior,* 78, 269–275.

Nevill, A. M., Balmer, N. J. and Williams, A. M. (2002). The influence of crowd noise and experience upon refereeing decisions in football. *Psychology of Sport and Exercise,* 2, 261–272.

Ommundsen, Y. and Vaglum, P. (1991). Soccer competition anxiety and enjoyment in young boy players: the influence of perceived competence and significant others' emotional involvement. *International Journal of Sport Psychology,* 22, 35–49.

Ostrov, J. M. and Keating, C. F. (2004). Gender differences in preschool aggression during freeplay and structured interaction: an observational study. *Social Development,* 13, 255–277.

Partridge, J. A. (2003). Effects of peer influence on psychosocial outcomes in the sport domain. Unpublished doctoral dissertation, University of Northern Colorado.

Partridge, J. A., Brustad, R. J. and Babkes Stellino, M. (2008). Social influence in sport. In T. S. Horn (ed.), *Advances in sport psychology* (3rd edn, pp. 269–291). Champaign, Ill.: Human Kinetics.

Partridge, J. A. and Elison, J. (2009). Shame in sport: issues and directions. *Journal of Contemporary Athletics,* 3, 197–210.

Passer, M. W. (1983). Fear of failure, fear of evaluation, perceived competence and self-esteem in competitive trait-anxious children. *Journal of Sport Psychology,* 5, 172–188.

Patrick, H., Ryan, A. M., Alfeld-Liro, C., Fredricks, J. A., Hruda, L. Z. and Eccles, J. S. (1999). Adolescents' commitment to developing talent: the role of peers in continuing motivation for sports and the arts. *Journal of Youth and Adolescence,* 28, 741–763.

Pensgaard, A. M. and Roberts, G. C. (2000). The relationship between motivational climate, perceived ability and sources of distress among elite athletes. *Journal of Sports Sciences,* 18, 191–200.

Pierce, W. J. and Stratton, R. K. (1981). Perceived sources of stress in youth sport participants. In G. C. Roberts and D. M. Landers (eds), *Psychology of motor behavior and sport–1980* (pp. 116–134). Champaign, Ill.: Human Kinetics.

Plessner, H. (1999). Expectation biases in gymnastics judging. *Journal of Sport and Exercise Psychology,* 21, 131–144.

Power, T. G. and Woolger, C. (1994). Parenting practices and age-group swimming: a correlational study. *Research Quarterly for Exercise and Sport,* 65, 59–66.

Price, M. S. and Weiss, M. R. (2000). Relationships among coach burnout, coach behaviors and athletes' psychological responses. *The Sport Psychologist,* 14, 391–409.

Raedeke, T. D. (1997). Is athlete burnout more than just stress? A sport commitment perspective. *Journal of Sport and Exercise Psychology,* 19, 396–417.

Riemer, H. A. and Chelladurai, P. (1995). Leadership and satisfaction in athletes. *Journal of Sport and Exercise Psychology,* 17, 276–293.

Ruble, D. N. and Goodnow, J. J. (1998). Social development in childhood and adulthood. In D. T. Gilbert, S. T. Fiske, and G. Lindzey (eds), *The handbook of social psychology* (4th edn, pp. 741–787). New York: Oxford University Press.

Sagar, S. S. and Lavallee, D. (2010). The developmental origins of fear of failure in adolescent athletes: examining parental practices. *Psychology of Sport and Exercise,* 11, 177–187.

Scanlan, T. K. (1975). The effects of competition trait anxiety and success–failure on the perception of threat in a competitive situation. Unpublished doctoral dissertation. University of Illinois, Urbana-Champaign.

Scanlan, T. K. (1977). The effects of success–failure on the perception of threat in a competitive situation. *Research Quarterly*, 48, 144–153.

Scanlan, T. K. (1984). Competitive stress and the child athlete. In J. M. Silva III and R. S. Weinberg (eds), *Psychological foundations of sport* (pp. 118–129). Champaign, Ill.: Human Kinetics.

Scanlan, T. K., Babkes, M. L. and Scanlan, L. A. (in press). Participation in sport: a developmental glimpse at emotion. In J. L. Mahoney, R. W. Larson, and J. S. Eccles (eds), *Organized activities as contexts of development: Extracurricular activities, after-school and community programs*. Mahwah, N.J.: Erlbaum.

Scanlan, T. K., Carpenter, P. J., Lobel, M. and Simons, J. P. (1993a). Sources of sport enjoyment for youth sport athletes. *Pediatric Exercise Science*, 5, 275–285.

Scanlan, T. K., Carpenter, P. J., Schmidt, G. W. and Keeler, B. (1993b). An introduction to the Sport Commitment Model. *Journal of Sport and Exercise Psychology*, 15, 1–15.

Scanlan, T. K. and Lewthwaite, R. (1984). Social psychological aspects of competition for male youth sport participants: I. Predictors of competitive stress. *Journal of Sport Psychology*, 6, 208–226.

Scanlan, T. K. and Lewthwaite, R. (1986). Social psychological aspects of the competitive sport experience for male youth sport participants: IV. Predictors of enjoyment. *Journal of Sport Psychology*, 8, 25–35.

Scanlan, T. K. and Passer, M. W. (1978). Factors related to competitive stress among male youth sport participants. *Medicine and Science in Sports*, 10, 103–108.

Scanlan, T. K. and Passer, M. W. (1979). Sources of competitive stress in young female athletes. *Journal of Sport Psychology*, 1, 151–159.

Scanlan, T. K., Russell, D. G., Beals, K. P. and Scanlan, L. A. (2003a). Project on elite athlete commitment (PEAK): II. A direct test and expansion of the Sport Commitment Model with elite amateur sportsmen. *Journal of Sport and Exercise Psychology*, 25, 377–401.

Scanlan, T. K., Russell, D. G., Magyar, T. M. and Scanlan, L. A. (2009). Project on elite athlete commitment (PEAK): III. An examination of the external validity across gender, and the expansion and clarification of the sport commitment model. *Journal of Sport and Exercise Psychology*, 31, 685–705.

Scanlan, T. K., Russell, D. G., Wilson, N. C. and Scanlan, L. A. (2003b). Project on elite athlete commitment (PEAK): I. Introduction and methodology. *Journal of Sport and Exercise Psychology*, 25, 360–376.

Scanlan, T. K. and Simons, J. P. (1992). The construct of sport enjoyment. In G. C. Roberts (ed.), *Motivation in sport and exercise* (pp. 199–215). Champaign, Ill.: Human Kinetics.

Scanlan, T. K., Stein, G. L. and Ravizza, K. (1989). An in-depth study of former elite figure skaters: II. Sources of enjoyment. *Journal of Sport and Exercise Psychology*, 11, 65–83.

Scanlan, T. K., Stein, G. L. and Ravizza, K. (1991). An in-depth study of former elite figure skaters: III. Sources of stress. *Journal of Sport and Exercise Psychology*, 13, 103–108.

Seidman, E., Chesir-Teran, D., Friedman, J. L., Yoshikawa, H., Allen, L. and Roberts, A. (1999). The risk and protective functions of perceived family and peer microsystems among urban adolescents in poverty. *American Journal of Community Psychology*, 27, 211–237.

Shields, D. L. Bredemeier, B. L., LaVoi, N. M. and Power, C. F. (2005). The behavior of youth, parents, and coaches: the good, the bad and the ugly. *Journal of Research on Character Education*, 3, 43–59.

Smith, A. L. (1999). Perceptions of peer relationships and physical activity participation in early adolescence. *Journal of Sport and Exercise Psychology*, 21, 329–350.

Smith, A. L., Balaguer, I. and Duda, J. L. (2006). Goal orientation profile differences on perceived motivational climate, perceived peer relationships, and motivation-related responses of youth athletes. *Journal of Sports Sciences*, 24, 1315–1328.

Smith, A. L., Sampson, M., DeFreese, J. D., Blankenship, B. T. and Templin, T. J. (2009). Peer victimization and student motivation in middle-school physical education. *Journal of Sport and Exercise Psychology*, 31(Suppl), S218–219.

Smith, A. L., Ullrich-French, S., Walker II, E. and Hurley, K. S. (2006). Peer relationship profiles and motivation in youth sport. *Journal of Sport and Exercise Psychology*, 28, 362–383.

Smith, R. E. (1986). Toward a cognitive-affective model of burnout. *Journal of Sport Psychology*, 8, 36–50.

Smith, R. E., Cumming, S. P. and Smoll, F. L. (2008). Development and validation of the Motivational Climate Scale for Youth Sports. *Journal of Applied Sport Psychology*, 20, 116–136.

Smith, R. E. and Smoll, F. L. (1997). Coach-mediated team building in youth sports. *Journal of Applied Sport Psychology*, 9, 114–132.

Smith, R. E., Smoll, F. L. and Barnett, N. P. (1995). Reduction in children's sport anxiety through social support and stress-reduction training for coaches. *Journal of Applied Developmental Psychology*, 16, 125–142.

Smith, R. E., Smoll, F. L. and Curtis, B. (1979). Coaching effectiveness training: a cognitive behavioral approach to enhancing relationship skills in youth sport coaches. *Journal of Sport Psychology*, 1, 59–75.

Smith, R., Zane, N., Smoll, F. L. and Coppel, D. (1983). Behavioral assessment in youth sports: coaching behaviors and children's attitudes. *Medicine and Science in Sports and Exercise*, 15, 208–214.

Spielberger, C. D. (1966). *Anxiety and behavior.* New York: Academic Press.

Spielberger, C. D. (1973). *Preliminary test manual for the State-Trait Anxiety Inventory for Children.* Palo Alto, Calif.: Consulting Psychologists.

Stuntz, C. P. and Spearance, A. L. (2007). Coach–athlete and teammate holistic relationships: measurement development and prediction of motivational factors. *Journal of Sport and Exercise Psychology*, 29 (Suppl), S206.

Stuntz, C. P. and Spearance, A. L. (2010). Cross-domain relationships in two sport populations: measurement validation including prediction of motivation-related variables. *Psychology of Sport and Exercise*, 11, 267–274.

Terry, P. (1984). The coaching preferences of elite athletes competing at Universiade '83. *Canadian Journal of Applied Sport Sciences*, 9, 201–208.

Triplett, N. (1898). The dynamogenic factors in pacemaking and competition. *American Journal of Psychology*, 9, 505–523.

Van Yperen, N. W. (1995). Interpersonal stress, performance level and parental support: a longitudinal study among highly skilled young soccer players. *The Sport Psychologist*, 9, 225–241.

Wankel, L. M. and Kreisel, P. S. J. (1985a). Factors underlying enjoyment of youth sports: sport and age group comparisons. *Journal of Sport Psychology*, 7, 51–64.

Wankel, L. M. and Kreisel, P. S. J. (1985b). Methodological considerations in youth sport motivation research: a comparison of open-ended and paired comparison approaches. *Journal of Sport Psychology*, 7, 65–74.

Wankel, L. M. and Sefton, J. M. (1989). A season-long investigation of fun in youth sports. *Journal of Sport and Exercise Psychology*, 11, 355–366.

Weiss, M. R. and Amorose, A. J. (2008). Motivational orientations and sport behavior. In T. Horn (ed.), *Advances in sport psychology* (pp. 99–114). Champaign, IL: Human Kinetics.

Weiss, M. R. and Petlichkoff, L. M. (1989). Children's motivation for participation in and withdrawal from sport: identifying the missing links. *Pediatric Exercise Science*, 1, 195–211.

Weiss, M. R. and Smith, A. L. (1999). Quality of youth sport friendships: measurement development and validation. *Journal of Sport and Exercise Psychology*, 21, 145–166.

Weiss, M. R. and Smith, A. L. (2002). Friendship quality in youth sport: relationship to age, gender, and motivation variables. *Journal of Sport and Exercise Psychology*, 24), 420–437.

Weiss, M. R., Smith, A. L. and Theeboom, M. (1996). "That's what friends are for": Children's and teenagers' perceptions of peer relationship in the sport domain. *Journal of Sport and Exercise Psychology*, 18, 347–379.

Wiersma, L. D. (2001). Conceptualization and development of the sources of enjoyment in youth sport questionnaire. *Measurement in Physical Education and Exercise Science*, 5, 153–177.

Wiersma, L. D. and Fifer, A. M. (2008). "The schedule has been tough but we think it's worth it": the joys, challenges, and recommendations of youth sport parents. *Journal of Leisure Research*, 40, 505–530.

Zarbatany, L., Ghesquiere, K. and Mohr, K. (1992). A context perspective on early adolescents' friendship expectations. *Journal of Early Adolescence*, 12, 111–126.

Zarbatany, L., Hartmann, D. P. and Rankin, D. B. (1990). The psychological functions of preadolescent peer activities. *Child Development*, 61, 1067–1080.

7

KEY MOVEMENTS IN DIRECTIONAL RESEARCH IN COMPETITIVE ANXIETY

Christopher Wagstaff, University of Portsmouth,
Rich Neil, University of Wales Institute, Cardiff,
Stephen Mellalieu, Swansea University and
Sheldon Hanton, University of Wales Institute, Cardiff

> I had ten or fourteen caps under my belt by this stage and was able to rationalise my emotional state a lot better and realised what they (physical symptoms) were there for. I had learnt that they (physical symptoms) just emphasised a 'buzz' indicating that I was excited and ready for the game. This enabled me to control the symptoms mentally and overcome the negative effects experienced previously.
>
> *(Dan Carter, 2007, fly-half for the New Zealand All Blacks rugby union team)*

Competitive anxiety has been defined as 'a specific negative emotional response occurring when a performer appraises competitive stressors as uncertain threats, with this response including such symptoms as worry along with a heightened perception of physiological arousal' (Hanton, Neil and Mellalieu, 2011). Given the negative connotations of this definition, it is of no surprise that early research was informed by the notion that competitive anxiety had detrimental effects on performance. Specifically, Martens, Vealey and Burton (1990b) proposed that cognitive anxiety (symptoms of worry) had a negative linear relationship with performance, and somatic anxiety (perceptions of physiological arousal) had a positive effect on performance up to an optimal level of somatic anxiety, beyond which performance decrements would occur. These propositions were, however, weakly supported by this body of research, perhaps because of the sole focus on the negative effects of competitive anxiety. That is, researchers have posited that, in certain circumstances, the experience of anxiety symptoms can be beneficial to performance (see Fazey and Hardy, 1988; Jones and Swain, 1992; Mahoney and Avener, 1977). Through this premise, two main research avenues have emerged. One advocated and tested an anxiety–performance model where the interactive effects of cognitive anxiety and physiological arousal were proposed to be beneficial to performance (Fazey and Hardy, 1988). The other avenue considered the notion of 'direction', which posits that the experience of anxiety-related symptoms could be viewed by athletes as either debilitative (that is, detrimental) or as facilitative (that is, beneficial) towards performance (Jones, 1991; Jones and Swain, 1992).

Focusing on the latter avenue, the research that has examined how individuals interpret their anxiety symptoms in relation to upcoming performance has gone beyond a model approach and offered insight into the individual difference variables and mechanisms that may positively mediate the anxiety–performance relationship. This has been accomplished though three key movements of inquiry. The first movement is of a quantitative nature, where researchers have primarily explored performers' interpretations of anxiety symptoms in relation to upcoming performance as a function of individual difference variables. The second movement involves research that has investigated the perceived mechanisms underpinning anxiety symptom interpretation through the use of qualitative methods. The third movement incorporates applied designs used to restructure symptom interpretations from negative (debilitative) to positive (facilitative). The purpose of this chapter is to provide insight into the contribution to knowledge of each movement with consideration of how knowledge from one movement has influenced the research direction of another, culminating with a discussion of how existing knowledge may be used to inform future research in existing and new anxiety direction movements.

The quantitative movement

To help promote the concept of direction, Jones and Swain (1992) introduced a directional scale to the Martens et al. (1990) Competitive State Anxiety Inventory-2 (CSAI-2), which measured anxiety intensity alone. Specifically, Jones and Swain included a facilitative–debilitative directional continuum scale to each questionnaire item on CSAI-2 to collect ratings of whether the intensity of cognitive and somatic anxiety symptoms experienced was interpreted as being beneficial or detrimental to upcoming performance. A large body of research subsequently used this revised CSAI-2 (CSAI-2D) to examine performers' interpretations of anxiety symptoms as a function of both situational and individual difference variables. In the current section we review this movement and provide an overview of the key developments that have emerged.

The first studies to adopt CSAI-2D examined directional interpretations as a function of competitiveness (Jones and Swain, 1992), performance (Jones, Swain and Hardy, 1993) and skill level (Jones, Hanton and Swain, 1994; Jones and Swain, 1995). Focusing first on Jones and Swain's (1992) study, they investigated the intensity and direction of anxiety symptoms in high and low competitive performers from a range of sports. Whilst no significant group differences on anxiety intensity were found, the highly competitive group reported their anxiety as more facilitative than the low competitive group. Jones et al. (1993) then examined relationships between intensity and direction scales and good and poor performance in gymnastics. Results showed no significant group differences in anxiety intensity scores, but the good–performance group did report their cognitive anxiety levels as being more facilitating and less debilitating to performance than the poor-performance group. Interestingly, further analyses showed that only self-confidence was a significant predictor of performance. The findings provided initial support for the proposal that performers' directional interpretations of their anxiety symptoms may provide further understanding of the competitive state anxiety response, and emphasized the importance of self-confidence in predicting performance.

In an attempt to expand their initial research on direction, Jones and colleagues (Jones et al., 1994) also employed CSAI-2D to examine the role of skill level on anxiety intensity and direction. The findings showed no difference between the two groups on the intensity of anxiety symptoms, but the elite performers interpreted anxiety symptoms as more facilitative for performance than did the non-elite performers. Additionally, self-confidence was higher in the elite group. In a follow-up to Jones et al. (1994), Jones and Swain (1995) examined the intensity and direction of trait anxiety symptoms in elite and non-elite cricketers using a trait version of CSAI-2D, the competitive trait anxiety inventory (CTAI-2D). In line with previous findings, no differences existed between the two groups' intensity response, but elite performers interpreted these symptoms as being more facilitative for performance than did non-elite performers. Collectively, this early research supported the value of distinguishing between the intensity and direction of symptoms associated with competitive anxiety in both state and trait contexts. Specifically, the interpretation of symptoms was found to be more sensitive to the individual difference variables under examination than the level at which performers experienced these symptoms (cf. Mellalieu, Hanton and Jones, 2003).

Following these initial inquiries into the nature of anxiety interpretation, a significant development emerged within the quantitative movement through the publication of Jones's (1995) control model of competitive anxiety symptom interpretation. Specifically, Jones proposed a model explaining directional interpretations based on the work of Carver and Scheier (1986, 1988), and predicted that a performer's perceived ability to control a stressor was the central factor in how performers interpret anxiety symptoms, with personal and situational factors deemed to affect this perception of control. Jones (1995) proposed that individuals who appraise themselves as having a degree of control over a threatening situation are better able to cope with their anxiety symptoms and achieve their goals (coping or positive expectancy of goal achievement), and consequently are more likely to interpret anxiety symptoms as facilitative for performance. In contrast, performers who appraise that they are not in control, cannot cope with the situation at hand and possess negative expectancies regarding goal attainment, are predicted to interpret anxiety symptoms in a negative manner (Jones, 1995). These suggestions were supported by Jones and Hanton (1996), who found competitive swimmers with positive expectations of goal achievement reported their cognitive and somatic anxiety symptoms as more facilitative than those who had negative goal expectations. Further analyses showed that the predictions of Jones's model were best supported in the case of goals perceived to be under the performer's control.

Ntoumanis and Jones (1998) furthered this line of inquiry by examining the differences in performers' interpretation of competitive anxiety symptoms as a function of locus of control beliefs. Discriminant function analysis showed that although there were no significant differences in the intensity of cognitive and somatic anxiety symptoms between those with an internal and those with an external locus of control, those with an internal locus of control viewed their trait cognitive and somatic anxiety as significantly more facilitative and less debilitative than the comparative external locus group. These results provided support for part of Jones's control model, in that an internal locus of control was associated with more facilitative interpretations of anxiety symptoms.

Further support for Jones's model came from Hanton, O'Brien and Mellalieu's (2003) goal attainment study, where they examined anxiety direction in a dispositional context as a function of the situational variable of skill level. Elite and non-elite participants from open-skilled sports completed a range of quantitative measures of perceived control, goal attainment expectations and competitive trait anxiety. Multivariate analyses provided support for Jones's (1995) predictions at a trait level, and highlighted the role of perceptions of control in moderating the relationship between goal attainment expectancy and anxiety direction. Moreover, the findings emphasized the importance of dispositional goal orientations when considering the strategies athletes employ to cope with competitive stressors and subsequent anxiety responses. Following this initial support for the notion of direction and Jones's (1995) control model, subsequent quantitative inquiries largely explored the individual difference element of the control model, in an attempt to distinguish which personal and situational variables influenced the interpretation of anxiety symptoms (Hanton, Neil and Mellalieu, 2008).

With regards to personal variables, researchers within the quantitative movement identified such factors as hardiness, coping use, psychological skill use and cognitive bias, as possible influences on anxiety interpretation. These variables were considered due to their theoretical association with positive and negative emotional and behavioural outcomes. Focusing first on hardiness, this form of dispositional resilience has been proposed to lower the intensity of such stress responses as anxiety and facilitate effective behaviour through the use of helpful coping strategies (Kobasa, 1979). Consequently, Hanton, Evans and Neil (2003) examined the effects of hardiness and skill level on competitive trait anxiety intensity and direction and self-confidence intensity. Findings partially supported the hypothesis that elite athletes high in hardiness would demonstrate lower levels of worry and a more facilitative interpretation of the anxiety response. These findings identified hardiness as an important dispositional construct in relation to anxiety interpretation, and led the authors to propose the need for research into the coping responses associated with high-hardiness individuals who view anxiety as facilitative for upcoming performance.

Although not related to the construct of hardiness, the types of coping strategies employed by facilitators (who view symptoms as beneficial to performance) and debilitators (who view them as detrimental) have been explored. For example, both Eubank and Collins (2000) and Jerome and Williams (2000) found that facilitators employed problem-focused and emotion-focused coping strategies, and debilitators were limited in their use of coping. Ntoumanis and Biddle (2000) examined how coping strategies related to anxiety symptom interpretation, and found that facilitative interpretations of cognitive anxiety were related to the use of problem-focused coping. In addition, high levels of cognitive anxiety intensity were related to emotion-focused coping and avoidance coping. The findings of these studies suggest that facilitative interpretations of competitive anxiety are a strong indicator of effective coping, which supports the same premise in Jones's (1995) control model.

A similar line of inquiry focused on the relationship between psychological skill use and anxiety interpretation. For example, Fletcher and Hanton (2001) examined these variables in a non-elite sample of competitive swimmers, and found significant differences in competitive anxiety intensity and direction scores between high and low-use groups. Specifically, those high in the use of relaxation strategies reported lower levels of cognitive and somatic anxiety, and interpreted these levels as more facilitative than the low-use group. Self-confidence was also significantly greater for the high-use group. In addition, those high in self-talk use reported lower levels of cognitive anxiety intensity, somatic anxiety direction and self-confidence than the low-self-talk-use group. Only self-confidence was higher for the high-imagery-use group. The findings of this study suggest that relaxation strategies should be used to reduce anxiety intensity and increase facilitative interpretations in non-elite performers. However, the authors were reluctant to generalize the use of relaxation for interventions to elite athletes, because of the non-elite sample used. Neil, Mellalieu and Hanton (2006) attempted to address this limitation by examining these variables in elite and non-elite rugby union players. Analyses revealed the elite group to report more facilitative interpretations of competitive anxiety symptoms, higher levels of self-confidence, lower relaxation use and greater imagery and self-talk use than their non-elite counterparts. These findings illustrate the different strategies used by elite and non-elite performers to manipulate their anxiety responses. Nevertheless, it is unclear whether such use is actually effective in influencing anxiety intensity and direction.

In line with the tenet of Jones's (1995) control model that individual difference variables influence anxiety interpretation, Eubank, Collins and Smith (2002) aimed to establish whether cognitive processing bias was a function of anxiety interpretation. To test this proposal, debilitators and facilitators performed a modified Stroop test, reacting to neutral and ambiguous words when in negative, neutral and positive moods. The findings of this study lent some support to the premise that debilitators show a processing bias for threatening information, and facilitators are biased toward emotionally positive stimuli. In a similar study, Jones, Smith and Holmes (2004) examined whether a performer's tendency to interpret anxiety symptoms as facilitative was more indicative of being classified as a repressor than being classified as high or low trait anxious. Repressors have been defined by Williams and Krane (1992) as those who 'avoid disturbing cognitions in an attempt to minimize distress and negative emotions... [and] typically deny having elevated levels of anxiety even though their behavior and physiological symptoms suggest otherwise' (p. 136). The findings of Jones et al.'s study demonstrated that repressors and those low in trait anxiety reported lower levels of competitive state anxiety than those high in trait anxiety. However, repressors did not interpret these anxiety symptoms as more facilitative than the two trait anxiety groups. A secondary purpose of the study was to examine the influence of the cognitive biases of high anxious and repressor groups on future performance expectations. Analyses showed that repressors were found to be overly optimistic about future performance and predicted better performance than they actually achieved, while the performance expectations of the high-anxious group did not differ from the level of performance actually achieved. In an attempt to extend these findings, Mullen, Lane and Hanton (2009) investigated anxiety interpretation as a function of four different coping styles: high-anxious, defensive high-anxious, low-anxious and repressors. Findings revealed that low trait anxious performers reported lower intensities of anxiety and higher self-confidence, and interpreted these as more facilitative, than did their high trait anxious counterparts. In line with results from Jones et al. (2004), the authors did not find support for their prediction that performers with a repressive coping style would interpret state anxiety symptoms as more facilitative than would performers with non-repressive coping styles.

Whilst there has been a wealth of research examining individual difference variables and anxiety symptom interpretation, fewer studies have explored the situational influences on this dimension. The types of situation variables considered include sport type, skill level and competitive experience. Sport type was examined first by Hanton, Jones and Mullen (2000) in the sports of rugby (an explosive sport) and pistol shooting (a fine-motor-skilled sport). Contingency analysis yielded a significant difference in the number of explosive sport performers who reported somatic anxiety as facilitative and the number of fine-motor-skill performers who reported somatic states as debilitative. No such differences were evident for cognitive anxiety. There were differences between the two sport types in the intensity of cognitive and somatic anxiety, but the performers competing in the explosive sport interpreted both states as more facilitative for performance. These performers also had higher scores on self-confidence than their fine-motor-skill counterparts. Mellalieu, Hanton and O'Brien (2004) then examined competitive trait anxiety interpretations as a function of sport type (using rugby and golf) and competitive experience. Performers' responses showed the main effects for experience and sport type, with those competing in rugby reporting that anxiety symptoms were viewed as more facilitative for performance than those who competed in golf. Evidently, the findings of these two studies suggest that consideration of the nature of sport activity is important when designing interventions to help performers who experience anxiety symptoms that may be viewed as detrimental for performance.

A key variable that has consistently been found to distinguish between facilitative and debilitative interpretations of competitive anxiety is skill level. The influence of skill level has already been touched upon when we discussed the effects of hardiness and psychological skill use. However, those studies that have focused primarily on skill level have generally found that cognitive and somatic anxiety intensity levels are similar in elite and non-elite performers, with elite athletes reporting more facilitative interpretations of their anxiety response and higher levels of self-confidence (see, e.g., Hanton and Jones, 1997; Jones et al., 1994; Jones and Swain, 1995; Perry and Williams, 1998). Informed by these findings, researchers suggested that self-confidence might protect against the debilitating effects of anxiety in elite performers, leading to facilitative interpretations of anxiety (Mellalieu, Hanton and Fletcher, 2006). Along with explanatory findings from the qualitative movement (which are discussed later), these propositions (Hanton and Connaughton, 2002; Hanton et al., 2004) led Mellalieu et al. (2006) to investigate whether self-confidence mediated the relationship between elite performers' competitive anxiety intensity symptoms and subsequent directional interpretations. The findings showed a mediating effect for self-confidence between cognitive anxiety intensity and direction in elite athletes, with the analysis for the non-elite group demonstrating that low levels of competitive anxiety and high levels of confidence are needed to experience less debilitative and more facilitative interpretations of anxiety symptoms. The results of this study reinforce those that examined psychological skill use as a function of skill level, as it seems that non-elite athletes would favour anxiety reduction techniques such as relaxation when experiencing anxiety symptoms. In contrast elite athletes cope with their levels of anxiety through the use of confidence-related strategies such as self-talk and imagery.

A recent study by Lundqvist, Kenttä and Raglan (in press) has provided support for the body of research by Hanton and associates that demonstrated skill level as a determining factor in anxiety interpretation. Specifically, Lundqvist et al. examined the extent to which individual intensity items on a revised CSAI-2D (Cox, Martens and Russell, 2003) are recognized by athletes as facilitative or debilitative to upcoming performance. Findings showed that elite athletes rated a higher percentage of items as facilitative for their performance, whereas sub-elite athletes rated a higher number of items as debilitative. A significant difference in anxiety interpretation was also found when anxiety was reported as low in intensity, with elite athletes demonstrating more facilitative interpretations. However, there were no significant differences in interpretation between skill level groups when anxiety was rated as moderate or high in intensity. Lundquist et al.'s findings suggest the value of considering both anxiety intensity and interpretation dimensions of anxiety for youth athletes. To elaborate, their integrated approach of pairing individual item intensity and direction ratings may provide information about the frequency with which specific anxiety symptoms are labelled as debilitative or facilitative. Such information may provide a more comprehensive understanding of the relationship between anxiety and its perceived impact as debilitative or facilitative (Lundqvist et al., in press).

Similar to Mellalieu et al.'s (2006) mediation study, the quantitative research that has examined the influence of competitive experience on anxiety interpretation has been influenced by findings within the qualitative movement. These are discussed in more detail later, but focusing briefly on Hanton and Jones's (1999a) qualitative study into the development of anxiety interpretation, they showed that elite swimmers developed facilitative interpretations over time and with experience through the acquisition and effective use of mental skills. Mellalieu et al. (2004) also considered competitive experience alongside sport type. In this study, both rugby union and golf performers with more experience reported lower intensity and more facilitative interpretations of competitive anxiety symptoms than their less experienced counterparts. Hanton et al. (2008a) then examined the influence of competitive experience (high versus low) and performance status (current-elite versus past-elite) on performers' trait anxiety, self-confidence and coping responses. Analyses revealed that current-elite athletes high in experience reported the highest levels of self-confidence and the most facilitative interpretations of competitive anxiety. The main effects demonstrated that the high-experience group reported lower somatic anxiety levels than their low-experience counterparts and viewed the use of problem- and avoidance-focused coping strategies as more and less effective, respectively. Current-elite performers reported lower worry intensity and more facilitative interpretations of somatic anxiety than past-elite performers, and used more effective problem-focused and positive-emotion-focused coping. These findings further emphasize the association between self-confidence and facilitative interpretations in elite athletes, and demonstrate the importance of competitive experience in the development of effective coping strategies.

In addition to the research that has focused on the influence of individual difference variables on the competitive anxiety direction response, empirical study within the quantitative movement has considered the temporal patterning of anxiety responses. The rationale for this line of inquiry is that competitive anxiety is a product of competition stress, and the stress and emotion process is proposed to change over time (see Lazarus, 1999). The first temporal study to consider anxiety direction was conducted by Wiggins (1998), who studied the changes in high-school and college athletes' anxiety intensity and direction at 24 hours, two hours and one hour prior to competition. He found that whilst anxiety intensity symptoms showed a predicted increase as competition neared (see Martens et al., 1990b), anxiety interpretation, self-confidence and performance expectations did not change significantly in the lead-up to competition. Hanton, Thomas and Maynard (2004b) conducted a similar study, but also considered skill level as an independent variable across a broader range of data collection times (one week, two days, one day, two hours and 30 minutes prior to competition). Their analyses indicated that elite athletes were more facilitative in their interpretation of cognitive and somatic symptoms than their non-elite counterparts, with these differences remaining stable across the two groups as competition approached. In line with Wiggins (1998), temporal effects indicated that intensities of cognitive and somatic anxiety increased from seven to two days, one day to two hours, and two hours to 30 minutes pre-competition for both groups of athletes. The findings of Wiggins (1998) and Hanton et al. (2004b) provided support for the separate measurement of competitive anxiety intensity and direction, and emphasized the need for practitioners and performers to consider the change in these dimensions in the lead-up to competition. Thomas, Maynard and Hanton (2004) also explored competitive anxiety and self-confidence temporally in 'facilitators', 'debilitators' and 'mixed interpreters'. No differences were evident for anxiety intensity responses as a function of direction, but facilitators reported increased self-confidence and more positive interpretations of cognitive and somatic anxiety symptoms as competition approached. Collectively, the research on temporal patterning emphasizes the importance of shaping the content of interventions to change directional interpretations depending on the proximity to competition.

The body of quantitative research that has examined the different facets of Jones's (1995) control model offers insight into performers' experiences of competitive anxiety and, in particular, the factors that may mediate the anxiety–performance relationship through influencing anxiety interpretation. Within this quantitative movement, some consistent findings arose that led authors to provide some interesting suggestions for applied practice. For example, the variables of skill level, competitive experience, self-confidence and psychological skill use seemed to be related to and have similar effects on anxiety interpretation, while time to competition also had an influence on how individuals interpret symptoms. Whilst the findings from this research have contributed to the understanding of anxiety direction, a major criticism has been directed towards the quantitative movement. That is, within the items of the modified CSAI-2 the word 'concern' is used instead of 'worry' to represent cognitive anxiety. This may, therefore, suggest that the studies that used this scale have not actually measured cognitive anxiety (Craft, Magyar, Becker and Feltz, 2003; Lane et al., 1999; Lundquist and Hassmén, 2005). Despite this criticism, some of the research described has incorporated other scales such as the Sport Anxiety Scale (SAS) Smith, Smoll and Shutz (1990) and the Immediate Anxiety Measure (IAMS) Thomas, Hanton and Jones (2002), all of which are proposed to be valid measures of such constructs as worry and somatic anxiety. Before bringing this section to a close, it is worth emphasizing that a strength of the research discussed is the description of what seems to be influencing the anxiety direction response. Researchers have attempted to address this question through testing facets of Jones's (1995) control model, which itself aimed to give some insight into the mechanisms that produce a facilitative interpretation of anxiety. Despite this, the findings do not give in-depth insight into why and how some performers view their anxiety symptoms as beneficial for performance. In line with our attempts to provide an overview of the contribution to knowledge of anxiety direction research, we now give attention to the numerous qualitative-based investigations in this area.

The qualitative movement

The qualitative examinations into anxiety interpretation were conducted to explain the findings from quantitative studies (Neil, Hanton and Mellalieu, 2009). The first investigation was born out of the quantitative findings of strong relationships between skill level and anxiety symptom interpretation (e.g. Hanton and Jones, 1997; Jones et al., 1994; Jones and Swain, 1995; Perry and Williams, 1998). Specifically, Hanton and Jones (1999a) sought to explore why elite performers consistently interpreted their anxiety symptoms as facilitative towards upcoming competition. Through interviewing elite swimmers who demonstrated facilitative interpretations, Hanton and Jones found that such interpretations were developed over time due to the gradual acquisition of such strategies as pre-competition and pre-race routines, and effective rationalization of thoughts and feelings through self-talk and imagery. The rationalization strategies allowed the elite performers to accept the anxiety symptoms they experienced as a natural part of competition. This possibly explains the findings of quantitative research that elite athletes reported similar intensity levels to their non-elite counterparts, yet viewed these symptoms as more facilitative.

Hanton, Wadey and Connaughton (2005) extended these findings by interviewing elite athletes who demonstrated debilitative anxiety profiles prior to competition. The rationale behind this study was that a very small proportion of elite athletes within the skill-level research had reported debilitative interpretations. They found that some performers reported symptoms as debilitative early in their careers, and became of an inability to use psychological skills effectively, these symptoms became habituated. Interestingly, the elite athletes also stated that they were still able to compete at a high level by attempting to overcome debilitative interpretations through focusing on training harder. Nevertheless, debilitative interpretations were stated to negatively influence performance. Together, the findings from these two studies demonstrated the importance of trying to teach elite performers how to use their anxiety symptoms to their advantage and make their 'butterflies fly in formation' (see Hanton and Jones 1999a, 1999b).

The next group of qualitative studies focused on explaining how perceptions of control and self-confidence influenced anxiety interpretation. Informed by such studies as Jones and Hanton (1996) and Ntoumanis and Jones (1998), Hanton and Connaughton (2002) examined elite and non-elite swimmers' beliefs about the link between anxiety symptoms and performance by considering perceptions of control and anxiety interpretation. Using causal networks to illustrate their findings they provided support for Jones's (1995) control model. That is, they found perceptions of control over the environment and over anxiety symptoms were interpreted as having facilitative consequences for performance through the belief that achievement of goals was possible even when anxious. The opposite was found for symptoms that were viewed as being outside the performers' control. The authors also suggested that the performers were able to remain in control of the environment through the high levels of self-confidence associated with such coping strategies as effective rationalization of thoughts and feelings. These findings led Hanton, Mellalieu and Hall (2004a) to investigate the specific role of self-confidence when elite performers experience anxiety symptoms. They found that high levels of self-confidence protected against debilitative interpretations of competitive anxiety through the use of strategies such as mental rehearsal, thought stopping and positive self-talk. Specifically, the use of these strategies helped to regulate self-confidence levels and promote a perception of control over anxiety symptoms. These findings further demonstrate the importance of self-confidence when experiencing anxiety, and extend the quantitative literature by providing insight into the underpinning mechanisms of self-confidence in the anxiety intensity–direction relationship.

Researchers have also adopted qualitative approaches to investigate the role of competitive experience in relation to anxiety interpretation. Specifically, to explain the more facilitative interpretations of highly experienced performers identified within the quantitative movement, Hanton et al. (2007) interviewed a number of experienced elite performers who interpreted their symptoms as facilitative towards performance. Findings revealed that specific critical incidents influenced performers' interpretations of anxiety symptoms. That is, positive and negative incidents affected future interpretations of cognitive and somatic symptoms through effective reflective practice, where the performers learned how to control symptoms and gradually interpret them as more facilitative. More recently, Hanton, Cropley and Lee (2009) examined these reflective processes in more detail with six experienced elite athletes. Again looking at reflections post positive and negative critical incidents, Hanton and associates showed distinctions between the effects of both types of incidents on the athlete's reflective and learning processes, and illustrated how such processes influenced the interpretation of competitive anxiety symptoms. Specifically, the findings highlighted that by reflecting, the athletes generated knowledge and understanding of competitive experiences, which initiated developmental changes to allow performers to interpret anxiety symptoms as more facilitative for performance. That is, they gradually learned that their experiences were natural, therefore they rationalized their competitive anxiety symptoms in an attempt to interpret them as more facilitative. These findings emphasize the importance of reflective practice as a framework for experiential learning when encountering competitive anxiety symptoms in sport.

All of the aforementioned research has suggested that confidence-related psychological strategies influence anxiety interpretation. This premise supports research within the quantitative movement which has shown that elite athletes use more cognitive restructuring-related strategies when experiencing anxiety, and non-elite performers use more anxiety-reduction approaches. Such findings led researchers to explore elite performers' perceptions of the underlying mechanisms involved in basic (Wadey and Hanton, 2008) and advanced (Hanton, Wadey and Mellalieu, 2008b) psychological skill use when experiencing competitive anxiety symptoms. Using a semi-structured interview approach, Wadey and Hanton found that when performers experienced anxiety prior to competition they reported using goal setting, imagery and/or self-talk strategies to achieve facilitative interpretations. Such strategies were associated with high levels of self-confidence and an optimistic outlook toward forthcoming competition, and promoted increased effort and motivation, attentional focus and perceived control over the anxiety response. In order to expand on these findings, Hanton et al. (2008b) examined the relationship between four advanced psychological strategies (simulation training, cognitive restructuring, pre-performance routines and over-learning of skills) and anxiety symptom interpretation. Semi-structured interviews were employed with eight elite athletes who reported that the use of each strategy enabled them to interpret their anxiety response as facilitative for performance. For example, over-learning of skills helped to lower performance-related cognitive anxiety symptoms, while cognitive restructuring transformed irrational concerns into more adaptive thought patterns. This latter transformational process involved the participants broadening their perspectives and then introducing positive statements and images of previous sporting accomplishments. As in Wadey and Hanton (2008), such strategies were associated with heightened attentional focus, increased effort and motivation, and perceived control over anxiety-related symptoms. Taken together, the findings of these studies have implications for the practice of sport psychology with elite athletes debilitated by competitive anxiety in stressful situations, and offer further support that teaching a range of psychological skills can promote facilitative interpretations of anxiety symptoms, along with higher levels of motivation and effort.

In the time since Wiggins's (1998) initial examination of the temporal patterning of anxiety symptom interpretation, research in this area has been advanced by a number of qualitative studies that have attempted to explain the changes in intensity and direction in the lead up to competition. Hanton, Mellalieu and Young (2002) were the first to do so when they examined retrospective interpretations of, and causal beliefs about, temporal experiences of anxiety, identifying six causal networks that supported underpinning theoretical predictions. Specifically, data analysis found anxiety symptoms to increase as competition approached, with changes in symptom interpretation dependent on self-confidence levels. For example, increases in precompetitive symptoms combined with low self-confidence were reported to result in a loss of perceptions of control, problems with focus and concentration, and were viewed as debilitating or harmful to preparation for forthcoming performance. In contrast, increases in precompetitive symptoms accompanied by high self-confidence were perceived to enhance control of cognitions, and were viewed as facilitating preparation for performance.

As the first part of an ongoing programme of research exploring temporal patterning in pre-competition anxiety experiences, Thomas, Hanton and Maynard (2007a) adopted an interview approach to track anxiety changes in facilitators and debilitators during a seven-day competition cycle, whilst noting the psychological strategies used to attain and/or maintain a positive psychological state. To facilitate recall during the interviews, participants in this study completed an anxiety symptom booklet over the seven days. This approach was underpinned by the Experience Sampling Method (ESM), which has been used to alleviate recall concerns (Cerin, 2004; Voelkl and Nicholson, 1992). Analysis of transcripts distinguished between three temporal phases during the competition cycle, within which the intensity of cognitive and somatic symptoms increased. Using composite sequence analysis, the authors were able to represent the perceived underlying mechanisms of performers' facilitative anxiety interpretations over these time periods. The findings illustrated that the facilitators used effective strategies and thought processes to influence future interpretations of anxiety symptoms. These included positive imagery techniques to manipulate negative images, cognitive restructuring to alter negative thoughts, and the use of physical warm-ups and listening to music. Conversely, debilitators did not possess this sophisticated repertoire of psychological skills, and relied solely on external strategies (such as physical warm-up routines and social support) to stabilize the negative symptoms experienced. The findings emphasize the dynamic nature of competitive anxiety, and provide a framework for the structure, timing and content of psychological skills interventions for use with performers (Thomas et al., 2007a).

Collectively, the findings of the studies within the qualitative movement suggest that elite performers maintain a facilitative perspective through high levels of self-confidence which are underpinned by the effective use of a combination of basic (such as relaxation) and advanced (such as cognitive restructuring and reflection) psychological skills. Research within this movement has also highlighted the idiosyncratic and dynamic nature of competitive anxiety by depicting the experience of symptom interpretation in a temporal manner. Moreover, the qualitative movement has provided researchers with an insight into how performers interpret the anxiety symptoms they encounter in competitive sport, through approaches that focus on the subjective experience of performers, the findings of which can guide the design, content and timing of applied interventions to promote facilitative perceptions of anxiety symptoms.

The applied movement

The quantitative and qualitative movements highlighted the importance of identifying and understanding the individual differences that influence performers' anxiety symptom interpretation, and the mechanisms by which this may occur. The research that has explored these processes has generated a wealth of information that is valuable to applied practitioners who aim to help performers view their anxiety symptoms as facilitative for upcoming performance. Indeed, a third movement within the anxiety-direction literature has recently begun to flourish by integrating this information into applied intervention designs aimed at modifying anxiety interpretation. In line with these developments, this section outlines the key messages to emerge from direction research within this applied movement.

Initial direction intervention research was conducted by Maynard and colleagues, who explored the efficacy of somatic (Maynard, Hemmings and Warwick-Evans, 1995a), cognitive (Maynard, Smith and Warwick-Evans, 1995b) and multimodal (Maynard et al., 1998) intensity-reduction techniques on anxiety and performance in semi-professional soccer players. Whilst these studies incorporated the direction scale in their measurement of anxiety, their approach was underpinned by the 'matching hypothesis' (see, for a review, Maynard et al., 1995b) rather than applied suggestions from the competitive anxiety direction literature (e.g. Jones and Swain,

1992; Jones, Hanton and Swain, 1994). The matching hypothesis suggests a compatibility notion where the nature and content of the intervention should be 'matched' to the most prominent form of anxiety being experienced by the athlete. Mellalieu and Lane (2009) suggest that while these findings provide practitioners with information regarding the efficacy of certain intervention approaches, a closer inspection of the findings indicates that the matching hypothesis is only partially supported by Maynard and colleagues' studies. Despite later support for the potential benefit of anxiety-reduction interventions for non-elite performers by Fletcher and Hanton (2001), future research is required to elucidate the value of such approaches because of their largely exploratory nature and non-directional conceptual foundations. In addition to Maynard and colleagues' early intervention studies, Page, Sime and Nordell (1999) conducted an anxiety direction intervention using mental imagery to manipulate interpretations. Although also not informed by previous anxiety direction research, Page et al. suggested that imagery might have value in reducing precompetitive anxiety levels and promoting facilitative interpretations. Adopting a switched replication design, anxiety interpretations of intercollegiate swimmers were measured weekly over the course of five weeks. Following random exposure to imagery, findings suggested that interpretations of anxiety might be modified by imagery.

The first intervention study to be informed by previous anxiety direction research was conducted by Hanton and Jones (1999b), who implemented a multi-component intervention with three elite swimmers who reported debilitative interpretations of cognitive and somatic anxiety symptoms. The intervention was guided by the emergent data from Hanton and Jones's (1999a) interview study, which itself was informed by earlier research from the quantitative movement (e.g. Jones et al., 1994; Jones and Swain, 1995). The approach involved teaching swimmers a number of psychological skills aimed at altering cognitions about anxiety symptoms (such as goal setting, imagery and self-talk). Hanton and Jones (1999b) found all three participants changed from debilitative to facilitative interpretations following treatment. They also reported post-intervention increases in self-confidence and performance in all participants, which were sustained during a follow-up assessment five months post-intervention. Mamassis and Doganis (2004) used a similar design with two elite junior tennis players. Specifically, the participants were exposed to five different psychological skills: goal setting, positive thinking and self-talk, concentration and routines, arousal regulation techniques and imagery. The results indicated an increase in facilitative interpretations of somatic anxiety, cognitive anxiety and self-confidence at post-test. Moreover, self-confidence and overall tennis performance increased in both tennis players.

Due to the encouraging findings of Hanton and Jones (1999b) and Mamassis and Doganis (2004), Cumming, Olphin and Law (2007) examined in more detail the types of imagery that may influence anxiety responses. Specifically, Cumming et al. considered anxiety intensity and interpretation following different motivational general arousal (MGA) and motivational general mastery (MGM) imagery (that is, MGA anxiety imagery, MGA psyching-up imagery, MGA relaxing imagery, and

MGM imagery and coping imagery). Significant increases in the intensity of cognitive and somatic anxiety and more debilitative interpretations of such symptoms were found following the anxiety imagery script, while MGM and coping imagery resulted in significantly higher ratings of self-confidence than with MGA anxiety and MGA relaxing imagery, and more facilitative interpretations of symptoms associated with precompetition anxiety than MGA anxiety imagery. Cumming et al. suggested that MGM and coping imagery enabled athletes to be confident and view anxiety symptoms as under their control and facilitative in nature, therefore supporting previous qualitative research into self-confidence and anxiety interpretation (e.g. Hanton et al., 2004).

The use of multimodal interventions to restructure symptoms has also been tested across various temporal phases in the lead-up to performance. Specifically, Thomas et al. (2007b) conducted an intervention study with elite performers as the final part of their series of investigations into temporal anxiety responses during the pre-competition period. Similar to Hanton and Jones (1999b), Thomas et al. based the content and structure of their single-subject intervention on preceding interview findings (i.e. Thomas et al., 2007a). The intervention taught to three female field hockey players who consistently displayed debilitative interpretations of anxiety, imagery, rationalization and restructuring, goal-setting and self-talk skills at different phases using a three-phase multiple-baseline intervention design. Phase I covered the post-match review period (seven to five days preceding next performance). Phase II covered the temporal phase of two days to one day pre-competition and Phase III covered the temporal phase of match day. The effects of the intervention were measured over a ten-match cycle in relation to the players' performance (via notational analysis) and competition-related anxiety symptoms within a rolling seven-day competitive cycle (six days, two days, one day, one hour pre-competition). The findings indicated that the intervention was successful at restructuring the performers' interpretations of anxiety and confidence symptoms, increasing self-confidence, decreasing cognitive anxiety symptoms and decreasing somatic anxiety for two of the three players. Finally, the notational analysis findings suggested that performance improvements were evident for all three performers.

Most recently, Mellalieu et al. (2009) investigated the efficacy of a motivational general-arousal based imagery strategy to enhance self-confidence and protect against debilitative symptom interpretations. A second aim of this study was to provide specific intervention content informed by previous findings from the qualitative movement (Hanton and Connaughton, 2002; Hanton et al., 2004) which have highlighted the importance of self-confidence. To elaborate, previous restructuring interventions had provided multi-modal interventions, incorporating a range of techniques that may leave readers unable to identify the specific technique that worked. In line with previous interventions (Hanton and Jones, 1999b; Thomas et al., 2007b) Mellalieu et al. subsequently adopted a single-subject multiple-baseline design with a sample of five male collegiate rugby union players. Precompetitive anxiety and affect were measured over a full competitive season with follow-up social validation procedures. Post-intervention, participants reported more facilitative interpretations of symptoms associated with competitive anxiety, greater self-confidence and changes in positive and negative affect. The findings highlighted the benefit of employing idiosyncratic imagery and motivational general-arousal interventions to modify performers' perceptions of their precompetitive experiences (Mellalieu et al., 2009). The authors proposed that the intervention effects occurred in two ways; directly, via adaptive changes in performers' psychological response systems, and indirectly, through the protective mechanisms of enhanced efficacy associated with intervention expectations.

When considered as a collective body of literature, the findings from the applied movement indicate that intensity-reduction interventions may have benefit but are unlikely to be as efficacious as those based on learning psychological skills to restructure cognitions. Indeed, it seems that temporally defined, idiosyncratic interventions which target basic and advanced psychological skills and motivational general-arousal may be the most efficacious intervention technique for promoting facilitative interpretations of anxiety symptoms. Further, the findings emanating from the applied movement based on preliminary results from the quantitative and qualitative movements provide further insight into the possible mechanisms behind the relationship between psychological skills use and subsequent modification of cognitions. Such findings have value for academics and practitioners alike when designing optimal interventions for those encountering pre-performance competitive anxiety symptoms that are viewed as detrimental to performance.

Future movements and directions

The increasingly demanding nature of the competitive sport environment and the pressure to sustain optimal performance ensure that effective emotion management remains an important theoretical and applied domain within sport psychology (Cerin et al., 2000; Mellalieu et al., 2009). In accordance with the significance of this area, research questions as well as the methods to address them must continually develop to provide cutting-edge knowledge. Therefore, the final section of this chapter provides a number of suggestions for future research within the existing and new movements.

The area of anxiety direction has relied predominantly on two forms of measurement. That is, the quantitative and applied movements have almost solely employed the modified CSAI-2, and the qualitative movement has largely used semi-structured interviews to collect data. These measurement methods have provided a wealth of knowledge regarding competitive anxiety, and have often been selected in the absence of suitable alternative measures or techniques. However, as with alternative measures (such as SAS), limitations associated with CSAI-2 have been identified which may impact on perceptions of the quantitative movement's contribution to knowledge and applied practice. As discussed and debated elsewhere (cf. Burton and Naylor, 1997; Hardy, 1998; Lane et al., 1999; Mellalieu et al., 2006; Mellalieu and Lane, 2009; Woodman and Hardy, 2001), the reliance on CSAI-2D to measure competitive anxiety is a potential obstacle to the future development of this field. Indeed, literature has discussed the difficulties associated with measurement of intensity and direction in psychometric scales (Burton, 1998).

In line with Cerin (2004), future research within the quantitative movement may wish to consider the multilevel nature of stress and anxiety phenomena. Multilevel modelling involves statistical models of parameters that vary at more than one level and could be used to complement qualitative data collection procedures (cf. Cerin, 2004). These models can extend linear models to incorporate the individual and situational variables that might influence anxiety intensity, direction and subsequent performance by allowing researchers to control for individual and group differences within a participant sample (such as hardiness, achievement goals and coping). Specifically, the prevalence of groups within sport (such as teams and organizations) means that researchers may gain further insight into anxiety interpretation by considering within- and between-group differences which, in turn, may be mediated or moderated by the wealth of individual and situational variables explored within the quantitative movement. For example, based on extant literature, researchers may expect performers' anxiety to decrease with increases in ability. However, multilevel analyses have provided findings that suggest that this relationship may not be so straightforward. Goetz et al. (2008) found that the worry component of test anxiety was more highly reactive to the effects of individual achievement than the emotionality component in the achievement/anxiety relationship, and that this effect was largely mediated by participants' academic reference group and their own academic self-concept. Although not a new idea (see Cerin, 2004), the use of such approaches to data analysis is becoming increasingly popular as computer technology develops. It is also possible that multilevel modelling can shed light on the mediating role through which a number of skills and competencies (such as leadership, emotion regulation and experience) influence different individuals' anxiety direction within teams, and how this differs between teams.

Future directions within the qualitative movement may also enhance knowledge within the anxiety direction literature. Semi-structured interviews have long been the technique of choice within the qualitative movement in stress and anxiety research (cf. Biddle et al., 2001; Neil et al., 2009). Such methods allow for in-depth exploration of performers' experiences, appraisals and affective responses to stressors. However, as highlighted by Neil et al. (2009), the application of a predetermined and deductive structure to meaning-based and exploratory methods may inadvertently impose researchers' theoretical assumptions on participants. Additionally, interview methods are often used in cross-sectional 'snap-shot' designs, which might influence the trustworthiness of data through inaccuracies or biases in performers' recollection of affective phenomena (because of retrospective recall bias). In light of such observations, it is important to develop and adopt more innovative research designs and data collection methods that promote more unbiased recall. Qualitative researchers should also continue to stringently evaluate the trustworthiness of their research, and consider recently provided guidelines for quality assurance (e.g. Sparkes and Smith, 2009; Weed, 2009).

As noted earlier, direction researchers have recently begun to adopt alternative approaches to data collection (e.g. Thomas et al., 2007a). Indeed, Thomas et al.'s use of anxiety symptom booklets provided a novel data collection method that can be used to continue knowledge development within the qualitative movement. In addition to anxiety logs, researchers might also explore the use of their own reflexive journals to provide an insight into their observations and interpretations throughout data collection and analysis. This may also go some way to enhancing transparency regarding the influence of researcher or theoretical bias in data treatment. Further, longitudinal prospective designs are being adopted with increasing prevalence in sport psychology, and can be used to advance knowledge about anxiety direction. Such approaches could include systematic observation (e.g. Smith and Smoll, 1990), case studies (e.g. Anderson et al., 2002), action research (e.g. Evans, Hardy and Fleming, 2000), ethnography (see Krane and Baird, 2005) and diaries (e.g. Thomas et al., 2007a), all of which offer exciting opportunities for future explorations of anxiety direction. Moreover, it is possible that the methods outlined in this section could coalesce to formulate a fourth movement under the banner of an applied-qualitative movement. Within this movement, a wealth of data-collection techniques could be employed to evaluate the efficacy of anxiety direction interventions, including research logs, diaries, systematic observation, video recordings and audio diaries. For example, in ethnographic enquiries the researcher might employ a selection of these techniques whilst becoming the conduit through which context-specific knowledge is interpreted and imparted to the reader, providing an alternative movement from which we currently research the psychosocial phenomena.

In addition to an applied-qualitative movement, future research should also adopt the methods that have been successfully employed in mixed-methods studies examining direction (e.g. Cerin, 2004). For example, using a mixed-method approach, Cerin (2004) examined the relationships between affective states, proximity of competition and personality traits as predictors of anxiety direction, and the role of personality characteristics in moderating these relationships. An idiographic/nomothetic approach to data collection and treatment was adopted to reveal that cognitive anxiety intensity; positive affect, proximity to competition and extraversion were significant predictors of cognitive anxiety direction. Significant interaction effects were also observed between proximity to competition on neuroticism, and neuroticism and negative affect on cognitive anxiety direction. Additionally, somatic anxiety direction was a function of positive affect, somatic anxiety intensity, proximity to competition, and the interaction effects of neuroticism and somatic anxiety intensity, and neuroticism and proximity to competition. The author concluded by proposing that a multilevel mixed idiographic/nomothetic interactional approach may substantially assist in the explanation of intra- and inter-individual differences in anxiety direction. Therefore, by combining methods from extant movements such as contemporary measurement scales (such as IAMS or CSAI-2D) and explanatory inquiry (such as diaries or ESM) in one study, researchers may provide a fuller picture of the cognitive processes surrounding anxiety experience and responses.

Whilst innovative future directions may extend our understanding of anxiety direction and encourage the development of new movements, we should not forget the questions that remain within the extant movements. Despite significant advances in our understanding of anxiety direction, very few studies (e.g. Hanton and Jones, 1999b, Lundquist et al., 2010; Swain and Jones, 1996; Thomas et al., 2007b) have examined the relationship between anxiety direction and performance. Whilst numerous studies have demonstrated associations between facilitative anxiety symptom interpretation and past or predicted performance (e.g. Jones et al., 2004; Robazza and Bortoli, 2007; Jones et al., 1993), much remains unknown about how anxiety direction relates to current performance. Therefore, whilst the current body of literature is encouraging, there is need for experimental research – under the banner of an applied–performance movement – to better elucidate this relationship through ecologically valid designs. In doing so, future applied research should look to unravel this relationship, and will likely be a continuation of the current quantitative, qualitative and applied movements discussed above as part of a trans-theoretical research movement.

Concluding remarks

This chapter has attempted to provide an insight into competitive anxiety direction research and the encapsulating movements into which this research can be categorized. The three movements outlined have each provided researchers and practitioners with valuable knowledge and understanding of the competitive anxiety experience. Specifically, the extant body of literature indicates three things.

First, a wealth of individual and situational variables have been identified as important in performers' anxiety symptom interpretation. For example, this research base has indicated relationships between anxiety interpretation and skill level, experience, psychological skill use, motivation and hardiness.

Second, the research examining these differences has informed and stimulated explorations within the qualitative movement. This body of research has aimed to illuminate the underpinning mechanisms that mediate and moderate interpretations of competitive anxiety symptoms and, in turn, expectations about performance. Indeed, this research has highlighted the importance of retaining a high level of self-confidence and control over stressors using basic (such as imagery) and advanced (such as cognitive restructuring) psychological skills in a dynamic and individual manner prior to competition.

Third, in an attempt to apply the insightful findings from the qualitative movement, researchers have designed interventions to promote facilitative interpretations of competitive anxiety symptoms. Specifically, research has suggested that temporally defined, idiosyncratic interventions that target psychological skills are effective in promoting such outcomes in a variety of sport samples.

To sum up this chapter, we have attempted to demonstrate how quantitative individual and situational difference research has led to the emergence of qualitative inquiries exploring the mechanisms underpinning relationships between such variables, which subsequently informed applied interventions to promote facilitative interpretations of anxiety symptoms. Despite these encouraging conclusions, it is possible that anxiety direction research has come to a crossroads. Whilst our understanding of competitive anxiety has developed significantly over the past twenty years within three distinct movements, we must now look to the future and the continuing development of extant movements, as well as encouraging the emergence of innovative and novel approaches to data collection and interpretation. It is possible that the next significant development in this area is perhaps now overdue. Such a breakthrough could be in the form of a measurement tool, a new movement incorporating the use of mixed and alternative methods, or an unforeseen development that propels this field forward into a new era.

References

Anderson, A. G., Miles, A., Mahoney, C. and Robinson, P. (2002). Evaluating the effectiveness of applied sport psychology practice: making the case for a case study approach. *The Sport Psychologist,* 16, 432–453.

Biddle, J. H., Markland, D., Gilbourne, D., Chatzisarantis, N. L. D. and Sparkes, A. C. (2001). Research methods in sport and exercise psychology: quantitative and qualitative issues. *Journal of Sports Sciences,* 19, 777–809.

Burton, D. (1998). Measuring competitive state anxiety. In J. L. Duda (ed.), *Advances in sport and exercise psychology measurement* (pp. 129–148). Morgantown, W.V.: Fitness Information Technology.

Burton, D. and Naylor, S. (1997). Is anxiety really facilitative? Reaction to the myth that cognitive anxiety always impairs performance. *Journal of Applied Sport Psychology,* 9, 295–302.

Carver, C. S. and Scheier, M. F. (1986). Functional and dysfunctional approaches to anxiety: the interaction between expectancies and self-focused attention. In R. Schwarzer (ed.), *Self-related cognitions in anxiety and motivation* (pp. 111–146). Hillsdale, N.J.: Erlbaum.

Carver, C. S. and Scheier, M. F. (1988). A control–process perspective on anxiety. *Anxiety Research,* 1, 17–22.

Cerin, E. (2004). Predictors of competitive anxiety direction in male Tae Kwon Do practitioners: a multilevel mixed idiographic/nomothetic interactional approach. *Psychology of Sport and Exercise,* 5, 497–516.

Cerin, E., Szabo, A., Hunt, N. and Williams, C. (2000). Temporal patterning of competitive emotions: a critical review. *Journal of Sports Sciences,* 18, 605–626.

Cox, R. H., Martens, M. P. and Russell, W. D. (2003). Measuring anxiety in athletics: The Revised Competitive State Anxiety Inventory-2. *Journal of Sport and Exercise Psychology,* 25, 519–533.

Cumming, J. L., Olphin, T. and Law, M. (2007). Self-reported psychological states and physiological responses to different types of motivational general imagery. *Journal of Sport and Exercise Psychology,* 29, 629–644.

Eubank, M. and Collins, D. (2000). Coping with pre- and in-event fluctuations in competitive state anxiety: a longitudinal approach. *Journal of Sports Sciences,* 18, 121–131.

Eubank, M., Collins, D. and Smith, N. (2002). Anxiety and ambiguity: it's all open to interpretation. *Journal of Sport and Exercise Psychology,* 24, 239–253.

Fazey, J. and Hardy, L. (1988). *The Inverted-U hypothesis: A catastrophe for sport psychology*. British Association of Sport Sciences Monograph No. 1. Leeds: National Coaching Foundation.

Evans, L., Hardy, L. and Fleming, S. (2000). Intervention strategies with injured athletes: an action research study. *The Sport Psychologist*, 14, 188–206.

Fletcher, D. and Hanton, S. (2001). The relationship between psychological skills usage and competitive anxiety responses. *Psychology of Sport and Exercise*, 2, 89–101.

Goetz, T., Preckel, F., Zeidner, M. and Schleyer, E. (2008). Big fish in big ponds: a multilevel analysis of test anxiety and achievement in special gifted classes. *Anxiety, Stress and Coping*, 21, 185–198.

Hanton, S. and Connaughton, D. (2002). Perceived control of anxiety and its relationship with self-confidence and performance: a qualitative explanation. *Research Quarterly for Exercise and Sport*, 73, 87–97.

Hanton, S. and Jones, G. (1997). Antecedents of competitive state anxiety as a function of skill level. *Psychological Reports*, 81, 1139–1147.

Hanton, S. and Jones, G. (1999a). The acquisition and development of cognitive skills and strategies. I: Making the butterflies fly in formation. *The Sport Psychologist*, 13, 1–21.

Hanton, S. and Jones, G. (1999b). The effects of a multimodal intervention program on performers. II: Training the butterflies to fly in formation. *The Sport Psychologist*, 13, 22–41.

Hanton, S., Cropley, B. and Lee, S. (2009). Reflective practice, experience and the interpretation of anxiety symptoms. *Journal of Sports Sciences*, 27, 517–533.

Hanton, S., Cropley, B., Neil, R., Mellalieu, S. D. and Miles, A. (2007). An in-depth examination of experience in sport: competitive experience and the relationship with competitive anxiety. *International Journal of Sport and Exercise Psychology*, 5, 28–53.

Hanton, S., Evans, L. and Neil, R. (2003). Hardiness and the competitive trait anxiety response. *Anxiety, Stress and Coping*, 16, 167–184.

Hanton, S., Jones, G. and Mullen, R. (2000). Intensity and direction of competitive anxiety as interpreted by rugby players and rifle shooters. *Perceptual and Motor Skills*, 90, 513–521.

Hanton, S., Mellalieu, S. D. and Hall, R. (2004a). Self-confidence and anxiety interpretation: a qualitative investigation. *Psychology of Sport and Exercise*, 5, 379–521.

Hanton, S., Mellalieu, S. D. and Young, S. (2002). A qualitative investigation into the temporal patterning of the precompetitive anxiety response and its effects on performance. *Journal of Sports Sciences*, 20, 911–928.

Hanton, S., Neil, R. and Mellalieu, S. D. (2008a). Recent developments in competitive anxiety direction and competition stress research. *International Review of Sport and Exercise Psychology*, 1, 45–57.

Hanton, S., Neil, R. and Mellalieu, S. D. (2011). Competitive anxiety theory and research. In T. Morris and P. C. Terry (eds), *Sport and exercise psychology: The cutting edge*. Morgantown, W.V.: Fitness Information Technology.

Hanton, S., O'Brien, M. and Mellalieu, S. D. (2003). Individual differences, perceived control and competitive trait anxiety. *Journal of Sport Behavior*, 26, 39–55.

Hanton, S., Thomas, O. and Maynard, I. (2004b). Competitive anxiety responses in the week leading up to competition: the role of intensity, direction and frequency dimensions. *Psychology of Sport and Exercise*, 5, 169–181.

Hanton, S., Wadey, R. and Connaughton, D. (2005). Debilitative interpretations of competitive anxiety: a qualitative examination of elite performers. *European Journal of Sport Science*, 5, 123–136.

Hanton, S., Wadey, R. and Mellalieu, S. D. (2008b). Advanced psychological strategies and competitive anxiety responses in sport. *The Sport Psychologist*, 22, 472–490.

Hardy, L. (1998). Responses to the reactants on three myths in applied consultancy work. *Journal of Applied Sport Psychology*, 10, 212–219.

Jerome, G. J. and Williams, J. M. (2000). Intensity and interpretation of competitive state anxiety: relationship to performance and repressive coping. *Journal of Applied Sport Psychology*, 12, 236–250.

Jones, G. (1991). Recent issues in competitive state anxiety research. *The Psychologist*, 4, 152–155.

Jones, G. (1995). More than just a game: research developments and issues in competitive state anxiety in sport. *British Journal of Psychology*, 86, 449–478.

Jones, G. and Hanton, S. (1996). Interpretation of anxiety symptoms and goal attainment expectations. *Journal of Sport and Exercise Psychology*, 18, 144–158.

Jones, G., Hanton, S. and Swain, A. B. J. (1994). Intensity and interpretation of anxiety symptoms in elite and non-elite performers. *Personality and Individual Differences*, 117, 657–663.

Jones, G. and Swain, A. B. J. (1992). Intensity and direction dimensions of competitive state anxiety and relationships with competitiveness. *Perceptual and Motor Skills*, 74, 467–472.

Jones, G. and Swain, A. B. J. (1995). Predispositions to experience facilitating and debilitating anxiety in elite and non-elite performers. *The Sport Psychologist*, 9, 201–211.

Jones, G., Swain, A. B. J. and Hardy, L. (1993). Intensity and direction dimensions of competitive state anxiety and relationships with performance. *Journal of Sports Sciences*, 11, 533–542.

Jones, K. A., Smith, N. C. and Holmes, P. S. (2004). Anxiety symptom interpretation and performance predictions in high-anxious, low-anxious and repressor sport performers. *Anxiety, Stress and Coping*, 17, 187–199.

Kobasa, S. C. (1979). Stressful life events, personality and health: an inquiry into hardiness. *Journal of Personality and Social Psychology*, 37, 1–11.

Krane, V. and Baird, S. M. (2005). Using ethnography in applied sport psychology. *Journal of Applied Sport Psychology*, 17, 87–107.

Lane, A. M., Sewell, D. F., Terry, P. C., Bartram, D. and Nesti, M. S. (1999). Confirmatory factor analysis of the competitive state anxiety inventory-2. *Journal of Sports Sciences*, 17, 505–512.

Lazarus, R. S. (1999). *Stress and emotion: A new synthesis*. London: Free Association Books.

Lundqvist, C., Kenttä, G. and Raglin, J. S. (in press). Directional anxiety responses in elite and sub-elite young athletes: intensity of anxiety symptoms matters. *Scandinavian Journal of Medicine and Science in Sports*.

Mahoney, M. J. and Avener, M. (1977). Psychology of the elite athlete: an exploratory study. *Cognitive Therapy and Research*, 1, 135–141.

Mamassis, G. and Doganis, G. (2004). The effects of a mental training program on juniors pre-competitive anxiety, self-confidence and tennis performance. *Journal of Applied Sport Psychology*, 16, 118–137.

Martens, R., Burton, D., Vealey, R. S., Bump, L. A. and Smith, D. E. (1990a). Development and validation of the Competitive State Anxiety Inventory-2. In R. Martens, R. S. Vealey and D. Burton (eds), *Competitive anxiety in sport* (pp. 117–190). Champaign, Ill.: Human Kinetics.

Martens, R., Vealey, R. S. and Burton, D. (1990b). (eds). *Competitive anxiety in sport*. Champaign, Ill.: Human Kinetics.

Maynard, I. W., Hemmings, B., Greenlees, I. A., Warwick-Evans, L. and Stanton, N. (1998). Stress management in sport: a comparison of unimodal and multimodal interventions. *Anxiety, Stress and Coping*, 11, 225–246.

Maynard, I. W., Hemmings, B. and Warwick-Evans, L. (1995a). The effects of a somatic intervention strategy on competitive state anxiety and performance in semi-professional soccer players. *The Sport Psychologist*, 9, 51–64.

Maynard, I. W., Smith, M. J. and Warwick-Evans, L. (1995b). The effects of a cognitive intervention strategy on competitive state anxiety and performance in semi-professional soccer players. *Journal of Sport and Exercise Psychology*, 17, 428–446.

Mellalieu, S. D., Hanton, S. and Fletcher, D. (2006a). A competitive anxiety review: recent directions in sport psychology research. In S. Hanton and S. D. Mellalieu eds), *Literature reviews in sport psychology* (pp. 1–45). Hauppage, N.Y.: Nova Science.

Mellalieu, S. D., Hanton, S. and Jones, G. (2003). Emotional labeling and competitive anxiety in preparation and competition. *The Sport Psychologist*, 17, 157–174.

Mellalieu, S. D., Hanton, S. and O'Brien, M. (2004). Intensity and direction dimensions of competitive anxiety as a function of sport type and experience. *Scandinavian Journal of Science and Medicine in Sport*, 14, 326–334.

Mellalieu, S. D. and Lane, A. M. (2009). Studying anxiety interpretations is useful for sport and exercise psychologists (debate). *Sport and Exercise Psychology Review*, 5, 48–55.

Mellalieu, S. D., Neil, R. and Hanton, S. (2006b). An investigation of the mediating effects of self-confidence between anxiety intensity and direction. *Research Quarterly for Exercise and Sport*, 77, 263–270.

Mullen, R., Lane, A. and Hanton, S. (2009). Anxiety symptom interpretation in high-anxious, defensive high-anxious, low-anxious and repressor sport performers. *Anxiety, Stress and Coping*, 22, 91–100.

Neil, R., Hanton, S. and Mellalieu, S. D. (2009). The contribution of qualitative inquiry towards understanding competitive anxiety and competition stress. *Qualitative Research in Sport and Exercise*, 1, 191–205.

Neil, R., Mellalieu, S. D. and Hanton, S. (2006). Psychological skills usage and competitive anxiety as a function of skill level in rugby union. *Journal of Sports Science and Medicine*, 6, 415–423.

Ntoumanis, N. and Biddle, S. J. H. (2000). Relationship of intensity and direction of competitive anxiety with coping strategies. *The Sport Psychologist*, 14, 360–371.

Ntoumanis, N. and Jones, G. (1998). Interpretation of competitive trait anxiety symptoms as a function of locus of control beliefs. *International Journal of Sport Psychology*, 29, 99–114.

Page, S. J., Sime, W. and Nordell, K. (1999). The effects of imagery on female college swimmers' perceptions of anxiety. *The Sport Psychologist*, 13, 458–469.

Perry, J. D. and Williams, J. M. (1998). Relationship of intensity and direction of competitive trait anxiety to skill level and gender in tennis *The Sport Psychologist*, 12, 169–179.

Robazza, C. and Bortoli, L. (2007). Perceived impact of anger and anxiety on sporting performance in rugby players. *Psychology of Sport and Exercise*, 8, 875–896.

Smith, R. E. and Smoll, F. L. (1990). Athletic performance anxiety. In H. Leitenberg (ed.), *Handbook of social and evaluation anxiety* (pp. 417–454). New York: Plenum.

Smith, R. E., Smoll, F. L. and Schutz, R. W. (1990). Measurement correlates of sport-specific cognitive and somatic trait anxiety: The Sport Anxiety Scale. *Anxiety Research*, 2, 263–280.

Sparkes, A. and Smith, B. (2009). Judging the quality of qualitative inquiry: criteriology and relativism in action. *Psychology of Sport and Exercise*, 10, 491–497.

Swain, A. B. J. and Jones, G. (1996). Explaining performance variance: the relative contributions of intensity and direction dimensions of competitive state anxiety. *Anxiety, Stress and Coping*, 9, 1–18.

Thomas, O., Hanton, S. and Jones, G. (2002). An alternative approach to short-form self-report assessment of competitive anxiety. *International Journal of Sport Psychology*, 33, 325–336.

Thomas, O., Hanton, S. and Maynard, I. (2007a). Anxiety responses and psychological skill use during the time leading up to competition: Theory to practice I. *Journal of Applied Sport Psychology*, 19, 379–397.

Thomas, O., Maynard, I. and Hanton, S. (2004). Temporal aspects of competitive anxiety and self-confidence as a function of anxiety perceptions. *The Sport Psychologist*, 18, 172–187.

Thomas, O., Maynard, I. and Hanton, S. (2007b). Intervening with athletes during the time leading up to competition: theory to practice II. *Journal of Applied Sport Psychology*, 19, 398–418.

Voelkl, J. E. and Nicholson, L. A. (1992). Perceptions of daily life among residents of a long term care facility. *Activities, Adaptation and Aging*, 16, 99–114.

Wadey, R. and Hanton, S. (2008). Basic psychological skills usage and competitive anxiety responses: perceived underlying mechanisms. *Research Quarterly for Exercise and Sport,* 79, 363–373.

Weed, M. (2009). Research quality in sport and psychology: Introduction to the collection. *Psychology of Sport and Exercise,* 10, 489–490.

Wiggins, M. S. (1998). Anxiety intensity and direction: preperformance temporal patterns and expectations in athletes. *Journal of Applied Sport Psychology,* 10, 201–211.

Williams, J. M. and Krane, V. (1992). Coping styles and self-reported measures on state anxiety and self-confidence. *Journal of Applied Sport Psychology,* 4, 134–143.

Woodman, T. and Hardy, L. (2001). Stress and anxiety. In R. Singer, H. A. Hausenblas and C. M. Janelle (eds), *Handbook of research on sport psychology* (pp. 290–318). New York: Wiley.

8

ENHANCING POSITIVE EMOTION IN SPORT

Paul McCarthy, Glasgow Caledonian University

> I'm going to try and adopt the same attitude over the last two days as I did
> the first two, go over there and still just try and enjoy myself.
>
> *(Lee Westwood's comments at the HSBC Championship in Shanghai, his first
> tournament after becoming world No. 1 in golf (Simpson, 2010, p. 19).*

Competitive sport is a tapestry of ambition and emotion. Some athletes are driven
to excel continuously on a rising tide of seemingly insurmountable standards; yet
those impulses to better oneself and one's achievements have driven athletes like
Lee Westwood to extraordinary triumph with positive emotion at its core. When
journalists invite champion athletes to reveal the ingredients of their success, at least
one common denominator emerges: the role of emotion control. To illustrate this
point, when Jessica Ennis won gold for Great Britain in the heptathlon at the 2010
European championships, she said,

> Going into that 800m, I just wanted to win. I wanted to do everything
> I could to stay in the lead, to take the gold medal. And I did. There is a lot
> of pressure on me. But I am so happy and proud of myself that I have dealt
> with it.
>
> *(Longmore, 2010, pp. 2–3).*

Because athletes weave this common thread of emotional control through their
tales of triumph, it cements sport psychologists' assertion that victory or defeat
teeter on controlling emotions when it matters most (Jones, 2003; Uphill,
McCarthy and Jones, 2009).

If we accept that claim and put it aside for now, we can inspect more closely
those emotions associated with victory and defeat. Empirical evidence from
research on emotional experience in competitive sport suggests that positive and

negative emotions are juxtaposed – hope and excitement are balanced by fear and worry which intensify and weaken in the crucible of competition (Martinet and Ferrand, 2009; Robazza, Pellizzari and Hanin, 2004; Sève et al., 2006). Until recently, sport psychologists have known most about negatively toned emotions such as fear and anxiety but much less about positively toned emotions such as hope and excitement, even though positive emotions colour the fabric of competitive sport as much as negative emotions (Cerin, 2003; Cerin et al., 2000; Jackson, 2000; Sève et al., 2006). For example, the 2006 World Indoor 60m hurdles champion, Derval O'Rourke, explained, 'I don't think sport is worth being completely miserable for …. You cannot run quick if you're not happy' (Walsh, 2009). Similarly, Paula Radcliffe, the world champion marathon runner stated, 'it isn't just the competition that appeals to me. Running is something I enjoy, full stop' (Radcliffe, 2004, p.13).

In the ensuing argument, I invite sport psychologists to appraise positive emotions in their research because both positive and negative emotions are constantly modified through the process of cognitive appraisal (Lazarus, 1999, 2000; Martinet and Ferrand, 2009). Thus the emotion–performance relationship changes over time, when positive emotions such as resilience and pride may be dragging a flagging performer across the winning line (Sève et al., 2006). Any dispassionate analysis of research on positive emotions within sport psychology would persuade most researchers that at least two related challenges are set before us. The first is to understand positive emotions better by identifying their influence on performance and psychological well-being in competitive sport. Once this step is taken, applied sport psychologists can harness the energy of positive emotions such as happiness, pride, hope, resilience, passion, excitement and enjoyment within their professional practice. Fulfilling both these aims would add considerably to the growing body of research on emotion in sport.

This chapter debates the value of positive emotion for sport performers' well-being and performance, but more crucially, outlines how sport psychologists can enhance positive emotion in sport. I begin by illustrating the value of positive emotions in people's lives and their relative obscurity in sport psychology research. Next, I briefly introduce a theory of positive emotion, because although several emotion theories cater for negative emotions, such theories conflict with the nuances of positive emotion (Fredrickson, 1998). Then, I explain how sport psychologists can boost positive emotion in sport settings whilst recognising that positive emotions can have drawbacks and negative emotions can have benefits. I conclude by offering some ideas for further study in this relatively uncharted field of research.

Understanding emotion

Darwin's classic work on the expression of the emotions in humans and animals generated and continues to generate interest among psychologists, not least because the prominence of emotion is apparent when we consider a world without it.

William James captured this notion impressively at the start of the last century: 'No one portion of the universe would then have importance beyond another; and the whole character of its things and series of its events would be without significance, character, expression, or perspective' (1902, p. 150). Sport in many ways represents a microcosm of the world; it infuses players and spectators with a distillation of emotions without which the drama of sport would resemble a paltry distraction. But when researchers begin to study emotion in sport, they are confronted by differences in definition and measurement discrepancies that impede understanding of how emotions can influence sport performers and their performances (Hanin, 2000). On further inspection, it appears impractical to define emotion in a way that adequately satisfies its complexity (Vallerand and Blanchard, 2000); nevertheless, Deci proposed a helpful definition to understand what emotion means:

> An emotion is a reaction to a stimulus event (either actual or imagined). It involves change in the viscera and musculature of the person, is experienced subjectively in characteristic ways, is expressed through such means as facial changes and action tendencies and may mediate and energise subsequent behaviours.
>
> *(Deci, 1980, p. 85)*

Even the term 'emotion' is used interchangeably with 'affect' and 'feeling' (e.g. Isen, 2000); however, researchers also distinguish these terms from each other (e.g. Fredrickson, 2001; Russell and Feldman Barrett, 1999). Affect refers to 'the experience of valence, a subjective sense of positivity or negativity arising from an experience' (Carver, 2003, p. 242), and many sport psychologists have and continue to explore emotion in sport with reference to affect (Gaudreau, Blondin and Lapierre, 2002; McCarthy, 2009; Robazza et al., 2000). Affect can be categorised using valence (positive versus negative) and activation (low versus high) (Feldman Barrett and Russell, 1998; Russell and Carroll, 1999). Low-activation positive emotions include emotions such as happiness and satisfaction, and reflect one's achievement of valued goals and the absence of a need for action (Fredrickson, 1998; Skinner and Brewer, 2004). High-activation positive emotions include emotions such as excitement and enthusiasm, and reflect one's anticipation of favourable outcomes (Skinner and Brewer, 2004). It is these low- and high-activation positive emotions that are the central feature of this chapter, with some analysis of definitions and measurement tools, but I avoid getting embroiled in their mechanics because these issues are discussed cogently elsewhere (Hanin, 2000). First we consider the value of positive emotions in society and sport.

What good are positive emotions?

It seems logical to ask, 'What good are positive emotions in our lives?' especially when we compare these emotions with fear, aggression or anxiety, because the latter emotions helped us to survive. A perplexing conundrum arises when we try to answer this question, because if we experience positive emotions in our lives, their evolutionary passage implies that they contributed to our survival as a species, though at first this may not appear obvious. Over the past decade, researchers have begun to review the positive aspects of people's lives such as hope, optimism, happiness and well-being with greater fervour (Boniwell, 2008), and a remarkable study published in 2001 demonstrated the enduring potency of positive emotions in our lives. To explain the context of this study, a group of young nuns were asked to write autobiographical sketches when they joined the congregation at the School Sisters of Notre Dame in Milwaukee in the 1930s. These essays described their lives to that point, and their religious experiences that had led them to join the convent. Though these essays were archived for more than sixty years, three researchers from the University of Kentucky, Danner, Snowdon and Friesen (2001) uncovered the nuns' writings as part of a larger study on ageing and Alzheimer's disease. They scored the essays for emotional content, and recorded illustrations of happiness, interest, love and hope. A substantial discovery emerged: nuns communicating the most positive emotions lived up to ten years longer than those communicating the fewest. Most notably, however, the nuns' survival was unrelated to their lifestyle but depended on their positive emotions, because they lived almost identical lives from their early twenties onwards. Many other studies have suggested that thinking positively and feeling good helps people to live longer (Fredrickson, 2003). But what could explain the relation between positive affect and survival?

One argument proposes that the immune system is responsible. Davidson et al. (2003) demonstrated that people with a positive affective style (positive trait affect) display better immune function than those with a negative affective style (negative trait affect). They revealed this link practically by training volunteers in mindfulness meditation before injecting them with a flu vaccine. Mindfulness meditation involves moment-by-moment, detached awareness and observation of a continually changing field of perception and its contents (Speca et al., 2000). Six months later, the researchers examined the strength of the antibody response produced by the participants to the vaccine. Compared with a control group, the meditation group produced almost twice as many antibodies, reinforcing the claim that positive emotional states can raise immune function. In short, mindfulness–meditation can be used as an intervention to increase positive emotions, which is associated with enhanced functioning of the immune system.

It would appear, therefore, that positive emotions assemble an ability to survive; yet this notion is challenged by emotion theorists such as Ekman (1992), Frijda (1986) and Lazarus (1991), who argue that emotions are associated with urges to act (Fredrickson, 1998). Fear, for example, creates the urge to escape, and anger, the urge to attack (Fredrickson, 2003). Such urges do not impel people to act; rather they guide people about specific possibilities (such as stay and fight or run and hide). These urges are associated with specific physiological changes to enable one to act (such as greater blood flow to the large muscle groups to run). The theorists' models of emotion suggest that negative emotions have evolutionary currency because they narrow thought–action repertories to those that paid greatest dividends for our ancestors' survival when their lives were threatened. From this perspective, however, positive emotions do not appear to confer survival instinct. On the other hand, if we accept that all emotions present an evolved capacity of biological organisms (Cosmides and Tooby, 2000; Plutchik, 1980), positive emotions, like negative emotions, also increased our chances of survival. Fredrickson (1998, 2003) insisted that positive emotions solve problems about personal growth and development. In short, they confer states of mind and modes of behaviour that indirectly prepare a person for challenging times ahead. Despite this persuasive proposal, positive emotions were marginalised in emotion literature, and there are at least three reasons for this (Fredrickson, 1998).

First, not only do scientific taxonomies of basic emotions (Ekman, 1992; Izard, 1977) usually identify one positive emotion for every three or four negative emotions (Ellsworth and Smith, 1988), the English-language emotion words also reflect this difference (Averill, 1980). Across the world, different cultures smile when happy, frown when sad and wrinkle their brow when angry (Ekman et al., 1987; Smith and Mackie, 2007). Facial configurations associated with specific negative emotions can be recognised universally (Ekman et al., 1987); however, positive emotions do not share this unique signal value (Ekman, 1992). Negative and positive emotions can also be distinguished based on autonomic responding, and some negative emotions can be distinguished from each other, but positive emotions show a lack of autonomic activation (Cacioppo et al., 1993; Levenson, 1992; Levenson, Ekman and Friesen, 1990).

Second, negative emotions such as anger, fear and anxiety create problems in our lives. To the extent that these emotions influence our daily functioning, they require consideration and management, and therefore have been the focus of research attention for many years.

Third, theorists developed models to fit specifications of prototypic (an original type serving as a basis for others) emotions (such as negative emotions like fear and anger) because understanding these emotions should help explain less prototypic emotions, including the positive emotions (Fredrickson, 1998). Researchers surveying positive emotions have struggled to establish a suitable theory to describe their findings because existing models of emotion present a suitable backdrop for negative emotions but rarely incorporate the minutiae of positive emotion (for instance, in contrast to negative emotions, positive emotions broaden rather than narrow action tendencies).

Because positive emotions did not fit existing models of emotions, this encouraged Fredrickson (1998) to advance a new model, which specifically included a subset of positive emotions: joy, interest, contentment and love. The model is referred to as the broaden–and–build model of positive emotion. In her hypothesis, positive emotions broaden an individual's momentary thought–action repertoire, and this effect builds that individual's physical, intellectual and social resources. The usefulness of positive emotions, therefore, can be witnessed in many facets of our lives within and outside sport, especially for our psychological well-being and physical health. For example, positive emotions have a clear role in the stress process because strong research evidence illustrates that these emotions co-occur with negative emotions even in intensely stressful situations (Folkman, 2008). More heartening perhaps is that positive emotions restore physiological, psychological and social coping resources. Positive emotions emerge from coping processes such as benefit finding and reminding, reordering priorities, adaptive goal processes and permeating ordinary events with positive meaning. These coping processes have the capacity to add richly to sport and exercise contexts as sport psychologists widen the scope of basic and applied research. In the following section, I briefly highlight how positive emotions such as enjoyment; happiness, pride, hope and optimism add substance to a growing field of emotion research in sport and exercise.

Positive emotions in sport

Since the Second World War, research on emotion in psychology clustered around a desire to realise how negative emotions alter people's lives and which psychological strategies work best to diminish their harmful influence. This focus seems prudent when, for example, we reflect on the distress caused by depression and anxiety in people's lives. But this spotlight on problems and pathology largely ignored wellness and prevention until recently, when the positive psychology movement persuaded researchers to consider character strengths (such as resilience) and positive emotions (such as happiness) rather than weaknesses. Recent developments in psychology have witnessed a burgeoning concentration on building positive qualities in one's life rather than repairing the worst things in life (Seligman and Csikszentmihalyi, 2000). At a subjective level, the field of positive psychology is concerned with valued subjective experiences such as well-being, satisfaction, optimism, flow and happiness.

Research in sport psychology followed a similar trend to other areas of psychology, with the strongest research emphasis on emotions such as anxiety and aggression; however, some researchers have begun to examine positive emotions in sport and exercise contexts (Hanin, 2000; McCarthy et al., 2010; Robazza et al., 2004; Vast, Young and Thomas, 2010), but only sport enjoyment has received equitable scrutiny (McCarthy and Jones, 2007; Scanlan and Simons, 1992). One likely reason for this neglect of positive emotions lies in the struggle to conceptualise and measure such emotions. For instance, researchers have contested the conceptual definition and measurement of sport enjoyment, arguing that it should be conceptualised as flow (e.g. Kimiecik and Harris, 1996), while others advocate that it is synonymous with intrinsic motivation (e.g. Deci and Ryan, 1985). Beyond this equivocation, researchers sought to identify the antecedents of sport enjoyment and positive affect, including:

- perceptions of competence (Scanlan, Stein and Ravizza, 1989)
- mastery-orientated motivational climate (Kavussanu and Roberts, 1996)

- task orientation (Boyd and Yin, 1996; Duda et al., 1992)
- social and life opportunities gained from participating in sport (Bakker et al., 1993; Scanlan et al., 1989).

As well as the motivational role served by sport enjoyment, research on mental factors linked to optimal performance has also stressed the relevance of sport enjoyment (Orlick and Partington, 1988). For instance, flow, an optimal psychological state that occurs when there is a balance between perceived challenges and skills of an activity (Csikszentmihalyi, 1990; Jackson et al., 2001), is associated with sport enjoyment. Jackson (1992) recorded that enjoying what they are doing was one of the five factors identified by elite figure skaters to augment the likelihood of accomplishing a flow state. Equally, research on peak performance has indicated that this psychological state is associated with psychological characteristics such as feeling highly self-confident, a narrow focus of attention, an absence of fear, and feeling physically and mentally relaxed, and that these experiences are linked with fun or enjoyment (Cohn, 1991). Apart from sport enjoyment and flow, however, other positive emotions such as happiness, pride, hope and optimism linger on the periphery of emotion researchers' curiosity in sport psychology. I shall briefly consider these emotions and associated empirical research because although they are relatively unexamined in sport emotion research, they represent emotions that confer energy, vivacity and striving among sport performers and harbour untapped utility within sport and society (Seligman and Csikszentmihalyi, 2000).

Happiness is a positively toned emotion that remains contemporary among society's goals despite cultural changes, secular trends and the passage of time. It resonates with our social milieu as much now as when Aristotle considered it as the complete use of a person's physical and mental resources (Lazarus, 1999). Perhaps its acclaim endures today because Thomas Jefferson, in penning the United States Declaration of Independence, proclaimed the 'pursuit of happiness' as an 'an unalienable right of all men [sic]'. He did not state that we have a right to happiness; rather, we have a right to *pursue* happiness, and research abounds to clarify this distinction (Diener and Oishi, 2005). Aristotle and Jefferson shared a common understanding about happiness that is widespread in today's psychology literature – happiness represents a process rather than an outcome, a fulfilment through journeying rather than arriving. Though an archetypal sketch of the meaning of happiness might prompt pictures of successful outcomes, such as winning Olympic medals, major tournaments or grand slams, we skip unknowingly over the richness of the process. Unquestionably, happiness is a helpful, positive emotion (Hanin, 2000) that psychologists know relatively little about in a sport context, except that it has influence over critical constructs such as attention, motivation, self-efficacy and attribution (Vast et al., 2010).

A classic example of the influence of counterfactuals on happiness emerged from Medvec, Madey and Gilovich (1995). Counterfactuals are alternatives to reality (for instance, if only I had started better I could have won this race). They asked students to watch videotaped footage of the 1992 Summer Olympics and judge the happiness of the medallists after their events or on the podium. Even though silver medallists performed better than bronze medallists, on average bronze medallists appeared happier. Medvec et al. (1995) claimed that the Olympic athletes' emotional reactions were steered by comparing the actual outcome with the easily imagined alternative. For example, the bronze medallists could have finished in fourth place and the silver medallists could have won gold. When Great Britain's Christian Malcolm was beaten on the line by French sprinter Christophe Lemaitre in the 200m at the final of the 2010 European championships, he said:

> I've come through with a medal but I can't believe he caught me on the line. It's hard being so close to winning it. To take a medal, I can't argue with that, but I have mixed emotions. Later on I'll be so happy to have a medal.
>
> *(Hart, 2010, p. 3)*

Perhaps most surprisingly, Medvec et al.'s study examined expectations and showed that these did not have a significant effect on emotions – a finding that contrasts with much previous research and theory (Atkinson, 1958; Weiner, 1985). More recently, McGraw, Mellers and Tetlock (2005) re-examined the predictors of the emotional reactions of Olympic athletes using results from the 2000 Summer Olympics in Sydney. The only difference between the methods for the two studies was that McGraw et al. added gold medallists and non-medallists to the existing set of silver and bronze medallists. They reported that expectations (defined by media predictions or qualifying event finishes) influenced emotions. Athletes with lower expectations were happier than those with higher expectations.

One emotion that features in newspapers excerpts and sports fans' interviews, but which is rarely discussed in the literature, is pride. Sports fans expect their team to play with pride, and when asked to rationalise why their team lost a match, many fans declare that their team lacked pride. But what exactly is pride? Pride is a secondary emotion, similar to embarrassment or shame, rather than a 'basic' emotion like happiness (Sauter, 2010; Tracy and Robins, 2007). An intriguing study by Tracy and Matsumoto (2008) examined non-verbal expressions of pride among athletes following a win in Olympic judo matches. Those who won a fight exhibited behaviours associated with pride such as smiling, tilting their head back, raising their arms and expanding their chest. To counter arguments that these indicators of pride were not learned from visual observation, they reported that congenitally blind Olympic athletes produced similar displays after winning matches. Systematic coding of detailed affective cues holds promise for researchers of affective communication, and especially for researchers in sport who explore intensely emotional situations (Sauter, 2010).

Because sport is intensely emotional and often unpredictable, athletes must believe that they are capable of succeeding, regardless of the challenge set before them. According to Scheier and Carver's (1985) theory of dispositional optimism, if people expect positive outcomes, they will work for the goals set, but if they expect failures, they disengage from the goals set. This behaviour pattern explains why optimists achieve more goals than pessimists (Diener et al., 1999) and why optimists respond to adversity more adaptively than pessimists (Carver, Scheier and Segerstrom, 2010). Researchers have linked optimism with better emotional well-being, more effective coping strategies and better outcomes in many aspects of physical health (Carver et al., 2010). Clearly, optimism represents a construct with much value for sport performers, and the following study illustrates the influence of optimism on performance in a sport context. Seligman and his colleagues (Seligman, 1990) examined whether pessimistic explanatory style predicted poorer than expected athletic performance among university varsity swimmers. They administered the Attributional Style Questionnaire (Peterson et al., 1982; Seligman et al., 1979) to two university varsity-swimming teams at the beginning of the season. Compared with optimistic swimmers, swimmers with a pessimistic explanatory style showed more unexpected poor performances during competition throughout the season. The authors also experimentally simulated defeat, giving each swimmer falsely negative times. Swimmers with a pessimistic explanatory style for bad events deteriorated in performance on their next swim, whereas swimmers with an optimistic explanatory style did not.

Collectively, happiness, pride, hope and optimism, along with passion and resilience, are emotions worth researching in sport contexts because these emotions should help athletes to cope with adversity. They also echo the language of sports fans, coaches and athletes. They feature in pre- and post-match interviews, pre-game and half time pep talks, in newspaper reports and in the sport arena. But more importantly, these emotions contour the pathway to successful performances and psychological well-being (Carver et al., 2010). From this standpoint, I present the next section and heart of this chapter.

Putting psychological strategies to good affect

Travails through competitive sport shape the balance of emotions that brings each performer success; yet re-establishing this emotional blend or zone of optimal functioning (Hanin, 2000; Robazza et al., 2004) for each performance proves elusive for many. Poor performances intensify the performer's will to eliminate or at least reduce the malaise associated with those emotions that linger in the memory when the contest ends. Sometimes, those memories never fade. When Doug Sanders, who lost the British Open in 1970 by missing a short putt that would have crowned his achievement, was asked if he ever thinks about the putt now, he replied, 'Only once every four or five minutes' (Gordon, 2005). According to Bower's (1981) theory of mood and memory, each performance is associated in memory with the emotion that predominated at that time. Our emotional state activates memories consistent with that state, so good performances and positive beliefs are easier to recall when people feel happy, but poor performances reflect our failures and breed disappointment when we feel sad (Kavanagh and Hausfeld, 1986). These emotions, then, arise not only as a feature of the preceding contest but also serve a foretaste of the following contest. When golfer Tom Watson asked fellow professional Lee Trevino if he ever got nervous playing golf, Lee replied, 'Some days I wake up and I'm so nervous I cannot hold the fork steady at breakfast' (Elliot, 2009, p. 10).

It seems axiomatic that sport psychologists should ease the effects of negative emotions such as unwanted anxiety on performance; but lateral thought would suggest to accentuate the positive – focus on increasing those emotions that serve a performance benefit whilst discounting those emotions that serve a performance deficit. In other words, rather than 'fixing' a gymnast's unconstructive response to competitive anxiety, it might be timely to enhance her positive emotions and generate good memories of past successes (Boyer, 1981; Kavanagh and Hausfeld, 1986). The impetus of research on positive emotion in mainstream psychology hints at the prudence of this suggestion (Fredrickson, 2000). To illustrate this point, a recent fMRI study explained that athletes who fail are susceptible to negative affect and impaired performance in future; however, a cognitive intervention may alleviate the harmful effects of negative affect (Davis et al., 2008). During fMRI, thirteen elite swimmers first engaged in negative self-reference by watching their failed races which resulted in negative affect, as predicted by Beck's (1967) cognitive model of depression. After a brief cognitive intervention designed to reappraise the event and planning for future performances, the swimmers then viewed the failed performance again, and this gave rise to considerably less negative affect.

Based on findings from numerous experiments, Isen (2009) concluded that inducing even a mildly positive mood greatly benefits social interactions, thinking and problem solving. If we accept this claim that emotions are amenable to change, perhaps sport performers' exploits and psychological well-being would profit from engendering more positive emotional experiences using psychological strategies. For example, promises of a reward, listening to music pieces or watching comical sketches can increase our experience of positive emotions. Psychological techniques such as goal setting, mental imagery, self-talk and relaxation can also achieve this goal in two ways. First, they can improve performance, which is enjoyable and fulfilling in itself, and second, they enhance a sport performer's perceived competence and control, which in turn enhances the subjective experience of positive emotion (Barker and Jones, 2008; McCarthy, 2009).

In basic and applied research, researchers manipulate emotions by asking participants to watch film clips or listen to music. Although listening to music triggers appropriate emotional changes, the physiological changes associated with watching a film are much greater, while knowing the story of a film induces the greatest emotional reaction (Gross and Levenson, 1995). One popular method to induce a positive emotion such as amusement is using video clips of penguins waddling, swimming and jumping, and watching particular clips of the film *Cliffhanger* (1993) (which portrayed mountain climbers scaling treacherous peaks in the Rocky Mountains) elicits anxiety and fear (Fredrickson and Branigan, 2005). That films manipulate our emotions has implications for coaches and managers whose teams watch motivational tales of winning against all odds (such as *Any Given Sunday* (1999) and *Invictus* (2009)) whilst travelling to matches. By establishing the emotions fashioned by these movies, sport psychologists could gauge whether these movies advance or impede performance.

Apart from movies, many sport performers listen to music as they prepare for performance, and in some sports, listening to music at the appropriate time can significantly influence readiness to perform well (Karageorghis et al., 2009; Rauscher, Shaw and Ky, 1993). Anecdotes from professional athletes hint that listening to music before performing could improve performance. For example, the England rugby team listened to 'Lose yourself' by Eminem before their success in the 2003 World Cup final. Before her double-gold-medal success at the 2004 Olympics Games in Athens, Kelly Holmes listened to 'If I ain't got you' by Alicia Keys (Kremer and Moran, 2008). Music serves sport performers in at least three ways (Karageorghis, Terry and Lane, 1999). First, music can alter psychomotor arousal, thereby stimulating or relaxing the performer. Second, music narrows a performer's attention and can divert attention away from fatigue. Finally, music can enhance the positive dimensions and moderate the negative dimensions of mood. Music, however, is seldom structured or used systematically in sport (Simpson and Karageorghis, 2006), and despite its use among sport performers preparing for competition, few studies have specifically investigated how individuals engaged in sporting activity use music to prepare for performance (Bishop, Karageorghis and Loizou, 2007). We know that adolescents use music to regulate mood, but what we need to know is how sport performers select pre-performance music, and its intended or actual affective and motivational consequences (Bishop et al., 2007).

In addition to using film clips and music excerpts to induce positive emotions, I now elaborate on my earlier proposal that basic psychological skills could enhance positive emotions in two ways: by improving performance and/or by increasing perceived competence and perceived control. I limit my proposal to the four basic psychological skills outlined in Hardy, Jones and Gould (1996): goal setting, mental imagery, self-talk and relaxation.

Goal setting

Goal setting presents a popular technique to improve performance in sport (Gould, 1998). Although researchers (Locke et al., 1981) have demonstrated the beneficial influence of goal setting on performance in many settings (such as business), they have observed only small to moderate effects in sport (Kyllo and Landers, 1995), perhaps because methodological and conceptual problems have plagued this research (Moran, 1996). Accumulating research proposes that having goals, making progress towards goals and concord among one's goals predict subjective well-being (Emmons, 1986; Myers and Diener, 1995). This proposal sounds conceivable for a few reasons. First, numerous researchers exploring the relation between emotion and goal orientation have demonstrated that task orientation is associated with positive affect. Second, Csikszentmihalyi (1990) explained that happiness emerges from mindful challenge rather than mindless passivity (Myers and Diener,

1995). Finally, when researchers scratch the surface of goal setting, they recognise the difference between goal setting – committing oneself to reaching desired outcomes or performing desired behaviours – and goal attainment, solving problems related to starting and persisting until the goal is attained (Gollwitzer, 1999). It is goal attainment rather than goal setting that allows one to feel a sense of achievement, which generates positive emotions.

Goals offer a direct strategy to enhance motivation by focusing attention on a task, increasing effort and intensity, encouraging persistence when failure looms, and promoting new task strategies (Burton and Weiss, 2008; Locke and Latham, 1990). Altering self-confidence is a second strategy that produces changes in a performer's beliefs about themselves and their ability (Burton and Weiss, 2008). Setting and attaining goals boosts a performer's confidence because through progressive goal attainment, performance accomplishments accumulate over time. Subsequently these feelings of increased confidence and motivation evoke positive emotions.

But which goals best induce these positive emotions? The consistent findings from over 500 goal-setting studies (Burton and Weiss, 2008; Kyllo and Landers, 1995; Locke and Latham, 1990; Weinberg, 1994) suggest that specific, difficult goals trigger better performances than vague do–your–best goals or no goals. Cumulatively, as a performance enhancement tool within and outside sport, it boasts few rivals. But what accounts for its potency? And are all goals created equal? To answer these questions satisfactorily, we need to examine goal types and disassemble their machinery.

Three goal types feature in the goal-setting literature: process, performance and outcome (Burton and Weiss, 2008). Process goals denote improving form, technique and strategy. Performance goals emphasise improving general performance relatively independently of others (such as running a race within a particular time). Outcome goals represent achieving objective outcomes (such as winning). The swell of support among goal-setting researchers in sport favours process and performance goals over outcome goals; yet outcome goals are vital to develop goal commitment (Hardy, 1997). It seems that although outcome goals matter, they matter less than process and performance goals, because outcome goals such as winning are vulnerable to the vagaries of competitive sport. Few athletes can win each time they play, because sport is typically a zero-sum game. In other words, if one athlete wins, the other loses. And if athletes base their self-confidence on winning or outperforming others, their self-confidence might destabilise without continued success. To address this concern, athletes should overhaul their goals and put winning into perspective with realistic performance and process goals. When goals become controllable, the disappointment and dejection lessens because performers gain more positive competitive cognitions and performance (Burton, 1989). Controllable goals bestow security on the performer because specific behaviours, if executed well, transport the performer towards objective success. The level of each challenge can be raised or lowered by the performer to ensure each challenge is optimal, stretching to maintain motivated behaviour and enduring positive emotions. When a performer achieves a goal, that goal signals and endows motivational resilience and emotional strength. The outcome goal lists the coordinates on the achievement map, but process and performance goals contain the specific directions to those coordinates.

In summary, most theories of motivation suggest that emotions have motivational consequences that influence beliefs, goal orientations, goal types, processes and responses (Burton and Weiss, 2008). When athletes engage successfully in goal setting, positive emotions amass to catalyse functional motivation. The role of emotion, therefore, ought to be considered seriously in goal-setting research because positive emotions (such as enjoyment and happiness) pull us towards challenges and higher levels of functioning in sport that support both performance and psychological well-being (Jones et al., 2009; Myers and Diener, 1995).

Mental imagery

Mental imagery, or the ability to create or recreate an experience in the mind, offers a fashionable and effective psychological technique to enhance motor control, fuel motivation and regulate emotion (Casby and Moran, 1998; Murphy, Nordin and Cumming, 2008). Mental imagery figures prominently in athletes' diaries while they prepare for competition. For instance, Liz McColgan, former 10,000m world champion, explained:

> I do visualize myself running with people around me, no faces, just people. I visualize myself and how I feel in the race and how I see the race developing and things like that. I visualize how I finish the race, how I feel after the race and the recovery after it.
>
> *(Beattie, 1998, p. 95)*

Added to athletes' anecdotal support, much research has accumulated to support the constructive influence of imagery on athletic performance, and sport psychologists endorse its effect on mental attributes such as self-confidence and motivation to secure athletic success (Gould, Damarjian and Greenleaf, 2002; Martin, Moritz and Hall, 1999). The folly of many unsuccessful athletes witnesses them falter in the cauldron of competitive sport because they have not used mental imagery effectively. Ostensibly, imagery grants the sport performer a means to exploit what the mind has to offer, and strengthening emotional control seems paramount in this endeavour. But could imagery fortify positive emotions among sport performers?

Proposed models of imagery in sport suggest emotion as a function and outcome of imagery (Murphy et al., 2008). Functions of imagery include understanding and solving problems, developing motor control, enhancing motivation and self-confidence, and changing arousal and affect. The outcomes emanating from the imagery process can be cognitive (such as improved decision making), behavioural (such as a more consistent routine), or affective (such as increased enjoyment).

However, the benefits of the affective dimension of imagery are twofold, as enjoyment can be used to illustrate. Enjoyment might be a goal or a by-product of imagery. It would be a goal of imagery if the athlete aimed to boost her enjoyment by imagining enjoying the challenge of competing against difficult opponents or in unpredictable environments. It would be a by-product of imagery if the process of imagery was enjoyable in and of itself. The available research supports this point (Cumming and Hall, 2002; Cumming, Hall and Starkes, 2005), thus, not only could imagery confer greater enjoyment to an athlete, also the experience itself is enjoyable.

Much of the research interest on affect and imagery in sport converged on one emotion: performance anxiety. The zeitgeist in sport psychology over the past thirty years rationalises why this emotion received empirical scrutiny while other emotions were eclipsed. The outcome of this research illustrated that imagery can reduce anxiety symptoms or alter how performers interpret such symptoms to perceive them as more facilitative for performance (Fletcher and Hanton, 2001; Hanton and Jones, 1999; Vadocz, Hall and Moritz, 1997). Related to this function, research also implies that imagery serves as a psyching up and calming down strategy (Munroe et al., 2000; White and Hardy, 1998). A recent surge of interest in imagery perspectives holds promise for imagery research on positive emotion in sport. To explain, we can adopt two perspectives to image visually. When we imagine looking at ourselves, we operate an observer (or external) perspective, and when we imagine looking at ourselves through our own eyes, we operate a field (or internal) perspective. From an emotional standpoint, these two perspectives vary in emotional intensity. For example, cognitive and clinical theories advocate that observer perspective imagery reduces emotional intensity compared with field perspective imagery (Holmes, Coughtrey and Connor, 2008). A recent study by Holmes et al. (2008) explored the relation between imagery perspective and positive emotion. Participants imagined 100 positive descriptions either from a field perspective or an observer perspective, or thought about their verbal meaning. Field imagery generated more positive affect than observer imagery, and verbal conditions and mood deteriorated in the latter two. Many elite athletes favour a field imagery perspective, though task type might influence this view. At face value, perhaps as athletes advance to elite or expert status, the field perspective amplifies the emotional charge in the mind's eye of the performer fulfilling the elaborate context of high-performance sport. But why do athletes use imagery? And how is emotion involved?

Hall et al. (1998) developed the Sport Imagery Questionnaire to measure why athletes use imagery. They identified five functions of imagery that operate on a general or specific level. Cognitive general imagery (CG) refers to imaging successful strategies, game plans, or routines while cognitive specific imagery (CS) involves imaging specific sport skills. The motivational specific (MS) function of imagery includes imaging individual goals such as winning a medal. The motivational general (MG) function comprises MG-arousal (MG-A), which involves imaging feelings associated with arousal and stress, and MG-mastery (MG-

M), which includes imagery related to being confident and mastering challenging situations. In sport, only a few studies have specifically examined whether imagery can generate positive emotions (Jones et al., 2002; McCarthy, 2009). Jones et al. (2002) used MG-M and MG-A imagery with novice rock climbers to modify their cognitions and eliminate distress when placed under stress. MG-M and MG-A offer a way to generate positive emotions among sport performers, and in youth sport, athletes tend to use MG-M imagery more than any other type of imagery (Cumming et al., 2002; Harwood, Cumming and Hall, 2003). At least one theoretical backcloth could clarify this proclivity for MG-M imagery among youth athletes. Children and adolescents display a natural tendency to demonstrate mastery in achievement domains such as sport (Harter, 1978, 1981). When they overcome challenges and master skills they demonstrate competence within that achievement domain, which is intrinsically enjoyable. Such positive emotion begets greater positive emotion by seeking and mastering greater challenges.

Self-talk

Self-talk implies the voice or internal dialogue that sounds in our mind (Cornelius, 2002). It resonates overtly or covertly, and not only does self-talk feature integrally in psychological interventions (e.g. Hanton and Jones, 1999), scholars also propose self-talk as the key to unlock cognitive control (Zinsser, Bunker and Williams, 1998). With such espousal, it seems surprising that until recently, self-talk lacked systematic scrutiny in the sport and exercise psychology literature and endured at least one other recurring quandary: failing to define the construct satisfactorily (Hardy, 2006). But we have witnessed conceptual ambiguity blight other fields of research in sport and exercise psychology such as mental imagery, and it inevitably knots the threads of self-talk research. On this occasion, however, compromised conceptual clarity could be avoided because relevant theories to study self-talk emerged in previous research (e.g. Landin, 1994). Perhaps the most interesting mark of self-talk for this chapter is that self-talk is critical to emotional state, and because we can regulate self-talk, we can regulate our emotional state (Ellis, 1977). We shall pluck the thread of this argument later. First, however, we ought to gauge the precise nature and function of self-talk among athletes.

Self-talk functions to help athletes to learn skills, correct bad habits, prepare for performance, focus attention, craft an appropriate mood for performance and build confidence (Hardy, 2006; Williams and Leffingwell, 2002). Its applications deepen and widen the athlete's toolbox to support performance in competitive sport. The character of self-talk separates successful athletes from less successful athletes because successful athletes seem to have fewer negative thoughts, more task-related thoughts, greater focus and positive expectancies (Cornelius, 2002). Several studies including elite and non-elite sport performers attest to its value. For instance, Orlick and Partington (1988) interviewed seventy-five Canadian Olympians from the 1984 Olympic Games, where the best athletes reported using self-talk to 'feel the way they wanted to feel' to prepare for competition. When Hardy, Gammage and Hall (2001) surveyed 150 college athletes about their use of self-talk, they explained that they developed and used self-talk to control their emotional state in sport. These strategies have been used successfully in meaning-focused coping to generate positive emotion. Meaning-focused coping is appraisal-based coping in which the person calls upon beliefs, values and existential goals to sustain coping and well-being during a difficult time (Folkman, 2008; Park and Folkman, 1997). Such meaning-focused coping could be applied in sport and exercise contexts, especially to cope with stress.

The cumulative research on the functions of self-talk implies that athletes draw on this skill for instructional and motivational functions. The instructional function comprises skills and strategy, whereas the motivational functions include arousal, mastery and drive (Hardy, 2006; Hardy and Hall, 2001). The arousal function refers to psyching up, relaxation and controlling arousal. The motivational mastery function is related to confidence, focus and mental preparation, and the motivational drive function helps athletes to commit to achieving their goals. Research on how often a performer uses self-talk – self-talk frequency – unearthed a surprising discovery in the literature: increasing exertion and performance was associated with growing use of negative self-talk (Hardy, Hardy et al., 2001). The authors suggested that mood was a covariate in this relationship, and greater exertion generated greater negative mood (e.g. Parfitt, Eston and Connolly, 1996; Parfitt, Markland and Holmes, 1994); however, clarifying the instructional and motivational nature of self-talk seems prudent. From a practical perspective, simply reframing adverse events in a positive light and permeating ordinary events with positive value can help create more positive emotions (Fredrickson, 2000).

Relaxation

The final psychological technique we examine in relation to positive emotion is relaxation. Relaxation is used to reduce arousal in sport performers, and perhaps it is sensible to first distinguish between mental and physical relaxation (Hardy et al., 1996). Mental relaxation refers to quieting the mind (for instance, reducing worry) to focus on the task at hand, whereas physical relaxation focuses on reducing physiological arousal manifest in indicators such as blood pressure, respiration rate, heart rate and muscle tension. To help a performer reduce unnecessary worry or tension, we can use cognitive techniques and relaxation exercises. Cognitive techniques might include thought stopping, attentional control strategies or imagery. But perhaps the most widely recognised techniques for relaxing an athlete aim to reduce physiological arousal. These techniques include breathing exercises, progressive relaxation, autogenic training and meditation, and have been described thoroughly elsewhere (e.g. Gill and Williams, 2008; Williams, 2010). Relaxation techniques, therefore, rarely focus on increasing positive emotion; however, one could argue that the relaxation response imbues at least one helpful positive emotion: contentment (Fredrickson, 2000). Based on Fredrickson's (1998) broaden–and–build model, learning how to relax offers a personal resource to help a person to cope in the future, but research to qualify this statement has yet to be conducted in a sport context.

Several sport psychologists have intervened with sport performers to ease the harmful effects of anxiety on their performances, and demonstrated the merits of relaxation strategies for this purpose (Maynard et al., 1998). These scholars proceeded thoughtfully because the most effective relaxation treatments are those directed at the type of symptoms experienced by the client (Davidson and Schwartz, 1976). For instance, a cognitive relaxation procedure might be most appropriate for unhelpful cognitive anxiety, and a somatic relaxation procedure might be most effective for somatic symptoms (Maynard et al., 1998). This 'matching hypothesis' aims to treat the most prominent form of anxiety suffered by the client, and to treat cognitive and somatic anxiety concurrently (Maynard, Smith and Warwick-Evans, 1995). Successful sport performers appear to use relaxation strategies more than less successful athletes. For instance, Bois et al. (2009) studied the psychological characteristics of forty-one male professional golfers and their relation to golf performance the day before an official competition. Players who made the 'cut' (a procedure to select the best-performing golfers after the first two days of a typical four-day tournament) were labelled 'successful golfers', and those who missed the cut were labelled 'unsuccessful golfers'. Successful golfers scored higher than unsuccessful golfers on their use of relaxation strategies, and a multiple regression analysis revealed that more frequent use of these strategies was associated with better players' rankings at the end of competition. A remarkable finding also emerged – successful golfers reported higher cognitive and somatic anxiety than unsuccessful golfers. In this study, players who made the cut were cognitively and somatically more anxious at the beginning of the competition than those who did not make the cut. This does reinforce two findings from the literature. First, increases in cognitive anxiety do not necessarily produce impaired performance (Hardy, Woodman and Carrington, 2004; Jokela and Hanin, 1999), and more skilled performers worry earlier as they prepare to perform (Epstein and Fenz, 1965; Fenz and Epstein, 1967; Fenz and Jones, 1972). To illustrate the last point, Epstein and Fenz (1965) showed that novice and experienced parachutists reported reliable patterns of heart rate, respiration rate and skin conductance when recordings were taken during a jump sequence. Recordings were taken when the parachutists arrived at the airport to the time when they prepared to jump: the ride up in the aircraft, reaching the exit point, and after landing. A gradual increase in reactivity emerged on all three measures in inexperienced parachutists until the last point immediately before jumping. In contrast, among experienced jumpers, an increase in autonomic activity emerged early in the jump sequence, followed by a decrease with arousal levels almost at baseline levels at the moment of the jump.

One technique with a relaxation component that offers multiple benefits for sport performers, especially to boost positive emotions, is hypnosis. Hypnosis alters long-term behaviour by changing thoughts, feelings, perceptions and sensations using hypnotic suggestions. These suggestions dissociate executive control from monitoring functions within the brain. This works conveniently because the non-conscious part of the cognitive control structure acts in response to suggestions and images without involving likely critical conscious awareness (Barker, Jones and Greenlees, 2010; Hilgard, 1994). Barker and Jones (2008) used a hypnosis intervention with a professional soccer player to overcome low self-efficacy and negative mood state relating to his soccer performance. The hypnosis intervention used eight hypnosis sessions comprising ego-strengthening suggestions. A substantial increase in positive affect and decrease in negative affect emerged over the course of the intervention.

In summary, relaxation strategies aim to reduce negative emotions rather than increase positive emotions; however, these strategies could infuse at least one positive emotion: contentment. Understanding whether relaxation strategies increase contentment or other positive emotions in sport settings seems sensible because these strategies are used more by successful than less successful sport performers.

Research directions

It seems reasonable to suggest that positive emotions have yet to receive the status they merit in emotion research in sport psychology; however, interest in positive emotions is gathering pace (Jones et al., 2005; Martinet and Ferrand, 2009; Robazza et al., 2004; Skinner and Brewer, 2004). The next challenge is to widen the contours of emotion research by explicitly examining how emotions such as happiness, pride, hope, resilience, passion and excitement influence psychological well-being and performance in sport. This research should resonate with coaches and fans who wax polemical for passion, resilience and optimism; coaches want athletes to enjoy themselves and deliver superlative performances, fans yearn for athletes to share the hope and optimism they have and to play with pride. Perhaps sport psychologists could attend to these words, which are as yet not properly understood conceptually or methodologically in a sport setting (Woodman et al., 2009). Fortunately, some researchers have blazed a trail for others to follow, such as Vallerand and his colleagues' study of passion in sport (Vallerand et al., 2006).

Some notable findings from contemporary research proposed that positive emotions could help sport performers to concentrate better and execute sport skills efficiently (Vast et al., 2010). When people experience positive emotion, they broaden their attention, which fosters openness, flexibility and an efficient integration of information (Derryberry and Tucker, 1994; Fredrickson, 2001). Because positive emotions can also occur without disrupting task execution (Carver, 2004; Carver and Scheier, 1990), unlike unwanted anxiety, increasing their prominence among sport performers might also alleviate choking. This suggestion could be tested empirically within a laboratory setting. Recently, Vast et al. (2010) explored attentional patterns associated with positive and negative emotions during sport competition among national and international softballers. They reported that excitement and happiness were positively correlated with concentration, whereas dejection and anger were negatively correlated with concentration, dejection and anger. The softballers perceived positive emotions as more likely to produce a performance-relevant focus. Because positive emotions can also occur without disrupting task execution (Carver, 2004; Carver and Scheier, 1990), unlike unwanted anxiety, increasing their prominence among sport performers might also alleviate choking.

Only a few studies have explicitly examined whether psychological skills such as goal setting, mental imagery, self-talk and relaxation can generate positive emotions such as happiness or resilience among sport performers (McCarthy, 2009; McCarthy et al., 2010). There is sound evidence to support the contention that these psychological skills improve performance and constructs necessary for successful performance (such as self-efficacy), but less obvious is their effect on positive emotions. It seems reasonable to assume that athletes would feel happy or satisfied with improved performance, or at least with progress towards outcome goals which would spawn greater interest and commitment towards those goals. Seligman et al. (2005) insisted that psychological interventions to increase individual happiness are in many ways the core of work in positive psychology. Perhaps such interventions will become the core of sport psychologists' work in professional practice if they generate improved performance and psychological well-being.

Positive emotions also benefit sports teams because when we are in a good mood, we are more likely to help others (Carlson, Charlin and Miller, 1988). It might be likely, therefore, that players work harder to help each other when they are in a good mood. One reason this may be the case is that people who feel good undergo greater self-awareness, prompting them to match their behaviour with their internal values (Carlson et al., 1988). Indeed, people looking at themselves in the mirror are more cooperative than those who are not (Batson et al., 1999). This strategy of looking at one's face in the mirror makes us more aware of the differences between our behaviour and salient personal standards (Wicklund, 1975). But if we are feeling good, can those around us link with this positive feeling? Totterdell's (2000) study of mood linkage among professional cricketers suggested that players perform better when their team mates are happier. And this mood linkage was larger for those players who were older, more committed to the team and more vulnerable to emotional contagion. Unfortunately, just as good moods spread among team members so too do bad moods (Totterdell et al., 1998).

Finally, meaning-focused coping generates positive emotions through at least five strategies: benefit finding, benefit reminding, adaptive goal processes, reordering priorities and infusing ordinary events with positive meaning (Folkman and Moskowitz, 2007). Some of these strategies intertwine with psychological skills such as goal setting, mental imagery, self-talk and relaxation. In their own right, these strategies have successfully improved mental and physical well-being during difficult times (Folkman and Moskowitz, 2007; Tugade and Fredrickson, 2006). Sport researchers could begin to establish whether these five strategies are fruitful in sport settings, and how exactly they regulate positive rather than negative emotions.

Summary

When we examine the potted history of emotion research, we notice that positive emotions have remained on the periphery not only in sport and exercise psychology, but also in other areas of psychology. In 1991, Susan Harter expressed her delight that psychologists now consider affect in their research:

> It is refreshing to see that psychologists have recently discovered affect. Emotion is now in. Hedonic tone is legitimate. We've reinvented another wheel. And we feel good about it ...! I would like to convince others that any compelling theory must make room for affect as well as cognition and behaviour. Lots of room. In fact, affect should be given center stage.
>
> *(Harter, 1991, p. 5)*

Although negatively toned emotions have dominated the emotion research in sport and exercise psychology (Hanin, 2000; Cerin, 2003), recent developments in other areas of psychology mean that positive emotions warrant attention – positive emotions are now in (Fredrickson, 2003). In sport and exercise psychology, we need to understand the efficacy and effectiveness of interventions such as goal setting, mental imagery and finding positive meaning to generate positive emotions. Generating positive emotions might benefit sport performance as well as psychological well-being, and we are fortunate to have Fredrickson's (1998) broaden-and-build model to test in the sport arena. No doubt we will encounter conceptual and methodological issues again, but by addressing them we can advance the field of emotion research in sport and exercise psychology.

References

Atkinson, J. W. (1958). *Motives in fantasy, action and society*. Princeton, N.J.: Van Nostrand.

Averill, J. R. (1980). A constructivist view of emotion. In R. Plutchik and H. Kellerman (eds), *Emotion: Theory, research and experience: Vol. I. Theories of emotion* (pp. 305–339). New York: Academic Press.

Bakker, F. C., De Koning, J. J., Van Ingen Schenau, G. J. and De Groot, G. (1993). Motivation of young elite speed skaters. *International Journal of Sport Psychology*, 24, 432–442.

Barker, J. B. and Jones, M. V. (2008). The effects of hypnosis on self-efficacy, affect and sport performance: a case study from professional English soccer. *Journal of Clinical Sport Psychology*, 2, 127–147.

Barker, J., Jones, M. and Greenlees, I. (2010). Assessing the immediate and maintained effects of hypnosis on self-efficacy and soccer wall-volley performance. *Journal of Sport and Exercise Psychology*, 32, 243–252.

Batson, C. D., Thompson, E. R., Seuferling, G., Whitney, H. and Strongman, J. A. (1999). Moral hypocrisy: appearing moral to oneself without being so. *Journal of Personality and Social Psychology*, 77, 525–537.

Beattie, G. (1998). *Head to head: Uncovering the psychology of sporting success*. London: Victor Gollancz.

Beck, A. T. (1967). *Depression: Clinical, experimental and theoretical aspects*. New York: Harper & Row.

Bishop, D. T., Karageorghis, C. I. and Loizou, G. (2007). A grounded theory of young tennis players' use of music to manipulate emotional state. *Journal of Sport and Exercise Psychology*, 29, 584–607.

Bois, J. E., Sarrazin, P. G., Southon, J. and Boiché, J. C. S. (2009). Psychological characteristics and their relation to performance in professional golfers. *The Sport Psychologist*, 23, 252–270.

Boniwell, I. (2008). *Positive psychology in a nutshell*, 2nd edn. London: PWBC.

Bower, G. H. (1981). Mood and memory. *American Psychologist*, 36, 129–148.

Boyd, M. P. and Yin, Z. (1996). Cognitive-affective sources of sport enjoyment in adolescent sport participants. *Adolescence*, 31, 383–395.

Burton, D. (1989). Winning isn't everything: examining the impact of performance goals on collegiate swimmers' cognitions and performance. *The Sport Psychologist*, 3, 105–132.

Burton, D. and Weiss, C. (2008). The fundamental goal concept: the path to process and performance success. In T. S. Horn (ed.), *Advances in sport psychology*, 3rd edn (pp. 339–375). Champaign, Ill.: Human Kinetics.

Cacioppo, J. T., Klein, D. J., Berntson, G. G. and Hatfield, E. (1993). The psychophysiology of emotion. In R. Lewis and J. M. Haviland (eds), *The handbook of emotion* (pp. 119–142). New York: Guilford Press.

Carver, C. S. (2003). Pleasure as a sign you can attend to something else: placing positive feelings within a general model of affect. *Cognition and Emotion*, 17, 241–261.

Carver, C. S. (2004). Negative affects deriving from the behavioural approach system. *Emotion*, 4, 3–22.

Carver, C. S. and Scheier, M. F. (1990). Origins and functions of positive and negative affect: a control–process view. *Psychological Review*, 97, 19–35.

Carver, C. S., Scheier, M. F. and Segerstrom, S. C. (2010). Optimism. *Clinical Psychology Review*, 30, 879–889.

Carlson, M., Charlin, V. and Miller, N. (1988). Positive mood and helping behaviour: a test of six hypotheses. *Journal of Personality and Social Psychology*, 55, 211–229.

Casby, A. and Moran, A. P. (1998). Exploring mental imagery in swimmers: a single-case study. *Irish Journal of Psychology*, 19, 525–531.

Cerin, E. (2003). Anxiety versus fundamental emotions as predictors of perceived functionality of pre-competitive emotional states, threat and challenge in individual sports. *Journal of Applied Sport Psychology*, 15, 223–238.

Cerin, E., Szabo, A., Hunt, N. and Williams, C. (2000). Temporal patterning of competitive emotions: a critical review. *Journal of Sports Sciences*, 18, 605–625.

Cohn, P. J. (1991). An exploratory study of sources of stress and athlete burnout in youth golf. *The Sport Psychologist*, 4, 95–106.

Cornelius, A. (2002). Intervention techniques in sport psychology. In J. M. Silva III and D. E. Stevens (eds), *Psychological foundations of sport* (pp. 177–196). Boston, Mass.: Allyn & Bacon.

Cosmides, L. and Tooby, J. (1995). From evolution to adaptations to behaviors. In R. Wong (ed.), *Biological perspectives on motivated activities* (pp. 11–65). Norwood, N.J.: Ablex.

Csikszentmihalyi, M. (1990). *Flow: The psychology of optimal experience*. New York: Harper & Row.

Cumming, J. and Hall, C. (2002). Athletes' use of imagery in the off-season. *The Sport Psychologist*, 16, 160–172.

Cumming, J. C., Hall, C. J., Harwood, C. and Gammage, K. (2002). Motivational orientations and imagery use: a goal perspective. *Journal of Sports Sciences*, 20, 127–136.

Cumming, J., Hall, C. and Starkes, J. L. (2005). Deliberate imagery practice: examining the reliability of a retrospective recall methodology. *Research Quarterly for Exercise and Sport*, 76, 306–314.

Danner, D. D., Snowdon, D. A. and Friesen, W. V. (2001). Positive emotions in early life and longevity: findings from the nun study. *Journal of Personality and Social Psychology*, 80, 804–813.

Davidson, R. J., Kabat-Zinn, J., Schumacher, J., Rosenkranz, M., Muller, D., Santorelli, S. F., et al. (2003). Alterations in brain and immune function produced by mindfulness meditation. *Psychosomatic Medicine*, 65, 564–570.

Davidson, R. J. and Schwartz, G. E. (1976). The psychobiology of relaxation and related states: a multiprocess theory. In D. I. Mostofsky (ed.), *Behavioural control and modification of physiological activity*. Englewood Cliffs, N.J.: Prentice–Hall.

Davis IV, H., Liotti, M., Ngan, E. T., Woodward, T. S., Van Snellenberg, J. X., van Anders, S. M., Smith, A. and Mayberg, H. S. (2008). fMRI BOLD signal changes in elite swimmers while viewing videos of personal failure. *Brain Imaging and Behavior*, 2, 84–93.

Deci, E. (1980). *The psychology of self-determination*. Lexington, Mass.: DD Heath.

Deci, E. L. and Ryan, R. M. (1985). *Intrinsic motivation and self-determination in human behaviour*. New York: Plenum Press.

Derryberry, D. and Tucker, D. M. (1994). Motivating the focus of attention. In P. M. Niedenthal and S. Kitayama (eds), *The heart's eye: emotional influences in perception and attention* (pp. 167–196). San Diego, Calif.: Academic Press.

Diener, E. and Oishi, S. (2005). The nonobvious social psychology of happiness. *Psychological Inquiry*, 16, 162–167.

Diener, E., Suh, M., Lucas, E. and Smith, H. (1999). Subjective well-being: three decades of progress. *Psychological Bulletin*, 125, 276–302.

Duda, J. L., Fox, K. R., Biddle, S. J. H. and Armstrong, N. (1992). Children's achievement goals and beliefs about success in sport. *British Journal of Educational Psychology*, 62, 313–323.

Ekman, P. (1992). An argument for basic emotions. *Cognition and Emotion*, 6, 169–200.

Ekman, P., Friesen, W. V., O'Sullivan, M., Chan, A., Diacoyanni-Tarlatzis, I., Heider, K., Krause, R., LeCompre, W. A., Ritcairn, T., Ricci-Bitti, P. E., Scherer, K., Tomita, M. and Tzavras, A. (1987). Universals and cultural differences in the judgments of facial expressions of emotions. *Journal of Personality and Social Psychology*, 53, 712–717.

Ellsworth, P. C. and Smith, C. A. (1988). Shades of joy: patterns of appraisal differentiating pleasant emotions. *Cognition and Emotion*, 2, 301–331.

Elliot, B. (2009). Tom Watson interview: a jewel of a duel. *Observer (Sport)*, p. 10.

Ellis, A. (1977). The basic clinical theory of rational-emotive therapy. In A. Ellis and R. Grieger (eds), *Handbook of rational–emotive therapy* (pp. 3–34). New York: Springer.

Emmons, R. A. (1986). Personal strivings: an approach to personality and subjective well-being. *Journal of Personality and Social Psychology*, 51, 1058–1068.

Epstein, S. and Fenz, W. D. (1965). Steepness of approach and avoidance of gradients in humans as a function of experience: theory and experiment. *Journal of Experimental Psychology*, 70, 1–12.

Fenz, W. D. and Epstein, S. (1967). Gradients of physiological arousal in parachutists as a function of an approaching jump. *Psychosomatic Medicine*, 29, 33–51.

Fenz, W. D. and Jones, G. B. (1972). Individual differences in physiologic arousal and performance in sport parachutists. *Psychosomatic Medicine*, 34, 1–8.

Feldman Barrett L. and Russell J. A. (1998). Independence and bipolarity in the structure of current affect. *Journal of Personality and Social Psychology*, 74, 967–984.

Fletcher, D. and Hanton, S. (2001). The relationship between psychological skills usage and competitive anxiety responses. *Psychology of Sport and Exercise*, 2, 89–101.

Folkman, S. (2008). The case for positive emotions in the stress process. *Anxiety, Stress, and Coping*, 21, 3–14.

Folkman, S. and Moskowitz, J. T. (2007). Positive affect and meaning-focused coping during significant psychological stress. In M. Hewstone, H. Schut, J. d. Wit, K. v. d. Bos and M. Stroebe (eds), *The scope of social psychology: Theory and applications* (pp. 193–208). Hove, UK: Psychology Press.

Fredrickson, B. L. (1998). What good are positive emotions? *Review of General Psychology*, 2, 300–319.

Fredrickson, B. L. (2000). Cultivating positive emotions to optimize health and well-being. *Prevention and Treatment* 3. [online] http://journals.apa.org/prevention/volume3/pre0030001a.html (accessed 18 March 2011).

Fredrickson, B. L. (2001). The role of positive emotions in positive psychology: the broaden-and-build theory of positive emotions. *American Psychologist*, 56, 218–226.

Fredrickson, B. (2003). The value of positive emotions: the emerging science of positive psychology is coming to understand why it's good to feel good. *American Scientist*, 91, 330–335.

Fredrickson, B. L. and Branigan, C. A. (2005). Positive emotions broaden the scope of attention and thought–action repertoires. *Cognition and Emotion,* 19, 313–332.

Frijda, N. H. (1986). *The emotions.* Cambridge: Cambridge University Press.

Gaudreau, P., Blondin, J.-P. and Lapierre, A.-M. (2002). Athletes' coping during a competition: relationship of coping strategies with positive affect, negative affect and performance–goal discrepancy. *Psychology of Sport and Exercise*, 3, 125–150.

Gill, D. L. and Williams, L. (2008). *Psychological dynamics of sport and exercise*, 3rd edn. Champaign, Ill.: Human Kinetics.

Gollwitzer, P. M. (1999). Implementation intentions: strong effects of simple plans. *American Psychologist*, 54, 493–503.

Gordon, P. (2005). Sanders still haunted by that missed putt. *The Times (Sport)*, p. 59.

Gould, D. (1998). Goal setting for peak performance. In J. M. Williams (ed.), *Applied sport psychology: Personal growth to peak performance* (3rd ed., pp. 182–196). Mountain View, Calif.: Mayfield.

Gould, D., Damarjian, N. and Greenleaf, C. (2002). Imagery training for peak performance. In J. Van Raalte and B. W. Brewer (eds), *Exploring sport and exercise psychology*, 2nd edn (pp. 49–74). Washington, DC: American Psychological Association.

Gross, J. J. and Levenson, R. W. (1995). Emotion elicitation using films. *Cognition and Emotion*, 9, 87–108.

Hall, C. R., Mack, D. A., Paivio, A. and Hausenblas, H. A. (1998). Imagery use by athletes: development of the Sport Imagery Questionnaire. *International Journal of Sport Psychology*, 29, 73–89.

Hanin, Y. L. (2000). Successful and poor performance emotions. In Y. L. Hanin (ed.), *Emotions in sport* (pp. 157–187). Champaign, Ill.: Human Kinetics.

Hanton, S. and Jones, J. G. (1999). The acquisition and development of cognitive skills and strategies: I. Making the butterflies fly in formation. *The Sport Psychologist*, 13, 1–21.

Hardy, J. (2006). Speaking clearly: a critical review of the self-talk literature. *Psychology of Sport and Exercise*, 7, 81–97.

Hardy, J., Gammage, K. and Hall, C. R. (2001). A description of athlete self-talk. *The Sport Psychologist*, 15, 306–318.

Hardy, J., Hall, C. R. and Hardy, L. (2005). Quantifying athlete self-talk. *Journal of Sports Sciences*, 23, 905–917.

Hardy, J., Hardy, L. and Hall, C. R. (2001). *Self-talk and perceived exertion in physical activity.* Poster presented at the meeting of the Association for the Advancement of Applied Sport Psychology, Orlando, Fla.

Hardy, L. (1997). Three myths about applied consultancy work. *Journal of Applied Sport Psychology*, 9, 277–294.

Hardy, L., Jones, G. and Gould, D. (1996). *Understanding psychological preparation for sport: Theory and practice of elite performers.* Chichester, UK: John Wiley & Sons.

Hardy, L., Woodman, T. and Carrington, S. (2004). Is self-confidence a bias factor in higher-order catastrophe models? An exploratory analysis. *Journal of Sport and Exercise Psychology*, 26, 359–368.

Hart, S. (2010). When lightning strikes Malcolm. *Daily Telegraph (Sport)*, p. 3.

Harter, S. (1978). Effectance motivation reconsidered: toward a developmental model. *Human Development*, 21, 34–64.

Harter, S. (1981). The development of competence motivation in the mastery of cognitive and physical skills: is there still a place for joy? In C. H. Nadeau (ed.), *Psychology of motor behaviour and sport* (pp. 3–29). Champaign, Ill.: Human Kinetics.

Harwood, C. G., Cumming, J. and Hall, C, (2003). Imagery use in elite youth sport participants: reinforcing the applied significance of achievement goal theory. *Research Quarterly for Exercise and Sport*, 3, 292–300.

Hilgard, E. R. (1994). Neo-dissociation theory. In S. J. Lynn and J. W. Rhue (eds), *Dissociation: Clinical, theoretical and research perspectives* (pp. 83–104). New York: Guilford Press.

Holmes, E. A., Coughtrey, A. E. and Connor, A. (2008). Looking through or at rose-tinted glasses? Imagery perspective and positive mood. *Emotion*, 8, 875–879.

Isen, A. M. (2000). Positive affect and decision making. In M. Lewis and J. Haviland-Jones (eds), *Handbook of emotions*, 2nd edn (pp. 417–435). New York: Guilford.

Isen, A. M. (2009). A role for neuropsychology in understanding the facilitating influence of positive affect on social behaviour and cognitive processes. In S. J. Lopez and C. R. Snyder (eds), *Oxford handbook of positive psychology* (2nd ed., pp. 503–518). New York: Oxford University Press.

Izard, C. (1977). *Human emotions*. New York: Plenum Press.

Jackson, S. A. (1992). Athletes in flow: a qualitative investigation of flow states in elite figure skaters. *Journal of Applied Sport Psychology*, 4, 161–180.

Jackson, S. A. (2000). Joy, fun and flow state in sport. In Y. L. Hanin (ed.), *Emotions in sport* (pp. 135–155). Champaign, Ill.: Human Kinetics.

Jackson, S. A., Thomas, P. R., Marsh, H. W. and Smethurst, C. J. (2001). Relationships between flow, self-concept, psychological skills and performance. *Journal of Applied Sport Psychology*, 13, 129–153.

James, W. (1902). *Varieties of religious experience: A study in human nature*. New York: Longman.

Jokela, M. and Hanin, Y. L. (1999). Does the individual zones of optimal functioning model discriminate between successful and less successful athletes: a meta-analysis. *Journal of Sports Sciences,* 17, 873–887.

Jones, M. V. (2003). Controlling emotions in sport. *The Sport Psychologist*, 17, 471–486.

Jones, M. V., Lane, A. M., Bray, S. R., Uphill, M. and Catlin, J. (2005). Development and validation of the Sport Emotion Questionnaire. *Journal of Sport and Exercise Psychology*, 27, 407–431.

Jones, M. V., Mace, R. D., Bray, S. R., MacRae, A. and Stockbridge, C. (2002). The impact of motivational imagery on the emotional state and self-efficacy levels of novice climbers. *Journal of Sport Behaviour*, 25, 57–73.

Jones, M., Meijen, C., McCarthy, P. J. and Sheffield, D. (2009). A theory of challenge and threat states in athletes. *International Review of Sport and Exercise Psychology*, 2, 161–180.

Karageorghis, C. I., Terry, P. C. and Lane, A. M. (1999). Development and initial validation of an instrument to assess the motivational qualities of music in exercise and sport: the Brunel Music Rating Inventory. *Journal of Sports Sciences*, 17, 713–724.

Karageorghis, C. I., Mouzourides, D. A., Priest, D. L., Sasso, T. A., Morrish, D. J. and Walley, C. J. (2009). Psychophysical and ergogenic effects of synchronous music during treadmill walking. *Journal of Sport and Exercise Psychology*, 31, 18–36.

Kavanagh, D. and Hausfeld, S. (1986). Physical performance and self-efficacy under happy and sad moods. *Journal of Sport Psychology*, 8, 112–123.

Kavussanu, M. and Roberts, G. C. (1996). Motivation in physical activity contexts: the relationship of perceived motivational climate to intrinsic motivation and self-efficacy. *Journal of Sport and Exercise Psychology*, 18, 264–280.

Kimiecik, J. C. and Harris, A. T. (1996). What is enjoyment? A conceptual/definitional analysis with implications for sport and exercise psychology. *Journal of Sport and Exercise Psychology*, 18, 247–263.

Kremer, J. and Moran, A. (2008). *Pure sport: Practical sport psychology*. London: Routledge.

Kyllo, L. B. and Landers, D. M. (1995). Goal setting in sport and exercise: a research synthesis to resolve the controversy. *Journal of Sport and Exercise Psychology*, 17, 117–137.

Landin, D. (1994). The role of verbal cues in skill learning, *Quest*, 46, 299–313.

Lazarus, R. S. (1991). Progress on a cognitive–motivational–relational theory of emotion. *American Psychologist*, 46, 819–834.

Lazarus, R. S. (1999). *Stress and emotion: A new synthesis*. New York: Springer.

Lazarus, R. S. (2000). How emotions influence performance in competitive sports. *The Sport Psychologist*, 14, 229–252.

Levenson, R. W. (1992). Autonomic nervous system differences among emotions. *Psychological Science*, 3, 23–27.

Levenson, R. W., Ekman, P. and Friesen, W. V. (1990). Voluntary facial action generates emotion-specific autonomic nervous system activity. *Psychophysiology*, 27, 363–384.

Locke, E. A. and Latham, G. P. (1990). *A theory of goal setting and task performance*. Englewood Cliffs. N.J.: Prentice Hall.

Locke, E. A., Shaw, K. N., Saari, L. M. and Latham, G. P. (1981). Goal setting and task performance. *Psychological Bulletin*, 90, 125–152.

Longmore, A. (2010). Golden girl Jessica caps week of glory. *Sunday Times (Sport)*, pp. 2–3.

Martin, K. A., Moritz, S. E. and Hall, C. (1999). Imagery use in sport: a literature review and applied model. *The Sport Psychologist*, 13, 245–268.

Martinet, G. and Ferrand, C. (2009). A naturalistic study of the directional interpretation process of discrete emotions during high-stakes table tennis matches. *Journal of Sport and Exercise Psychology*, 31, 318–336.

Maynard, I. W., Hemmings, B., Greenlees, I. A., Warwick-Evans, L. and Stanton, N. (1998). Stress management in sport: a comparison of unimodal and multimodal interventions. *Anxiety, Stress and Coping*, 11, 225–246.

Maynard, I. W., Hemmings, B. and Warwick-Evans, L. (1995). The effects of a somatic intervention strategy on competitive state anxiety and performance in semi-professional soccer players. *The Sport Psychologist*, 9, 51–64.

McCarthy, P. J. (2009). Putting imagery to good affect: case study among competitive youth swimmers. *Sport and Exercise Psychology Review*, 5, 27–38.

McCarthy, P. J. and Jones, M. V. (2007). A qualitative study of sport enjoyment in the sampling years. *The Sport Psychologist*, 21, 400–416.

McCarthy, P. J., Jones, M. V., Harwood, C. G. and Davenport, L. (2010). Using goal setting to enhance positive affect among junior multievent athletes. *Journal of Clinical Sport Psychology*, 4, 53–68.

McGraw, A. P., Mellers, B. A. and Tetlock, P. E. (2005). Expectations and emotions of Olympic athletes. *Journal of Experimental Social Psychology*, 41, 438–446.

Medvec, V. H., Madey, S. F. and Gilovich, T. (1995). When less is more: counterfactual thinking and satisfaction among Olympic medalists. *Journal of Personality and Social Psychology*, 69, 603–610.

Moran, A. P. (1996). *The psychology of concentration in sport performers: A cognitive analysis*. Hove, East Sussex: Psychology Press/Taylor &Francis.

Munroe, K. J., Giaccobi, P. R., Jr, Hall, C. R. and Weinberg, R. (2000).The four w's of imagery use: where, when, why and what. *The Sport Psychologist*, 14, 119–137.

Murphy, S., Nordin, S. and Cumming, J. (2008). Imagery in sport, exercise and dance. In T. S. Horn (ed.), *Advances in sport psychology* (3rd ed., pp. 297–324). Champaign, Ill.: Human Kinetics.

Myers, D. G. and Diener, E. (1995). Who is happy? *Psychological Science*, 6, 10–19.

Orlick, T. and Partington, J. (1988). Mental links to excellence. *The Sport Psychologist*, 2, 105–130.

Parfitt, G., Eston, R. and Connolly, D. (1996) Psychological affect at different ratings of perceived exertion in high- and low-active women: a study using production protocol. *Perceptual and Motor Skills*, 82, 1035–1042.

Parfitt, G., Markland, D. and Holmes, C. (1994). Responses to physical exertion in active and inactive males and females. *Journal of Sport and Exercise Psychology*, 16, 178–186.

Park, C. L. and Folkman, S. (1997). Meaning in the context of stress and coping. *Review of General Psychology*, 2, 115–144.

Peterson, C, Semmel, A., von Baeyer, C., Abramson, L. Y., Metalsky, G. I. and Seligman, M. E. P. (1982). The Attributional Style Questionnaire. *Cognitive Therapy and Research*, 6, 287–299.

Plutchik, R. (1980). A general psychoevolutionary theory of emotion. In R. Plutchik and H. Kellerman (eds), *Emotion: Theory, research and experience: Vol. 1. Theories of emotion* (pp. 3–33). New York: Academic.

Radcliffe, P. (with David Walsh) (2004). *Paula: My story so far: Paula Radcliffe*. London: Simon & Schuster.

Rauscher, F. H., Shaw, G. L. and Ky, K. N. (1993). Music and spatial task performance. *Nature*, 365, 611.

Robazza, C., Bortoli, L., Nocini, F., Moser, G. and Arslan, C. (2000). Normative and idiosyncratic measures of positive and negative affect in sport. *Psychology of Sport and Exercise*, 1, 103–116.

Robazza, C., Pellizzari, M. and Hanin, Y. (2004). Emotion self-regulation and athletic performance: an application of the IZOF model. *Psychology of Sport and Exercise*, 5, 379–404.

Russell, J. A. and Carroll, J. M. (1999). On the bipolarity of positive and negative affect. *Psychological Bulletin*, 125, 3–30.

Russell, J. A. and Feldman Barrett, L. (1999). Core affect, prototypical emotional episodes and other things called emotion: Dissecting the elephant. *Journal of Personality and Social Psychology*, 45, 513–523.

Sauter, D. (2010). More than happy: The need for disentangling positive emotions. *Current Directions in Psychological Science*, 19, 37–40.

Scanlan, T. K. and Simons, J. P. (1992). The construct of sport enjoyment. In G. C. Roberts (ed.), *Motivation in sport and exercise* (pp. 199–215). Champaign, Ill.: Human Kinetics.

Scanlan, T. K., Stein, G. L. and Ravizza, K. (1989). An in-depth study of former elite figure skaters: II. Sources of enjoyment. *Journal of Sport and Exercise Psychology*, 11, 65–83.

Scheier, M. F. and Carver, C. S. (1985). Optimism, coping and health: assessment and implications of generalized outcome expectancies. *Health Psychology*, 4, 219–247.

Seligman, M. E. P. and Csikszentmihalyi, M. (2000). Positive psychology: an introduction. *American Psychologist*, 55, 5–14.

Seligman, M. E. P., Abramson, L., Semmel, A. and von Baeyer, C. (1979). Depressive attributional style. *Journal of Abnormal Psychology*, 88, 242–247.

Seligman, M. E. P., Steen, T. A., Park, N. and Peterson, C. (2005). Positive psychology progress: empirical validation of interventions. *American Psychologist*, 60, 410–421.

Seligman, M. E. P., Nolen-Hoeksema, S., Thornton, N. and Thornton, K. M. (1990). Explanatory style as a mechanism of disappointing athletic performance. *Psychological Science*, 1, 143–146.

Sève, C., Poizat, G., Saury, J. and Durand, M. (2006). A grounded theory of elite male table tennis players' activity during matches. *The Sport Psychologist*, 20, 58–73.

Simpson, P. (2010). Strong start to high life 'surprises' Westwood. *Independent Sport*, Saturday 6 November, p. 19.

Simpson, S. D. and Karageorghis, C. I. (2006). The effects of synchronous music on 400m sprint performance. *Journal of Sports Sciences*, 24, 1095–1102.

Skinner, N. and Brewer, N. (2004). Adaptive approaches to competition: challenge appraisals and positive emotion. *Journal of Sport and Exercise Psychology*, 26, 283–305.

Smith, E. R. and Mackie, D. M. (2007). *Social psychology*, 3rd edn. Philadelphia, Pa.: Psychology Press.

Speca, M., Carlson, L. E., Goodey, E. and Angen, M. (2000). A randomized, wait-list controlled clinical trial: the effect of a mindfulness meditation-based stress reduction program on mood and symptoms of stress in cancer patients. *Psychosomatic Medicine*, 62, 613–622.

Totterdell, P. (2000). Catching moods and hitting runs: mood linkage and subjective performance in professional sport teams. *Journal of Applied Psychology*, 85, 848–859.

Totterdell, P., Kellett, S., Teuchmann, K. and Briner, R. B. (1998). Mood linkage in work groups. *Journal of Personality and Social Psychology*, 74, 1504–1515.

Tracy, J. L. and Matsumoto, D. (2008). The spontaneous expression of pride and shame: evidence for biologically innate nonverbal displays. *Proceedings of the National Academy of Sciences, USA*, 105, 11655–11660.

Tracy, J. L. and Robins, R. W. (2007). Emerging insights into the nature and function of pride. *Current Directions in Psychological Science*, 16, 147–150.

Tugade, M. M. and Fredrickson, B. L. (2006). Regulation of positive emotions: emotion regulation strategies that promote resilience. *Journal of Happiness Studies*, 8, 311–333.

Uphill, M. A., McCarthy, P. J. and Jones, M. V. (2009). Getting a grip on emotion regulation in sport: conceptual foundations and practical applications. In S. Hanton and S. Mellalieu (eds), *Advances in applied sport psychology* (pp. 162–194). London: Routledge.

Vadocz, E. A., Hall, C. R. and Moritz, S. E. (1997). The relationship between competitive anxiety and imagery use. *Journal of Applied Sport Psychology*, 9, 241–253.

Vallerand, R. J. and Blanchard, C. M. (2000). The study of emotion in sport and exercise. In Y. L. Hanin (ed.), *Emotions in sport* (pp. 3–37). Champaign, Ill.: Human Kinetics.

Vallerand, R. J., Rousseau, F. L., Grouzet, F. M. E., Dumais, A., Grenier, S. and Blanchard, C. B. (2006). Passion in sport: a look at determinants and affective experiences. *Journal of Sport and Exercise Psychology*, 28, 454–478.

Vast, R. L., Young, R. L. and Thomas, P. R. (2010). Emotions in sport: perceived effects on attention, concentration and performance. *Australian Psychologist*, 45, 132–140.

Walsh, D. (2009). Getting over the hurdles. *Sunday Times* (Sport), p. 16.

Weinberg, R. S. (1994). Goal setting and performance in sport and exercise settings: a synthesis and critique. *Medicine and Science in Sport and Exercise*, 26, 469–477.

Weiner, B. (1985). An attributional theory of achievement motivation and emotion. *Psychological Bulletin*, 92, 548–573.

Williams, J. M. (2010). *Applied sport psychology: Personal growth to peak performance*. New York: McGraw-Hill.

Williams, J. M. and Leffingwell, T. R. (2002). Cognitive strategies in sport and exercise psychology. In J. Van Raalte and B. W. Brewer (eds), *Exploring sport and exercise psychology*, 2nd ed (pp. 75–98). Washington, DC: American Psychological Association.

White, A. and Hardy, C. (1998). An in-depth analysis of the uses of imagery by high-level slalom canoeists and artistic gymnasts. *The Sport Psychologist*, 12, 387–403.

Wicklund, R. A. (1975). Objective self-awareness. In L. Berkowitz (ed.), *Advances in experimental social psychology* (Vol. 8, pp. 233–275). New York: Academic Press.

Woodman, T., Davis, P. A., Hardy, L., Callow, N., Glasscock, I. and Yuill-Proctor, J. (2009). Emotions and sport performance: an exploration of happiness, hope and anger. *Journal of Sport and Exercise Psychology*, 31, 169–188.

Zinsser, N., Bunker, L. and Williams, J. M. (1998). Cognitive techniques for building confidence and enhancing performance. In J. M. Williams (ed.), *Applied sport psychology: Personal growth to peak performance*, 3rd edn (pp. 270–295). Mount View, Calif.: Mayfield.

9

COPING AND EMOTION IN DISABILITY SPORT

Jeffrey Martin, Wayne State University

Introduction

> At the elite level of any sport, there are so many physically talented players
> .... What often separates the winners from the losers is the mental toughness
> they acquired, the ability to maintain their focus under pressure when the
> outcome of the game is on the line.
>
> *(Berger, 2008, p. 326)*

In the last 10 to 20 years sport psychology and adapted physical activity scholars
have started to examine sport psychology theories and research questions with
athletes with disabilities. In particular, there has been a growing body of research
that directly and indirectly reflects coping processes and emotional reactions in
disability sport. The quote introducing this chapter illustrates the value of coping
skills under the emotional pressure of competition.

The current chapter is organized as follows. First, I examine how individuals
cope with an acquired disability. Second, societal sources of stress (such as prejudice)
are examined. Third, a review of the social milieu that people with disabilities live
in is provided. Fourth, I review literature on sport marginalization. Fifth, research
is presented that suggests that training for sport is often difficult. Sixth, research into
competition-specific stressors and coping (that is, psychological skills) is reviewed.
Seventh, research on mood and emotion is examined. Eighth, I examine the
challenges associated with leaving sport. Finally, a summary with some concluding
statements is provided so the reader can have a succinct series of take-away
messages.

The information included in the current chapter reflects my perspective,
favoring a holistic human development model. Such an approach acknowledges
that disability (and pain), general sport considerations (such as sport anxiety),

disability sport (including its classification) and non-sport considerations (such as relationship issues) all influence an athlete's ability to cope and manage challenges that influence their ability to train and compete optimally (see Bawden, 2006; Martin, 1999a, 2005).

General coping and emotion

Coping with an acquired disability

> Now I am nothing. Life moves on, without me. That is how it is. How it will always be. I just survive. No ambitions. Nothing .... Sometimes I don't think I can go on.
>
> *(Smith and Sparkes, 2005, p. 1101)*

Given that about 85 percent of athletes with disabilities have had a serious traumatic injury (in other words, theirs is an acquired disability), it is important to understand how people with disabilities cope with their accident. Many people who experience a spinal cord injury (SCI) eventually adjust to their injury through rehabilitation, social support, and adaptive coping skills (Galvin and Godfrey, 2001). Recently researchers (Chevalier, Kennedy, and Sherlock, 2009) have indicated that individuals with SCI employ a number of adaptive strategies in order to cope. For instance, having a 'sense of coherence' or seeing the world as manageable, understandable and meaningful is related to positive coping. Similarly, locus of control, having purpose in life, and social reintegration are associated with adjustment (Chevalier et al., 2009).

Over time many people eventually adjust to an acquired disability and enjoy a high quality of life. However, a major ramification of an unexpected and permanent injury is a significant disruption of psychological well-being (Smith and Sparkes, 2005; Trieschmann, 1988). As the quote introducing this section illustrates, some people are devastated and may consider suicide as a result of the life-changing nature of their injury. A primary characteristic of experiencing a significant and permanent injury is a loss of function, and people often become defined by others as their disabilities (Hutchinson and Kleiber, 2000). This loss of function often becomes the most dominating feature of the disability experience.

Sparkes and Smith (2002) and Smith and Sparkes (2005) described men's SCI-related experiences. Able-bodied male athletes with strong masculine athletic identities and who depend on sport for substantial self-esteem benefits have both elements of their identities damaged when they became disabled. One participant indicated, 'Your masculinity is gone, broken, you just struggle to live up to it [being a man]' (Sparkes and Smith, 2002, p. 269). A few athletes will dismiss disability sport as an option. For example, one athlete stated, 'How can you play sports like that? I mean I can understand people using sport for rehabilitation and everything. For me though, they aren't real sports, not really' (Sparkes and Smith,

2002, p. 270). A related sentiment was expressed by a former able-bodied basketball player who noted, 'No way would I settle for less with a sport I had excelled in on my feet. So in the hospital I set my mind on the triathlon' (Hutchinson and Kleiber, 2000, p. 50). The above evidence suggests identity grounded in athletics and masculinity can undergo tremendous change.

In addition to broad based adjustment issues (such as daily personal care), when individuals with disabilities leave the hospital setting for the first time they must make significant adjustments. For instance, they automatically encounter reduced social support from hospital staff and go from a built environment that is designed specifically for them to one in which it is often difficult to move around (Rees, Smith, and Sparkes, 2003).

In sum, experiencing an acquired disability is world-changing and requires significant coping.

Coping with misperceptions and prejudice

> Other people can't understand why I am so happy. They don't have the same appreciation of life. They would have to understand the satisfaction of using all my resources to conquer each day of challenges.
>
> *(Albrecht and Devlieger, 1999, p. 983)*

One way in which people with disabilities are marginalized (and disparaged) is through the assumption by able-bodied people that they must inevitably have 'terrible' lives. In contrast, many people with disabilities experience a high quality of life. The two different viewpoints held by people with and without disabilities are often referred to as the disability paradox. This describes the apparent contradiction that people who have a disability also simultaneously report enjoying a high quality of life. Dunn (2000), for instance, reported that able-bodied individuals regularly believe that the influence of a disability on life quality is far greater than that reported by persons with a disability. Contrary to this perspective over 50 percent of people with disabilities indicate that they have a good to excellent quality of life.

Albrecht and Devlieger (1999) examined the factors that differentiated respondents reporting a good to excellent quality of life participants from those reporting a poor to fair quality of life. People with disabilities reporting a high quality of life expressed a balanced view of the value of the mind, body, and spirit. In other words one of the ways that they coped with their disability was to appreciate and value their minds and spirits. They also felt supported by and integrated with their family and communities, and they coped by eliciting and relying on social support. Participants with poor-quality lives often reported that the mind, body, spirit, and feelings of connectedness to the larger world were regularly interrupted by pain and fatigue.

Able-bodied people overemphasize the value of the body and marginalize the importance of the mind, spirit, and social worlds (Albrecht and Devlieger, 1999).

These beliefs then contribute to their opinions that all people with disabilities must have a poor quality of life. This dynamic means that individuals with disabilities routinely have to endure and cope with social situations where people inappropriately convey pity. One outcome of this perspective is the notion that life is not worth living. The award-winning film *Million Dollar Baby* (2004), about a quadriplegic boxer, unfortunately conveys this attitude that death is better than life with a disability (Gard and Fitzgerald, 2008). Finally, people with disabilities also have to cope with inappropriate behaviors by able-bodied people on a quite regular basis. For example, in the documentary film *Murderball* (2005), members of the US Paralympic Wheelchair Rugby team faced questions from strangers about their abilities to perform sexually (Lindemann, 2008).

The disability world

> Your friendships are greatly affected by your disability. I don't have any friends except maybe two from the pre-disability days.
>
> *(Lyons, Ritvo, and Sullivan, 1995, p. 38)*

People with disabilities share much in common with people without disabilities. Nevertheless, they still move through a world that is different from the able-bodied world. Disability affects almost every aspect of a person's life, and this includes self-esteem, employment, education, travel, relationships, parenthood, and well-being. People with disabilities have fewer friends and less extensive social networks than people without disabilities. Friendships, marriage, and parenthood often undergo extreme strain, especially immediately after a traumatic accident (Lyons et al., 1995). People with disabilities see their friends less, have difficulty relating to established friendships, and often experience rejection by old friends. Marriages are often severely disrupted, and disability is a risk factor for divorce. For adult athletes with disabilities who are parents, parent–child relationships are also affected.

One parent stated that 'another thing that makes it hard is the fact that I can't run with [his children]' (Kleiber et al., 1995, p. 293). Young children who are cognitively immature cannot understand the permanency of disability, and this exacerbates the frustration that parents feel in coping with the changes in their relationships with their children. For example, discussing his daughter, this man noted that 'She's not accepting the fact, I don't think, that I can't walk, she'll tell me to put on my shoes, and I can walk. So, see, that makes it hard on me' (p. 293).

People with disabilities have lower incomes and less education than people without disabilities, and higher rates of poverty. Hence, individuals with lifestyles commensurate with an upper-income bracket prior to disability may have to make serious downward adjustments. Individuals with disabilities are also more likely to be the victims of crime, with disabled women having a 40 percent greater chance of being assaulted than women without disabilities. Simple tasks for able-bodied athletes, such as getting in a car to go to practice or competition, take more time for athletes with disabilities. In brief, athletes with disabilities live in a world that is often profoundly different from the one in which an able-bodied person lives. Challenges such as fewer friends and less income can clearly influence an athlete's ability to train and perform and require coping skills.

Sport-related coping and emotion

Coping with sport marginalization

> Our athletic accomplishments are just as good athletically as able bodied people are and it's not because I have super human powers that I go out and play a sports [sic] everyday.
>
> *(Hargreaves and Hardin, 2009)*

Although the Paralympics are the largest sporting event in the world, after the Olympics, they receive mixed media coverage. For instance, four major British newspapers published sixty-two articles on the 2000 Paralympics (Thompson and Smith, 2003). However, about a quarter of them reinforced common stereotypes by framing athletes as victims, suffering or heroic. Other researchers found that French and German media coverage of the Paralympics trivialized Paralympic performances (Schantz and Gilbert, 2001). There is virtually no mainstream media coverage of the Paralympics in the United States (Schell and Duncan, 1999). For instance, in 2002 NBC provided one hour of Paralympic coverage, showing the opening ceremonies 48 hours after they happened. The print media also fails to cover disability sport adequately. According to Golden (2003), sport journalists do not see disability sport as 'real' sport because they fail to understand how athletes with disabilities can be competitive.

In particular, female athletes with disabilities are less prominent in the media than male athletes. For instance, even the disability sport publication *Sports n' Spokes* used male images of athletes approximately 80 percent of the time (Hardin and Hardin, 2005). Furthermore, women are portrayed in fewer competitive and non-sporting situations than men (Hardin and Hardin, 2005). Even the limited amount of disability sport coverage of elite Paralympians by the mainstream media tends to ignore athletes' accomplishments in favor of focusing on how they cope with their disability (Hardin, 2006). Hargreaves and Hardin (2009) interviewed ten female wheelchair athletes who expressed frustration at having their athletic accomplishments portrayed as inspirational and as being labeled as 'supercrips.'

Research has demonstrated that although many athletes with disabilities view themselves as committed and serious athletes, they typically feel that the public does not view them as legitimate athletes (Martin, Mushett, and Eklund, 1994; Martin, Mushett, and Smith, 1995; Wickman, 2007). One reason is that individuals with disabilities are often identified by their disabilities, and their athletic capabilities go unrecognized. Being an athlete is thought to counteract the stereotype of a helpless disabled person (Hardin and Hardin, 2003; White, Gordon, and Jackson, 2006) and as a result make them somewhat immune from negative attitudes and prejudice (Hardin and Hardin, 2003). Unfortunately, researchers have shown that even athletes with disabilities face strong negative biases when implicit attitude measures are used (White et al., 2006).

Contrary to the above view is the 'supercrip' stereotype, whereby athletes with disabilities are viewed as heroes simply because they play a sport. As the quote opening this section indicates, most athletes with disabilities do not view themselves as heroes, or feel that their achievements represent a personal victory over their disabilities. Athletes perceive the supercrip and hero labels as inaccurate because they view their sporting successes as normal athletic achievements (Hardin and Hardin, 2004). In brief, most elite-level athletes with disabilities do not want to be reduced to a 'supercrip' stereotype, a hero, or be viewed as a pseudo-athlete. They simply want their legitimate athletic accomplishments to be recognized as such (Berger, 2008).

Coping with training difficulties

Training

> Accessible transport and training facilities are major problems. If athletes cannot get to training on a regular basis and/or cannot use a facility, they cannot prepare for top-level competition.
>
> *(Ferreira, 2006, p. 345)*

Based on the age range and mean age of elite athletes with disabilities (e.g. Groff, Lundberg, and Zabriskie, 2009; Martin, Malone, and Hilyer, in review) it would appear that most elite disability sport athletes are adults. Hence more disabled than able-bodied athletes are likely to be juggling marriage, families, careers, and their sport. This can be particularly problematic for team sport athletes, where the ability to practice together is critical. For instance, the 2009 US National Wheelchair Rugby Team came from eleven different states and could only train together at national training camps. Many sport psychologists have found that athletes receive social support as a result of team sport involvement, and sport friendships are one reason to continue playing sport. Clearly the sport-related support obtained from training partners and teammates can be critical in helping athletes adhere to demanding training schedules. Martin (2002, 2008) suggested that one reason disabled athletes' training self-efficacy for overcoming common training barriers was less than optimal was because they faced many social (such as lack of training partners) and environmental (such as inaccessible exercise facilities) barriers to training.

Many athletes train in less than ideal settings. Rimmer et al.'s line of research examining fitness and health clubs suggests that athletes who wish to train for their sport in such locations would have difficulty doing so (Rimmer et al., 2005, 2004). Rimmer et al. (2005) examined thirty-five health clubs across the United States in urban and suburban settings. Many facilities did not allow adequate room for wheelchair users to exercise equipment transfers although they had adequate access to the exercise area in general. Also, many of the exercise facilities had no adaptive exercise equipment.

Even outdoor areas, which are often designed to facilitate and support play and sport, can present barriers to individuals with disabilities. Poorly lit walking paths or wooded walking trails with rocks or fallen branches can be barriers to individuals with vision loss (Rimmer, 2006). Without audible signals at traffic lights and curb cuts with high-contrast markings that make them distinctly visible, individuals with vision loss cannot train outside without a partner (Rimmer, 2006).

Spivock, Gauvin, and Brodeur (2007) surveyed 112 neighborhoods in Montreal, Canada for their activity friendliness for people with disabilities. They examined walking surfaces (such as paths wide enough for a wheelchair), signs (such as auditory signals on the crosswalks) and surrounding areas (for issues such as access ramps and parking). Participants' mean scores on the activity friendliness scale were under the scale mid-point, and significantly lower than reference items on the same scale for non-disabled individuals.

Finally, even when athletes are members of disabled sport teams and can train in sport facilities they still rate difficulties with accessing and using toilet and changing facilities as their primary complaint. Few ramps and a lack of room to accommodate wheelchairs are also common barriers in sport facilities (French and Hainsworth, 2001). However, in a study of deliberate practice and sport expertise, Boxell (2009) found high levels of practice. Boxell examined ten National level quad rugby players from the United States and found they practiced as much (on average, 8,309 hours) or more than able-bodied high-level performers (such as violinists and wrestlers) over the course of a ten-year period. She suggested that athletes in her study might have sacrificed other daily life activities for training, which seems plausible given the elite athlete status of the quad rugby players she studied. To reach elite-level status most athletes must persevere, give up other valuable activities, overcome various obstacles to training, and maintain consistent motivation over time (Martin, 2002; Smith, 2003).

Travel

> the biggest thing ... you've got to travel half way across the country and then you've got to pay for the taxi at the other end, it's a cost, and it takes up all your time.
>
> *(Macbeth, 2009, p. 461)*

Travelling to practice and competition is often more difficult and time-consuming for athletes with disabilities than for those without disabilities (Bawden, 2006,

Macbeth, 2009). Visually impaired athletes, for example, often do not have a driver's license and must rely on friends and family or public transportation (Macbeth, 2009). When travelling long distances for major competitions, athletes often worry about time away from their spouses, and this can lead to relationship difficulties (Campbell and Jones, 2002a). In turn, relationship-related stress can lead to a lack of self-confidence (Campbell and Jones). Long periods of time sitting, such as on an overnight flight, can also exacerbate existing pressure sores (Campbell and Jones). Finding and using bathrooms is an additional difficulty associated with travel (Bawden, 2006).

Pain

> I never listened or respected my body and what it was doing. I saw through them (injuries) ... . I just had incredible pain ... It was winning or nothing. I was going to die trying; that was what I was going to do.
>
> *(Wheeler et al., 1996, p. 389)*

All athletes will at times have to cope with pain in training and competition. Preliminary evidence suggests that the role of pain in the sporting lives of athletes with disabilities is significant, and may play a larger role in their lives than in that of non-disabled athletes. For instance, up to 94 percent of people with SCI indicate that they have pain (Martin Ginis et al., 2002, 2003). Other researchers have reported that pain limits physical activity (PA; Henderson and Bedini, 1995) and in some cases individuals have indicated that their pain limits their PA more than their disability (Goodwin and Compton, 2004). Even PA itself can be painful (Rollins and Nichols, 1994). Finally, athletes with disabilities report more sport-related muscle pain (SRMP) as their training volume increases (Bernardi et al., 2003). Furthermore, 18 percent reported that SRMP interrupted their training for from one to four weeks.

Injury and illness

> When you get these little injuries, and you know you've got a hard training session coming up, and you think – Is it going to stand up to it? Having a boney bum and big muscley shoulders and not being able to stand up to relieve the pressure all the time, you can get pressure sores. This causes me concern and stress. It's because, if I get one, it means I will have to be off my bottom and laid up in bed for about 2 weeks, and that means no training.
>
> *(Campbell and Jones, 2002a, p. 87)*

Training is also disrupted by injury and illness. Relative to their able-bodied counterparts, athletes with disabilities lose more training time through injury (Davis and Ferrara, 1995). Researchers examining athletes at the 1996 Paralympics found that visually impaired runners experienced lower-leg overuse injuries that were similar in nature to non-visually impaired athletes (Nyland et al., 2000). Athletes with unilateral amputations (leaving only one leg) suffered more injuries in the ankle area of the non-amputated foot/leg. Bernardi et al. (2003) speculated that the everyday demands of wheeling, combined with wheeling for sport, did not allow enough time for rest and adaptation to occur. Athletes with disabilities may also be at risk for upper respiratory tract infections (URTI). For instance, 19 percent of wheelchair marathon racers compared with 15.4 percent of able-bodied control subjects experienced URTIs in the two weeks after a race. Finally, it is important to understand the increased risk of heat exhaustion and related outcomes (such as heat stroke) for athletes with SCI because they have difficulty regulating body temperature, particularly when competing in high temperatures (Filho et al., 2006).

Classification

> It is the waiting and uncertainty that bothers me with regard to classification. From time to time the classification process has been engaged too close to my races ...
>
> *(Howe, 2008, p. 502)*

Most able-bodied athletes (such as wrestlers) who are classified (for instance, by weight) usually know their classifications and thus can reasonably predict or control them. However, athletes with disabilities are functionally classified, which means they are graded based on their abilities to perform physical tests. As a result, athletes with different disabilities may compete against each other. Hence, a swimmer with cerebral palsy (CP) may race against a swimmer missing a limb. Being classified, which occurs prior to competition, can be stressful for several reasons. First, athletes may fear being reclassified at a different level from previously. Second, if athletes are reclassified at a more functional level they may face tougher competition. It is certainly plausible that competing against more functional athletes may reduce confidence and increase anxiety at a critical time (especially the 48 hours before competition). Functional classification is clearly a potential stressor.

Competition-related coping

Self-efficacy

> other players are sitting looking at me thinking – He's not playing well, get him off, give him a rest, talk to him, do whatever, and then put him back on. If I miss shots, my confidence nose dives, and then that affects my all round performance.
>
> *(Campbell and Jones, 2002a, p. 87)*

Athletes with disabilities, like all athletes, need to feel confident in their capabilities in order to cope with performance stress and perform well. For instance, Lowther, Lane, and Lane (2005) examined self-efficacy, psychological skills, and performance for fifteen elite amputee male soccer players over a six-game Amputee World Cup tournament. Higher self-efficacy was also associated with stronger psychological skills, and athletes with the strongest self-efficacy performed better than soccer players with weaker efficacy. In a study of Greek athletes participating in the National Wheelchair Basketball Championships, self-efficacy (along with past performance) predicted passing performance (Katartzi et al., 2007).

Training self-efficacy, performance self-efficacy, efficacy for overcoming barriers to successful racing, and positive affect were all positively linked with wheelchair road-racing performance (Martin, 2002). Athletes with stronger multidimensional efficacy and positive affect raced faster than 'wheelers' who were less efficacious, and reported lower positive affect. In a similar study with wheelchair basketball players, Martin (2008) also found positive relationships among training efficacy, performance self-efficacy, thought control self-efficacy, and resiliency self-efficacy. Basketball players who could control distressing thoughts and maintain positive self-talk also had greater ability to play basketball and train well, despite barriers, than players who had less ability to manage their negative thoughts.

Swimmers with disabilities who had strong training self-efficacy also reported receiving high levels of emotional and technical challenge support from their coaches and parents. This finding affirms the value of a strong support system (Martin and Mushett-Adams, 1996). As might be expected, quad rugby athletes had much stronger quad rugby skill self efficacy than non-quad rugby players (Adnan, McKenzie, and Miyahara, 2001). Of additional importance however is that athletes' sport self-efficacy likely transferred to feelings of efficacy for activities of daily living (ADL). In particular, athletes expressed much stronger self-efficacy for transferring from wheelchair to bed and seat (and vice versa) than non-athletes. Adnan et al.'s findings supported earlier research on wheelchair tennis players (Greenwood, Dzewaltowski, and French, 1990). Greenwood et al. (1990) found that wheelchair tennis self-efficacy was correlated with wheelchair mobility self-efficacy. They suggested that participation in wheelchair tennis lead to enhanced efficacy for non-sport tasks such as wheeling up ramps and going down curbs (Greenwood et al., 1990). Cumulatively, as for able-bodied athletes, these findings support the relevance and important role of efficacy, confidence, and positive affect in sport performance, and the research by Adnan et al. (2001) and Greenwood et al. (1990) suggests that sport participation has non-sport-specific benefits for helping athletes cope with ADL.

Coping, stress, and anxiety

> About 50 percent of my anxiety before a major competition is concerned with my performance, and the other 50 percent is related to organizational issues, such as transport, accommodation and disabled access.
>
> *(Bawden, 2006, p. 673)*

Stress and coping have been a prominent theme in disability sport research. In a series of three studies, Campbell and Jones (1997, 2002a, 2002b) examined stress and anxiety in elite wheelchair athletes. They found that athletes' stressors were as follows:

- pre-competition issues (such as team selection)
- negative competition readiness (such as concerns about faulty equipment)
- performance worries (such as playing time)
- post-match performance concerns (such as playing badly)
- downside of participating in major events (such as being away from home)
- low group cohesiveness (such as conflict with teammates)
- negative coaching (such as insufficient encouragement)
- relationship worries (such as concern about a partner's well-being)
- sport demands (such as limited funds for expensive equipment)
- poor disability awareness (such as inaccessible toilets).

It is clear that athletes' worries ranged from unique disability sport stressors (such as equipment concerns) to disability specific worries (such as concern about pressure sores), and finally, common sources of sport anxiety (such as a lack of fitness).

In a follow-up study with the same athletes, Campbell and Jones (2002b) asked participants to appraise these sources of stress. Athletes who viewed stressors as challenges saw them as in their control. This finding suggests that framing stressful events as challenges to overcome, instead of uncontrollable problems, is a helpful coping strategy. Athletes who viewed stressors as severe were also likely to rate them as threatening and harmful. The most severe stressors were negative coaching behaviors, relationship issues, and the financial costs of wheelchair basketball. The demands of wheelchair basketball were the most frequent stressors.

Pensgaard, Roberts, and Ursin (1999) found that Norwegian Paralympians reported moderate use of functional coping skills such as planning and redefining stress as an opportunity for growth. Scores for more ineffective coping skills such as behavioral disengagement and denying stress were substantially lower. In general, Paralympians and Olympians reported similar levels of coping.

In short, athletes with disabilities experience both sport-specific and disability-specific anxiety. In addition, limited evidence suggests that elite-level athletes with disabilities develop skills for coping effectively with sport stress. Sport may also contribute to the development of coping skills, particularly in committed athletes, that can extend to stressful non-sport situations.

Emotion

> It was an unbelievable feeling to know that I was among the 12 best
> wheelchair basketball players in the entire country, chosen to represent the
> U.S.A. in front of the whole world.
>
> *(Berger, 2008)*

As most sport psychologists and athletes know, sport can be the catalyst for a wide
range of feelings stemming from ecstasy to profound disappointment. Disability
sport research has mostly been limited to examinations of athletes' mood states
with the Profile of Mood States (POMS; McNair, Lorr, and Droppleman, 1971).
Most researchers have sought to determine whether athletes report an 'iceberg
profile' indicative of positive mental health. The iceberg profile is supported when
athletes have scores below the norm for anger, confusion, depression, fatigue, and
tension, with vigor, the only positive mood state, above the norm.

Campbell and Jones (1994) found that wheelchair athletes reported lower anger,
confusion, depression, and tension scores, and higher vigor scores than wheelchair
users who were inactive. Additionally, athletes exhibited iceberg profiles, indicative
of mental health. The most accomplished athletes reported the strongest feelings of
vigor. Similar results have been obtained with wheelchair tennis players and non-
tennis players with disabilities (Greenwood et al., 1990). Tennis participants
reported higher than the norm on vigor scores and lower than the norm on tension,
anger, confusion, fatigue, and depression, indicative of the iceberg profile of mental
health. Tennis players also scored higher on vigor and lower on the negative states
than non-tennis players (Greenwood et al., 1990). Fung and Fu (1995) compared
150 Chinese wheelchair athletes who were finalists in the National Games with
150 non-finalists, and found that collectively, mood scores for vigor, confusion,
tension, and sport commitment distinguished finalists from non-finalists in 78
percent of the cases. Finalists were less tense and confused, and expressed having
more vigor and commitment than non-finalists.

Jacobs et al. (1990) compared wheelchair athletes and non-athletes with able-
bodied athletes. Both groups of athletes reported greater feelings of vigor whereas
non-athletes reported higher scores for depressed mood. Jacobs and colleagues
speculated that sport participation provides physiological benefits leading to
increased feelings of vigor. Horvat et al. (1989) compared able-bodied athletes with
athletes with disabilities who were similar in years of sport experience and in
training habits. Again, athletes with disabilities exhibited iceberg profiles, and the
authors concluded that sport helps athletes with disabilities learn to cope with their
disability.

Campbell (1995) compared mood states between wheelchair athletes with
congenital and acquired disabilities. Both groups reported iceberg profiles, but
athletes with acquired disabilities reported lower scores for anger, confusion,
fatigue, and depressed mood, and higher scores for vigor, than those with congenital

disabilities. Athletes did not differ on tension. Campbell suggested that athletes with an acquired disability may learn coping skills in order to manage their affect, compared with athletes with congenital disabilities.

Mastro et al. (1987) examined forty-nine visually impaired, national-level athletes, and found that male athletes reported iceberg profiles. Female athletes tended to report profiles similar to non-athletic populations. Masters et al. (1995) also examined mood responses among elite athletes with CP or comparable levels of brain trauma. Athletes reported reduced tension and anger from the beginning to the end of a six-day training camp, followed by an increase in tension and anger one month later at the Paralympic trials. Mastro, Canabal, and French (1988) compared seventy-five male visually impaired and forty-six sighted beep baseball players competing in the World Series of beep baseball. Unsighted athletes were higher in depressed mood and tension. Visually impaired athletes may have experienced more tension because of limited time to adjust to an unfamiliar competition site.

In summary, athletes with disabilities have usually reported iceberg mood profiles, suggesting that athletic participation might be associated with positive moods, coping ability, and a buffer against negative mood states. One path of influence is that sport participation provides physiological benefits leading to increased feelings of energy and vigor. Mastery experiences from sport as well as increased social support are two other plausible mechanisms acting to reduce negative mood states. Of course individuals with positive mood states may simply be drawn to sport. Given that individuals with disabilities are prone to higher levels of depression than individuals without disabilities, the potential mood enhancement abilities of sport for coping with disability-related difficulties should not be underestimated.

Leaving sport

> I honestly believe it is very closely related … as if you were to lose a baby. Just like a miscarriage. It is just the sorrow inside and it is something that you have looked forward to and planned for and boom it is taken away …
> *(Wheeler et al., 1996. p. 389)*

Leaving sport can be difficult, as exemplified in the quote above. A few authors have suggested that athletes with disabilities face unique challenges when leaving sport (such as Martin, 1996, 1999a, 2000). Athletes may acquire a 'secondary disability' (such as overuse injuries in the shoulder) as a function of overcommitment and overtraining (e.g. Burnham et al., 1993). Such a situation may have significant consequence for coping with the post-sport world and functional aspects such as mobility (Wheeler et al., 1996; Wheeler et al., 1999). Athletes with disabilities may face coping with their disability for the first time as well as with transition-related emotional issues. This may be a function of a rapid transition to sport and 'promotion' to elite sports after an acquired disability combined with a short athletic career (Asken, 1989; Martin, 1996, 1999b). Asken (1989) suggested that in some cases sport can act as a way for athletes with disabilities to avoid dealing with their disability, hence after retirement they may have to cope more overtly with it.

Despite difficulties in the retirement process, disability sport transition research has shown that athletes may also be either ambivalent or relieved to be leaving the stresses and strains of the competitive sport environment, and having the opportunity to take time for other important aspects of life (Wheeler et al., 1996, 1999). However, leaving sport may represent a period of grieving for psychological, social, and physiological losses. Athletes may report symptoms consistent with unresolved grieving and clinical depression long after they have retired. Whereas the majority of athletes interviewed in the Wheeler et al. (1996, 1999) studies coped well with their daily lives, for many the memories of the transition out of sport were poignant, and many were angry at sports organizations simply allowing them to drift away from sport.

A number of factors are probably important in the athlete's ability to cope with the transition from sport. These include:

- level of commitment (maintaining a balanced approach to sport and other life interests)
- avoiding overtraining and managing sports injuries (resting an injured shoulder)
- identity (identifying self with diverse aspects or roles in life)
- coping style (emotional or problem solving)
- support structures (family, sports organizations)
- remaining involved in sports (such as through coaching or as a sports ambassador; Martin, 1996).

Sport psychologists should speak with their athletes early in their careers about such matters. They should also help athletes monitor their training regimens closely, and minor injuries should be taken care of quickly to avoid chronic overuse injuries. Another important strategy is remaining engaged in sports in some capacity. Mentoring or sports ambassador roles have been suggested as a means of keeping athletes involved. Finally, it is important to note that whereas many athletes will experience some degree of loss upon leaving sports, not everyone will have significant emotional difficulties. Nor will every athlete wish to take part in a career transition intervention program.

Chapter summary

Sport psychologists can best support athletes' efforts to train and reach their potential if they understand the disability world, sport psychology, and how disability sport is different from able-bodied sport. Knowledge of the disability paradox, coping with a disability, disability stereotypes, and disability culture are just a few salient considerations. Researchers investigating confidence and efficacy, coping, stress and anxiety, and mood states have reported results that mostly parallel research with able-bodied athletes. A few findings specific to the disability sport or disability condition illuminate the subtle differences between disability and non-disability sport. Disability sport challenges requiring coping also span the areas of identity, training, travel, pain, injury, illness, coaching, classification, and leaving sport.

Finally, as the reader will note, most of the research discussed only implicitly reflects connections between coping and emotion. For instance, researchers have rarely examined whether training pain from a disability causes an emotional reaction (such as frustration) which then elicits some type of adaptive or maladaptive coping response. The links established in this chapter reflect my thinking, in which I have used theory, logic, and empirical findings to inform my perspective. However, the literature presented, for the most part, remains to be empirically supported by research focused specifically on coping and emotion and their links. I hope the current chapter might serve as a catalyst for such research.

References

Adnan, Y., McKenzie, A. and Miyahara, M. (2001). Self-efficacy for quad rugby skills and activities of daily living. *Adapted Physical Activity Quarterly*, 18, 90–101.

Albrecht, G. G. L. and Devlieger, P, J. (1999). The disability paradox: high quality of life against all odds. *Social Science and Medicine*, 48, 977–988.

Asken, M. J. (1989). Sport psychology and the physically disabled athlete: Interview with Michael D. Goodling, OTR/L. *The Sport Psychologist*, 3, 166–176.

Bawden, M. (2006). Providing sport psychology support for athletes with disabilities. In J. Dosil (ed.), *The sport psychologist's handbook: A guide for sport-specific performance enhancement* (pp. 665–683). Malden, Mass.: John Wiley & Sons.

Berger, R. J. (2008). Disability and the dedicated wheelchair athlete: beyond the 'Supercrip' critique. *Journal of Contemporary Ethnography*, 37, 647–678.

Bernardi, M., Castellano, V., Ferrara, M. S., Sbriccoli, P., Sera, F. and Marchetti, M. (2003). Muscle pain in athletes with locomotor disability. *Medicine and Science in Sports and Exercise*, 35, 199–206.

Boxell, L. R. (2009). An examination of the deliberate practice framework in quad rugby, Master's thesis. http://trace.tennessee.edu/utk_gradthes/23 (accessed on 21 March 2011).

Burnham, R. S., May, L., Nelson, E., Steadward, R. D. and Reid, D. (1993). Shoulder pain in wheelchair athletes: The role of muscle imbalance. *American Journal of Sports Medicine*, 21(2), 238–242.

Campbell, E. (1995). Psychological well-being of participants in wheelchair sports: Comparison of individuals with congenital and acquired disabilities. *Perceptual and Motor Skills*, 81, 563–568.

Campbell, E. and Jones, G. (1994). Psychological well-being in wheelchair sport participants and nonparticipants. *Adapted Physical Activity Quarterly*, 11, 404–415.

Campbell, E. and Jones, G. (1997). Precompetition anxiety and self-confidence in wheelchair sport participants. *Adapted Physical Activity Quarterly*, 14, 95–107.

Campbell, E. and Jones, G. (2002a). Sources of stress experienced by elite male wheelchair basketball players. *Adapted Physical Activity Quarterly*, 19, 82–99.

Campbell, E. and Jones, G. (2002b). Cognitive appraisal of sources of stress experienced by elite mate wheelchair basketball players. *Adapted Physical Activity Quarterly*, 19, 100–108.

Chevalier, Z., Kennedy, P. and Sherlock, O. (2009). Spinal cord injury, coping and psychological adjustment: a literature review. *Spinal Cord*, 47, 778–782.

Davis, R. W. and Ferrara, M .S. (1995). Sports medicine and athletes with disabilities. In K. P. DePauw and S. J. Gavron (eds), *Disability and sport* (pp. 133–149). Champaign, Ill.: Human Kinetics.

Dunn, D. S. (2000). Social psychological issues in disability. In R. Frank and T. R. Elliott (eds), *Handbook of rehabilitation psychology* (pp. 564–584). Washington, DC: American Psychological Association.

Ferreira, S. (2006). The preparation of athletes with cerebral palsy for elite competition, doctoral dissertation. http://scholar.sun.ac.za/bitstream/handle/10019.1/1459/Ferrei. pdf (accessed on 4 April 2011).

Filho, J. A. O., Salvetti, X. M., de Mello, M. T., da Silva, A. C. and Filho, B. L. (2006). Coronary risk in a cohort of Paralympic athletes. *British Journal of Sports Medicine*, 40, 918–922.

French, D. and Hainsworth, J. (2001). 'There aren't any buses and the swimming pool is always cold!' Obstacles and opportunities in the provision of sport for disabled people. *Managing Leisure*, 6, 35–49.

Fung, L. and Fu, F. H. (1995). Psychological determinants between wheelchair sport finalists and non-finalists. *International Journal of Sport Psychology*, 26, 568–579.

Galvin, L. R. and Godfrey, H. P. D. (2001). The impact of coping on emotional adjustment to spinal cord injury (SCI): review of the literature and application of a stress appraisal and coping formulation. *Spinal Cord*, 39, 615–627.

Gard, M. and Fitzgerald, H. (2008). Tackling murderball: Masculinity, disability, and the big screen. *Sport, Ethics and Philosophy*, 2, 126 – 141.

Golden, A. V. (2003). An analysis of the dissimilar coverage of the 2002 Olympics and Paralympics: frenzied pack journalism versus the empty press room. *Disability Studies Quarterly*, 23. www.dsq-sds.org/article/view/437/614 (accessed on 21 March 2011).

Goodwin, D. L. and Compton, S. G. (2004). Physical activity experiences of women aging with disabilities. *Adapted Physical Activity Quarterly*, 21, 122–138.

Greenwood, C. M., Dzewaltowski, D. A. and French, R. (1990). Self-efficacy and psychological well-being of wheelchair tennis participants and wheelchair non-tennis participants. *Adapted Physical Activity Quarterly*, 7, 12–21.

Groff, D. G., Lundberg, N. R. and Zabriskie, R. B. (2009). Influence of adapted sport on quality of life: perceptions of athletes with cerebral palsy. *Disability and Rehabilitation*, 31, 318–326.

Hardin, M. (2006). Disability and sport. In A. A. Raney and J. Bryant (eds), *Handbook of Sports and Media* (pp. 577–585. Mahwah, N.J.: Lawrence Erlbaum Associates.

Hardin, B. and Hardin, M. (2003). Conformity and conflict: wheelchair athletes discuss sport media. *Adapted Physical Activity Quarterly*, 20, 246–259.

Hardin, M. and Hardin, B. (2004). The 'supercrip' in the sport media: wheelchair athletes discuss hegemony's disabled hero. *Sociology of Sport Online*, 7, 1–10.

Hardin, M. and Hardin, B. (2005). Performance or participation ... pluralism or hegemony? Images of disability and gender in *Sports n' Spokes* magazine. *Disability Studies Quarterly*, 25. www.dsq-sds.org/article/view/606/783 (accessed on 21 March 2011).

Hargreaves, J. A. and Hardin, B. (2009). Women wheelchair athletes: competing against media stereotypes. *Disability Studies Quarterly*, 29. www.dsq-sds.org/article/ view/920/1095 (accessed on 21 March 2011).

Henderson, K. A. and Bedini, L. A. (1995). 'I have a soul that dances like Tina Turner but my body can't': physical activity and women with mobility impairments. *Research Quarterly for Exercise and Sport*, 66(2), 151–161.

Horvat, M., Roswal, G., Jacobs, D. and Gaunt, S. (1989). Selected psychological comparisons of able-bodied and disabled athletes. *Physical Educator*, 5, 202–207.

Howe, P. D. (2008). The tail is wagging the dog: classification and the Paralympic movement, *Ethnography*, 9, 499–518.

Hutchinson, S. L. and Kleiber, D. A. (2000). Heroic masculinity following spinal cord injury: implications for therapeutic recreation practice and research. *Therapeutic Recreation Journal*, 34(1), 42–54.

Jacobs, D. P., Roswal, G. M., Horvat, M. A. and Gorman, D. R. (1990). A comparison between the psychological profiles of wheelchair athletes, wheelchair nonathletes, and able bodied athletes. In G. Doll-Tepper, C. Dahms, B. Doll, and H. von Selzam (eds), *Adapted Physical Activity: An interdisciplinary approach* (pp. 75–79). New York: Springer-Verlag.

Katartzi, E., Theodorakis, Y., Tzetzis, G. and Vlachopoulos, S. P. (2007). Effects of goal setting and self-efficacy on wheelchair basketball performance, *Japanese Journal of Adapted Sport Science*, 5, 50–62.

Kleiber, D., Brock, S., Lee, Y., Dattilo, J. and Caldwell, L. (1995). The relevance of leisure in an illness experience: realities of spinal cord injury. *Journal of Leisure Research*, 27, 283–299.

Lindemann, K. (2008). 'I can't be standing up out there': communicative performances of (dis)ability in wheelchair rugby. *Text and Performance Quarterly*, 28, 98–115.

Lowther, J., Lane, A. and Lane, H. (2002). Self-efficacy and psychological skills during the amputee soccer world cup. *Athletic Insight: The online journal of sport psychology*, 4, 23–34.

Lyons, R. F., Ritvo, P. G. and Sullivan, M. J. L. (1995). *Relationships in chronic illness and disability*. Thousand Oaks, Calif.: Sage.

Macbeth, J. L. (2009). Restrictions of activity in partially sighted football: Experiences of grassroots players. *Leisure Studies*, 28, 455–467.

Martin, J. J. (1996). Transitions out of competitive sport for athletes with disabilities. *Therapeutic Recreation Journal*, 30, 128–136.

Martin, J. J. (1999a). A personal development model of sport psychology for athletes with disabilities. *Journal of Applied Sport Psychology*, 11, 181–193.

Martin, J. J. (1999b). Loss experiences in disability in sport. *Journal of Loss and Interpersonal Loss*, 4, 225–230.

Martin, J. J. (2000). Sport transitions among athletes with disabilities: In D. Lavallee and P. Wylleman (eds), *Career transitions in sport: International perspectives* (pp. 161–168). Morgantown, W.V.: Fitness Information Technology.

Martin, J. J. (2002). Training and performance self-efficacy, affect, and performance in wheelchair road racers. *The Sport Psychologist*, 16, 384–395.

Martin, J. J. (2005). Sport psychology consulting with athletes with disabilities. *Sport and Exercise Psychology Review*, 1, 33–39.

Martin, J. J. (2008). Multidimensional self-efficacy and affect in wheelchair basketball players. *Adapted Physical Activity Quarterly*, 25(3), 1–15.

Martin, J. J., Malone, L. A. and Hilyer, J. C. (in review). Personality and mood in women's Paralympic basketball champions. *Journal of Clinical Sport Psychology*.

Martin, J. J., Mushett, C. A. and Eklund, R. C. (1994). Factor structure of the Athletic Identity Measurement Scale with adolescent swimmers with disabilities. *Brazilian International Journal of Adapted Physical Education Research*, 1, 87–99.

Martin, J. J., Mushett, C. A. and Smith, K. L. (1995). Athletic identity and sport orientation of adolescent swimmers with disabilities. *Adapted Physical Activity Quarterly*, 12, 113–123.

Martin, J. J. and Mushett-Adams, C. (1996). Social support mechanisms among athletes with disabilities. Adapted *Physical Activity Quarterly*, 13, 74–83.

Martin Ginis, K. A., Latimer, A. E., Francoeur, C., Hanley, H., Watson, K, Hicks, A. L. and McCartney. (2002). Sustaining exercise motivation and participation among people with spinal cord injuries: lessons learned from a 9 month intervention. *Palaestra*, 18, 38–50, 51.

Martin Ginis, K. A., Latimer, A. E., McKenzie, K., Ditor, D. S., McCartney, N., Hicks, A. L., Bugaresti, J. and Craven, B. C. (2003). Using exercise to enhance subjective well-being among people with spinal cord injury: the mediating influences of stress and pain. *Rehabilitation Psychology*, 48, 157–164.

Masters, K. S, Wittig, A. F., Cox, R. H., Scallen, S. F. and Schurr, K. T. (1995). Effects of training and competition on mood state and anxiety among elite athletes with cerebral palsy. *Palaestra*, 11, 47–52.

Mastro, J. V., Canabal, M. Y. and French, R. (1988). Psychological mood profiles of sighted and unsighted beep baseball players. *Research Quarterly for Exercise and Sport*, 59, 262–264.

Mastro, J. V., Sherrill, C., Gench, B. and French, R. (1987). Psychological characteristics of elite visually impaired athletes: The iceberg profile. *Journal of Sport Behavior*, 10, 39–46.

McNair, D. M., Lorr, M. and Droppleman, L. F. (1971). *Profile of Mood States manual*. San Diego, Calif.: Education & Industrial Testing Services.

Nyland, J., Snouse, S. L., Anderson, M., Kelly, T. and Sterling, J. C. (2000). Soft tissue injuries to USA Paralympians at the 1996 summer games. *Archives of Physical Medicine and Rehabilitation*, 81, 368–373.

Pensgaard, A. M., Roberts, C. G. and Ursin, H. (1999). Motivational factors and coping strategies of Norwegian Paralympic and Olympic winter sport athletes. *Adapted Physical Activity Quarterly*, 16, 238–250.

Rees, T., Smith, B. and Sparkes, A. C. (2003). The influence of social support on the lived experiences of spinal cord injured sportsmen. *The Sport Psychologist*, 17, 135–156.

Rimmer, J. H. (2006). Building inclusive physical activity communities for people with vision loss. *Journal of Visual Impairment and Blindness*, 100, 863–865.

Rimmer, J. H., Riley, B., Wang, E. and Rauworth, A. (2005). Accessibility of health clubs for people with mobility disabilities and visual impairments. *American Journal of Public Health*, 95(11), 2022–2028.

Rimmer, J. H., Riley, B., Wang, E. and Rauworth, A. (2004). Development and validation of AIMFREE: accessibility instruments measuring fitness and recreation environments. *Disability and Rehabilitation*, 26(18), 1087–1095.

Rollins, R. and Nichols, D. (1994). Leisure constraints, attitudes and behavior of people with activity restricting physical disabilities. In I. Henry (ed.), *Leisure: Modernity, postmodernity and lifestyles* (pp. 277–290). Eastbourne, UK: Leisure Studies Association.

Schantz, O. J. and Gilbert, K. (2001). An ideal misconstrued: newspaper coverage of the Atlanta Paralympic games in France and Germany. *Sociology of Sport Journal*, 18, 69–94.

Schell, L. A. and Duncan, M. C. (1999). A content analysis of CBS's coverage of the 1996 Paralympic Games. *Adapted Physical Activity Quarterly*, 16, 27–47.

Smith, B. and Sparkes, A. C. (2005). Men, sport, spinal cord injury, and narratives of hope. *Social Science and Medicine*, 61, 1095–1105.

Smith, D. (2003). A framework for understanding the training process leading to elite performance. *Sports Medicine*, 33, 1103–1126.

Sparkes, A. C. and Smith, B. (2002). Sport, spinal cord injury, embodied masculinities, and the dilemmas of narrative identity. *Men and Masculinities*, 4, 258–285.

Spivock, M., Gauvin, L. and Brodeur, J. J. (2007). Neighborhood-level active living buoys for individuals with physical disabilities. *American Journal of Preventive Medicine*, 32, 224–230.

Thompson, N. and Smith, A. (2003). Pre-occupied with able-bodiedness? An analysis of the British media coverage of the 2000 Paralympic Games. *Adapted Physical Activity Quarterly*, 20, 166–181.

Trieschmann, R. B. (1988). *Spinal cord injuries: Psychological, social and vocational rehabilitation* (2nd edn). New York: Demos.

Wheeler, G., Malone, L. A, VanVlack, S., Nelson, E. R. and Steadward, R. (1996). Retirement from disability sport: a pilot study. *Adapted Physical Activity Quarterly*, 13, 382–399.

Wheeler, G. D., Steadward, R.D., Legg, D., Hutzler, Y., Campbell, E. and Johnson, A. (1999). Personal investment in disability sport careers: An international study. *Adapted Physical Activity Quarterly*, 16, 219–237.

Wickman, K. (2007). "I do not compete in disability": how wheelchair athletes challenge the discourse of abel-ism through action and resistance. *European Journal for Sport and Society*, 4, 151–167.

White, M. J., Gordon, P. and Jackson, V. (2006). Implicit and explicit attitudes towards athletes with disabilities. *Journal of Rehabilitation*, 72, 33–40.

10

THE CONSEQUENCES AND CONTROL OF EMOTIONS IN ELITE ATHLETES

Mark Uphill, Canterbury Christ Church University and Marc Jones, Staffordshire University

> Inside I was saying, 'Keep yourself together. This is the Ryder Cup. You have to perform. You are going to perform. Please let me hit the ball.' My heart was racing and all sorts of emotions were going through every part of my body.
>
> *(Clarke, 2006)*

The quote above from Darren Clarke describes the occasion, when in 2006, he teed off on the first hole playing for Europe against America less than four weeks after his wife passed away from cancer. Many of sport's most memorable moments are those of athletes displaying their emotions in the heat of competition. Who can forget Paul Gascoigne's tearful response to receiving a yellow card that would see him miss the final if England triumphed against Germany in the semi-final of the 1990 Football World Cup; or the anger of Greg Rusedski who contested a disputed line call at 5–3 up in the third set against Andy Roddick at the 2003 Wimbledon tennis tournament, and went on to lose five consecutive games and the match?

Although rarely as intense and as public as the above episodes, athletes experience a wide variety of emotions prior to, during and after performance (Hanin, 2000; Uphill and Jones, 2007). Further, there is, first, a widespread belief that emotions influence sports performance (Prapavessis and Grove, 1991), and second, an appreciation that athletes' emotional displays have implications for how opponents, coaches, spectators and the media react to such episodes (cf. Crocker et al., 2002). Perhaps symptomatic of these beliefs about emotions, athletes such as tennis player Bjorn Borg have been, or are, famed for their apparent lack of emotion; or perhaps more precisely, for their lack of emotional expression during competitive sport. Despite the widespread belief that emotions influence performance, and the probability that athletes use a range of strategies to control their emotions, surprisingly little is known about these twin aspects of athletes' sporting experience.

This chapter begins by providing a review of literature, concerning the consequences and control of a broad range of emotions in elite athletes, highlighting the limitations in this body of knowledge. Based on the identified limitations in the extant literature, the second section of this chapter reports on elite athletes' perceptions of the consequences and control of emotions experienced during sport. We conclude by discussing the data and considering implications for further research.

Given the growing body of evidence suggesting that emotions influence sport performance, it is perhaps not surprising that the ability to control emotions is considered an important psychological skill (Thomas, Murphy and Hardy, 1999). Yet there is surprisingly little literature directed toward these twin aspects of athletes' experience. Of the literature that does bear upon questions regarding the consequences and control of emotions in athletes, described in Chapter 2, much has been extrapolated from understanding of the consequences of emotions in general, and understanding the interrelations between anxiety, coping and performance. Accordingly, the extent to which either of these bodies of knowledge relates to the consequences and control of a broad range of emotions in athletes should be treated circumspectly. Some authors for instance have advised caution when a theory developed in one domain is 'borrowed' and applied in another (Whetten, Felin and King, 2009). Similarly, while an 'emotion-general' theory would imply that all emotions influence performance by similar processes, literature suggests that discrete emotions differ in their antecedents and consequences (cf. Lazarus, 2000).

The literature that has examined relations between discrete emotions (besides anxiety) and performance is characterised by several limitations. First, many studies have used pre-competitive assessments of athletes' emotions (cf. Cerin, Szabo and Williams, 2000). However, because emotions are transient and players' emotions can be influenced by events during competition (cf. Sève et al., 2007), assessments of emotions within competition may explain more variance in performance than pre-competitive assessments of emotion (cf. Jones, Mace and Williams, 2000). Second, studies that rely on global indices of performance (such as finishing position), have been criticised for being insensitive to fluctuations in emotion, and accordingly recommendations to examine subcomponents of sport performance have been made (Jones, 1995). Third, several studies have been conducted in a laboratory setting (e.g. Murphy, Woolfolk and Budney, 1988; Woodman et al., 2009). Although desirable, the extent to which laboratory research translates to the 'heat of competition' is questionable, particularly when a myriad of other variables are no longer controlled.

One approach that arguably does extend to the 'heat of competition' is the individual zones of optimal functioning model (IZOF: Hanin, 2000), originally developed to explain the association between anxiety and sport performance, but extended to include a range of emotions. The IZOF model has in part redressed the 'anxiety-centric' literature, and proposes that there is an idiosyncratic relationship between athletes' 'psychobiosocial state' (of which emotions comprise a part) and performance levels (see Chapter 3 for elaboration). Briefly stated, to understand relations between athletes' psychological state and their performance, IZOF are derived, typically based on athletes' retrospective reports of emotional experiences. Athletes' psychobiosocial states are classified into one of four categories – pleasant-functional, unpleasant-dysfunctional, unpleasant-functional, and pleasant-dysfunctional – and then related to indices of performance such as perceived good and poor performance (e.g. Hanin, 2000; Robazza et al., 2008). Functional states are described as generating enough energy to initiate and maintain the task, alongside the efficient use of available resource. In contrast, dysfunctional states are described as those that result in too much or too little energy for the task, and an inefficient, erroneous or inappropriate use of resources (Hanin, 2000). Emotions impact on performance by influencing the amount and allocation of resources. Satisfaction for instance may be dysfunctional insofar as it may lead to complacency, less effort and striving for success. This model has contributed to a growing recognition that a range of pleasant and unpleasant emotions are central to athletes' experiences, and that idiosyncratic relations between emotions and performance are typically reported. However, several limitations of this approach persist (see Chapter 2), not least concerns about whether some of the adjectives athletes use to describe their psychological state (such as lethargic and purposeful) are ones that describe emotions (e.g. Lazarus, 2000).

One theoretical perspective that may hold some promise in understanding emotion–performance relations is Lazarus's (1991, 2000) cognitive motivational relational (CMR) theory. As described in more detail in Chapter 2, Lazarus (1991) contends that athletes' emotions can be represented by a core relational theme comprising a summary of up to six separate appraisal judgements. The core relational theme in essence describes an assessment of the significance of what is happening to a person in a given situation. For example, for anger, the core relational theme is a 'demeaning offence against me and mine', whereas for happiness the core relational theme is 'making reasonable progress towards the realisation of a goal' (Lazarus, 2000, p. 234). Lazarus (2000) describes three components of performance that could be influenced by emotions generally: motivation, attention to what is happening in a competition, and concentration on the task. Closer inspection of Lazarus's description of these components suggests that concentration on the task, 'that is, on the actions and competitive strategies needed to defeat an opponent' (p. 240), approximates the process of decision making. Lazarus goes on to suggest that each emotion requires a 'mini-theory' that must be consistent with principles employed for emotions generally. From this perspective, each core relational theme evokes an associated action tendency that will influence performance according to the interplay between the individual and situation (cf. Woodman et al., 2009). For example, if guilt following a mistake is associated with an inclination toward reparation of the situation, one might anticipate heightened task-related motivation. However, as others have argued, whether such action tendencies are manifest behaviourally depends on a complex interplay between coping styles, impulse control, cultural norms and situational factors that can either inhibit or increase the likelihood of emotion expression (Frederickson, 1998). For example, a rugby fly half who is angry at being impeded by an opposition forward may not retaliate aggressively because of the likelihood of incurring a penalty and/or injury.

From this perspective, understanding how individuals control, or in Lazarus's terms cope with, emotions, is important to understand the association between emotions and performance. Not only is coping central to the appraisal process, and therefore it influences which emotions are experienced and with what intensity (see Chapter 2), coping also plays a role in how emotions influence performance. Thus Lazarus's CMR theory is potentially useful as a theoretical framework from which to explore both the consequences and control of emotions in athletes.

Folkman and Lazarus (1988) and Lazarus (1991, 2000) suggest that coping behaviours can be classified into one of either two categories. Problem-focused coping involves taking action to change an aspect of the person–environment relationship, either by altering an aspect of the environment (such as verbally challenging a line-judge's call in tennis) or by changing one's situation within it (such as taking a 'comfort break'). Emotion-focused coping alters only what is in the mind of the athlete (Lazarus, 1991). Strategies to cope may involve, but not be limited, to redirecting attention, or a reinterpretation of the significance of the situation. For instance, a cricket batter anxious about facing a fast bowler may redirect attention to ensure that they are correctly positioned in relation to the wicket, or perhaps see this as an opportunity to score quickly because the ball will travel faster off the bat. According to Lazarus (1991), coping can both flow from an emotion (that is, it can occur temporally after an emotion has been elicited), and/or temporally precede an emotion following an initial appraisal of harm, threat or challenge, in effect 'short-circuiting' the emotional reaction and inhibiting the elicitation of the emotion. In turn athletes' attempts at controlling emotions may have both costs and benefits (see Uphill, McCarthy and Jones, 2009), and thus attempts to diminish anger, for instance, may mean that performance is either enhanced or impaired.

Considerable literature has been directed towards coping in sport (see Chapter 2 and Nicholls and Polman, 2007 for reviews). Most of this has been directed to how individuals cope with stressors generally, and less directed towards how individuals cope with emotions specifically. Literature does suggest however that the strategies individuals use to cope with stressful situations can influence their emotional response. For example, Ntoumanis and Biddle (2000) observed that emotion-focused coping (venting) and avoidance coping (behavioural disengagement, distancing) were associated with high levels of cognitive anxiety intensity, whereas problem-focused strategies (such as suppression of competing activities, increasing effort) were associated with a positive interpretation of cognitive anxiety symptoms. With regard to somatic anxiety, individuals with high and facilitative levels of somatic anxiety were more likely than those with similarly high but debilitative levels of anxiety to suppress competing activities and increase effort, and less likely to use behavioural disengagement and venting.

In addition, Gaudreau, Blondin and Lapierre (2002) examined the coping strategies used and affect experienced before, during and after a golf competition. Positive reappraisal was effective in enabling golfers who had not performed to expectations to reduce the negative affect experienced. To facilitate goal attainment and a positive emotional state, Gaudreau et al. (2002) suggested athletes should engage in active coping, planning and positive reappraisal during competition, but refrain from engaging in behavioural disengagement. In summary, although Lazarus's CMR theory may provide a useful framework for exploring emotion–performance relationships in sport, little research has examined the central tenets of this theory.

In a qualitative study with elite athletes, Uphill and Jones (2007) explored the association between athletes' appraisals and experienced emotions. In this study, twelve international athletes (of whom eleven were men), representing a number of team and individual sports including rugby union, athletics, badminton, golf, archery, sailing and snooker, each participated in a semi-structured interview (typically lasting around one or one and a half hours). The interviews were guided by a phenomenological perspective consistent with Lazarus's CMR theory, and consistent with the desire to obtain rich and detailed data (e.g. Hanton, Mellalieu and Young, 2002; Patton, 1990). Although CMR theory provided the framework for the investigation, its efficacy was not preconceived, and its use not considered tantamount to having a priori hypotheses (cf. Krane, Andersen and Strean, 1997).

The interview schedule comprised lead questions and elaboration probes (Patton, 1990), in three related, but distinct sections: an introductory section (designed to orient the participants to the interview; a section containing lead questions and elaboration probes in relation to eight of Lazarus's fifteen emotions (designed to elicit understanding of the antecedents and consequences of emotions); and a final section asking participants to consider in detail any emotions not previously addressed that were pertinent to their sport participation. With the exception of sadness, these eight emotions (anger, anxiety, guilt, happiness, pride, relief, sadness and shame) were considered by Lazarus (2000) to be applicable to sport. Pilot interviews established that sadness was an emotion experienced by athletes who performed below expectations, and that the length of time required to ask questions relating to all fifteen emotions was impractical. Transcribed interviews were subject to concurrent inductive and deductive analysis. Deductive analysis was concerned with identifying data themes associated with Lazarus's theory, while inductive data analysis identified raw data themes not specifically accounted for by Lazarus's theory.

Uphill and Jones (2007) found that all eight expressly targeted emotions were reported by athletes to have occurred while competing, and some athletes reported experiencing others. All athletes reported experiencing relief, while other positively toned emotions reported included happiness (8), excitement (3), pride, satisfaction and joy (1). Negatively toned emotions reported were anger (11), anxiety (10), disappointment (5), guilt (3), embarrassment (3), shame (2), sadness, annoyance and regret (1).

Uphill and Jones reported that athletes' appraisal dimensions (goal relevance, goal congruence, ego-involvement, blame/credit, coping potential and future expectations) were associated with a range of emotions, although the construct of 'core relational themes' was less evident within the data. Although this study provided some evidence that athletes' appraisal judgements were associated with emotions, the consequences and control of emotions (for reasons of parsimony and length constraints within a single manuscript) were not addressed. Below we return to the data, and using the analytic method described above, report athletes' perceptions about the consequences and control of emotions in sport.

Consequences and control of emotions: moving forward

In the light of limitations in the extant literature highlighted above we examine athletes' perceptions of the impact of emotions experienced during competitive sport on sub-components of sport performance. Although it is acknowledged that athletes' self-report of the influence of emotions on performance may be subject to bias (cf. Brewer et al., 1991), the advantage is that the experiential aspect of emotions is retained. Specifically, in the absence of any objective changes in performance, emotions may influence athletes' experience of how the performance felt (for instance, more effortful, less focused, less confident), and this may make an important contribution to understanding the emotion–performance relationship.

Elite athletes' perceptions of how emotions influence performance

Athletes reported performance changes to be associated with all eight emotions (anger, anxiety, guilt, happiness, pride, relief, sadness and shame). Of the processes by which emotions were perceived to influence performance, 32 per cent of the raw data themes were indicative of attentional change (for instance, 'My focus went'), 25 per cent illustrated changes in physiological parameters (such as 'Makes me feel more tense'), 16 per cent were associated with alterations in motivation (such as 'Want to make amends'), and a further 21 per cent were related to changes in decision making (for instance, 'Just shy away from something'). In some instances the same emotion was associated with improvements or impairments in a particular process (so anger could either enhance or impair concentration).

Figure 10.1 provides a summary of the consequences of specific emotions on performance. Although these consequences are illustrated separately for clarity, it should be noted that there is a strong likelihood that cognitive, motivational and physiological processes interact to influence performance. For example, an increase in motivation may require a concomitant increase in the physiological substrates underlying behavioural change. Similarly, changes in athletes' decision making may manifest themselves in overt behaviour, as described by a rugby player recounting feeling anxious during the game, 'You might just shy away from something if things haven't been going your way.' Five athletes remarked that they did not become very emotional during competition, echoing a sentiment from the sailor who expressed a desire to remain calm and emotion-free during competition regardless of whether the emotions experienced were positive or negative:

> I try and not succumb to any of the emotions …. I try and stay very calm, so I can gather all the information that I need and therefore make the right decision …. I tend to think of any emotion that gets me away from a concentrated state of mind is detracting from my decision making.

Indeed, the sailor was one of two athletes who perceived all emotions experienced during the competitive event to be detrimental to performance, regardless of the emotion's valence. Despite this desire to remain emotion-free, emotions at least occasionally punctuated all athletes' competitive experience and were frequently reported as influencing sport performance. Figure 10.1, together with data reported below, also lends credence to the inter- and intra-individual differences in the emotion–performance relationship reported by others (e.g. Hanin, 2000).

Raw Data Theme	Higher Order Theme	General Component
Anger • Wasn't thinking clearly • You're still thinking about the line call • Thoughts aren't channelled to the goal of shooting • Thinking, "I shouldn't have done that." • Makes you concentrate on what you're doing • My focus went	Concentration	Cognitions
• Shot selection • I rushed things • A split second when I lash out	Decision making	
• Gets me going • You can go the other way and not give a loss	Motivation	
• Makes me feel more tense • I'm not fluid, there's no rhythm • Still moving well	Physical perceptions	
Relief • Relaxes me • I feel relaxed • It felt like a release	Physical perceptions	
• Don't do that again	Decision making	
Shame • Thinking this is getting worse... • You're not concentrating on the game • Thinking about letting the opponents back in • Thinking about losing the rally	Concentration	

Raw Data Theme	Higher Order Theme	General Component
Anxiety		
• Start thinking about things that aren't to do with the game • I don't switch off, I dwell on things • You're not thinking purely about your role • I lost perspective • Your mind starts to wander • "Do without this" • Chaos in your head • Worried about making a mistake • Focussed fully on what I had to do • Lose concentration • Can make you zoom in, more alert • Concentrates the mind a little more	Concentration	Cognitions
• Sense of pacing went • I started off fast • Just shy away from something • Start to do things you wouldn't normally do • I don't want to see the ball in case I make another mistake	Decision making	
• I was shaking • My legs felt heavy • A little bit tense • Not completely relaxed • Butterflies in the stomach • Wasn't able to play shots; holding back • The more erratic I get • It affects your mechanics • Your hands can be shaky • Legs wobble	Physical perceptions	
• Try a little harder • Try too hard • Almost trying too hard • Holding back a bit	Motivation	
Sadness	Concentration	
• It can be a distraction		
Pride	Motivation	
• Go for my shots more		
• More focus and attention	Concentration	
Happiness	Concentration	Cognitions
• Affects my concentration • Concentrated better		
• Construct rallies better • There's no hesitation • Don't worry about anything • All strategies go out the window • You can win from any direction • Go for my shots, not play safe • Continue trying things	Decision making	

Raw Data Theme	Higher Order Theme	General Component
Anxiety (cont)		
• Takes out the effort • Push yourself to the limit	Motivation	
• I just freed up • I feel in control • Exaggerate your technique	Physical perceptions	
Guilt		
• Want to make amends, repair the damage that you've done • You grit your teeth and try twice as hard • Wanted to get home	Motivation	
• The focus really goes • Think about it for the next couple of rallies	Concentration	

FIGURE 10.1 The consequences of specific emotions on performance

Cognitive consequences

A common theme across four of the emotions (anger, anxiety, guilt and happiness) was that these emotions were repeatedly identified as influencing the content of athletes' attention, with thoughts redirected to task-irrelevant information. Feeling guilty after wrongly judging a line call out, one badminton player recalled experiencing concerns about others' negative evaluations. Another badminton player stated about happiness, 'I see the [winning] posts too soon .... I am thinking, Yes we've won, but I shouldn't have, my expectations change but they shouldn't.' Further, a rugby player indicated that when anxious, 'You're not thinking 100 per cent purely on your role within the team's performance.' He went on to observe that if there was a period in which he was not directly involved in play, anxiety may be exacerbated, 'You've got more time on your hands to think about things which isn't a good thing.'

The archer in the study recounted an occasion when he was angry with himself for not shooting as well as he would have liked: 'Your thoughts aren't channelled to the goal of shooting correctly ... your mind's constantly trying to find something to get back on track and perform well.'

Although in the majority of instances athletes recalled that emotions had a negative impact on their attention, there were several occasions when athletes reported that emotions had a positive influence on their focus. One professional golfer described an occasion when he felt happy following an unexpected eagle (scoring two shots below par) although he was missing the cut: 'I remember laughing that it was ironic that I holed such a tough shot when I was struggling big time ... [After the eagle] I was thinking more about the cut and playing well rather than how badly I had been playing.'

He went on to observe the following about anxiety, 'It's a good feeling ... it concentrates the mind a little more .... I want to stand up on the first tee with a few butterflies .... If anything it [anxiety] might improve it [performance] because you're just a little more careful about what you are doing.' This latter quote indirectly supports the idea that anxiety is associated with an attentional narrowing effect (e.g. Janelle et al., 1999), and also lends support to previous research highlighting that elite performers often have a facilitative perception of anxiety (Jones and Swain, 1995), and that anxiety may aid concentration (Eysenck and Calvo, 1992).

At least one athlete reported that guilt, pride, sadness and shame had an impact on attention and focus. The failure to identify a more consistent influence of these emotions on attention is probably because both sadness and pride were reported by athletes predominantly after a competitive event, while guilt and shame were experienced less frequently by participants. With regards to sadness for example, one golfer recalled an occasion when thoughts 'would pop into [his] head' about a recent family bereavement and understandably caused him to become saddened: 'I hate to call it a distraction because it makes it sound unimportant and trivial, but not trying to put that down at all, it is a distraction and any form of distraction isn't good on a golf course.' One possible explanation for the deleterious impact emotions sometimes have on athletes' attention is that when emotional, an athlete's attention is directed towards the task of managing the emotion at the expense of focusing on task-relevant cues. Because working memory has a limited capacity (Baddeley, 2001), performance that is reliant on working memory is likely to be impaired by emotions 'using up' valuable resources of working memory. Such a contention is consistent with the proposition that the conscious experience of emotion is represented in working memory (Le Doux, 1998).

Athletes also reported that some emotions influenced their decision making while competing. In particular, athletes' decisions during competitive performance were impacted by the emotions of anger, anxiety, happiness and pride (see Figure 10.1). For example, one badminton player described the impact of anger on shot selection: 'You lose control and you don't think. You've got to build rallies up ... but more errors came into the game [through] selecting the wrong shots.' Happiness appeared to coincide with a feeling of automaticity, in which decisions about performance strategies were much less pervasive: The archer commented, 'There's no hesitation ... all strategies go out of the window.' Similarly, another badminton player indicated that he would 'Just go for my shots.' Although research examining the impact of emotions on athletes' decision making is scant at best, some indirect evidence suggests that criticality of game situations may influence the quality of basketball players' decision making (Bar-Eli and Tractinsky, 2000). Although emotions were not assessed in this study, the criticality of game situations has been associated with heightened anxiety (Smith et al., 2001), and in the light of the evidence above, it is not unreasonable to suggest that a range of emotions may influence athletes' decision making.

Motivational consequences

Comparable to the instances described above, several emotions (anger, anxiety, guilt, relief) were reported as having a beneficial and/or detrimental impact on athletes' motivation. Guilt was associated with a positive motivational influence. One rugby player commented, 'You want to make amends, repair the damage you've done,' and similarly another suggested, 'you try twice as hard'. With regards to anger one golfer noted, 'It helps me if I get nasty with myself ... swear a lot .... Sometimes you've got no fight, if you start having a go, it just gets you going.' Equally, he reported that, 'sometimes you can go the other way and not give a t***.'

The above quotes illustrate intra-individual differences in the impact of discrete emotions on motivation, and suggest that how athletes attempt to manage their emotions can impact performance. The positive and negative impact of emotions on athletes' motivation is also illustrated in anxiety. As mentioned before, one rugby player described feeling anxious and withdrawing involvement a little during the course of a competition, 'You might just shy away from something if things haven't been going your way.' In contrast, one rugby player commented that he sometimes tried too hard when anxious: 'When I'm relaxed going into a game, it [performance] just happens, it's instinctive ... if I'm anxious I think I try a little bit harder to get performance back to where it was ... you just try too hard.' Collectively, these observations support the motivational impact of a range of emotions in sport as suggested by others (Hanin, 2000; Isberg, 2000; Vallerand and Blanchard, 2000).

Physiological consequences

A change in athletes' physiological state as a result of experiencing an emotion (anger, anxiety, happiness) appeared to exert a direct impact on performance, both positive and negative, by altering athletes' coordination and muscular tension (see Figure 10.1). For example, a golfer alluded to a reduction in muscular tension when feeling happy, 'I just freed up ... it felt better .... I mean to the eye it doesn't look any different, to you it feels like a millimetre is a mile.' A decrease in coordination associated with anger was noted by the archer, 'I'm not fluid, there's no rhythm,' but conversely, a badminton player noted that while angry he was 'still moving well'. Interestingly, the least reported influence of emotion on performance reported by athletes was on physiological symptoms (see Figure 10.1). Possibly because the effects of physiological arousal may be masked by the physical exertion required in many sports, except for those emotions characterised by a strong physiological component, emotions generally may influence performance by impacting athletes' cognitions and motivation.

Elite athletes' strategies to cope with emotions experienced during sport

Results depicted in Figure 10.2 illustrate that strategies used by athletes to cope with emotions could be broadly categorised as either problem focused or emotion focused. Problem-focused coping accounted for 24 per cent and emotion-focused coping 76 per cent of all reported strategies. Anshel et al. (2001) have voiced concerns over this dichotomy, suggesting that, on occasion, the same coping strategy could be problem focused and/or emotion focused. For example, individuals may use social support for instrumental reasons such as seeking advice, or for emotional reasons, for instance, attaining sympathy or understanding (Carver, Scheier and Weintraub, 1989). Although it is acknowledged that making fine distinctions between problem-focused and emotion-focused coping may occasionally be problematic, distinctions are nonetheless frequently possible, as evidenced in the data. Within the problem-focused/emotion-focused dichotomy other distinctions could be made, supporting previous research (cf. Carver et al., 1989; Gould, Finch and Jackson, 1993). Specifically, problem-focused strategies used to cope with emotions included attempts to modify the situation (12 per cent of all strategies), and increased task-related effort (12 per cent of all strategies). Emotion-focused coping strategies included attentional control (19 per cent), suppression (12 per cent), reappraisal (21 per cent), imagery (3.5 per cent), breathing techniques (3.5 per cent) and expression (17 per cent). The large proportion of emotion-focused strategies reported in the present study may reflect the transient characteristic of many stressors experienced during sport (such as a contentious line call, personal error or injury) and that many of the stressors may be outside athletes' perceived control, particularly at the moment the incident occurs. Each of the higher-order themes depicting coping strategies emerging from the present analysis is discussed in more detail below.

Problem-focused strategies

Attempts to modify the situation or one's place within it

Athletes reported making attempts to modify the situation to cope with emotions experienced prior to, during and after competition. Experiencing anger after being held back by an opponent, one rugby player commented that he lashed out. 'I think, why hasn't the referee reacted to that? And you sort of snap and take it out on the guy holding you back because you can't take the anger out on the referee.' Lashing out, far from being a mere reaction to a provocation, served a much more instrumental purpose. The rugby player went on to explain, 'I want to prevent it [being held back] from happening again, to make the point that he can't do that to me and expect to get away with it.' The desire to prevent a similar incident unfolding in the future was also evident in a golfer's account of anger during one tournament. Recalling an

Raw Data Theme	Higher Order Theme	General Component
• Go for a game of golf • I do lash out • If I'm embarrassed, I'll just have a shower and go • I confronted him about what he'd said • I've adapted my schedule to suit • Told by an external person, that you're getting anxious, that you want to ease down	Attempts to modify my situation or place within it	Problem focused coping
• Repair the damage that you feel you have done, to try harder • You focus more, become more critical of your performance...see where you went wrong and try and iron things out • Search for a feeling within the mechanics of the swing • We worked and battered ourselves for the next 3 or 4 weeks • Try to do something special to make up for it	Increase task-related effort	
• Breathing techniques	Breathing	Emotion focused coping
• Imagine what's going to happen	Imagery	
• You're concentrating so hard that you don't really [have any emotions] • You get straight back in concentrating • Concentrate on the job in hand • I try and put it out straightaway • Try not to dwell on it • Concentrate on your technique • I tend not to dwell on things • I'm quite good at putting events out of the way; I think that's the same with positive events as well	Attentional Control	Emotion focused coping
• You learn to suppress emotions...channel them out • You don't want to cry in front of people, I didn't want anyone else in the team to see me crying • After one race I bottled it in • I tend not to show any emotion, don't give no body language away	Suppression	

Raw Data Theme	Higher Order Theme	General Component
• It can't be any worse than that • Try and make everything that makes you anxious into a positive thing • I can't do anything about it…anything out of your control, don't worry about it • I came from a new approach…just enjoy that I was shooting • It's just a sport, it's not my life • It was a nice feeling, cause you've earned it • The goal was to get to the tournament, not to make the final and I'd achieved that • We all miss balls and you can't go through life without missing anything • Best thing to do was to play the next hole well	Reappraisal	Emotion-focused coping
• Everyone's going wild, grabbing hold of each other • Laughing to myself • That person has to shout and look really angry • Sometimes you need a release, it's no good bottling things up • Lashed out at the bag • We just lost it, we went mental shouting at him… • I showed my anger at a bad line call	Expression	Emotion-focused coping

FIGURE 10.2 Elite athletes' strategies to cope with emotions experienced during sport

occasion when he became angry at a fellow golfer's unprofessional behaviour and comments made behind his back that 'became a bit personal,' he remarked that, 'I confronted him about what he'd said …. I didn't want to let it carry on ticking away without doing anything about it …. I didn't want to be annoyed any more, so that's why I tried to clear things up.' The golfer went on to say:

> It didn't solve anything and in a way it didn't improve the relationship, but it improved things for me because at least I said my piece and that's all you can do in a way isn't it? The fact that he didn't care just shows what a lack of perspective he's got, but I kind of laid it to rest in a way.

As indicated by others, the effectiveness of particular coping strategies may be assessed at a variety of levels (e.g. Anshel et al., 2001). For example, drinking alcohol to calm pre-competitive anxiety may be effective in controlling anxiety, but impair coordination and decision making.

Examples of attempts at modifying one's situation within an environment were provided by a badminton player and a runner. The badminton player described feeling embarrassed after performing poorly. He remarked, 'As soon as I lose and I'm embarrassed about it I just have a shower and go; any other time I usually stay around and watch.' The runner in contrast described recognising his experience of pre-competitive anxiety (that he was pacing up and down), and channelling this behaviour in a positive manner. 'You are walking up and down, and you think that it's not going to do me any good because I'm going to be tired by the time of the race .... I force myself to sit down, to keep all this nervous energy inside me.'

Increased task-related effort

For many athletes, increasing on–task effort was a coping strategy used in association with negatively valenced emotions. Recalling an experience of guilt following a mistake, one rugby player indicated that he 'wanted to make up for the mistake, to make amends ... repair the damage that you feel you have done and try harder'. Similarly, a golfer unhappy about the mechanics of his golf swing described 'searching for a feeling within the mechanics of the swing' to bring back a more positive feeling. In one of the few instances of shame reported by athletes, one rugby player described feeling ashamed about his contribution to a particularly poor team performance: 'We were absolutely awful, and I just felt, as a side, we gave up. We knew we weren't going to win and we just let them walk all over us .... I was ashamed personally, as well as for the side.' Although the rugby player believed that the occurrence of shame was associated with a decrement in effort during the game itself, the manner of the defeat galvanised effort during training in the coming weeks, 'We worked and battered ourselves ... and basically turned our season around on that one game.' Whether or not increased effort was directed toward coping with the stressor (incurring a heavy defeat) or represented an attempt to cope with the symptoms of shame (such as feelings of personal incompetence or inadequate performance: Izard and Ackerman, 1999), remains unclear. Providing such processes are accessible to conscious awareness, clarifying the intent of athletes' coping behaviours may help to elucidate these processes.

Increasing on-task effort in response to negatively valenced emotions such as embarrassment, guilt or shame is at least intuitively an adaptive coping strategy. However, performance may be impaired in a performer who, by investing additional effort in a motor skill, overrides otherwise automatic processes (e.g. Masters and Maxwell, 2008).

Emotion-focused strategies

Attentional control

Controlling attention emerged as a further strategy to cope with emotions experienced during sport. One runner believed that his ability to concentrate on task-relevant cues during the race diminished the likelihood of emotions occurring. Other athletes commented on the importance of 'concentrating on the job in hand' of, 'putting it [the event which elicited the emotion] out of the way' and not to 'dwell on it'. Precisely how athletes were able to redeploy attention onto task-relevant cues remains intriguing, and warrants further scrutiny. For example, one archer recalled trying to concentrate on his technique to cope with the experience of anger. While this may enable the athlete to cope with the emotion, consciously focusing on aspects of technique may not help performance if it involves consciously trying to control a movement (Masters and Maxwell, 2008). Controlling one's thoughts may also be problematic. Attempts to suppress certain thoughts may paradoxically exacerbate the very thoughts one is attempting to suppress, particularly when under stress (Wegner et al., 1990).

Expression and suppression

One postulated function of emotion expression is to inform others about the expressers' feelings and motives, which may in turn motivate actions by the perceiver (Ekman and Davidson, 1994). A sailor described simulating the expression of anger to achieve a specific objective:

> Quite often when two boats come together there's a bit of an argument about who's in the right and it's quite often the case that who shouts the loudest in that situation comes out best …. I allocate one person on the boat, either me or the crew to be a 'shouter' in those situations and we practice it, shouting and looking really angry to scare the other bloke off. But inside you've got to be thinking, 'I've got to be doing this now' rather than becoming emotional about things and losing yourself in that shout.

Although this was the only reported strategic use of emotion expression in the apparent absence of emotional feeling other athletes discussed expressing anger in response to specific stimuli. One badminton player described an occasion when he and his partner lost control following one decision and were eventually beaten by their opponents:

> We were well up, 13–10 in the final game and I hit it [the shuttlecock] onto the net and it hit the line, we were sure of it. The umpire couldn't actually see it, it was right underneath him, he had his pad in front of him and he called it out! … Me and my partner both lost it, went mental because it was plainly in …. I don't think we started playing for about another five or six minutes.

Although the expression of emotion may perform a communicative function, and in some cases influence others' behaviour, expression of anger in response to a contentious line call is unlikely to impact the umpire's behaviour (that is, their decision). Accordingly, athletes may also express emotions as a form of catharsis, a form of emotional release, akin to Carver et al.'s (1989) venting of emotion. While the expression of anger had a negative effect on the performance of the badminton player, one golfer suggested that he needed to release his anger. 'If you can outburst and finish, get it out of your system and get on with playing that's good … it's the one which keeps bubbling up and you don't show it outwardly …. You've got to lose it sometimes, although we're not meant to.'

Conversely, on occasions, athletes also reported a desire to suppress emotions during competition. One badminton player remarked that he tried not to display any emotion, 'I tend not to show any emotion, I try to stay as calm as possible and remain the same all the time if I can.' A runner demonstrated that her decision to express or suppress emotions was influenced by the presence of significant others:

> I don't want people to see faults in my characteristics, especially in front of people who I have to compete against …. You have to portray yourself in a way as invincible, as a confident, level-headed person …. After one race I bottled my disappointment in. The person who I was with, I didn't want to see me in that state, I just held it in.

While suppressing emotions can have important social consequences there is growing evidence that suppression may not be that effective and may even be costly as a strategy. To explain, suppressing emotions may not change how the person is feeling and may use up important cognitive resources (Richards and Gross, 2000).

Imagery

The sailor described using imagery to cope with anxiety:

> I spend most of my time thinking about what's going to happen in the race … whether it be wind patterns, the position of the fleet … you've just got to think of every conceivable option and have all the options in your head so that when you see something happen, you can immediately go to that scenario and take advantage of it. It's basically lack of knowledge about what might happen that makes you anxious and frustrated.

Imagery has been proposed as one strategy that may be used to control emotions (Martin, Moritz and Hall, 1999). The use of motivational general mastery (MG-M) imagery, which represents effective coping and mastery of challenging situations, is implied within the sailor's quote. The use of MG-M imagery is proposed to alter an athlete's appraisal of a situation (Jones et al., 2002; Martin et al., 1999). By using MG-M imagery an athlete has dealt successfully with situations that may arise. This positive (albeit virtual) experience results in a more appropriate emotional state as the athlete feels better prepared for competition.

Breathing techniques

The archer used breathing techniques in combination with attentional control ('concentrating on your technique') and reappraisal ('It's just a sport, it's not my life') to manage his anger. Breathing techniques may be useful for reducing physiological arousal, which may have a positive effect in reducing the intensity of the emotion experienced (Zillman, 1971). As highlighted by previous research, athletes often use different strategies simultaneously to cope with stressors (Gould, Eklund and Jackson, 1993; Gould et al., 1993).

Reappraisal

As depicted in Figure 10.2, reappraisal was the singular coping strategy most frequently used by these athletes to control their emotions. One golfer recounted the following episode:

> I'd made a bogey [scoring a six] on a par five hole, and at the time I was in with a chance of winning. To drop a shot on that hole was pretty poor, especially compared to the rest of the field .... I wasn't very happy about bogeying the hole, but I thought the best thing to do was to play the next hole well .... The only shot you can do anything about is the one you're about to play. You can't do anything about the one you just hit.

It is perhaps not surprising that reappraisal is such a frequently used strategy given its flexibility. Reappraisal involves reinterpreting a stimulus in ways that change its emotional 'punch', and can both reduce or increase an emotion's intensity and/or its quality (Uphill et al., 2009). For instance, a rugby player who re-evaluates a 'handling error' as something that was related to the pass of a teammate, rather than a personal transgression, may be more inclined to feel anger or disappointment toward a teammate rather than self-directed guilt or embarrassment. Many cognitive strategies, such as imagery and self-talk, can be used for reappraisal in that they can be used to change the way an event is viewed (Jones, 2003).

Attempts to reappraise a stimulus event may not, however, always be successful. One rugby player described making a mistake, 'If you've let the side down terribly, obviously you're going to feel guilty ... but then you think that you can't put losing a game down to one incident ... but you can't help it, you feel guilty for making a mistake and letting the team down.'

Although Figure 10.2 depicts strategies instigated by athletes themselves to cope with emotions, seeking the support of others to either manage the situation or regulate the emotional response has been identified as one coping strategy in previous research (Carver et al., 1989). Indeed, the role of others was instrumental in helping one runner's reappraisal of pre-competitive anxiety:

I'd won this particular race [she names the competition] the previous two years and I really wanted to get the hat-trick. One of the girls had run faster than me that season ... and she was jogging past me and everything and I was thinking she was faster than me. It was a fear of her beating me .... I almost 'lost it' in the warm-up, had to go to the toilet, and my coach had a real go at me, really told me off. He told me that I'd trained a lot faster, I was capable of running a lot faster and that I could win the race. He told me to go for a jog and sort my head out. I was a lot better after that .... It was literally ten minutes when I was really, really, nervous.

Alongside athletes' own strategies to manage emotions, significant others can play an active role in shaping the emotions of the athletes with whom they interact.

Discussion and future research

Collectively, the data provide some support for the applicability of Lazarus's CMR theory as they describe broadly the impact of emotions on performance, and the coping strategies athletes employ to control their emotions. The data suggest that a range of discrete emotions may influence athletes' performances by altering cognitive functioning (such as attention and decision making), motivation and/or physiological processes. An 'emotion-specific' impact on performance did not emerge from the data, however, and there remain several issues to be reconciled with the coping data, as discussed below.

Issue 1: Can coping occur prior to an appraisal of harm, threat or challenge?

From a CMR perspective, coping mediates the emotional response. However data in the present chapter suggest that athletes may use various coping strategies much earlier in the emotion-generative process than suggested by Lazarus. Specifically, they may invoke strategies to minimise the occurrence of emotions prior to an appraisal of harm, threat or challenge. As reported earlier, the sailor used imagery to 'play out' the occurrence of likely scenarios to reduce potential anxiety at the time of competition. Whether it was an appraisal of challenge that initially prompted this engagement in imagery, or indeed whether the construct of coping is sufficiently broad to accommodate such activities within its rubric, remains a question that would benefit from resolution.

Issue 2: Do athletes need to cope with events perceived as positive?

Not only do athletes experience negatively valenced emotions, they also experience positively valenced emotions that they perceive as impairing and/or improving performance. From a CMR perspective, only stressful appraisals of harm, threat or challenge warrant the use of coping strategies; events appraised as positive or benign do not (Anshel et al., 2001). This represents a difficulty for CMR theory, particularly in an environment where it may be necessary to 'cope' with intense excitement or happiness, for example. Understanding how athletes may cope with or 'downplay' positive events and emotions has seemingly been ignored within the extant literature.

Issue 3: Do strategies that are invoked automatically without an athlete's awareness constitute 'coping'?

There has been considerable debate about this issue, in relation to coping generally and the regulation of emotions in particular (e.g. Cramer, 2000; Gross, 1999; Hardy, Jones and Gould, 1996). Although a full discussion of this issue is beyond the scope of this chapter (see also Chapter 2 of this book), it is important to consider the implications of this debate for the control of emotions in sport. As opposed to viewing conscious versus unconscious strategies as a dichotomy or categorical distinction, it may be favourable to view emotion-regulation strategies as a continuum of processes that vary in the degree to which they are conscious, effortful and automatic (Gross, 1999). Indeed, it is probable that strategies that were once conscious and effortful, over time, with continued practice, become automatic and executed without conscious deliberation. The automaticity of coping has been associated with how effective the strategy is in some sport research (e.g. Gould et al., 1993), and the automaticity of emotion regulation strategies has been associated with a reduction in emotion experience and less maladaptive cardiovascular responses (cf. Mauss, Cook and Gross, 2007).

Issue 4: How can the unfolding emotion–coping–performance relationship be explored?

Methodologically, the present chapter examined the emotion–performance and coping strategies in isolation. This analytic approach can be defended on the basis that attaining some (additional) understanding of the elements involved in the emotion–performance relationship may be a useful precursor to understanding the process itself. However, given the theorised mediating or moderating role of coping within this relationship it is desirable to use designs that facilitate understanding of how coping influences this relationship. As identified in issue 3 above, understanding the characteristics of 'coping' has implications for how we understand the emotion–performance relationship. This study for example points to overlap in the consequences of emotion, and some coping strategies (such as change in attentional focus). As others have argued (cf. Gross and Thompson, 2007), separating the generation and consequences of emotions from attempts to regulate emotions can be difficult, and there remains a need to be (more) explicit about the grounds for assuming emotion-regulatory efforts are occurring. Research of a longitudinal nature has been advocated to examine coping processes (Lazarus, 1993), and it is logical that the same argument extends to consideration of the emotion–coping–performance relationship. Each methodological decision brings to bear its own strengths and limitations, and thus building an 'edifice' of knowledge (cf. Forscher, 1963), requires embracing and valuing an eclectic range of approaches to address this question.

In conclusion, the data provide some support for the notion that Lazarus's CMR theory may provide a useful framework for examining the emotion–performance relationship. Although a range of discrete emotions may influence athletes' performances by altering cognitive functioning (such as attention and decision making), motivation and/or physiological processes, an 'emotion-specific' impact on performance did not emerge from the data. These qualitative data also lend insight into the processes by which emotions may influence sport performance, and include aspects (such as decision making) which are rarely explicit within theories of emotion–performance relationships (e.g. Hanin, 2000).

There also remain several questions that future theoretical development and research may help to reconcile. Such advances are both desirable and necessary if a more complete understanding of the consequences and control of emotions in athletes is to be attained.

References

Anshel, M. H., Kim, K-W., Kim, B-H., Chang, K-J. and Eom, H J. (2001). A model for coping with stressful events in sport: theory, application, and future directions. *International Journal of Sport Psychology*, 32, 43–75.

Baddeley, A. D. (2001). Is working memory still working? *American Psychologist*, 56, 849–864.

Bar-Eli, M. and Tractinsky, N. (2000). Criticality of game situations and decision making in basketball: an application of performance crisis perspective. *Psychology of Sport and Exercise*, 1, 27–39.

Brewer, B. W., Van Raalte, J. L., Linder, D. E. and Van Raalte, N. S. (1991). Peak performance and the perils of retrospective introspection. *Journal of Sport and Exercise Psychology*, 13, 227–238.

Carver, C. S., Scheier, M. F. and Weintraub, J. K. (1989). Assessing coping strategies: a theoretically based approach. *Journal of Personality and Social Psychology*, 56, 267–283.

Cerin, E., Szabo, A., Hunt, N. and Williams, C. (2000). Temporal patterning of competitive emotions: a critical review. *Journal of Sports Sciences*, 18, 605–626

Clarke, D. (2006). *Heroes all: My 2006 Ryder Cup story*. London: Hodder & Stoughton.

Cramer, P. (2000). Defence mechanisms in psychology today: further processes for adaptation. *American Psychologist*, 55, 637–646.

Crocker, P. R. E., Kowalski, K. C., Graham, T. R. and Kowalski, N. P. (2002). Emotion in sport. In J. M. Silva III and D. E. Stevens (eds), *Psychological foundations of sport* (pp. 107–131). London: Allyn & Bacon.

Dale, D. A. (1996). Existential phenomenology: emphasising the experience of the athlete in sport psychology research. *The Sport Psychologist*, 10, 307–321.

Ekman, P. and Davidson, R. J. (1994). Afterword: what is the function of emotions? In P. Ekman and R. J. Davidson (eds), *The nature of emotion: Fundamental questions* (pp. 137–139). Oxford: Oxford University Press.

Eysenck, M. W. and Calvo, M. G. (1992). Anxiety and performance: the processing efficiency theory. *Cognition and Emotion*, 6, 409–434.

Folkman, S. and Lazarus, R. S. (1988). Coping as a mediator of emotion. *Journal of Personality and Social Psychology*, 54, 466–475.

Forscher, B. K. (1963). Chaos in the brickyard. *Science*, 142, 339.

Frederickson, B. L. (1998). What good are positive emotions? *Review of General Psychology*, 2, 300–319.

Gaudreau, P., Blondin, J. P. and Lapierre, A. M. (2002). Athletes' coping during a competition: relationship of coping strategies with positive affect, negative affect, and performance–goal discrepancy. *Psychology of Sport and Exercise*, 3, 125–150.

Gould, D., Eklund, R. C. and Jackson, S. A. (1993). Coping strategies used by U.S. Olympic wrestlers. *Research Quarterly for Exercise and Sport*, 64, 83–93.

Gould, D., Finch, L. M. and Jackson, S. A. (1993). Coping strategies used by national champion figure skaters. *Research Quarterly for Exercise and Sport*, 64, 453–468.

Gross, J. J. (1999). Emotion regulation: past, present, future. *Cognition and Emotion*, 13, 551–573.

Gross, J. J. and Thompson, R. A. (2007). Emotion regulation: conceptual foundations. In J. J. Gross (ed.), *Handbook of emotion regulation* (pp. 3–24). London: Guilford Press.

Hanin, Y. L. (2000). Individual zones of optimal functioning (IZOF) model: emotion–performance relationships in sport. In Y. L. Hanin (ed.), *Emotions in sport* (pp. 65–89). Champaign, Ill.: Human Kinetics.

Hanton, S., Mellalieu, S. and Young, S. G. (2002). A qualitative investigation of the temporal patterning of the precompetitive anxiety response. *Journal of Sports Sciences*, 20, 911–928.

Hardy, L., Jones, G. and Gould, D. (1996). *Understanding psychological preparation for sport: Theory and practice of elite performers.* Chichester: Wiley.

Isberg, L. (2000). Anger, aggressive behaviour, and athletic performance. In Y. L. Hanin (ed.), *Emotions in sport* (pp. 113–133). Champaign, IL: Human Kinetics.

Izard, C. E. and Ackerman, B. P. (1999). Motivational, organisational, and regulatory functions of discrete emotions. In M. Lewis and J. M. Haviland-Jones (eds), *Handbook of emotions*, 2nd edn (pp. 253–264). London: Guilford Press.

Janelle, C. M., Singer, R. N. and Williams, A. M. (1999). External distraction and attentional narrowing: visual search evidence. *Journal of Sport and Exercise Psychology*, 21, 70–91.

Jones, G. and Swain, A. (1995). Predispositions to experience debilitative and facilitative anxiety in elite and nonelite performers. *The Sport Psychologist*, 9, 201–211.

Jones, J. G. (1995). More than just a game: research developments and issues in competitive state anxiety in sport. *British Journal of Psychology*, 86, 449–478.

Jones, M. V. (2003). Controlling emotions in sport. *The Sport Psychologist*, 17, 471–486.

Jones, M. V., Mace, R. D., Bray, S. R., MacRae, A. and Stockbridge, C. (2002). The impact of motivational imagery on the emotional state and self-efficacy levels of novice climbers. *Journal of Sport Behaviour*, 25, 57–73.

Jones, M. V., Mace, R. D. and Williams, S. (2000). Relationship between emotional state and performance during international field hockey matches. *Perceptual and Motor Skills*, 90, 691–701.

Krane, V., Andersen, M. and Strean, W, B. (1997). Issues of qualitative research methods and presentation. *Journal of Sport and Exercise Psychology*, 19, 213–218.

Lazarus, R. S. (1991). *Emotion and adaptation.* Oxford: Oxford University Press.

Lazarus, R. S. (1993). Toward better research on stress and coping. *American Psychologist*, 55, 665–673.

Lazarus, R. S. (2000). How emotions influence performance in competitive sports. *The Sport Psychologist*, 14, 229–252.

LeDoux, J. E. (1998). *The emotional brain: The mysterious underpinnings of emotional life.* New York: Simon & Schuster.

Martin, K., Moritz, S. E. and Hall, C. R. (1999). Imagery use in sport: a literature review and applied model. *The Sport Psychologist*, 13, 245–268.

Masters, R. and Maxwell, J. (2008). The theory of reinvestment. *International Review of Sport and Exercise Psychology*, 1, 160–183.

Mauss, I. B., Cook, C. L. and Gross, J. J. (2007). Automatic emotion regulation during an anger provocation. *Journal of Experimental Social Psychology*, 43, 698–711.

Murphy, S. M., Woolfolk, R. L. and Budney, A. J. (1988). The effects of emotive imagery on strength performance. *Journal of Sport and Exercise Psychology*, 10, 334–345.

Nicholls, A. R. and Polman, R. C. J. (2007). Coping in sport: a systematic review. *Journal of Sports Sciences*, 25, 11–31.

Ntoumanis, N. and Biddle, S. J. H. (2000). Relationship of intensity and direction of competitive anxiety with coping strategies. *The Sport Psychologist*, 14, 360–371.

Patton, M. Q. (1990). *Qualitative evaluation methods*. Newbury Park, Calif.: Sage.

Prapavessis, H. and Grove, J. R. (1991). Precompetitive emotions and shooting performance: the mental health and zone of optimal function models. *The Sport Psychologist*, 5, 223–234.

Richards, J. M. and Gross, J. J. (2000). Emotion regulation and memory: the cognitive costs of keeping one's cool. *Journal of Personality and Social Psychology*, 79, 410–424.

Robazza, C., Pellizzari, M., Bertollo, M. and Hanin, Y. L. (2008). Functional impact of emotions on athletic performance: comparing the IZOF model and the directional perception approach. *Journal of Sports Sciences*, 26, 1033–1047.

Sève, C., Ria, L., Poizat, G., Saury, J. and Durand, M. (2007). Performance-induced emotions experienced during high-stakes table tennis matches. *Psychology of Sport and Exercise*, 8, 25–46.

Smith, N. C., Bellamy, M., Collins, D. J. and Newell, D. (2001). A test of processing efficiency theory in a team sport context. *Journal of Sports Sciences*, 19, 321–332.

Thomas, P. R., Murphy, S. M. and Hardy, L. (1999). Test of performance strategies: development and preliminary validation of a comprehensive measure of athletes' psychological skills. *Journal of Sports Sciences*, 17, 697–711.

Uphill, M. A. and Jones, M. V. (2007). Antecedents of emotions in elite athletes: a cognitive motivational relational perspective. *Research Quarterly for Exercise and Sport*, 78, 79–89.

Uphill, M. A., McCarthy, P. J. and Jones, M. V. (2009). Getting a grip on emotion regulation in sport: conceptual foundations and practical applications. In S. Hanton and S. Mellalieu (eds), *Advances in applied sport psychology* (pp. 162–194). London: Routledge.

Vallerand, R. J. and Blanchard, C. M. (2000). The study of emotion in sport and exercise: historical, definitional, and conceptual perspectives. In Y. L. Hanin (ed.), *Emotions in sport* (pp. 3–37). Champaign, Ill.: Human Kinetics.

Wegner, D. M., Shortt, J. W., Blake, A. W. and Page, M. S. (1990). The suppression of exciting thoughts. *Journal of Personality and Social Psychology*, 28, 409–418.

Whetten, D. A., Felin, T. and King, B. G. (2009). The practice of theory-borrowing in organisational studies: current issues and future directions. *Journal of Management*, 35, 537–563.

Woodman, T., Davis, P. A., Hardy, L., Callow, N., Glasscock, I. and Yuill-Proctor, J. (2009). Emotions and sport performance: an exploration of happiness, hope and anger. *Journal of Sport and Exercise Psychology*, 31, 169–188.

Zillmann, D. (1971). Excitation transfer in communication-mediated aggressive behaviour. *Journal of Experimental Social Psychology*, 7, 419–434.

11

THE EMOTIONAL RESPONSE TO ATHLETIC INJURY

Re-injury anxiety

Natalie Walker, University of Northampton and Joanne Thatcher, Aberystwyth University

> Being injured is like being in someone else's body. It is the worst thing you have to cope with as a player, and of course there is then the worry of doing it again and going through it all over again.
>
> *(quote from professional Soccer player; Walker, 2006)*

Reports of athletes experiencing fears, or anxieties, about re-injury during rehabilitation from athletic injury and the return to training and competition have become increasingly common (Hare, Evans and Callow, 2008; Hunt and Short, 2006; Mankad, Wallman and Gordon, 2009; Monsma and Mensch, 2009; Niven, 2007; Podlog and Eklund, 2006, 2007a, 2007b; Podlog, Lochbaum and Stevens, 2010; Thatcher et al., 2007; Walker, Thatcher and Lavallee, 2007, 2010; Fear of re-injury is a prominent emotion associated with returning to sport following an athletic injury (Johnston and Carroll, 1998). Athletes have also identified fear of re-injury as one of their most salient sources of stress on return to sport (Bianco, Malo and Orlick, 1999; Gould et al., 1997). Re-injury anxiety is a particularly common response to injury, particularly for injured athletes who require surgery, experience a long rehabilitation period, and/or those who sustained severe injuries (Cassidy, 2006). Re-injury has been defined as 'an injury occurring after an initial injury of the same type and location' (Hägglund et al., 2005, p. 343).

This chapter outlines the proposed impact of fears and anxieties related to re-injury, and offers conceptual clarity about these two concepts. The chapter then summarises key re-injury anxiety research findings, and considers the limitations of research that has attempted to measure re-injury anxiety. Thus the chapter describes a valid and reliable method of measuring re-injury anxieties by practitioners and in future research. Following a discussion of the limited research examining the usefulness of psychological interventions for reducing re-injury anxiety, the chapter considers the application of the research and understanding gained to date. An applied case study example is presented, and concluding sections focus on how to help athletes cope with re-injury anxiety.

It must be noted that much of the literature on fear of re-injury and re-injury anxiety is anecdotal. The majority of studies also do not offer conceptual clarification on fear of re-injury and re-injury anxiety, and this should be addressed in future research (Walker et al., 2010). Conceptual clarity (on the lines outlined in this chapter) means that coaches, athletes, practitioners and researchers will 'speak the same language' and discuss the same concepts, leading to increased shared understanding.

Fear of re-injury or re-injury anxiety: conceptual clarity

Fear of re-injury (Kvist, Sporrstedt and Good, 2005; Podlog and Eklund, 2007a, 2007b; Tracey, 2003) and re-injury anxiety (Podlog et al., 2010) are often mentioned in contemporary sports injury literature. However, authors rarely define their conceptual framework (Cassidy, 2006; Kleinert, 2002).

Providing initial insight into this debate, the emotional response to athletic injury was explored by Walker (2006) using a longitudinal, case-study approach. Injured athletes (n = 5) ranging from university standard, semi-professional through to professional status, were sampled from rugby league (n = 2), rugby union (n – 1), professional football (n = 1) and martial arts (n = 1), and were interviewed fortnightly, using an existential phenomenological interview approach (Dale, 1996). The interviews produced concurrent information regarding the athletes' lived experiences of their injuries. Interviews commenced at the onset of injury and followed each athlete through the recovery process, including the return to sport competition. In addition, all athletes were interviewed three months following their return to sports performance to allow reflection on issues raised previously and discussion of the athlete's experiences in recommencing competition. All interviews were transcribed and analysed using inductive content analysis procedures. Temporal changes in emotions and individual responses in experiences of athletic injury were explored.

Walker (2006) argued against fear of re-injury as a prominent emotional response to injury, and stated that a more common response is re-injury anxiety. The injured athletes used terms such as nervousness, worry and unease when discussing emotions related to re-injury thoughts, in contrast to fear terminology such as terror, dread and panic. Therefore, as illustrated below, all athletes described emotions that appeared to manifest *re-injury anxiety* as opposed to *fear of re-injury*.

The fear–anxiety debate was summarised by Hackfort and Schwenkmezger (1993). These authors concluded that with fear there is certainty regarding the sources of danger, and therefore actions of escape occur. Athletes within Walker's (2006) study did not take actions of escape, despite being worried about re-injury during rehabilitation exercises. For example, they continued to participate in rehabilitation throughout the recovery process, although often with some hesitation. Anxiety is associated with the 'development of the higher nervous system and the abilities of abstraction and anticipation' (p. 330). Fear is defined as stimulus-specific and associated with definite danger, whereas anxiety is connected to the anticipation and imagination of ambiguity and uncertainty. Therefore, anxiety is more a feeling of what might happen rather than a response to an obvious fear-provoking situation (Hackfort and Schwenkmezger, 1993). This can be seen in Walker's (2006) findings, as the athletes in this study were anticipating possible re-injury and imagining scenes of the injury recurring rather than being aware of a definite danger that would cause re-injury.

Fear is a fundamental biological mechanism, whereas anxiety is composed of different elements (cognitive and somatic) and is associated with learning (Hackfort and Schwenkmezger, 1993). Cognitive and somatic state anxiety were evident in the emotional responses to injury for the athletes in Walker's (2006) research. Within the cognitive state dimension the athletes reported thinking about the injury recurring during rehabilitation exercises, functional rehabilitation exercises, and on the return to practice and competition. They reported images of the injury playing over repeatedly in their minds in various clinical and sport-specific situations. They also reported that, in conjunction with their cognitive state anxiety, they felt nauseous, sweaty and tense, reflecting their experience of somatic state anxiety.

Although injury is a definite danger in sports participation, there is no certainty or clarity regarding the extent of injury risk and the character of injury situations, therefore athletes associate the risk of injury with situations of varying general characteristics and degrees of uncertainty (Kleinert, 2002). The response to athletic injury has been proposed to be individual and dynamic (Wiese-Bjornstal et al., 1998). For all the athletes in Walker's (2006) study, re-injury anxiety was evident throughout the injury process, including both rehabilitation and re-entry to practice/competition. However, for these athletes, re-injury anxiety was more salient towards re-entry to competition, as has been suggested by Taylor and Taylor (1997). Re-injury anxiety was also more salient for the more severely injured athletes in the sample. The two more severely injured athletes stated that they were anxious about re-injury because they believed their injury site was more vulnerable and weakened as a result of the severity of their injury, so they anticipated that minor blows might cause re-injury. They also reported feeling unable to cope with the lengthy rehabilitation, the pain suffered and the daily hassles the injury imposed.

A high degree of ambiguity remains regarding injury situations and the injury itself, hence a more accurate term for the most part appears to be re-injury anxiety rather than fear of re-injury. Moreover, it is stated that injury-related concerns and anxieties in many respects result from learning processes and are not fundamental or biological. They derive from previous experience (such as the original injury experience) and other developmental factors (such as personality, injury severity, injury location and rehabilitation time; Kleinert, 2002). This kind of emotional development is more typical of anxiety than fear. Re-injury has been defined as 'an injury occurring after an initial injury of the same type and location' (Hägglund et al., 2005, p. 343). Hence, re-injury anxiety can be defined as worries over the possibility of an injury recurring after an initial injury of the same type and location.

However, it is important to note that we do not propose that fear of re-injury does not exist. For the reasons suggested above we propose that within a competitive sports context the most common response of the two is re-injury anxiety. Nevertheless some athletes may exhibit a response more akin to fear of re-injury. Walker (2006) reported how one male case study participant kept replaying his injury scenario in his mind and endured frequent nightmares where he saw the injury occurring repetitively. The images were reported to be significant enough to cause him to wake on many occasions. The athlete used avoidance strategies to cope with his injury. These included avoiding team mates, avoiding reminders of his sport and injury status, and avoiding rehabilitation activities that he perceived would put the injured site at risk and potentially cause further injury or re-injury. This athlete appeared to be experiencing fear of re-injury rather than re-injury anxiety.

Much of the existing research discusses fear of re-injury as opposed to re-injury anxiety. This section outlines the impact of fear of re-injury on the athlete. However, the same principles can also be applied to re-injury anxiety (Walker et al., 2010).

The impact of fear of re-injury

Fear of re-injury is always present for the injured athlete and the athlete who has just recovered from injury (Draper and Ladd, 1993; Heil, 1993a; Gould et al., 1997). This suggestion has been supported by previous research in this context (e.g. Draper and Ladd, 1993; Gould et al., 1997). Klavora (1976) was one of the earliest authors to discuss emotions related to re-injury and their effects. He proposed that emotions related to re-injury thoughts can actually predispose athletes to re-injury, although he did not provide any empirical evidence in support of this. Fear of re-injury also has a detrimental effect on performance when the athlete returns to competition (Pargman, 1999).

Fear of injury results in physiological and psychological changes that impact performance and ultimately increase the risk of injury (Heil, 1993a). This concept could also be applied to fear of re-injury (e.g. Taylor and Taylor, 1997). Fear of injury diminishes concentration and self-confidence (psychological changes) and produces increased muscle tension and over-arousal (physiological changes) (Heil, 1993a). The athlete who fears injury is also said to be preoccupied with the physical sensations arising from the site of the injury or with slight reductions in performance (such as brief loss of balance). These perceptions affect performance through decreased efficiency in the biomechanics of skill execution, poor use of energy resources and decreased attention. This may then intensify the initial psychological and physiological effects, which leads to a mutually reinforcing, self-perpetuating cycle (Heil, 1993a; Williams and Andersen, 1998). Taylor and Taylor (1997) stated that fear of re-injury produces the responses proposed by Heil (1993a). These include psychological decrements such as reduced confidence and poor focus which inhibit progression in the return to sport (Chase, Magyar and Drake, 2005; Taylor and Taylor, 1997; Tripp et al., 2007). Furthermore, individuals complain that their performance was worse after injury than before, and fear of re-injury may contribute to an athlete's failure to return to their sport (Kvist et al., 2005).

Re-injury fears also cause physiological changes, such as muscular bracing, which can increase the likelihood of re-injury (Heil, 1993). Muscular bracing (also called muscular guarding or splinting) is a common protective response to injury which can isolate or decrease the mobility of the injured area through postural adjustment (Heil, 1993a). Fear of re-injury is an expected reaction following injury, and develops from a lack of confidence and trust in the injured area (Taylor and Taylor, 1997). The emotions related to re-injury affect rehabilitation adherence, and are reported to reduce adherence to rehabilitation when re-injury anxiety is experienced by athletes (Pizzari et al., 2002).

A lack of confidence and trust in the injured site and fear of re-injury can produce a tentative performance (Chase et al., 2005; Johnston and Carroll, 1998; Petitpas and Danish, 1995; Taylor and Taylor, 1997). Hesitancy could also cause decreased coordination and increased muscle tension and bracing, which are linked to re-injury occurrence (Gould and Udry, 1994; Taylor and Taylor, 1997). Distractions as a consequence of fear of re-injury (such as perceptions of discomfort or pain) may also occur and thus increase the fear of re-injury further.

On return to competition athletes often report being 'rusty', and a challenge for them is to return to the comfort and ease of skill execution that was evident prior to injury (Podlog and Eklund, 2006; Taylor and Taylor, 1997). They often report preoccupation with details of technique to the detriment of natural feelings associated with well-practised and autonomous skill execution. Focusing on the technique can also cause a lack of movement flow and contribute to muscular bracing, which increases the likelihood of re-injury and decreases confidence in skill execution (Taylor and Taylor, 1997).

Where re-injury fears are greater and more long-term, this is likely to be disruptive enough to affect the athlete's speed of recovery and mental readiness for sports performance (Heil, 1993a). However, there are no studies at present that have quantified different levels of fear of re-injury. Hence, it is currently impossible to state that fear of re-injury ranges along a continuum of intensity levels. Despite researchers failing to outline their conceptual framework when discussing fear of re-injury or re-injury anxiety, there are some key research findings which it is important to outline. The next section of the chapter summarises them, and concludes with a critical overview of this body of research.

Re-injury anxiety research findings

Re-injury anxiety behavioural responses

A qualitative study on taping conducted by Hunt and Short (2006) revealed insight into the relationship between protective behaviours and re-injury anxiety. Eleven collegiate athletes were interviewed. The athletes represented three injury groups: recent injury, past injury and no prior injury. All participants were taping their ankles at the time of the study. The most common feeling among all the athletes was worry about injury or re-injury. The athletes reported that taping resulted in feelings of increased confidence, increased strength, and decreased injury and re-injury anxiety.

Changes in re-injury anxiety through rehabilitation

Walker's (2006) phenomenologically driven interviews provide some detailed information about re-injury anxiety at different stages of injury recovery. During rehabilitation, athletes described feeling vulnerable and worried about causing further damage through the incorrect execution of rehabilitation activities. Re-injury anxieties also caused these athletes to question the functional properties of their injured limb (for instance, 'Is it strong enough?') and often led to statements that they were worried the injured site would always carry a weakness. Re-injury anxiety during rehabilitation was manifest in caution, apprehension and hesitation, particularly in relation to activities (such as tackling, leaping, bounding, twisting, turning) that would test the injured site. When athletes attempted to test the injured site and re-injury did not occur, re-injury anxiety was reported to decrease and confidence in the injured site increased. The athletes participated in a follow-up interview three months after their return to training and competition, and described their anxieties regarding their first training session and competitive match after successful rehabilitation, particularly recurrence of the incident causing the original injury (for example, breaking an ankle in a tackle in the first training session).

Types of re-injury anxiety

A large number of athletes were surveyed by Cassidy (2006) to determine the types of anxiety they experienced when injured, or thought they might experience if injured. They reported anxieties associated with the loss of athleticism, being perceived as weak, experiencing pain, loss of social support, letting down important others, impaired self-image and re-injury. This author reported that re-injury anxiety appeared to be particularly problematic for female athletes, athletes whose injuries required surgery, athletes who perceived that their injuries were severe, and athletes who were unable to participate in their sport for a prolonged period of time (Cassidy, 2006).

Re-injury appraisals and emotions

More recently, Podlog et al. (2010) tested hypotheses grounded in self-determination theory (Ryan and Deci, 2000) regarding athletes' cognitive appraisals and emotional reactions when returning to competition following a serious injury. They presented

225 athletes with hypothetical scenarios that varied in degree of self-determination and salience of re-injury concerns. The descriptive results tended to fall in predicted directions: hypothetical scenarios that featured an apparent re-injury concern resulted in less positive appraisals and more negative emotional responses. Inferential analyses, however, revealed that this manipulation only produced a single statistically significant result: athletes exposed to hypothetical scenarios with no apparent re-injury concern indicated greater relief at being able to return to sport.

Critical overview of the body of research

Although findings from the research summarised above are useful, these studies are not without limitations. These typically centre on the design of the studies (retrospective and hypothetical scenarios). Retrospective designs are prone to memory bias and recall inaccuracies (e.g. Hunt and Short, 2006). Responses to hypothetical injury scenarios (e.g. Podlog et al., 2010) are unlikely to be the same as to a 'real' injury experience. The use of a single-item dependent measure (for cognitive appraisals and emotional responses) and a lack of manipulation checks also limited the work by Podlog et al. (2010). Research in this field also tends to use small sample sizes (e.g. Walker, 2006), and this reduces the generalisability of the findings.

Measuring re-injury anxiety

Research measuring re-injury anxiety has tended to employ single-item Likert type scales (Cupal and Brewer, 2001) or other instruments, such as the Competitive State Anxiety Inventory-2 (CSAI-2, Martens et al., 1990), which were designed to measure other constructs. A lack of appropriate measures to accurately assess athletes' responses to injury has necessitated a reliance on non-population-specific measures (Brewer, 2001; Evans, Hardy and Mullen, 1996; Evans et al., 2006). As a result, the measures used may lack content and predictive validity (Evans et al., 2008). Brewer (2001) suggested that the development of psychological measures specific to the sport injury rehabilitation setting will help to provide researchers with standardised instruments and enable specific research questions to be answered.

Given the need for a specific measure of re-injury anxiety, initial validation of a scale to assess re-injury anxiety in injured athletes was conducted by Walker et al. (2010). Their proposed Re-Injury Anxiety Inventory (RIAI) is a twenty-eight-item multidimensional measure of two constructs. The items in construct one, rehabilitation re-injury anxiety (RIA-R) (n = 13), relate to rehabilitation, and those in construct two, re-entry into competition re-injury anxiety (RIA-RE) (n = 15), relate to re-entry into competition. Separate scores are calculated for the two constructs, and a minimum score of 0 indicates a complete absence of re-injury anxiety. Maximum RIA-R and RIA-RE scores of 39 and 45 respectively indicate extreme anxiety in both contexts. The internal consistency for both factors was above the 0.70 criterion value (Tabachnick and Fidell, 1996; Nunally and Bernstein, 1994): RIA-R, alpha = 0.98; RIA-RE, alpha = 0.96.

It is accepted that establishing the validity of an instrument is an ongoing process (Anastasi and Urbina, 1997). Walker et al. (2010) recommended further analyses of the RIAI, and also suggested that it could be used to test the causal relationships discussed in this chapter (such as proposed links between re-injury anxieties and physiological and psychological effects such as muscle tension and distraction, as suggested by Heil, 1993a). This tool could also be employed to explore the usefulness of psychological interventions to help athletes cope with their re-injury anxieties, and to identify athletes who may need further support with their re-injury anxieties (Walker et al., 2010). To date we know of only two studies into the usefulness of psychological interventions, which are considered in detail below.

Re-injury anxiety interventions

Little empirical research has examined psychological intervention strategies in an injury context (Evans, Mitchell and Jones, 2006). Despite some progress, developments have been slow and intervention studies have predominantly focused on behavioural issues (for instance, adherence) and clinical outcomes (such as range of movement; Evans et al., 2006). Thus researchers are encouraged to implement intervention studies that examine a variety of emotional outcomes such as re-injury anxiety (Evans et al., 2006).

The usefulness of a cognitive-behavioural intervention for improving knee strength, pain perceptions, and re-injury anxiety following anterior cruciate ligament (ACL) reconstruction was explored by Cupal and Brewer (2001). All athletes (n = 30) participated in physical therapy, and re-injury anxiety and pain were assessed using single-item eleven-point Likert-type scales (ranging from *no anxiety/pain* (0) to *a high level of anxiety/pain* (10)). Knee strength was examined using the Cybex 6000 isokinetic dynamometer. Participants were randomly assigned to one of three groups (treatment, placebo and control groups). Comparisons of their initial means for age, activity level, re-injury anxiety and pain revealed no significant differences. Athletes completed the re-injury and pain scales two and twenty-four weeks post surgery. Knee strength was measured twenty-four weeks post surgery.

The treatment group received ten individual sessions of relaxation and guided imagery in addition to a normal course of physical therapy. Sessions were two weeks apart over the course of a six-month recovery period. Each session was designed to provide mental rehearsal of the physical rehabilitation goals after ACL reconstruction, as determined by the rehabilitation personnel. Each session began with breath-assisted relaxation. Although imagery content varied from session to session depending on recovery goals, overall the treatment group participants' imagery content was identical. These sessions were audiotaped, and participants within the treatment group were asked to listen to the tape at least once daily. Participants in the placebo group received attention, encouragement and support from the clinician in addition to pursuing a normal course of physical therapy. Each participant was asked to devote 10 to 15 minutes daily to visualising a peaceful scene, and all were reminded during physical rehabilitation to do this. Control group participants followed a normal course of physical therapy, receiving no treatment or attention from the researcher during the rehabilitation period. Throughout the rehabilitation the physical therapists were not informed of the participants' group allocation.

Reductions in re-injury anxiety over time were evident for all groups. However, the treatment group demonstrated more greatly reduced anxiety at twenty-four weeks post surgery than the placebo and control groups. Variance effect size calculations demonstrated that the treatment accounted for approximately 62 per cent of the variance in reduction of re-injury anxiety ($\acute{\eta}^2 = .62$). Although this study demonstrated reductions in re-injury anxiety, using a single-item scale to assess perceptions of anxiety is a limitation. Single-item scales have lower reliabilities than multiple item scales, thus the authors recommended that future studies should adapt a multi-item scale with demonstrated psychometric properties.

The use of a relaxation technique to reduce re-injury anxiety was explored by Castillo, Cremedes and Butcher (2002). Four injured participants were randomly assigned to either a treatment (n = 2) or a control group (n = 2), and participated in a pre-test imagery session to recall the injury. All participants completed CSAI-2 (Martens et al., 1990) as a measure of re-injury anxiety. The treatment group were asked to follow relaxation instructions on audio CD for one hour on three separate days for one week. Both groups were asked to return seven days after their initial visit for a post-test recall session, in which re-injury anxiety was measured using CSAI-2. Pre and post-test in-depth interviews were also conducted. Contrary to expectations, the control group's cognitive anxiety decreased by 15 per cent and somatic anxiety decreased by 22 per cent from pre to post intervention compared with the treatment group. Furthermore, a 24 per cent increase in self-confidence was observed in the control group. Interviews revealed that the control group had successfully returned to competition during the study period, and they reported feeling more confident and less anxious. The authors suggested that the results implied a successful return to competition reduced re-injury anxiety more than relaxation techniques.

One limitation of this research which puts its validity in question is that although the authors claimed to be measuring re-injury anxiety, CSAI-2 is designed to measure competitive anxiety. Re-injury anxiety differs from sports performance anxiety, which is associated with a failure to achieve a skill without the implication of injury (Heil, 1993b). Competitive state anxiety could possibly differ between the control and experimental groups without this reflecting re-injury anxiety. It could also have been more suitable to employ a multiple-baseline rather than a between-group design in view of the small sample size. In addition, the authors do not provide any participant information on injury type, participant gender, injury severity, sport participation, injury location, injury rehabilitation details, and whether the same rehabilitation personnel carried out each athlete's rehabilitation. Such extraneous variables could have had a confounding effect on the study's results. Cupal (1998) recommended, as far as possible, that homogeneous samples are used in intervention research for this reason.

Managing re-injury anxieties: an applied example

Although limitations are apparent in the research discussed above, preliminary evidence suggests that re-injury anxiety can be reduced using psychological strategies such as imagery and relaxation. These research studies do not, however, provide a detailed picture of exactly how the intervention was conceived, implemented and received by the athlete. The applied case study below offers a more detailed discussion of a psychological intervention to help an athlete overcome re-injury anxiety.

A 21-year-old national-level female soccer player, playing in the Nationwide Women's Premier League, contacted the first author for help in coping with re-injury anxiety. The client had a total of ten years competitive soccer experience, including three years at an elite level. Her injury, which is classified as moderate according to the National Athletic Injury/Illness Reporting System (NAIRS) (Coddington and Troxel, 1980), occurred during a competitive match. She and an opposing player 'both went up for it [the ball] and missed. I really went for it and bang, the front of my head, all around my eyebrow smacked against the back or side of her head as she came back and went for it.' She went on to describe the injury: 'It was awful. The cut was massive, I felt dazed and there was blood everywhere. All over my shirt, my face, her and the pitch.' The gash across her left eyebrow required twenty stitches, of which ten were visible on the outside of the wound. She described the pain and the reactions of her team mates and the referee: 'The pain came after the initial shock and it was agony. I knew it was bad because of everybody's face. They all looked so shocked.' The day following the injury, she said, 'I couldn't look in the mirror. I was so worried about what my face would look like, how big the stitches were and worried about how big my scar was going to be.'

It was two weeks before she was given permission to return to training (excluding heading or competition) by the team doctor. She was told she could begin competitive match play and go for headers after three weeks, at which time she contacted the author for psychological support. At this point the physical injury was healing well, but as she explained, 'I'm training again and just can't go in for a header when challenged. I just don't commit. I'm worrying about it more as I'm making progress to regaining my place, apart from the heading, and we've games coming up.' She explained that she had been working on headers during training:

> Heading the ball with no challenge is OK, that's fine. It's just when I'm against an opponent, even against a team mate. Then I just chicken out because I think I'm going to get hit again, the pain, the worry that the scar would be worse with a second hit and the missing training. I jump for it but just don't commit. I've no intention of making the header. I'm more concerned about where the other player's head is, that my arms are up to protect me and so my eyes aren't even on the ball.

She claimed that heading had used to be a natural skill for her, and now she was worried of losing her reputation as a 'powerful midfield player who dominates the air'. She frequently experienced visions of the incident that injured her, was worried about it recurring, felt tense and sick when executing challenged headers, and commented that 'this makes my performance worse'. She reported feeling:

> so sick when the coach mentions anything to do with heading drills. My hands shake and I get these visions of heads clashing, seeing the blood and my hands up at my face. I feel dizzy like I did when it happened and I just can't pull it off. I go up for it like a fairy and never get near the ball. I'm too worried about protecting myself and where the other player's head is. I'm so stiff too I don't even jump right. If I did get my head to it, my body is so tense the ball would go straight up in the air and come right back down again. The technique isn't right because I'm worried and paying attention to things I shouldn't be.

The anxiety experienced was becoming more salient as re-entry into competition approached, and was detrimentally impacting her performance, supporting the suggestions made by Taylor and Taylor (1997) and Walker et al. (2002).

Also in support of Taylor and Taylor (1997), the client demonstrated muscular tension and was focusing on the injured site, directing her attention away from the cues that she should have been taking from the game in progress. This then negatively impacted her performance, confidence and could have increased the risk of actual re-injury. She appeared frustrated that she could not play headers as easily as before the injury. Both cognitive and somatic anxiety were evident when she clearly described her thought processes and somatic responses to images of injury and re-injury. She also associated the risk of re-injury differently with different situations; she was comfortable executing a header in training under no challenge, but experienced anxiety when executing a header in training under challenge and was becoming increasingly anxious about executing a header under challenge during competitive match play. This offers further support for the term re-injury anxiety as opposed to fear of re-injury, in that athletes associate the risk of injury with situations of variable uncertainty and contextual characteristics.

In managing the client's re-injury anxiety, Heil's (1993b) suggested six steps were followed.

1. The client was reassured that re-injury anxiety was a common response following injury. It was explained to her that it is normal to experience this. Crossman (2001) also advocates informing the athlete what to expect during rehabilitation and encouraging them to ask questions. It is important to provide detailed answers/explanations at a level suitable to the age of the athlete, their sport and injury status and their understanding of injury/healing processes.

2. The consultant reassured the client that the re-injury anxiety could be managed with the aid of psychological interventions. Any suggestion that the emotion itself is not a problem can be misconstrued, because as has been shown, the anxiety can have a major impact on rehabilitation, performance and the likelihood of actual re-injury. The point to get across is that the problem can be addressed. If the athlete is encouraged to perceive their anxiety as a problem, the situation likely to be exacerbated. For example, the athlete might not fully adhere to the rehabilitation routine, and might pull out of exercises because of their anxiety about being re-injured, both of which may actually increase the likelihood of re-injury.

3. The adaptive role of the re-injury anxiety was explained in view of setting safe limits in rehabilitation and re-entry to training and competition to reduce the risk of actual re-injury.

4. The medical staff were consulted to ensure that the consultant was fully aware of the player's current physical state. Their reassurance that she had recovered and was able to recommence competitive play was communicated to her. This was intended to reassure her that she had no reason for any anxiety regarding the weakness of the area around her eyebrow.

5. Safe limits were identified. The medical doctor had already ruled out heading for the first three weeks following the injury, and also specified that the client should wear a head bandage and use a lubricant on the injured site for a further three weeks to reduce the possibility of further injury.

6. Psychological skills were integrated in the form of systematic desensitization (Wolpe, 1958).

The intervention implemented to help to reduce the athlete's re-injury anxiety was systematic desensitization (SD: Wolpe, 1958), which has been demonstrated to be an effective method to reduce fears (e.g. Ost, 1989; Zinbarg et al., 1992). SD is a clinical procedure for the treatment of phobias such as fear of flying, heights and public speaking (Crossman, 2001). Crossman (2001) reports the usefulness of SD within her practice for treating athletes who have re-injury anxiety. Its usefulness has also been reported in a case study discussed by Rotella and Campbell (1983). The technique, also termed counter-conditioning, pairs relaxation with images of the anxiety-provoking stimulus (Crossman, 2001). Counter-conditioning involves reducing a conditional response (such as re-injury anxiety) by establishing an incompatible response (such as relaxation) to the conditioned stimulus (in this case, heading the ball when challenged by another player). Wolpe (1958) stated that most abnormal behaviour is learned like normal behaviour, so it can be unlearned and replaced with more adaptive reactions (Tredget, 2001). Wood (1981) believes that pairing relaxation with the anxiety-provoking stimulus causes a new learned response to be developed, which is incompatible with anxiety. To conduct systematic desensitization the athlete must recognize the anxiety that is preventing them from full participation. This seems in conflict with Heil's (1993a) suggestion that the consultant should reassure the athlete that re-injury anxiety is not a problem. This conflict was addressed by advocating that the anxiety can be managed, therefore it should not be viewed as a problem. In the female soccer player's case the athlete recognized that her anxiety over re-injury and visions of re-injury were preventing her from full participation in soccer, as she was unable to execute a header when challenged by another player.

Recognition of anxiety response

During consultation with the athlete, SD was adopted as a coping strategy. First, to encourage the athlete to recognize her anxiety, she was asked to describe situations that were related to the anxiety-provoking stimulus. She was then asked to write each one down on a separate card in as much detail as possible (see Table 11.1). She described eight anxiety-provoking situations with regard to heading the ball, and the description on each card enabled her to construct vivid images of each situation. Next she was asked to rate each situation on a scale from 0 (comfortable/relaxed) to 10 (extremely anxious). This produced an anxiety hierarchy, from the least anxiety-producing to the most anxiety-producing of the situations.

TABLE 11.1 Anxiety hierarchy for an elite female soccer player

Anxiety-Provoking Situation	Anxiety Rating
Heading a ball that I have thrown in the air.	0
Heading a ball that someone else has thrown in the air.	1
Heading a ball with a teammate standing next to me.	3
Heading a ball with a teammate jumping up next to me but not challenging for the ball.	5
Heading a ball with a teammate challenging.	7
Heading a ball with a member of the opposition standing next to me.	8
Heading a ball with a member of the opposition challenging	9
Heading the ball with the same opposing player challenging as when the original injury occurred.	10

Counter-conditioning

The player then imagined, as vividly as possible, the least anxiety-provoking situation. The image was paired with progressive muscular relaxation (PMR: Jacobson, 1938). The client was familiar with PMR as she had used this tool in performance-enhancement sessions with the consultant prior to sustaining the head injury. When she could imagine the situation and remain in a relaxed state, she then progressed to imagining the next situation in the anxiety hierarchy. No more than two anxiety-provoking situations were dealt with in any one session. The client and sport psychologist then worked through the hierarchy, pairing imagery and relaxation, until the player was able to overcome her anxiety when presented with images of the situations that were identified as the root of her anxiety.

Application to competition

Following completion of the hierarchy (achieved in approximately three weeks) the client then went on to carry out (not just imagine) each of the anxiety-provoking situations (which was achieved in approximately four weeks). For example, she had a low to moderate anxiety rating of 3/10 regarding heading the ball when a team mate was next to her. During a normal training session the client, the consultant, the coach and a team mate worked at counter-conditioning the anxiety response. While she headed the ball with a team mate standing next to her, she used progressive muscular relaxation when she experienced anxiety. The aim was to reduce the conditional response (anxiety) by establishing an incompatible response (relaxation) to the conditional stimulus (heading the ball with a team mate standing next to her). This technique was repeated in several sessions until she felt that the conditional stimulus no longer caused the conditional response of anxiety. Then the next conditional stimulus (in this case, heading the ball while her team mate jumped up next to her but did not challenge for the ball) was counter-conditioned, and so forth. Finally all anxiety-provoking situations were counter-conditioned and the client could perform a header without experiencing anxiety in any of the situations that had previously caused an anxious response. Within seven weeks she was playing competitive soccer again and executing challenged headers effectively and with self-confidence, as she reported during a follow-up interview.

A summary of the client's interpretation of the intervention

The client quickly engaged in the intervention and had approximately three months of mental skills training experience prior to her injury. In a follow-up meeting the day prior to a competitive match against the team that hers had been playing when the original injury occurred (her most anxiety-provoking situation) she reported on the benefits of the intervention:

> Having to describe situations that caused me to be anxious actually was the first step in confronting how I felt. I knew I was anxious about heading the ball but when prompted to think about specific situations I realized how anxious I was.

She stated of the preparatory work, identifying her anxiety hierarchy:

> Having this plan in front of me showing me when my anxiety was highest
> gave me goals to work towards. After I was told how the thing [SD] worked
> I knew where I was going and knew each one would be tackled. Achieving
> each in small steps, first using my imagination and then actually doing each
> scene, was a great confidence boost that helped my belief and confidence
> that the next one would be solved too.

The client reported, 'Using your imagination first doesn't put you into too
threatening a situation either. But you know that the real life scenarios will be
tackled soon so the real problem is being dealt with. It's like having this little
confidence builder.' When asked about her re-injury anxiety regarding the game
on the next day, she said:

> I'm ready for it. I've imagined the scene of going up for a header against the
> same girl as the original injury and all I see are clear images of me making
> good contact with the ball and no injury. I'm confident I can do it because
> I've seen the images in my head and I've not got injured. Now it's time for
> me to show I can in tomorrow's game. I've even performed challenged
> headers in training and in the last few games without worrying about getting
> re-injured so I know I can.

After the game the client reported the benefits of SD again, 'It worked. Did you
see me? Banging headers all over the park I was.'

Coping with re-injury anxiety

Given the potential implications of re-injury anxiety for performance and
psychological readiness during rehabilitation and return to competition, and the
increased likelihood of re-injury, it seems important to address coping strategies to
help athletes with re-injury anxieties. Surprisingly however, this has not been
explored to date.

Coping is a dynamic process that involves a person's efforts (cognitive and
behavioural) to manage (that is, reduce or tolerate) demands that are perceived as
stressful (Lazarus, 1999). Appraisal of harm, loss, or threat to one's well-being is
often followed by negative emotions such as anxiety. Negative emotions (in this
case, re-injury anxiety) are typically followed by a coping response (problem-
focused, emotion-focused and avoidance-focused coping; Sagar, Busch and Jowett,
2010). These coping strategies are used to control the stressor or its effects (Lazarus,
1999, 2000). Problem-focused coping (PFC) aims to reduce emotional distress by
directing efforts to alter or manage the stressor (such as planning, making decisions,
gathering information, acquiring skills to help deal with the problem; Sagar et al.,
2010). PFC strategies tend to be associated with positive affect and well-being

during stressful situations. This is because they allow the individual to focus their attention and to assert control over the stressor (Carver and Scheier, 1998; Folkman and Moskowitz, 2000; Sagar et al., 2010). Emotion-focused coping (EFC) strategies (such as self-talk and social support) are often employed when the individual appraises that nothing can be done to modify the stressor (Sagar et al., 2010). They are used to help reduce the emotional distress caused by the stressor. Avoidance-focused coping (AFC) strategies (cognitive or behavioural avoidance) are used to attempt to weaken emotions that are distressing by the avoidance of dealing with the problem (Carver, Scheier and Weintraub, 1989). However, AFC coping strategies are considered ineffective for managing long-term threats (Carver et al., 1989).

A preliminary study by Walker and Freed (unpublished) explored strategies employed by athletes in their attempts to cope with their re-injury anxieties. Four injured athletes all experiencing re-injury anxieties (with high scores on the RIAI; Walker et al., 2010) were interviewed, using a semi-structured interview, towards the end of their injury rehabilitation. Interview questions were retrospective in nature and asked athletes to describe their coping responses to re-injury anxiety. The interviews were transcribed verbatim and were inductively content analysed. The findings represent one of the first attempts to document the coping strategies employed by a group of injured athletes experiencing re-injury anxiety.

The athletes employed a combination of all three types of coping strategy. However, it should be noted that only cognitive avoidance coping was evident with respect to AFC. Cognitive disengagement was used as a typical cognitive avoidance strategy. The athletes reported trying not to think about the possibility of re-injury. They tried to distract themselves by thinking about anything other than re-injury, and remaining positive about a successful injury-free return to training and competition. There was no evidence of behavioural AFC employed by the athletes participating in the study (such as not talking about the anxieties related to re-injury or avoiding rehabilitation activities perceived as risky). This could be further evidence that athletes experience re-injury anxiety and not fear of re-injury, where behavioural avoidance (actions of escape) would be more likely.

Seeking emotional support was the only EFC strategy reported. The athletes sought emotional support from friends, family and team mates. PFC was also employed, and included increasing effort in rehabilitation, taking care of their body (for example, healthy eating), and seeking instrumental support from the medical team and fellow injured athletes. Despite employing effective coping strategies (PFC) to deal with re-injury anxieties, these athletes also employed some ineffective strategies (AFC; Carver et al., 1989; Folkman and Moskowitz, 2000). AFC does not address the root of the problem, and the same has also been reported of EFC in the long term (Sagar et al., 2010). Practitioners should encourage the use of more PFC strategies in the long term (such as questioning the rationale/logic of re-injury anxieties), and work with the athlete on ways to address the problem. However, research has also supported the notion of not relying on one type of coping strategy. It has been suggested that the use of multiple coping strategies, or having a repertoire of coping strategies, is important for healthy adjustment to a stressor (Kerr and Miller, 2004). Therefore, an athlete can be expected to cope much better with the adjustment to injury if they have a range of EFC and PFC strategies at their disposal (Kerr and Miller, 2004).

Implications for the practitioner

Understanding the emotional responses to injury, such as re-injury anxiety, is essential for sport psychologists, coaches, management, and the medical personnel involved with any injured athlete. 'Sport trainers, sport therapists and physiotherapists are required to address the psychological factors when treating injured athletes and apply various psychological strategies if complete holistic recovery is to occur' (Ford and Gordon, 1998, p. 80). By having an awareness of the responses to injury these individuals can assist the injured athlete effectively in both their physical and mental recovery, and help to prevent or modify adverse responses, such as re-injury anxiety, that can disrupt rehabilitation and the return to training and competition.

Those individuals involved in the injured athletes' recovery play an important role in helping the athlete develop and adopt effective coping strategies to manage their re-injury anxieties. Practitioners should encourage the development of PFC to help reduce emotional distress by directing the athletes' efforts to manage their re-injury anxieties. PFC allows the athlete to assert some control over their injury and their responses to the injury. This is important as athletes often report a perceived lack of control over their injury rehabilitation and recovery (Walker, 2006). One method of developing an athlete's coping skills, and sense of control, is through the use of psychological interventions. Those who engage in psychological interventions which enable them to perceive themselves as active agents in their recovery are more likely to have better recovery outcomes (Cupal, 1996). Using psychological interventions also promotes communication between the individuals involved in the rehabilitation process. If an athlete feels that they are actively involved in the decision-making process, and that their needs are both understood and are being cared for, their overall performance in rehabilitation is said to improve (Ray and Wiese-Bjornstal, 1999). Good communication increases the understanding of the injury, the process of the injury, and recovery outcomes (Hemmings and Povey, 2002). This can then increase treatment compliance, which affects athletes' coping skills and injury recovery.

The most widely adopted psychological interventions employed in an injury context are goal setting, imagery, relaxation, and positive self-talk (Brown, 2005; Arvinen-Barrow, 2009). It is beyond the scope of this chapter to discuss each of these techniques in detail, or their detailed application. However, we offer a brief summary of how psychological skills might be employed in injury rehabilitation to help athletes develop PFC in an attempt to help them to manage their re-injury anxiety effectively. One key PFC strategy is planning (Sagar et al., 2010). Goal setting is an appropriate technique for this purpose as it encourages the athlete to focus on the present and the future, and not the past and its problems (White and Black, 2004).

It is imperative when planning goal setting for rehabilitation that the practitioner has an awareness of different types of rehabilitation goals (physical, psychological, and performance goals). According to Taylor and Taylor (1997), physical goals can enable a clear direction for the physical aspects of recovery. Psychological goals can assist with motivation, self-confidence, focus, stress and anxiety, all of which can have a negative effect on the rehabilitation process and the final outcome of holistic recovery (Arvinen-Barrow, 2009). Performance goals can benefit the athlete by identifying areas for improvement related to performance (such as technical and tactical development, physical conditioning, mental training, and return-to-form), which, during regular training might not have been a priority. It is necessary to think about how these goals can be accomplished (Flint, 1998).

With the intention of achieving full recovery, Taylor and Taylor (1997) propose that different levels of goals should also be considered: *recovery, stage, daily*, and *lifestyle goals*. In relation to the general principles of the goal-setting theory (Locke and Latham, 1990), recovery goals are associated with full recovery (long-term goals), stage goals consist of specific objectives for each of the different stages of rehabilitation (medium-term goals), and daily goals relate to daily objectives and targets for each rehabilitation session (short-term goals). Daily goals are often not planned into a goal-setting programme but should be set to ensure that stage and recovery goals will be successfully attained as planned. In addition, it is recommended that goals should also be set in relation to the athlete's lifestyle (Taylor and Taylor, 1997). Existing lifestyle factors (sleep, diet, alcohol, relationships, work and school commitments) can either assist or hinder rehabilitation adherence, and ultimately have an effect on recovery outcomes. The goals set should be constantly monitored, evaluated and adjusted (Flint, 1998). Also in line with previous goal-setting proposals, rehabilitation goals should include process goals (actions and tasks required to achieve performance goals) and be linked to outcome goals (focused on achieving a particular personal level of performance). However, it is argued that a greater emphasis should be placed on process goals because they are more likely to be within the athlete's personal control, and are directly linked with personal effort (Flint, 1998). Furthermore, it is important to set both short and long-term goals and to link goals with aspects of the athletes' performance with which they are familiar (that is, designing goals specific to aspects of their sport).

In addition, three main principles should be employed when setting goals for injured athletes (Arvinen-Barrow, 2009). First, rehabilitation practitioners need to work together with the injured athlete to establish realistic goals for the rehabilitation programme (Kolt, 2000). The process for setting goals should begin with a conversation between the practitioner and the athlete in which rehabilitation is discussed and explained (Taylor and Taylor, 1997). This should then be followed by setting clear goals for each of the component of recovery (for example range of motion, strength, stability). Psychological goals should then be discussed in a similar manner. For this purpose, the practitioner might consider adopting performance profiling (Butler, 1989) in a rehabilitation context (called rehabilitation profiling) as suggested by Taylor and Taylor (1997). Second, strategies for achieving goals need to be agreed upon and learned by athletes. By doing this, the athlete is more likely to feel a sense of control, and this has been found to have a positive effect on rehabilitation adherence (Kolt, 2000). Finally, to be effective goals need to be revised and assessed on a regular basis (Gould, 1986). Butler (1997) mentions various methods such as diaries and contracts.

When applied to an injury context the psychological technique of social support has been proposed as an integral part of injury, stress and coping (Taylor and Taylor, 1997). Instrumental social support is a useful PFC strategy, and should be encouraged. Instrumental social support is one method the athlete can use to gather information related to their injury and their responses to it. The practitioners involved with the injured athlete can offer instrumental support by providing advice and information related to the injury and the injury process. Specifically related to re-injury anxiety, the practitioner could advise the athlete that re-injury anxiety is a common response, and in many cases an expected reaction. They can make clear that hesitancy, caution and apprehension are common reactions when testing the injured site, and encourage the athlete to test the injury location when physically ready in an attempt to increase confidence. Richman et al. (1989) made three specific suggestions on how best to enhance social support in sport. It is best provided by a network of individuals, needs to be developed and nurtured, and works best as part of a ongoing programme rather than when simply employed as a reaction to a crisis.

Acquiring the skills to help deal with the problem is a key aspect of PFC (Sagar et al., 2010). Practitioners might encourage their injured athletes to use imagery, relaxation and cognitive restructuring. Relaxation techniques can help reduce the negative effects of anxiety by reducing tension, lowering heart rate, slowing breathing, and increasing blood flow (O'Connor et al., 2005). Muscular tension and worries are reported outcomes of re-injury anxiety (Walker, 2006), thus, by using relaxation techniques (such as centring and progressive muscular relaxation) the athlete may be more able to manage their anxiety and its associated effects. Pre-recorded audio recordings of a relaxation script and the use of audio equipment (such as a CD or MP3 player) during the rehabilitation process can be beneficial in facilitating relaxation (Taylor and Taylor, 1997). Relaxation techniques should form an integral part of the rehabilitation process (Flint, 1998). Relaxation is a skill, and as with any other skill, it must be learned and practised for it to be effective (Flint, 1998). Rotella (1982) believes that the first step in relaxation training should be education. The athlete should be educated about the purpose, the benefits, and the rationale for the use of relaxation, and any possible questions and worries about the technique should be highlighted and resolved. It is also vital to ensure that relaxation takes place in a quiet, calm, and comfortable area (Taylor and Taylor, 1997). Relaxation is most effective when integrated into the structure of daily physical sessions (for instance, using deep breathing during the times when re-injury anxiety is present and hindering the rehabilitation process; Taylor and Taylor, 1997).

Cognitive restructuring could be used to challenge the rationale of re-injury anxieties, to help the athlete to identify negative cognitions and subsequently reframe these into a positive counter response. Cognitive restructuring does not downplay or encourage athletes to ignore their negative and troublesome experiences. It allows them to switch to a more positive frame of mind, to programme the subconscious for success and lay down the foundations for progress and change in the future. Altering the appraisal of the situation effects a change in the way emotions are attached to that situation (Hill, 2001). As a result of the change, behaviour is likely to change.

Imagery has also been recommended as a means of coping for injured athletes (Rotella, 1982; Gould et al., 1997). Imagery might be employed specifically with injured athletes who are experiencing re-injury anxiety and are familiar with the use of imagery. It could be used in this context to regain confidence in the injured site, for recalling successful skill execution, and as an attentional focus tool. Four types of imagery have been suggested as beneficial for sport injury rehabilitation:

- *healing* (visualising and feeling the injured body part healing)
- *pain management* (assisting the athlete to cope with the pain associated with the injury)
- *rehabilitation process* (helping to cope with challenges that they may encounter during the rehabilitation programme)
- *performance imagery* (practising physical skills and imagining themselves performing successfully and injury free; Walsh, M. (2005). Injury rehabilitation and imagery. In T. Morris, M. Spittle & A. P. Watt (Eds.), *Imagery in sport* (pp. 267–284). Champaign: Human Kinetics.

Identifying possible areas of development for rehabilitation should be of primary importance, according to Taylor and Taylor (1997). Once the key areas have been identified, goals for rehabilitation imagery should be set. These should then form the basis of the rehabilitation imagery programme.

Practitioners involved in the injured athlete's rehabilitation can discourage them from using AFC. Practitioners should be aware that the use of multiple coping strategies, or having a repertoire of coping strategies, is important for healthy adjustment to a stressor such as re-injury anxiety. However, they should also be aware that PFC offers more effective strategies in the long term. By encouraging the development and adoption of PFC strategies the practitioner is arming the athlete with effective coping skills not only for the rehabilitation environment but also for the return to training and competition. It is at this point that the support from the rehabilitation team is withdrawn, so it is important that athletes are self-aware and able to employ effective coping skills themselves. Also of applied importance is the need for practitioners not only to focus on clinical and behavioural outcomes but also to monitor the emotional outcomes of an injured athlete, such as re-injury anxiety.

Summary

Preliminary studies (e.g. Cassidy, 2006; Hunt and Short, 2006; Podlog et al., 2010) have demonstrated that re-injury anxiety is a salient emotional response to athletic injury. Re-injury anxiety can impact performance during rehabilitation and on return to competition, and increase the risk of actual re-injury through attentional changes and muscular tension. Although some studies have used the term fear of re-injury, the terminology used by athletes describing their emotional responses to injury tends to be more synonymous with anxiety than fear (for example, they are worried or nervous). There is no certainty regarding re-injury and in the case of anxieties related to the potential of re-injury there are no actions of escape as a consequence. Therefore, re-injury thoughts appear to be more related to anticipation of what might happen, a factor associated with anxiety and not fear. Fear is a fundamental biological mechanism, whereas anxiety is more complex, and this is evident in re-injury thoughts identified in preliminary research (e.g. Walker, 2006), where athletes experience cognitive and somatic symptoms of anxiety. Re-injury concerns are more typical of anxiety because they result from previous experience and other developmental factor, and are therefore not biological or fundamental factors that typically underpin fear responses.

An initial body of research (e.g. Castillo et al., 2002; Cupal and Brewer, 2001) has demonstrated the application of psychological interventions to help athletes cope with re-injury anxiety. However, this lacked a valid or reliable assessment tool capable of measuring re-injury anxiety. Future research in this area should use the RIAI (Walker et al., 2010). Furthermore, given the suggested implications of re-injury anxiety on rehabilitation performance, performance upon re-entry and increasing the likelihood of actual re-injury, future studies should address the usefulness of PFC strategies targeted towards reducing emotional distress by directing efforts to alter or manage re-injury anxiety.

The use of multiple coping strategies is important for healthy adjustment to a stressor such as re-injury anxiety. However, PFC should mainly be used by the injured athlete with re-injury anxiety to direct efforts to alter or manage the stressor and reduce the emotional distress experienced. Effective coping can be achieved through the development and use of psychological techniques such as goal setting, relaxation, imagery and cognitive restructuring.

References

Anastasi, A. and Urbina, S. (eds). (1997). *Psychological testing*, 7th edn. New Jersey: Prentice Hall.

Arvinen-Barrow, M. (2009). Psychological rehabilitation from sports injury: issues in training and development of chartered physiotherapists. Unpublished doctoral dissertation, University of Northampton, UK.

Bianco, T., Malo, S. and Orlick, T. (1999). Sport injury and illness: elite skiers describe their experiences. *Research Quarterly for Exercise and Sport*, 70, 157–169.

Brewer, B. W. (2001). Psychology of sport injury rehabilitation. In R. N. Singer, H. A. Hausenblas and C. M. Janelle (eds), *Handbook of sport psychology*, 2nd edn (pp. 787–809). New York: Wiley.

Brown, C. (2005). Injuries: The psychology of recovery and rehab. In S. Murphy (ed.), *The sport psych handbook* (pp. 215–235). Champaign, Ill.: Human Kinetics.

Butler, R. J. (1989). Psychological preparation of Olympic boxers. In J. Kremer and W. Crawford (eds), *The psychology of sport: Theory and practice* (pp. 74–84). Leicester: British Psychological Society.

Butler, R. J. (1997). Psychological principles applied to sports injuries. In S. French (ed.), *Physiotherapy: A psychosocial approach*, 2nd edn (pp. 155–168). Oxford: Butterworth-Heinemann.

Carver, C. S. and Scheier, M. F. (1998). *Self-regulation of behavior.* New York: Cambridge.

Carver, C. S., Scheier, M. F. and Weintraub, J. K. (1989). Assessing coping strategies: a theoretically based approach. *Journal of Personality and Social Psychology*, 56, 267–283.

Castillo, R., Cremades, J. G. and Butcher, M. (2002). Relaxation techniques as a method to reduce re-injury anxiety in athletes. *Journal of Sport and Exercise Psychology*, 24, 42.

Cassidy, C. M. (2006). Understanding sport-injury anxiety. *Athletic Therapy Today*, 11, 57–58.

Chase, M., Magyar, M. and Drake, B. M. (2005). Fear of injury in gymnastics, self-efficacy and psychological strategies to keep on tumbling. *Journal of Sports Sciences*, 23, 465–475.

Coddington, R. D. and Troxell, J. R. (1980). The effect of emotional factors on football injury rates: a pilot study. *Journal of Human Stress*, 6, 3–5.

Crossman, J. (2001). *Coping with sports injuries: Psychological strategies for rehabilitation*. Oxford: Oxford University Press.

Cupal, D. (1996). The efficacy of guided imagery for recovery from anterior cruciate ligament (ACL) replacement. *Journal of Applied Sport Psychology*, 8(suppl), S56.

Cupal, D. D. (1998). Psychological interventions in sport injury prevention and treatment. *Journal of Applied Sport Psychology*, 10, 103–123.

Cupal, D. D. and Brewer, B. W. (2001). Effects of relaxation and guided imagery on knee strength, re-injury anxiety and pain following anterior cruciate ligament reconstruction. *Rehabilitation Psychology*, 46, 28–43.

Dale, G. A. (1996). Existential phenomenology: emphasizing the experience of the athlete in sport psychology research. *The Sport Psychologist*, 10, 307–321.

Draper, V. and Ladd, C. (1993). Subjective evaluation of function following moderately accelerated rehabilitation of anterior cruciate ligament reconstructed knees. *Journal of Athletic Training*, 28, 38–41.

Evans, L., Hardy, L., Mitchell, I. and Rees, T. (2008). The development of a measure of psychological responses to injury. *Journal of Sport Rehabilitation*, 16, 21–37.

Evans, L., Hardy, L. and Mullen, R. (1996). The development of the psychological responses to sport injury inventory. *Journal of Sport and Exercise Science*, 14, 27–28.

Evans, L., Mitchell, I. and Jones, S. (2006). Psychological responses to sport injury: a review of current research. In S. Hanton and S. D. Mellalieu (eds), *Literature reviews in sport psychology* (pp. 289–319). New York: Nova Science.

Flint, F. A. (1998). Specialized psychological interventions. In F. A. Flint (ed.), Psychology of sport injury (pp. 29–50). Leeds: Human Kinetics.

Fisher, L. A. and Wrisberg, C. A. (2006). What athletic training students want to know about sport psychology. *Athletic Therapy Today*, 11, 32–33.

Folkman, S. and Moskowitz, J. T. (2000). Positive affect and the other side of coping. *American Psychologist*, 55, 647–654.

Ford, I. W. and Gordon, S. (1998). Perspectives of sport trainers and athletic therapists on the psychological content of their practice and training. *Journal of Sport Rehabilitation*, 7, 79–94.

Gould, D. (1986). Goal setting for peak performance. In J. Williams (ed.), *Applied sport psychology: Personal growth to peak performance* (pp. 133–148). Palo Alto, Calif.: Mayfield.

Gould, D. and Udry, E. (1994). The psychology of knee injuries and injury rehabilitation. In L. Y. Griffin (ed.), *Rehabilitation of the injured knee* (2nd ed., pp. 86–98). St. Louis, Miss.: Mosby.

Gould, D., Udry, E., Bridges, D. and Beck, L. (1997). Down but not out: athlete responses to season-ending injuries. *Journal of Sport and Exercise Psychology*, 19, 229–248.

Hackfort, D. and Schwenkmezger, P. (1993). Anxiety. In R. N. Singer, M. Murphy and L. K. Tennant (eds), *Handbook of research on sport psychology* (pp. 328–364). New York: Macmillan.

Hägglund, M., Waldén, M., Bahr, R. and Ekstrand, J. (2005). Methods for epidemiological study of injuries to professional football players: developing the UEFA model. *British Journal of Sports Medicine*, 39, 340–346.

Hare, R., Evans, L. and Callow, N. (2008). Imagery use during rehabilitation from injury: a case study of an elite athlete. *The Sport Psychologist*, 22, 405–422.

Heil, J. (1993a). Sport psychology, the athlete at risk, and the sports medicine team. In J. Heil. (ed.), *Psychology of sport injury* (pp. 1–14). Champaign, Ill.: Human Kinetics.

Heil, J. (1993b). Mental training in injury management. In J. Heil (ed.), *Psychology of sport injury* (pp. 151–174). Champaign, Ill.: Human Kinetics.

Hemmings, B. and Povey, L. (2002). Views of chartered physiotherapists on the psychological content of their practice: a preliminary study in the United Kingdom. *British Journal of Sports Medicine*, 36, 61–64.

Hill, K. L. (2001). Frameworks for sport psychologists Champaign, Ill.: Human Kinetics.

Hunt, H. and Short, S. (2006) Collegiate athletes' perceptions of adhesive ankle taping: a qualitative analysis. *Journal of Sport Rehabilitation*, 15, 280–298.

Jacobson, E. (1938). *Progressive relaxation*. Chicago: University of Chicago Press.

Johnston, L. H. and Carroll, D. (1998). The context of emotional responses to athletic injury: a qualitative analysis. *Journal of Sport Rehabilitation*, 7, 206–220.

Kerr, G. A. and Miller, P. S. (2004). Coping strategies. In J. Crossman (ed.), *Coping with sports injuries: Psychological strategies for rehabilitation* (pp. 83 – 102).

Klavora, P. (1976). Effects of injury history on pre-competitive anxiety in competitive athletics. *Proceedings of the International Congress on Physical Activity Sciences, USA*, 7, 297–303.

Kleinert, J. (2002). An approach to sport injury trait anxiety: scale construction and structure analysis. *European Journal of Sport Science*, 2, 1–11.

Kolt, G. S. (2000). Doing sport psychology with injured athletes. In M. B. Andersen (ed.), *Doing sport psychology* (pp. 223–236). Champaign, Ill.: Human Kinetics.

Kvist, J., Ek, A., Sporrstedt, K. and Good, L. (2005). Fear of re-injury: a hindrance for returning to sports after anterior cruciate ligament reconstruction. *Knee Surgery, Sports Traumatology, Arthroscopy*, 13, 393–397.

Lazarus, R. S. (1999). *Stress and emotions: A new synthesis*. London: Free Association.

Lazarus, R. S. (2000). How emotions influence performance in competitive sports. *The Sport Psychologist*, 14, 229–252.

Locke, E. A. and Latham, G. P. (1990). *A theory of goal setting and task performance*. Englewood Cliffs, N.J.: Prentice Hall.

Mankad, A., Gordon, S. and Wallman, K. (2009). Perceptions of emotional climate among injured athletes. *Journal of Clinical Sports Psychology*, 3, 1–14.

Martens, R., Burton, D., Vealey, R. S., Bump, L. A. and Smith, D. E. (1990). Development and validation of the Competitive State Anxiety Inventory – 2. In R. Martens R. S. Vealey and D. Burton (Eds.) *Competitive anxiety in sport* (pp. 117–190). Champaign, IL: Human Kinetics.

Monsma, E. and Mensch, J. (2009). Keeping your head in the game: sport-specific imagery and anxiety among injured athletes. *Journal of Athletic Training*, 44, 410–417.

Niven, A. (1997). Rehabilitation adherence in sport injury: Sport physiotherapists' perceptions. *Journal of Sport Rehabilitation*, 16, 93–110.

Nunally, J. and Bernstein, I. (1994). *Psychometric theory*. New York: McGraw-Hill.

O'Connor, E., Heil, J., Harmer, P. and Zimmerman, I. (2005). Injury. In J. Taylor and G. Wilson (eds), *Applying sport psychology: Four perspectives* (pp. 187–206). Champaign, Ill.: Human Kinetics.

Ost, L. G. (1989). One-session treatment for specific phobias. *Behavioral Research and Therapy*, 27, 1–7.

Pargman, D. (ed.) (1999). *Psychological bases of sport injuries.* Morgantown, W.V.: Fitness Information Technology.

Petitpas, A. and Danish, S. (1995). Caring for the injured athlete. In S. Murphy (ed.), *Sport psychology interventions* (pp. 255–284). Champaign, Ill.: Human Kinetics.

Pizzari, T., McBurney, H., Taylor, N. and Feller, J. (2001). Adherence to ACL rehabilitation: a qualitative analysis. In *Proceedings of the Australian Conference of Science and Medicine in Sport and Exercise* (pp. 135). October 24–27, Perth, Western Australia.

Podlog, L. and Eklund, R.C. (2006). A longitudinal investigation of competitive athletes' return to sport following serious injury. *Journal of Applied Sport Psychology*, 18, 44–68.

Podlog, L. and Eklund, R.C. (2007a). The psychosocial aspects of a return to sport following serious injury: a review of the literature from a self-determination perspective. *Psychology of Sport and Exercise*, 8, 535–566.

Podlog, L. and Eklund, R. C. (2007b). Professional coaches' perspectives on the return to sport following serious injury. *Journal of Applied Sport Psychology*, 19, 207–225.

Podlog, L., Lochbaum, M. and Stevens, T. (2010). Need satisfaction, well-being, and perceived return-to-sport outcomes among injured athletes. *Journal of Applied Sport Psychology*, 22, 167–182.

Ray, R. and Wiese-Bjornstal, D. M. (eds). (1999). *Counseling in sports medicine.* Champaign, Ill.: Human Kinetics.

Richman, J. M., Hardy, C. J., Rosenfeld, L. B. and Callanan, R. A. E. (1989). Strategies for enhancing social support networks in sport: a brainstorming experience. *Journal of Applied Sport Psychology*, 1, 150–159.

Rotella, R. J. (1982). Psychological care of the injured athlete. In D. N. Kulund (ed.), *The injured athlete* (pp. 213–224). Philadelphia, Pa.: Lippincott.

Rotella, R. J. and Campbell, M. S. (1983). Systematic desensitization: psychological rehabilitation of injured athletes. *Athletic Training*, 18, 149–152.

Ryan, R. and Deci, E. L. (2000). Self-determination theory and the facilitation of intrinsic motivation, social development and well-being. *American Psychologist*, 55, 68–78.

Sagar, S. A., Busch, B. K. and Jowett, S. (2010). Success and failure, fear of failure, and coping responses of adolescent academy football players. *Journal of Applied Sport Psychology*, 22, 213–230.

Tabachnick, B. G. and Fidell, L. S. (1996). *Using multivariate statistics*, 3rd edn. New York: Harper Collins.

Taylor, J. and Taylor, S. (1997). *Psychological approaches to sports injury rehabilitation.* Maryland: ASPEN.

Thatcher, J., Kerr, J. Amies, K. and Day, M. (2007). A reversal theory analysis of psychological responses during sports injury rehabilitation. *Journal of Sport Rehabilitation*, 16, 343–62.

Tracey, J. (2003). The emotional response to injury and rehabilitation process. *Journal of Applied Sport Psychology*, 15, 279–293.

Tredget, J. (2001). A systematic desensitization programme for agoraphobia. *Nursing Times*, 97, 39–40.

Tripp, D. A., Ebel-Lam, A., Stanish, W. and Brewer, B. W. (2007). Fear of reinjury, negative affect, and catastrophizing predicting return to sport in recreational athletes with anterior cruciate ligament injuries at 1 year postsurgery. *Rehabilitation Psychology*, 52, 74–81.

Walker, N. (2006). *The meaning of sports injury and re-injury anxiety measurement and intervention.* Unpublished doctoral dissertation, Aberystwyth University, UK.

Walker, N., Thatcher, J., Lavallee, D. and Golby, J. (2002). A longitudinal study of emotional responses to sports injury. *Proceedings of the British Psychological Society*, 10 (2), 106.

Walker, N., Thatcher, J. and Lavallee, D. (2007). Psychological responses to injury in competitive sport: a critical review. *The Journal of Royal Society for the Promotion of Health,* 127, 174–180.

Walker, N., Thatcher, J. and Lavallee, D. (2010). A preliminary development of the Re-Injury Anxiety Inventory (RIAI). *Physical Therapy in Sport,* 11, 23–29.

Webster, K. E., Feller, J. A. and Lambros, C. (2008). Development and preliminary validation of a scale to measure the psychological impact of returning to sport following anterior cruciate ligament reconstruction surgery. *Physical Therapy in Sport,* 9, 9–15.

White, C. A. and Black, E. K. (2004). Cognitive and behavioral interventions. In G. S. Kolt and M. B. Andersen (eds), *Psychology in the physical and manual therapies* (pp. 93–109). London: Churchill Livingstone.

Wiese-Bjornstal, D. M., Smith, A. M, Shaffer, S. M and Morrey, M. A. (1998). An integrated model of response to sport injury: psychological and sociological dynamics. *Journal of Applied Sport Psychology,* 10, 46–69.

Williams, J. M. and Andersen, M. B. (1998). Psychosocial antecedents of sport injury: review and critique of the stress and injury model. *Journal of Applied Sport Psychology,* 10, 5–25.

Wolpe, J. (1958). *Psychotherapy by reciprocal inhibition.* Stanford, Calif.: Stanford University Press.

Wood, M. M. (1981). Psychological and behavioral techniques in facilitating sports performance. *Sports Coach,* 5, 10–12.

Zinbarg, R. E., Barlow, D. H., Brown, T. A. and Hertz, R. M. (1992). Cognitive-behavioral approaches to the nature and treatment of anxiety disorders. *Annual Review of Psychology,* 43, 235–267.

12

LOSING TO WIN

A clinical perspective on the experience of loss among elite athletes

Corinne Reid, Murdoch University

England won the World Cup because they were mentally tougher than any other side. That sort of mental toughness is born out of experience, both of winning competitions and of losing. It was by losing Grand Slam games, by losing every now and then at the final hurdle despite the fact that people are calling you the best team in the world, and going through those lows together that England built up that experience. When you get to that stage again you know what you have to do not to slip up.

Josh Lewsey, England rugby player

Introduction

Loss is a theme that runs through the life stories of most elite athletes – we could go so far as to say that in many cases it is the thread that holds the story together. When we think of champions we like to think of those who have overcome adversity, who have come back from monumental defeat. But it is also true that the experience of loss can be the weak link that relegates potential champions to mediocrity. What is it then that determines whether an athlete's experience of loss will be formative or destructive? Why do some exceptional juniors become paralysed by fear of failure and fail to make the transition to elite status? Why is injury-related 'depression' an increasingly common referral for psychologists working with elite athletes? This chapter examines the 'loss experience' of the elite athlete based on clinical observations from the author's work with elite athletes and their coaches. The second part reflects on a model for intervention forged during seven years of working with the Australian Women's Hockey Team as they reconciled to a disappointing Olympic campaign in Barcelona in 1992 and moved toward two consecutive gold-medal Olympiads. Specifically, it considers the challenge of how to develop a team 'culture' that recognizes, values and utilizes the experience of loss in the pursuit of excellence. Such a culture understands intense emotional experiences as the bedrock of both compelling personal motivation and paralyzing inertia. It recognizes that these states of being are never far removed from one another, and that emotional regulation is one of the core skills required of elite athletes. In its most encompassing clinical sense, emotional regulation is knowing when, where and how to use emotion. Well-managed emotional processing of loss can manifest in a growing armory of personal coping resources as well as significant personal growth more broadly.

The experience of loss can be usefully considered as a sense of compromised connection with something of significance. If we consider 'loss' in the broad sense proposed by Peretz (1970), it may involve being deprived of, or disconnected from:

- significant or valued people
- some aspect of self
- objects or possessions
- and/or some significant aspect of the process of human growth and development.

Each of these types of loss can be found routinely, and multiply, in the life of elite sportspeople. Significant career transition points that both highlight and threaten a sportsperson's identity as an athlete have been identified as times when the potential for loss, and hence the experience of loss, comes into sharpest focus (Lavallee et al., 1998). Points of transition thus provide the canvas for the current discussion of the nature of the loss experience for the elite athlete.

Transitions

Perhaps the most widely studied transition in sport is, paradoxically, the transition *out of sport,* that is, athlete retirement. There is considerable literature suggesting that this can be a distressing and personally challenging experience involving the loss of athletic identity and hence, a loss of a core element of 'self' (for a review see Fortunato and Marchant, 1999; Ogilvie and Taylor, 1993). Many athletes grieve this loss for many years after retirement, others make repeated comeback attempts as they struggle to come to terms with their new life circumstances. Even those who adjust well to life after sport often develop a growing awareness, a retrospective appreciation or wistfulness, for aspects of their former life that are no longer achievable in their new life.

> I have never missed hockey – I can honestly say that ... but being involved with something that you are the best in the world at, passionate about, that is hard to excel in, surrounded by motivated people, is what you start to miss – having to start all over again in the corporate [world], while at times feeling

the world owed me something and wishing that financially I had gained from being so good at something.

(Jenny Morris, hockey player, dual Olympic gold medallist)

Injury and performance slumps are two other frequently identified critical incidents for athletes that are associated with both actual and symbolic loss, and considerable distress (Brewer, 1999; Ford and Gordon, 1999; Grove and Stoll, 1999; Lavallee et al., 1998; Rees, Smith, and Sparkes, 2003). Athletes commonly consider these experiences to be an immediate threat to their physical competence and hence, potentially challenging to their success as an athlete, to their athletic identity and to their broader sense of self-confidence.

I felt as though the bottom had fallen out of my world … like suddenly a fog was lifting and there was a nothingness on the other side …. I didn't know what I would do if my leg didn't heal …. I felt as though there were nothing out there for me if I couldn't compete. I wanted the fog to wrap back around me so that all I could see was the track again.

(Reflections of an injured Olympic track athlete)

Notwithstanding the strength of such reactions, the research literature is perhaps most noteworthy for identifying that in fact, despite the almost universal distress engendered by such events, only a minority of athletes go on to experience chronic 'highly distressful reactions' to retirement (37 per cent reported by Lavallee, Gordon, and Grove, 1997). Fewer still develop 'clinically meaningful' levels of distress associated with injury (5–13 per cent reported by Brewer, 1999). In understanding these and other loss experiences of the elite athlete – in neither underestimating the power of loss-related grief, nor overlooking the resilience of athletes in the face of significant loss – it is helpful to consider the experience of transition and loss throughout an athlete's career as both a chronic force and an acute stressor.

By its very nature an athletic career has as its *primary focus*, constantly, actively and urgently, seeking improvement. With growth, necessarily, according to Baltes (1987), comes loss and the threat of future loss. This fact both prepares the athlete in unique ways for handling loss, that is, it builds resilience, but also taxes the coping resources of the athlete by confronting them with numerous challenges, often concurrently or in quick succession (such as being injured and consequently not being selected for a team). From the moment of entering the elite domain there are an endless series of events that constitute marked transitions. The following clinical scenarios are just a selected few cases, to illustrate in more detail the breadth and pervasiveness of the loss experience for elite athletes. These, perhaps less obvious (or less researched) transitions, will broaden the basis for this discussion of the issue of loss in the life of an athlete.

Becoming elite and staying elite

The struggling 'novice'

> I have wanted to be in this squad for so long that I thought I would be on a permanent high, but now I am just miserable ..., I don't understand it.... I am working harder than I ever have but I am running on the spot ... no, it's worse than that, I am going backwards .... I don't think I am cut out for this.
>
> *(new national squad member, 1994, Olympian in 2000)*

By entering the elite domain, athletes choose to make sport their priority, in many cases giving up work, study, family, peers and sometimes relationships to focus full-time on their sporting development – it is a rite of passage that identifies and defines the individual as an athlete. Unfortunately, at a time when the individual's identity is becoming closely bound up with their sporting competence (Miller and Kerr, 2003), their performance (relative to their new peers) will often seem below par as they move from being on the top rung of the ladder as an 'exceptional junior' to the bottom rung as a 'novice elite' athlete. This can lead to frustration, self-doubt and even a retreat to junior ranks. Geographic dislocation from family and friends can amplify this experience. An additional challenge for female athletes is the physical changes resulting from intensified training requirements. Many young female athletes feel that becoming 'muscle-bound' challenges their femininity. Body image dysphoria is an important indicator of a particular sense of loss and distress in this transition to elite status, and may result in disordered eating if not addressed.

Post-tournament blues

> But we won ... why do I feel like crying?... since we came back I just can't seem to get it together ... nothing is the same ... if I never see [training venue] I won't care ... but I want to go to Sydney [Olympics]
>
> *(Olympic medallist, six months after Atlanta Olympics)*

Non-selection or poor-tournament performance at a major event generally manifests in an explicit sense of loss. This is the most widely recognized and commonly accepted form of loss, but it often outlives the expectations of both athlete and coach. Loss of self-efficacy in future ability is commonly reported, but also a sense of retrospective loss of the effort and resources invested in the attempt, and loss relating to personal and interpersonal sacrifices made in the pursuit. *Winning* a major tournament, however, does not ensure freedom from feelings of loss. Following the Atlanta Olympics, the term 'post-Atlanta blues' was coined by a journalist to describe the feeling of 'flatness' associated with 'coming down' after a major success. This loss is often described as a fear of not being able to recapture that moment of ultimate achievement, and of the feeling of being 'aimless' in the absence of the intense, structured, goal-directed, pre-tournament training programme. Other symptoms can include alternating bursts of energy and exhaustion, and general 'tetchiness'. The symptom most fearful to athletes is an associated loss of desire to play their chosen sport, which, however, is usually short-lived if handled appropriately. Normalizing this experience as part of a *process* of 'grieving' in the let-down after a major victory can prevent impulsive acts by athletes – notably this is a high risk time for premature retirement announcements. This process is discussed in greater detail later in the chapter. With many sports moving toward a more densely packed competition and touring schedule, the time for psychological as well as physical recovery between tournaments is also decreasing, leading to an increased risk of chronic hypervigilance about performance, almost continual anticipatory anxiety and potentially, exhaustion.

Post-injury 'malingering'

> I want to be back at the top ... but I don't want to get back on the track ... they tell me I am ready to go, I have given 100 per cent to my rehab [sic] ... but something is wrong, it doesn't show on the x-rays, it doesn't hurt when I run, but I know it ... somehow ...
>
> *(Olympic athlete prior to Olympic trials)*

The sense of loss associated with injury has been well documented in the literature and interpreted using such models as Hobfoll's (1988) conservation of resources model. This model suggests that an athlete's injury can be understood as representing a threat to their personal and physical resources and hence to the achievement of desired conditions (such as selection into a team) or objects (such as an Olympic medal). However, when such injuries are receding and such threats reducing, injured athletes, seemingly counter-intuitively, often display increasing ambivalence toward their rehabilitation programme and their return to training. When explored further, they report feelings of trepidation that they will not regain their premorbid level of ability (even in the face of strong contradictory evidence), that they are more vulnerable to future injury, or that things have changed or 'moved on' in their team and that they will not 'fit in'. This perhaps coincides with a perceived loss of status in the eyes of their coach and peers. These factors can contribute to an over-riding sense of loss of control (helplessness) and of self-doubt, which can manifest in self-sabotage in the form of reduced or ineffectual effort in rehabilitation and variable motivation to return to competition.

These case stories illustrate some of the ways in which an athlete is particularly vulnerable to perceived threats to their sporting ability. Moreover, in a context where the identity of the athlete is so closely bound with their sporting performance, this may challenge their *general* self-efficacy, their sense of control over their destiny, their sense of self (Lavallee et al., 1998). As the literature on self-efficacy has demonstrated, this in turn may affect behaviour (Bandura, 1982; Seligman, 1991). More specifically it can adversely affect competition performance, but can also manifest itself in less obvious ways such as variable commitment to training and amplification of the athlete's fear of future failure (termed *anticipatory* loss by Janis, 1982). This, in turn, can constrain the athlete's development. Compromised self-efficacy can also be expressed in displacement activities such as coach–athlete conflict or intra-team conflict. This effect can be compounded when anticipatory fear of loss is relevant for an entire team, such as just prior to team selection or prior to a tournament.

Given the fact that experiences of loss are a pervasive feature of life as a career athlete, understanding individual resilience to loss would seem to be paramount. This will become increasingly important as the demands of being an elite athlete grow. In the past decade, more training programmes have become full-time, more are residential, more travelling is involved, more tournaments are contested. Concurrently, in many sports, elite athletes are becoming younger and hence, developmentally less well equipped to cope with these increasing demands. This is not to say that we should necessarily protect our charges by preventing such experiences even if it were possible! Instead we should find ways to support their instinctual tendency toward survival by providing an environment in which they can work to increase their resilience to these challenging aspects of the sporting experience (Charlesworth, 2001; Shatte and Rievitch, 2002). It is worth noting that each of the athletes quoted above went on to achieve Olympic selection. Journeying through these experiences was perhaps a fundamental part of their preparation – forging the 'champion psyche'.

What do we know about loss that can help us get the balance right?

Most of the psychological research on loss in the sporting arena has focused on defining problematic reactions to loss, identifying events or stressors that might induce a sense of loss and the risk factors that might predispose someone to 'react negatively' to loss or the threat of loss. Such studies have been critical in turning a spotlight on the issue of loss in sport. However, mostly they have been implicitly predicated upon static models of the experience of loss. This is best illustrated by the fact that most studies do not consider the time that has elapsed since the critical event (such as injury) when assessing the impact of the loss. Nor do questions focus on exploring the *changing* nature of an individual's responses over time. It is also common for questions to focus (often exclusively) on the negative aspects of the experience. At best, changes in an athlete's response to their injury or retirement have been acknowledged tangentially or implicitly rather than considered as the primary source of data in understanding the degree of resilience in the face of loss, or the degree of progress in managing the loss. Perhaps we are now at a point where we can take the next step and consider loss in sport as *primarily* a process – a chronic, repetitive process at that. Moreover, in considering loss as an ever-changing experience we can also turn our attention to the growth that accompanies such experiences.

Loss and grief: a process

Perhaps a helpful, dynamic approach to the understanding of loss can best be gleaned from the bereavement literature. How do people cope with the most significant loss experience – the death of a loved one? While there are obvious differences between death and other forms of loss, there are also many similarities. Elisabeth Kübler-Ross's (1973) seminal work identified five key emotional stages of grieving:

- *Denial and isolation*, characterized by emotional and intellectual avoidance of the loss.
- *Anger*, or externalizing the feelings of loss and often accompanied by blame.
- *Bargaining*, or attempts to change the reality of the loss as a means of regaining a sense of control.
- *Depression*, characterized by great sadness or hopelessness, and, eventually:
- *Acceptance*, or learning to accept feelings and reality as they are, neither minimizing the loss nor feeling overwhelmed by it.

While individuals vary in the order in which they experience these stages and in the length of each stage (they are not mutually exclusive and are often iterative), her widely accepted thesis is that each stage is a necessary part of the recovery process, a way of coming to terms with a significant loss. When the loss is expected, as in the case of terminal illness (or anticipatory loss in sport), this process often begins before death has actually occurred. She also recognized that while death is the most extreme form of loss, other significant loss experiences followed the same path. The task for clinicians then is to assist people to recognize this process as normal and necessary, to validate their emotional experiences, and to assist the individual to anchor their understanding of often confusing and contradictory behaviour (such as feeling angry at a dead spouse, or feeling angry with a coach or team mate after non-selection) to a process that begins with distress and travels toward resolution.

This is no easy feat when working with elite athletes and coaches. For the athlete and coach, emotional responses to significant loss are often considered 'acceptable' only when manifestly related and temporally contiguous with a poor performance. As we saw in our earlier examples, things are rarely this clear cut – as mentioned above, some aspects of the loss process may precede the event, others may follow months, or even years later. Even when they are clearly performance-related, sporting culture dictates a short outburst, it does not typically accommodate a 'response process'. In this context it is understandable that a coach might react defensively to an athlete's angry response to a less obvious loss (such as blaming the coach) or become frustrated when an athlete swings between depression and anger. In all likelihood, however, this response would be transient except for the reaction it engendered, which can then make it a 'sticking point' in their relationship and in the process of the athlete accepting the loss and accepting responsibility for rectifying the situation. In team sports this can quickly escalate to general dissatisfaction with the coach, when several players experience this reaction simultaneously (such as after a poor tournament performance). Teams can get 'stuck' at various stages of this process, when consonant expressions of grief are taken as affirmation of the validity of a particular viewpoint, rather than a shared grieving experience.

Kübler-Ross's (1973) model of bereavement helps us to understand the *normal* emotional journey of responding to loss, and provides a clear framework for facilitating this process through acknowledgment of the reactions to loss as part of a new personal growth and acceptance of responsibility for our own future. It also helps us to understand how, in settings where the threat of loss is ever-present, that pre-emptive anticipatory loss, such as the threat of non-selection, can trigger a debilitating, demotivating grieving process that contributes to a self-fulfilling prophecy (poor performance and non-selection). Even for those few athletes who do go on to develop 'clinically significant' responses to loss (that may well meet the *Diagnostic and Statistics Manual of Mental Disorders* (DSM-IV; American Psychiatric Association, 1994) or *International Statistical Classification of Diseases and Related Health Problems* (ICD-10; National Center for Health Statistics, 1992) diagnostic criteria for adjustment disorder or even post-traumatic stress disorder as indicated by excessive and prolonged reaction that interferes with functioning or performance), a process-focused model assists in maintaining fluidity and change in the perception of the loss. Central to this model is the potential for things to be different, for people to recover no matter what their initial reaction to the event.

When is loss an issue? Mediating and moderating factors in elite sport

As mentioned earlier there are several aspects of the loss experience of the elite athlete that make it significantly different from the case of death, bereavement or unexpected trauma. First and most importantly, elite athletes make a *choice* to participate in an activity and a lifestyle in which adversity and loss are clearly and explicitly going to be part of the experience. Indeed most athletes choose to seek elite status after already having first-hand experience of painful performance-related losses (such as non-selection or competition defeat). Second, the experience of loss of control and the challenge to self-efficacy does not always result directly from, or result in, a crisis experience (performance loss), but can also be the gradual result of chronic, cumulative, lifestyle factors such as alienation from support systems (for instance, moving interstate for training), loss of privacy (such as when touring or from constant performance evaluation), financial constraints or time pressure that function more as 'background stressors'. Third, the experience of death and bereavement are infrequent for most of us – they are *exceptions* to our life experience.

In the case of the elite athlete, loss experiences take many forms and are frequent experiences. This may affect, perhaps truncate, the 'normal' response process. For example, chronic anticipation of loss may indicate an incomplete grieving process for non-athletes but may be merely a different, realistic, and still functional resolution point in the life of an athlete. Thus it seems there are a number of factors that may mediate or moderate the process of recovery after a loss experience for elite athletes.

In better understanding the athlete's transition through loss, we must turn to research from 'like' environments, that is, those marked by: chronic threat (and thus loss as an ever-present process); the very real potential for significant loss (and hence, anticipation of loss and fear of loss); the presence of chronic background stressors (lifestyle factors and so on), and, in spite of this, voluntary participation! In addition to the broader research on high achievers in other domains, a number of less obvious research areas have proven informative – primarily, the literature on the functioning of military combat teams but also studies of people living in high-risk natural disaster zones or facing serious medical intervention. The point of interface of these domains is the 'stress' literature (Driskell and Salas, 1996; Meichenbaum and Fitzpatrick, 1993) and more recently, the resilience literature (Seligman, 1991). Both address the effect of high demand factors on human performance. From this literature it seems that the likely key mediating factors in successfully facing adversity and dealing with loss in sport include:

- individual differences in personal resources
- expectations and preparation for loss
- response and recovery skills
- the accessibility of support.

Individual differences in personal resources

Personality

At the broadest level, twin studies from the behaviour-genetics literature demonstrate that from infancy, we actively influence the environments that we choose to inhabit, selecting those that have 'goodness of fit' with, and allow expression of, desired aspects of our personality (Scarr and McCartney, 1983). Further, choosing environments that involve a degree of risk, personal threat or challenge is a common feature of the personality of high achievers in a range of life domains, and is associated with high self-efficacy and a persistent nature (Bloom, 1985; Gagne, 1993; Sulloway, 1996). Therefore, athletes for the most part are not passive victims of a fickle environment, but bring with them a range of potential resources suited to navigating such difficulties. Based on studies investigating the efficacy of particular personality *types* for coping with the stress of potential failure and perceived threat, Hogan and Lesser (1996) advocate selection of personnel for hazardous performance (such as working with chemicals or military combat crews) based on personality. These authors consider those who score highly on conscientiousness, emotional stability and openness to experience – three of McRae and Costa's (1987) Big Five personality factors – to be most suited to performing in environments in which there is a realistic expectation of danger.

While we are not yet at the point of knowing this much about the specific function of personality in elite sport, current studies undertaken for the author's doctoral research would suggest that indeed elite athletes are different from the general population on a number of the Big Five personality dimensions, and that some elite athletes have a 'sporting personality' that differs significantly from their general personality. Moreover, athletes differ from each other in their personality profiles. So while there is not one 'optimal sporting personality', athletes do seem to come armed with resources different from those in the general population, and/ or to develop resources to adapt to the demands of their environment. Being aware of the different reactive styles of individual athletes and the different resources they bring to the situation should help us to better predict and understand their reaction to loss and the threat of loss. It might also help us to identify the particular points in the process of loss where an individual might get stuck, and what personality-consonant manifestations we might expect to see at different points in that process. For example, someone extremely high on the trait of Openness might, in situations of stress, get caught in a frantic search for new solutions or be uncritically swayed by suggestions from others. Contrastingly, someone low on Openness may, under pressure, revert to old habits rather than considering new and different response options.

Developmental stage

Another mediating factor in coping with loss experiences is the developmental stage of the athlete (Baltes, Rees and Lipsitt, 1980; Brewer, Van Raalte and Linder, 1993). Elite athletes are becoming younger and younger, with many athletes competing at high levels during their adolescent years. Normal developmental progress will constrain the athlete's likely response to performance-related losses and to lifestyle changes. Adolescence, for example, is marked by a sense of invincibility, and is a time of volatile and turbulent emotions. Losing a major tournament is likely to accentuate these features. Normal development during this phase is also associated with being sensitive to criticism and challenging authority, which makes for a potentially volatile relationship between coaches and athletes. However, moving through a loss experience can also be a maturing transition for adolescent athletes – being confronted with vulnerability and personal distress can encourage new resourcefulness and a sense of personal responsibility. Addressing the athlete as 'adult' while being aware of the 'child' (and cognizant of developmental regression associated with stress), can encourage a more mature response to stressful experiences. Adopting a process (future) orientation is particularly important for work with athletes who are developmentally more likely to be transfixed in the 'here and now'.

Expectations and preparation for loss: identifying threat and 'the work of worrying'

The experience of loss as well as the spectre of loss can have a positive impact on performance depending on the participants' expectation and preparation for the event. The perceived importance of an experience impacts on how many of the individual's resources are actually made available to deal with the situation. While the individual may have sufficient latent personal resources to deal with a loss situation, they must *perceive* the loss in order to 'enable' and utilize those resources. Janis (1982) reports that the psychological effects of *warning* in instances of imminent disaster (such as bombing raids, floods, cyclones) is a moderating factor in effective responding. When the threat is perceived to be moderate (and therefore real but controllable), the most optimal reaction, vigilance, is likely to occur, rather than denial, overwhelming anxiety or demoralization, which are associated with insurmountable threat or when no threat is perceived. Action is most likely to follow if there is perceived to be no escape route (no way of avoiding the threat), if there is no one else to act, if there is anticipated restriction to access of own or other resources, and if there is clear role assignment (the individual knows what is required). False alarms artificially decrease the perceived threat, while near-miss experiences (such as being spared in a bombing raid) are likely to result in vigilance. Similarly, increased exposure to potential loss in combat soldiers resulted in the participants becoming more discriminating about where the danger lay, and also resulted in judgements and actions becoming more appropriate. They adopted a 'vigilance set' that involved both cognitive and behavioural changes in scanning, attending and planning for threat. In response to these findings, Janis coined the phrase the 'work of worrying', and discusses the cost of not experiencing loss or the threat of loss. He suggests that the absence of actual experience or mental rehearsal of impending danger leads to feelings of helplessness if danger occurs.

The value of the 'work of worrying' can be implicitly seen in sport in the often motivational effect of uncertain selection. A late selection policy can see the 'work of worrying' manifested as an increased training commitment leading up to a tournament for those athletes who perceive a moderate likelihood of non-selection. The incorporation of performance self-evaluation into the training routine can also systemically instigate the positive 'work of worrying' by routinely focusing an athlete's attention on both their strengths and weaknesses. Getting the balance wrong, however, by over-focusing on potential disasters or avoiding them altogether, can lead to some of the unhelpful effects outlined above.

The question of whether to prepare athletes in advance for the possibility of non-selection evoked considerable debate amongst national coaches of Olympic sports prior to the Sydney Olympics. The position argued strongly by some coaches was that discussing the consequences of non-selection (such as experiencing symptoms of grief and depression) could be pre-emptively demoralizing. Others (including the author) argued that this position ignores the reality that athletes are very aware of this potential threat whether it is spoken about or not – the value of preparing for this and other potential losses *at the outset* of an Olympic campaign outweighs the immediate discomfort that may be caused by making the potential threat explicit. The valuable 'work of worrying' is also often overlooked where loss experiences are genuinely not readily identifiable, as in the case of the 'post-Atlanta blues', where the issue of loss seems almost antithetical. Our task is to assist athletes and coaches to accurately assess the risk, and the perceived risk, associated with each situation to assist them in developing a commensurate response.

After the storm: response and recovery skills

Attributional style

The learned helplessness and resilience literature has identified that attributing poor performance outcome or other loss experiences to stable causes can lead to a sense of pessimism about future changeability of such experiences (Seligman, 1991). This is particularly so when this attribution is accompanied by an external locus of control, or perceived lack of personal agency in effecting outcomes. Moreover, if such events and personal resource limitations are considered to be pervasive, general self-efficacy is affected, a sense of helplessness follows and performance is chronically diminished. Resilient individuals, on the other hand, are those who challenge unhelpful and inaccurate habitual personal assumptions about agency, who do not see external constraints as all-encompassing (that is, they understand that they always have control over changing some things even if it is just the way they view the situation), who realistically appraise the consequences of each event and use a problem-solving approach to gather evidence and challenge beliefs about outcomes.

Ellis (1962) identified ten irrational attributions that often occur under stressful situations. These include generalizing or 'catastrophizing' from a single event, thinking in black and white (all-or-none) terms, personalizing, magnification of undesirable elements, minimization of desirable elements, and blaming. We know that these rules of thinking apply to athletes and that, to some extent, post-performance attributions assist us in predicting emotional adjustment and future achievements in both the short and long term (Biddle, 1993; Brewer, 1999; Ford and Gordon, 1999; Grove and Stoll, 1999; Rettew and Reivich, 1995). Challenging irrational attributions is known as cognitive reappraisal. However, cognitive reappraisal is not just about training athletes in 'positive thinking'. It involves honest self-evaluation, developing a sense of personal responsibility and accountability for life choices, and challenging narrow beliefs about what constitutes 'success' and 'failure'. It has at its core an assumption that we may not be able to change events in life, but we can always change how we respond to them. The resilience literature embodies a process orientation that encourages evidence gathering as the basis for differentiating between current performance, past actions and future achievements. An athlete who has missed selection for the Olympics is only temporarily assisted in diminishing their distress by attributing the cause of non-selection to external factors such as a biased coach or misperceived lack of opportunity. A more resilient athlete will move through their initial distress to acknowledge their role in the non-selection (for instance, 'I know that I didn't really put in at all of the training sessions'), unchangeable factors in their selection (such as 'Although I completed all of the training requirements, my competitor was faster/fitter/stronger/more tactically aware') but also to moderate their initial impression of the impact of this loss (for instance, 'I am disappointed but there is another selection in twelve months' time – I will work hard to be in a better position for selection') and to acknowledge the broader context in which it has occurred (as, 'As an elite athlete it is inevitable that I will experience loss and disappointment as I spend all of my life competing – these opportunities can help make me stronger' and 'I am more than just an athlete'). Schinke and Jerome (2003) have recently outlined a programme for teaching resilience skills to athletes. This would seem to be a promising new approach to preventative intervention.

Stress inoculation skills

The military combat literature is clear that the perceived ability to effectively assess and respond to a potential threat is the most effective means of being inoculated against the negative aspects of the situation and of optimizing performance (Orasanu and Backer, 1996). Responding to a critical event is optimized by two elements of preparation: recognizing and managing the symptoms of stress, and developing appropriate situation-relevant skills.

Recognizing and managing symptoms of stress requires education about the cognitive, behavioural, emotional and physiological indicators of stress. Physiological arousal reduction procedures include an array of relaxation techniques in addition to the cognitive reappraisal techniques discussed earlier. Cognitive reappraisal can be effectively used with athletes to reinterpret anxiety and distress-related symptoms as expectable but not inherently threatening responses to a stressful situation.

Developing appropriate situation-relevant skills in combat teams (such as responding to enemy fire) has traditionally meant training skilled responses in threatening circumstances, that is, overlearning specific situation-relevant skills (such as target shooting) by repetitive practice under pressure so that the response will become automatic, requiring few cognitive resources and therefore being more resistant to stress-related decrements. However, Orasanu and Backer (1996) showed that while the resultant skills are easily and accurately invoked under stress, they are rigid and non-responsive to unexpected or changing circumstances. The alternative is to overlearn an *approach to crisis management* rather than a specific skill. That is, to develop process skills such as communication and decision making that, once mastered, can be transferred to training and performance under a range of threat conditions. This is particularly relevant in the sporting context. Overlearning specific 'plays' will only ensure success if there is no opposition to challenge the practised sequence. Overlearning communication and problem-solving skills under pressure maximizes the likelihood that athletes can respond to any eventuality. Similarly, self-management skills such as cognitive reappraisal and arousal control can be translocated by the athlete to any situation. They are as relevant on the field ('I messed up that play badly. I just have to stay calm and focused. I have the skills to do it better next time the next time the ball comes my way') as off the field ('The coach is yelling at me again – but I know he is trying to help me improve my skills. It isn't personal').

The accessibility of support

Access to support when experiencing loss or fearing loss is a strong buffer to stress. Janis (1982) noted that under conditions of extreme threat, combat soldiers reported that group identification increased. Group affiliation functioned by providing reassurance (through sharing of fear and correction of baseless fears) and role clarification (through discussion of tasks). Interestingly, if superiors were perceived not to be contributing to this process of support, combat soldiers perceived them instead to be contributors to the feeling of threat, and were more likely to exclude them from the protective group boundary.

Interviews with elite sportspeople suggested to Rees and Hardy (2000) and others (Ford and Gordon, 1999; Rees et al., 2003) that four types of social support are particularly important in this domain in times of stress – emotional support (or feeling cared for), bolstering of self-esteem, informational support (or advice) and tangible support (such as financial assistance or physical help). A well-functioning team can act as a support network and potentially fulfil each of these functions, but unlike the combat soldiers, competition for selection within the team can make the process of peer support even more fraught (Bowers, Weaver and Morgan, 1996). Athletes often do not see their coach as a support person (even if they have tried hard to foster this image) because they are in a position of potentially using the athlete's display of 'vulnerability' against them when it comes to selection. In addition, the athlete often has limited access to more traditional forms of support away from the sporting context (such as family and friends and workmates) because of geographic distance or training commitments. The challenge is to ensure that each athlete has some form of support available – addressing obstacles to accessing support explicitly with athletes can be helpful in moderating impediments.

Where to from here? Putting it into practice

It seems then that loss experiences, and the anticipation of loss, can be seen as a primary, and necessary facet of the career of the elite athlete. It is not just necessary in the sense of a 'necessary evil' to be endured or overcome, but perhaps an essential ingredient in enhancing motivation and developing the resilience required for an athlete to reach their potential and perform well under pressure. Ed Moses's comment that 'I just didn't think about it as *losing*. I was *preparing*' (*Sports Illustrated*,

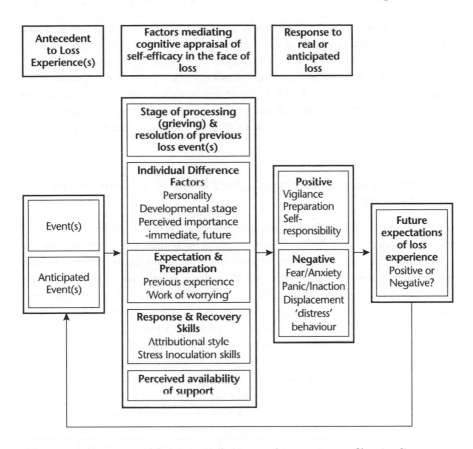

FIGURE 12.1 Summary of factors contributing to the experience of loss in elite athletes

30 July 1984) illustrates the essence of such a stance. It is likely that athletes as a group are more capable of handling significant, recurrent loss experiences than the general population. Beyond this there are a range of factors that facilitate or disrupt the transition through the loss process. Taken together the factors outlined in Figure 12.1 contribute to the stress resilience of the individual in the face of repeated loss experiences and the chronic threat of loss. Developing a culture that is responsive to these factors is our primary task. The rest of this chapter utilizes a case study to explore the process of developing such a culture.

The Australian Women's Hockey Team (1994–2000): a case study

Consideration of the issues discussed above underpinned the working model developed by the author in her work with the Australian Women's Hockey Team during two successful Olympic cycles. This model incorporated both a preventive and a responsive approach to the issue of loss in sport, and involved organizational education, group work and individual sessions with coaches, support staff and athletes. At the time of initial involvement with the team, a new coach had been recently appointed and the team's Olympic experience in Barcelona some two years earlier was still a remarkably 'raw' loss experience for many players and staff – the team had come fifth despite being tournament favourites. This unfortunate event provided a platform for addressing with the team, the far-reaching impact of such a significant and unexpected loss, and for developing a culture that was more responsive to loss experiences.

Preparing for loss: developing a culture in which loss is an integral part of success

The starting point in developing such a culture must be a coach who is open to the view of recovery from loss as a *process*, and who is thus not threatened by the expression of strong emotions (and sometimes accusations) in the progress toward resolution. Richard Charlesworth, coach of the women's team, was fortunately one such coach, as was assistant coach Chris Spice, and former coach Brian Glencross, who was still working with the team. The Barcelona result, still a defining experience for a core of the group, provided an invaluable opportunity to observe the potentially destructive impact of significant loss. Some members of the Olympic squad acknowledged raw anger and distress about their experience. External attributions were expressed by some, placing responsibility for the result variably with coaching staff, other players and officials. Others expressed significant self-blame. Others still, who had not been part of the Olympic team, felt unable to penetrate 'the Barcelona group'. The experience had started to become somewhat of a toxic 'glue' that was binding the team to a sense of distress and to a time exemplified by poor performance and team conflict. It provided a powerful experience as the basis for a team discussion of the nature of loss, and an opportunity to introduce the notion of recovery as a grieving process.

Athletes were invited to express their views about what had happened. Validating unique (sometimes conflicting) as well as shared impressions of the issue was a necessary part of an individual and group process of making sense of the event and of recovering strength after such an unexpected loss. Giving voice to these issues in a non-judgemental context (with coaches present) provides an opportunity to externalize some of the emotional power of the experience and to contextualize this response as part of an important grief process. It also provides a platform from which to move forward in a self-determining manner, accepting the experience (or exclusion from the experience) as a fact, a part of history which cannot be undone, but which can be understood more fully and thus demoted to a position of lesser importance where it is less constraining of the future place in their sporting psyche. Recognizing the strength and growth associated with such experiences involves reframing defiant persistence (a reaction against another which is inherently tied to the past) as renewed commitment to improved performance (reflecting growth and a forward looking self-determining response to loss). Athletes were inducted into recognizing the loss response as a 'process', and encouraged to see it as a transition from distress to positive expression through self-development.

The 'Barcelona experience' opened the door to discuss other examples of loss situations in a group context so that athletes and coaches could check the validity of this model by exploring its robustness in explaining their particular experiences. While some events had wide face validity (such as non-selection or injury), others were more a function of individual experience (such as the sense of loss following the retirement of a particular coach, or personal dissatisfaction with a new approach to training). Some team members were initially more reluctant than others to contribute to such discussions. Most often such resistance is related to fear of admitting any perceived vulnerabilities, and can be overcome with a performance-focused explanation of the benefits of this model. Choosing an appropriate language for exploring issues of loss and grief is vital. The language of 'adversity' is familiar to coaches and athletes – indeed they embrace the notion of 'facing adversity', 'taking on challenges' and accepting that there is 'risk' (implicitly, of loss) associated with that choice. They talk about 'persistence', which maps onto a process-oriented view of the world. Similarly, they talk about 'coming from behind', 'fighting the odds' and 'hitting rock bottom'.

Skills development

Regular group sessions were also good forums for skills development in a non-crisis response context. Symptom recognition and stress management skills such as visualization (to change responses to difficult elements of stressful experiences), thought stopping and relaxation (Meichenbaum and Fitzpatrick, 1993) can be effectively imparted in this environment. However, perhaps the most important use of group sessions for this team was to develop cognitive reappraisal skills (finding meaning in the loss) so that all team members could participate in challenging each other's beliefs and attributions. This was a far more powerful mechanism than a coach or psychologist directly challenging the athlete's strongly held convictions. An important example of the power of this process was revealed on two occasions when major structural and tactical changes in on-field play were proposed: specifically, the abolition of the traditional 'starting line-up' identified as the eleven best players, and the associated change to a 'revolving bench' system, meaning less field time for experienced players. Group discussions allowed expression of a range of feelings and opinions about these changes, which reflected a significant sense of loss from members of the existing starting line-up and from those who aspired to become part of it. A tradition of the game had been changed, and its loss was felt keenly. With regard to the revolving bench, increased uncertainty about playing time on the field was initially interpreted through traditional belief sets – 'If I am taken from the field, I must be performing poorly.' Over time, responses spanned all of Kübler-Ross's (1973) stages, which at times challenged the coaches to reconsider their decision. Understanding these strong emotional responses as part of a grieving process and a reflection of uncertainty about the future allowed coaches to persist with the changes, and allowed the athletes to express their distress as it manifested without fear of reprisal. It provided an opportunity to challenge attributions and to provide alternative explanations. Over time, athletes came to focus on the positive outcomes associated with this change and even to advocate it when it was challenged by others! By 2000, these strategies had become tradition, indeed the hallmark of success despite the fact that initially, they presented a destabilizing force.

The importance of developing stress-inoculation skills specific to the sporting context were also discussed in group sessions – for example the importance of overlearning under stressful conditions. Athletes were encouraged to be actively involved in the process of translating these beliefs into pre-emptive behaviours such as training in high-pressure, high-intensity situations so as not to be taken by surprise during competition. This active participation fostered their sense of control over their own development, and had the added benefit of increasing their commitment to these (often unpopular!) training techniques. Finally, the group setting provided an opportunity for athletes to generate 'maps' of known situations where there is a high likelihood of loss, or where anticipation of loss is likely to be a factor (such as not getting selected, being injured or experiencing a slump in form), and to discuss likely symptomatology (often quite an educative and revealing experience in itself!) and appropriate responses for the individual and/or for the team (for example, identifying their key support people). These conversations formed a core part of our preparation for the Olympics. In 2000 we extended this preparation by inviting partners or significant others to shadow the team for several days – to observe training, competition and group sessions, and to participate in discussions such as planning for the possibility of non-selection and post-Olympic 'blues'.

Athletes were also encouraged to take a role in acknowledging and responding to distress in their team mates. Policies were developed in group sessions to accommodate individual loss experiences through the introduction of such things as post-selection debriefing sessions and 'wildcards' that could be used by athletes to exclude themselves from training with no explanation after a personally distressing event such as non-selection. Interestingly, very few athletes used their wildcard – it seems that the possibility of using it, and the associated acknowledgment of the significance of such a loss, was sufficient to provide the support needed in most cases.

Individual work

In the context of the organizational and group work outlined above, individual, preparatory work with athletes could then fruitfully involve exploring their history of loss experiences, expectations regarding future losses, and personality characteristics that may help or hinder their particular responses to those situations. Some athletes typically showed delayed reactions to loss; others, quite emotionally violent reactions that subsided rapidly. The aim of individual sessions was for the athlete to become aware of their own tendencies rather than to advocate a 'correct response'. Further, it was not to deny, minimize or distort past loss experiences but rather to examine how they were contributing formatively or destructively to the athlete's current situation. Finally, it was to highlight the conflicting and changing nature of emotions and responses over time as each athlete developed ways of coming to terms with their loss.

Responding to loss: debriefing and guided mourning

Developing a culture that incorporates loss as an integral part of the athlete's life experience lays the foundations for reducing the potential for pathological loss experiences. However, once a major loss has occurred, such as missing out on Olympic selection after four years of full-time commitment, there are additional steps that will facilitate the supported movement of individuals and teams through the process of grief. The trauma literature is clear that immediate debriefing should be available, and that talking through the experience assists in the processing of difficult, confronting and emotionally laden information (Joseph, Williams and Yule, 1997). Debriefing sessions were used routinely and effectively in this group. Moreover, after each team selection, counseling was offered, and coaching staff made themselves available to players who wished to talk through the issue of their non-selection. Often the initial effect of such discussions is to open emotional wounds expressed as overwhelming sadness, anger, fear or confusion – such reactions can dissuade some coaches and staff from raising the topic. However, in considering loss as a *process,* there was less fear amongst support staff that these emotions would represent a permanent response (though they felt pretty powerful at the time!). Group debriefing provided an opportunity to normalize a diverse range of post-trauma or loss responses so that the affected individual(s) could identify them as a normal part of the process of recovery. However, individuals differ in their receptiveness to debriefing, and participation should be a choice. Often it is a matter of timing.

In the same way that the work of worrying was discussed earlier in the chapter, so the grief literature tells us that approaching (rather than avoiding) discussion of the experience of loss is most effective in 'un-sticking' people in their journey of recovery – but such work must be undertaken in a supportive environment. This approach is called guided mourning (Mawson et al., 1981). A guided approach to loss recovery does not paint the individual as a 'victim' or as helpless in the face of loss. Rather, it is predicated on a belief that each individual has a range of personal resources available to them that they will bring to the process of their own recovery. Moreover, the job of a support person is to provide a 'safe' (non-judgemental) environment in which they can work their way toward accessing those resources as they acknowledge and respond to their sense of loss and distress. Personal resolution of a loss does not negate or deny the conflicting feelings and distress felt, it accepts that awareness of such distress remains as part of the 'memory trace' when acceptance of loss (in Kübler-Ross's terms) is achieved. Moreover, each response element is part of the rich tapestry of experience that is potentially helpful in contributing to future strength and resilience, most fundamentally as a contrasting point of evidence of personal growth. This ethos is clearly captured in the reflections of Clover Maitland, hockey goalkeeper and dual Olympic gold-medallist regarding several significant loss experiences:

Post-Atlanta blues

After having such a fantastic experience in Atlanta [1996 Olympics] in so many ways once the excitement died down I came to the point of realizing it was over. I suppose I doubted whether that experience could ever be beaten or reached again (and it wasn't mind you – so I was right) … and I felt sad when reminded of it because it was gone. Recovering the enthusiasm to play on was a struggle even though at no point did I think of not continuing.

Non-selection

My only major non-selection was for the 1998 Commonwealth Games …. I think I went for a run every day of the Games and didn't watch a match. It was partly ignoring the situation yet being pissed off about it too and wanting to get out and do something about it.

Not playing in the Sydney Olympics gold medal game

Crying outside the Olympic Village on a rainy night before one of our last games is what I remember most about the Sydney Olympics. I guess I searched for things that would give me solace at the time – that fact that I had really had to work hard and push myself to get selected in the team the second time around and had been pleased with myself for doing that, the fact that as part of a team I still wanted to win a gold medal and contribute in any way I could, and the fact that I had been in the reverse situation four years earlier. I had worked hard to be there and had been given the chance in the earlier rounds to play to my best or better than the other goalkeeper and hadn't done it. I wasn't as though I could blame anyone – it was the decision I would have made.

Retirement

I don't think I felt loss until some time later. Getting a real job, buying a house, being able to be normal was very exciting for some time. Once the new life started being routine then I started searching for the next thing to excite me … to Excite, Challenge, Engulf me, to be passionate about, be outstanding at, be special in the eyes of others, be recognized for, be the very best at – I'm not sure exactly what the right words are. But I think I am still searching for that and probably getting back into hockey in another way reflects that. I still hate the same things but I also get similar positive things from coaching that I used to from playing … even if it is a fairly average Perth Premier League Team.

Loss in a team

The experience of loss in a team does not just affect individuals – it must be considered at a systemic level (Walsh and McGoldrick, 1998). When one or more members of a team experience non-selection, the individual experiences a very direct sense of loss, but the group also experiences the loss of one of its elements. Even if this element has been peripheral in terms of on-field performance, the non-selected player may have been a major contributor to the life of a team in other domains such as off-field wellbeing, group cohesion or training tempo. Moreover, team mates experience the loss of a team member, a friend, a supportive competitor. In both group and individual sessions, expressed sadness throughout this process was not discouraged as a sign of weakness or dissent, but acknowledged such that the 'wounded' group could move forward to re-heal and re-strengthen itself. Gaining a workable balance between acknowledgement and valuing of all team members in such circumstances without compromising the cohesion of the newly selected unit is a challenge, but one that is not helped by pretending that the new absences are not being felt.

Concluding remarks

The Australian Women's Hockey Team brought together a diverse group of very talented individuals, each with a different history of loss and different personal style in the face of loss. During this time, they melded into a resilient team. Developing a team culture that acknowledged loss, and the threat of loss, as integral to the experience of all its members was one feature of this resilience. Awareness of this ever-present threat did not undermine the strength of the team, rather it garnered creativity and systemic strength in responding to it. Developing such a culture is a difficult and long-term task which requires extensive collaboration with a committed coach and committed players. However, there is a high return, particularly in team sports where there are significant benefits for a large number of individuals and also for the effective functioning of the team. The effects are not just in the optimal management of key events, but in the development of a process for dealing with difficult experiences more generally. Resilience in this context was the ability to accurately assess and confront challenging experiences (rather than downplaying or being hyper-vigilant to threat), respond from a position of confidence and rebound from challenges that tested the athletes' personal resources with minimal permanent compromise or damage to sense of self or self-efficacy. As a clinician, it was rewarding to see both individuals and a team evolve to a point where they got the best out of each experience – win, lose … or both.

References

American Psychiatric Association APA). (1994). *The diagnostic and statistical manual of mental disorders*, 4th edn. Washington, DC: APA.

Baltes, P. (1987). Theoretical propositions of life-span developmental psychology: on the dynamics between growth and decline. *Developmental Psychology*, 23, 611–626.

Baltes, P., Reese, H. and Lipsitt, L. P.(1980). Lifespan developmental psychology. In M. Rosenzweig and L. Porter (eds), *Annual Review of Psychology,* 31, 65–110.

Bandura, A. (1982). Self efficacy mechanism in human agency. *American Psychologist*, 37, 122–147.

Biddle, S. J. H. (1993). Attribution research in sport psychology. In R. M. Singer, M. Murphey and L. K. Tennant (eds), *Handbook of research on sport psychology* (pp. 437–464). New York: Macmillan.

Bloom, B. S. (ed.). (1985). *Developing talent in young people*. New York: Ballantine Books.

Bowers, C., Weaver, J. and Morgan, B. (1996). Moderating the performance effect of stressors. In J. Driskell and E. Salas (eds), *Stress and human performance*. Mahwah, N.J.: Lawrence Erlbaum

Brewer, B. W. (1999). Causal attribution dimensions and adjustment to sport injury. *Journal of Personal and Interpersonal Loss*, 4, 215–224.

Brewer, B. W., Van Raalte, J. L. and Linder, D. E. (1993). Athletic identity: Hercules' muscles or Achilles' heel? *International Journal of Sport Psychology*, 24, 237–254.

Charlesworth, R. (2001). *The coach: Managing for success*. Sydney: Macmillan.

Driskell, J. and Salas, E. (1996). *Stress and human performance*. Mahwah, N.J.: Lawrence Erlbaum.

Ellis, A. (1962). *Reason and emotion in psychotherapy*. New York: Lyle Stuart.

Ford, I. W. and Gordon, S. (1999). Coping with sport injury: resource loss and the role of social support. *Journal of Personal and Interpersonal Loss*, 4, 243–256.

Fortunato, V. and Marchant, D. (1999). Forced retirement from elite football in Australia. *Journal of Personal and Interpersonal Loss*, 4, 269–280.

Gagne, F. (1993). Constructs and models pertaining to exceptional human abilities. In K. A. Heller, F. J. Monks and A. H. Passow (eds), *International handbook of research and development of giftedness and talent* (pp. 69–87). Oxford: Pergamon Press.

Grove, J. R. and Stoll, O. (1999). Performance slumps in sport: personal resources and perceived stress. *Journal of Personal and Interpersonal Loss*, 4, 203–214.

Hobfoll, S. E. (1988). *The ecology of stress*. New York: Hemisphere.

Hogan, J. and Lesser, M. (1996). Selection of personnel for hazardous performance. In J. Driskell and E. Salas (eds), *Stress and human performance*. Mahwah, N.J.: Lawrence Erlbaum.

Janis, I. (1982). *Stress, attitudes and decisions: Selected papers*. New York: Praeger.

Joseph, S., Williams, R. and Yule, W. (1997). *Understanding post-traumatic stress: A psychological perspective on PTSD and treatment*. Chichester: Wiley.

Kübler-Ross, E. (1973). *On death and dying*. London: Tavistock.

Lavallee, D., Gordon, S. and Grove, J. (1997). Retirement from sport and the loss of athletic identity. *Journal of Personal and Interpersonal Loss*, 2, 129–148.

Lavallee, D., Grove, J., Gordon, S. and Ford, I. (1998). The experience of loss in sport. In J. Harvey (ed.), *Perspectives on loss: A sourcebook* (pp. 241–252). Philadelphia: Taylor & Francis.

Lewsey, J. (2004). *The Independent*, 24th November.

McCrae, R. and Costa, P. (1987). Validation of the five factor model of personality across instruments and observers. *Journal of Personality and Social Psychology*, 56, 586–595.

Mawson, D., Marks, I., Ramm, L. and Stern, R. (1981). Guided mourning for morbid grief: a controlled study. *British Journal of Psychiatry*, 138, 185–193.

Meichenbaum, D. and Fitzpatrick, D. (1993). A constructive narrative perspective on stress and coping: stress inoculation applications. In L. Goldberger and S. Breznitz (eds), *Handbook of stress: Theoretical and clinical aspects* (pp. 706–723). New York: Free Press.

Miller, P. and Kerr, G. (2003). The role experimentation of intercollegiate student athletes. *The Sport Psychologist*, 17, 196–219.

National Center for Health Statistics (1992). *International statistical classification of diseases and related health problems*, 10th revision. Geneva: World Health Organization Publications.

Ogilvie, B. C. and Taylor, J. (1993). Career termination in sports: when the dream dies. In J. M. Williams (ed.), *Applied sport psychology: Personal growth to peak performance* (pp. 356–365). Mountain View, Calif.: Mayfield.

Orasanu, J. and Backer, P. (1996). Stress and military performance. In J. Driskell and E. Salas (eds), *Stress and human performance*. Mahwah, N.J.: Lawrence Erlbaum.

Peretz, D. (1970). Development, object–relationships and loss. In B. Schoenberg, A. C. Carr., D. Peretz, and A. H. Kutscher (eds), *Loss and grief: Psychological practice in medical practice* (pp. 3–19). New York: Columbia University Press.

Rees, T. and Hardy, L. (2000). An investigation of the social support experiences of high level sports performers. *The Sport Psychologist*, 14, 327–347.

Rees, T., Smith, B. and Sparkes, A. (2003). The influence of social support on the lived experiences of spinal injured sportsmen. *The Sport Psychologist*, 17, 135–156.

Rettew, D. and Reivich, K. (1995). Sports explanatory style. In G. McClellan Buchanan and M. Seligman (eds), *Explanatory style* (pp. 173–186). Mahwah, N.J.: Lawrence Erlbaum.

Scarr, S. and McCartney, K. (1983). How people make their own environments: a theory of genotype greater than environment effects. *Child Development*, 54, 424–435.

Schinke, R. and Jerome, W. (2003). Understanding and refining the resilience of elite athletes: an intervention strategy. *Athletic Insight*, 14. http://athleticinsight.com/Vol14Iss3/ResilienceIntervention.htm

Seligman, M. (1991). *Learned optimism: How to change your mind and your life*. New York: Pocket Books.

Shatte, A. and Reivitch, K. (2002). *The resilience factor*. New York: Random House.

Sulloway, F. (1996). *Born to rebel: Birth order, family dynamics and creative lives*. New York: Vintage.

Walsh, F. and McGoldrick, M. (1998). A family systems perspective on loss, recovery and resilience. In P. Sutcliffe, G. Tufnell and U. Cornish (eds), *Working with the dying and bereaved*. London: Macmillan Press.

13

ELITE ATHLETES' EXPERIENCES OF COPING WITH STRESS

Remco Polman, Victoria University

> The team was physically as well prepared as any other team but we had Olympic phobia constantly present in our preparations... We need a stronger coach development programme offering greater depth of experience to coaches and to include as a priority, big-meet psychology development ... It's not what you do, it's how you do it.
>
> *Bill Sweetenham, the National Performance Director of British Swimming talking in 2004*

There has been consistent interest in the mental aspects associated with sport performance. In the last few decades researchers have tried to identify psychological as well as physical factors which might be detrimental or beneficial to athletic performance. There is some evidence to suggest that successful athletes have a different psychological profile from less successful athletes (e.g. Gould, Dieffenbach and Moffett, 2002; Thomas and Over, 1994). Similarly, mental preparation has been considered to be a key to success (e.g. Krane and Williams, 2010). Sport psychology, in this respect, can provide athletes with tools to achieve their true potential and make sport a satisfactory experience rather than leaving this down to chance.

An area of particular interest has been the influence of stress and the coping strategies athletes use to deal with stressful situations. Athletes can be said to experience stress when circumstances place them in situations that tax or exceed their resources and endanger their well-being, and when they make appraisals of threat, harm, challenge or benefit (Lazarus, 1999; Lazarus and Folkman, 1984). While stress is an inevitable aspect of the competitive sporting environment, it is coping that makes the difference in performance outcomes (Lazarus, 2000; Levy, Nicholls and Polman, in press). It is well reported that sport settings include a number of potential stressors for athletes (e.g. Anshel and Kassidis, 1997; Nicholls and Polman, 2007a). Inability to cope with these stressors has been associated with decrements in performance (Haney and Long, 1995), diminished satisfaction (Scanlan and Lewthwaite, 1984), increases in the probability of physical injury (Smith, Ptacek and Smoll, 1992), burnout (Smith, 1986), sport withdrawal (Klint and Weiss, 1986) and preventing athletes from pursuing careers in professional sport (Holt and Dunn, 2004).

The process by which an athlete attempts to reduce the unpleasant feelings and emotions following stress is called coping. Due to the possible consequences of experiencing stress (such as decreased performance) it is important for both researchers and practitioners (such as coaches or sport psychologists) working with athletes to have a greater understanding of stress and coping in sport, in order to design effective interventions to help athletes to cope with stress and to make sport a successful as well as a satisfying experience (Nicholls and Polman, 2007a).

This chapter focuses on stress and coping in elite athletes. There is no accepted definition in the literature on what 'elite' athlete status entails, and many studies have not explicitly provided information on the achievement level of the athletes included or controlled for this factor in their statistical analysis. This chapter mainly covers papers that have investigated stress and coping in junior or senior athletes who play their sport professionally or have represented their country in national or international events. Inevitably this means that many of the studies included in this chapter deal with relatively small samples, making generalizations difficult. Although this is a limitation, it has to be remembered that the number of elite athletes is limited, and it is hoped that this will provide valuable information for aspiring or developing athletes and their support personnel on factors that might enable future athletes to achieve an elite status.

Theoretical framework

A number of different theoretical frameworks exist within the stress and coping literature. The most dominant model in stress and coping research in sport has been Lazarus's (1999) cognitive–motivational–relational theory of stress and coping (Crocker, Kowalski and Graham, 1998; Nicholls, 2010a; Nicholls and Polman, 2007a). This theoretical model views coping with stress as a dynamic and recursive process involving transactions between environmental and personal variables, where an individual makes an appraisal of the situation, known as primary and secondary appraisal (Lazarus, 1999).

Primary appraisal is the process of assessing the impact of the event (such as an important competition) in relation to the individual's physical and psychological well-being. The stress appraisals include harm/loss, threat, challenge and benefit. Harm/loss appraisals are characterized by the athlete evaluating and interpreting previous experiences (such as losing a match) as damaging. Threat appraisals refer to harm or loss that has not happened yet, but may happen in the near future (for example, playing an opponent ranked much higher). Challenge is associated with a beneficial outcome (such as engaging in a hard training session to improve fitness).

Finally, benefit occurs when the person perceives that they have benefited from a situation. It reflects a potential gain or growth inherent in an encounter.

If the athlete perceives the encounter as causing harm/loss, a threat, challenge or benefit, they will engage in secondary appraisal (Lazarus, 1999). Secondary appraisal refers to a complex evaluative process which involves consideration of the available coping options in relation to the specific situation, focusing on minimizing harm and maximizing gains or favourable outcomes (Lazarus and Folkman, 1984). The secondary appraisal process includes judgements of the resources available to the athlete, such as coping strategies and the degree of control they perceive that they have in meeting the demands of the situation (Zakowski et al., 2001).

Coping has been defined as 'constantly changing cognitive and behavioural efforts to manage specific external and/or internal demands that are appraised as taxing or exceeding the resources of the person' (Lazarus and Folkman, 1984, p. 141). Coping responses start in an emotional environment, and normally the first coping task is to down-regulate negative emotions that are stressful in themselves and can possibly interfere with more active ways of coping (Folkman and Moskowitz, 2004). However, as noted by Compas (1987), coping merely reflects a strategy and does not ensure the reduction of unpleasant emotions. In this way, it is important to underline that the act of coping does not assure a beneficial outcome or a reduction of distress.

Coping responses have been classified into higher-order categories or dimensions (Gaudreau, Ali and Marivain, 2005). There has been a lack of consistency in the terminology used by different authors, making comparisons between studies difficult (see Skinner et al., 2003 for a review). In addition, a limitation of assessing coping within higher-order dimensions is that a single coping strategy could be classified within more than one dimension (Compas et al., 1996). That said, three common higher-order categories or dimensions are often identified in the sport psychology literature. *Problem-focused coping* (PFC) involves efforts to alter the situation: an athlete obtains information about what to do and then mobilizes actions for the purpose of changing the person–environment relationship (Lazarus, 1999). Examples of PFC strategies are problem solving, planning, increasing efforts, time management, goal setting and seeking information. *Emotion-focused coping* (EFC) strategies involve efforts to regulate the emotional distress associated with the situation (Lazarus, 1999). Examples of EFC strategies include relaxation, acceptance, seeking social support, and wishful thinking. Avoidance coping includes both behavioural (such as removing oneself from the situation) and cognitive (such as cognitive distancing) efforts to disengage from a stressful situation (Krohne, 1993).

The last stage in the transactional model refers to emotions. These are an integral part of the coping process during a stressful situation, as an outcome of coping, as a response to new information, and as a result of reappraisals during the status of the event (Folkman and Moskowitz, 2004). As suggested by Lazarus (2000), an emotion is 'an organized psycho-physiological reaction to ongoing relationships with the environment, most often, but not always, interpersonal or social' (p. 230). According to Lazarus (1999) there are fifteen emotions, which he classified into:

- nasty emotions (anger, hostility, envy and jealousy)
- existential emotions (anxiety, guilt and shame)
- emotions provoked by unfavourable life conditions (relief, hope and sadness-depression)
- empathic emotions (gratitude and compassion)
- emotions provoked by favourable life conditions (happiness, pride and love).

Sources of stress in elite sport

The sport psychology literature is awash with descriptions of the sources of sport-specific stressors athletes face. Using mainly qualitative research methods, researchers initially provided some support for the suggestion of McRae (1992) that athletes could experience an infinite number of stressors (e.g. Anshel, 2001; Noblet and Gifford, 2002). However, more recent studies using diaries and concept maps suggest that there are a small number of stressors that are experienced by most athletes, and these stressors recur over time. For example, in a study of elite adolescent golfers who kept a daily diary over a thirty-one-day competitive period, four stressors: physical error (29.5 per cent), making a mental error (23.8 per cent), observing an opponent play well (13.3 per cent) and difficult weather conditions (8.7 per cent) accounted for 75.3 per cent of all stressors reported over the four-week period (Nicholls et al., 2005a). Similar findings have been reported for elite adolescent and professional rugby union athletes. Using a daily diary methodology over thirty-one days, players representing the England under-18 rugby union team reported five stressors (physical error, criticism of coach or parent, mental error, sustaining an injury, and observing an opponent perform well) which accounted for 73 per cent of all stressors reported (Nicholls and Polman, 2007b). Using the same methodology, but over twenty-eight days, Nicholls et al. (2006) found that professional elite rugby union players reported twenty-four different stressors. However, three stressors (injury, mental error, physical error) accounted for 44 per cent of the responses, and nine stressors for 79 per cent of the responses.

Nicholls et al. (2007c) conducted a study with a large number of athletes (n = 749) of whom ninety-five were classified as national/international athletes. This study used concepts maps to assess stress and coping. The national/international athletes in this study reported a total of eighteen stressors. However, seven of these stressors (injury, error, performance, outcome, training, opponent, fitness) were reported by most of the athletes. A similar number of stressors was generated by Gan, Anshel and Kim (2009) with elite Chinese athletes. This provides further support for the notion that athletes are more likely to encounter a relatively small number of stressors over time.

More recently there has also been increased interest in sport coaching, as coaching at the elite level has the potential to be extremely demanding. A number of studies have retrospectively investigated the stressors experienced by elite coaches (e.g. Frey, 2007; Thelwell et al., 2008). For instance, Thelwell et al. (2008) interviewed eleven coaches who worked with elite athletes with regard to the performance and organizational stressors they experienced. They found eighty-eight performance-related stressors, which were associated with struggling to meet session outcomes, having to make decisions, getting results, delivering athletes at the highest level, expectations of self and stakeholders, and poor officiating. The coaches in this study experienced ninety-four organizational stressors, which could be classified as related to environment (such as training resources), leadership (managing athletes), personal (being away from home for long periods), and team (arguments between athletes). In a longitudinal diary study with an elite swimming coach, Levy et al. (2009) replicated findings from those obtained from elite competitive athletes. That is, the five organizational stressors (administration, overload, competition environment, athletes and team atmosphere) most cited by the coach accounted for approximately 60 per cent of the number of stressors experienced over a twenty-eight-day period.

The way stressors are assessed might provide the impression that there are a large number of potential stressors. However, longitudinal research designs provide evidence that only a small number of these stressors are experienced on a regular basis by both athletes and coaches.

Lazarus (1999) stated that stressors are situation-specific. Support for this theoretical assumption in the sport context comes from comparisons of studies of athletes participating in different sports, and studies that have made comparisons between training and competition situations. There are some differences in the type of stressors reported by athletes participating in different sports. For example, the elite rugby athletes in the studies by Nicholls and colleagues reported injury as the most significant stressor. The weather and score/outcome were reported as sources of stress by the golfers but not the rugby players. The concept map study by Nicholls et al. (2007c) also showed some differences between athletes participating in individual and team sports. Individual athletes were more concerned with training (for instance its volume and scheduling) whereas team athletes were more concerned with selection and team mates. Most of the differences reported in stressor type are in line with the demands of different sports. For example, in rugby union injury rates have increased significantly over the last decade (Bathgate et al., 2002; Brooks et al., 2005). The incidence of injury in the professional game has been found to be 218 and 6.1 injuries per 1,000 hours of competitive performance and practice respectively, and the injuries required on average seventeen days of rehabilitation (Brooks et al., 2005). It is therefore not surprising that injury is of considerable concern to rugby players.

Studies that have compared training with competition days also provide support for Lazarus's (1999) assertion that situational specificity plays a role in the stressors encountered. For example, in a longitudinal study by Nicholls et al. (2009a) with five professional rugby union athletes, a wrong call from an official and crowd were much more likely to be match-specific stressors and less likely to occur in training situations. On the other hand, the rugby union athletes reported physical error and injury as stressors more frequently experienced during training than in match situations. Similarly, in a study by Nicholls et al. (2009c) with ten international cross-country runners, differences were observed between training and competition days in relation to stressor type. Fatigue and environment were more often reported on training days, whereas ability and outcome were more frequently reported on competition days. Although different situations elicited specific stressors in these studies, an additional important observation was that the athletes encountered more stressors during training days than on match days. However, the cross-country runners rated the intensity of the stressors higher during competition than in training situations.

A study by Nicholls et al. (2009b) examined sources and symptoms of life stress (rather than sport-specific stressors) during training, competition and rest days. Sixteen professional rugby union athletes completed the Daily Analysis of Life Demands for Athletes scale (DALDA; Rushall, 1990) for twenty-eight consecutive days. This study showed differences in sources and symptoms of life stress between match, competition and rest days. In particular, the professional athletes experienced more stress and increased symptoms on training days than on competition or rest days. In addition, on the day after a competitive game the number of stressors and symptoms reported as worse than normal was greater than on match days or days before a match (see also Polman et al., 2007).

There are also some temporal variations in the number of stressors experienced by athletes or coaches. As would be expected, athletes and coaches tend to report more stressors during important periods of the season (e.g. Nicholls et al., 2005a). Elite athletes must cope with a range of competitive and non-competitive stressors which might vary over time, in number and intensity, in order to achieve high levels of performance. However, the sources of stress experienced over time tend to be relatively small in number. Surprisingly, many athletes are not aware of which specific situations trigger stress. In order to help athletes to cope better, it is essential to establish what causes stress (Folkman et al., 1991). There are a number of techniques that could be employed to enhance awareness, including keeping a journal or a daily diary. Asking athletes to monitor stressors over a period of time provides a relatively easy and structured method for the assessment of potential stressors encountered and their possible consequences (Ravizza, 2010). In addition, athletes do not only need to develop coping skills to deal with stressors encountered during competitions. Because more stressors are experienced by athletes during training days, interventions should also be tailored toward these days. Finally, stressors have been rated with higher levels of intensity during competitive situations. If stress levels are too great, it might become difficult for the athletes to make rational decisions and invoke adaptive coping strategies to deal with the situation. Athletes regularly react to stressful encounters in competitive situations with behaviours that are less than optimal and appropriate, which might subsequently interfere with performance (Gill, 1986). This includes verbal abuse of opponents or referees, and aggressive behaviour towards opponents (or their own team mates). It would therefore seem important for athletes to learn coping strategies which down-regulate emotional states (such as deep breathing). Only after this has occurred can the athlete invoke adaptive coping strategies to deal effectively with the stressful encounter.

Coping response and coping effectiveness

The most obvious way to deal with stress is to avoid situations and people who cause stress in the first place. However, certain stressors are inherent in sport, and thus inevitable and unavoidable. This includes playing in front of an audience, making technical or tactical mistakes, and officials making wrong calls. Although social engineering might help athletes to avoid certain situations (such as venues for practice) or people (for example, changing their coach or not allowing parents to watch) it seems that athletes also need to develop an effective coping repertoire to deal with stress.

There has been an increase in the examination of the coping strategies employed by athletes since the early 1990s. An important reason for this increased attention to coping is that coping research has the potential to significantly impact athletic performance and satisfaction. In their systematic review, Nicholls and Polman (2007a) identified a number of PFC strategies used by athletes of all abilities when encountering a stressful event. These included task-oriented coping, concentrating on goals, time management, learning about opponents, and practice or training. EFC strategies included seeking social support, imagery, venting emotions, humour and remaining confident. Finally, athletes made use of behavioural (removing oneself from a stressor) and cognitive (blocking) avoidance coping strategies. This systematic review included sixty-four studies with athletes from a range of athletic abilities. Twenty of these studies exclusively assessed coping in elite athletes, and an overview follows of the coping strategies used by elite athletes in the higher-order categories of PFC, EFC and avoidance coping.

Problem-focused coping

It is widely accepted that PFC strategies are generally more adaptive in nature than EFC and avoidance coping strategies. Active problem solving, in this respect, requires engagement and ownership of solutions which will help athletes to cope better with similar events in the future, and also results in greater positive affect (e.g. Ntoumanis and Biddle, 2000; Polman, Borkoles and Nicholls, 2010). It is therefore not surprising that most studies report that athletes use more PFC strategies than EFC or avoidance coping strategies.

As with stressors there are differences in coping behaviours between elite athletes competing in different sports, and between training and competition situations. Such findings are in line with Lazarus and Folkman's (1984) assertion that coping is a dynamic process which is shaped by the interaction between the person and the environment. For example, in the study by Nicholls et al. (2006)

with professional rugby union players, a number of coping strategies were reported to deal with the three most reported stressors. For injury, ten different strategies were reported, with reducing symptoms of injury and warm-up as the two most frequently used coping strategies. For both mental and physical error eleven different coping strategies were reported, with increased concentration on the task being favoured by most players to deal with these two stressors. Increased concentration, as well as increased effort, were also the most frequently reported PFC strategies by England under-18 rugby union players (Nicholls and Polman, 2007b). Similarly, increased concentration was a frequently reported coping strategy by international adolescent golfers (Nicholls, Holt and Polman, 2005b). However, the golfers also reported the use of technical adjustment, swing thoughts, sticking to their strategy and focusing on their own game. International cross-country runners on the other hand reported problem solving and planning as their most frequently used coping strategies (Nicholls et al., 2009c).

The study on cross-country runners also demonstrated that training and competition were associated with the use of different coping strategies. Problem solving (22.1 per cent) and planning (16.7 per cent) were the dominant strategies used during training, whereas the top strategies were increasing effort (14.5 per cent) and strategy orientation (14.5 per cent) during competition. Differences in coping behaviour between training and competition situations have also been observed in professional rugby union players. In particular, they reported increased effort more often during competition days, and focused on their own role and increased concentration more on training days (Nicholls et al., 2009a).

Few studies have compared differences in coping between athletes at different achievement levels, although one exception is a study by Nicholls et al. (2007b). In this large scale cross-sectional study, using concept maps to assess stress and coping, athletes were classified as either national/international (n = 95), county (n = 202), university (n = 202) or club (n = 303). Comparisons between athletes at different playing standards showed that the national/international athletes made more use of the PFC strategies of problem solving and increasing effort than did athletes at lower playing standards. Of course such a cross-sectional study does not provide information about causal relationships. It is therefore unclear whether differences in coping behaviour between athletes of different standards are the result of participation in sport or of some innate difference. However, such findings provide opportunities for future longitudinal studies to examine whether coping changes as a consequence of participating in sport at different standards.

Emotion-focused coping

In general, EFC strategies are used as a result of experiencing greater negative affect (Ntoumanis and Biddle, 2000). For example, Hammermeister and Burton (2001), in a sample of endurance athletes, found a relationship between greater use of EFC strategies and cognitive anxiety. Like PFC, the use of EFC strategies varies between athletes competing in different sports, between different situations (training or competition) and at different standards. For elite rugby players visualization, taking advice (Nicholls and Polman, 2007b) and acceptance (Nicholls et al., 2006) have been the most frequently reported EFC strategies. In addition, elite rugby athletes report more use of visualization during competition than training (Nicholls et al., 2009a). For elite adolescent golfers, positive (re)appraisal (Nicholls et al., 2005a; Nicholls and Polman, 2008) has been the most common EFC strategy reported. International cross-country runners also report acceptance as well as positive self-talk during training and visualization during competition (Nicholls et al., 2009c) as frequently used EFC strategies.

Differences between national/international athletes and lower-level athletes were found for the use of visualization in the study by Nicholls et al. (2007b). In particular, the higher the playing standard, the more use the athletes made of visualization as a coping strategy. This observation is in line with research which has compared successful with less successful athletes, and suggests that successful athletes are more likely to make more and more systematic use of visualization techniques (see Vealey and Greenleaf, 2010 for a review). Although EFC strategies are considered less adaptive than PFC strategies, there appears some variation within this higher-order coping dimension. Visualization might be considered an adaptive EFC strategy which should be utilized by athletes. Venting emotions, on the other hand, is generally considered to be an ineffective coping strategy (Kaiseler, Polman and Nicholls, 2009; Kristiansen, Roberts and Abrahamsen, 2008).

Avoidance coping

Avoidance coping has been used on a regular basis by athletes to deal with acute stress. For example, in the longitudinal study by Nicholls et al. (2006) with professional rugby union players, blocking (such as stopping thinking about the stressful event) was the second most reported coping strategy during training and competition. In a more recent longitudinal study, also with professional rugby union athletes, cognitive avoidance coping and in particular blocking was found to be the second most frequently used strategy during training, and the most frequently reported strategy during competition. Only on one occasion did a player report using behavioural avoidance (walking away) as a coping strategy (Nicholls et al., 2009a). Similarly, Anshel and Kaissidis (1997) reported avoidance coping as a regularly used strategy by basketball athletes when dealing with bad decisions by referees.

The use of avoidance coping strategies is not limited to elite team sport athletes. Cognitive avoidance was reported to be the most frequently used coping strategy by eleven elite adolescent golfers over a thirty-one-day period (Nicholls et al., 2005a). The main cognitive avoidance strategy reported was again blocking. The golfers in this study also used the cognitive avoidance coping strategies of ignoring other people and laughing, but less frequently. Only on one occasion was behavioural avoidance (leaving the course) used by a golfer as a coping strategy. Similar results were reported by Nicholls et al. (2005b). In this qualitative study, blocking was used by thirteen of the eighteen elite golfers. This included 'stop thinking about the match being over' or 'really just block it out and play my own shot'.

Avoidance coping is said to be used in situations where an individual perceives little control over the outcome of the situation (Carver, Scheier and Weintraub, 1989). In particular, avoidance coping strategies will be adaptive when goals are out of reach for the individual irrespective of investment of effort. In such situations commitment to alternative goals might increase (Wrosch et al., 2003a; Wrosch et al., 2003b). This appears to be the case in a number of sporting situations. These include poor refereeing decisions or an opponent's score in golf. As such, avoidance coping appears to be an adaptive coping strategy for athletes when dealing with acute stressors in either training or competitive situations. However, it has been suggested that avoidance coping is maladaptive in the long term (Mullen and Suls, 1982; Carver et al., 1989). For example, in the health psychology literature, avoidance coping has been associated with reduced resistance to disease and immunocompetence (Suls and Fletcher, 1985), prolonged cardiovascular reactivity (Vitalino et al., 1993), increased negative affectivity (Ingledew, Hardy and Cooper, 1997), higher levels of symptoms of burnout (Polman et al., 2010) and higher levels of stress. Avoidance coping, in this respect, is considered to be a relatively passive coping strategy (Finset et al., 2002). Most avoidance coping strategies provide temporal relief from a stressful situation, and as such might be useful strategies in the sport context to deal with an acute stressor (for instance, moving away when a referee has made a bad decision, or blocking out when a tactical or technical mistake is made). In a recent study by Carson and Polman (2010), it was also found that the use of avoidance coping was beneficial to the rehabilitation process in injured (anterior cruciate ligament damage) professional rugby union players. Avoidance coping in this longitudinal study was effective in the short term for controlling emotional states and in relation to long-term rehabilitation from injury by committing to alternative goals.

However, using avoidance coping strategies also indicates that the athlete has chosen to not deal with the problems as they arise but postpone problem solving to a later date. There are a number of instances when cognitive or behavioural removal from stressful situations can only be maintained for a limited period of time (for example when the same technical error is made repeatedly). Also, if an athlete wants to disengage from a situation that cannot be avoided (for example, by walking off the course in golf), they are likely to experience increased levels of stress because they cannot invoke this coping strategy without serious consequences (Carver and Scheier, 1998).

Lack of coping

An interesting observation in several studies has been the notion that in a number of stressful encounters athletes did not invoke coping strategies. For example, in a study by Reeves, Nicholls and McKenna (2009), twenty out of forty elite adolescent soccer players reported a lack of coping. Similar results have been found for elite adolescent golfers, as illustrated by comments made by these athletes such as 'I was not attempting to cope. I was plodding along not thinking of anything' and 'I didn't do anything to cope' (Nicholls et al., 2005b). Similarly, in the longitudinal study with professional rugby union players, on fourteen occasions where stressors were experienced, no coping strategies were reported (Nicholls et al., 2006). Finally, in the study on international cross-country runners, 2.7 per cent of the athletes' responses to stress during training and 2.4 per cent during competition were classified as lack of coping; the athletes reported that they did not use a coping strategy to deal with the stressor they encountered (Nicholls et al., 2009c).

In the qualitative study by Nicholls et al. (2005b), some of the elite adolescent golfers only started to realize that they had not coped with the stressful encounter during the interview with the researcher. Not coping with a stressful encounter is not an adaptive strategy, and is associated with frustration (Nicholls et al., 2005b) and performance decrements (Haney and Long, 1995). As such athletes must acquire the appropriate coping skills to deal effectively with situations in which they were unable to use a coping strategy.

Coping effectiveness

Relatively few studies have addressed the issue of coping effectiveness in sport. However, this is an important issue, as one of the main reasons to examine coping is that some strategies are more effective than others, and appreciating this will help in the design and implementation of effective coping interventions (Folkman and Moskowitz, 2004). Nicholls (2010b, p. 264) recently defined coping effectiveness as the 'degree in which a coping strategy or combination of strategies is or are successful in alleviating stress'.

The most frequently used coping strategies reported by athletes are not necessarily the most effective. In addition, the effectiveness of coping strategies might be situation-specific. The aforementioned studies in rugby, golf and cross-country running all provide evidence for these assertions. That is, strategies that were reported the most frequently were not always rated as being the most effective. For example, the coping strategies rated as most effective by international cross-country runners in training (increasing effort (4.33 out of 5), positive orientation (4.22) and channel emotion (4.50)) were only reported to be used 4.8 per cent of the time (Nicholls et al., 2009c). Problem solving (3.77) on the other hand was reported to be used 22.1 per cent of the time to deal with stress.

A number of theoretical explanations and models have been put forward to explain coping effectiveness, including the outcome model, goodness-of-fit approach (Folkman, 1984, 1992), automaticity (Gould et al., 1993), choice of coping strategy (Eubank and Collins, 2000), and path analysis model (Haney and Long, 1995). In a recent review, Nicholls (2010b) suggest that the 'choice of coping strategy' hypothesis provides the best explanation to date. The choice of coping strategy suggests that the effectiveness of a coping strategy is related to the type of strategy the athlete deploys (Eubank and Collins, 2000), which implies that some strategies are more effective than others. Support for this theory was provided by Nicholls et al. (2005b) in their qualitative study with international adolescent golfers. In particular, the golfers rated blocking, reappraisal, positive self-talk, rationalizing, following a routine, breathing, physical relaxation and seeking on-course support as effective coping strategies. Trying too hard, speeding up, routine changes, negative thoughts and lack of coping were seen as ineffective coping strategies. Some of the studies on golf, rugby and cross-country running also provide tentative support for this theory. That is, these studies report coping strategies that are generally seen to be effective or ineffective. However, there is variation over time and between different situations in ratings of the effectiveness of individual coping strategies.

Ultimately, athletes need to develop coping strategies that are effective in dealing with the stressors they encounter. To date relatively few intervention studies have been reported that have investigated the efficacy of coping effectiveness training. An exception is a study by Nicholls (2007) with an international adolescent golfer. This study was successful in increasing the golfer's use of effective coping strategies (committing to all shots, trusting swing, maintaining a routine) whilst decreasing their use of ineffective coping strategies (trying to hit the ball further, making technical adjustment, focusing on opponent). However, the study was limited by a lack of performance data and the fact that it included only one participant.

Moderators and mediators in the stress and coping process

A number of factors have been found to have an influence on the coping strategies used by elite athletes. In a study by Kristiansen et al. (2008), it was found that elite wrestlers who had a task-mastery motivational orientation were more likely to use adaptive coping strategies during competition. In particular, active coping, emotional support, instrumental support and positive reframing were positively correlated with a task-mastery orientation. Similarly, Lane, Jones and Stevens (2002), in a sample of national tennis players, showed that higher levels of self-esteem were associated with the use of more PFC strategies. Low self-esteem, on the other hand, was associated with the use of behavioural disengagement, self-blame and humour. Similar results have recently been obtained for sport confidence. In addition, the relationship between sport-confidence and subjective performance was mediated by PFC and disengagement-oriented coping. Whereas higher levels of sport confidence resulted in the use of more task-oriented coping strategies and higher subjective performance ratings, lower levels of self-confidence were associated with increased use of disengagement-oriented coping and lower subjective performance ratings (Levy et al., in press).

A potential factor influencing coping behaviour is the athlete's personality. One personality variable that has received increased interest is mental toughness. An important characteristic of a mentally tough athlete is their ability to cope effectively with the stressors encountered. Two recent studies provide evidence for the notion that more mentally tough athletes use more PFC strategies and less EFC and avoidance strategies (Kaiseler et al., 2009; Nicholls et al., 2008). In addition, coping effectiveness was influenced by the coping strategy used. That is, only those strategies that were reported to be used more frequently by the mentally tough athletes were rated as more effective (Kaiseler et al., 2009). However, these studies did not distinguish between athletes at different playing standards.

A number of additional factors could influence stress appraisal, coping and coping effectiveness. These include gender (Kaiseler and Polman, 2010), coping self-efficacy beliefs (Nicholls et al., 2010c), personality (Polman, Clough and Levy, 2010) and culture (Anshel, 2010). However, studies that have examined the role of these factors have generally used heterogenic groups of athletes (different sports and different ability or athletic achievement), making it difficult to establish their role in elite sport. These are all fruitful avenues for future research.

Practical implications

Stress appears to be an inherent aspect of athletic performance, so it essential that athletes cope with the stress they encounter to circumvent the negative effects of stress on performance and satisfaction. Previous research has described the stressors encountered and the coping strategies employed and their effectiveness. In addition, some effort has been directed towards understanding possible underlying mechanisms that may shape coping (such as personality, self-confidence and coping self-efficacy beliefs). The current overview provides some guidelines to help athletes to cope more effectively with the stressors they encounter. In particular, it is useful to establish which stressors a particular athlete encounters in their environment. Such an analysis should not be limited to competitive stressors, but should also include training stressors and possibly stressors experienced on rest days. In addition, athletes need to be taught coping strategies from all three higher-order dimensions: PFC, EFC and avoidance coping.

Although PFC strategies are generally more adaptive, athletes should also make use of EFC strategies. For example, EFC strategies are essential in the down-regulation of intense emotional states (such as deep breathing). Down-regulation of intense emotional states is essential before effective PFC can be used to deal with a problem. In addition, visualization appears to be an adaptive EFC strategy which is also associated with greater use by athletes competing at higher levels. The cognitive avoidance coping strategy of blocking appears to be useful to deal with acute stressors. However, athletes have to be aware that in a number of circumstances avoidance strategies do not solve the problem. This is particularly the case when the athlete continues to make the same technical or tactical error. In such an instance ignoring the problem is not desirable, and the athlete is required to invoke PFC strategies to remedy the underlying problem.

Future research directions

A limitation of much of the literature is that it has only investigated certain aspects of the stress and coping process in isolation. Thus future research could adopt a more holistic approach by assessing appraisal of stressful events (such as whether appraised as a challenge or a threat), accompanying emotions (negative or positive), coping strategies employed, their effectiveness, and performance and affective consequences. A further limitation of the current body of work is the lack of comparisons of athletes of different ability. For example, it is unclear whether elite athletes perceive different stressors from non-elite athletes or the same stressors but less frequently. Also, it is unclear whether elite athletes appraise stressful events in a different way from non-elite athletes (for example, with greater perceptions of control and lower levels of stress intensity). Finally, elite athletes might use different coping strategies from less elite athletes, or they might use the same strategies but more effectively. Future research is required to address these questions. A difficulty with the cross-sectional designs that are often used in studies in this area is that it is not possible to establish cause and effect. Therefore, longitudinal studies are also needed which establish whether possible differences between athletes of different abilities are due to developmental processes or more stable factors (such as personality). Such studies can also shed light on possible intra-individual and inter-individual differences in the stress and coping process over time.

Conducting research with elite athletes is not without difficulties. For example, it is not easy to obtain athletes' permission and willingness to be included in a research study, and if initial agreement is secured, adherence might be an obstacle. For example, in some of the diary studies by Nicholls et al. (e.g. 2007, 2006) there was a significant drop-out of participants throughout the studies. Building rapport with coaching staff and the athletes themselves is one way to build trust and engagement in the research process. In addition, there is a lack of studies that have investigated the efficacy of coping interventions. Studies addressing this issue are needed as they could inform both practical application and theoretical understanding, and thus be beneficial to both the athlete and the researcher.

Conclusion

Stress appears to be an inherent aspect of athletic performance, so it essential that athletes cope with the stress they encounter to circumvent potential negative effects on performance and satisfaction. Previous research has described the stressors encountered, coping strategies employed and their effectiveness in elite athletes. In addition, some effort has been directed towards possible underlying mechanisms that may shape coping (such as personality, self-confidence and coping self-efficacy beliefs). Although some research has investigated what elite athletes do to cope in their sports, there is still relatively little research into whether elite athletes differ from their less elite counterparts in their appraisal of stressful events, coping or coping effectiveness. In addition, it is unclear whether possible differences are learned through participation in sport and other life domains, or are due to relatively stable innate factors, and whether any differences may provide an explanation for athlete level of success and achievement. Although the current literature provides some useful practical information for athletes, coaches and sport psychologists to improve performance and manage satisfaction, there is still considerable scope to advance our knowledge in this field.

References

Anshel, M. H. (2001). Qualitative validation of a model for coping with acute stress in sport. *Journal of Sport Behavior*, 24, 223–246.

Anshel, M. H. (2010). Cultural differences in coping with stress in sport: theory and practice. In A. R. Nicholls (ed.), *Coping in sport* (pp. 119–138). New York: Nova Science.

Anshel, M. H. and Kassidis, S. N. (1997). Coping style and situational appraisals as predictors of coping strategies following stressful events in sport as a function of gender and skill level. *British Journal of Psychology*, 88, 263–276.

Bathgate, A., Best, J. P., Craig, G. and Jamieson, M. (2002). A prospective study of injuries in elite Australian rugby union players. *British Journal of Sports Medicine*, 36, 265–269.

Brooks, J. H. M., Fuller, C. W., Kemp, S. P. T. and Reddin, D. B. (2005). Epidemiology of injuries in English professional rugby union. *British Journal of Sports Medicine*, 39, 757–775.

Carson, F. and Polman, R. C. J. (2010). The facilitative nature of avoidance coping within sport injury rehabilitation. *Scandinavian Journal of Medicine and Science in Sport*, 20, 235–240.

Carver, C. S. and Scheier, M. F. (1998). *On the self-regulation of behavior*. Cambridge: Cambridge University Press.

Carver, C. S., Scheier, M. F. and Weintraub, J. K. (1989). Assessing coping strategies: a theoretically based approach. *Journal of Personality and Social Psychology*, 56, 267–283.

Compas, B. E. (1987). Coping and stress during childhood and adolescence. *Psychological Bulletin*, 101, 393–403.

Compas, B. E., Worsham, N., Ey, S. and Howell, D. C. (1996). When mom or dad has cancer: II. Coping, cognitive appraisals, and psychological distress in children of cancer patients. *Health Psychology*, 56, 405–411.

Crocker, P. R. E., Kowalski, K. C. and Graham, T. R. (1998). Measurement of coping strategies in sport. In J. L. Duda (ed.), *Advances in sport and exercise psychology measurement* (pp. 149–161). Morgantown, W.V.: Fitness Information Technology.

Eubank, M. and Collins, D. (2000). Coping with pre- and in-event fluctuations in competitive state anxiety: a longitudinal approach. *Journal of Sports Sciences*, 18, 121–131.

Finset, A., Steine, S., Haugli, L., Steen, E. and Laerum, E. (2002). The brief approach/avoidance coping questionnaire: development and validation. *Psychology Health and Medicine*, 7, 75–85.

Folkman, S. (1984). Personal control and stress and coping processes: a theoretical analysis. *Journal of Personality and Social Psychology*, 46, 839–852.

Folkman, S. (1992). Making the case for coping. In B. N. Carpenter (ed.), *Personal coping: Theory, research and application* (pp. 31–46). Westport, Conn.: Praeger.

Folkman, S., Chesney, M., McKusick, L., Ironson, G., Johnson, D. S. and Coates, T. J. (1991). Translating coping theory into practice. In J. Eckenrode (ed.), *The social context of coping* (pp. 239–260). New York: Plenum Press.

Folkman, S. and Moskowitz, J. T. (2004). Coping: pitfalls and promise. *Annual Review of Psychology*, 55, 745–774.

Frey, M. (2007). College coaches' experiences with stress: problem solvers have problems, too. *The Sport Psychologist*, 21, 38–57.

Gan, Q., Anshel, M. H. and Kim J. K. (2009). Sources and cognitive appraisal of acute stress as predictors of coping style among male and female Chinese athletes. *International Journal of Sport and Exercise Psychology*, 9, 68–88.

Gaudreau, P., El Ali, M. and Marivain, T. (2005). Factor structure of the Coping Inventory for Competitive Sport with a sample of participants at the 2001 New York marathon. *Psychology of Sport and Exercise*, 6, 271–288.

Gill, D. L. (1986). *Psychological dynamics of sport*. Champaign, IL: Human Kinetics.

Gould, D., Dieffenbach, K. and Moffett, A. (2002). Psychological characteristics and their development in Olympic champions. *Journal of Applied Sport Psychology*, 14, 172–204.

Gould, D., Eklund, R. C. and Jackson, S. A. (1993). Coping strategies used by US Olympic wrestlers. *Research Quarterly for Exercise and Sport*, 64, 83–93.

Hammermeister, J. and Burton, D. (2001). Stress, appraisal, and coping revisited: examining the antecedents of competitive anxiety with endurance athletes. *The Sport Psychologist*, 15, 66–90.

Haney, C. J. and Long, B. C. (1995). Coping effectiveness: a path analysis of self-efficacy, control, coping and performance in sport competitions. *Journal of Applied Social Psychology*, 25, 1726–1746.

Harris, N. (2004). *The Independent*, 23rd August.

Holt, N. L. and Dunn, J. G. H. (2004). Grounded theory of the psychosocial competencies and environmental conditions associated with soccer success. *Journal of Applied Sport Psychology*, 16, 199–219.

Ingledew, D. K., Hardy L. and Cooper, C. L. (1997). Do resources bolster coping and does coping buffer stress? An organizational study with longitudinal aspect and control for negative affectivity. *Journal of Occupational Health Psychology*, 2, 118–133.

Kaiseler, M. and Polman, R. C. J. (2010). Gender and coping in sport: do male and female athletes cope differently? In A. R. Nicholls (ed.), *Coping in sport* (pp. 79–94). New York: Nova Science.

Kaiseler, M., Polman, R. C. J. and Nicholls, A. R. (2009). Mental toughness, stress, stress appraisal, coping and coping effectiveness in sport. *Personality and Individual Differences*, 47, 728–733.

Klint, K. A. and Weiss, M. R. (1986). Dropping in and dropping out: participation motives of current and former youth athletes. *Canadian Journal of Applied Sport Sciences*, 11, 106–114.

Krane, V. and Williams, J. M. (2010) Psychological characteristics of peak performance. In J. M. Williams (ed.), *Applied sport psychology: Personal growth to peak performance* (6th edition, pp. 169–188). New York: McGraw-Hill.

Kristiansen, E., Roberts, G. C. and Abrahamsen, F. E. (2008). Achievement involvement and stress coping in elite wrestling. *Scandinavian Journal of Medicine and Science in Sports*, 18, 526–538.

Krohne, H. W. (1993). Vigilance and cognitive avoidance as concepts in coping research. In H. W. Krohne (ed.), *Attention and avoidance: Strategies in coping with aversiveness* (pp. 19–50). Seattle, Wa.: Hogrefe and Huber.

Lane, A. M., Jones, L. and Stevens, M. J. (2002). Coping with failure: the effects of self-esteem and coping on changes in self-efficacy. *Journal of Sport Behavior*, 25, 331–345.

Lazarus, R. S. (1999). *Stress and emotion: A new synthesis*. New York: Springer.

Lazarus, R. S. (2000). How emotions influence performance in competitive sports. *The Sport Psychologist*, 14, 229–252.

Lazarus, R. S. and Folkman, S. (1984). *Stress, appraisal and coping*. New York: Springer.

Levy, A., Nicholls, A., Marchant, D. and Polman, R. (2009). Organisational stressors, coping, and coping effectiveness: a longitudinal study with an elite coach. *International Journal of Sports Science and Coaching*, 4, 31–45.

Levy, A. R, Nicholls, A. R. and Polman, R. C. J. (in press). Pre-competitive confidence, coping, and subjective performance in sport. *Scandinavian Journal of Medicine and Science in Sports*, available online.

McCrae, R. R. (1992). Situational determinants of coping. In B. N. Carpenter (ed.), *Personal coping: Theory, research, and application* (pp. 65–76). Westport, Conn.: Praeger.

Mullen, B. and Suls, J. (1982). The effectiveness of attention and rejection as coping styles: a meta-analysis of temporal differences. *Journal of Psychosomatic Research*, 26, 43–49.

Nicholls, A. R. (2007). Can an athlete be taught to cope more effectively? The experiences of an international level adolescent golfer during a training program for coping. *Perceptual and Motor Skills*, 104, 494–500.

Nicholls, A. R. (2010a). *Coping in sport*. New York: Nova Science.

Nicholls, A. R. (2010b). Effective versus ineffective coping in sport. In A. R. Nicholls (ed.), *Coping in sport* (pp. 263–276). New York: Nova Science.

Nicholls, A. R., Backhouse, S. H., Polman, R. C. J. and McKenna, J. (2009b). Stressors and affective states among professional rugby union players. *Scandinavian Journal of Medicine and Science in Sports*, 19, 121–128.

Nicholls, A. R., Holt, N. L. and Polman, R. C. J. (2005b). A phenomenological analysis of coping effectiveness in golf. *The Sport Psychologist*, 19, 111–130.

Nicholls, A. R., Holt, N.L., Polman, R. C. J. and Bloomfield, J. (2006). Longitudinal analyses of stress and coping among professional rugby players. *The Sport Psychologist*, 20, 314–329.

Nicholls, A. R., Holt, N. L., Polman, R. C. J. and James, D. W. G. (2005a). Stress and coping among international adolescent golfers. *Journal of Applied Sport Psychology*, 17, 333–340.

Nicholls, A. R., Jones, R., Polman, R. C. J. and Borkoles, E. (2009a). Acute sport-related stressors, coping, and emotions among professional rugby union players during training and matches. *Scandinavian Journal of Medicine and Science in Sports*, 19, 113–120.

Nicholls, A. R., Levy, A. R., Grice, A. and Polman, R. C. J. (2009c). Stress appraisals, coping, and coping effectiveness among international cross-country runners during training and competition. *European Journal of Sport Science*, 9, 285–293.

Nicholls, A. R. and Polman, R. C. J. (2007a). Coping in sport: a systematic review. *Journal of Sports Sciences*, 25, 11–31.

Nicholls, A. R. and Polman, R. C. J. (2007b). Performance related stressors, coping, and coping effectiveness among international adolescent Rugby Union Football players: a 31-day diary study. *Journal of Sport Behavior*, 30, 19–218.

Nicholls, A. R. and Polman, R. C. J. (2008). Think aloud: acute stress and coping strategies during golf performances. *Anxiety, Stress, and Coping*, 21, 283–294.

Nicholls, A. R., Polman, R. C. J., Levy, A. and Backhouse, S. (2008). Mental toughness, optimism, pessimism and coping among athletes. *Personality and Individual Differences*, 44, 1182–1192.

Nicholls, A. R., Polman, R. C. J., Levy, A. R. and Borkoles, E. (2010c). The mediating role of coping: a cross-sectional analysis of the relationship between coping self-efficacy and coping effectiveness among athletes. *International Journal of Stress Management*, 17, 181–192.

Nicholls, A. R., Polman, R. C. J., Levy, A., Taylor, J. A. and Cobley, S. P. (2007c). Stressors, coping, and coping effectiveness: gender, sport type, and ability differences. *Journal of Sports Sciences*, 25, 1521–1530.

Noblet, A. J. and Gifford, S. M. (2002). The sources of stress experienced by professional Australian footballers. *Journal of Applied Sport Psychology*, 14, 1–13.

Ntoumanis, N. and Biddle, S. J. H. (2000). Relationship of intensity and direction of competitive anxiety with coping strategies. *The Sport Psychologist*, 14, 369–371.

Polman, R. C. J., Borkoles, E. and Nicholls, A. R. (2010). Type D personality, stress and symptoms of burnout: the influence of avoidance coping and social support. *British Journal of Health Psychology*, 15, 681–696.

Polman, R. C. J., Clough, P. J. and Levy, A. R. (2010). Personality and coping in sport: the big five and mental toughness. In A. R. Nicholls (ed.), *Coping in sport* (pp. 139–140). New York: Nova Science.

Polman, R. C. J., Nicholls, A. R., Cohen, J. and Borkoles, E. (2007). The influence of game location and outcome on behaviour and mood states among professional rugby league players. *Journal of Sports Sciences*, 25, 1491–1500.

Ravizza, K. (2010). Increasing awareness for sport performance. In J. M. Williams (ed.), *Applied sport psychology: Personal growth to peak performance*, 6th edn (pp. 189–200). New York: McGraw-Hill.

Reeves, C. W., Nicholls, A. R. and McKenna, J. (2009). Stressors and coping strategies among early and middle adolescent premier league academy soccer players: differences according to age. *Journal of Applied Sport Psychology*, 21, 31–48.

Rushall, B. R. (1990). A tool for measuring stress tolerance in elite athletes. *Journal of Applied Sport Psychology*, 2, 51–66.

Scanlan, T. K. and Lewthwaite, R. (1984). Social psychological aspects of competition for male youth sport participants: Predictors of competitive stress. *Journal of Sport Psychology*, 6, 208–226.

Skinner, E. A., Edge, K., Altman, J. and Sherwood, H. (2003). Searching for the structure of coping: A review and critique of category systems for classifying ways of coping. *Psychological Bulletin*, 129, 216–269.

Smith, R. E. (1986). Toward a cognitive-affective model of athletic burnout. *Journal of Sport Psychology*, 8, 36–50.

Smith, R. E., Ptacek, J. T. and Smoll, F. L. (1992). Sensation seeking, stress, and adolescent injuries: a test of stress-buffering, risk-taking, and coping skills hypotheses. *Journal of Personality and Social Psychology*, 62, 1016–1024.

Suls, J. and Fletcher, B. (1985). The relative efficacy of avoidant and non-avoidant coping strategies: a meta-analysis. *Health Psychology*, 4, 247–288.

Thelwell, R. C., Weston, N. J. V., Greenlees, I. A. and Hutchings, N. V. (2008). Stressors in elite sport: a coach perspective. *Journal of Sports Sciences*, 26, 905–918.

Thomas, P. R. and Over, R. (1994). Psychological and psychomotor skills associated with performance in golf. *The Sport Psychologist*, 8, 73–86.

Vealey, R. S. and Greenleaf, C. A. (2010). Seeing is believing: understanding and using imagery in sport. In J. M. Williams (ed.), *Applied sport psychology: Personal growth to peak performance*, 6th edn (pp. 267–304). New York: McGraw-Hill.

Vitalino, P. P., Russo, J., Bailey, S. L., Young, H. M. and McCann, B. S. (1993). Psychosocial factors associated with cardiovascular reactivity in older adults. *Psychosomatic Medicine*, 55, 164–177.

Wrosch, C., Scheier, M. F., Carver, C. S. and Schulz, R. (2003a). The importance of goal disengagement in adaptive self–regulation: when giving up is beneficial. *Self and Identity*, 2, 1–20.

Wrosch, C., Scheier, M. F., Miller, G. E., Schulz, R. and Carver, C. S. (2003b). Adaptive self-regulation of unattainable goals: goal disengagement, goal reengagement, and subjective wellbeing. *Personality and Social Psychology Bulletin*, 29, 1494–1508.

Zakowski, S. G., Hall, M. H., Klein, L. C. and Baum, A. (2001). Appraisal control, coping, and stress in a community sample: a test of the Goodness-of-Fit hypothesis. *Annals of Behavioral Medicine*, 23, 158–165.

14

WORKING AS A SPORT PSYCHOLOGIST AT TWO OLYMPIC GAMES

A humanistic approach

Peter Clarke, Chartered Psychologist

> Greatness (in football) is not just about winning trophies, it is also to do with how you react to defeat and disappointment.
>
> *(Brian Clough, legendary and unique Nottingham Forrest manager, typically magnanimous in victory after his team had defeated Liverpool FC, cited in Smith, 2008, p. 428)*

It was over eighteen years since Great Britain had won an Olympic Winter gold medal, and no Olympic medal of any colour had ever been won before in curling, so the achievement of the Great British (GB) women's curling team in 2002 was both historic and memorable. The work reported here is not intended to be an exhaustive account of coping behaviours within the context of a major tournament (like some other studies, such as Bond, 2002; Dugdale, Eklund and Gordon, 2002; Holt and Hogg, 2002; Miller, 1997), rather it is an overview of some of the difficulties encountered by the groups in the lead-up to, and participating in, the Olympic Games in Salt Lake City (2002) and Turin (2006). This account essentially employs a case study approach, following examples of similar work by Gordon (2001) and Holt and Sparkes (2001), based on the perceptions of the author, who was an active participant as team sport psychologist for over five years prior to the Salt Lake City Olympic success, and was involved with the Turin group for approximately fifteen months prior to the 2006 Games. As a personal account it can therefore be challenged for accuracy, personal bias and an impressionistic approach, though Miller (1997), in his book *Golden Minds*, presented a similar analysis of his work at various Olympics, and this report in some ways reflects his approach.

I hope this account will be insightful and capture a snapshot of some of the processes involved in gaining an Olympic gold medal, and in the failure to achieve a medal after entering the tournament as current Olympic champions. It discusses coping with the emotions inherent in elite performance. Other approaches to reporting consultancy work with teams have been used (e.g. Bond, 2002; Gordon, 2001; Gould, 2000, 2001), and Gilbourne (2002), and Tuckman (1993) offered similar insights from a personal viewpoint. I hoped it will help to show some of the stresses and strains of involvement at the elite level, and perhaps some strategies can be designed to help other elite performers cope with the inevitable stresses on both them and support personnel at such prestigious events. The chapter also gives background detail about the psychological work carried out with both sets of curlers in order to set the scene for player behaviour, and how they attempted to use their acquired mental skill set to cope with the demands of elite competition.

The aim of this chapter is to make a comparison of my work as an applied sport psychologist to the GB women's curling teams at Salt Lake City and Turin. The chapter considers how the GB women's curling team and support staff prepared for competing at Salt Lake City, won the gold medal, then attempted to cope with the consequences of that success. That success is then contrasted with the resultant performance at the Turin Games, where the team did not gain a medal. The chapter comments on coping with the demands of my role and my operating philosophy, and discusses how the players attempted to cope with the emotional demands of Olympic involvement. Entering the Turin Games as current Olympic champions brought its own pressures, which were added to by a change in selection system which also impacted on team dynamics. This is an example of the longitudinal involvement of a sport psychology consultant at the elite level, something that has received relatively little attention in the literature. While this is a personal reflective account, it is a genuine attempt to present an objective and truthful account of events that took place.

Emotions, coping and group behaviour

The Olympic Games are arguably the most significant athletic event in world sport in both size and prestige. Gould (2001) has testified to difficulties inherent in Olympic performance, as has Miller (1997), who states that though the events are somewhat like normal world championships, they are 'taking place within the context of a much bigger, multi-sport festival. This is a unique setting and presents many new challenges to the athletes and officials associated with the Olympic experience' (p. 88). It is not just the players and coaching staff who might feel the stresses and strains of Olympic competition. Gould (2001) emphasizes that 'sport psychology consultants have few resources to help them prepare for the Olympic consulting experience' (p. 49), and unlike the professional practice of counsellors/ psychotherapists (certainly in Great Britain), sport psychologists do not always have a system of ongoing supervision of their work in which a supportive, professional relationship can be of immense value. The world's attention seems relentlessly focused on the events during the period of Olympic competition, and the exposure the Games receive from the media continues to grow remorselessly. Consequently, living closely together with a small group of athletes in such a cauldron for up to five weeks brings immense pressures, difficulties, expectancies and a myriad of other demands upon all those who are involved. Much has been written in the sport psychology literature on emotions and coping, and the vast area of group (team) behaviour has been written about extensively (cf. Carron, Bray and Eys, 2002a; Carron et al., 2002b; Widmeyer, Brawley and Carron, 2002). It is not the intention of this chapter to delve into the minutiae of all the emotions one might investigate, or attempt to describe in great detail individual or group attempts to deal with such matters. Rather it offers comment from a personal point of view on how emotional reactions to events within the group developed and were expressed, and how individuals might have appraised resulting interactions and attempted to cope with them.

The ability to cope with emotional demands of major athletic competition would seem to be a crucial aspect of the successful athlete. Lazarus (2000) points out that coping is an integral aspect of the emotional process, though defining such behaviour has proved problematic for many years (Hardy et al., 1996). After reviewing the more prominent theories in the coping literature, Hardy et al. suggest that the transactional process model is perhaps the most dominant approach today. One of the advantages of this position 'is its process orientation in that it views coping as a dynamic sequence of steps involving both cognitive and behavioural efforts to manage stress' (Hardy et al., p. 206). Katz and Hemmings (2009, p. 53) also describe coping in terms of an ongoing process by stating that coping is 'any process a person uses to manage the demands and pressures they experience that threaten the "sense of equilibrium/balance"'. A great deal of research in coping behaviour has emphasized the appraisal aspect of coping, though Lazarus (1999, p. 101) states that coping behaviour:

> has been generally misunderstood because the emphasis has been on appraisal. Many emotion theories, although not being unfriendly to the concept of coping ignore the coping process. My position is that, in addition to appraisal, coping is an essential aspect of the emotion process and emotional life.

Most research on coping behaviour with elite athletes has been carried out either from a theoretical perspective or 'after the event', mainly because the demands of the tournament and the role definition of the sport psychology consultant preclude undertaking research at that point. However, Gould, in a series of papers with co-workers (Gould, 2000, 2001; Gould, Eklund and Jackson, 1993a, 1993b) has pointed out how sport psychology consultants (and indeed coaches) working at major events, such as the Olympics and world championships, need to facilitate the awareness of coping in athletes and help them learn coping strategies so that each athlete can use the appropriate strategy for the relevant situation.

I undertook detailed work with the players over the months before the actual Games in Salt Lake City and Turin, developing individual profiles of their psychological skills, using Repgrid methods (see examples of such work in Clarke, 1996, 2007) to ascertain the athletes' own unique perceptions of the group. I provided workbook examples of mental skills that they could practise and refine for their unique needs. This work was focused on enabling the players to devise their own ways of coping with adversities (such as poor personal performances, disappointments and media pressure). Though the development of a skill set for performance was not solely directed at coping with stress per se, it was quite clear that performing at such a high-profile tournament was going to involve many stressors, and having a well-refined way of dealing with such events was crucial in their overall mental repertoire.

However, the practical realities of the curling tournament meant that there was very limited time to have, for example, group discussions of events (suggested by Hardy et al., 1996, as one way of coping with the pressures of the event), as the time demands of travelling, playing – sometimes twice a day – and inevitable (technical) team meetings took precedence. Consequently, it was down to the individual to seek out psychological support from myself, if the individual so desired, though this only happened in a very limited way at both Olympics. This made it extremely difficult to gauge the extent to which players were able to cope with the ongoing demands of performance during the Olympic tournament, except through observation, which is fraught with problems.

The game of curling

It is first necessary to provide some background details on the sport of curling and the team. Teams consist of four players (an 'alternate' is attached for major championships such as the Olympics, world and European championships, and this was perhaps the main reason why the issue of group dynamics played such an important part in the preparation for and performance at Salt Lake City). The four players have quite distinctive, specialized roles, and throw their stones in strict order, with the team skip (the captain) always playing the last stone. This puts considerable pressure on the skip, and it is vital that they have the technical and mental abilities to cope with the demands of such a role. It is also of particular importance for the skip and third player to be able to communicate effectively, as they are often faced with considerable pressure(s) to make crucial strategic decisions throughout a game. A high level of task cohesion is of paramount importance, and communication between all four players is both crucial and fundamental in the game. An acceptance of, and trust in, fellow players' abilities is also critical, as is the case in most team games, though the interactive nature of each shot in curling places even greater emphasis on these factors. Major curling championships, such as the Olympics, take approximately ten days to complete, and often at major championships teams have to play two games in one day. With any single game lasting as long as three hours there can be an immense toll on a player's physical and mental capacities.

The players

Five players were chosen to represent Great Britain at Salt Lake City. They were drawn from 'rinks' (clubs) from different parts of Scotland. (Curling is played almost exclusively in Scotland rather than elsewhere in Great Britain, so the GB team and the Scottish team are all but synonymous.) Coming from different parts of the country meant that it was quite difficult to get practice time together on ice with the coach or to engage in psychological work as a team. Often, though, time spent at tournaments, in Scotland, in Europe and Canada, was used to maintain their mental skills preparation. We engaged in mini workshops and discussed material relevant to both individual and team preparation. Previously the same team had won the Scottish Championships, had gained a silver medal at the European Championship, and had finished fourth in the World Championships in 2000, so all the members had been exposed to high-level competition.

At the Salt Lake City Games there was a virtual schism within the group: four players were in one camp and one separate, which meant it was extremely difficult to achieve group cohesion. At Turin the main issue seemed to be that four of the five players had been skips of teams in their own right, which was always going to prove problematic, even dysfunctional. Local club rivalry and the impact of previous elite-level performances (one player was the current Olympic champion going into the Turin Games and another had been a previous world champion in her own right) were evident, and certainly did not help in the development of task cohesion.

The coaching staff

The team coach had been involved with the team for over six years prior to the Olympic Games in Salt Lake City, and had been an elite player himself over many years. He attended, as I did, about 95 per cent of games that the team played over his years of involvement, and consequently had a very sound understanding of the players' abilities as well as a strong, positive relationship with them. He, together with the skip, was solely responsible for team selection, tactics and overall direction. I was fortunate to be able to form a positive relationship with him, and his acceptance of the role of sport psychology in the overall preparation of the players was crucial to my involvement and work with the team. During major championships, such as the Olympics, the national coach was on hand to offer support to the group, though his work was split between the men's and women's teams at the Salt Lake City Games, which meant that he essentially adopted the role of adviser, which was important nevertheless. At certain critical points his input was vital (such as in finalizing selection of the group that would travel to the Games), and he was able to sit with the team coach throughout all the games in Salt Lake City, offering helpful and insightful support. At the Turin Games the coaching set-up changed somewhat. The national coach took a much more hands-on approach, and essentially there was a dual selection and instructional system, which had not happened at the Salt Lake City Games.

The sport psychologist

As consultant sport psychologist I had worked with the team for approximately five years prior to the Salt Lake City Games. The composition of the team changed over this period, but four of the team had been playing together for over three years and the fifth player joined approximately two years before the Olympics, when the team took part in and placed fourth in the World Championships. This five-player squad then played together for the two years leading up to, as well as at the Salt Lake City Games. My main work with the squad over the period largely followed the normal pattern of mental skills training, similar to that reported by Gordon (2001) and Gould (2001). Of crucial importance was my insistence on total confidentiality in the individual exchanges I had with players. Even the coach was not party to these interactions, and though at times it might have been important for the coach to be aware of player concerns, if an individual player did not want the coach to be aware of an issue, I did not tell him. The coach was in total agreement with this way of working, and never once questioned me about my discussions with a player, even though at times it was obvious that a player might need psychological support. Various writers have commented on the importance of having a sound and productive relationship with a team's coach (e.g. Baillie and Ogilvie, 1996; Gordon, 2001; Gould, 2001; Miller, 1997), although it was also very important for the players to accept my role within the group. This became especially salient when there was clearly a major breakdown in relations between the players just prior to the Games.

My background in sport was a tremendous help in my work. (I had been a coach in professional soccer and had spent approximately twelve years as national coach to the Scottish women's football team.) My experience as a trained counsellor/psychotherapist was also important. I follow the principles of person-centred therapy (PCT) expounded by Carl Rogers (e.g. 1951, 1967). Attempting to be empathetic, accepting and congruent is at the very centre of the Rogerian approach, though it is often misrepresented and misunderstood. It can be an extremely demanding and exacting, though immensely rewarding, operational style. It is important to state that I did not ever attempt to work with the group as a therapist, as I firmly believe that such behaviour would be unethical and a clear conflict of interest. I realize that some writers believe sport psychologists can act as therapists so long as they have the requisite competencies. Anderson and Clarke (2002) highlight the dangers faced by sport psychologists because of the role boundary difficulties often inherent in contemporary sport psychology consultations, and suggest that it is unethical for a sport psychologist to attempt to act as a therapist even when they are suitably qualified to fulfil both roles. In my view there is a need for clearly defined boundaries, and although I was able to utilize my counselling skills in my interactions with players and support staff, I did not venture beyond the performance-enhancement role of a sport psychologist.

My personal situation was somewhat different with the Turin group. I had to formally apply for the role as sport psychologist to the team. I had not worked directly with many of the players in the original group of eleven selected, and had worked with only two of the final Olympic squad. I felt there was some resistance to me and my role: I was seen as being the psychologist to 'the gold medal winners of Salt Lake', and it was quite an onerous task to move beyond this perception. My personal coping was made more difficult as a result of this.

Personal approach to my role as sport psychologist

My training as a Rogerian psychotherapist and my use of Kelly's personal construct theory (Kelly, 1955) in terms of research heavily influence my teaching, consultancy and simply being. Both Rogers and Kelly emphasize a humanist, phenomenological approach, and in many ways their underlying philosophies are complementary in character. Kirschenbaum and Henderson (2005) highlight the basic tenets of Rogerian philosophy, in which 'three conditions were necessary and sufficient' for personal growth. Though largely targeted at the client–therapist interaction, these conditions have much wider implications. The conditions are empathy (active listening), unconditional positive regard (accepting clients for what they are without necessarily liking them) and congruence (being as genuine, honest and open with clients as one can be). This approach is definitely not a simple 'nodding donkey style of involvement', as characterized by some detractors of the approach, and is demanding, though very powerful.

Kelly's work also emphasizes the idiosyncratic nature of individuals, and though this is not the place for a full investigation of Kelly's theory, perhaps some explanation of the approach is in order. Kelly (1955) described individuals as personal scientists trying to make sense of their own world. Fransella, Bell and Bannister (2004, p. 6) stated that 'We are scientists who derive hypotheses from our theories', and as a result the views (constructs) so generated have personal meaning and value to the individual concerned. We try to understand and make sense of our unique universes and interpret them through situations we encounter. This is a phenomenological view, and puts the individual at the very centre of any engagement. Combining these two complementary philosophies was at the core of my approach, though working with elite athletes who may not really wish to engage can make consultancy very demanding at times.

The selection system for the Games

There was a considerable and crucial difference in the selection system for the two Games. The original team that represented Great Britain in Salt Lake City was essentially a local club team that had played together for a number of years and whose members had qualified to take their place as Great Britain's representatives. There was disharmony within the group a few weeks before the 2002 Games, and funding bodies and officials were alert to the dangers of such an event and determined to prevent its happening again. This had massive repercussions on the selection of the team for Turin, where a very different system of selection was introduced. In addition, the national curling performance director (the national coach) took a much more hands-on approach to the coaching of the team at Turin, whereas at Salt Lake he was mostly involved with the men's team (which had its own internal problems) and had little involvement with the women's team's pre-game discussions and post-game debriefs. In Turin there was in effect a joint coaching set-up with the women's coach and the national coach working in parallel.

The new approach to preparation for the Turin Olympics involved the selection of eleven players approximately fifteen months before the Games. The staff worked with these players over a prolonged period, so that when a final decision was taken on the squad of five who would compete in Turin, a range of alternative groupings had been examined. It was hoped that the final set of five would be best suited to compete as a team.

In the context of the sport of curling this was rather visionary and well thought-out, though it had some awkward consequences. Because of the number of players in the squad, some players who travelled to tournaments did not play in them at all. For example, the squad played a number of competitions in Canada. Normally two teams of four players were selected, so three players were not chosen for either team. The coaching staff decided not to give technical coaching input to these players on an individual basis, because 'this might give the players a reason for formally objecting when they were not selected'. (This issue had roots in another Olympic sport, where an appeal was successfully lodged against selection procedures.) This left some players feeling aggrieved and somewhat confused. I (quite rightly) had no input into the decisions that led to this situation (and found it a difficult one), but did my best to counsel athletes who felt aggrieved or upset. Ravizza (2001) emphasizes this point, and though he clearly states that he 'is not a psychologist' (p. 198), his background in providing educational services to sports teams which 'focuses (sic) on [the] mental and emotional side of performance enhancement' is extensive and well noted. He points to the inherent dangers to client confidentiality when stating 'I do not want to be involved in team selection or playing time because if the players know my input is considered, they are going to tell me what they think I want to hear' (p. 198). In hindsight, I feel that although the decision not to offer specific, individual technical advice to those not selected for teams was made in good faith by the coaching staff, it might have been explained better. It did not help issues of team cohesion, or to use Kremer and Moran's (2008) term, 'team identity'.

The coaches did engage with helping the players technically and tactically in game situations and when all players were involved in practice sessions, so it was mainly when players were not selected for a team during an overseas trip that they felt their needs were not being attended to. My own view of the coach as both educator and selector has always been deep-rooted, and this dual role never gave me problems in my coaching career. Nor had I ever experienced an appeal situation of the kind the coaches were anxious to avoid, so although I understood the coaches' reasoning, I shared something of the players' unhappiness at the situation.

Though it is very common in most international sports for relatively large squads to be chosen and for their members to compete for places in the final team, this had never happened in Scottish (British) curling before. Thus, it lead to some misunderstanding, difficulties regarding the nature of selection and suspicion of the motives of coaches.

The pre-Olympic years for both games

Salt Lake City

As has been testified by many writers (e.g. Baillie and Ogilvie, 1996; Bond, 2002; Gould, Jackson and Finch, 1993b; Miller, 1997), performance at major championships, such as the Olympics, can be extremely stressful. To understand the sequences of events that led up to the Olympic gold, and the aftermath of disharmony and break-up, it is essential to report on the pre-Olympic year.

Once the players had been selected to represent Great Britain (the details of the selection are too complex to discuss here), a crucial decision was made by the players and the coach to expand the squad from four to five players. There were a number of reasons. It was of prime importance to have a substitute (alternate) player if someone became injured. It was also important that all five players were able to play in various positions if it became necessary to alter the team line-up for such reasons as performance decrement or tactical necessity. This in effect meant that it would also be possible to alter the team based on individual performances, as happens in many other sports, though very few teams in curling have adopted such an approach. The decision to follow this path was quite innovative, and received the backing of the five players in the squad, though this led to unforeseen negative consequences, especially in terms of social cohesion within the players, in the period prior to the Games, at the Games itself and in the aftermath of winning the gold medal.

The competitive period prior to the Games was spent attempting to accommodate this new way of playing as a squad, and assessing its utility and acceptability. At various competitions both in Scotland and throughout Europe each player in turn dropped out of the team as 'fifth player'. A variety of options were devised in case of unforeseen circumstances that might have necessitated different combinations in the team. Of crucial importance in curling is the rapport between third player and skip, who both have a tactical input into the choice of shot the skip should make, and the skip relies heavily on the influence, knowledge and tactical awareness of the third player. If there is not a sense of mutual compatibility between third and skip, or trust in the validity of information exchanged, there can be major problems. The question of which player would perform the role of third became a central point of contention within the group.

Because one squad member did not play in each game, there were inevitably perceptions of threat by some players ('Which position will the new player really want?'), concerns over reasons for change ('Why should we really alter a proven system just because we might need someone else in an emergency?') or straightforward selection concerns ('I will not be selected now if I have one poor performance as there is always someone to take my place'). Although the players had expressed their agreement with the decision to have a squad of five, an attitude of 'I agree with the new system so long as I am one of the four selected' seemed apparent at times.

Over a number of months prior to the European Championships in Finland in December 2001, the team attempted to cope with the new system, but there were obvious teething problems. Deciding on the best team combination was obviously going to take a lot of time and consideration, and the process of experimenting was not without its drawbacks. A variety of problems arose during this period, from the magnification of personal dislikes of one particular individual (often manifest by a refusal to talk or to room with this person) as the Games drew closer, to having to make decisions about which four players to start on the ice. That I was neither qualified to make selections nor in a role that made it appropriate for me to do so was a help to my role as psychologist. It meant I was able to deal openly with questions of selection disappointment, personal upset and individual concern. I could provide committed yet professionally objective support for all players regarding their needs. I gave the players details of a variety of emotional and problem-focused coping strategies, such as those outlined by Madden (1995), and this work became a central aspect of the players' preparation (although the precise details of their individual coping styles are beyond this text). The players knew and accepted that matters of selection were the domain of the coach and skip, and such a situation was beneficial all round.

Greenleaf, Gould and Dieffenbach (2001) present an account of some of the difficulties experienced by US Olympians at the Nagano and Atlanta Games. Some of the problems they reported, such as negative team atmosphere, poor interaction between team mates and selection problems, became evident with the GB curling group over this period. Individual confrontations and group disharmony began to emerge to such an extent that one player considered leaving the team almost a year before the Olympics. Only I and the player concerned were aware of this. The view of Bond (2002) is worth noting: '[Surely] the role of the sport psychologist is to understand, assist and support the development of the whole person not just the athlete' (p. 23). I would have supported the individual in whatever action she wanted to take, but in this instance she was strong enough psychologically to deal with and overcome her difficulties. It is important to realize that the athlete's views are of paramount importance, even if it seemed this was not totally understood by a number of administrators in the post-Olympic period.

In the initial part of the season prior to the Games (in September 2001) the conflict was particularly concerned with perceived infractions of accepted group norms of behaviour. One player was perceived as not being as fully committed to the group as the rest of the players, not training enough, and so on. This festered to such an extent that normal psycho-educational training (mental skills work) and on-ice technical work suffered. Debate centred round the problem of internal group disharmony, which (from my perspective) was largely brought on by this player's behaviour and the rest of the group's reaction to it. It seemed that at every major competition an enormous amount of time was spent on how to cope with and resolve the major problem of group harmony. The players, the coach and I had numerous discussions about this. Matters came to a head during the European Championships in Finland (December 2001). The team's results were very disappointing (they only achieved sixth position when they had expected a medal), and interpersonal relationships began to fracture. Eventually it was decided to convene a meeting of the five players, team coach, national team coach and myself.

My role in the meeting was as facilitator. It was probably the most important, and taxing, meeting of the whole period of my involvement with the team. It lasted several hours, and all the players agreed that the decision it reached must be accepted by everyone. In many ways the meeting resembled a Rogerian encounter group in that everyone was expected to openly and honestly express their views, which they did, often quite brutally, so that the group as a whole could learn from the experience and develop a better working relationship. The whole experience was quite demanding, even debilitating. The rest of the group tackled the player who was perceived to be the problem, over matters such as her approach to physical conditioning, rehydration, psychological preparation and communication issues. She insisted that she would change her behaviour, improve her attitude and be ready for the challenges of the Olympics. I found it very difficult to be part of such a meeting, but my experiences of similar events during my psychotherapy training were enormously helpful to me. They provided me with a systematic approach that enabled me to cope with the demands of the situation, to properly fulfil my role as facilitator and be supportive of the group as a whole. I feel this was much appreciated by the staff involved in this session.

After the meeting a decision was eventually made, after much heart-searching and consultation with appropriate Olympic officials, to continue with the five-player squad system. In spite of the commitments made to accept the decision, this was not initially accepted by all the players, largely because of the acrimonious nature of the interpersonal exchanges that had taken place. A great deal of further discussion took place with the players before an agreement was reached to continue as a group. The whole Olympic experience was in grave danger of going under in Finland, and it was perhaps the realization of the likely impact that brought the group back from the brink. Two players in particular found it hard to accept the decision to allow the fifth player to continue as a member of the team that would travel to Salt Lake City, but they agreed after much soul searching to abide by the outcome.

Essentially the squad now became a group of four starting players plus an alternate (substitute), which meant that in reality this player was now aware that she would travel to Salt Lake not as a rotating player but as a substitute to be used only in exceptional circumstances. A number of conditions were set in place to ensure that she was both aware of this fact and able to meet the demands that all the players had to accept, regarding physical conditioning, practice and commitment to the group. She agreed to accept these stipulations, and continued as a member of the team.

Turin

I applied formally for the post of psychologist to the Turin squad; I was not 'shooed in' because I had worked with the previous gold medal winners in Salt Lake City. I had not actually worked with most of the original group of eleven players, even though I had met and talked with all of them over a number of years, mainly at competitions in Scotland and throughout Europe. Three had been members of the Salt Lake City team. It was important for me to get a better understanding of the remainder of the squad, so I could work with all the players on an equal footing, and to explain my modus operandi to them. My approach was to use a Repgrid analysis, produce a mental skills workbook and carry out a player performance profiling check. These areas focused on helping the players gain a better understanding of themselves, their group, and providing them with mechanisms (strategies) for dealing with emotional difficulties that inevitably arise in the cauldron of Olympic competition.

It was important for me to demonstrate what my role of consultant sport psychologist entailed. One member of the squad seemed happy to rely on a sport psychologist she had previously engaged with, and one assumed that knowing a 'motivational guru' was possibly just as important for her. Besides meeting with the squad as a group, throughout the year I also ensured that I met with each individual member. This entailed travelling many miles throughout Scotland to engage with the players, mostly at their convenience, to discuss issues relating to their performance and group membership.

One major approach I adopted was to issue to each player a mental skill training workbook. These had been developed for use with the Indian national cricket team by Gordon, and adapted, with permission, for curling. Though one fundamental aspect of Rogerian theory is the importance of the non-directive nature of interaction (between client and therapist generally, and in this context between athlete and sport psychologist), only a very rigid interpretation of such an approach would prohibit a sport psychologist from offering an athlete a choice of mental skills. My approach was to explain the variety of skills that might be useful, and allow the curlers to choose which ones most suited their needs, rather than imposing skills I thought they should work on. The mental skills handbook was similar in vein to what many sport psychologists would see as fundamental preparation strategies, and it provided detailed explanations and exercises that the players were encouraged to follow.

Though I met each player personally to discuss the book in detail, it was never a realistic objective to ensure that the players actually used it. I got the feeling that unless the individual player really bought into the psychological side of preparation, this might have been seen as another unnecessary imposition on valuable preparation time. However, it was an extremely detailed resource for players to use at their own discretion, and as with many other areas of scientific approaches to sport involvement (such as nutrition or lifestyle management), it is the athlete's personal responsibility to make use of what is available to help them maximize their preparation.

I also used Kelly's (1955) PCT approach. As a sport psychology consultant, meeting with new clients always presents different challenges. I tend to avoid using standard psychometric tests with athletes. Andersen (2009) suggests that coaches often have misguided views on, and understanding of, the limitations of such tests. I favour a more qualitative approach. Brustad (2008, p. 32), examining the role of qualitative research in contemporary sport psychology, states that:

> qualitative researchers have relatively little interest in trying to discover universal laws of nature because they generally conduct research that focuses (sic) on knowledge that is situated and constructed by people in interaction with others, in relation to the meaning and purpose that this interaction has for them in a given context.

Applying a similar principle in my consultancy, I believed that I was able to attend to individual needs more closely and thus be better prepared to help the athletes deal with any issues without recourse to standard psychometric interventions. A similar phenomenological approach (using a daily diary) has been reported by Pensgaard and Duda (2002) when attempting to gain an understanding of how a Norwegian Olympian footballer (soccer player) coped with the stressors and demands of Olympic competition.

Kelly's humanist approach is directly focused on the individual, though it can also be used in group settings if this is deemed necessary. It combines qualitative and quantitative analysis, and Kelly's Repgrid methodology enables the researcher (or consultant) to use either as is deemed appropriate. There are two different approaches to the analysis of grids, the qualitative ('storytelling' approach) and the quantitative ('statistical' approach). Fromm (2007) states that both can be used depending on the needs and circumstance of the investigation. Believing that statistics give structure not meaning, Fromm nevertheless argued for the appropriate use of either approach.

Kelly's approach has been used in a wide range of contexts, from business (Fromm, 2004; Stewart and Stewart, 1982), education (Ravenette, 1999; Rossi, 1997), and medicine (Vogt, Armstrong and Marteau, 2010) to mental health (Winter, 2003). Sport psychologists have mostly been slow to use Kelly's approach, and only recently have many articles appeared in the sport and exercise literature. Mental toughness was the subject of a number of studies by Gordon and his colleagues, in an Australian sporting context (e.g. Gordon, Gucciardi and Chambers, 2007; Gucciardi, Gordon and Dimmock, 2009). In Britain, Cripps (1999) investigated how athletes construct their world; Clarke produced studies from swimming (1996) and football coaching (1995, 1999, 2007); and Feixas, Marti and Villegas (1989) produced a rare example of an examination of a football team.

This is essentially a tool for engaging with the idiosyncratic world of each athlete. Shaw (1980, p. 9) describes the technique as 'A hard tool for soft psychologists and indeed to date is one of the best attempts to examine and bring into awareness the conceptual system of the individual.' Jankowicz (2004, p. 14) explains that a grid is a 'structured form of interviewing, with ratings or without, which arrives at a precise description uncontaminated by the interviewer's viewpoint'. It can be tailored quite precisely to the individual or group involved.

The immediate pre-Olympic periods

Salt Lake City

Immediately after Christmas 2001 the group had a preparation week at the Great Britain Winter Olympics training camp at Lofur in Austria. In general it appeared that a number of team-related issues pertaining to individual player concerns were resolved and a specific behavioural plan of action for player preparation was put in place. Such an approach was seen as one way of enabling all players to establish a personalized format for coping with the obvious difficulties of interpersonal conflict, which was, in reality, the main preparation difficulty facing the group. There seemed to be general understanding and agreement within the group about what was expected from each player, even to the extent of specifying small though significant aspects of team behaviour, such as details of warm-ups and physical conditioning routines as well as the more common practices of not drinking alcohol during competition and maintaining confidentiality on group matters.

Superficially this seemed to have repaired any damage within the group, and there was agreement on how the details of the next few weeks would be organized. The polarized positions that had developed within the group meant that great care had to be taken at the social level, to ensure that the alternate player was not treated in a discourteous manner. A semblance of group solidarity was maintained, while the focus was on ensuring that the main group goals pertaining to Olympic preparation were met.

The entire British Olympic team had a camp at Calgary in the week immediately prior to the Games. It was a change to be involved in a wider group setting, meeting athletes from events such as skiing, bobsleigh and ski-jumping, as well as being free from media infringements or demands from well-meaning though often intrusive individuals. The camp was also very beneficial to the group in terms of finalizing technical work, completing physical conditioning and reflecting on mental skills practices. Unfortunately one member of the curling team – the skip – was suddenly taken ill. It happened during a weekend. The hospital in Calgary was unable to offer immediate treatment and a decision was taken to fly her to Salt Lake City. I accompanied her there, though this meant that the players and coach were left without my support in Calgary. More importantly, it seemed that the team might have to perform without its leader, and the alternate was liable to be required to play. This was extremely upsetting to the players. Fortunately the skip recovered after approximately five days of recuperation at Salt Lake City. She had obviously lost a lot of technical time on ice, but most of the players, and the coaching staff, were relieved and glad to have her back in position. The team line-up that was considered strongest was restored, and the entire squad met up in Salt Lake City for the tournament itself.

Turin

Throughout the twelve months leading up to the Turin Games the squad had a comprehensive training/practice programme. Initially a training camp was established in Cyprus in May 2005, where basic fitness levels were examined and I had the opportunity to meet, sometimes with the coach, though normally just with the individual player or squad as a whole. The warm weather and relaxed atmosphere (the men's Olympic squad were also present during this camp, though usually they would travel to separate tournaments throughout the year) contributed a great deal to the development of a positive group atmosphere and establishment of a winning mind set for the coming year.

Because of the disparate geographic locations of the eleven players – these ranged throughout the length and breadth of Scotland – it was virtually impossible for the squad to get together to train/practise once the competitive season began (approximately late August), so team integration and growth could only happen during actual competition. Consequently my own involvement entailed being at as many of these competitions as possible, and these often took place in Canada, Scandinavia and other parts of Europe. It was extremely demanding and time-consuming, and as a number of players had children it was even more stressful for them.

The Cyprus training camp

Training camps usually provide a very useful opportunity for engaging with players on both an informal and formal basis. At the camp in Cyprus, beside the normal routine of involvement (group psycho-educational sessions, individual consultations and so on) the players each undertook a profiling exercise which the coach and I had used many times previously. We had worked together for more than eight years and were very comfortable with each other's philosophy and approach. Player profiling has been used extensively in athletic preparation (see Butler, 1992; Butler and Hardy, 1992). Butler's work has been seminal here, and is quite clearly based on Kelly's approach. The system used with the women's curling team entailed the player and coach completing, independently, a profile sheet with twenty constructs relating to psychological aspects of performance, using a ten-point scale. Both the team coach and I had undertaken this task over the many years that we had worked with women's curlers, and the checklist used was essentially one that we had constructed through discussion with a number of curlers over previous years. Both forms were returned to me, then the player, coach and I discussed the resultant profiles and investigated any major discrepancies (a differential of two points was used) for further discussion. Often players would under-rate themselves initially and then through debate a final target score was agreed by all concerned. From this it was possible to suggest to the athlete some strategies for improving scores in particular areas, such as enhancing concentration skills or visualization practices, and a relevant time scale for development was established. The relatively flexible training timescale and the relaxed atmosphere at the Cyprus camp enabled much more personal interaction between all staff and players, and clear goals and objectives for the period prior to the Games were established.

The final group of five players was selected by the coaching staff in early December, so that the team could play in the upcoming European Championships and begin to operate as a unit. Clearly it was going to take a period of time to establish any proper understanding and set up appropriate strategies in areas such as format, individual roles and communication strategies.

Much has been written about sports teams, though perhaps the most useful notion comes from Kremer and Moran (2008), when they stress the importance of team identity. Though there appears to be a dearth of research on this topic, it was obvious that valuing and developing identity would be fundamental in forging the final group of five players into a successful performing unit. The team performed only moderately well at the European Championships (coming joint fifth out of a field of ten), though as a new team this was not thought to be unduly worrying or of great concern.

The Games at Salt Lake City

In order to deal with the reality of competing at the Games it was imperative that a number of strategies were put in place. By now it was quite clear that in terms of social cohesion there was a fissure within the group which was often exemplified with two of the players being polite to the alternate but interacting no further with this player, especially in social situations off the ice, one being able to manage the situation through her own coping strategies, and the other was really concerned that the group should be harmonious, though this was really an unlikely possibility. One player was so opposed to the fifth player's behaviour that she had to develop a range of coping strategies that suited and worked for her though this meant that she almost totally ignored the fifth player at the ice arena, as this was the only way that she could block out the difficulties she had in accepting her as part of the group. This was similar to the tactics used by previous US Olympians (Greenleaf et al., 2001).

The situation became so fraught that when the matches began, the starting players established a set of rules to minimize group upset. They did not want the alternate to interfere (in their perception) with their preparation, and to this end they ensured that the fifth player did not walk out with the group on to the ice before matches, did not sit at the end of the ice sheet (as was the norm for other teams) and was not allowed to warm up on ice with the other players before games. It might be felt that this behaviour was petty or narrow-minded, but the starting team saw it as their individual and collective way of approaching the enormous demands of the Olympic matches. Although these methods proved effective in terms of task performance, they did not contribute to overall group harmony. Achieving optimal performance at the Olympics was the clear goal of the team, and as the players had made many sacrifices to be at the Games, they were prepared to sacrifice social cohesion in order to achieve this.

This coping behaviour extended to room-sharing arrangements (the fifth player roomed with the physiotherapist), eating arrangements and even aspects of travel to and from the ice arena. All these aspects were designed to ensure that the pressures of Olympic competition were dealt with effectively and that the starting four players were not needlessly upset. Many other, seemingly minor, issues caused some upset, but one crucial issue perhaps gives a true flavour of the group disharmony, or the strength of feeling towards the alternate player. When it became apparent (halfway through the Olympic tournament) that the alternate would have to throw two stones during a match in order to receive a medal – assuming the team reached a medal-winning position – other team members fiercely expressed their viewpoints about whether she should be enabled to do so. Some thought disrupting the group on ice would be a dangerous move as the team had not yet qualified for a place in the playoff stages; others thought it would be difficult to justify politically a return home in which four but not five players displayed their medals. Eventually the four players and coaching staff agreed to allow the fifth player to throw two stones. Unfortunately the game in which she participated was lost (although this was not entirely her fault). This caused some upset in the group, but generally the four players who formed the core team showed little negative behaviour and continued to focus on their future games. They eventually succeeding in winning the gold medal.

Arguably the four members involved in playing the games displayed what has been called 'emotional contagion' (Hatfield, Cacippo and Rapson, 1993). Barsade (2002) suggests how collective emotions can result from shared cognitions. However, it is difficult to see how emotional contagion was not directly influenced by cognitive contagion, whereby purposeful processing of information, such as observing behaviours that were contrary to group norms, was concurrent with emotional reactions to such behaviours.

In order to achieve the Olympic gold it is quite obvious that a variety of coping strategies were needed. Hammermeister and Burton (2000) emphasize this point when they state that different types of stress require different coping strategies. Lazarus (2000) has reported on the importance of personal appraisal in the coping strategies adopted by individuals. This chapter does not discuss individual players' coping strategies in detail, but it is clear that some of the players engaged in either problem-focused (typically using such behaviours as goal setting or time management skills) or emotion-focused coping strategies (such as relaxation or using cognitive efforts to change the meaning that the individual attaches to the particular environmental stressor). Details are reported elsewhere (Gould, 2000; Gould et al., 1993a; Gould et al., 1993b; Holt and Hogg, 2002). Each player had her own individual way of coping with stressful situations, and though the alternate player really did not believe in, nor accept the value and usefulness of the mental preparation work in any meaningful way, the other four athletes generally accepted the importance of the area for their own preparation.

A more obvious coping strategy was the use of avoidance behaviour, in which an individual physically and mentally disengages from a situation in order to deal with a stressor. This was suggested by Hardy, Jones and Gould (1996) as one possible coping strategy. Indeed it had particular relevance to at least two of the players, and was especially effective for them in dealing with their perceived difficulties of existing in the same group as the alternate player. Finally, in line with the evidence reported by Holt and Hogg (2002), there are examples of how different players were able to reappraise situations in order to assess the effectiveness of their individual coping strategies and make changes where necessary. Of course, such coping strategies vary from person to person and from time to time, and a detailed account of individual responses is beyond the scope of this chapter.

Overall, the issue of dealing with the perceived problem of player polarization dominated the preparation work. It meant that the more normally reported issues of pre-tournament anxiety and nerves received very little attention. This is in contrast to the evidence produced by authors such as McCann (2000), who states that performance at this level inevitably produces great tension and subsequent raised anxiety levels, and goes as far as to suggest that an 'Olympic pathology' (p. 212) results from the intensity of the competition. This was not evident in the curling team. It was as if the normal reported increased performance anxiety and enhanced stress levels reported by many writers (e.g. Dugdale et al., 2002; Gould, 2001) had been superseded by the over-riding issue of the internal disruption to the group harmony largely brought about by the ways in which the four players in the group perceived the alternate's approach to preparation for elite performance.

The Games in Turin

In the week prior to the Games in Turin, both the men's and women's teams had a last training and practice camp in Switzerland. The training camp was enjoyable from a social point of view, and the on-ice preparation enabled the team to get to know each other more fully. Previously the players had played for three separate club teams, and it was important that they begin to gel collectively as a single unit.

As a squad the players seemingly demonstrated an acceptable amount of social cohesion. Living together in a house close to the Olympic venue (along with the GB men's team) inevitably brings up small logistical issues and complaints, but the domestic arrangements passed by without any real difficulty – particularly in comparison with the nightmarish experiences in Salt Lake City. However, the easy nature of the social environment was not matched by task cohesion. Having four players in the squad of five who had been skips in their own right proved to be a difficulty, especially once results started to deteriorate. The strains that had in a sense been papered over began to surface and now became cracks. It was abundantly clear that some members of the team still viewed me as sport psychologist to the two players who had played at Salt Lake City. They seemed suspicious of my role, and never really bought into the psychological work in a meaningful way as I had I hoped they would.

In the auditorium during the matches I could not hear the conversation between the players. A number used microphones (for television purposes), so viewers on television heard them, but not spectators at the ice rink. It later became apparent that on-ice (verbal) behaviour did not match the perceptions that we, as support staff, had of the team when they were competing. We had felt the team had achieved a good level of social cohesion off-ice, but this did not seem to be the case on the ice. Since we (the support staff) had not anticipated this, and were not fully aware of it at the time, it was not possible to counteract it. It simply appeared that performance was not reaching the standard we had expected.

The role of a sport psychologist at major sporting events such as the Olympic Games can be diverse – from coach driver, odd job man to close confidant to players – and in curling there is very little time to engage in detailed psychological consultation, either to individuals or to the team collectively. There is generally little time to engage with the players as a whole. Meeting with individual players is much easier, though this depends on the way that players engage with the sport psychologist, and with this particular team that did not happen to a large extent.

The team did not live up to the highest hopes people had had of them, although their performance was probably in line with their overall world standing prior to the Games. The players themselves were extremely disappointed with the performance outcome, as were all the staff involved.

Coping with the aftermath of winning a gold medal

Here I discuss the period immediately after the Games, even though most of the team continued to play together in the year following the Salt Lake City success. As Jackson (2000) points out, most sport psychology research in emotions tend to focus on the negative aspects of performance, such as anxiety, and little is written about the joy and pleasure of success. A replay of the moment when the gold medal was won shows clearly emotions such as joy, exhilaration, relief and happiness. The group received a huge, and totally unexpected, amount of media coverage on returning home to Scotland. The details of their internal dissensions remained private, but on returning home the core four players and the coach decided that the best way forward was to return to a four-player formation. (The week after returning the group were due to play in the Scottish Championships, the winner of which would go to the World Championships a few weeks later.) The alternate player left the group, and another player voluntarily decided to stop curling at the end of the season for reasons of her own.

Coping at the Turin Games

Having to meet the needs of players and other support staff at the Olympics is always going to prove demanding for any sport psychologist. Katz and Hemmings (2009, p. 53) point out that:

sport psychologists are required to deliver support within a wide range of professional relationships (i.e., collaborating and interacting with athletes, coaches, managers, and other sport science and medicine practitioners). Accordingly, the quality of these professional relationships is central to the effectiveness of interventions undertaken.

Clearly having definite boundaries and established practices is vital in any team environment, and when this is not transparent – such as when the coach of the team suddenly becomes subsidiary to the team manager in terms of selection and pre and post-match debrief – the quality of the professional relationships between all concerned suffers somewhat. The power of the sport psychologist within a team environment is always going to be limited in terms of inputs to selection, personnel management or coaching strategy, and taking a person-centred view of the resulting team dynamics can be extraordinarily difficult. Knowing the boundaries – and concomitant aspects of my role as a sport psychologist – enabled me to accept and therefore cope with such scenarios even though other aspects of my experience (former professional coaching roles, for example) meant that such situations were difficult for me to come to terms with. However, it was crucial to me to follow my own principles in treating all concerned from a congruent and an unconditional regard (accepting) standpoint.

I found it unusual and surprising to realize that a number of players really did not wish to use my support, and indeed dealt with me in an almost superficial manner. It was still vital, though, for me to treat all these people in a Rogerian way, in which my own viewpoint as sport psychologist (agenda, some writers would suggest) is secondary to the perceptions of the client. Rogers's precept of unconditional positive regard (or acceptance of others for what they are, not what you would like them to be) was crucial to me in my professional interactions, even if it was not straightforward or easy to accomplish this. Years of psychotherapy practice (sometimes dealing with life and death scenarios, particularly with prisoners in a major Scottish prison) enabled me to make sense of these seemingly less earth-shattering difficulties (even though these may have been immensely important to the athletes concerned) and therefore enhanced my own coping strategies.

Coping with the emotional demands of working with a variety of different athletic personalities in the cauldron of Olympic competition demands a solid and well-practised set of philosophical principles. In my own case, being able to use the humanist approaches of Kelly and Rogers was of immense support and sustenance. This in no way is meant to imply that dealing with the demands of the role of sport psychologist at such an event as the Olympics is any way easy – though not having such a well-developed professional underpinning for my work would have been emotionally debilitating for me.

In addition, having a personal supervisor (who was not at the Games in Turin, though very much in touch through the modern wonder of mobile telephones) was of enormous importance. Such a formal relationship, while essential in psychotherapy work, is still not seen (in a British context at least) as crucial for applied sport psychologists once they have become chartered (by the British Psychological Society). It was clearly impossible to discuss any of the individual athletes' psychological needs with the coaching staff, so access to an objective, supportive other person was of immense value. Reflection on one's practice – be it with a support group or ongoing supervision – is seen as a central part of psychotherapy practice, and considered vital for ongoing professional development. By undertaking such reflection I was able in some way to attempt to cope with the demands of my Olympic involvement, even if this reflection, and therefore coping, did not take place until a number of weeks after the event.

Reflections on personal effectiveness

An examination of one's perceived effectiveness is central to the coping behaviour of the sport psychologist. Sport psychology, being a rather imprecise and some would say 'soft' science, often has problems of proving definitively that the use of a sport psychologist with a team has been measurably effective. Even members of the harder sciences – physiologists, biomechanics and physiotherapists – might also have difficulty in making claims concerning the precise effectiveness of their programmes, though clearly it is easier to witness such things as increase in muscle bulk and thus increases in power and reduced sprint times than it is to observe or even accept that development of mental toughness or improved mental skills practices may have had a direct influence on performance. Consequently trying to evaluate the relevance and importance of any sport psychology intervention has always proved hazardous. However, funding bodies have the right to see that their funds are being spent appropriately and they are getting value for money. Unfortunately, definitive proof is impossible to guarantee.

Tod and Andersen (2005) suggest that the perception that sport psychology has limited value might partly be influenced by the difficulty of separating applied sport psychology services from the individual providing the product. They go further and believe that 'Although conscientious consultants evaluate themselves and their service delivery, their influence on performance often cannot be assessed in an objective, quantitative manner' (p. 305). This indeed is often replicated in such activities as coaching and teacher behaviour, where personal interaction is crucial and standardized psychometric instruments do not yet appear to be sufficiently sophisticated to successfully tease out which variables are of most importance. Often it might be as simple as examining the degree to which athletes feel happy with the sport psychology services they receive, though even discovering this can be hazardous and difficult. Clearly the personality of the sport psychology consultant can be central to any successful interaction. Approaches that might be successful with individual athletes may not work with teams, and it is a challenge to sport psychologists in general to continue to examine this area of concern, perhaps in line with the case study approach suggested by Anderson et al. (2002) or the phenomenological approach of Pensgaard and Duda (2002).

In attempting to evaluate my professional involvement at both Games it is very difficult to be objective. However, reflecting on one's professional practice is essential, and the notion of reflexivity which is central to all Kelly's thinking is most useful here. Fransella (2005, p. 43) points to the importance of reflexivity in such situations by stating that reflexivity is essential 'for anyone wanting to apply personal construct psychology in a professional capacity'. Citing Fransella's (2005) belief that that there is widespread acceptance of reflexivity as a core feature in any application of PCT, Butler (2009, p. xviii) states that it 'rarely provokes more than a fleeting reference in the literature'. Reflexivity, according to Bannister (2003, p. 37), 'is the bedrock of personal construct theory' and is of immense help in permitting, for example, a professional sport psychology consultant to check and evaluate their personal experience. According to Butler (2009, p. xv), 'Reflexivity can be understood as an act of self reference whereby a person examines the nature of their own actions, beliefs, idiosyncrasies and emotions – an exploration as it were, of one's psychological stance.' One aspect of my self-evaluation of involvement at the Turin Games involved completing another personal Repgrid (a formal, more detailed report of my work was submitted to the relevant authorities, as is normally the case) of my views of the players post Olympics, so that my constructs could be compared with my original ones, devised when the group was formed some twelve months earlier. In this way I was able to systematically observe how my perceptions of the players had altered, and how such changes were manifest, making the ensuing discussions with my personal supervisor much more relevant and helpful in terms of debriefing and thus coping with the aftermath of my work at the Turin Games.

Summary

Comparing behaviour, by athletes and support staff alike, at elite-level events is always going to be onerous. Each sporting group/team is different, and from a sport psychologist's point of view varying demands and pressures arise from different environmental contexts. Being involved in the winning of the gold medal at Salt Lake City had its own consequences, while working with a team that did not achieve any medal resulted in other considerations.

The work of a sport psychologist certainly cannot be measured simply by the success of the team, and Mark Twain's aphorism that distance lends enchantment to the view may not always be correct. A deeper analysis of professional involvement is instead needed. While my own approach is based fundamentally on humanist principles, other practitioners will understandably favour different approaches. Adopting a humanist approach as suggested by Rogers and Kelly is demanding, often time-consuming, but ultimately rooted in the desire to focus on the needs of the individual (even in a group context). It is certainly not an 'easy way out', although it puts the onus on the individual to take responsibility for their actions. The athlete has to buy in to the idea of having to undertake the work necessary for their own improvement – the sport psychologist can only outline possible alternatives, as Bruce Ogilivie (1979), one of the original doyens of applied sport psychology, often used to comment. One of Rogers's guiding principles is that unless a client is ready (for therapy), growth and movement (in personal growth terms) are not possible.

In the situation at Turin it could be argued that the players were not ready to buy into my approach, or just not ready for me as their sport psychologist, especially in terms of the way that I might have operated. With the Salt Lake City group it is safe to say that the majority (four out of five curlers) actively engaged in the psychological aspect of preparation – in their own ways – but this did not happen with the players at the Turin event, and the real reasons will probably never be known.

In Turin, the situation was quite different. The details presented did not provide a theoretical analysis of coping behaviour, though they followed the transactional process model suggested by Hardy et al. (1996). Coping behaviour was discussed in terms of how the players practically should have been able to use their psychological preparatory work to deal with Olympic pressure, and a truncated description of the use of Kelly's personal construct psychology to help my own reflections of practice throughout the Games was also presented. Not being able to undertake a formal data-gathering session after the Games was unfortunate, though understandable. Playing and consulting at an Olympic tournament brings many pressures, as well as positive experiences, and perhaps a more precise, objective and exact way of ascertaining exactly how the players did indeed attempt to cope with the various pressures that they endured needs to be established.

Concluding remarks: a personal postscript

Attempting to recount the precise emotions that I experienced and coped with over both Olympic involvements presents considerable difficulties, especially after such a time lapse. However, some were so powerful that they still remain vivid. The periods covered by this chapter fitted neatly into three phases: pre-Olympic, at the Games themselves, and the post-Olympic period. My recollection of the pre-Olympic training and competition period for the Salt Lake City Games is one mainly of frustration at not being able to solve properly the growing issue of team disharmony, the factor that became so central to the whole Olympic experience, and annoyance that an opportunity to spend quality time developing a thorough psychological training programme was being wasted. At the Olympics the task of keeping the team together as a viable, successful unit was fraught with difficulties, and having to cope personally with individuals without any direct support for my own position was extremely stressful. Being an advocate of developing appropriate mental training strategies for athletes to deal with stressful situations meant that I was able to use my own coping skills to deal with my cognitive appraisal of the stressful situation within the group and with my emotional reactions to this. However, it was my genuine belief in and ongoing practice of the Rogerian principles of behaviour (such as active listening, unconditional positive regard and congruence) that was of immense importance and value in coming to terms with the demands experienced during this acutely difficult time.

Being present at and playing a part in supporting the team's success was an enormously gratifying experience, and one that still lives with me. It was one of professional pride as well as immense pleasure at seeing the players' joy and exhilaration. However, witnessing this achievement, of fulfilling an Olympic dream, was also tinged with sadness that it had occurred under a cloud of such interpersonal upset and stress. Numerous writers have pointed to the negative impact of dysfunctional emotional reactions on performance levels (Hanin, 2000; Weinberg and Gould, 1999), though in this particular case the players were mentally strong enough to counter these stresses, and that continues to give me pleasure.

My perceptions of the performance at Turin were quite different. Trying to evaluate one's own contribution to the performance is hazardous. My own feelings regarding my work with the team in Turin during the period of the Games, from observation, engagement and interaction with the group, were fundamentally ones of great disappointment and even sadness. This was in general not because of the poor level of achievement; rather, it reflects a sense of what might have been. The majority of the players clearly did not value the psychological aspect of their preparation, probably did not engage with the process, and continued to see me as sport psychologist as a sort of peripheral adjunct rather than an essential and beneficial resource. This was completely contrary to my experiences at the Salt Lake City Games in 2002, and it was not totally clear to me why this was the reaction of the squad. Perhaps only a thorough and open discussion with the players involved at some period after the Games had finished would have thrown light on this situation.

Future directions

To date most research on coping behaviour has investigated individual athletes (Gould, 2001; Gould et al., 1993a; Gould et al., 1993b), and few studies besides Holt and Sparkes (2001) and Holt and Hogg (2002) have attempted to provide detailed information of how teams cope with emotions at major events. Perhaps future researchers might focus on the question of how teams cope with such pressures at major competitions, and develop 'more psychometrically valid coping inventories for competitive sports' (Anshel et al., 2001, p. 70). These might enable players, coaches and support staff to gain a better appreciation of emotional reactions at major events, and enable sport psychology consultants to help groups cope with such emotions in a more informed way.

Working with a group of Olympic athletes over a long period of time, where the prime goal was to win the ultimate prize, necessitated a great deal of commitment from all sides – players, the coach and the sport psychologist – and was a profoundly rewarding experience. Throughout the period of the Olympic preparation for the Salt Lake City Games, one issue virtually dominated the proceedings – the resolution of intra-group conflict. Although Lenk (1960), working with East German Olympic rowers, has offered some evidence that groups that are seemingly dysfunctional can produce effective medal-winning performances, the orthodox view would suggest that harmonious groups are more likely to be productive (e.g. Widemeyer et al., 2002). Groups are of necessity evolving entities, and in the highly charged arena of elite sport, coping with both internal and external demands can result in disharmony and even break-up.

Carron et al. (2002) believe 'that the cohesion–performance relationship is present when cohesion is operationally defined as commitment to task (i.e. analogous to task cohesion) but not when it is operationally defined as interpersonal attraction (i.e. analogous to social cohesion) or group pride' (p. 169). The case of the Salt Lake Games would seem to verify this view, as on-ice (task) cohesion was positive and rewarding, while the obvious lack of social cohesion did not seem to interfere with the eventual success. Gill (2000) states that 'We know little about how cohesiveness is developed and maintained in sport and exercise groups' (p. 315), and the question of which processes are involved remains a matter of concern for future sport psychology researchers and consultants alike. The issue of internal dissent started as a nagging inconvenience, became an annoyance, and developed into an irritation, until eventually it became a major, ongoing problem that led to definite stress within the group. Thankfully, the four players who eventually acted as the team on ice at Salt Lake were able to make use of their own particular coping mechanisms that they had developed and practised over the previous years. They were able to set aside the stresses and strains experienced at the Games, focus on the task at hand and win the gold medal. For those athletes who performed at Turin, internal rivalry was eventually more important than task cohesion, and it appears that one consequence of this was a level of performance much below what was expected by athletes and support staff alike. Clearly, there were many factors involved in their perceived underachievement, though having a strong sense of team identity might have been more productive than allowing personal animosities to fester and thus impact on performance outcome. Increasing knowledge of the correlates of and how best to develop team identity seems to be an important forward step in helping teams to cope with the stress of major athletic competition.

References

Andersen, M. (2009). Sport psychology in practice. In B. W. Brewer (ed.), *Sport psychology*. Chichester, UK: Wiley-Blackwell.

Anderson, A. and Clarke, P. (2002). Afterword. In D. Lavallee and I. Cockerill (eds), *Counselling in sport and exercise contexts* (pp. 69– 73) Leicester: British Psychological Society.

Anderson, A. G., Miles, A., Mahoney, C. and Robinson, P. (2002). Evaluating the effectiveness of applied sport psychology practice: making the case for a case study approach. *The Sport Psychologist*, 16, 432–453.

Anshel, M. H., Kim, K. W., Kim, B. H., Chang, K. J. and Eom, H. J. (2001). A model for coping with stressful events in sport: theory, application and future directions. *International Journal of Sport Psychology*, 32, 43–75.

Baillie, P. H. F. and Ogilvie, B. C. (1996). Working with elite athletes. In J. L. Van Raalte and B. W. Brewer (eds), *Exploring sport and exercise psychology* (pp. 335–354). Washington, DC: American Psychological Association.

Bannister, D. (2003). Kelly and clockwork psychology. In F. Fransella (ed.), *International handbook of personal construct psychology* (pp. 33–40). Chichester, UK: John Wiley.

Barsade, S. G. (2002). The ripple effect: emotional contagion and its influence on group behaviour. *Administrative Science Quarterly*, Dec. www.findarticles.co./cf (accessed 12 January 2004).

Bond, J. W. (2002). Applied sport psychology: philosophy, reflections and experience. *International Journal of Sport Psychology*, 33, 19– 37.

Brewer, B. R. (2009). (Ed.) *Sport psychology.* Chichester, UK: Wiley-Blackwell.

Brustad., R. J. (2008). Qualitative research approaches. In T. Horn (ed.), *Advances in sport psychology*, 3rd edn (pp. 31–43). Champaign, Ill.: Human Kinetics.

Butler, R. J. (1992). *Sport psychology in action.* Oxford: Butterworth-Heinemann.

Butler, R. J. (ed.) (2009). *Reflections on personal construct theory.* Chichester, UK: Wiley-Blackwell.

Butler, R. J. and Hardy, L. (1992). The performance profile: theory and application. *The Sport Psychologist*, 6, 253–264.

Carron, A. V., Bray, S. R. and Eys, M. A. (2002). Team cohesion and success in sport. *Journal of Sports Sciences*, 20, 119–126.

Carron, A. V., Coleman, M. C., Wheeler, J. and Stevens, D. (2002). Cohesion and performance in sport: a meta analysis. *Journal of Sport and Exercise Psychology*, 24, 168–188.

Clarke, P. T. (1995). The perception of coaching qualities held by professional soccer players. In F. H. Fu and M. L. Ng (eds), *Sport psychology: Perspectives and practices: Towards the 21st century* (pp. 273–284). Hong Kong: Hong Kong Baptist University.

Clarke, P. T. (1996). An analysis of competitive stress over a swimming season. Paper presented at the International Congress on Stress and Health, Sydney, Australia, 5–8 October 1996.

Clarke, P. T. (1999). The use of the laddering technique to asses the perceived qualities of soccer coaches. Paper presented at the 4th Conference of Science and Football, Sydney, Australia, November 1999.

Clarke, P. T. (2007). A comparison of coaching qualities between a neophyte and experienced soccer coach. Poster presentation at the VIth World Congress on Science and Football, Antalya, Turkey, January 2007.

Cripps, B. (1999). Constructing the athlete's world: the early period. In H. Steinberg and I. Cockerill, *Sport psychology in practice* (pp. 8–15). Leicester, UK: British Psychological Society.

Dugdale, J. R., Eklund, R. C. and Gordon, S. (2002). Expected and unexpected stressors in major international competition: appraisal, coping and performance. *The Sport Psychologist*, 16, 20– 33.

Feixas, G., Marti, J. and Villegas, M (1989). Personal construct assessment of sport teams. *International Journal of Personal Construct Psychology*, 2, 49–54.

Fransella, F. (2003). *International handbook of personal construct psychology*, Chichester, UK: John Wiley.

Fransella, F. (ed.) (2005). *The essential practitioner's handbook of personal construct theory.* Chichester, UK: Wiley.

Fransella, F., Bell, R. and Bannister, D. (2004). *A manual for the repertory grid technique*, 2nd edn. London: John Wiley.

Fromm, M. (2004). *Introduction to the repertory grid interview.* Munster, Germany: Waxman.

Fromm, M. (2007). Meaning making in repertory grid elicitation and analysis. Workshop at the School of Psychology, University of Hertfordshire, England, 28 February.

Gilbourne, D. (2002). Sport participation, sports injury and altered images of the self: an autobiographical narrative of a lifetime legacy. *Reflective Practice*, 3, 71–87.

Gill, D. L. (2000). *Psychological dynamics of sport and exercise*. Champaign, Ill.: Human Kinetics.

Gordon, S. (2001). Reflections on providing sport psychology services in professional cricket. In G. Tenenbaum (ed.), *The practice of sport psychology* (pp. 17– 36). Morgantown, W.V.: Fitness Information Technology.

Gordon, S., Gucciardi, D. and Chambers., T. (2007). A personal construct perspective on sport and exercise psychology research: the example of mental toughness. In T. Morris, P. Terry, and S. Gordon (eds), *Sport and exercise psychology: International perspectives*. (pp. 43–55). Morgantown, W.V.: Fitness Information Technology.

Gould, D. (2000). Stress management at major games. Paper presented to the Scottish Sport Psychology Group. November, Edinburgh, Scotland.

Gould, D. (2001). Sport psychology and the Nagano Olympic Games: the case of the US freestyle ski team. In G. Tenenbaum (ed.), *The practice of sport psychology* (pp. 49–76). Morgantown, W.V.: Fitness Information Technology.

Gould, D., Eklund, R. C. and Jackson, S. A. (1993a). Coping strategies used by U.S. Olympic wresters. *Research Quarterly for Exercise and Sport*, 64, 63–93.

Gould, D., Eklund, R. C. and Jackson, S. A. (1993b). Coping strategies used by national champion figure skaters. *Research Quarterly for Exercise and Sport*, 64, 453–468.

Greenleaf, C., Gould, D. and Dieffenbach, K. (2001). Factors influencing Olympic performance: interviews with Atlanta and Nagano U. S. Olympians. *Journal of Applied Sport Psychology*, 13, 154–184.

Gucciardi, D. F., Gordon, S. and Dimmock, J. A. (2009). Advancing mental toughness research and theory using personal construct psychology. *International Review of Sport and Exercise Psychology*, 2, 54–72.

Hammermeister, J. and Burton, D. (2001). Stress, appraisal and coping revisited: examining the antecedents of competitive state anxiety with endurance athletes. *The Sport Psychologist*, 15, 66– 90.

Hanin, Y. L. (2000). *Emotions in sport*. Champaign, Ill.: Human Kinetics.

Hardy, L., Jones, G. and Gould, D. (1996). *Understanding psychological preparation for sport: Theory and practice of elite performers*. Chichester, UK: John Wiley & Sons.

Hatfield, E., Cacioppo, J. T. and Rapson, R. L. (1993). *Emotional contagion*. Cambridge: Cambridge University Press.

Holt, N. J. and Hogg, J. M. (2002). Perceptions of stress and coping during preparations for the 1999 Women's Soccer World Cup finals. *The Sport Psychologist*, 16, 251–271.

Holt, N. L. and Sparkes, A. C. (2001). An ethnographic study of cohesiveness in a college soccer team over a season. *The Sport Psychologist*, 15, 237–259.

Jackson, S. A. (2000). Joy, fun, and flow state in sport. In Y. L. Hanin (ed.) *Emotions in sport* (pp. 135–155). Champaign, IL: Human Kinetics.

Jankowicz, A. D. (2004). *The easy guide to repertory grids*. Chichester, UK: Wiley.

Katz, J. and Hemmings, B. (2009). *Counselling skills handbook for the sport psychologist*. Leicester, UK: British Psychological Society.

Kelly, G. (1955). *The psychology of personal constructs, Volumes 1 and 2*. New York: Norton (repr. London: Routledge, 1991).

Kirschenbaum, H. and Henderson, V. L. (eds) (2005). *The Carl Rogers reader*. London: Constable & Robertson.

Kremer, J. and Moran, A. P. (2008). *Pure sport: Practical sport psychology*. London: Routledge.

Lazarus, R. S. (1999). *Stress and emotion: A new synthesis*. London: Free Association Books.

Lazarus, R. S. (2000). How emotions influence performance in competitive sports. *The Sport Psychologist*, 14, 229–252.

Lenk, H. (1960). Top performance despite internal conflict: an antithesis to a functional proposition. In J. Loy and G. Kenyon (eds), *Sport, culture and society: A reader in the sociology of sport* (pp. 393–397). Toronto, Ont.: Macmillan.

Madden, C. (1995). Ways of coping. In T. Morris and J. Summers (eds), *Sport psychology: Theory, applications and issues* (pp. 288– 310). Chichester: John Wiley & Sons.

McCann, S. C. (2000). Doing sport psychology at the really big show. In M. B. Andersen (ed.), *Doing sport psychology* (pp. 209– 222). Champaign, Ill.: Human Kinetics.

Miller, B. (1997). *Golden minds.* Wiltshire, UK: Crowood Press.

Ogilvie, B. (1979). Seminar on the psychology of coaching behaviour. Art and Science of Coaching Conference, Wingate Institute for Physical Education and Sport, Natanya, Israel, 18–23 December.

Pensgaard, A. M. and Duda, J. L. (2002). 'If we work hard, we can do it': a tale from an Olympic (Gold) medallist. *Journal of Applied Sport Psychology,* 14, 219–236.

Ravenette, T. (1999). *Personal construct theory in educational psychology: A practitioner's view.* London: Whurr.

Ravizza, K. (2001). Reflections and insights from the field on performance enhancement consultation. In G. Tenenbaum (ed.), *The practice of sport psychology* (pp. 197–216). Morgantown, W.V.: Fitness Information Technology.

Rogers, C. R. (1951). *Client centred therapy: Its current practice, implication and theory.* London: Constable.

Rogers, C. R. (1967). *On becoming a person: A therapist's view of psychotherapy.* London: Constable.

Rossi, T. (1997). Seeing it differently: physical education, teacher education and possibilities of personal construct theory. *Sport, Education and Society,* 2, 205–220.

Shaw, M. L. G. (1980). *On becoming a personal scientist.* New York: Academic Press.

Smith, T. (2008). *Tommy Smith: Anfield iron – the autobiography* (p. 428). London: Bantam Books.

Stewart, V. and Stewart, A. (1982). *Business applications of repertory grid.* London: McGraw Hill.

Tod, D. and Andersen, M. (2005). Success in sport psychology: Effective sport psychologists. In S. Murphy (ed.), T*he sport psych handbook: A complete guide to today's best mental training techniques* (pp. 305–314). Champaign, Ill.: Human Kinetics.

Tuckman, B. W. (1993). I cried because I had no shoes...: A case study of motivation applied to rehabilitation. In D. Pargman (ed.), *Psychological bases for sport injuries* (pp. 285–295). Morgantown, W.V.: Fitness Information Technology.

Vogt, F., Armstrong, D. and Marteau, T. M. (2010). General practitioners' perceptions of the effectiveness of medical interventions: an exploration of underlying constructs. *Implementation Science,* 5, 17.

Weinberg, R. and Gould, D. (1999). *Foundations of sport and exercise psychology,* 2nd edn. Champaign Ill.: Human Kinetics

Widmeyer, W. N., Brawley, L. R. and Carron, A. V. (2002). Group dynamics in sport. In T. Horn (ed.), *Advances in sport psychology,* 2nd edn (pp. 285–308). Champaign, Ill.: Human Kinetics.

Winter, D. A. (2003). Repertory grid technique as a psychotherapy research method. *Psychotherapy Research,* 13, 25–42.

15

LEARNING TO COPE IN EXTREME ENVIRONMENTS

Solo endurance ocean sailing

Neil Watson, University of Portsmouth

> Paradoxically environmental psychologists have, to a great extent, ignored the most fascinating environments: those that lie outside the common everyday situations encountered by most of us. Descriptions of how people cope with such conditions attract a much wider and more enthusiastic readership than the painstaking analysis, the meticulous research, and the ingenious theories published in professional journals. As a matter of fact, I suspect that many environmental psychologists themselves enjoy the tales of solitary sailors, polar explorers, and deep-sea divers more than they do the monthly issue of even their favourite scientific periodical.
>
> *(Suedfeld, 1987, p. 863)*

Although this quote is over twenty years old, it is still as relevant today as it was then. Scientists, psychologists and the general public enjoy listening to, or reading about the experiences of those individuals who test themselves in environments alien to their own. For instance, mountaineers attempting to climb the highest peaks in the world, solo sailors trying to sail non-stop around the globe, and explorers testing their mental and physical endurance in isolated hot or cold environments; in each of these examples it is intuitively interesting to learn about the motives for participating, stressors faced, coping strategies employed and successes, or in some case, fatal failures. Indeed, a significant number of successful book publications over the years have centred on individuals recounting their experiences and opening up a world that the general population can only dream about experiencing.

The author's own interest in this area began when examining the psychology of single-handed round the world ocean sailing through Sir Robin Knox-Johnson's book *A World of My Own* (2004) which detailed the first ever non-stop solo round the world voyage in 1968/69. The inaugural *Sunday Times* Golden Globe non-stop round the world event threw up numerous interesting stories, including the presumed suicide of Donald Crowhurst whilst participating in the event, which has since been chronicled in a scientific publication (Bennet, 1974) and more recently a film *Deep Water* (2006) (Osmond and Rothwell, 2006).

Contrary to the wealth of autobiographical literature in the area, there is less available scientific research examining stress and coping associated with activities performed in extreme environments. The isolation and complexity of these environments result in numerous difficulties associated with adopting rigorous scientific methodology. However, if these problems are minimised, such research can provide a unique insight into how humans survive and perform at the limits of their mental and physical capabilities. Indeed, this research could provide important knowledge and information to help prepare future explorers, solo sailors and the like to perform to their optimum and more importantly, to survive when it matters most.

This chapter draws on the recent research and applied practitioner experiences of the author in solo endurance ocean sailing (SEOS). The principal aim is to review existing stress and coping research in this sport in order to identify specific practical recommendations or future research opportunities in the area. Inherent within this review is the discussion of stress and coping-related literature conducted in other extreme environment sports to help to contextualise and explain the findings obtained in solo sailing.

The chapter begins by defining key terms including stress, coping and an extreme environment. An overview of the stress and coping-related research that has been undertaken in SEOS with reference to research conducted in other extreme environment sports is then provided. Next, an applied consultation with a female elite solo endurance sailor entered into a non-stop round the world event is described. The discussion focuses on the tools used to monitor the psychological state of the performer, and includes a reflection on the coping strategies that enabled successful completion of the event. The final parts of the chapter outline general practical recommendations and future research opportunities in extreme environment sports.

Key definitions and categorisations

Imagine driving a car, fast, off-road at night in lashing rain. You're forced to hang on to the steering wheel just to stay in your seat, and you have no idea what's coming next, as you have no headlights. To make matters worse, you have no windscreen wipers clearing your view. In fact, you have no windscreen. No roof. That's how it feels sailing fast in the Southern Ocean at night.

(MacArthur, 2006, p. 13)

Given that this chapter is dedicated to examining stress and coping in a sport performed in an extreme environment, it is important to define each of these key terms at the outset. For key terms relating to the topics of stress, stressors and strain, we adopt the definitions provided by Fletcher, Hanton and Mellalieu (2006, p. 329):

- *Stress* is 'an ongoing process that involves individuals transacting with their environments, making appraisals of the situations they find themselves in, and endeavouring to cope with any issues that may arise'.
- *Stressors* are 'environmental demands encountered by an individual' which have been categorised into competitive (i.e. primarily related to competitive performance), organizational (i.e. principally related to the organization within which the performer is participating), and personal stressors (i.e. mainly associated with the individual's non-sporting life events)'.
- *Strain* is 'an individual's negative psychological, physical and behavioural responses to stressors'.

Coping is defined as 'constantly changing cognitive and behavioural efforts to manage the specific external and/or internal demands that are appraised as taxing or exceeding the resources of the person' (Lazarus and Folkman, 1984, p. 141). Nicholls and Polman (2007), in their review of coping in sport, identify five coping dimensions:

- problem-focused coping, which refers to actions initiated to remove/lessen a threatening event by altering an aspect of the environment itself
- avoidance coping, which relates to actions chosen to disengage the person from the situation
- emotion-focused coping, which refers to actions to manage an individual's emotions
- appraisal coping, which entails the re-evaluation of the situation and desensitising of its importance
- approach coping, which involves the person confronting the stressor and initiating direct action to lessen its effects.

Paulus et al. (2009, p. 1081) state that:

> extreme environments are characterised as those situations which place a high demand on the physiological, affective, cognitive, and/or social processing resources of the individual ... strongly perturb the body and mind, which in turn initiate complex cognitive and affective response strategies.

Suedfeld (1987) suggests that the term 'extreme' is associated with the 'physical characteristics related to danger and discomfort' (p. 864) and can be categorised in relation to three important parameters:

- Physical parameters such as the temperature, air composition and pressure, humidity, terrain, day–night cycles of the environment are likely to impact upon the 'extremeness' of the setting.
- person–environment interactive parameters will also influence the extremity of the environment: for example, the availability and ease of communication, the degree of physical mobility or restriction, the extent of isolation from others, and the level of control and predictability of the environment.
- Internal psychological parameters such as how the person perceives and copes with the environment, and their motivation, personality and affective reactions, in addition to how they perceive themselves within the setting, will also impact upon the extremity of the environment.

Paulus et al. (2009) also point out that performance in a variety of different types of extreme environment may share key characteristics. However, each extreme environment will possess unique stressors that will impact upon the performer.

To summarise the above comments, for the purposes of this chapter an extreme environment is defined as:

> A setting that an individual encounters which is distinctly different from their normal daily life in terms of its physical characteristics (temperature, humidity, isolation, terrain, and so on), lacking in predictability and control, and results in a significant taxing of the individual's physical, cognitive and affective resources thus forcing them to initiate cognitive, affective and behavioural response strategies to perform and/or survive.

In his review into the psychology of extreme and unusual environment activities, Suedfeld (1987) states that there are plenty of examples of people encountering extreme, unusual environments in the world, yet there is little rigorous academic study of these situations. Suedfeld's tone is one of surprise as to the lack of research, yet given the complex, dynamic and difficult environment in which solo sailors, rowers, mountaineers and explorers find themselves, it is not surprising that scientists struggle to conduct and publish rigorous scientific studies in the area. Indeed, often competitors in extreme environments are working at the limits of their human functioning towards very specific and important goals (such as winning a particular competition, or becoming the fastest person to achieve an extreme feat), where performance and survival are a far greater priority than participating in scientific research. This is certainly the author's own experience of conducting research in this area; hence it is my strong opinion that the researcher and participant must work closely to establish a programme of research that is both feasible and beneficial for both parties (the researcher obtains ecologically valid and reliable findings whilst the participant gains greater self-awareness of how they have coped/ performed in the activity).

Because of the lack of a substantial body of published scientific research in this area, the majority of literature has come from the performers themselves through autobiographical accounts of their struggles to survive and perform under sometimes enormous environmental pressures (e.g. Caffari, 2007; Knox-Johnson, 2004; MacArthur, 2006). Suedfeld (1987) acknowledges this situation, and reinforces the need to view the personal and scientific literature as complementary rather than competing when attempting to understand more of individuals' endeavours in such extreme, unusual environments. Hence the remainder of the chapter will draw from the existing scientific literature as well as the autobiographical accounts of the performers themselves.

Stress and coping in solo endurance ocean sailing

> I felt very depressed on getting up .... The future does not look particularly bright, sitting here being thrown about for the next 150 days, with constant soakings as I take in or let out sail, is not an exciting prospect. After four gales my hands are worn and cut about badly and I am aware of my fingers on account of the pain from skin tears and broken fingernails. I have bruises all over from being thrown about. My skin itches from constant chafing with wet clothes, and I forgot when I last had a proper wash .... I feel altogether mentally and physically exhausted and I've been in the southern ocean only a week .... A prisoner in Dartmoor doesn't get hard labour like this .... I wonder how the crime rate would be affected if people were sentenced to sail round the world alone, instead of going to prison. It's ten months solitary confinement with hard labour.
>
> *(Knox-Johnston, 2004, pp. 69–70)*

The sport of SEOS is one that pitches the skipper at the mercy of a dynamic and sometimes volatile environment, requiring significant energy reserves under sustained levels of sleep deprivation (Myers et al., 2008). Skippers sailing in the southern ocean can often encounter high sea states, strong winds, cold rainy weather and icebergs whilst isolated from any physical support and rescue. Such conditions place the skipper and their yacht in an extremely perilous position which could result in the yacht capsizing at any moment and thus endangering the skipper's life.

Examination of the SEOS literature reveals very few published scientific articles which can enlighten the stress and coping involved in the sport. Early research by Lewis et al. (1964) and Bennet (1973) attempted, with some success, to examine the physical and psychological state of skippers entered into two transatlantic solo ocean sailing events. The findings revealed a number of stressors that they had to cope with, including injuries, sea sickness, hunger, isolation, physical and mental fatigue and difficult environmental conditions. The authors also highlighted the prevalence of hallucinations or sensory impairment, where skippers stated that they had heard (for instance hearing a radio when it was not on), smelled (for example, coffee when there was none on board) or seen (for example, seeing their father in law at the top of the mast) things that could not possibly have happened yet they felt were very real. Explanations forwarded to explain these strange sensory experiences included sleep deprivation, sea sickness and anxiety, in addition to the relatively monotonous sensory input of the sport where the environment stays relatively similar (the sea and sky visual scenery remaining relatively constant and empty), thus increasing the likelihood that individuals will start to create sensory experiences from within (Bennet, 1973).

Whilst coping was not the central focus of either paper, skippers did mention the importance of completing tasks on board to overcome fear and depression, in addition to reading books to combat boredom (Lewis et al., 1964). Furthermore, examination of each skipper's responses revealed a distinctly individual emotional and psychological response to the activity, which was assumed to result from the differing personalities and circumstances faced throughout each race. Lazarus (1999) supports this contention, suggesting that it is a person's unique way of construing a stressor (assigning their own psychological meaning to the stressor) that results in the idiosyncratic cognitive and emotional response. Indeed, stress-based research studies in sport have found this to be the case (e.g. Nicholls et al., 2009a).

Despite the interesting insights into the psychological characteristics of SEOS offered by Lewis et al. (1964) and Bennet's (1973) research, both were limited by a lack of scientific rigor and detail in the data analysis phase. What was clear from both these studies was that SEOS did put significant pressure on the resources of the sailors, a factor that Gunnarsson et al. (2004) attempted to quantify in their physiological assessment of stress levels in a yacht crew entered into the 2001 Volvo Ocean Race. It is important to point out at this stage that what Gunnarsson et al. (2004) termed mental stress is in actual fact strain, and hence for clarity the word 'stress' has been replaced by 'strain' when discussing their findings. Over a nine month period the researchers found elevated levels of glycosylated hemoglobin (HbA$_{1c}$, a measure of blood glucose), and lowered levels of saliva testosterone during periods of sustained mental strain whilst at sea. Similar changes observed in each of these variables have been recorded in other stressful contexts (such as students revising for examinations, Schuck, 1998; people working in highly stressful occupations, Kawakami, et al., 2000; athletes participating in sustained periods of endurance training, Zitzmann and Nieschlag, 2001). Thus these markers offer a useful way of physiologically quantifying strain. Gunnarsson et al. (2004) further assert that they may also provide a useful mechanism to monitor the speed of recovery from stressful events at sea.

Despite these findings, Gunnarsson et al's (2004) study was limited by the lack of scientific rigour with which the researchers recorded the perception of strain during the race. This appears to have come from general reports from the crew as opposed to specific daily monitoring of the crew's perception of strain in line with the acquisition of the physiological strain markers. A more systematic, combined physiological and perceptual daily analysis of strain is needed to fully establish whether Gunnarsson et al's (2004) findings are accurate and to identify the extent to which different strain measures are correlated. Such research would provide scientists, practitioners, skippers and shore teams with a greater understanding of the extent to which certain critical events at sea impact upon levels of actual (as measured by the physiological markers) and perceived strain.

Participation in SEOS has grown markedly since the inaugural Golden Globe event in 1968. What has not necessarily changed in that time is the inherent danger of the sport. With increasing participation numbers, the need to develop knowledge of how skippers deal with the various demands they are likely to face is fundamental in order to ensure safety. It is therefore surprising that it took until 2009 for the first detailed study into how skippers cope with the stressors they experience at sea. Employing a two-stage qualitative interview design, Weston et al. (2009) investigated the stressors faced, and related coping strategies adopted, by single-handed skippers entered into the 2006/07 Velux 5 Oceans Round the World yacht race. A central aim in this study was to provide information for practitioners, skippers and their support team to help prepare skippers for the rigors of SEOS.

The race itself was a three-stage single-handed circumnavigation of the world, in which the sailors travelled approximately 29,400 miles, starting and finishing in Bilbao (Spain) via Fremantle (Australia) and Norfolk (USA). Although seven skippers entered, only four finished on time, taking between 103 and 159 days. Skippers were interviewed before and after the race to ascertain their experiences of the stressors they had faced, and related coping strategies they adopted, both in their prior solo sailing experiences, and in the race itself. Following an inductive and deductive content analysis of skipper interview transcripts, fourteen first-order stressors were identified in addition to twenty-six first-order coping strategies. Whilst it could be argued that the stressors identified (such as difficult environmental conditions, isolation, sleep deprivation, physical exertions, sea sickness, lack of progress, yacht-related problems, communication difficulties and monotonous tasks) are reasonably obvious given the nature of sport, what is more helpful is the range of coping strategies that skippers employed to deal with the various demands.

Skippers reinforced the importance of meticulous pre-race preparation in order to develop a plan to deal with the likely onset of difficult environmental conditions, poor progress, technical problems, and to respond to physical exhaustion and sleep deprivation. The attention to detail in terms of preparing for every eventuality ensured that skippers were confident that they could deal with these stressors should they arise. Such detailed pre-event planning (also known as anticipatory coping) has been advocated in short-duration land-based sports (e.g. Nicholls et al., 2005a; Thelwell, Weston and Greenlees, 2007). In the light of the complex, dangerous and isolated nature of SEOS, and the fact that participation in the sport is growing, it is essential that detailed recommendations on how to best prepare for this type of sport are established.

Communication with a skipper's support team or others (such as family, friends and supporters) was an important coping strategy. This strategy was employed to deal with the isolation and loneliness associated with the activity, concerns around technical problems or possible threats, frustration over poor progress and when struggling to deal with difficult environmental conditions. Social support has been proposed as a useful strategy to help protect an individual against the harmful effects of stress. Indeed, research examining the coping strategies employed by individuals climbing Mount Everest (Burke and Orlick, 2003) and during polar expeditions (Devonport et al., in review; Leon, List and Magor, 2004) have found that social support plays a significant role in helping the individual deal with stressors within these activities.

Known as the stress-buffering hypothesis (Cohen, 1988), researchers assert that social support helps athletes deal with stress by helping them to functionally appraise the stressor and/or to identify and initiate better coping strategies (Cohen, Gottlieb and Underwood, 2000; Cohen and Wills, 1985). It is important to acknowledge and take into consideration an athlete's own preference for how and from whom support is provided, in relation to a particular stressor and in the context of the support network that is currently available to them (Gottlieb, 2000). Given the above findings, it is clear that skippers and their shore team should spend sufficient time identifying the specific social support needs of the performer. Indeed, given the physically isolated and dangerous nature of SEOS, one could argue that social support is of greater importance in this type of sport than in safer land-based sports where there are few periods of sustained isolation and generally no threat to a performer's life.

Other coping strategies adopted by skippers included the need to remain focused on actions or factors that they could influence or control during times when they started to worry about possible threats (such as rolling the yacht or hitting an iceberg), bad weather coming, or the lack of wind. It would be quite easy to dwell on these various stressors and allow them to negatively influence one's mood and fail to initiate any tangible actions. However, skippers reinforced the need to focus the mind on completing tasks and actions that are within their control and thus help to best prepare themselves and their yacht for when it matters most (such as when a storm arrives). Successful Mount Everest climbers have similarly reinforced the importance of maintaining a clear and directed focus on specific tasks that will enable them to fulfil their overall goal (Burke and Orlick, 2003). Moreover, these climbers emphasised the importance of keeping their emotions intact and not allowing self-doubts to enter their mind. Thus skippers finding themselves in stressful situations in the future should try to minimise their frustration and worry by staying in the 'here and now' and focusing on controllable activities that will positively contribute to their continued safe passage.

Sleep deprivation and physical exhaustion are inevitable consequences of the solo nature of this sport. Indeed, Stampi (1989) asserts that when sailing solo the skipper is more at risk when they are asleep because of the increased chances of the yacht going off course, problems emerging on board or collisions with ships, containers or icebergs. As a consequence solo skippers sleep less in total than is usual, and normally in short accumulated naps when and where they deem it is most appropriate. Skippers in the Weston et al. (2009) study accumulated up to five hours of sleep a day. This compares favourably with similar sailing research which has found 6.33 (Stampi, 1989), 3.5 (Weston and Thelwell, 2009), 2.8 (Groslambert, Candau and Millet, 2008), and 2 (Myers et al., 2008) hours of accumulated sleep in a 24-hour period. Interestingly, one skipper in the Weston et al. (2009) study initiated a sleep deprivation training programme of 20 minutes of sleep every four hours for five weeks prior to the race start, with the aim of developing a quick and effective deep sleep. Whilst the effectiveness of this skipper's sleep strategy, known as 'prophylactic polyphasic sleep' (Dinges et al., 1980 cited in Stampi, 1989), was not evaluated, there is some evidence to suggest that such sleep patterns during an event may lead to more successful sailing performance. For instance, Stampi (1989) observed sleep strategies in ninety-nine solo and double-handed ocean sailors during three different sailing events. The highest-performing skippers tended to sleep less and have shorter naps than their less successful competitors. More specifically, the successful skippers were napping for between 20 and 60 minutes, totalling an average of five hours in a 24-hour period.

Hence, it appears that the demands of SEOS result in prolonged periods of sleep deprivation that physically exhaust skippers and therefore must be managed effectively (Groslambert et al., 2008; Stampi, 1989; Weston et al., 2009). The amount of sleep necessary to fulfil one's duties adequately and safely is likely to be specific to the individual. Furthermore, the unique, dynamic and often unpredictable nature of the environment will influence a skipper's ability to initiate any form of sleep strategy effectively. That being said, sleep patterns have been linked to performance success (Léger et al., 2008; Stampi, 1989); hence skippers should attempt to develop an effective during-race sleep strategy, tailored to their own preferences, which allows them to maintain a high-performing but safe yacht. Simulating different sleep approaches prior to an event may provide skippers with a better understanding of how to maximise their sleep. However, more experimental research is needed that examines the effectiveness of different pre-race sleep strategies on sailing performance before definitive recommendations can be made (Weston et al., 2009).

Skippers also reinforced the need to rationalise a number of the stressors experienced, including lack of progress, sea sickness, possible threats, yacht-related problems and family issues. Critical to dealing with these stressors was the skipper's ability to functionally appraise the situation and thus ensure first, a more positive and optimistic mindset, and second, the initiation of actions within their control to facilitate performance and ensure safety. Skippers voiced the importance of drawing on prior experience to rationalise situations appropriately and thus encourage a more proactive attitude towards each particular situation, a strategy that has been reinforced by other solo skippers (Bennet, 1973) and mountaineers (Burke and Orlick, 2003).

In summary, solo endurance ocean sailors encounter numerous difficult and dangerous stressors which require a range of problem, approach, appraisal and emotion-focused coping strategies to ensure a safe, optimally performing yacht. The coping research examining this sport is minimal despite the evident increase in participation numbers. Several coping strategies appear to be available to the skipper, but the selection of which coping strategy (or strategies) are used is dependent on the specific situation encountered, in addition to the skipper's individual preferences. Given that the sport tests athletes to the limits of their mental and physical capabilities, and in some instances has resulted in fatalities, it is important that more research is conducted to develop a comprehensive knowledge base from which to educate performers on how to cope when it matters most.

In order to examine the individual nature of stress and coping in SEOS and how such information could help educate a skipper to cope more effectively, the next section details an applied consultation led by the author with an elite solo endurance ocean sailor entered into a non-stop round the world event. An important part of this process was the development and implementation of a daily psychological monitoring tool from which key lessons could be learned.

Solo ocean sailing case study

> At its peak the tropical storm flayed Aviva and me with hurricane force winds that reached 68 knots ... the seas were enormous, crests heaped on crests and crushed at their tops by the force of the wind .... I was shocked by the violence of the storm .... I was alert, anxious and exhausted all at the same time but there was no way I could sleep: the noise was too distressing.
>
> *(Caffari, 2007, p. 116)*

Lane et al. (2004) assert that detailed monitoring of the psychological state of individuals participating in extreme environments may provide valuable insights into how the person reacts and responds to adverse environmental conditions. Bearing this in mind and acknowledging the early psychological monitoring work of Lewis et al. (1964) and Bennet (1973), in addition to the qualitative stress and coping research of Weston et al. (2009), the present case study reflects upon the applied work conducted by the author with a female professional ocean sailor during the 2008/09 Vendée Globe event (parts of this work have been presented elsewhere; see Weston and Thelwell, 2009). The purpose of the work was to quantify the psychological demands of SEOS by monitoring the skipper's psychological state during ninety-nine days alone at sea. A second important aim was to identify the factors that contributed to her mindset and critically identify the coping strategies she adopted to deal with the stressors that were encountered.

Although yachts are now more sophisticated and communication systems significantly improved from the inaugural Golden Globe event in 1968, modern-day skippers still face a wide range of stressors which they must deal with in order to perform and survive. The Vendée Globe, held every four years, is the world's premier SEOS event. It starts and ends in Les Sables d'Olonne, France and requires skippers to sail non-stop around the world. Of the thirty entrants to this particular race, only eleven successfully completed the event, with the skipper in question finishing sixth.

While not underestimating the importance of long and reliable questionnaires, Tenenbaum, Kamata and Hayashi (2007) surmise that researchers must seek out more ecologically valid measures in order that a scientific study can better fit situational practicalities. Tenenbaum et al. further argue that the use of short, convenient, task-specific questionnaires can provide important scientific and practical information for athletes, coaches and scientists alike.

With these statements in mind, the author sought to develop and use a short, ecologically valid measure for monitoring the daily psychological responses of the skipper. A short Excel-based bipolar questionnaire (termed the Solo Ocean Psychological Questionnaire, SOPQ, see Figure 15.1) was developed in tandem with the skipper and in line with the client-centred philosophy of performance profiling (Butler and Hardy, 1992). Drawing on Deci and Ryan's (1985) cognitive evaluation theory, Butler and Hardy assert that autonomy-supportive approaches which encourage athlete input to the decision-making process will result in greater intrinsic motivation to engage in any future work. Given that the present skipper was being asked to complete the SOPQ every 24 hours for 99 days, it was important that she felt involved in the development of the scale and thus more likely to adhere to completing it.

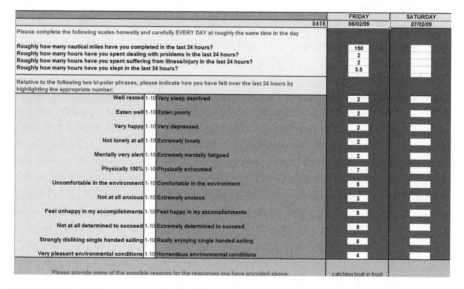

FIGURE 15.1 Solo ocean psychological questionnaire (SOPQ; Weston & Thelwell, 2009)

The SOPQ was developed through a combination of a detailed literature review and discussion with the skipper. The consultant reviewed literature which had examined the psychology of human performance in long-duration activities performed in extreme environments including solo ocean sailing (e.g. Bennet, 1973, 1974; Lewis et al., 1964). This produced a list of psychological attributes that had been identified as influential when engaging in these unique environmentally challenging activities. These attributes were then discussed with a second academic, knowledgeable in the area, revised and then presented to the skipper to review, add and/or amend as she felt appropriate given her experience of solo ocean sailing. Some items were removed, with minor changes made to the wording of two items. The newly formulated SOPQ was then piloted in two transatlantic sailing events to ensure that the skipper was happy with the structure and content of the questionnaire, in addition to the way in which the data were input and communicated back to the consultant. No additional changes to the SOPQ were required following this pilot testing.

The resulting questionnaire contained three sections. The first involved general daily information (such as the number of nautical miles sailed and the number of hours she spent sleeping, dealing with problems, and suffering from illness/injury). The second section focused on the participant's psychological responses, and asked her 'relative to the following two bi-polar phrases, please indicate how you have felt over the last 24 hours by highlighting the appropriate number'. Twelve bipolar items were rated on a 1 to 10 Likert scale (1 = very happy to 10 = very depressed). The third section asked the skipper to briefly provide some possible reasons for the responses that she had provided.

Two forms of data analysis were conducted on the SOPQ responses. First, mean scores for each attribute were calculated for the duration of the event. Second, the 1 to 10 scale was used to categorise the skipper's responses to each item: a score of 1–3 was low, 4–6 moderate and 7–10 a high response. This enabled the consultant to quantify the percentage of time the skipper was experiencing low, moderate or high levels of the various psychological attributes.

A detailed report summarising the SOPQ findings was supplied to the skipper one week after she had completed the event. Three days later the consultant conducted a face to face interview (lasting approximately 90 minutes) with the skipper to discuss the findings. The general aim of this interview was to raise the skipper's awareness of how her psychological state had changed over the course of the event, what factors had contributed to either positive or negative states, and what coping strategies she had employed to deal with some of the difficult periods whilst alone at sea.

To the author's knowledge, the analysis provided the first published detailed daily monitoring of the psychological state of an extreme environment sport performer. Findings revealed that the skipper was highly physically exhausted 48 per cent of the time and highly sleep deprived 31 per cent over the course of the ninety-nine days at sea (an overview of the descriptive psychological responses can be found in Table 15.1). The skipper averaged 3.5 hours of accumulated sleep per day, which is in line with reports elsewhere in the solo sailing literature (Groslambert et al., 2008; Myers et al., 2008; Stampi, 1989; Weston et al., 2009). Sleep deprivation and physical exhaustion appeared to be closely related throughout the duration of the race in that sleep deprivation was linked to periods of heightened physical exhaustion (Figure 15.2). Furthermore, it was apparent that when she ate poorly she tended to be highly physically exhausted.

TABLE 15.1 Skipper's SOPQ descriptive perceptual responses

SOPQ Bipolar Item *	Mean	Low Percentage Response **	Moderate Percentage Response **	High Percentage Response **
Well rested – very sleep deprived	4.3	53	16	31
Eaten well – eaten poorly	3.0	83	9	8
Not at all lonely – extremely lonely	3.9	60	24	16
Very happy – very depressed	3.0	83	14	3
Mentally very alert – extremely mentally fatigued	3.7	57	38	5
Physically 100% - physically exhausted	6.2	0	52	48
Not at all anxious – extremely anxious	5.2	26	38	36
Feel unhappy in my accomplishments – feel happy in my accomplishments	6.8	6	19	75
Not at all determined to succeed – extremely determined to succeed	7.3	0	13	87
Strongly disliking solo sailing – really enjoying solo sailing	6.6	0	45	55
Very pleasant environmental conditions – horrendous environmental conditions	4.2	38	48	14
Uncomfortable in the environment – comfortable in the environment	6.5	6	19	75

* Bipolar Likert scale from 1 (first phrase) to 10 (second phrase)
** Low, moderate and high percentage responses reflect the percentage of scores between 1-3, 4-6, and 7-10 respectively on the bipolar Likert scale.

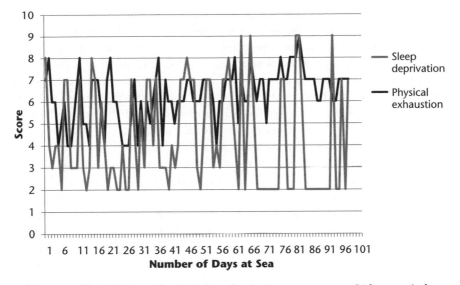

FIGURE 15.2 Physical exhaustion and sleep deprivation responses per 24 hour period

These findings reinforced to the skipper the importance of maintaining a consistent sleep and eat routine to amass sufficient energy reserves to fulfil the various physically demanding tasks on board. Indeed, she had set a provisional target to achieve an average of five hours of sleep per day, and indicated that completing the SOPQ had raised her awareness of her low-sleep pattern, which had then prompted her to sleep more. Integral to this process was the need to have confidence in her own ability to set the yacht up safely enough to allow for sleep. She also emphasised that a dangerous situation could emerge at any time, thus it was important to bank sleep whenever possible to ensure she had sufficient energy to make key decisions and complete actions that would maintain a safe yacht. These approach-focused coping strategies align closely with those identified by skippers in Weston et al.'s (2009) study, and emphasise that the participants must take responsibility for their sleep to ensure they have sufficient energy to fulfil key actions and make critical decisions when it matters most.

The skipper experienced low to moderate levels of mental fatigue on average, and in many instances throughout the ninety-nine days perceived herself to be generally mentally alert (defined by her as the ability to make effective decisions) despite experiencing moderate to high levels of physical exhaustion. Although some extreme environment research suggests that high levels of cognitive performance can be maintained in physically fatigued individuals (Hockey and Sauer, 1996; Maruff et al., 2006), intuitively one would expect the opposite. Indeed, research by Reed et al. (2001) found cognitive performance significantly declined over the course of a four-month Antarctic residency. However, Paulus et al. (2009), in their review of the impact of extreme environment exposure on cognitive performance, conclude that there is insufficient research to suggest 'uniform deterioration' of cognitive performance in extreme environments. They also point out that the unique and specific characteristics of the environment and activity will dictate the relationship between physical exhaustion and cognitive performance. In the case of this skipper, she stated that the solo isolated nature of the sport combined with the potential life-threatening environment forced her to remain mentally alert throughout irrespective of how physically depleted she was. In essence she respected her environment and understood the potentially fatal consequences should she not maintain her mental alertness.

Despite the present findings, previous research has suggested that the physically demanding nature of solo sailing has resulted in detrimental cognitive and sensory impairment in the form of hallucinations (Lewis et al., 1964; Bennet, 1973). The complexity and severity of the environment combined with the physical fatigue necessitates that solo sailors make clear and effective decisions in order to maintain a safe and high-performing yacht (Weston et al., 2009). Despite this assertion no research has specifically examined the relationship between the perception of physical fatigue and cognitive performance over the course of a long-duration sporting event. This research would provide the skippers, support team and practitioners with valuable information about how the demands of the sport impact on cognitive performance. This may lead to the development of specific and targeted coping strategies to facilitate effective cognitive performance when under stressful, physically depleting situations.

Examination of the coping strategies employed by the skipper to deal with the physical exhaustion revealed the importance of sleeping and eating regularly and properly, accepting each situation that materialises, taking control and getting on with the tasks in hand, realising that the effort was being rewarded with progress, receiving acknowledgement from others (such as her support team, partner and family) for her efforts, communicating with others to vent her frustration, in addition to taking inspiration from the comments of supporters (via e-mails). Based on the current findings and those presented elsewhere (e.g. Bennet, 1973; Lewis et al., 1964; Myers et al., 2008; Weston et al., 2009), solo skippers need to prepare for the fact that they will experience sustained levels of physical exhaustion throughout the event, and that they will need to identify, and then draw upon, a range of coping strategies to deal with such difficulties.

Affective responses recorded throughout the event revealed a skipper who was very determined to succeed, generally enjoying her sailing and was happy in her accomplishments. Furthermore, her levels of depression remained relatively low throughout, only rising to high levels 3 per cent of the time. Perceptions of loneliness fluctuated throughout the event but also remained relatively low to moderate, elevating to high levels 16 per cent of the time. Key coping strategies adopted to deal with periods of depression included communicating with her partner, drawing strength from the messages of supporters, solving problems, listening to music and generally trying hard to rationalise her predicament to ensure a more optimistic state.

The strategies adopted by the skipper to improve her depressive mood states align closely to those found in general settings (Thayer, Newman and McLain,

1994) and other extreme sport settings. For example, Knox-Johnson (2004) in his autobiographic account of his 1968 solo sailing circumnavigation, cited several strategies to alleviate a depressed mood state, including engaging in mentally challenging tasks, listening to music, eating and drinking, and visualising other historic sailing patriots looking down and urging him on. Cracknell and Fogle (2006), in their account of a 2,930 mile Atlantic Ocean row, cite favourable progress in comparison to competitors, eating treats, communication from friends, supporters or family, and allowing their mind to wander off to past events or future plans all helped to raise their spirits. Hadow (2005), a solo polar explorer, also cited the importance of focusing on the future and using creative and positive visualisation as effective strategies in improving his mood and distracting him from the rigours of his sport. He also stated that the use of self-talk and communication with others helped to lift his mood and give him the strength to carry on.

Periods of loneliness tended to last only 24 hours, principally due to the dynamic and variable nature of the environment, which would produce a new problem or task that needed solving. However, the skipper did use music, communication with her shore team and partner, and reading e-mails from supporters to cope with the loneliness experienced. General coping strategies used to help deal with loneliness have identified a number of approaches, including accepting and reflecting on the sources of the loneliness, drawing on a social support network, gaining strength through religious faith, engaging in activities, and denying and distancing oneself from the loneliness feelings (Rokach and Brock, 1998). Given the lack of literature examining the experience of loneliness in sporting activities, further investigations into the levels of, and factors contributing to, loneliness in long-duration, isolated environments would be worthwhile. It would also be beneficial to identify specific strategies to combat this feeling.

The most significant affective response experienced by the skipper related to her perception of anxiety. She averaged moderate levels throughout the race, recording high levels of anxiety around a third of the time at sea. These elevated levels of anxiety predominantly occurred on three occasions lasting six to ten days (Figure 15.3). On the first occasion the skipper experienced a significant technical problem on the yacht which caused her concern until she managed to fix it. The second high bout of anxiety was experienced when she received e-mails almost every day regarding the misfortune, injuries and withdrawals of her fellow competitors. This created a great deal of anxiety in her as she began to question whether her yacht would be able to withstand the rigours of the event. The third, and probably most significant, period of elevated anxiety occurred immediately prior to entering the waters around Cape Horn when her weather systems were predicting dangerous weather conditions ahead. The anticipation of these challenging conditions led the skipper to remain highly anxious for several days prior to the storm arriving, as she worried about whether she and her yacht could cope with the conditions she was likely to face. The skipper revealed that when she was in these bad weather conditions her mind was very much focused on dealing with the situation and making the most of the opportunities available. She felt more in control under those situations as she could influence what was happening, whereas immediately prior to the bad weather, the unpredictability and lack of control that she had over the impending situation caused her significant anguish and worry. Such comments align closely to several of the underlying properties of stress (such as event uncertainty, predictability, imminence and temporal uncertainty) that Lazarus and Folkman (1984) assert are likely to lead to an individual perceiving a situation as stressful.

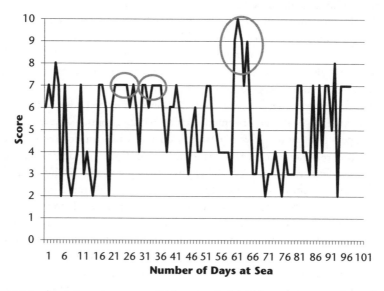

FIGURE 15.3 Anxiety responses per 24 hour period (circles represent prolonged periods of heightened anxiety that were experienced)

Coping strategies employed by the skipper to deal with anxiety included setting various flexible goals to help her through difficult times, taking confidence from past experiences where she had coped in similar or worse conditions, and talking situations over with the shore team. Furthermore, she tried to stay in the 'here and now' to ensure a safe, performing yacht rather than worrying about the perils of fellow competitors or what weather system might materialise in 24 hours' time.

Research examining the affective or emotional impact of prolonged exposure to extreme environmental activities suggests more significant affective responses than those found in the present case study. For instance, early research examining individuals in polar environments found increased depression, irritability and hostility (Gunderson, 1966, cited in Paulus et al., 2009). Research examining military personnel in various extreme environments either in simulated training exercises or full deployment have found significant deterioration in mood states (Lieberman et al., 2005; Vasterling et al., 2006), in some instances reaching clinical levels (Bardwell, Ensign and Mills, 2005). Despite these findings, research has found that exposure to extreme polar environments can result in quite significant mood variability, which includes both positive and negative fluctuations in mood responses (Palinkas and Houseal, 2000; Palinkas, Houseal and Miller, 2000; Palinkas, 2003). These authors conclude that it is the individual's cognitive appraisal of their current situation that will significantly influence the mood state reported. Thus despite the difficulty of the environment encountered, if an individual is accomplishing goals set or developing more effective coping strategies, their mood state will be protected or indeed improved.

In the case of this skipper, she was making excellent progress and achieving a good position in her first Vendée Globe event, which was reflected in her positive enjoyment and performance accomplishment responses. Furthermore, the data revealed that she experienced extremely difficult environmental conditions only 14 per cent of the time she was at sea. Hence for the majority of the time she was experiencing environmental conditions with which she was familiar, and while they were challenging, they were unlikely to represent significant threat to her well-being. Therefore, despite difficult and often highly stressful situations occurring, the skipper adopted a predominantly challenge appraisal approach to each situation, reflecting more positive affective responses.

In line with the propositions of Lazarus (1991, 1999; Lazarus and Folkman, 1984), it was clear from the post-event skipper interview that her appraisals of various stressors encountered markedly influenced the psychological responses that she recorded. The more effective she was in appraising the stressor, the more positive her psychological response. There were of course situations where she struggled to adopt a positive appraisal of the situation and indeed did fear for her life. However, it was also noticeable that over time the skipper developed a greater ability to adopt coping strategies to suit the demands faced and indeed to positively influence her emotional state. By her own admission, prior to the event she was not into 'psycho babble' and almost reluctantly got involved in the psychological monitoring as part of a larger sport science support programme (see O'Hara et al., 2009). However, through the process of monitoring her psychological state and reflecting on the responses in the interview, she did acknowledge the important role psychology can play in influencing her performance, and indeed learned a number of key lessons that will serve her well in future races. Such lessons included the need to maintain clear and effective communication with the shore team, being wary of difficult impending environmental conditions but making sure to sail in the 'here and now', ensuring that every human's fundamental desire for food and sleep are fulfilled on a daily basis, and taking confidence from performing well and surviving in the toughest of environments and events. Finally, the most important lesson related to her improved awareness of how the environment and the physically demanding nature of SOES influences the way in which she thinks, feels and behaves.

In summary, whilst acknowledging the principal limitations of case study methodology (such as the difficulty in generalizing the findings to a wider population), the present example provided the first thorough and systematic examination of a solo ocean skipper's psychological state throughout a long-duration circumnavigation event. The client–centred electronic daily monitoring combined with the production and discussion of a detailed client report enabled the skipper and her shore team to become more aware of how the demands of the activity impacted on the skipper's psychological and affective state. Importantly this approach also provided a basis from which to discuss the effectiveness of coping strategies employed, and thus act as a useful learning tool to facilitate more effective planning for, and performance in, future events.

Practical implications for activities performed in extreme environments

Drawing upon the theoretical propositions of Lazarus (1999) and stress literature in sport (Nicholls et al., 2009a,b), it is apparent that people appraise, respond and react to stressful activities in an idiosyncratic manner. This is influenced by the participant's past experiences, their personality and the specificity of the environment that they encounter. However Weston et al.'s (2009) research suggests there is also some commonality in the coping strategies that individuals adopt to deal with specific stressors. It is also evident from the case study outlined and other related research (e.g. Lane et al., 2004) and theory (Lazarus, 1991, 1999), that an individual's appraisal of environmental demands will influence their emotional state. Furthermore, the identification of effective coping strategies to deal with specific stressors and regulate an athlete's emotional state will be critical in ensuring high performance and safety.

Clearly individuals wishing to participate in activities performed in extreme environments require meticulous planning to prepare themselves and their equipment for the rigours of the environment they are about to enter. Participants and their support team must plan for the worst possible scenarios in the knowledge that such a situation might arise and that their preparation may be the difference between their living or dying. It is recommended that the planning should involve compiling a list of possible 'what if' scenarios relating to possible technical, physical, psychological and tactical eventualities (Weston et al., 2009). Should the participant or support team have insufficient experience or expertise in the sport, they should enlist the assistance of elite performers to draw from their experience (Devonport et al., in review).

Planning tactics may be significant in helping the athlete to chart a course out of a potentially difficult situation (such as a difficult weather system), and therefore discussions with experts knowledgeable in the terrain or weather systems would be advisable both before and during the particular event (as observed in Caffari, 2007). Technical scenarios may include various forms of equipment breaking down in either isolation or a possible sequence (Caffari, 2007). Hence advice needs to be obtained from specialists relating to each of the various technical parts of the yacht and a detailed plan to solve potential technical problems drawn up for the skipper. Indeed, it would be worthwhile having these specialists on call during the event should a problem emerge. Physical preparation/difficulties may relate to the various physical demands or tasks that will be required of the individual (such as sustained walking in -40°C, and requiring dexterity to solve problems in cold, dark environments) in order to maintain performance and in some extreme instances save their life. The skipper in the case study acknowledged the support she received from strength and conditioning specialists in addition to physiotherapists prior to the event to maximise her physical preparation (O'Hara et al., 2009). Furthermore, advice was sought from biomechanists to optimise the ergonomic aspects of her performance on the yacht (such as in grinding and winching). Given the extent of the physical demands of performing in extreme environments, it would be useful for performers to elicit sports science and medicine support to prepare their body for the specific rigours of their sporting activity.

In order to prepare a performer's mind for an extreme environment, it would be invaluable for the performer to engage in a practice event which simulates the type of environmental demands (physical, technical, tactical, psychological) they are likely to face. This would be beneficial for a number of reasons. First, such an event would force the person to experience the physical hardship, psychological strain and related negative emotional reactions (such as loneliness, depression, anxiety and mental fatigue) associated with the activity. This would help the performer to establish the limits of their personal capabilities, be more aware of the consequences of their actions, and identify the line between optimal performance and safety. These have been found to be important in helping solo skippers to cope in extreme environments (Caffari, 2007; Weston et al., 2009). Second, the simulated practice would offer performers the opportunity to initiate different coping strategies and evaluate their effectiveness in helping to deal with demands faced and their related emotional responses. This would then provide a useful basis from which to discuss stress and general emotion management strategies with a sport psychologist to facilitate psychological adaptation to the extreme environment. Finally, and importantly, evidence suggests that drawing on successful past experiences can provide confidence and motivation when challenging situations occur and difficult decisions need to be made (Knox-Johnson, 2004; Weston et al., 2009). Successfully achieving various tasks within a simulated practice run may have a positive impact on confidence and motivation going into the targeted event. Indeed, the use of simulated stress training has been strongly advocated and employed within military settings, where similar mental and physical hardship, in addition to a direct threat to an individual's life, are particularly evident (Driskell et al., 2008).

Staying in the 'here and now' and drawing on problem-focused coping strategies have been identified as essential in helping performers to deal with a situation (Weston et al., 2009). Time wasted focusing on problems or eventualities that the performer has no control over will only lead to heightened anxiety and more negative emotional responses. Hence, whilst it is important that performers are aware of the terrain, weather or difficulties ahead, they must stay focused on actions, behaviours and decisions that can be influenced at any one moment in time.

Social support has also been cited as an important psychological resource which can facilitate performance (Freeman, Rees and Hardy, 2009; Rees and

Hardy, 2000; see Chapter 5). Indeed, a variety of different forms of social support have been identified in the general sport literature including emotional (for example, for dealing with difficult times), esteem (for instance, to reinforce confidence and help cope with worry or apprehension), informational (such as to help with performance difficulties), and tangible (for example, to reduce worries associated with practical problems) support (Rees and Hardy, 2000). It is clear from the available extreme environment research that a performer's support team can play an essential role in facilitating safe and effective performance. More often than not the support team will be physically remote from their performer, therefore it is vital that performers and their support team establish the most effective methods of communication in order to maximise the performer's cognitive and emotional state throughout the event. This may involve specific training in communication styles and social support strategies prior to the event, or at least discussing possible scenarios and the best ways in which the support team can assist their performer.

Finally, it was clear from the case study presented that monitoring the skipper's psychological state and then discussing how to cope during difficult times was a worthwhile exercise. However the methodological approach adopted was limited to discussing the data after the event had been completed. Clearly it would be more beneficial to the client if such detailed discussion could be initiated at regular intervals throughout long-duration events in order to facilitate more effective coping, and thus performance and safety during the actual event.

Future research

Given the paucity of rigorous scientific research examining sporting performance in extreme environments, there is a wealth of important further research that is necessary. It would be useful to begin by extending the qualitative stress and coping work of Weston et al. (2009) to other extreme environmental sports (such as mountaineering, desert or Antarctic explorations) by employing similar one-to-one interviews or focus group methodologies. The development of in-depth knowledge associated with coping in these sports would provide an excellent basis from which more quantitative intervention-based research designs could be utilised.

Fundamental to this initial research is the need to specifically link the coping strategies employed to each particular stressor in order that the findings can be directly applied within the specific sport setting (Weston et al., 2009).

One of the critical limitations of qualitative enquiry conducted out with the duration of an event relates to the retrospective recall of information. Hence the employment of during-event psychological monitoring strategies would provide a more temporally accurate representation of the coping process. Indeed, recent research in rugby union (Nicholls et al., 2006) and golf (Nicholls, et al., 2005a) has found electronic daily diary approaches to be useful in describing the stress and coping process.

An important advancement in the recent coping research has been to focus on evaluating the effectiveness of coping strategies in addition to the situations when and where the strategies are most effective (Nicholls et al., 2005b; Nicholls et al., 2009b). Given the distinct lack of coping effectiveness research in extreme environment sports, it is important that future research attempts to examine when, where and how effective various coping approaches are in order that more accurate advice and support can be provided to performers.

Lazarus's (1991, 1999) cognitive motivational relational (CMR) theory asserts that emotions have a strong role to play in the stress and coping process. CMR hypothesises that emotions are determined by an individual's cognitive appraisal of various stressors, in addition to the coping actions enacted by that individual. CMR emphasises the importance of examining stress, coping and emotions together in order to fully understand how an individual reacts and responds to a stressful event (Lazarus, 1999). However, little research in sport has done so (Nicholls, Hemmings and Clough, 2010). Hence, further innovative research is needed to examine the interplay between stress, coping and emotions to fully explain how individuals respond to stressful events in extreme environment sports.

If these research suggestions can be realised within a sport or collection of sports, they would provide a knowledge base from which specific, targeted coping intervention research could be initiated. Given the unique extreme sport complexities and the idiosyncratic nature of each performer's personality and coping preferences, the employment of a single-subject, multiple-baseline-across-individuals design (Martin and Pear, 2003) would provide an appropriate means of examining the efficacy of specific coping interventions.

Sports in extreme environments often involve performers being isolated from any physical support. Furthermore, given the range and severity of the stressors experienced in these sports, remote social support is likely to form an important strategy in helping athletes perform, cope and survive. Despite performers indicating that they receive social support whilst engaging in their chosen extreme environment sport (e.g. Caffari, 2007; Cracknell and Fogle, 2006; MacArthur, 2006), to the author's knowledge, no scientific research has examined the characteristics of providing effective social support to athletes performing in remote extreme environments. Hence qualitative research examining the type, function and benefits of different social support strategies employed within extreme environment sports may help to uncover recommendations on how to optimise remote social support. In order to achieve this objective, it is necessary that the perceptions not only of the performer, but of those individuals who provide the support (such as the race director, support team, key family members or friends) are examined in tandem. Furthermore, given the recent successful implementation of social support interventions within land-based sports (e.g. Freeman, et al., 2009), it would be worthwhile examining the impact of such interventions in extreme sport activities.

In line with these research suggestions, it is essential that a detailed set of evidence-based coping recommendations is compiled for each extreme environment sport in order to maximise safety. The focus of such recommendations would be to provide clear guidelines for performers (and their support staff) as to how best prepare for, react to, and cope with the stressors they are likely to encounter in their sport. Clearly, given the lack of research in extreme environment sports and the number of further research suggestions outlined above, the development of such detailed guidelines is some way off. However this must be the ultimate goal in order to minimise fatalities and ensure safe and successful participation in sports that are becoming ever more popular.

General summary

Sporting performers who participate in extreme environments are required to deal with a range of often unpredictable and uncontrollable stressors. Learning to cope in such challenging environments is important not only to successful performance but in some instances to survival. Given the complexity and sometimes volatile nature of extreme environments, research examining stress, coping and emotions in these contexts has been difficult to conduct, resulting in a lack of academic literature to draw upon. Given the potentially fatal consequences of sports in these environments, more innovative research is needed to understand the stress and coping experience, in addition to providing important practical advice for performers wishing to participate in the future.

Acknowledgements

The author would like to thank Dee Caffari for completing the SOPQ each day for ninety-nine days at sea, an unbelievable feat in itself! He would also like to acknowledge the support of Jo Uffendell, who played an important role in facilitating the data collection.

References

Bardwell, W. A., Ensign, W. Y. and Mills, P. J. (2005). Negative mood endures after completion of high-altitude military training. *Annals of Behavioral Medicine*, 29, 64–69.

Bennet, G. (1973). Medical and psychological problems in the 1972 singlehanded transatlantic yacht race. *The Lancet*, 2, 747–754.

Bennet, G. (1974). Psychological breakdown at sea: hazards of singlehanded ocean sailing. *British Journal of Medical Psychology*, 47, 189–210.

Burke, S. M. and Orlick, T. (2003). Mental strategies of elite high altitude climbers: overcoming adversity on Mount Everest. *Journal of Human Performance in Extreme Environments*, 7, 15–22.

Butler, R. J. and Hardy, L. (1992). The performance profile: theory and application. *The Sport Psychologist*, 6, 253–264.

Caffari, D. (2007). *Against the flow: The inspiring story of a teacher turned record-breaking yachtswoman*. London: Adlard Coles Nautical.

Cohen, S. (1988). Psychosocial models of the role of social support in the etiology of physical disease. *Health Psychology*, 7, 269–297.

Cohen, S., Gottlieb, B. H. and Underwood, L. G. (2000). Social support and health. In S. Cohen, L. G. Underwood and B. H. Gottlieb (eds), *Social support measurement and intervention: A guide for health and social scientists* (pp. 3–25). New York: Oxford University Press.

Cohen, S. and Wills, T. A. (1985). Stress, social support and the buffering hypothesis. *Psychological Bulletin*, 98, 310–357.

Cracknell, J. and Fogle, B. (2006). *The crossing: Conquering the Atlantic in the world's toughest rowing race.* London: Atlantic Books.

Deci, E. F. and Ryan, R. M. (1985). *Intrinsic motivation and self determination in human behavior.* New York: Plenum Press.

Devonport, T. J., Lane, A. M., Davies, K. A. and Lloyd, J. (in review). *Keeping your cool: A case study of a female explorers solo North Pole expedition.*

Dinges, D. F., Orne, M. T., Orne, E. C. and Evans, F. J. (1980). *Voluntary self-control of sleep to facilitate quasi-continuous performance* (NTIS N. AD-A102264). Maryland, USA: US Army Medical Research and Development Command.

Driskell, J. E., Salas, E., Johnston, J. H. and Wollert, T. N. (2008). Stress exposure training: an event-based approach. In P. A. Hancock and J. L. Szalma (eds), *Performance under stress* (pp. 271–286). Aldershot, UK: Ashgate.

Fletcher, D., Hanton, S. and Mellalieu, S. D. (2006). An organizational stress review: conceptual and theoretical issues in competitive sport. In S. Hanton and S.D. Mellalieu (eds), *Literature reviews in sport psychology* (pp. 321–373). New York: Nova Science.

Freeman, P., Rees, T. and Hardy, L. (2009). An intervention to increase social support and improve performance. *Journal of Applied Sport Psychology*, 21, 186–200.

Gottlieb, B. H. (2000). Selecting and planning support interventions. In S. Cohen, L. G. Underwood and B. H. Gottlieb (eds), *Social support measurement and intervention: A guide for health and social scientists* (pp. 195–220). New York: Oxford University Press.

Groslambert, A., Candau, R. B. and Millet, G. P. (2008). Effect of sleep deprivation on anxiety and perceived fatigue during a one-man Atlantic Ocean crossing on a sport catamaran. *Environment and Behavior*, 40, 96–110.

Gunderson, E. K. (1966). *Adaptation to extreme environments: Prediction of performance* (Rep No. 66-17). San Diego, USA: Navy Medical Neuropsychiatric Research Unit.

Gunnarsson, I., Bäck, H., Jones, I. and Olsson, T. (2004). Stress recovery during an ocean boat race. *Stress and Health*, 20, 165–171.

Hadow, P. (2005). *Solo: The North Pole: Alone and unsupported.* London: Penguin.

Hockey, G. R. and Sauer, J. (1996). Cognitive fatigue and complex decision making under prolonged isolation and confinement. *Advances in Space Biology Medicine*, 5, 309–330.

Kawakami, N., Akachi, K., Shimizu, H., Haratani, T., Kobayashi, F., Ishizaki, M., Hayashi, T., Fujita, O., Aizawa, Y., Miyazaki, S., Hiro, H., Hashimoto, S. and Araki, S. (2000). Job strain, social support in the workplace, and haemoglobin A_{1c} in Japanese men. *Occupational and Environmental Medicine*, 57, 805–809.

Knox-Johnson, R. (2004). *A world of my own: The first ever non-stop solo round the world voyage.* London: Adlard Coles Nautical.

Lane, A. M., Terry, P.C., Stevens, M. J., Barney, S. and Dinsdale, S. L. (2004). Mood responses to athletic performance in extreme environments. *Journal of Sports Sciences*, 22, 886–897.

Lazarus, R. S. (1991). *Emotion and adaptation.* New York: Oxford University Press.

Lazarus, R. S. (1999). *Stress and emotion: A new synthesis.* New York: Springer.

Lazarus, R. S. and Folkman, S. (1984). *Stress, appraisal and coping.* New York: Springer.

Léger, D., Elbaz, M., Raffray, T., Metlaine, A., Bayon, V. and Duforez, F. (2008). Sleep management and the performance of eight sailors in the Tour de France à la voile yacht race. *Journal of Sports Sciences*, 26, 21–28.

Leon, G. R., List, N. and Magor, G. (2004). Personal experiences and team effectiveness during a commemorative trek in the high Arctic. *Environment and Behavior*, 36, 386–401.

Lewis, H. E., Harries, J. M., Lewis, D. H. and de Monchaux, C. (1964). Voluntary solitude: studies of men in a singlehanded transatlantic sailing race. *The Lancet*, 1, 1431–1435.

Lieberman, H. R., Bathalon, G. P., Falco, C. M., Kramer, F. M., Morgan III, C. A. and Niro, P. (2005). Severe decrements in cognition function and mood induced by sleep loss, heat, dehydration, and under nutrition during simulated combat. *Biological Psychiatry*, 57, 422–429.

MacArthur, E. (2006). *Race against time*. London: Penguin.

Martin, G. and Pear, J. (2003). *Behavior modification: What it is and how to do it*. Englewood Cliffs, N.J.: Prentice-Hall.

Maruff, P., Snyder, P., McStephen, M., Collie, A. and Darby, D. (2006). Cognitive deterioration associated with an expedition in an extreme desert environment. *British Journal of Sports Medicine*, 40, 556–560.

Myers, S. D., Leamon, S. M., Nevola, V. R. and Llewellyn, M. G. L. (2008). Energy expenditure during a single-handed transatlantic yacht race. *British Journal of Sports Medicine*, 42, 285–288.

Nicholls, A. R., Hemmings, B. and Clough, P. J. (2010). Stress appraisals, emotions, and coping among international adolescent golfers. *Scandinavian Journal of Medicine and Science in Sports*, 20, 346–355.

Nicholls, A. R., Holt, N. L., Polman, R. C. J. and Bloomfield, J. (2006). Stressors, coping and coping effectiveness among professional rugby union players. *The Sport Psychologist*, 20, 314–329.

Nicholls, A. R., Holt, N. L., Polman, R. C. J. and James, D. W. G. (2005a). Stress and coping among international adolescent golfers. *Journal of Applied Sport Psychology*, 17, 333–340.

Nicholls, A. R., Holt, N. L., Polman, R. C. J. and James, D. W. G. (2005b). Stress, coping, and coping effectiveness among international adolescent golfers. *Journal of Sports Sciences*, 23, 166–167.

Nicholls, A. R., Jones, C. R., Polman, R. C. J. and Borkoles, E. (2009a). Acute sport-related stressors, coping and emotion among professional rugby union players during training and matches. *Scandinavian Journal of Medicine and Science in Sports*, 19, 113–120.

Nicholls, A. R., Levy, A. R., Grice, A. and Polman, R. C. J. (2009b). Stress appraisals, coping, and coping effectiveness among international cross-country runners during training and competition. *European Journal of Sports Science*, 9, 285–293.

Nicholls, A. R. and Polman, R. C. J. (2007). Coping in sport: a systematic review. *Journal of Sports Sciences*, 24, 1–21.

O'Hara, J., Fearnley, D., Sutton, L., Tomlinson, E., King, R. F. G. J., Radley, D., Wright, A., Brightmore, A., Hind, K., Weston, N. J. V., Thelwell, R. C., King, A., Isted, A. and Cooke, C. B. (2009). Sport science support for a female competitor in the Vendée Globe 2008 single handed sailing race. *Journal of Sports Sciences*, 27 (S2), S18.

Osmond, L. and Rothwell, J. (Directors). (2006). *Deep Water* [motion picture]. United Kingdom: IFC Films.

Palinkas, L. A. (2003). The psychology of isolated and confined environments: understanding human behavior in Antarctica. *American Psychologist*, 58, 353–363.

Palinkas, L. A. and Houseal, M. (2000). Stages of change in mood and behavior during a winter in Antarctica. *Environment and Behavior*, 32, 128–141.

Palinkas, L. A., Houseal, M. and Miller, C. (2000). Sleep and mood during a winter in Antarctica. *International Journal of Circumpolar Health*, 59, 63–73.

Paulus, M. P., Potterat, E. G., Taylor, M. K., Van Orden, K. F., Bauman, J., Momen, N., Padilla, G. A. and Swain, J. L. (2009). A neuroscience approach to optimizing brain resources for human performance in extreme environments. *Neurosciences and Biobehavioral Reviews*, 33, 1080–1088.

Reed, H. L., Reedy, K. R., Palinkas, L. A., Van Do, N., Finney, N. S., Case, H. S., LeMar, H. J., Wright, J. and Thomas, J. (2001). Impairment in cognitive and exercise performance during prolonged Antarctic residence: effect of thyroxine supplementation in the polar triiodothyronine syndrome. *Journal of Clinical Endocrinology and Metabolism*, 86, 110–116.

Rees, T. and Hardy, L. (2000). An investigation of the social support experiences of high-level sports performers. *The Sport Psychologist*, 14, 327–347.

Rokach, A. and Brock, H. (1998). Coping with loneliness. *Journal of Psychology*, 132, 107–127.

Schuck, P. (1998). Glycated haemoglobin as a physiological measure of stress and its relations to some psychological stress indicators. *Behavioral Medicine*, 24, 89–94.

Stampi, C. (1989). Polyphasic sleep strategies improve prolonged sustained performance: a field study on 99 sailors. *Work and Stress*, 3, 41–45.

Suedfeld, P. (1987). Extreme and unusual environments. In D. Stokols and I. Altman (eds), *Handbook of environmental psychology* (pp. 863–887). New York: Wiley.

Tenenbaum, G., Kamata, A. and Hayashi, K. (2007). Measurement in sport and exercise psychology: a new outlook on selected issues of reliability and validity. In G. Tenenbaum and R. C. Eklund (eds), *Handbook of sport psychology* (3rd ed., pp. 757–773). N.J.: Wiley & Sons.

Thayer, R. E., Newman, R. and McLain, T. M. (1994). Self-regulation of mood: strategies for changing a bad mood, raising energy, and reducing tension. *Journal of Personality and Social Psychology*, 67, 910–925.

Thelwell, R. C., Weston, N. J. V. and Greenlees, I. A. (2007). Batting on a sticky wicket: identifying sources of stress and associated coping strategies for professional cricket batsmen. *Psychology of Sport and Exercise*, 8, 219–232.

Vasterling, J. J., Proctor, S. P., Amoroso, P., Kane, R., Heeren, T. and White, R. F. (2006). Neuropsychological outcomes of army personnel following deployment to the Iraq war. *Journal of the American Medical Association*, 296, 519–529.

Weston, N. J. V. and Thelwell, R. C. (2009). Psychological profiling during the Vendée Globe 2008 single handed sailing race. In A. Abraham (ed.), Proceedings of the British Association of Sport and Exercise Sciences Conference, 27, S2, (S21). *Journal of Sports Sciences*

Weston, N. J. V., Thelwell, R. C., Bond, S. and Hutchings, N. (2009). Stress and coping in single handed around the world ocean sailing. *Journal of Applied Sport Psychology*, 21, 460–474.

Zitzmann, M. and Nieschlag, E. (2001). Testosterone levels in healthy men and the relation to behavioural and physical characteristics: facts and constructs. *European Journal of Endocrinology*, 144, 183–197.

16

COPING AND EMOTION IN SPORT

Future directions

Joanne Thatcher, Marc Jones and David Lavallee

I have a big picture outlook .... I am willing to fall, and I understand that it's OK to fall, but I am going to get back up. I may take a step back, but in the end I am going to take a giant leap forward.

(Tiger Woods quoted in Owen, 2006, p. 26)

The preceding chapters in this book illustrate that coping and emotion in sport is a vibrant area of study, and this is reflected in the diversity of topics covered, theoretical approaches employed, and the geographical spread of the authors. Collectively the chapters provide a full description of 'what we know' that informs practice and guides future study in coping and emotion in sport. In this chapter we outline some of the themes for future work in sport on coping and emotion. These are our current thoughts on the area having been involved in editing this book for eighteen months. This is not an exhaustive list of areas for future work, nor a summary of the research suggestions highlighted in each chapter, but rather a reflection of key themes that we feel emerge from the body of work as a whole in this book.

Performance issues

Understanding the relationship between emotion and sport performance is an important endeavour. However, many studies have considered the association between emotion and global sport performance (e.g. Jones, Mace and Williams, 2000). Unfortunately such research is limited in that it does not tell us how emotions impact performance. Future research should focus specifically on the relationship between emotion and sub-components of performance, and importantly the mechanisms by which this occurs. Research has explored the relationship between anxiety and sub-components of performance (e.g. Collins et al., 2001; Parfitt and Pates, 1999; Wilson, Vine and Wood, 2009). However more work needs to be done, considering a broad range of emotions in line with that exploring the relationship between hope, anger and sub-components of performance (Woodman et al., 2009). While anxiety is an emotion that many athletes have experienced, and some experience frequently, it is by no means the only one. What may be considered an overemphasis on anxiety is not peculiar to sport psychology. Over twenty years ago, Lazarus, Coyne and Folkman (1984) suggested that it seemed as if anxiety had become the prime emotion for all efforts in psychology research. With this in mind, a movement towards positive psychology (e.g. Seligman, 2003) and research which considers a broader range of emotions (e.g. Hanin and Syrjä, 1995) are developments to be welcomed (see also McCarthy, Chapter 9; Babkes, Partridge and Moore, Chapter 7).

Notwithstanding the need for more research into the emotion–performance relationship there is currently enough theoretical and research evidence to suggest that emotions can impact the performance levels of athletes (e.g. Hanin, 2000; Lazarus, 2000; Vallerand and Blanchard, 2000). It is hardly controversial to suggest that for nearly all athletes at some time, some emotions may have some impact on some aspects of performance. Sport psychologists will therefore encounter athletes who experience debilitating emotions during competition, and it is therefore essential to have a range of strategies that can be used to regulate emotions (e.g. Jones, 2003; Uphill, McCarthy and Jones, 2009). Emotion regulation refers to 'the processes by which individuals influence which emotions they have, when they have them, and how they experience and express these emotions' (Gross, 1998, p. 275). As such, emotion regulation is considered to be distinct from coping, in that the primary focus of coping is on decreasing negative emotional experience, while emotion regulation may include processes such as maintaining or augmenting positive emotions (Gross, 1998).

Adopting strategies to regulate emotions may in fact be costly for individuals (see Hagger et al., 2010). Self-control – that is, any attempt to override one's responses – draws on, and depletes, a limited pool of resources that is available for controlling all emotions, thoughts and behaviours (Baumeister and Heatherton, 1996). For example, participants required to suppress emotions performed worse on a subsequent anagram task (Baumeister et al., 1998, study 3). There may even be physical consequences from cognitive self-regulation (e.g. Bray et al., 2008). The potential cost of regulating emotions in athletes, coaches and officials is an underexplored area in sport. Future research could consider whether using techniques to regulate emotions that are well learned and automatic deplete the central resource for self-control in the same way as emotion-control techniques that are novel and under conscious control. Further, if emotion-control techniques that are new and effortful deplete the central resource for self-control, but ones that are well learned do not, it would be useful to understand at what point this change occurs. On a broader scale, if costs to emotion regulation are identified, it may not always be worthwhile to try to regulate emotions. For example, suggesting to an anxious athlete that efforts must be made to control anxiety may, at times, be worse for performance than simply allowing the anxiety to occur. Future studies that explore this more fundamental proposition may represent the first step in this research endeavour.

Determining the usefulness of the strategies proposed for emotion regulation is also an area worthy of further research. In common with many other psychological strategies, the evidence points towards the effectiveness, rather than the efficacy, of emotion–regulation strategies. To explain, the efficacy of an intervention is determined when an intervention group is compared with a comparison group under controlled conditions (see Seligman, 1995), and in general the research in sport fails to achieve some of the criteria required to test the efficacy of an intervention (for example, that participants in a control group are exposed to placebos). Rather, most of the research demonstrates that strategies can be effective in the way they would normally be delivered out in the field under less controlled conditions (such as pre and post data with a specific group or individual).

The antecedents of emotions and the role of coping

It is important for sport psychologists to be able to answer the question 'why do athletes respond emotionally?' Understanding how emotions arise has implications for the efficacy of emotional control strategies. Interventions that 'stop' an emotion occurring are likely to be more desirable than those that aim to deal with an emotion when it occurs. For example, because reappraising a stimulus stops the emotion occurring and requires less cognitive processing than strategies which suppress an emotion once it occurs (Richards and Gross, 2000), it may be considered a more advantageous strategy for athletes. Accordingly, research which untangles and clarifies the cognitive processes involved in emotion generation (e.g. Pensgaard and Duda, 2003; Uphill and Jones, 2007; Vallerand, 1987) is to be welcomed.

Of particular interest in sport is the perception of emotional symptoms in relation to performance. Sport psychologists have led the way in research exploring perceptions of anxiety symptoms (see Wagstaff, Mellalieu and Hanton, Chapter 8). Yet, understanding of whether positive perceptions of anxiety change the nature of the emotional experience is still unclear (e.g. Jones and Uphill, 2004). Further, the conceptual worth of research into perceptions of anxiety symptoms has recently been questioned, and a positive perception of symptoms may simply represent the absence of any perceived anxiety (Lundqvist, Kentta and Raglin, 2010). Further research is needed to understand whether anxiety, and in particular high levels of anxiety, can ever be perceived as helpful to performance, and whether perceiving anxiety as helpful changes the valence of the emotion (for instance, anxiety perceived as helpful to performance becomes excitement).

In understanding the cognitive processes involved in emotion generation it is necessary to consider the role of coping. It could be argued that the distinction made between coping and emotion is artificial and does not mirror what occurs in the 'real world'. Throughout this volume authors have illustrated the integration between the two concepts (although emotion and coping are dealt with separately in the chapters on theoretical perspectives). Greater emphasis on the integration of coping and emotion as evidenced in some studies (e.g. Pensgaard and Duda, 2003; Ntoumanis and Biddle, 2000) and many of the chapters in this volume is both necessary and fitting.

While understanding how emotions arise is an important endeavour, it is also a difficult one. First, athletes may not be able to articulate why they respond emotionally because they lack the linguistic ability to do so. Second, athletes may not be aware why they respond emotionally. Jones (2003) suggested that understanding the role of conscious and unconscious processing in emotion generation is an important avenue for sport psychologists, and cites an example provided by Lazarus (1991) to illustrate this point. Lazarus outlined that although most people know that flying is the safest form of travel (statistically at least), it does not stop the same people being very anxious when they fly. The appraisal of stimuli at different levels may help explain why cognitive-behavioural modification techniques do not always work, as they may change the conscious appraisal of a situation but do little to alter the subconscious appraisal of the stimulus that might determine the emotional reaction (Jones, 2003). For example, a soccer player recovering from a broken leg may believe that when the bone is healed it will be as strong as it was before the break, and therefore no more likely to break in subsequent challenges than it was previously. Yet the same player may still feel anxious and reticent about engaging in challenges on their return to competition. Unconscious processing of stimuli may help explain why athletes are not aware why they respond emotionally. Further, not only may unconscious processing influence emotions, the autonomic arousal associated with an emotion may guide decision making and performance in performance settings for reasons of which we are unaware (c.f. Bechara et al., 1997). Yet there has been no research of that nature in performance settings. Exploring this area may help explain why performers often rely on their instinct (for instance, a baseball pitcher who just 'feels' what the right pitch is for his opponent). See Kihlstrom et al. (2000) for a detailed discussion of conscious and unconscious processing in emotion.

Neglected populations and environments

As with many other areas of psychology, our understanding of coping and emotion in sport is based mostly on data collected from university populations. There are populations and environments not covered in this book, or in sufficient detail in the extant literature, where there is the potential for future work.

As noted in the future research section in Weston's chapter (Chapter 16), studies examining the interplay between stress, coping and emotions in extreme environment sports could help inform targeted interventions. We feel such research has the potential to go further and contribute to the growing research base on extreme and hostile environments across psychology. Research in military contexts (e.g. Norwood, Ursano and Gabbay, 1997) as well as situations such as the recent collapse of a mine in Chile (e.g. British Psychological Society, 2010) could be informed by well-designed research in sporting contexts. Conceptual exchange needs to be fostered among investigators who would otherwise be isolated in their specialisations. Unfortunately, most existing institutions for the dissemination of research findings (such as conferences and journals) promote communication with others within the same discipline, while fewer promote cross-fertilisation with those in quite different areas. One possible outlet for dissemination of work in the area is the *Journal of Human Performance in Extreme Environments*.

One population worthy of more research is children and young athletes. Understanding children and young athletes' affective responses to sport is an area of increasing research interest. Enjoyment is reported to be one of the most important predictors of sport commitment in youth athletes (Babkes, Partridge and Moore, Chapter 7; Carpenter and Scanlan, 1998). Accordingly, understanding sources of enjoyment in children and young athletes is an important area of research (e.g. McCarthy and Jones, 2007; McCarthy, Jones and Clark-Carter, 2008). Further, the use of psychological techniques such as attribution training (e.g. Sinnott and Biddle, 1998) may help children and young athletes cope with competition in a way that increases the likelihood of a positive affective response (such as enjoyment), which may have substantial benefits in increasing commitment and adherence to sport. This is clearly important, not only in sport but also in exercise settings, given growing concerns over the sedentary nature of the population in industrialised countries (Biddle and Mutrie, 2008). Further work, which considers the development of coping skills in children and young athletes, is also apt. Understanding how coping develops in children and young athletes and what coping strategies are effective at varying stages of development would provide valuable information for sport psychologists working with this specific population.

Sport officials can often have a substantial impact on competition outcome, and have to deal with a number of stressors. While research has outlined that a range of factors may impact the decisions made by officials (e.g. Frank and Gilovich, 1988; Jones, Paull and Erskine, 2002; Plessner, 1999) there is little work outlining how officials cope with the stress of competition, the emotions experienced, and their consequences. One exception has been Rainey's work on burnout and sources of stress in officials (e.g. Rainey and Hardy, 1999). Similar to sport officials, coaches can clearly have a substantial impact on competition outcome, and have to deal with a number of stressors, yet coping and emotion research in this population is equally scant.

Sport not only impacts individuals directly involved in the competition such as athletes, coaches and officials, it also impacts those who have an emotional investment in the athletes or teams involved, for example, fans, or the family and friends of the athlete. Some research has focused on fans' emotional responses to success and failure (e.g. Banyard and Shevlin, 2001), and involvement with a team (e.g. Wann, 2006). However in general these specific populations remain underrepresented in the coping and emotion research in sport.

Coping with positive experiences

Research has typically focused on athletes' abilities to cope with, and the consequences of, negative events. Yet understanding the emotions experienced following positive events and how to cope with positive emotions and positive events is both an interesting and relevant topic (Jackson, Mayocchi and Dover, 1998; Kreiner-Phillips and Orlick, 1993). As Reid (Chapter 13) outlined, even following successful events athletes may experience feelings of loss. A negative impact of a positive event, in this case becoming world snooker champion, is illustrated in the following quote by Mark Williams:

> After that win [World Championships 2000], I went downhill – rapidly. I was still getting to a few finals but I wasn't practicing at all. I was taking things for granted. I was also going a bit wild off the table then, to be fair. I was having some good drinking sessions regularly, which I never used to do. It caught up with me in the end and I didn't win a tournament for about two-and-a-half years.
>
> *(Reported by Nick Townsend in the*
> *Independent on Sunday, 1 February 2004, p. 10)*

In one regard, sport provides a unique environment to investigate the way in which individuals cope with positive emotions and events, as these are experienced by most, if not all, athletes, and often very frequently. Notwithstanding the benefits of positive emotions (e.g. Frederickson, 2001) athletes do report that positive emotions can be associated with performance decrements (Hanin, 2000) and that sources of stress may result from positive events (Gould, Jackson and Finch, 1993). While for many of us positive events and positive emotions are to be 'enjoyed', the reality for athletes, particularly during competition, may be different.

Social and cultural issues

The social and cultural environment of the athlete has an important role to play in the emotions experienced and the ways in which athletes cope (for examples, see Babkes, Partridge and Moore, Chapter 7; Richards, Chapter, 3; Clarke, Chapter, 15; Rees and Freeman, Chapter 6). One topic that would appear to be particularly relevant to sport settings is emotional contagion. Coaches, fans, officials, team mates and opponents may engage in overt displays of emotion which could increase the likelihood of an athlete experiencing that emotion. While some research has been conducted in this area (e.g. Totterdell, 2000) a more detailed understanding of this phenomenon would appear to have clear implications for the way in which significant others, such as coaches and officials, interact with athletes. The role of significant others in helping athletes cope with emotions is also of interest, and research in the area of social support by Rees and colleagues, outlined in Chapter 6, is relevant in this regard.

The culture, or ethos, of the sport which defines acceptable and appropriate behaviour may also have a significant impact on the emotions experienced by athletes and the way in which they cope. It may be interesting to investigate whether venting, to which some sports are more open than others, impacts the emotions experienced and/or the coping strategies employed by athletes. For example, researchers may wish to contrast sports such as soccer, where displays of verbal dissent to referees and opponents are commonplace, with sports such as rugby in which overt displays of verbal dissent to officials and opponents are less common. Similarly, examining differences in coping and emotion between contact sports such as rugby, which provide players with an opportunity to exorcise their emotions in a physical manner, with non-contact sports such as cricket or baseball, which do not, may be illuminating. The differing cultures and ethoi of sports may contribute to sport-specific antecedents of emotions. An example of this may be sport-specific self-presentation issues. Sports such as ice hockey, rugby union, rugby league, American football and Australian rules football are contact (in some cases collision) sports in which demonstrating physical dominance over an opponent is often considered to be an integral part of the game. Being seen to be dominated physically by an opponent may give rise to self-presentation concerns resulting in negative emotions (such as embarrassment and shame). Further, different self-presentation aspects of different sports may give rise to different emotions. For instance, anxiety may stem more from different self-presentation concerns in subjectively scored sports such as ice-skating than in objectively scored sports such as field athletics.

To conclude

The chapters in this book illustrate that coping and emotion in sport is a vibrant area of study, and this is reflected in the diversity of topics covered, theoretical approaches employed, and the geographical spread of the authors. While there are many exciting avenues for potential exploration and future research, this should not distract us from progress made and the knowledge accrued to date. We feel that, collectively, the chapters in this book provide a full description of 'what we know', and that this can both inform practice and guide future study in coping and emotion in sport.

References

Banyard, P. and Shevlin, M. (2001). Responses of football fans to relegation of their team from the English Premier League: post traumatic stress? *Irish Journal of Psychological Medicine*, 18, 66–67.

Baumeister, R. F., Bratslavsky, E., Muraven, M. and Tice, D. M. (1998). Ego depletion: is the active self a limited resource? *Journal of Personality and Social Psychology*, 74, 1252–1265.

Baumeister, R. F. and Heatherton, T. F. (1996). Self-regulation failure: an overview. *Psychological Inquiry*, 7, 1–15.

Bechara, A., Damasio, H., Tranel, D. and Damasio, A. R. (1997). Deciding advantageously before knowing the advantageous strategy. *Science*, 275, 1293–1295.

Biddle, S. J. H. and Mutrie, N. (2008). *Psychology of physical activity: Determinants, well-being and interventions*. London: Routledge.

British Psychological Society (2010). Still early days for Chilean miners. www.bps.org.uk/media-centre (accessed 13 October 2010),

Bray, S. R., Martin Ginis, K. A., Hicks, A. L. and Woodgate, J. (2008). Effects of self-regulatory strength depletion on muscular performance and EMG activation. *Psychophysiology*, 45, 337–343.

Carpenter, P. J. and Scanlan, T. K. (1998). Changes over time in the determinants of sport commitment. *Pediatric Exercise Science*, 10, 356–365.

Collins, D., Jones, B., Fairweather, Doolan, S. and Priestley, N. (2001). Examining anxiety associated changes in movement patterns. *International Journal of Sport Psychology*, 31, 223–242.

Frank, M. G. and Gilovich, T. (1988). The dark side of self- and social perception: black uniforms and aggression in professional sports. *Journal of Personality and Social Psychology*, 54, 74–85.

Gould, D., Jackson, S. and Finch, L. (1993). Sources of stress in national champion figure skaters. *Journal of Sport and Exercise Psychology*, 15, 134159.

Gross, J. J. (1998). The emerging field of emotion regulation: an integrative review. *Review of General Psychology*, 2, 271–299.

Hagger, M. S., Wood, C., Stiff, C. and Chatzisarantis, N. L. D. (2010). Ego depletion and the strength model of self-control: A meta-analysis. *Psychological Bulletin*, 136, 495–525.

Hanin, Y. L. (2000). Successful and poor performance and emotions. In Y. L. Hanin (ed.), *Emotions in sport* (pp. 155–187). Champaign, Ill.: Human Kinetics.

Hanin, Y. and Syrjä, P. (1995). Performance affect in junior ice hockey players: an application of the individual zones of optimal functioning model. *The Sport Psychologist*, 9, 169–187.

Jackson, S. A., Mayocchi, L. and Dover, J. (1998). Life after winning gold: II. Coping with change as an Olympic gold medallist. *The Sport Psychologist*, 12, 137–155.

Jones, M. V. (2003). Controlling emotions in sport. *The Sport Psychologist*, 17, 471–486.

Jones, M. V., Mace, R. D. and Williams, S. (2000). Relationship between emotional state and performance during international field hockey matches. *Perceptual and Motor Skills*, 90, 691–701.

Jones, M. V., Paull, G. C. and Erskine, J. (2002). The impact of a team's aggressive reputation on the decisions of association football referees. *Journal of Sports Sciences*, 20, 991–1000.

Jones, M. V. and Uphill, M. (2004). Responses to the competitive state anxiety inventory-2(d) by athletes in anxious and excited scenarios. *Psychology of Sport and Exercise*, 5, 201–212.

Kihlstrom, J. F., Mulvancy, S., Tobias, B. A. and Tobis, I. P. (2000). The emotional unconscious. In E. Eich, J. F. Kihlstrom, G. H. Bower, J. P. Forgas and P. M. Niedenthal (eds), *Cognition and emotion* (pp. 30–86). New York: Oxford University Press.

Kreiner-Phillips, K. and Orlick, T. (1993). Winning after winning: the psychology of on-going excellence. *The Sport Psychologist*, 7, 31–48.

Lazarus, R. S. (1991). *Emotion and adaptation*. Oxford: Oxford University Press.

Lazarus, R. S. (2000). How emotions influence performance in competitive sports. *The Sport Psychologist*, 14, 229–252.

Lazarus, R. S., Coyne, J. C. and Folkman, S. (1984). Cognition, emotion and motivation: the doctoring of Humpty-Dumpty. In K. R. Scherer and P. Ekman (eds), *Approaches to emotion* (pp. 221–237). London: Lawrence Erlbaum Associates.

Lundqvist, C., Kentta, G. and Raglin, J. S. (2010). Directional anxiety responses in elite and sub-elite young athletes: intensity of anxiety symptoms matters. *Scandinavian Journal of Medicine and Science in Sports*. doi: SMS1102 [pii] 10.1111/j.1600-0838.2010.01102.x

McCarthy, P. J., Jones, M. V. and Clark-Carter, D. (2008). Understanding enjoyment in youth sport: a developmental perspective. *Psychology of Sport and Exercise*, 9, 142–156.

McCarthy, P. J. and Jones, M. V. (2007). A qualitative study of sport enjoyment in the sampling years. *The Sport Psychologist*, 21, 400–416.

Norwood, A. E., Ursano, R. J. and Gabbay, F. H. (1997). Health effects of the stressors of extreme environments on military women. *Military Medicine*, 162, 643–648.

Ntoumanis, N. and Biddle, S. J. H. (2000). Relationship of intensity and direction of competitive state anxiety with coping strategies. *The Sport Psychologist*, 14, 360–371.

Owen, D. (2006). *Observer Sport Monthly*, November, p. 26.

Parfitt, G. and Pates, J. (1999). The effects of cognitive and somatic anxiety and self-confidence on components of performance during competition. *Journal of Sports Sciences*, 17, 351–356.

Pensgaard, A. M. and Duda, J. L. (2003). Sydney 2000: the interplay between emotions, coping, and the performance of Olympic-level athletes. *The Sport Psychologist*, 17, 253–267.

Plessner, H. (1999). Expectation biases in gymnastic judging. *Journal of Sport and Exercise Psychology*, 21, 131–144.

Rainey, D. W. and Hardy, L. (1999). Sources of stress burnout and intention to terminate among rugby union referees. *Journal of Sports Sciences*, 17, 797–806.

Richards, J. M. and Gross, J. J. (2000). Emotion regulation and memory: the cognitive costs of keeping one's cool. *Journal of Personality and Social Psychology*, 79, 410–424.

Seligman, M. E. P. (1995). The effectiveness of psychotherapy: the consumer reports study. *American Psychologist*, 50, 965–974.

Seligman, M. E. P. (2003). Positive psychology: fundamental assumptions. *The Psychologist*, 16, 126–127.

Sinnott, K. and Biddle, S. (1998). Changes in attributions, perceptions of success and intrinsic motivation after attribution retraining in children's sport. *International Journal of Adolescence and Youth*, 7, 137–144.

Totterdell, P. (2000). Catching moods and hitting runs: mood linkage and subjective performance in professional sport teams. *Journal of Applied Psychology*, 85, 848–859.

Townsend, N. (2004). I'd rather be in the bingo hall than in the players' lounge. *Sportsweek, Independent on Sunday*, 1 February, p. 10.

Uphill, M. A. and Jones, M. V. (2007). Antecedents of emotions in elite athletes: a cognitive motivational relational theory perspective. *Research Quarterly for Exercise and Sport*, 78, 79–89.

Uphill, M. A., McCarthy, P. J. and Jones, M. V. (2009). Getting a grip on emotion regulation in sport: conceptual foundations and practical application. In S. Mellalieu and S. Hanton, (eds), *Advances in applied sport psychology* (pp. 162–194). London: Routledge.

Vallerand, R. J. (1987). Antecedents of self-related affects in sport: preliminary evidence on the intuitive-reflective appraisal model. *Journal of Sport Psychology*, 9, 161–182.

Vallerand, R. J. and Blanchard, C. M. (2000). The study of emotion in sport and exercise: historical, definitional, and conceptual perspectives. In Y. L. Hanin (Ed.), *Emotions in sport* (pp. 3 – 37). Champaign, Ill.: Human Kinetics.

Wann, D. L. (2006). Understanding the positive social psychological benefits of sport team identification: the team identification–social psychological health model. *Group Dynamics: Theory, Research and Practice*, 10, 272–296.

Wilson, M. R., Vine, S. J. and Wood, G. (2009). The influence of anxiety on visual attentional control in basketball free throw shooting. *Journal of Sport and Exercise Psychology*, 31, 152–168.

Woodman, T., Davis, P. A., Hardy, L., Callow, N., Glasscock, I. and Yuill-Proctor, J. (2009). Emotions and sport performance: an exploration of happiness, hope, and anger. *Journal of Sport and Exercise Psychology*, 31, 169–188.

INDEX